W9-BXE-255

SECOND EDITION

PHYSICAL ACTIVITIES FOR COLLEGE WOMEN

MARYHELEN VANNIER, ED. D.
Professor and Director, Women's Division
Department of Health and Physical Education,
Southern Methodist University

HALLY BETH POINDEXTER, ED. D.
Professor, Department of Health Education and
Physical Education, Rice University

W. B. SAUNDERS COMPANY · Philadelphia · London · Toronto

W. B. Saunders Company: West Washington Square
Philadelphia, Pa.   19105

12 Dyott Street
London, WC1A   1DB

1835 Yonge Street
Toronto 7, Ontario

Physical Activities for College Women   SBN 0-7216-9006-8

Print No.:   9   8   7   6   5   4   3

PREFACE

This text and its many illustrations have been prepared primarily as a helpful guide and handbook for women college students enrolled in basic instruction courses in physical education. It has been designed to help each young woman gain a greater understanding and appreciation of the unique contributions physical education makes both to the curriculum of higher education and to life itself. It has also been written to help each student to develop a meaningful vocabulary of movement and a desire to continue to use these movements in later life, for any college course must be concerned with tomorrow as well as yesterday or today. Our book also has been created to help all students to gain a concept of the vital role physical activity plays in developing the total fitness and buoyant health needed for life's ever-changing and always demanding tasks.

In each of the seventeen chapters on Individual Sports and of the eight chapters on Team Sports detailed explanatory illustrations and written materials are included to give students a clearer understanding of the history, nature, and purpose of each sport; the facilities needed; the purchase, care, and proper use of equipment; each part of the basic movement skills inherent in each sport; game rules; scoring techniques; terminology; strategy for offensive and defensive play; courtesies needed as a participant as well as a spectator; suggested audio-visual aids and reference materials. Sample study questions are given at the end of each chapter; the appendix provides approximately 25 objective examination questions for each activity included in the book. Materials found in the chapters on Folk, Modern, Social, and Square Dance will help students to have a clearer concept of the rhythmic movement skills fundamental to each of these activities, as well as help them to develop a greater appreciation of dance as a rich part of our cultural legacy and as a means of creative self-expression.

The chapters Body Mechanics and Movement Fundamentals and Body Types, Weight, and Figure Control will help college women to understand that physical education is far more than just taking part in an active sport while in college, and is concerned with guiding each young but slowly maturing woman toward her fuller development as a unique but contributing individual member of a democratic society. Included in these chapters also are materials that will help each student to become more attractive, healthy, intelligent, and socially sensitive, and to have a fine proportioned, conditioned body, as well as to become more aware of the importance of routinized health habits, including those of daily exercise and proper nutrition, for keeping herself in good physical condition throughout life. Specific exercises are included in these materials for reducing, preserving, or developing various areas of the body, as well as suggested ways to avoid or eliminate tension through relaxation. Materials are also included to help each student to gain a greater understanding of and appreciation for the vital role that leisure time and its positive re-creative use play in re-energizing a person's mind, body, and spirit, in order to discover the balance, joy, and real satisfaction needed for living productively, abundantly, and happily in our time of ever-increasing drastic change, fearful tension, and uncertainty.

Many new materials have been included in the second edition of this widely adopted and popular textbook. Briefly stated, these include a discussion of the physiological benefits of exercise, a health habit check sheet, new exercises in the chapter on weight and figure control, including those for students with dysmenorrhea, the bringing up to date of all game rule changes and suggested references, and the inclusion of many new illustrations and photographs. The chapter on Recreational Activities now contains materials on playground golf, tether ball, horseshoes, table tennis and billiards. In the area of Sports Competition for Women the most recent policies devised by the Division of Girls' and Women's Sports of the American Association for Health, Physical Education, and Recreation have been included. Mention also has been made of the latest kinds of sport equipment now on the market, such as the new snow ski mat and newly styled tennis and badminton rackets. Finally, a new chapter on the popular activity of surfing has been provided.

MARYHELEN VANNIER
HALLY BETH POINDEXTER

Dallas, Texas
Houston, Texas

ACKNOWLEDGMENTS

The authors are indebted to many persons who have made this book possible. We wish to express our appreciation to our families, personal friends, professional colleagues, and students for their inspiration, suggestions, and reactions to the material in this book. We are especially grateful to the following colleagues, who wrote the chapters indicated:

Iris M. Carnell, Ithaca College: Skiing
M. Frances Dougherty, University of Oregon: Modern Dance
Aimée Loftin, Western Illinois University: Water Skiing
Lola Sadlo, San Fernando Valley State College: Folk Dance,
Social Dance, and Square Dance

Our thanks to Mrs. Barbara Wadsworth for her help on the skiing chapter and to Gabrielle Blockley, Carole L. Mushier, and R. Mildred Alford for their specialized suggestions and criticisms. We are also grateful to Edwin Ellis of the National Golf Foundation, Ted Banks of the Athletic Institute, David Boehm and Sylvia Link of Sterling Publications, Jerrold Russom of the Los Angeles Public Schools, Hollis Fait of the University of Connecticut, Clifford Lewis of the University of Georgia, and Dean Anne Schley Duggan, College of Health, Physical Education and Recreation, Texas Woman's University, Jean Jacobs of Springfield College, Mary Kate Miller of Mississippi State College for Women, and Agnes Michaels of State University College, Fredonia, New York, for the use of illustrative photographs. To the American Association of Health, Physical Education, and Recreation for permission to reproduce certain materials and especially to Rachael Bryant, their Consultant in Girls and Women's Sports, to William Osburn, who did the marvelous illustrations, and to the staff of the W. B. Saunders Company, our grateful appreciation.

Mrs Dorothy Good and Miss Patty Jo Allen deserve our special vote of thanks for typing the manuscript.

CONTENTS

Chapter Six

Chapter Seven

Chapter Ten

Chapter Eleven

Chapter Twelve

1

ORIENTATION

"A good education consists of giving to the body and to the soul all the beauty and all the perfection of which they are capable."

— *Plato*

CHAPTER ONE

Courtesy of Mary Kate Miller, Mississippi State College for Women.

THE UNIQUE CONTRIBUTION OF PHYSICAL EDUCATION TO EDUCATION AND TO LIFE

Just as all roads once led to mighty Rome, every subject in the school curriculum leads toward the goal of the total development of each student, and thus society. A morally strong, physically vigorous, and cultured nation can be made up only of citizens who have these qualities. Just as little drops of water and tiny grains of sand make a mighty ocean and a mighty land, what the present and future of the United States will be depends on the intelligent actions and dedicated beliefs and goals of each citizen. To this present and that future, you, as a part of the whole, can make a significant contribution. Your experience at college should help you to become a more cultured human being and world citizen prepared to better human life, and prepare you for your future personal and professional role in life and society. As a result of your many educational experiences both in and outside college classrooms, you should become better informed, more skilled in communicating with and understanding others, and acquire a more refined appreciation for beauty. Since what one does, believes in, and is dedicated to results from the amount and *depth* of education, your college experiences should inspire you to live a fuller, more joyous, and more meaningful life.

While in college you will be primarily concerned with learning, and with making new discoveries about yourself and the wonderful past, present, and possible future world of mankind. What you learn should enable you to find ways to make satisfying and meaningful choices in the many ever-changing situations in your own present and future life. Learning means changed behavior in obtaining desired goals. From the time you enter college, throughout your entire remaining stay on earth, you will be a part of a rapidly changing world. You, too, will change, both inwardly and outwardly, in what you care deeply about as well as how you will think, look, and act. Unless you gain experiences while in college that will help to prepare you for that future, you will have wasted four precious years (and there are just so many sand grains in every person's hourglass), much money, plus a great deal of precious energy. To educate means "to lead forth," but *where* depends largely on you. Through your many learning experiences at school you should:

1. Gain a new understanding of the true meaning of words and other symbols.
2. Be able to communicate better with others and have something of value to communicate, and be able to listen more intelligently.
3. Develop many new leisure-time skills that will enable you to discover and use free time in creative ways.
4. Form improved health habits and behavior patterns.
5. Develop finer attitudes, new understandings, and deeper appreciations of yourself, others, and the meaning of life.
6. Be able to make more mature, intelligent choices and to apply learned facts, concepts, and skills
7. Show greater concern for the human rights of other people.
8. Become better self-disciplined and more motivated to reach high personal and professional goals as a student and citizen.
9. Gain greater knowledge and appreciation of your own body and how to use it wisely.

In the final analysis, the real purpose of education is to improve the *quality* of living. To become well educated is a long, slow process that goes on for the entirety of one's existence. Since the average life span for all Americans is increasing, your chances are good for living to be at least 70 years old.*

---

*According to the forecasts by the experts in the Statistical Bureau of the Metropolitan Life Insurance Company, in the year 2000 the expectation of life at birth will be 71.2 years for males and 76.8 years for females. At the present time, a much greater number of Americans are reaching the seventies, eighties, and nineties. *Most college students have about two-thirds of their lives before them.* Since females outlive males, most women will live longer than men, and if married, most will survive their husbands.

Many of your classmates, and perhaps even you, will live to be 100 years old or more. Each year will bring new problems to be solved, new adjustments to be made. How well you meet those future changes depends greatly on how well you go about solving present problems and how well you are applying what you are learning from your college experiences. As Theodore Roosevelt once remarked, "What I am to be, I am now becoming." What you will be like, then, on your graduation day depends on your background, what you do and are becoming now at school, and how well you master skills and knowledges needed to obtain your present and future goals.

TAKE A LOOK AT YOURSELF

Using the following check list, make a general appraisal of your daily habits, assets and liabilities in order to discover if you are living, have acceptable health habits, or are merely existing.

HEALTH RATING SCALE—ARE YOU LIVING OR EXISTING?

or
Score Yourself

5 — Excellent   (always)
4 — Good   (most of the time)
3 — Fair   (half and half)
2 — Poor   (seldom)
1 — Very Poor   (never)

175-136 — Living
135-110 — Acceptable
109 and below — Existing

DO YOU:
____ Eat three meals every day?
____ Include the basic foods (meat, salad, vegetables, milk or milk products, fruit, and cereal) in your daily diet?
____ Drink six to eight glasses of water every day?
____ Limit your "between meal snacks" to fruit and milk?
____ Sleep at least six hours every night?
____ Relax at intervals during the day?

____ Exercise at least one hour every day (preferably out-of-doors)?
____ Keep healthy—free from colds, headaches, or sore throats?
____ Keep your smoking to a minimum (between three and five cigarettes a day)?
____ See your dentist at least twice a year?
____ Brush your teeth after every meal and when you get up or before you go to bed every day?
____ Wear shoes which fit properly and rarely cause your feet to ache?
____ Keep your feet clean and free from athlete's foot, corns or bunions?
____ Carry yourself well when standing, sitting, and walking?
____ Take exercise during your menstrual periods?
____ Bathe at least once a day while menstruating?
____ Have a menstrual period free from pain?
____ Have regular bowel movements?
____ Take a daily shower or bath?
____ Wear clean underwear and hose each day?
____ Use a deodorant every day?
____ Keep your hands and fingernails clean every day?
____ Take care of and have a clear complexion?
____ Dress appropriately for each occasion?
____ Keep your clothes neat and clean?
____ Keep yourself well-groomed, including having your shoes well shined daily?
____ Keep your weight normal for your age and height and are not more than three pounds under or overweight?

PERSONALITY AND CHARACTER RATING SCALE

ARE YOU:
____ Enthusiastic?
____ Cooperative?
____ Dependable?
____ Loyal?
____ Friendly?
____ Able to meet people and make friends easily?

____ TOTAL

CONCLUSIONS: I find from checking this list that I can improve my health and appearance if I _____
_____,
and that I am _____ living, _____ acceptable, or _____ existing.

YOUR COLLEGE PHYSICAL EDUCATION PROGRAM

Among the basic developmental courses you will take in college is physical education. The purposes of this field of study are the same as those of all others in the school curriculum—to develop well rounded, happy, healthy, skilled, intelligent, and productive human beings to their highest potential as individuals and democratic citizens. The courses you will take in physical education will help you to discover the joy found in movement. You will gain greater appreciation of our heritage through dance, rhythmical, and other physical experiences. In learning individual and dual sports such as golf or tennis, or team sports such as hockey and softball, or the skills needed in aquatic activities such as synchronized swimming you will develop your ability to solve physical and mental problems. Physical education, like education in general, is continuous. You can lay the foundation for becoming physically educated in college when you:

1. Learn to use your body in rhythmical, efficient movements as a young adult, and can carry over and modify those skills into the middle years and those in advanced age.
2. Know how and do play one or more individual and team sports with above average ability and gain satisfaction from doing so.
3. Can move gracefully whether you are doing folk, social, or modern dancing, or other movements to accompaniment.
4. Can swim well enough to save yourself or another from drowning.
5. Can use your body without undue fatigue and have an energy reserve for emergency situations.
6. Can move at different speeds and at different levels easily, change directions, and judge distances accurately.
7. Can throw and strike balls or other objects of varying size with a fair degree of accuracy.

8. Can hit, strike, kick, and catch moving objects of varying size with a fair degree of accuracy.
9. Can hit stationary and moving targets with a fair degree of accuracy.
10. Are generally happy and optimistic, and have a zest for living.
11. Do a wide variety of recreative activities during well planned leisure time.
12. Have periodic medical and dental checkups and have defects corrected.
13. Follow regulated daily health habits.

Your increased health and total fitness resulting from physical education should help you to succeed as a college student. You cannot develop your mind and neglect your body without soon encountering difficulties, for a sound mind, to work best, must be housed in a sound body. If, as a result of going to college, you become intellectually superior and well prepared professionally but also a physical wreck, many people will doubt if you are *really* educated. To consider the human body inferior to the mind is a throwback to the "dark" days of the Middle Ages. Your mind and body are inseparable and incomplete without each other. Of all the great wonders of the world, the human being is the most wonderful masterpiece of them all! As you will learn, the ideal life is found in properly balancing intellectual, moral, physical, and esthetic experiences.

Your college physical education program will be made up of carefully planned and progressively more challenging activities focusing on the development, use, and movement of the whole body. Since the body is the fundamental tool for any life task, movement is basic to growth, development, and all learning. When you no longer move, you will be dead indeed!

Your college years are a time for fun as well as study. Through sports and games you can share many good times with others—friends of the same or opposite sex. Many of the activities you will learn to play will have high carryover value for your later life as well. As a future wife and mother you will be concerned with family recreation. As a future employee you will probably be living in a large apartment complex in a large city. Knowing how to swim, or play volley ball or other sports will help you to gain friends more easily, whether this be through activities centering around an apartment swimming pool, a private club, a church-sponsored recreational center, or a Y.W. or Y.M.C.A.

In our sports-oriented society knowing how to take part in sports will give you a magic ticket which will help you belong as well as to contribute as a citizen to the health of our nation. The greater your skill in understanding of and appreciation for dance activities and individual and team sports, the greater your thrill will be as a participant or spectator while in college and later on with your own family.

By developing sport, dance, and recreational skills in your physical education class, or playing on an intramural team or a team representing your school, you can gain the following personal qualities:

Respect for others as well as rules
Perseverance
Better health status
Enjoyment of life
Leadership skills
Increased vigor and vim
Sportsmanship
Improved coordination
Increased understandings of people as well as sports
Character development
Team or followership skills

Play is the balance wheel of life. All work and no play makes Jane and Jack, regardless of age, not only dullards but also maladjusted individuals. Performing challenging, adventurous and refreshing physical activities can help to add joy, meaning, luster, and beauty to life.

"Play for the child is the gaining of life, play for the adult is the renewal of life." This concept, developed by Joseph Lee, the father of the American playground movement, carries much educational and physiological merit.

Your college physical education experiences will help you to develop (1) physical and total fitness, (2) movement skills, (3) finer social attitudes, (4) knowledges and appreciations, and (5) ability for better use of leisure time.

DEVELOPING PHYSICAL AND TOTAL FITNESS

Just as primitive people had to learn to use their bodies wisely or perish, so must we moderns. Differences are only in degree. There are those who claim that Americans are rapidly becoming a race of softies looking on, instead of doers. Others claim that we let our bodies rust out rather than wear out. Some declare that as a people we need to get off our seat onto our feet and do meaningful, vigorous activities. Man, primitive or modern, is an active animal, and as such his

Fig. 1-1. Skills learned in school have an important role to play in positive free time use both for the present and the future. (Courtesy of College of Health, Physical Education and Recreation, Texas Woman's University, Denton, Texas.)

basic physical needs are the same; but his emotional, social, and mental needs are greatly intensified. Failure to satisfy physical needs—the balance wheels of life—often throws him out of gear.

Buoyant health does not come naturally or without effort. It must be determinedly built and maintained, for fitness is a product of vigorous physical activity and a strong desire to possess it. Such well-being results from taking part in physical activities, following positive health habits, and maintaining a balance between work and play. The body increases in strength, efficiency, and beauty through just the right amount and kind of activity, for too little or too much can be equally detrimental. Total fitness (emotional, spiritual and physical) cannot be stored away for future use or emergency, like food or money, but must be maintained when once acquired and replaced when used. Since the human body is composed (along with many other things) of 639 muscles and 208 bones, exercise over and beyond the daily movement requirements of living is necessary for the development of an efficient, strong and attractive body.

One is physically fit when she is free from disease, does not deviate significantly in body structure or function, has sufficient strength, speed, agility, endurance, and skill to do the maximum daily life tasks, is mentally and emotionally adjusted, and has high moral and spiritual concepts. Such a person is not easily fatigued and does not wilt from strain or boredom, but is buoyant, happy and attractive. Exercise for at least 20 minutes daily, sports, games, dance, and other physical activities are the foundation upon which such fitness rests.

Physical signs of the lack of fitness are:

1. Fatty degeneration of body, heart, lungs, blood vessels, and brain
2. Shrunken and constricted capillaries in muscles, heart, lungs, and brain.
3. Poor muscle tone.
4. Abdominal ptosis (sag) and postural slouch.
5. Slowed reactions and reflexes.
6. Loss of flexibility, stiffness in joints.
7. Traumatic weakness in the sacroiliac, inguinal, spine, knee, and foot regions.
8. Persistent tension.

9. Lowered energy for work and social enjoyment—withdrawal from hard tasks, mental or physical.
10. Lowered metabolic rate and reduced sexual response, digestive capacity, and warmth of the body.
11. Psychological maladjustments, depression, feelings of inadequacy, loss of confidence, imaginary (psychogenic) illnesses, bad temperament, anxiety, cardiac neuroses, and neurasthenia (nervous exhaustion).
12. Inability to take stress and adjust to it, day by day, which is prerequisite to any real continued success.*

Since, as you know, fitness is necessary for the fullest enjoyment of living, you can quickly evaluate your own physical condition by answering yes or no to the following questions:

1. Do you wake in the morning tired and lethargic?
2. Are you frequently sleepy or drowsy during the day? Do you "fight sleep" in class?
3. Are you uncomfortably tired, mentally and physically, at bedtime?
4. Do you feel tired and dull in tackling difficult assignments after dinner at night?
5. Do you find it difficult to get to sleep at night?
6. Are you often "on edge," nervous, jittery? Is it difficult for you to relax?
7. Are you subject to worries? moods?
8. Are you troubled with indigestion? bad breath? constipation?
9. Are you troubled with headaches? twitching face and eyelids?
10. Are you subject to colds? sore throats? earache?
11. Do you have foot trouble? joint pains? backache?
12. Does climbing stairs leave you breathless?
13. When standing, is it difficult for you to maintain an upright, pleasing posture?
14. Are you irritable toward others? Do people generally "bother" you?

---

*American Association for Health, Physical Education, and Recreation: *Fit for College*, Washington, D.C., 1959, p. 22.

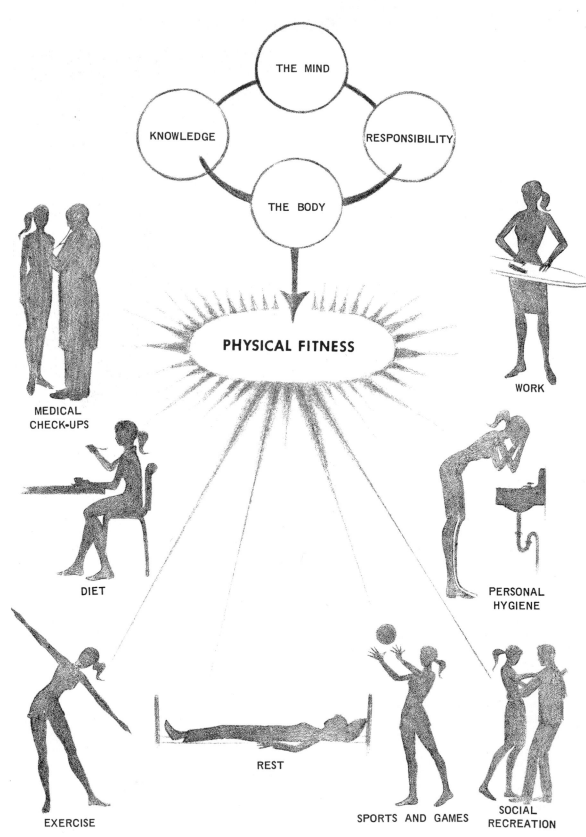

Fig. 1-2. The seven aspects of fitness.

Fig. 1-3. The Jump Reach Test is often included in physical fitness testing. As a test of explosive power, it is both challenging and revealing. (Courtesy of the Los Angeles Public Schools.)

15   Are you actually dissatisfied with your present physical condition?*

An answer of yes to any of the above questions indicates some degree of unfitness, while an answer of yes to more than two questions indicates that you should become concerned enough about your present physical state to improve it.

Another quick way to find out how fit you really are is to row, run, or swim vigorously for as long as you can. If you are in fairly good physical condition, you should be able to keep going for at least six minutes, and ten if you are in top form. Fitness, however, is far more than having the ability to answer yes or no to questions, or to move the body quickly for a certain number of minutes. The seven aspects of fitness are good nutrition, adequate rest and relaxation, health, physical activity and recreation, the proper amount of daily exercise, dental and physical care, and satisfying work.

———————

*American Association for Health, Physical Education, and Recreation: *Fit for College*, Washington, D.C., 1959, p. 9.

THE PHYSIOLOGICAL BENEFITS OF EXERCISE

Buoyant health results from effort and the motivated desire to become and stay healthy. Exercise throughout life over and beyond daily work requirements is necessary for the development and retention of an efficient, strong, attractive body. The older you become, the more you will sag and wilt unless you remain active. The human body rarely wears out. It can deteriorate, however, very rapidly.

The physiological benefits of exercise are that it:

1. Increases muscular strength and physical endurance.
2. Improves circulation and produces more red blood corpuscles.
3. Increases heart size and power.
4. Relieves tension and fatigue by providing an outlet for feelings of hostility and aggression.
5. Increases the function of all body

systems, especially those of circulation, respiration, and digestion.

6. Increases neuromuscular coordination and the use of the body through more skillful movements.

7. Produces greater strength and resiliency of the skeletal system of the body by increasing the size and the thickness of the bones.

8. Builds greater resistance to disease and fatigue.

9. Helps to keep weight normal when coupled with the reduction of food intake and the elimination of between-meal snacks.

10. Stimulates physical growth as well as redistributes weight and body fat.

11. Favorably affects the functions of each of the internal body organs and glands.

12. Helps to remove body waste products more quickly through perspiration, respiration and elimination.

13. Helps one to remain young and zestful throughout life by retarding the physical and mental effects of aging.

14. Increases the recovery rate after surgery and major illness.

15. Aids in childbirth ease.

16. Helps to make sleep more refreshing for healthful, joyful living.

INCREASING MOVEMENT SKILLS

Skills develop from movements ranging from simple to complex. Basic experiences in body control are found in running, jumping, landing, pushing, pulling, climbing, carrying, lifting, throwing, hitting, and catching. For mastery, all require body balance, control, and rhythm. The highest movement skills are those that combine any locomotor or axial movement with speed, accuracy, agility, rhythm, power, timing and beauty. Kinesiologists believe that such perfection can be reached through understanding how to control all body movements, and through sports and games and dance skills. How the body is used in everyday work and play has a great effect on one's figure. College women who have been well educated physically realize that sports, dance, and games can do more to help them acquire and keep a good figure than does going to a masseur to have him pound or roll away bulging hip fat, or

signing up for a slenderizing program with a jiggling machine.

The mastery of human movement patterns is an everchanging, adaptive, and lifelong process. The child is faced with the progressively difficult tasks of learning to walk, run, jump, and to coordinate hands, feet, and body. The early adolescent "skill-hungry years" are the best for beginning skill refinement. Later, still more complex skills must be learned.

From your college physical education experiences you will learn some of these skills:

I. Skills of maintaining and regaining equilibrium
II. Skills of moving one's own body
   A. On land or other solid surface
      1. Arm, leg and trunk movements
      2. Locomotion
      3. Rotary movements of the body as a whole
   B. In the water
      1. Swimming
      2. Aquatic stunts
      3. Boating
   C. In the air
      1. Diving
      2. Trampoline and tumbling activities
   D. In suspension
      1. Swinging activities on trapeze, flying rings, etc.
      2. Hand traveling on traveling rings, horizontal ladder, etc.
III. Skills of receiving impetus
   A. Of own body
      1. Landing from jumps and falls
   B. Of external objects
      1. Catching and trapping
      2. Receiving with an implement
      3. Receiving and spotting in stunts and apparatus events
IV. Skills of giving impetus to external objects
   A. Pushing, pulling, thrusting, lifting
   B. Throwing with hand or implement
   C. Striking, hitting, kicking, etc.
V. The selection and classification of skills related to prevention of injury
   A. The maintenance of equilibrium
   B. The range of motion
   C. The intensity and duration of muscular exercise
   D. The transmission of weight

Fig. 1-4. Ball handling routines help students to develop coordination, rhythm, and accuracy of movement. (Courtesy of Clifford Lewis, University of Georgia.)

Fig. 1-5. Balance is one aspect of body control. (Courtesy of College of Health, Physical Education and Recreation, Texas Woman's University, Denton, Texas.)

through the body segments and weight-bearing joints

E. The reception of one's own weight

~~The li~~fting and carrying of heavy

G. The impact of

' forces*

Learning motor skills involves the whole person; in reality there is no separate kind of learning that is strictly "motor" in nature. Although some individuals learn more easily than others, both sexes have the same potential for learning sport skills, within their structural and functional limits, for differences in the way the two sexes learn physical activities are largely due to cultural influences.† Women have not had so many opportunities to learn sports as men, and each sex has assumed the sex role set by society. Likewise, there is no evidence that people of any one race can learn some sports more rapidly than others, although those of any nationality will succeed in mastering more quickly those skills that their ancestors had acquired. Each individual, however, learns motor skills in her own way and according to her own pattern. Some may make no real apparent progress for some time, while others may improve steadily and gradually. Although people in their sixties can and do learn to play shuffleboard, golf, or other sports, they do so more slowly than young people, for after the age of 30 a person loses the ability to learn entirely new physical skills quickly.

You will acquire motor skills easily if you have the following qualities:

1. Insight into the nature of the skill: "catching on" to what is expected.

2. Ability to visualize spatial relationships.

3. The ability to make quick and adaptive decisions.

4. Sensory motor coordination: as in the coordination of the eye with the head, hand, or foot.

5. Sensory motor coordination: the adaptation of weight and force.

6. Judgment of the relationship of the subject to external objects in relation to time, height, distance, and direction.

7. Accuracy of direction and small angles of error.

8. General kinesthetic sensitivity and control.

9. Ability to coordinate a complex unitary movement.

10. Ability to coordinate a complex series of combinations of movements which follow one another in rapid succession.

11. Arm control.

12. Balance

13. Timing.

14. Motor rhythm.

15. Esthetic feeling.

16. The necessary prerequisites to effective motor learning, including:

a. Muscular strength.

b. Dynamic energy—the ability to throw oneself into a performance with full vigor.

c. Ability to change directions.

d. Flexibility of muscles, joints and ligaments.

e. Ability to move rapidly from one position in space to another.

f. Peripheral vision.

g. Good vision.

h. Concentration.

i. Understanding of the mechanics of the techniques of the activity.

j. Absence of disturbing or inhibitory complications.*

Thus your experiences in physical education will extend far beyond helping you to learn to play basketball successfully or to hit the archery target.

DEVELOPING FINER SOCIAL ATTITUDES

One great value of physical activities, especially in team sports, is in developing the attitudes of the individual, who, as a group member engaged in a united effort, both contributes and cooperates by substituting the finer "we" drives for selfish "I" drives. Through such endeavor one learns the

---

*Wells, Katharine: *Kinesiology.* 4th Ed., Philadelphia, W. B. Saunders Company, 1966, p. 336.

†Oberteuffer, Delbert, and Ulrich, Celeste: *Physical Education, A Textbook of Principles for Professional Students,* 3rd Ed., New York, Harper & Row, 1962, p. 282.

---

*McCloy, Charles: "A Preliminary Study of Factors of Motor Educability," *Research Quarterly*, May, 1946, pp. 28-39.

lessons of give and take, and of failure as well as success. It is while playing on a team that many of the techniques for successful group life are best learned. It is here that leaders as well as good followers are often developed. Likewise, it is here that one gains fuller appreciation of such American principles as "where there is unity there is strength," or "unite or perish." Just as our forefathers, whether they were members of a wagon train group rolling out to new glory and adventure on the way West or soldiers on the side of the Blue or the Gray, learned that in numbers there was safety, and that through united group effort dreams could become faster realities, you today must be aware of the importance of the individual in relation to a group.

The social value of physical activities is also inherent in games for the single player and in those for two. Even when playing alone on the golf course or archery range, one wishes to do her best. In all dual activities such common courtesies as taking turns, or rotating courts so one person does not always face into the sun, do much to develop respect and consideration for the rights of others. Play without a referee, wherein one calls her own games honestly, helps a person to develop habits of truthfulness. The best discipline is, or course, self-discipline rooted in self-control. Since today, more than ever before, we need more upright citizens in every age group, every method and activity that produces such individuals must be used to its utmost.

The development of social-mindedness will be one of the important results of your physical education. Like John Donne, centuries ago, you must be involved in all mankind, and see the wisdom of the following:

No man is an *Iland*, intire of its selfe; every man is a peece of the *Continent*, a part of the *maine*: if a *Clod* bee washed away by the *Sea, Europe* is the lesse, as well as if a *Promontorie* were, as well as if a *Mannor* of thy *friends* or *thine owne* were, any mans *death* diminishes *me*, because I am involved in *Mankinde*: and therefore never send to know for whom the *bell* tolls; it tolls for *thee*.

INCREASING KNOWLEDGES AND APPRECIATIONS

Self-understanding is the key to understanding others. It can be gained through physical activities, for one soon senses how she is regarded by her teammates and opponents — as a dub who cheats, or as one who plays according to the rules. One also develops new interests and hobbies enduring enough for later life. Those fortunate enough to acquire superior sport skills benefit as game spectators, for only they fully appreciate the beauty of the movements they watch, or know of the hard, long hours of practice that go into the making of such a finished performance.

It is important for you to know as much as possible about your own body and how to take care of it, for as the "house" in which you live, it must be well built, kept in good repair, and enduring enough to last you a lifetime.

FOSTERING BETTER USE OF LEISURE TIME

Although more people have more free time than ever before, this is only the beginning of a glorious new age of leisure. In this new era, brought about by the Industrial Revolution with its labor-saving devices, millions have benefited from shortened work hours. Yet the new age has its dangers. Many observers warn us that too many of us are living at too fast a pace both in work and play, and too few are finding the release, refreshment, or recreation inherent in this newly found free time. Others scoffingly ask "What leisure?" This remark is significant to the well trained ear, for it shows a failure to understand what planned free time can do to recreate a person after an exhausting day of work or study. Certainly there is evidence that Americans are as frenzied in their leisure time as in their work. We are all aware that more and more Americans are content to watch fewer and fewer play. Some experts claim that the "soft American" is more than just physically soft.

The number of those rejected for military service because of physical defects in all the wars of this century has been appallingly high. The failure of American children to pass certain fitness tests in comparison to European children resulted in President Eisenhower's National Conference on Physical Fitness and President Kennedy's Council on Youth Fitness. Likewise, obesity, heart diseases, mental illness and death from degenerative diseases are all on the increase. The constant threat of internal social upheaval, war, and tragedy undermines our morale. As a nation it is imperative that we be strong, healthy, and ready to maintain our position of world leadership, or even to survive, if need be, in time of still another great crisis.

In their free time people voluntarily do those things that bring them joy and satisfaction. They will choose to play only when they have an interest in doing so, a feeling that from such activity they can gain something of value, or when they possess enough skill to receive real satisfaction from doing so. Therefore it is important that while you are in college you learn sports and games that you can keep on playing in future life.

Every living person has the same amount of daily time—24 hours, no more, no less. What one *does* with these 24 hours is quite another matter. If one has not been taught to allow so many hours each day for recreational activities, she is not only ignorant of a revitalizing process necessary to maintain health, but also has developed detrimental, life-shortening habits.

Free time can be spent in positive or negative ways. The former are made up of those activities that benefit each person and society; the latter are detrimental both to the individual and the group. Recreation is not merely doing what one wishes when one has time, for both a game and a criminal act fit this description. How one's free time is spent is important to the individual and to civilization, for leisure time offers rich opportunities that benefit us all when rightly used. An upright citizen is more than one who votes in all elections or collects donations for the Heart Fund; she is hale, hearty, and healthy, and fully realizes the role physical activity plays in keeping her in that state. She not only pursues the good life, but *contributes*.

Leisure is not self-indulgence; along with man's other great physical drives, food, rest, elimination, and sex, it is a basic human need. The well educated find true leisure and use it in creative, self-expressive ways in such activities as art or dance. Those who learn to use leisure well can become the most productive and successful students of all. Leisure when used to its fullest will recreate the mind, body, and spirit through activities which have meaning, beauty, and value, and will bring forth re-energized effort necessary in the seeking of the *best* of life!

THE MODIFIED PHYSICAL EDUCATION PROGRAM

Those students with some kind of physical limitation or disability should be assigned to an adapted or modified physical education program. Although in the past these individuals were excused from physical education because no class could be provided for them, increasingly they are known today to be the very ones who, in many ways, most need to learn physical activity skills, especially if they are to live successfully and happily in a future world of expanded free time, in a more competitive, sports loving society and in a mechanized working world.

Since many students with physical problems (both temporary, as found in the postoperative patient, and permanent, as in the poliomyelitis or cerebral palsy victim) need increased personal attention, they should be placed in a small class group with others who also have physical limitations. Emphasis in this class should be placed upon teaching these students a variety of individual sports and games as well as team sports, when feasible, which others in their peer group can and do perform. High on the list of recommended activities for the class are archery, golf, bowling, table tennis, hiking, jogging, shuffleboard, weight training, fencing, billiards, deck tennis, swimming, and modified volleyball, softball, and even in some cases, basketball.

Acquiring game and sport skills can do much to increase both the physical and emotional health of these students and their social mobility chances, both within as well as outside the adapted physical education class.

In the class each student should also learn as much as possible about the nature of her limitations and potentialities, and the important role daily physical activity and exercise play in relation to gaining and maintaining health and happiness throughout life.

Suggested Readings

Allen, Robert: *Time for Everything*, New York, Thomas Y. Crowell Company, 1955.
Bucher, Charles: *Foundations of Physical Education*, 5th Ed., St. Louis, The C. V. Mosby Company, 1968.

Brightbill, Charles: *Man and Leisure*, Englewood Cliffs, N.J., Prentice-Hall, Inc., 1961.

Rodahl, Kaare: *Be Fit for Life*, New York, Harper and Row, 1966.

Slusher, Howard: *Man, Sport and Existence*, Philadelphia, Lea & Febiger, 1967.

Voeks, Virginia: *On Becoming an Educated Person*, 2nd Ed., Philadelphia, W. B. Saunders Company, 1964.

Suggested Study Questions

1. Summarize in your own words the result you should obtain from your learning experiences at college.

2. In what ways is physical education more than just learning to play basketball?

3. Define the following: physical fitness as a part of total fitness, education, leisure, free time, health, learning.

4. Keep a record of how you spend your free time away from the classroom every day for one week. Are you a well organized and self-disciplined student? Do you use your free time productively? Are you finding true leisure?

5. Explain the five aspects of physical fitness. Are you physically fit according to the 15 questions you have answered for yourself on pages 7 to 9?

CHAPTER TWO

Courtesy of Jean Jacobs, Springfield College, Springfield, Massachusetts

BODY MECHANICS AND MOVEMENT FUNDAMENTALS

"Posture is a perpendicular line connecting heaven with earth."

— MARTHA GRAHAM

Every one has her own rhythmic movement patterns and limitations, body build, and personality traits. Some of your classmates, you notice, move more gracefully than others. All of you will gain increased movement skill as well as a deeper understanding of correct body mechanics and the fundamentals of movement through your physical education classes. How a person moves is revealing to the trained observer. Even you, as an amateur, can detect shyness and unsurety in the mincing gait of an introvert, or see a fairly accurate personality image in the more rapid, definite stride of the extrovert. As the psychologist William James and the scientist Darwin discovered, good posture gives the outward impression of buoyancy and nobility in spirit, of courage and physical vigor, of

Fig. 2-1. Personality and movement.

cheerfulness and hope, whereas a moping posture and dismal voice increase melancholy feelings. Marcel Marceau, the great pantomimist, as well as any professional actor or actress, can masterfully express age and a wide variety of personality traits, emotions, and occupations through movement. To move expressively is an art even an amateur can learn with patience and determination. It is never too late to improve your movement patterns, and you have a lifetime in which to practice.

POSTURAL FITNESS

BODY STANDING

Plato defined the most beautiful motion as one that achieves the best results with the least effort. The body houses the soul, and therefore it should be kept beautiful. For beauty of movement, the body must be balanced over its supporting base (the feet) and center of gravity (slightly above the hips). Like a set of well laid bricks, each body part must be perfectly balanced over the feet, hips, and chest. If any body segment is not in balance, the result is poor posture, which often contributes to fatigue, constipation, menstrual difficulties, and impaired circulation and respiration. With a partner you can make a quick test of your own posture by dropping a weighted line from the tip of the ear across the shoulder. If you have good standing posture, the line will bisect the shoulder, hip, side of the leg at the knee joint, and ankle. The head should be perfectly balanced on its small connecting segment of the neck, so that the eyes can look squarely out at the world without the head's being raised or lowered. The shoulders should be relaxed, held down and wide, with each pointing directly to the side. The chest should be held high and relaxed, stomach and rear pulled in, the knees held loose and relaxed.

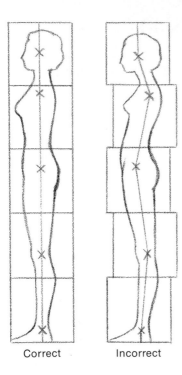

Correct　　　　Incorrect

Fig. 2-2. Alignment of body segments. (After Lee and Wagner.)

These are the points to remember:

Head
  Chin level
  Look straight ahead
Shoulders
  Hold them down and wide
Chest
  Move gracefully out from your chest
Knees
  Keep knees loose and relaxed
Abdomen
  Stomach in and hold
Hips
  Tuck in your rear
Feet
  Toes forward
  Step out straight ahead

Posture Reminders
  Stand tall
  Keep each part balanced

WALKING

Walking can be one of your best means of daily exercise. It is one of the few remaining forms of cost-free recreation that can bring lifelong enjoyment and healthful benefits. Walking is an alternate loss and recovery of balance as the body seeks a new base of support, for as one leg swings forward with the heel striking first, the rear foot and leg pushes forward and body weight transfers to

A　　B　　C　　D　　E　　F　　G　　H　　I

Fig. 2-3. Walking faults. For explanation, see text.

the forward foot in a continuously interchanging movement. The most common defects in walking are spraddle-footed, toes-out waddling (A); the pigeon-toed, awkward gait (B); the arm thrasher who pumps her way along (C); the bouncing head bobber (D); the heel thrower and rain splasher whose hose and shoes become well mud-caked in inclement weather (E); the lost-coin searcher who keeps her head down, hopefully looking for the penny she dropped as a child (F); the stomper (G); the shuffler (H); and the bent-knee, high-heel bobber whose Achilles tendon has become shortened from wearing high heels for too long a period (I).

The points you should remember about walking are:

1. Point toes ahead. Weight moves from heel, to outside of foot, to metatarsals.
2. Swing the legs alternately from the hips.
3. Swing the arms freely and rhythmically.
4. Keep tall and up.
5. Balance each body part.
6. Do not sway from side to side.
7. Walk in two imaginary lines, straight lines, one for each foot.
8. Move vigorously at a rhythmic gait.
9. Walk—do not ride—every chance you have; climb stairs instead of using an elevator if you want to have and keep a trim, attractive figure.
10. Walk briskly at least six blocks daily; hike at least three miles once a week.
11. Do not take a hike of 10 or more miles without first conditioning yourself.
12. On long hikes wear two pairs of socks—a wool pair over a cotton pair—and wear low-heeled shoes that are longer and wider than your street shoes.

STAIR CLIMBING

Stair climbing is one of the best hip reducers, for it eliminates muscle flabbiness and increases organic vigor and muscular strength. It takes 15 to 17.7 times more energy to climb an ordinary flight of stairs than it does to walk on the level a distance equal to the height of the flight of stairs. Although it takes only one-third the amount of energy to come down that it does to go up stairs, even this requires more energy than walking in a straight line.

Points to remember:

Correct

Incorrect

Fig. 2-4. Stair climbing.

1. Keep the body balanced.
2. Tuck in hips and pull in stomach.
3. Incline slightly forward from the ankles, keeping the back straight.
4. Plant the whole foot firmly on each step before moving the body.
5. Make your legs move you up or down; use the handrail for safety, not to pull yourself along.
6. Lower body gradually through the knees to the next stair.
7. Transfer weight over the whole foot, keeping toes straight ahead.

STANDING STATIONARY

Standing for a long time, in a cafeteria line, for example, is less fatiguing if you keep your

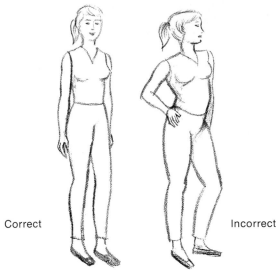

Correct   Incorrect

Fig. 2-5. Standing stationary.

Fig. 2-6. Running.

weight evenly distributed on both feet. For a short rest period, place one foot slightly in front of the other, keeping shoulders and weight balanced. Other points to remember are:

1. Be relaxed.
2. Stand tall, with rear tucked in and stomach pulled in.
3. Keep hands loosely at your sides, or clasped loosely in front.
4. Avoid having one hand on your hip, rocking, drooping, or standing with feet far apart.

RUNNING

Running requires a longer, more rapid stride and arm swing than walking, and a springing takeoff from the toes instead of the whole foot. Although the body leans slightly forward, the back should be in a straight line. Points to remember:

1. Keep body erect.
2. Swing legs rhythmically from the hip joint. Knees are flexed.
3. Lean slightly forward from the hips.
4. Avoid vigorously pumping the arms and shoulders; bend the elbows and let the swing be a natural movement as you run faster.

SITTING

The human anatomy was not designed for sitting. This is one reason we get tired when we sit for a long time. Because of automation we are fast becoming a sedentary nation, and "sititis" affects every age group. Since you will be sitting much of the time in college, you can avoid fatigue by following these suggestions:

1. Sit up straight with your shoulders parallel; pull in your stomach. Keep hips all the way to back of seat and sit evenly on both hips and legs.
2. When studying, sit up straight with rear touching the seat back. Sit at a desk of correct height so that you do not have to lean forward or down to read. Keep both feet on the floor.
3. Keep a relaxed but not tense position.
4. Keep your feet and knees closer together.
5. When leaning forward, keep your back straight, bend from the hips instead of from the waist.
6. Work and study with elbows close to your body.
7. Keep hands relaxed and close together.
8. Cross legs at the ankles or knees, and keep in good balance, distributing weight evenly.
9. To get up, move feet close to the chair, shift weight to forward foot, push with the back leg and rise.
10. To sit down, get close to the chair so that the calf of one leg touches it. Place the toes of the other foot back under the chair

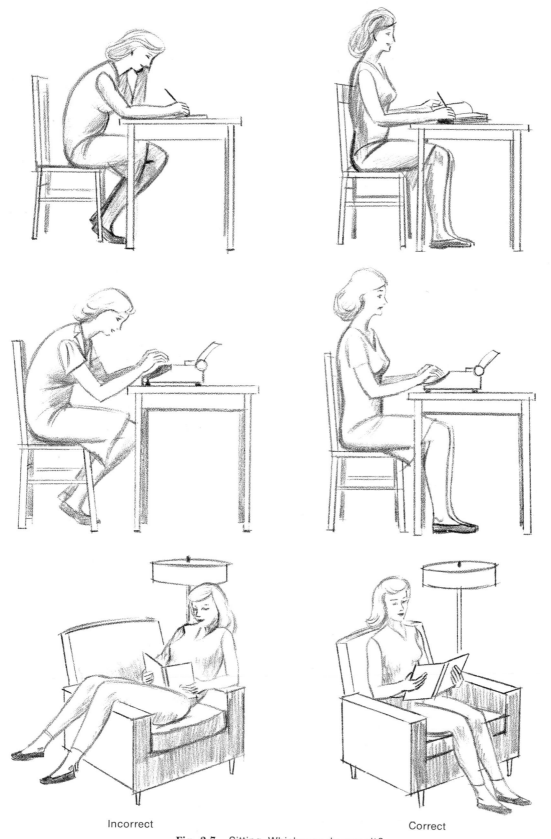

Incorrect   Correct

Fig. 2-7. Sitting. Which way do you sit?

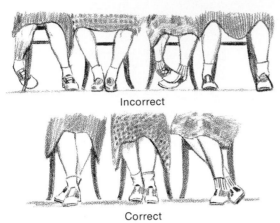

Incorrect

Correct

Fig. 2-8.   Position of feet in sitting.

Incorrect   Correct

Fig. 2-9.   Lifting with both hands.

edge. Sit down slowly, keeping body line straight.

11. When sitting on the floor, sit on both hips with weight evenly balanced, body line straight. For some, going down to one or both knees and getting up the same way is the best procedure. Do not use your hands or arms for assistance.

12. In driving a car, sit up straight, weight evenly distributed and your rear against the seat back. Relax, guide the car, and enjoy your trip!

LIFTING

This movement, when improperly done, often is damaging as well as painful to the body, especially to the back. Points to remember are:

1. First, stand tall, stomach in, body in a straight line.

2. Place feet close to object to be lifted, with one foot slightly forward. If object is heavy enough to require both hands to lift it, spread feet shoulder width apart.

3. Bend at the hips, knees, and ankles, keeping body erect. Grasp object, and lift with the *leg* muscles.

4. Do not try to lift loads too heavy for you. As Steinhaus warns, "because of the weakness of the female's pelvic floor, [a woman] should avoid jumping from heights, heavy lifting, and other activities which greatly increase intra-abdominal pressure."* If the object is

*Steinhaus, Arthur: "Fitness and How We May Attain It," *Journal of Health and Physical Education*, 14:456, October, 1943.

too heavy for you to lift, call someone to help you.

5. Put your hands under the object and lift slowly. If it is very heavy, lift it first to a knee, to the hip, then up to the chest. Easy does it. Set objects down by reversing the process.

CARRYING

Markets and book stores often supply women with carts for shopping. Unfortu-

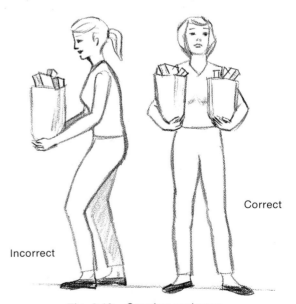

Correct

Incorrect

Fig. 2-10.   Carrying packages.

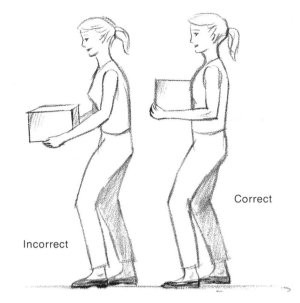

Fig. 2-11. Carrying a heavy box.

Incorrect

Correct

nately, there are times when we all have to carry heavy objects such as groceries or suitcases. According to orthopedic specialists, a woman should not lift or carry any load that weighs more than one-fourth of her own weight. Points to remember when doing so are:

1. Pull in your stomach and stand erect.
2. Carry a heavy load up on one shoulder or on one hip, but do change side positions often.

3. When carrying a suitcase with one hand, raise the opposite arm for better balance, keep shoulders even with body's straight line.
4. When carrying two heavy packages, carry one on each side of your body.
5. When carrying a load on your back, keep weight evenly distributed and in the middle of your back. Bend slightly forward from the hips, but keep back straight.
6. Do not push one hip out for a carrying shelf when carrying books. Change side carrying positions often.

Fig. 2-12. Carrying a suitcase.

Incorrect

Correct

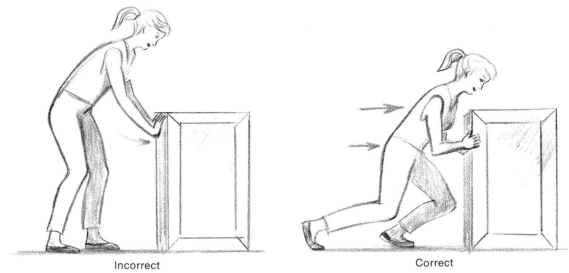

Incorrect   Correct

Fig. 2-13. Pushing.

PUSHING AND PULLING

When you clean house, you must move furniture around. It is easier for a woman to push or pull a heavy load than to carry it. The two movements are similar, for pushing is the reverse of pulling. When pushing:

1. Push mostly with your leg muscles.
2. Place both hands at center of object. Keep your back straight. Stand as close to object as possible.
3. Spread feet apart, with one foot forward, and push in the direction you want to move.

4. Relax knees, keep your back straight but lean slightly forward and push by walking forward slowly.

When pulling heavy objects, points to remember are:

1. Pull directly toward you from the front and center of the object.
2. Use a rope to pull things close to the ground, such as a sled or heavy box.
3. Pull mostly with your leg muscles, and bend your body slightly toward the direction you are pulling.

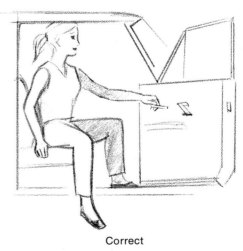

Incorrect   Correct

Fig. 2-14. Getting into a car.

Table 2-1.   *The Basic Movement Skills Used in Sports and Games**

Standing	Walking	Running and Stopping	Jumping, Leaping, Hopping, etc.	Landing and Falling	Sitting	Pushing and Pulling	Holding, Lifting, Carrying	Throwing† and Catching	Striking†
All activities except:	All activities except:	Badminton	Apparatus	Apparatus	Canoeing	Archery	Canoeing	Apparatus (spotting-catching)	Badminton
Canoeing	Archery	Baseball-Softball	Basketball	Baseball-Softball	Crew	Canoeing	Dance	Baseball-Softball	Baseball-Softball
Crew	Canoeing	Basketball	Dance	Basketball	Modern Dance	Crew	Tumbling	Basketball	Basketball
Riding	Crew	Dance	Diving	Dance	Riding	Dance	Weight Lifting	Bowling (throwing)	Boxing
Swimming	Riding	Football	Skiing	Football		Fencing	Wrestling	Deck Tennis	Football
	Shuffle-board	Handball	Track and Field	Skiing		Riding		Football	Golf
	Weight Lifting	Hockey	Tumbling	Tumbling		Shot Put	Also, carrying equipment for many activities such as Golf Skiing	Lacrosse	Handball
		Lacrosse	Volleyball	Track and Field		Shuffle-board		Track and Field	Hockey
	Note: use of walking coordination in crawl kick in swimming	Soccer		Volleyball		Swimming		Tumbling (spotting-catching)	Squash
		Speedball		Wrestling		Wrestling		Speed-A-Way	Rackets
		Speed-A-Way						Speedball	Soccer
		Squash							Speed-A-Way
		Rackets						Some application of throwing to: Hockey (Roll-in) Soccer (Goalie)	Speedball
		Tennis							Table-Tennis
		Track and Field							Tennis
									Volleyball

*Adapted from Broer, Marion, *Efficiency of Human Movement*, 2nd ed., W. B. Saunders Company, Philadelphia, 1966.
†Use the same basic movement patterns.

GETTING INTO AND OUT OF A CAR

This is easier to do in some makes of cars than others. It can be done gracefully when getting into most automobiles by remembering to:

1. First sit on the seat, face to the outside.
2. Swing one foot in and forward, then the next.
3. Swing the body around, facing forward with the second leg movement, sit erect, keep shoulders balanced, and your rear far back in the seat.
4. In getting out of car, reverse order of actions.

SUGGESTIONS FOR THE BEST USE OF THE BODY IN HOUSEHOLD TASKS

In spite of modern conveniences, most college girls who marry will do their own housework, at least during some part of their married life. Many of them, knowing that they have just so much energy, will learn how to use it wisely by knowing how to conserve and replenish it.

1. Take it slow and easy. Rest and relax at frequent intervals by wiggling, stretching, sitting down after standing over a long time period, or by rolling your head in a large circle on your shoulders, or becoming a rag doll by bending from the waist, shaking yourself in order to become as relaxed and "loose" as you can. Another easy method is to clench both fists as hard as you can, hold it, and then let go completely. Next, tighten and relax other body parts, then as many combinations or parts as you can.
2. Build strength and endurance by using brisk movements for sweeping, dusting, and other tasks.
3. Reach and stretch with your whole body when getting things off of high shelves. Stand on your tiptoes and s-t-r-e-t-c-h!
4. Pull in your stomach and hold it as long as you can (but not your breath) every time you brush your teeth, walk down the street, answer the phone, or at other times best for your daily scheduled routine.

5. Grasp or touch the top of a door sill when going into certain rooms as many times a day as you can. Stretch and hold this position for 10 or more counts. Do this one often, too.
6 Sit when ironing, peeling vegetables, and so forth, but be sure your work space is the right height and that you do not have to bend too far over. When necessary, bend from the hips, keeping the body in a straight line.
7. Stand on both feet, keeping shoulders and body balanced.
8. Use a long-handled mop for scrubbing rather than doing it on your hands and knees. Put a lot of vigor into each scrub!
9. Avoid backstrains by having sinks and work tables high enough so that you do not have to bend over. Stand with weight evenly distributed and pull "in and up" frequently as you work.
10. When picking up a baby or an object from the floor, kneel on one knee, keep your body erect and lift slowly.

APPLYING MOVEMENT SKILLS TO SPORTS

Most sports utilize the basic movement skills of standing, walking, running and stopping, jumping, sliding, landing, throwing, catching, and striking.* Most such physical activities require that you be on your feet, be able to move quickly, changing from one direction and position to another, and be able to remain balanced, triggered for anticipated action. Many sports, such as hockey, basketball, tennis, or lacrosse, are based upon each player's skill at starting and stopping quickly, as well as increasing and decreasing speed in order to catch, kick, or strike a fast moving, approaching object. Some activities, such as basketball, diving, and trampolining, can be done successfully only by having enough explosive power to project, fold, and thrust the body out into space, and sufficient control balance to land without injury on the floor or field, or in the water.

As Broer shows in Table 2-1, since certain

---

*Any of the movement skills not described in this chapter will be discussed farther on.

basic movement skills are common to many different sports, to be well skilled physically requires mastery of the many mechanics found in basic body movement.

Suggested Readings

Broer, Marion: *Efficiency of Human Movement*, 2nd Ed., Philadelphia, W. B. Saunders Company, 1966.

Cratty, Bryant: *Movement Behavior and Motor Learning*, 2nd Ed., Philadelphia, W. B. Saunders Company, 1967.

Shifferes, Justus: *Essentials of Healthier Living*, 3rd Ed., New York, John Wiley & Sons, Inc., 1967.

Wessel, Janet: *Movement Fundamentals*, 2nd Ed., Englewood Cliffs, N.J., Prentice-Hall, Inc., 1961.

Williams, Jesse F., and Kitzinger, Angela: *Health for the College Student*, 2nd Ed., New York, Harper and Row, 1967.

Suggested Study Questions

1. Determine whether or not you have good posture by checking it with the aid of a partner.
2. Describe the correct way to carry books, pick up a baby from the floor, or get into a car.
3. Demonstrate the correct way to walk, sit in a chair, and run.
4. According to Steinhaus, women should not lift heavy objects that are more than one-fourth of their total body weight. Why do you think this is a good recommendation?
5. Give five suggestions for the best use of the body in performing household tasks.

CHAPTER THREE

Courtesy of Jean Jacobs, Springfield College, Springfield, Massachusetts

BODY TYPES, WEIGHT, AND FIGURE CONTROL

Those who are physically fit usually get more real enjoyment out of living. They sparkle, they are enthusiastic, they are fun to be with, and usually do better work both in and out of school. They look better and feel better than their classmates who are less healthy. Anyone can become physically fit if she is willing to exercise 20 minutes daily, eat a controlled, balanced diet, have defects corrected, and follow a daily routine of good health habits. Fitness, however, must be maintained when reached. Being in a good physical condition while in college is no guarantee that you will still be fit at the age of 30. Your college physical education, however, can help you become healthier and happier as a student, help you to understand why daily exercise is necessary for good health, teach you a movement—exercise vocabulary that can be modified in later years, and teach you that health and fitness are a vital part of life. Whether or not you take care of your body now or in the future depends on the effectiveness of your physical education and on how much you want to master yourself and your appetite for food.

WHAT KIND OF SHAPE ARE YOU REALLY IN?

Every person has her own body build (somatotype), depending on fat distribution, muscularity, and linearity. There are three distinct body types.

The Endomorph (A Well-Padded, Square Box). This type is big, soft, and square, and has accumulated fat in the areas of the stomach, thighs and rear, neck, and upper arms, but usually has small hands, feet, wrists, and ankles, and relatively short arms and legs. Such a person moves slowly and often awkwardly because of her excessive bulk. She always has a girth and weight problem, and tends to be either happy-go-lucky and popular or a resentful left-outer.

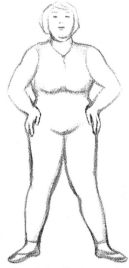

Fig. 3-1. Endomorph.

The Mesomorph (Ideal Average, Inverted Triangle). This type has a well formed, hard, well kept body with well proportioned legs. Although somewhat short, has firm muscles, slender waistline, narrow hips,

Fig. 3-2. Mesomorph.

29

Fig. 3-3. Ectomorph.

ties. Oddly enough, she frequently outlives those of the other two types because, throughout the years, she has learned to protect her health.

FINDING YOUR FIGURE TYPE

To analyze your figure type, stand in the nude, or in shorts or leotards, before a mirror. See if you look like a box, or an inverted triangle, or if you are pencil thin. Next, check for accumulated body fat by pinching the skin around your stomach, hips, neck, and the back of the neck. If you can pinch as much as half an inch around your stomach and hips, this is a sign of stored fat that should be discarded and of need for exercise. If, when you tightly tense your stomach, leg, or hip muscles and flex your arm or leg muscles, they feel hard and firm, you have good muscle tone. If they feel soft and flabby, your muscles lack tonus and are in poor condition, and you have much exercising to do to get them back into good shape.

topped by broader shoulders. She tends to be an extrovert and is especially good in sports that call for agility, balance, strength, and endurance.

The Ectomorph (Frail, Thin and Pencil-Like). This type has a tall, frail, and slim body; long, thin, graceful hands and feet; small, underdeveloped muscles; narrow, sloping shoulders; a long waistline; and long arms and legs. She is constantly trying to gain weight, but in spite of increased caloric intake remains frail and fragile. She tires easily and lacks the energy required for strenuous activi-

YOUR BODY MEASUREMENTS

Measure your neck, upper arm, waist, both thighs, calf, and ankle, using a tape measure. A well proportioned body should have:*

*Wessel, Janet: *Movement Fundamentals, Figure, Form, Fun*, 2nd Ed. Englewood Cliffs, N.J., Prentice-Hall, Inc., 1961, p. 42.

	NOW	1st MONTH	2nd MONTH	3rd MONTH	4th MONTH	GOAL
NECK Just Under Chin	12					
BUST At Fullest Part	34 7/8					
WAIST At Narrowest Part	25 3/8					
ARM Close to Armpit	10 1/4					
THIGH At Largest Part	22 3/4					
CALF At Largest Part	12 3/8					

Fig. 3-4. A chart for recording body measurements.

1. A waistline 8 to 10 inches smaller than the bust circumference (measured at maximum bust curve).

2. Hips (measured at the largest part of your buttocks) 1 to 2 inches larger than the bust. (Full hips measure 3 to 4 inches larger, while slim hips measure the same as the bust.)

3. Calf measurements (taken at largest part of the lower leg) 4 to 5 inches larger than your ankle.

4. Ankles 10 to 13 inches smaller than your thighs.

Record your measurements on a chart like the one in Figure 3-4, and if they need improvement, check the measurements monthly until you have reached your goal.

YOUR LEGS AND FEET

In front of a mirror, compare yourself with the illustrations on this page to see if your knees knock or sway too far back, or if you have bowed legs. Next, standing as you normally do, check to see if you carry your weight on the inner borders of your ankles (ankle pronation), on the outer borders (ankle supination), or through the center of your foot, which is the correct way. Now take a good look at your feet. See if you have hammertoe, corns, bunions, or flat or high arches. If so, you need to buy more comfortably fitting shoes.

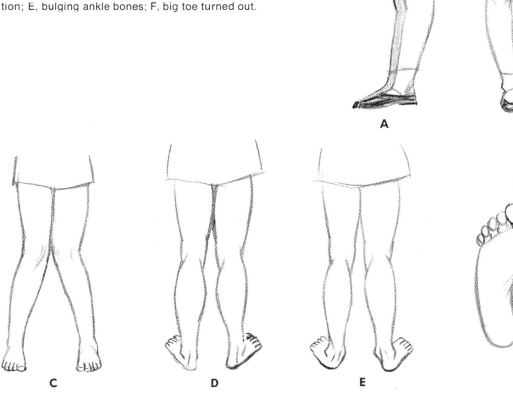

Fig. 3-5. Common leg and foot faults. A, Back knees; B, bowlegs, C, knock-knees, D, ankle pronation; E, bulging ankle bones; F, big toe turned out.

Table 3-1. Desirable Weights for Girls
18 Years of Age*

Height (with flat heels)		Weight (as ordinarily dressed)		
		Small Frame	Medium Frame	Large Frame
Feet	Inches			
4	10	98-106	105-113	112-122
4	11	100-108	107-115	114-124
5	0	103-111	110-118	117-128
5	1	106-114	113-121	120-131
5	2	109-118	117-125	124-135
5	3	112-121	120-128	126-138
5	4	116-125	123-133	131-143
5	5	119-129	127-137	135-147
5	6	122-132	130-140	138-151
5	7	126-136	134-144	142-155
5	8	129-140	138-148	145-159
5	9	132-143	141-151	148-162

*Adapted from tables prepared by the Metropolitan Life Insurance Company. Women between 18 and 25 should add one pound for each year over 18.

Weight Record

Date	Weight	Date	Weight

Fig. 3-6. A moderately active woman of medium frame who is five feet five inches tall should weigh about 134 pounds. If she weighs more, this is how she can calculate her daily calorie quota for losing one pound a week:

She finds her normal requirement . . .
    134 × 15 = 2010 calories
She subtracts 500 calories
(from her body fat)

She learns that . . .
    1510 calories is her daily quota for reducing

(American Institute of Baking: *Eat and Grow Slim.* By permission.)

YOUR HEIGHT AND WEIGHT

Next check your height and weight according to Table 3-1, which shows your ideal weight for your height and body frame. The table is for girls of 18. If you are older, add one pound for each year over 18, up to age 25.

Record your findings on a chart like that in Figure 3-6. Weigh youself at least once weekly, preferably in the morning, while in the nude or your underwear. You will be slightly heavier and shorter by nightfall!

WEIGHT CONTROL AND THE DIET

Because of the dangerous consequences of obesity, it is important that you acquire eating habits that will help you to maintain your most desirable weight, as calculated from Table 3-1.

Dr. Thomas Cureton, an expert on physical fitness, recommends that the fat person use as many as possible of the following methods for reducing fat:

1. Regulation of diet to reduce intake of fats and carbohydrates
2. Endurance running
3. Doubling up on periods of physical activity
4. Exercising in heavy sweat or rubber clothes
5. Relatively cold baths and showers
6. Massage of fat parts such as the abdomen (while contracting the muscles)
7. Drinking less water and adding more iodized salt to the diet*

TIPS ON NUTRITION

Most students gain weight in college, especially during the first year. Those goodie boxes from home make for wonderful room parties and can help you to make friends (at least the eating kind) fast. If you are concerned about having and keeping a good figure, however, avoid them as you would a rattlesnake.

It is also important that your diet contain essential proteins, vitamins, and minerals. The following list will guide you in selecting the protective foods you need each day:

*Cureton, Thomas: *Physical Fitness and Dynamic Health,* New York, The Dial Press, pp. 78-79.

Meat or an Alternate—*2 or more*
servings
(Total: 4 ounces)

Meat, fish, poultry, eggs, and cheese—along with dry peas and beans as alternates—supply needed top-quality protein. Some of these are good sources of B vitamins and iron as well. Be a Jack Sprat and select meats low in fat, for these are also lower in calories. Trim off whatever fat you can see. Avoid adding fat in cooking and in serving.

Here is a quick guide to judge cooked meat portions and their alternates:

2 ounces lean meat—2 thin slices,
     4-inch square
2-ounce meat patty—3-inch diameter,
     1/2-inch thick
2 ounces fish fillet—4-inch square,
     1/2-inch thick
2 ounces cottage cheese—1/4 cup
2 ounces cheddar cheese—2 thin
     slices, 4-inch square
2 ounces poultry—2 slices breast
     meat or its equivalent

Eggs belong in your diet, too.
One a day, or five a week will do.

Fats—*3 teaspoons daily*

Use your quota of fats where you like it most—as a spread on bread or as an oil in salad dressing. Foods prepared with extra fat or thickened sauces have no place in a reducing diet.

Vegetables and Fruits—*4 or more*
servings

Include a dark green or deep yellow vegetable or fruit—important for vitamin A—at least every other day. Many of these also provide worthwhile amounts of iron, calcium, and the B vitamin, riboflavin.

Include, daily, a vitamin C-rich fruit or vegetable, such as citrus fruit, tomato, raw cabbage, green pepper, broccoli, sweet potatoes, or cantaloupe.

Add other fruits and vegetables, including potatoes. Potatoes are eaten daily by many Americans and are an important source of vitamin C, iron, and the B vitamins, thiamine and niacin.

Vegetables, important for their vitamin and mineral content, are especially valuable in a reducing diet. Green and raw, they can be eaten in quantity and add their special flavor and crunch besides. Use vegetables plain or in a salad. Limit the dressings and flavorings, however, to spices, a dash of lemon juice, or vinegar.

Fruits add zest, but check them for calories. Some are sweeter than you think. Fresh fruits and those packed without sugar contain fewer calories than those packed in sirup.

Desserts

Desserts can be nutritious as well as delicious, but remember, they are part of your meal.*

EATING TO LOSE WEIGHT

Obesity is a vicious merry-go-round. The fatter you are, the more you eat; the more you eat, the fatter you get. Obesity shortens life; it is a self-imposed early death sentence resulting from the overuse of the suicide weapons knife, fork, and spoon. It is expensive, for fat people eat more and need expensive, outsize clothes. Overweight is also tiring, a fact you will fully appreciate if you pick up a suitcase weighing 20 pounds. With every 100 steps you will not only be tired, but you will have done 2000 foot pounds of work. Fat people tire more easily and tend to have emotional problems that prompt them to feed their damaged egos through compulsive but comforting eating. Obesity places a tremendous additional work load on the heart. Every pound of fat requires about 4500 feet of blood vessels, and expansion of the capillaries. Overweight, with its resulting possibilities of heart disease, gallbladder and liver trouble, hernia, and diabetes, is one of our major health problems. Heart disease is the chief cause of death among American adults. According to medical findings, out of every ten fat people aged 30, six will be alive at 60, and three at 70, whereas among ten normal weight people of 30, eight will be alive at 60, and five at 70. Between the ages of 20 and 65, the mortality rate for fat people averages 15 per cent higher than for normal people.†

Although weight can be lost quickly through the reduction of caloric intake and crash diets, such measures are extremely dangerous unless they are being carried out under medical supervision. Certainly there is much truth in the saying, "She who doctors

---

*American Institute of Baking: *Eat and Grow Slim*, Chicago, 1961, pp. 11-12. By permission.

†Williams, Andrew: *You Can Reduce*, Heathside Press, 303 Fifth Avenue, New York, 1962, p. 16.

herself is doctored by a fool." Excessive dieting brings only temporary results and leaves one physically soft and weakened. The scientific answer to weight reduction lies in *diet control together with increased exercise. People are fat because they eat too much and are underactive*; in fact, only 5 per cent of all obesity is due to glandular imbalance. Overeating is largely due to psychological, not physical, needs. Nor is obesity a family trait. Overstuffing may be a long-standing family habit, however. In order to eat less, new eating patterns must develop from a desire to become and stay slim. Such new habits take time and much real determination, for one cannot undo in a few days a routine that has been established for years. To reduce, one needs to develop her *won't power* ("No, I won't have an ice cream soda; I won't overeat") as well as her *will power* ("I am determined to lose weight; I will eat less at each of my three meals today"). Note in Table 3-2 how many calories you need daily.

If you want to reduce more than five pounds, do so only under the direction of a doctor. Weight loss should be slow and steady, not more than two pounds a week. Going without food, skipping breakfast, or eating only bananas or milk are all dangerous practices. Many people who think they can melt off extra pounds by strenuous exercise should know that this is a foolish and almost impossible thing to do. Table 3-3 shows how many calories various activities

Table 3-2. *Calorie Allowances for Women of Various Body Weights**

| | Calorie Allowances | | |
Desirable Weight	25 Years of Age	45 Years of Age	65 Years of Age
88	1750	1650	1400
99	1900	1800	1500
110	2050	1950	1600
121	2200	2050	1750
128	2300	2200	1800
132	2350	2250	1850
143	2500	2350	2000
154	2600	2450	2050
165	2750	2600	2150

*At a mean environmental temperature of 68 degrees F. and assuming moderate physical activity. Prepared by the Food and Nutrition Board of the National Academy of Sciences—National Research Council.

Table 3-3. *The Calories You Use per Hour per Single Pound of Your Weight**

Activity	Calories Used†
Sleeping	.43
Awake, motionless	.50
"Just sitting"	.65
Standing relaxed	.69
Hand sewing	.72
Typewriting rapidly	.91
Ironing, dishwashing	.93
"Light" exercise	1.10
Walking slowly	1.30
Carpentry	1.56
"Active" exercise	1.88
Walking downstairs	2.36
"Severe" exercise	2.92
Swimming	3.25
Running	3.70
"Very severe" exercise	3.90
Walking fast (5.3 mph)	4.22
Walking upstairs	7.18

*From *A New Figure in 30 Days*, New York, Dell Publishing Co. Dell Purse Book No. 6324.

†Multiply by your weight to find out how much energy you use.

require. As one of our leading physiologists, Steinhaus, has found, to lose a single pound a man weighing 155 pounds would have to walk 44 miles or run 129 separate 100-yard dashes in 10 seconds each. Furthermore, taking drugs to reduce is extremely risky unless one does so under a doctor's supervision. It is only when calorie intake balances energy output that one can keep weight steady. Consequently, self-discipline is needed. Dietary tips for reducing are:

1. Eat less, but be sure that you eat three well balanced meals daily.

2. Eat a light breakfast of 200 to 300 calories for this will help you eat less for lunch and dinner.

3. Reduce your daily number of calories by 500 (which would bring the loss of one pound in a week), but not more than 700, by eating filling foods low in calories such as skim milk, lean meat, eggs, deep yellow or dark green leafy vegetables, two thin slices of bread, and a potato each day.

4. Eat slowly.

5. If preparing your own meals, use a garnish of watercress for the meat, or paprika over cottage cheese, and so on, for color adds

to eye and appetite appeal, making nonfattening foods attractive.

6. Avoid the *snack* pit. It you must munch, nibble on unsalted celery stalks, carrot sticks, or fresh fruit.

7. Stay away from carbonated drinks, alcohol, peanuts, and anything made with chocolate, for they are all loaded with calories.

Whether you need to gain or lose weight, the calorie chart in Table 3-4 will prove helpful.

Table 3-4. *100-Calorie Portions**

Since there is some variation in the proportions of foodstuffs in given foods and in the size of servings, this table cannot be considered entirely accurate, but it shows in a general way how much of the various sorts of foods, as served, will provide about 100 calories.

Meat and Fish

Tenderloin steak	slice 2 × 1 × 1 inches
Hamburg steak	1 medium cake
Roast beef	slice 4 × 2 × ¼ inches
Corned beef	small serving
Lamb, roast	medium serving
Lamb chop	small chop
Pork, roast, lean	medium serving
Ham, boiled or roasted	small serving
Bacon, fried	4 or 5 small slices
Frankfurters	1
Chicken, roast	medium serving
Fish	medium to large serving
Sardines	3-6

Eggs

Raw or cooked	1 very large
	1⅓ medium

Vegetables

Asparagus	20 stalks
Beans, baked	⅓ cup
Beans, string	2 cups
Beets	1⅓ cups
Cabbage, shredded	5 cups
Carrots	1½ cups
Cauliflower	small head
Celery	1 bunch
Corn, canned	⅓ cup
Corn, on cob	2 small ears
Lettuce	2 large heads
Onions	3 to 4 (2 servings)
Peas	¾ cup
Potatoes	
boiled or baked	1 large
sweet	½

Spinach	2½ cups
Tomatoes	
canned	1¾ cups
fresh	4 medium

Fruits

Apple	2
Applesauce	⅜ cup
Apricots (canned)	3 halves with 2 tablespoonfuls of juice
Banana	1 large
Blueberries (fresh)	1 cup
Cantaloupe	1 melon (4½″ diameter)
Fig	1 large
Grapes, Concord	1 large bunch
Orange	1 very large
Peach	3
Pear	1 large
Pineapple (canned)	1 slice with juice
Prunes, stewed	3 medium, with juice
Strawberries (fresh)	1⅓ cups

Cereals

Cornflakes	1¼ cups
Grape Nuts	3 tablespoonfuls
Oatmeal, cooked	1 cup
Shredded wheat	1 biscuit

Dairy Products

Butter or margarine	½ oz. or 1 tablespoonful
Cream	¼ cup
Cheese, American	1½″ cube
Cheese, cottage	½ cup
Milk	small glass (⅝ cup)

Bread, Rolls, and Crackers

Bread	thick slice, medium size
Graham crackers	2
Saltines	6
Griddle cakes	1 cake (4½″ diameter)

Desserts

Custard	⅓ cup
Ice cream, average	2½ heaping tablespoonfuls
Chocolate sauce	1 tablespoonful
Sherbet and water ices	½ cup
Milk sherbet	¼ cup
Jello with cream	½ cup
Baked apple with sugar and cream	¼ large
Ric pudding with cream	½ serving
Pie	(1″-2″ sector (diam. 9″)
Doughnuts	½
Gingerbread	2″ cube
Macaroons	2
Fudge cake	slice (2 × 1 × 1 inches)

Accessories

Sugar	2 tablespoonfuls
Honey	1 tablespoonful
Maple syrup	1½ tablespoonfuls
Marmalade	3 teaspoonfuls

*From *Health and Fitness,* by Florence Meredith, Leslie Irwin, and Wesley Staton, Boston. D.C. Health and Company, 1962. By permission.

(Table 3-4 continued on page 36.)

Nuts

Peanuts	10-12 double
Walnuts	8-16
Peanut butter	2½ teaspoonfuls

Candy

Fudge	1 large piece
Caramels	1″ cube
Chocolate peppermint	one medium

Soups

Bouillon	4 cups
Cream soup, average	2 plates
Bean soup	large plate

Dressing

Mayonnaise dressing	1 tablespoonful
Olive oil	1 tablespoonful

Beverages

Cocoa, average	½ cup
Lemonade	large glass (1⅔ cups)
Orange juice	1 cup
Grape juice	½ cup

EATING TO GAIN WEIGHT

To gain weight, plan a diet that will provide from 500 to 1000 additional calories in excess of body needs. Try to gain one to two pounds a week steadily. Other recommendations for gaining weight include:

1. Eat more carbohydrates, fats, and other foods than you usually do.
2. Have between-meal snacks such as malted milk shakes, ice cream sundaes.
3. Drink a glass of milk with every meal.
4. Have a glass of milk with graham crackers and peanut butter or cookies before going to bed each night.

THE ROLE OF EXERCISE IN FITNESS

To be fit you should have:
1. Optimum organic health consistent with heredity and the application of present health knowledge;
2. Sufficient corrdination, strength, and vitality to meet emergencies, as well as the requirements of daily living;
3. Emotional stability to meet the stresses and strains of modern life;
4. Social consciousness and adaptability with respect to the requirements of group living;
5. Sufficient knowledge and insight to make suitable decisions and arrive at feasible solutions to problems;
6. Attitudes, values, and skills which stimulate satisfactory participation in a full range of daily activities;
7. Spiritual and moral qualities which contribute the fullest measure of living in a democratic society.*

Exercise, good nutrition, sufficient rest and relaxation, satisfying work, regular physical and dental examinations, and moderation in eating, drinking, and smoking are important in maintaining fitness. Since exercise is one of the most important factors contributing to health and total well-being, the ability to recuperate after vigorous physical activity is a good guide to the type and amount of exercise best for each age group. If ten minutes after exercising you are still breathless and your heart is pounding, if you feel persistent fatigue after a two-hour rest period, or if you still feel weary and worn out the next day, the exercise has been too severe or continued over too long a period. You should push yourself beyond your fatigue level when exercising daily, however, in order to build up endurance and strength. Consequently, contract your muscles at least once a day until they quiver, for only by reaching this maximum "overload" can they grow stronger in order to do a whole day's work more easily. Muscles thus contracted once daily for a week will become 4 per cent stronger, 8 per cent in two weeks, and so on.† Women who fear that exercise will make them look like Tarzan need to be reminded that behind every curve there must be a muscle. Exercise tends to distribute weight rather than bunching it. Other helpful exercise facts are:

1. Exercise tones the body and develops attractive lines in the right places. It cannot produce spot or overall reducing unless calorie intake is also decreased. It is one of two means of developing and keeping an attractive and efficiently working body, the other being through eating a controlled, balanced diet.
2. A vigorous daily workout of 20 minutes keeps the body in good working condition

---

*Statement prepared and approved by the 100 delegates to the AAHPER Fitness Conference, Washington, D.C., September 14-15, 1956.

†Steinhaus, Arthur: *How To Keep Fit and Like It*, Chicago, The Dartnell Corporation, 1957, p. 5.

and more flexible. It also increases health and zest for living.

3. It is much easier to keep a good figure than to regain it. Ninety days of inactivity will undo 60 days of training.

4. To be most effective, exercise must be done daily throughout life. It should become a routine health habit.

5. Swimming, skiing, vigorous walking, rope jumping, and running are excellent overall developmental activities and fast calorie burners.

6. Exercise, together with weight control, is the most successful means of preventing or retarding the degenerative diseases of later life.

7. Regular exercise keeps a person young, and probably exerts a favorable influence upon longevity.

8. Conditioning the body through daily exercise prepares one to meet emergencies better, and so in turn preserves health.*

9. Exercise helps one to gain strength, build endurance, and perfect movement skills.

10. Because of variations in body build, strength, physical constitution, and differences in experience and condition, diet and exercise must be geared to each individual's needs.

11. After the age of 40, frequent evaluation of a person's capacity and physical exercise program is imperative. Highly competitive sports should not be played after the age of 30 unless one has maintained or can attain an appropriate fitness.

12. Those who are "soft" and out of training should take part in a gradual conditioning program.

EXERCISES FOR BODY CONDITIONING AND FIGURE CONTROL

If your weight is just right for your age and height (see Table 3-1), vigorous daily physical activity will help you to keep it that way. Remember, though, that the proper kind and amount of exercise (which affects shape) must be accompanied by a well controlled diet (which affects weight). A total

*Hein, Fred, and Ryan, Allan: "The Contributions of Physical Activity to Physical Health," *The Research Quarterly*, 31:2, May, 1960, pp. 263-285.

body workout for 20 minutes daily is recommended. It is best to do movements to music; records with a strong 4/4 beat and a peppy tune such as "Oh, What a Beautiful Morning" are stimulating, for the swing of the music makes you want to move and keep time to it. Radio music can also be used, or you can set a steady rhythmic pattern of your own by counting, for example, *bend* 1-2-3-, *back* 1-2-3. It is also fun to work out with a partner or a group. Begin gradually, doing 8 to 10 minutes for the first several days, but increase your time to 20 or more minutes as soon as you can, judging by how refreshing you find your program.

BASIC CONDITIONING EXERCISES

RUNNING

Run in place 25 times, starting slowly, picking up speed, and then tapering off. Raise your legs high. Increase to 50 times, then to 100, 150, and finally 200.

Fig. 3-7. Running.

THE TWIST

Take a stride position, arms out at shoulder height. Twist right on 1, back to place on 2, left on 3. Repeat 25 times.

THE JUMPING JACK

Take a stride position, hands at side. On 1, bring feet together and clasp hands over

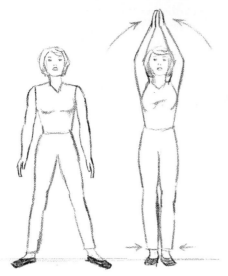

Fig. 3-8.   The jumping jack.

Fig. 3-10.   The star picker.

head. On 2, go back to stride position, hands at sides. Do 25 times.

KNEE AND ARM LIFT

Arms at sides. On 1, swing both arms up, pull in stomach, bend left leg as far as it will go. On 2, lower arms to side and bring leg down. On 3 and 4, do the same with arms and right leg. Do 25 times.

forward. On 2, lower it slightly and reach high with right arm while walking forward. Repeat 25 times.

THE SIT-UP (MODIFIED BY BENT KNEES)

Lie on your back, knees bent, hands clasped behind head. On 1, sit up, bend to touch right elbow to left knee; 2, lie back down; 3, sit up, bend touch left elbow to right knee; 4, lie back down. Do 6 to 8 times.

Fig. 3-9.   Knee and arm lift.

Fig. 3-11.   The sit-up.

THE STAR PICKER

On tiptoes stretch high with arms above head. On 1, thrust left arm higher and walk

JUMPING ROPE

With an individual rope, jump, stretching your arms high. Increase speed as you go

Fig. 3-12.   Jumping rope.

along, then taper off. Jump 50 times the first day, 60 the second, 75 the third, and so on.

LONG STRETCH

Sit with legs extended. On 1, bend to touch toes; on 2, return. Do 10 times.

Fig. 3-13.   Long stretch.

EXERCISES FOR HIPS AND LEGS

SCISSORS KICK

Lie on left side, with head resting on extended left arm. Stretch legs out. On 1, raise

Fig. 3-14.   Scissors kick.

right leg up; lower it on 2. Do 15 times. Change to right side and repeat.

THE HIP WALK

Sit, feet extended. Extend arms to front at shoulder level. On 1, shift weight to left hip and move right hip and leg forward. On 2, do the same for the left hip. Move in rhythm 10 times forward, then 10 times back.

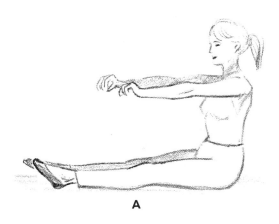

A

B

Fig. 3-15.   The hip walk.

TWISTER TOE TOUCH

Take wide stride position with arms extended over head. On 1, twist to touch right hand to left toe; 2, back to place; 3, touch left hand to right toe; 4, back to place. Do 15 times.

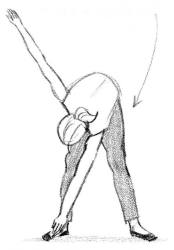

Fig. 3-16. Twister toe touch.

Do 20 times, speeding up and then slowing down again.

A

THE KNEE-TOE BALANCE

Stand straight, stomach in, hands on hips. Place instep of left foot on inside of right knee. On counts 1, 2, 3, slowly go up and down on toes. Repeat on left foot.

Fig. 3-17. The knee-toe balance.

B

Fig. 3-18. The dipsy doodle.

THE DIPSY DOODLE

With feet together, extend arms in front of you at shoulder height. On 1, touch feet; 2, return to erect position; 3, bend knees, arms extended to front; 4, back to erect position.

LEG SWINGS

Standing facing sideways, hang on to a chair or wall for support. Swing the left leg forward in rhythm, back to side, and return to front 15 times. Turn, and repeat this pattern with the right leg.

Fig. 3-19.   Leg swings.

Fig. 3-21.   Tuck and swing.

KNEE GRASP AND PULL

Stand tall. On 1, bend the left knee, grasp the lower leg, and pull toward chest as high as you can. On 2, return leg to position. Repeat with right leg on 3 and 4. Do 10 times for each leg.

touch your chin; on 2, arch back and extend leg straight back as far as possible. Do 10 times. Change legs and repeat 10 times.

LEG CIRCLE

Lie face down, chin on back of left hand, right arm straight to the side. Without turning the body, raise straightened right leg, and on counts 1, 2, 3, make 3 circles with it. Reverse positions and repeat with left leg. Do 10 times with each leg.

Fig. 3-22.   Leg circle.

Fig. 3-20.   Knee grasp and pull.

NIP OUT AND UP

Stand with feet slightly apart. On 1, squat, placing both palms on the floor. On 2, straighten knees and extend legs. On 3, return to position. Do 15 times, increasng speed between the sixth and twelfth times, then slowing down.

TUCK AND SWING

Stand erect, holding on to a practice bar or chair back. On 1, bend right leg, raise knee to

Fig. 3-23.   Nip out and up.

touch right elbow to it. On 2, uncurl slowly. Repeat with right knee bent on 3 and 4. Do 10 times. (Have someone hold your feet or place them under heavy furniture.)

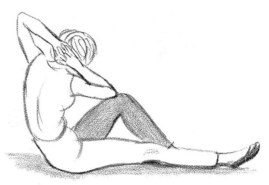

Fig. 3-25.   The curl-up.

EXERCISES FOR THE WAISTLINE

HAND AND TOE TOUCH

Stand with arms extended to the sides at shoulder level. On 1, swing left leg up to touch right hand, moving the hand as little as possible. On 2, return to place. Swing right leg to touch left hand on 3 and 4. Do 10 times.

THE JACKKNIFE

Lie flat on your back, back straight. On 1, curl body up, extend both arms forward and up, and raise both extended legs. On 2, touch ankles. On 3, slowly return to position. Do 10 times.

Fig. 3-24.   Hand and toe touch.

Fig. 3-26.   The jackknife.

NOSE TO KNEE

On hands and knees keep arms straight and head up. On 1, curl head in, bringing right knee to touch your nose. On 2, raise head back and stretch straightened leg back.

THE CURL-UP

Lie on back, hands clasped behind head, elbows out. On 1, curl trunk forward, bend left knee but keep foot on the floor, and

Fig. 3-27. Nose to knee.

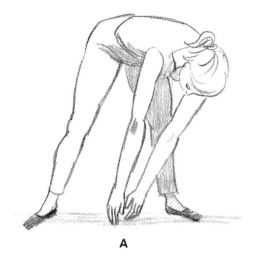

A

Do 10 times. Change, bringing left knee to touch nose, and repeat 10 times.

TWIST RIGHT AND LEFT

Stand with feet wide apart, arms out to side at shoulder level. Keep the whole of both feet, including heel, on the floor. On 1, twist to the left as far as possible. On 2, back to place. On 3, twist right; back to place on 4. Repeat with increased speed, twisting farther each time, for a total of 20 times.

B

Fig. 3-29. Eight-count stretch. A, Count 2; B, counts 5, 6, and 7.

Fig. 3-28. Twist right and left.

series with left arm down leg and right overhead for counts 5, 6, and 7. Do series 10 times on each side.

EIGHT-COUNT STRETCH

Stand erect, stomach in, hands on hips. On 1, stretch arms above head; 2, touch floor between legs with fingers or palms; 3, back to place. On 4, slide right hand as far down right leg as possible, stretch left arm overhead, bend at the waist and stretch on 5, 6, 7. On 8, return to erect position. Repeat

THREAD THE NEEDLE

Kneel, then distribute weight easily on knees and left hand. On 1, bring right shoulder to the floor and push right arm through the arch made by the left arm. On 2, withdraw right arm and stretch it briskly overhead, following movement with head and eyes. Do 10 times, thrusting arm farther

Fig. 3-30. Thread the needle.

on each through and up movement. Change position, using left arm, and repeat 10 times.

BICYCLING

Lying on your back, bicycle by stretching legs to full extension, toes pointed out. On 1, bend left leg as close to stomach as possible while extending right leg. On 2, reverse. Keep in rhythm, doing this one for the length of a whole record, pushing leg closer to the body and farther away from it each time.

Fig. 3-31. Bicycling.

THE STRETCHER

Lie on your stomach with hands clasped behind head. On 1, raise trunk to where waistband or navel touches the floor, and raise straightened legs up 7 to 10 inches from floor. Hold for 10 counts, counting 1000 and

Fig. 3-32. The stretcher.

1, 1000 and 2, and so on. Relax, rest, and repeat. Avoid overarching the back. A cushion may be used if desired.

THE TOE TOUCH, CENTERED BACK

Stand tall, stomach in. On 1, touch left toes; 2, touch floor between feet. On 3, reach way back between legs; 4, touch right toes; 5, straighten up. Do 10 times in slow rhythm, 10 in faster, and taper off with a set of 5 more.

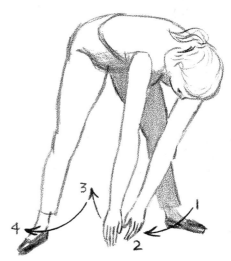

Fig. 3-33. The toe touch, centered back.

EXERCISES FOR THE FEET

The foot is an example of mastery in the engineering of the human body, for although it is composed of only 26 small bones, it is so constructed that the total weight of the body can be well supported on three small areas, the base of the big and little toes and the heel. There are seven ankle bones, the largest and strongest of which is that of the heel; all these tiny foot bones are held in place by strong ligaments, muscles, and tendons over the longitudinal and transverse arches. When body weight is incorrectly balanced, the result is ankle supination (weight carried on the outer foot borders) or ankle pronation (weight carried on the inner foot borders). Since the feet are farthest from the heart, circulatory problems often show up first in swollen feet and ankles. Shoes, especially those with high heels, are hard on the arches, for the extra elevation of the heel relieves the calf muscles of their function of supporting the longitudinal arch, causing it gradually to weaken. They also cause a redistribution of body weight, pushing it forward on the arch and spreading the toes. Consequently, those who wear high heels often should do foot exercises and change to low heels or walk around barefooted for a while every day. If you have serious foot difficulties, you should seek the services of a medical orthopedic specialist or podiatrist. Corns, bunions, hammertoe, and ingrown toenails result from wearing improperly fitting shoes, while trench foot and athlete's foot are signs of faulty foot hygiene.

Since faulty habits of walking and standing may cause weak feet, the following exercises are recommended for those whose feet hurt and whose leg muscles tire easily.

1. Sitting in a chair with one leg crossed, swing one foot to write the letters A to M. Recross your legs and finish writing the rest of the alphabet with the other foot.

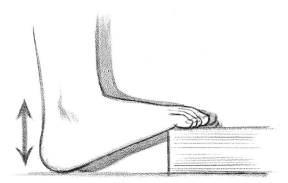

Fig. 3-35.   The heel lifter.

4. Sit barefooted on floor with legs extended. Bring both feet back toward you, then extend. Turn soles toward each other, without using your hands for assistance, and pat them 10 times. Repeat whole pattern, first slowly, then as fast as you can, until you have done it 10 times.

Fig. 3-34.   The alphabet writer.

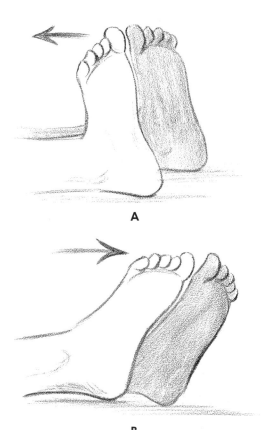

A

B

Fig. 3-36.   Back and out foot exercise. *(Continued on next page.)*

2. Standing straight with arms extended at sides, focus your eyes on a spot across the room. Raise yourself slowly to tiptoe position, then slowly lower yourself. Do 10 times.

3. Curl your toes over a large book such as a telephone directory, standing tall. Raise and lower yourself slowly. Do 10 times.

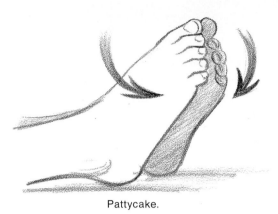

Pattycake.

C

Fig. 3-36. *(continued).*

5. Sit on floor or chair with legs crossed. On 1, extend left leg with foot turned in, flex ankle, making complete circle. As front of foot comes up, curl toes hard and push heel down. On 2, repeat with other foot. Do 20 times, alternating feet.

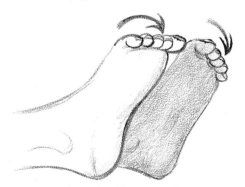

Fig. 3-37.   The toe curl.

6. Sit on floor with legs extended. On 1, spread toes far apart as possible. Relax on 2. On 3, curl toes under, relax on 4. Do 10 times.

7. Pick up a pencil or marbles with the

Fig. 3-38.   The pencil pick up.

toes. Write your full name with each foot, or pick up 10 marbles, one at a time, by using your toes and put them in a box.

8. Stand erect with feet apart. On 1, rise on toes; 2, lower body. On 3, lift front part of the feet; lower on 4. Do 15 times.

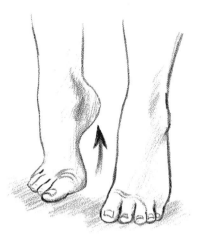

Toes up and down foot exercise.

A

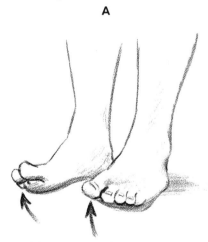

Toes up, toes down exercise.

B

Fig. 3-39.

9. Skip rope in place 25 times, clearing rope with one foot at a time. First spring from toes, then transfer weight from front to back of foot. Next jump with feet together, springing from your toes. Work up to doing this 50, 75, and finally 100 times.

and body tension with body relaxation. Americans live in an increasingly tension-filled world. If as a college student you learn how to relax and use your body well, you will have a knowledge, a skill, and an appreciation that will probably not only prolong your stay on earth, but help you to enjoy each day along the way to the fullest.

Signs of tenseness are pain at back of the neck, aching shoulders, headaches, burning eyes, and irritability. The tense person is touchy, fidgity, and drawn within herself. To relieve tension, exercises like the following are recommended:

THE WILTED DAISY

Stand with feet apart. Stretch on tiptoe with both hands over head. Then bend body and shake and wiggle both shoulders, arms and hands, becoming as limp as you can. Come up slowly on the count of 10. Repeat.

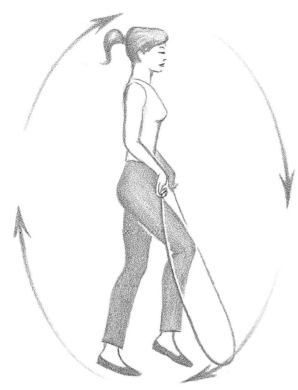

Fig. 3-40. Rope jumping.

10. Sit with heels drawn up close to the hips, feet and knees together, palms on the floor. Keeping feet on floor, advance by toe movement for 10 counts, then back. Do 20 times.

Fig. 3-41. The up and back toe crawl.

Fig. 3-42. The wilted daisy.

THE HEAD ROLL

(For shoulder tension.) Stand in a relaxed position. On 1, slowly roll head from front to left shoulder and back on 2. On 3, roll it over right shoulder and back to place on 4. On 5 and 6, slowly roll it all the way around, relaxing neck and shoulder muscles.

EXERCISES FOR RELAXATION

One secret of a happy, productive life is found in properly balancing work with play

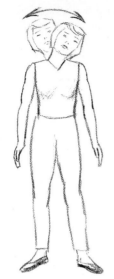

Fig. 3-43. The head roll.

Fig. 3-45. The tailor tuck.

BACK AND LEG RAISER

(For back tension.) Lie on floor. On 1, inhale slowly and raise back with body weight supported by your head and buttocks. On 2, relax. On 3, inhale and raise right knee to chest, clasping it with both hands. On 4, exhale and extend right knee to floor. On 5 and 6, raise and lower left leg in the same fashion.

trunk forward; then gradually straighten trunk, starting from lower back. Next, curve the back slowly, starting in the neck area.

THE ARM SWING

(For tension of the upper back.) Stand, swing left arm away from body and back, then both arms, and finally both arms in easy rhythm to music. For variation, raise and lower alternate legs as you swing both arms forward and back. This exercise also helps the circulation and the flexibility of the back.

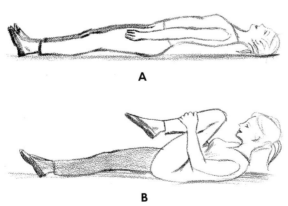

Fig. 3-44. Back and leg raiser. A, Count 1; B, count 5.

Fig. 3-46. The arm swing.

THE TAILOR TUCK

(For neck tension.) Sit tailor fashion, with legs crossed. Slowly circle head, keeping shoulders still. For variation, sitting in this position, clasp arms behind the head, relax

THE STANDING LEG SWING

(For lower back tension.) Stand erect. Swing left leg forward and back in easy

Fig. 3-47. The standing leg swing.

rhythm, then right leg. Next, move alternate legs in large circles.

THE STRETCHER

(For back tension.) Stand with feet apart, hands clasped overhead, arms fully extended. Moving left, make a big circle with clasped hands, bending slowly all the way around.

Fig. 3-48. The stretcher.

LETTING GO

Lie down, arms and legs out to the sides. On 1, tighten fists and pucker lips as tightly as

you can. Relax both as much as you can on 2. On 3, tighten muscles of buttocks, stomach, and legs. Relax on 4. Repeat.

SWINGING ALL THE WAY AROUND

(For general tension.) Swing arms forward and sideward, stopping sideward swing at the point where tension begins. Swing arms forward, sideward, crossing arms in front.

Next, swing arms forward and backward, using entire body. Flex knees and straighten them on both forward and backward swings. Then spread feet far apart, carry swings through the legs.

Next, swing both arms horizontally from side to side. Bend over with body relaxed and start a low swing, gradually straightening up and increasing the perimeter of the swing until the body is erect.

Finally, by experimenting, see how many different swings to music you can do with your arms, legs, and body.

Fig. 3-49. Swinging all the way around.

FROG SITTING

(For back and leg tension.) Sit with inside of knee touching floor, legs flexed, hands on hips. Inhale, slowly bend forward to touch head to floor in front of you on count of 1.

Fig. 3-50. Frog sitting.

Fig. 3-51. The daisy droop.

On 2, slowly exhale and come back to original position.

EXERCISES FOR THE RELIEF OF MENSTRUAL PAIN

Although today only a minority of girls and women suffer from menstrual pain (dysmenorrhea), partaking in the right types of exercise in sufficient amounts can work wonders to help those faced with this periodic problem. Those with severe pain should consult a physician (preferably a gynecologist).

Most girls and women suffering from cramps preceding or during menstruation have weak pelvic floor muscles supporting the visceral organs. Strengthening these muscles daily through specific exercises not only relieves menstrual difficulties but usually leads to ease in childbirth later. It is important to know, however, that performing a few of the following exercises will *not* help unless they are done daily for 15 to 30 minutes over an extended period of time. The following exercises are recommended:

THE DAISY DROOP

Stand straight, slump over and tighten stomach muscles on counts 1-2-3. On 4-5-6 return to erect position; on 7-8 return to slump position with stomach muscles tightened; on count 9-10, relax, return to erect position. Repeat 10 times.

FOOT-FEET PATTY CAKE

Lie on your back with arms bent out and up from your sides. Keep legs straight and raise them 3 inches from the floor. Bring feet together and apart in patty-cake fashion 25 times.

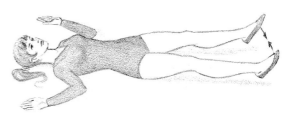

Fig. 3-52. Foot-feet patty cake.

THE BENT KNEE TWIST

Lie on your back as described in the previous exercise. Flex knees, tighten stomach muscles, and keep your shoulders flat on the floor while turning your lower body and legs over to the right, then to the left. Repeat 25 times.

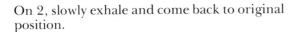

Fig. 3-53. The bent knee twist.

Fig. 3-55. The Mosher exercise.

THE CAMEL HUMP

With weight on your hands and knees, arch your back on counts 1-2-3-4, and tighten stomach muscles. Relax on 5-6-7-8; repeat 10 times.

Fig. 3-54. The camel hump.

THE GRASSHOPPER

Kneel supporting body weight on your hands and knees to suspend your internal organs while in this unnatural position for three minutes. Stand erect and then repeat for 10 times.

THE MOSHER EXERCISE

Called the "pumping" exercise, this exercise does just that: your hands become the pumping power. Lie on your back and flex your knees, keeping your feet flat on the floor. Place both hands on your stomach, take a deep breath, and push down with both hands. Exhale and relax. Repeat 10 times daily.

THE GOLUB EXERCISE

Stand with body and arms in full extension, and with knees locked. On count 1, twist, turn body; on count 2 bring fully extended left arm across your body to touch your outer right heel and fully extend your right arm back for balance. Repeat on other side. On 3 swing both fully extended arms forward, and at the same time, kick left leg backward. On 4 return. Repeat arm swing on 4 and then kick back with the right leg. Repeat 20 times.

Fig. 3-56. The Golub exercise.

THE BILLIG EXERCISE

Stand with feet together 18 inches from a wall. Lock knees and move hips forward. Place forearm against a wall at shoulder height. Place other hand against the hollow of the thigh joint. On count 1 slowly push your hips toward the wall as far as you can. On 2 return to place. On 3 and 4 repeat with body turned in the opposite way. Do this one at least 3 times.

Fig. 3-57. The Billig exercise.

PASSIVE RELAXATION

One can relieve tension by learning the kinesthetic difference between tenseness and relaxation. Deliberately tensing the muscles of the body, beginning with those of the face, then arms and hands, abdomen and buttocks, legs and feet, then letting them relax is one recommended way of learning to *feel* this difference. This exercise should be done several times. Next, lie on your back with eyes closed, and concentrate on extending your breathing span by inhaling and exhaling as slowly as possible. Finally, inhale slowly, simultaneously tensing the entire body; then relax completely as you exhale. Although the full benefit of such an exercise requires much practice, the results are well worth the effort.

Passive relaxation can be achieved in other ways. For each of the following exercises, lie on your back with eyes closed.

1. Count backward from 100 as slowly as you can, saying "One hundred . . . ninety-nine," and so on.
2. Imagine you are a big log floating slowly down a lazy stream. Say as slowly as you can, "Float . . . float."
3. Think of softly touching water or the velvet petals of a pansy, As you do so, slowly say, "Touch . . . touch."
4. With eyes closed, think of the most beautiful and restful place you know (a lake at sunset, a mountain peak with snow, and so on). Say slowly as you inwardly "see" this place, "Rest . . . rest."

MUSIC AND RELAXATION

Some students can relax best by lying in bed in a darkened room with eyes closed, listening to soothing music and letting their thoughts stray. If using this method for the first time, choose a record that has a slow rhythm and a pleasing melody. As you drift and dream, think of something serene. "Music for People Who Can't Sleep," by Richard Hayman, Mercury MG20184, is especially recommended for those who have great difficulty going to sleep. Other methods of inducing sleep include taking a long, warm (never hot) bath, drinking a glass of warm milk, reading an especially dull book, or going through a series of mild exercises. Sleeping pills and tranquilizers are both dangerous unless prescribed by a physician. Although the number of hours of sleep required varies for each individual, most people need from 7 to 10 hours nightly. Sleep is the great restorer. Since mental work is actually more de-energizing than physical work, college students especially need well-regulated sleep. Those who are "half asleep" most of the time soon get into all kinds of academic difficulties. The kind of sleep you get is actually more important than the amount. If your sleep habits are good, you can afford a late night occasionally. Studies show, however, that although it is not too serious to miss your accustomed amount of sleep for one night, missing one hour of sleep a night over a long period can do more harm than losing several hours of sleep on one night.*

---

*Hein, Fred, and Farnsworth, Dana: *Living*, 4th Ed., Scott, Foresman & Company, Dallas, 1965, p. 129.

Although many Americans work all day and worry most of the night, this is one practice college students must avoid. Likewise, taking pills, drinking coffee, or using other methods to stay awake can be extremely dangerous. It is best to remember, therefore, that if you are tired and sleepy, you should go to bed. By getting up earlier the next morning to study, you can accomplish far more in a shorter time, because your mind will be fresh. How well you sleep is a vitally important factor in how you feel, how well you do in your studies, and even in how long and happily you will live.

Suggested Readings

Brean, Herbert: *The Only Diet That Works*, New York, William Morrow & Company, 1965.

Drury, Blanche: *Posture and Figure Control Through Physical Education*, Palo Alto, California, National Press Publications, 1961.

Jacobson, Edmund: *You Must Relax*, New York, McGraw-Hill Book Co., 1948.

Maltz, Maxwell: *Creative Living for Today*, New York, Trident Press, 1967.

Rubin, Theodore: *The Thin Book by a Formerly Fat Psychiatrist*, New York, Trident Press, 1966.

Royal Canadian Air Force Exercise Plans for Physical Fitness, New York, Pocket Books, 1962.

Vannier, Maryhelen: *A Better Figure for You Through Easy Exercise and Diet;* and *Figure and Weight Control* (an instructor's manual to be used with *A Better Figure for You*), New York, Association Press, 1965.

Vannier, Maryhelen: *Slimnastics*, Belmont, California, Wadsworth Press, 1969.

Wells, Katherine: *Posture Exercise Handbook*, New York, The Ronald Press Company, 1963.

Suggested Pamphlets

(The following pamphlets are all available from the National Dairy Council, 111 North Canal Street, Chicago, Illinois.)

Personalized Weight Control (10¢)
The Food Way to Weight Reduction (10¢)
A Girl and Her Figure and You (20¢)
Go Places, Gal (20¢)
Guide to Good Eating (15¢)
Your Calorie Catalog (7¢)
It All Depends Upon You (10¢)
An Album of Snack Time Hits (3¢)

Suggested Exercise Records for Home and Class Use

Better Physical Fitness Record Album for Girls: Fitness for Teens; Marching Along with the Girls; Reduce In Record Time. All available from The Children's Music Center, 5373 West Pico Blvd., Los Angeles, California 90019.

Bucher, Charles; *Slimnastics*, Decca Records. (This is the best of all exercise records and can be ordered through a local record shop. No number is given for it on the jacket.)

Club 15 Exercise Record, Club 15, Box 1515, Maple Plain, Minnesota.

The Good Housekeeping Plan for Reducing off the Record, Columbia Records, HL7143.

Paul Fogarty's Famous Forty Exercises for Streamlining Your Figure. Paul Fogarty's Streamline Records, 555 North Sheridan Road, Chicago, Illinois.

Suggested Study Questions

1. Using the methods described in this chapter, determine your body type, your height and weight, and your figure faults.

2. If you want to lose or gain weight, keep a record of everything you eat and drink, and its calorie count, for a week. Show your instructor your record for the week and discuss with her the results of this experiment.

3. Explain why exercise alone will not cause a person to lose weight.

4. Describe in your own words the seven ways of losing weight suggested in this chapter.

5. List ten facts about exercise and discuss them in your own words.

2

INDIVIDUAL SPORTS

*"Personality is not so much like a structure
as like a river
  — it continuously flows,
and to be a person is to be engaged
in a perpetual process of becoming."*
— *Harry Emerson Fosdick*

CHAPTER FOUR

Courtesy of Kristie L. Kaiser, Arizona State University.

ARCHERY

Archery is a year-round sport for both sexes of all ages. Properly played either indoors or outdoors as an individual or group activity, it can improve posture and develop chest, abdominal, arm, and back strength as well as general physical fitness. Its carryover value is among the highest of all sports, for a beginning archer may develop into a hobbyist who makes her own arrows and leaves the stationary target for an occasional field shoot or a hunting trip.

This ancient sport of Robin Hood, William Tell, and Hiawatha has strong romantic appeal, especially to youth. Archery's history began with primitive men who fashioned the bow and arrow to protect themselves and to provide food. Its history contains the colorful panorama of Egyptian, Greek, Turkish, Japanese, English, and French armies with soldiers standing shoulder to shoulder or mounted on heavily padded horses shooting hundreds of arrows in unison at the approaching enemy. Museums in almost every nation have exhibits of these ancient weapons—the short, heavy bow of only $4\frac{1}{2}$ feet with even shorter arrows, the oddly shaped C bow from which 6 foot long arrows were shot, the highly polished English or Oriental crossbows, the unattractive but deadly weapons of the Indian hunters, or the poisoned arrows of uncivilized tribes.

Since the beginning of the 17th century, after gunpowder gained prominence as a means of warfare in most of the world, archery continued to gain popularity as a sport. In the United States today more than 4.5 million people of varying ages participate in target and field archery in schools, colleges, camps, forests, and parks. For more than 20 years the Camp Archery Association has granted proficiency certificates to youth in Y's, schools, and summer camps. The National Archery Association, organized in America in 1879, and the National Field Archery Association, founded in 1939, sponsor annual tournaments. The Division for Girls and Women's Sports of the American Association for Health, Physical Education, and Recreation sponsors an annual winter intercollegiate telegraphic tournament.

Archery is receiving additional emphasis through the preparation of instructors in clinics and workshops sponsored by the Outdoor Education Project of the American Association for Health, Physical Education, and Recreation.

NATURE AND PURPOSE OF THE SPORT

The skills basic to the sport of archery are used in many archery activities. The most common form of target archery leads to the development of field archery, flight shooting, archery games, and bow hunting.

TARGET ARCHERY

The purpose of *target archery* is to hit the target, preferably the "gold," with a prescribed number of arrows shot from specified distances. A set of six arrows constitutes an *end*. A *round* consists of a designated number of ends. In college competition the *Columbia round* is ordinarily used, which consists of shooting 24 arrows from each of three distances—50 yards, 40 yards, and 30 yards.

Some other competitive rounds are:

American round—30 arrows from 60 yards, 50 yards, and 40 yards, respectively.

Junior American round—30 arrows from 50 yards, 40 yards, and 30 yards, respectively.

Junior Columbia round—24 arrows from 40 yards, 30 yards, and 20 yards, respectively.

Scholastic round—24 arrows from 40 yards and 30 yards, respectively.

Junior scholastic round—24 arrows from 30 yards and 20 yards, respectively.

Range round—60 arrows from a single distance; 50 yards, 40 yards, 30 yards, or 20 yards on regulation targets.*

Miniature round—60 arrows from 15 yards on a *two-foot* target, scaled to the same proportions as the regulation target.*

A team in archery consists of four archers. *The team round* for women consists of 16 ends shot from 50 yards. The individual scores are totaled for the team score.

FLIGHT SHOOTING

Participants in flight shooting release a designated number of arrows from a shooting line in an attempt to send the arrows as far as possible. Competition is held for regular flight (bow held in the hands) and free-style flight (bow held by the feet and pulled by the hands and arms).

FIELD ARCHERY

Field archery includes hunting with bow, roving (shooting at various inanimate objects while walking in fields or woods), and shooting at established targets while walking over a designated course. In these activities the distances shot are unknown and the instinctive aiming method is generally used.

ARCHERY GAMES

Several archery games are increasing in popularity. Two of the most popular are archery golf and clout shooting.

Archery Golf. Archery golf is played under varying sets of rules but utilizes the terrain of a golf course.† One set of rules requires a bow and three arrows. The object is to use the flight, approach, and putting arrows to get to a designated disc or ball on the green in as few shots as possible. Archery golf par scores are usually one less per hole than the par scores for golf.

Clout Shooting. Clout shooting is accomplished by directing 36 arrows at a target 48 feet in diameter. The target, laid out in concentric circles, has values similar to those of a regular target. Men shoot from 180 yards; women from 140 and 120 yards.

---

*Designed particularly for indoor shooting.
†See D.G.W.S. *Archery Guide*, 1966-68, p. 54, for another description.

FACILITIES AND EQUIPMENT

THE TARGET RANGE

The outdoor range should be on well mowed, level ground in a remote spot (preferably inside a fenced or roped-off area when located in a heavily populated play space). The target backdrop may be a hill, a cliff, or bales of hay. An open area may be used as long as there is an open space of no less than 30 feet behind the farthest target. The range should be at least 75 yards long and marked with white shooting lines parallel to the line of the target at 20, 30, 40, and 50 yards. For additional safety when groups are shooting at different distances at one time, use the common shooting line and set the *targets* at various distances.

An indoor range of 35 to 45 feet may be used successfully. All room exits and entrances must be kept locked while shooting is in progress. Targets should be placed 10 feet apart and 3 feet from the back wall. For a beginning class, an area 30 feet × 50 feet can accommodate ten 36 inch targets placed close together. Backdrops made of canvas, of nylon netting, of plywood, or of heavy felt mats will protect the wall and arrows. Floor quivers made of tennis ball cans nailed to square boards can be used. A 20 foot and a 30 foot range can both be set up in such an area.

FIELD ARCHERY COURSE*

Field archery courses may be laid out on relatively rough, undeveloped land. The flint round is suggested as a beginning course.

The modified flint round was devised for use at an indoor field where only 20 yard distances are available.

---

*For information on construction consult the National Field Archery Association, Box 514, Redlands, California.

The Flint Round

Target No.	Shooting Distance	No. Arrows	Target Size
1	25 yards	4	12″
2	20 feet	4	6″
3	30 yards	4	12″
4	15 yards	4	6″
5	20 yards	4	12″
6	10 yards	4	6″
7	30, 25, 20, and 15 yds.	Walk up, shoot one at each distance	12″

The Modified Flint Round

Target No.	Shooting Distance	No. Arrows	Target Size
1	17 yards	4	8″
2	20 feet	4	6″
3	20 yards	4	8″
4	14 yards	4	6″
5	15 yards	4	8″
6	10 yards	4	6″
7	20, 17, 15, and 10 yds.	Walk up, shoot one from each distance	8″

TARGETS

Although bales of hay or heavy cardboard boxes stuffed with hay or straw can be used, rye straw and marsh grass tightly wound in a coil and held together by twine offer the best backing. The matte should be 48 inches in diameter, 4 to 6 inches thick and hung so that the center of the gold is 4 feet from the ground. The face is tilted slightly toward the sky.

Lightweight excelsior and plastic foam mattes are now available. Their light weight and convenient size of 36 inches make them useful both indoors and outdoors.

Target stands are made of three soft pine, cedar, or cypress boards, 6 feet long, 3 inches wide, and 1 inch thick, which are bolted into a tripod. On windy days ropes or ground hooks should be used to secure the target.

Preferably, the target face is made of oil cloth but may be made of canvas. The face should be painted in bright colors, with a gold center $9\frac{3}{5}$ inches in diameter and four concentric rings, each $4\frac{4}{5}$ inches in width, col-

ored red, light blue, black, and white. The outer edge (or petticoat) beyond the outer white ring should be 1 inch wide. A *skirt* encloses the target and is tied with a drawstring in back.

TACKLE

An archer's equipment is called *tackle*. Basic equipment includes a bow, bowstring, arrows, an arm guard, finger tab or glove, and quiver.

Bows. Fiberglass bows are excellent for beginners, for they are durable and have consistent shooting qualities. Bows are of two basic types: the *self bow*, made from one type of material, and the *laminated bow*, made from wood, plastic, felt, or other materials, glued together. Wooden self bows are usually of yew, lemonwood, hickory, and osage orange. Yew produces a smooth shooting bow; osage orange is an extremely hard wood and is used by many for hunting bows that must endure abuse. Lemonwood is used for modestly priced target and field bows. Lemonwood has a tendency to "follow the string," that is, it fails to return to its original shape when un-

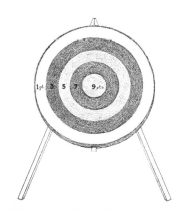

Fig. 4-1. A target showing scoring values.

Fig. 4-2. An archer's equipment is called tackle. (Courtesy of Clifford Lewis, University of Georgia.)

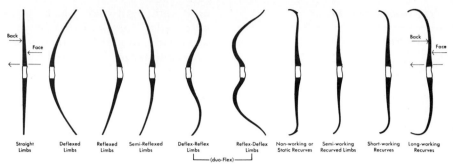

Fig. 4-3. Bow designs (From D.G.W.S. *Archery*Riding Guide.*)

strung. Hickory, though inexpensive, follows the string, has slow action, and has a great deal of kick or recoil. Because of its stretch qualities, hickory is excellent for backing other bow woods.

For durability many bows are backed with wood or fiberglass material along the back of the bow.

Many skilled archers are adopting a laminated recurved bow. Because this is a relatively new design, there is great variation among manufacturers in the bow length, weight, amount of recurve, and handle design. This efficient, smooth bow usually has a maple core with a fiberglass back and belly and handle sections of black walnut or tropical hardwoods.

The *length* of a bow is largely determined by arrow length. The following list indicates average lengths used by beginners:

Arrows 24″ to 25″ — Bow 5′0″ to 5′3″
Arrows 26″ to 27″ — Bow 5′4″ to 5′6″
Arrows 28″ to 30″ — Bow 5′7″ to 5′10″

Bow *weight* refers to the number of pounds required to draw the string a specific distance. Most bows are marked for bow weight at a 28 inch draw. For each inch over or under 28 the weight increases or decreases approximately 2 pounds. Weights range from 10 to 110 pounds, the heavier bows being used for hunting and fishing. Most women use 25 to 28 pound bows for target archery, 25 to 32 pounds for field archery, and 30 to 45 pounds for hunting. Beginners may choose a bow as light as 18 pounds until skill and strength are developed.

Arrow rests serve as guides when placing the arrow against the bow. Wooden plates are more durable, but leather deadens the sound of the arrow on release and therefore is helpful when hunting.

Bowstrings. The best string to use depends upon the bow weight, style, model, and length, and replacement orders should always indicate the length and weight of the bow. Those made of Fortisan and Dacron or of Dacron with a nylon serving are now con-

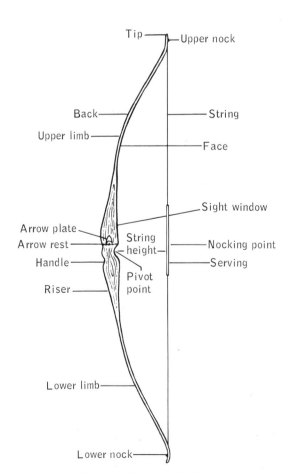

Fig. 4-4. Parts of the bow.

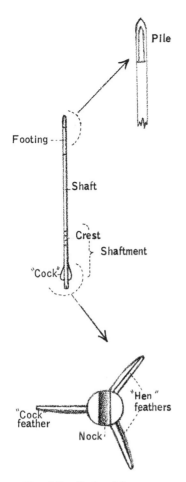

Fig. 4-5. Parts of the arrow.

will help to increase shooting accuracy, for it allows the archer to hook the arrow consistently at the same spot for each shot. A do-it-yourself nocking point can be made by folding, in opposite directions, a six inch piece of dental tape (which is heavier and flatter than dental floss). Plastic tape may also be used.

Arrows. Arrows should be true or straight and weigh between 250 and 300 grams. They are either "matched" (the set is all of the same spine) or unmatched (the set contains some which are not of the same weight or stiffness). Buying the best arrows will help archers to gain greater joy from shooting. Most wooden arrows are made of Port Orford cedar, which is superior to birch because it warps less easily. Fiberglass arrows are increasing in popularity because of their durability and lightness. Aluminum arrows cost more but are favored by advanced archers for their near perfect weight and construction.

Wooden arrows are classified as *self arrows*, those made of a single piece of wood, and *footed arrows*, those having a piece of hardwood spliced into the foreshaft for more strength and weight and better balance.

The point of the arrow is called the *pile*. These points vary in type and size and should be selected for their specific use. Light parallel points are used for beginning target archery. The notched end that fits the string is the *nock*.

The feathers on the arrow are called the *fletching*. There may be three or four feathers, and they may be set straight or spirally. They should be evenly spaced and be of the same shape, height, and length.

The shaftment includes the crest, or group of varicolored rings, which adds attractiveness and makes identification easy.

Women commonly use arrows 24 to 28 inches in length. Proper arrow length is very important, for an arrow too short may cause injury, while one too long results in inaccuracy. Correct length can be determined by placing an arrow against the breastbone and extending both arms and hands toward the tip. The arrow is proper length if the pile extends just beyond the fingertips of both hands. Some archers prefer to measure their arm spread from fingertip to fingertip and refer to an arrow-length chart based on arm spread. Thirty-eight per cent of the total

sidered superior to those made of linen or latex. All strings should be kept well waxed. The best strings are those which distribute stress from the draw evenly. When a single loop bowstring is attached, the timber hitch knot should be used to tie it to the bow at the lower nock. Both the double and single loop strings should be purchased only for specific bow types.

Bow tip protectors prevent scuffing of the bow tip and help to hold the bowstring in place while stringing or during storage. These can be bought and are usually made of plastic or pliable rubber. The archer can make her own easily, however, by twisting a small rubber band so that it will hold the bowstring in the nock.

A nocking point (a bowstring attachment)

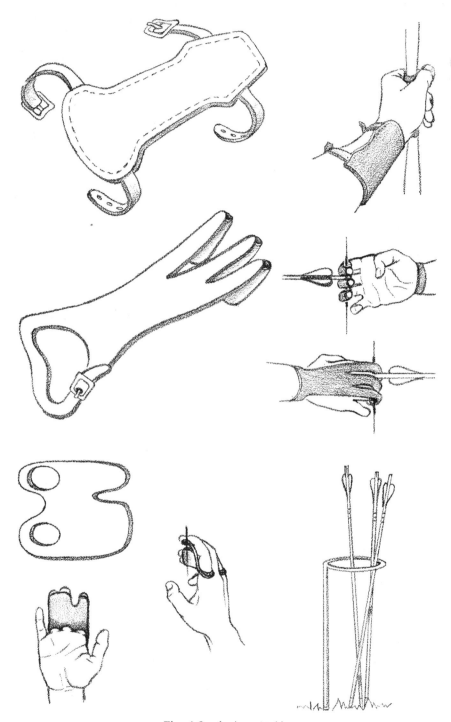

Fig. 4-6.   Archery tackle.

measurement is the recommended arrow length.

Finger Protection. Finger tabs or finger gloves are used for protection and to aid in a smooth release. There are two types of tabs: the Western style with two finger holes, and the Marshall style with a single finger hole. Finger tabs are more moderate in cost than finger gloves but do not offer maximum protection. Made of durable leather, the tab is designed to go between the shooting fingers and the string. The smooth leather glove surrounds the three shooting fingers and is secured around the wrist or hand.

Arm Guards. Guards should cover the inner forearm of the extended arm for protection against the recoil of the bowstring. Guards are usually made of leather or composition and are reinforced inside by metal ribs to assure firmness. The guards buckle or lace over the back of the forearm.

Quivers. The type of archery activity determines the kind of quiver necessary. Target archers use back and hip quivers but prefer ground quivers. Ground quivers are usually made of iron, have a pointed tip at the bottom, and are circle-shaped at the top, with a hook near the circle on which to rest the bow.

Back, hip, and pocket quivers made of leather are used by field archers. Hunters also use arm and bow quivers.

Points of Aim. A point of aim may be a piece of colored wood, a brightly painted ice pick, or a wooden block with a spike drive through it to push into the ground.

Bow Sights. Sight shooting involves a mechanical device attached to the bow. A simple sight can be devised by inserting a large-headed pin on the back of the upper limb of the bow. The location of the pin for various ranges is marked on a strip of adhesive tape. Glass-headed pins and sponge rubber glued to the bow serve as another simple sight. Commercial sights are available in a wide price range and in various designs.

PURCHASE AND CARE OF EQUIPMENT

As has been indicated, archery tackle should be bought for specific uses. Guidance by a competent instructor will be helpful,

whether purchasing modestly priced or individually constructed bows and arrows. Whether selecting a recurved fiberglass target bow or an osage orange hunting bow, make sure that:

1. The bow describes an arc with a flat center when drawn.

2. The bowstring bisects the bow the full length when strung.

3. The bow returns to its original shape when unstrung.

4. The bow is the proper weight and length for the archer and her purpose.

Bows may be protected by light cases when traveling or when stored for a period of time. After each use they should be unstrung and placed horizontally on two pegs (one at either end) or hung vertically in a slightly humid area. Wooden bows should be waxed occasionally and refinished every few years.

Bowstrings should be waxed frequently with paraffin on the serving and beeswax on the remainder of the string.

When selecting arrows, make certain they are the proper length, of a matched set (weight, fletching), marked with the same crest, and correct for the archer's purpose.

After use, arrows should be dried and stored vertically, tips down, to avoid bending the shaft. Destroy cracked or splintered arrows; feathers, points, and nocks, however, can be replaced with a "do-it-yourself" kit. Wooden arrows that are warped may be heated and bent to original shape. Aluminum arrows may be straightened by the manufacturer or by the hobbyist with an arrow tube straightener.

When retrieving arrows from the target, place the back of one hand against the target with the index and second fingers close to the arrow. The other hand grasps the arrow close to the target and pulls the arrow out at the angle it entered the target. The target hand exerts pressure on the face to prevent tearing. If the arrow is so deep in the target that the feathers are lodged, draw the arrow through the back of the target. If the arrow is in the dirt or grass with feathers out, remove straight backwards; if the feathers are caught, grasp the tip and pull forward.

Arm guards, gloves, and quivers are largely a matter of personal choice. They may be homemade or bought reasonably. All leather equipment should be dried slowly when wet

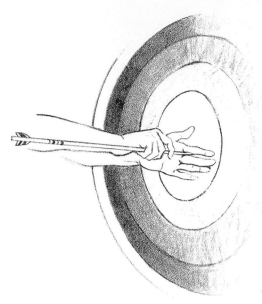

Fig. 4-7. Removing arrow from target.

and cleaned occasionally with saddle soap or commercial leather cleaners.

BASIC SKILLS

Many skills are basically the same for both target and field archery. Differences will be mentioned in the discussion that follows.

Prior to developing shooting skills, the beginner should determine her dominant eye. Although shooting is done with both eyes open, the dominant eye aligns with linear objects and consequently the shooting arm should be on the same side.

A simple method is to extend both arms in front of the body. The palms are facing away from the body and the fingers and thumbs overlap so that there is a small opening between the two hands. With both eyes open, focus on an object through the opening. Close the left eye; if the object remains in the opening, the right eye is dominant. To verify this, close the right eye and see if the object moves from focus. Occasionally a person may have "nondominance" and she may then shoot from the most natural side.

Bracing and Unbracing the Bow. A commercial bow stringer is a common and desirable accessory. Not only does it lessen the labor of bow stringing for the individual, it also lessens or equalizes the stress on the bow while being strung.

The *push-pull method* is frequently used on light target bows. The lower end of the bow is placed against the inside arch of the left foot with the back of the bow toward the body. The bow tip does not touch the ground but is pressed against the foot. The heel of the right hand is placed near the bow tip while the left

Fig. 4-8. In competitive archery the score made by each arrow should be carefully recorded before it is removed from the target. (Courtesy of the Los Angeles Public Schools.)

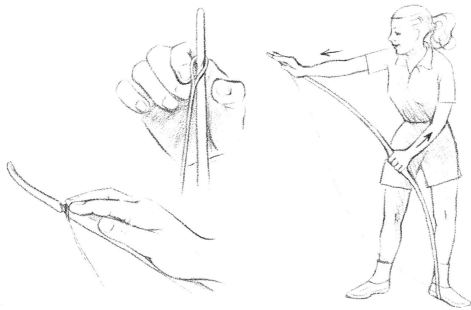

Fig. 4-9. Stringing the bow.

hand, on the handle, pulls the bow toward the body. The heel of the right hand presses the upper limb of the bow down while the thumb and index finger slide up the bow and slip the noose into the nock.

To unstring the bow, the same bow, hand, and body positions are used. The string is lifted from its nock by the index and middle fingers and slipped down the bow as the left hand pulls the bow toward the body.

For a heavier or recurve bow the *step-in* stringing method is often used. With the right leg between the string and the belly of the bow, belly facing forward, the lower end of the bow rests on the instep of the left foot. As the right hand pushes the bow forward at the top of the upper limb, the bow at the handle bends against the back of the right thigh. The left hand guides the string into the nock. Use of a commercial bow string for bows usually strung by the "push pull" method prevents twisting and possible damage to bow limbs.

The Stance. The target archer stands astride the shooting line, the field archer behind the shooting stake, with body weight equally distributed. For the right-handed archer the left shoulder and head are turned toward the target and the feet are spread shoulder width. The left foot is moved backward approximately 6 inches and the toe turns slightly to the target to complete the open stance. The body is held in a comfortable, relaxed, yet erect, position. The stance must be consistent.

The Grip and Bow Arm. The fingers and

Fig. 4-10. Step-in method of stringing bow.

Fig. 4-11. The grip.

Fig. 4-12. Drawing.

thumb of the bow hand lightly encircle the bow so that the "V" of the thumb and forefinger is at the pivot point of the handle. The bow is held parallel to the ground and pointing toward the target with string toward the body until the arrow is nocked.

The bow is raised upright, and in preparation for the draw the bow arm is raised to shoulder height. During the draw and release, the bow handle is pushed by the "V" formed by the fleshy part of the thumb and hand. The forefinger is around the back of the bow and the thumb may be resting lightly on the forefinger. The other three fingers no longer "hold" the bow but are relaxed in an extended position and point toward the target. The wrist is straight and firm. The arm is comfortably extended with the elbow turned out, away from the bowstring. The bow arm shoulder is kept down and back to avoid leaning toward the target.

Nocking. The bow is held horizontal to the ground with the back of the bow hand facing up. With the cock feather up, the drawing hand, holding the nock of the arrow between the thumb and index finger, slides the arrow across the arrow rest and places the nock on the serving. A 90 degree angle is formed by the arrow and the string. The thumb remains in contact with the arrow until the index finger and the other drawing fingers reach behind the string to stabilize the arrow. Often the index finger of the bow hand may be needed to support the arrow until it is partially drawn.

Drawing and Anchoring. The first three fingers of the right hand grasp under the string with the fingertips (no farther back than the first joint). The back of the hand remains straight, with flexion only in the first and second finger joints. The large knuckle joints are never flexed during the draw. The arrow is positioned between the first and

second fingers. At the same time the bow arm is raised, the drawing arm is pulled backward by the muscles of the back, shoulder, and arm. When fully extended, the right elbow is bent and parallel to the ground. During the draw take a deep breath and hold it.

Anchor Point. Anchor point refers to the point on the archer's face at which she places her hand when the bowstring is fully drawn. The point is often described as low, a point on or under the jaw bone, or high, a point on or directly under the cheek bone. The anchor

Fig. 4-13. Anchoring correctly is basic to scoring success in archery.

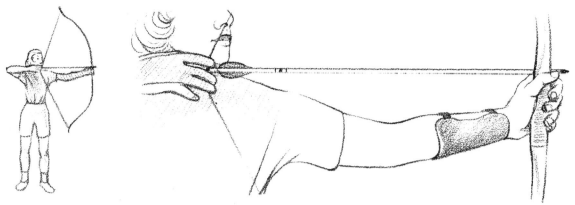

Fig. 4-14. Field archery draw.

point, once established, must be used consistently and constantly for all distances.

Target archers using point of aim or bow sight shooting usually prefer an anchor point under the chin. On each draw the string is drawn so that it bisects the tip of the nose and the chin. The hand is anchored under the jaw and against the neck with the forefinger against the chin.

Field archers, bow hunters, and instinctive shooters usually anchor at the back corner of the mouth. The upper surface of the index

finger rests snugly under the right cheekbone. Field archers often tip the upper limb of the bow and their heads 15 to 30 degrees to insure that the eye is over the arrow.

Aiming. Point of aim and "bow sight method" are used by most target archers. The instinctive method is gaining popularity and may replace the antiquated point of aim method. *Point of aim* involves using a spot on the ground, target, or background at which the archer sights over her arrow tip. This

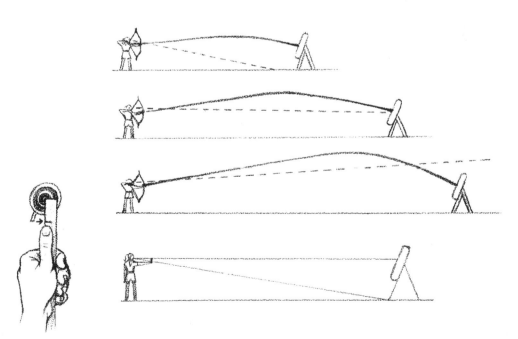

Fig. 4-15. Determining the point of aim.

point must be adjusted for each distance shot, bow weight, arrow design, and changing environmental conditions. For shooting long distances, the point of aim should be well above the target; on or near the target for medium distances; and in front of it for short range shooting. The point of aim should be lowered when arrows go over the target and raised when they go below it.

After a point of aim is found for a specific distance, it should be recorded on a range finder for future use. A short stick or tongue depressor can serve as a range finder when it is held by the extended bow arm in a shooting position with the top of the thumbnail matching a ground point of aim. The edge of the stick is aligned with the eye to the center of the gold.

When improvised or manufactured bow sights are used, the center of the target is the point of aim, regardless of distance. The sight is attached to the back of the bow slightly above the arrow rest. The "pin" extends to the left side of the bow. If possible, keep both eyes open, allowing the "master" eye to sight the pin and align it with the gold. Correct settings are found by trial and error. If arrows group anywhere other than at the center of the target, *move the sight in the direction of the error for correction.* That is, if the group is high and right, move the pin up and to the right.

Aiming in field archery differs from the previously mentioned target techniques. The field archer sights with both eyes on the smallest observable point in the middle of the target. If the archer sees the aiming spot immediately above the tip of the arrow and the released arrow hits the spot, the archer used point blank aim. Shooting with the same equipment at a closer target necessitates lowering the bow arm; at a farther target, raising the bow arm. The difficult part of "instinctive" shooting is knowing "how much." This is learned through practice and acquaintance with one's equipment. Many field archers and an increasing number of target archers learn through concentration and practice to adjust the vertical space between the arrow tip and the aiming spot by appraising the distance to the target.

Beginning archers will find the "pre-draw-gap" method an aid in learning instinctive shooting. The principle of the pre-gap method is that it sets the shooter's arm on a plane with the target and in the proper position, so that at full draw her concentration can be entirely on the spot she intends to hit. After the pre-gap spot is established, nothing moves except the draw to anchor. This method presents the mechanics and develops the security for learning instinctive shooting.

Release. In preparation for the release

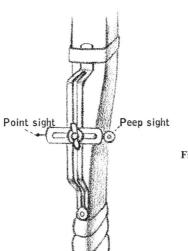

Point sight   Peep sight

Fig. 4-16. Bowsight.

Fig. 4-17. In preparation for the release, the body should be relaxed yet in readiness. (Courtesy of Clifford Lewis, University of Georgia.)

the body should be relaxed, yet in readiness. The fingers open smoothly to release the string and arrow. The right hand and elbow move *straight* back from the anchor position into the follow-through or *afterhold* position.

GAME RULES AND SCORING

TARGET ARCHERY

In target archery there are various competitive rounds, yet all are governed by the same basic rules and scoring.

BASIC RULES

1. Archers must straddle the shooting line.
2. Lady Paramount's whistle signals the beginning of shooting an end.
3. Archers must be three yards back of line when not shooting.

4. When a round requires shooting from several distances, begin shooting from the greatest distance.
5. An arrow leaving the bow is considered shot if the archer cannot reach it without her bow.
6. All shooting stops on two blasts of Lady Paramount's whistle.

SCORING

1. Score values are: gold—9 points; red—7 points; blue—5 points; black—3 points; white—1 point.
2. An arrow that cuts two colors is given the higher value.
3. An arrow that passes through the scoring face so it is not visible from the front counts 7 points, if shot from 60 yards or less.
4. An arrow rebounding from the scoring face shall count 7 points, if shot from 60 yards or less.
5. Arrows in the petticoat have no scoring value.

Table 4-1. *Shooting Chart Summary*

Causing arrows to go high or over the target	Causing arrows to go low or below the target	Causing arrows to go to the right	Causing arrows to go to the left
1. Straightening the bow arm	1. Creeping or pushing the arrow forward as it is released	1. Moving the bow arm to the right	1. Moving the bow arm to the left
2. Lifting the bow arm or index finger	2. Anchoring too high, failing to anchor under jaw, or holding anchor and draw position too long before releasing	2. Turning the bow to the right just before or during shooting	2. Incorrect anchor, usually at cheekbone or beside lips
3. Dropping the elbow or string hand	3. Lifting the chin forward to reach the string	3. Body weight carried on toes instead of whole foot	3. Hunching left shoulder
4. "Peeking" or looking up too soon to see arrow flight at short ranges	4. Using a point of aim that is too near, or not keeping the aiming position steady	4. Releasing too quickly (sometimes called shooting Indian style)	4. Gripping the bow and/or arrow too tightly thus "controlling" it to the left
5. Opening the mouth, causing the anchor point to be lowered	5. Dropping the bow arm	5. Jerking	5. Bending the bow arm too much
6. Overdrawing the bow by bringing the string back behind the anchor point	6. Holding too long before release	6. Wind blowing from the left	6. Moving the string hand away from the anchor point
7. Jerking the hand back and inward on the release	7. Hitting arm or clothing with string on release		7. Sighting with the left eye while shooting right-handed
8. Leaning away from target	8. Head wind		8. Weight on heels and body line held backward
9. Raising bow arm on or before release			9. Turning in wrist of bow arm instead of keeping it straight
10. Tail wind			10. Wind blowing from the right

1. Long distance (50 to 100 yards)—point of aim should be above the target
2. Medium distance (40 to 50 yards)—point of aim should be on the target
3. Short distance (20 to 40 yards)—point of aim should be in front of the target

Name: Audry Bullett			Name: Mary McGowan			Name: Joan Lord			Name: Nancy Hoag		
Round: Jr. Col. Round			Round: Jr. Col. Round			Round: Jr. Col. Round			Round: Jr. Col. Round		
Date: May 20, 1968			Date: May 20, 1968			Date: May 20, 1968			Date: May 20, 1968		
At 40 yds.	Hits	Score	At 40 yds.	Hits	Score	At 40 yds.	Hits	Score	At 40 yds.	Hits	Score
9 7 7 7 5	5	35	9 5 5 5 3	5	25	9 9 7 7 5 3	6	40	7 7 7 5 5	5	31
9 7 7 7 7 5	6	42	7 5 5 5 3 1	6	26	7 7 7 5 5 5	6	36		6	24
9 7 7 7 7	5	37	5 5 1 1	4	12	7 7 7 5 3 1	6	30	7 7 7 7 5 5	6	38
9 9 7 7 7 7	6	46	9 5 3	3	17	9 9 7 5 5 5	6	40	9 9 9 7 7 3	6	44
	22	160		18	80		24	146		23	137
At 30 yds.			At 30 yds.			At 30 yds.			At 30 yds.		
9 7 7 7 7 5	6	42	9 9 7 5 5 3	6	38	9 9 9 9 9 7	6	52	7 7 7 7 5 3	6	36
7 7 7 7 7 5	6	40	9 7 7 5 5 5	6	36	9 9 9 9 9 7	6	52	9 9 9 7 7 5	6	44
9 9 9 9 5 5	6	46	7 7 7 7 3 3	6	34	9 9 7 7 7 5	6	44	9 9 9 7 7 5	6	46
7 7 7 5 5 5	6	36	7 7 5 5 5 3	6	32	9 9 9 9 9 7	6	52	9 9 7 7 7	6	46
	24	164		24	142		24	200		24	172
At 20 yds.			At 20 yds.			At 20 yds.			At 20 yds.		
9 9 9 9 7 7	6	50	9 7 7 5 3	6	38	9 9 9 7 7 1	6	42		6	44
9 9 9 9 9 9	6	54	7 7 7 7 3	6	36	9 9 9 9 9 7	6	52	9 7 7 7 7 5	6	42
9 9 9 9 9 7	6	52	9 7 7 7 5 5	6	40	9 9 9 9 9 7	6	52	9 9 9 7 5 5	6	44
9 9 9 9 7 7	6	50	9 7 7 5 5 3	6	36	9 9 9 9 7 7	6	50	9 9 9 9 7 7	6	50
	24	206		24	150		24	196		24	180
Total Score	70	530	Total Score	66	372	Total Score	72	542	Total Score	71	489
									Team Score		279 – 1933

SAMPLE SCORE SHEET

Fig. 4-18.

Scores are recorded by listing the highest values first. Each score is recorded; a zero indicates misses or hits outside the scoring area.

FIELD ARCHERY

There are several suggested rounds in field archery. As mentioned earlier, the flint round is most appropriate for beginners. Simplified rules and scoring include:

BASIC RULES

1. Archers shoot in groups of four, with the target captain calling scores and pulling arrows. One person is the scorer.

2. "Timber" is the warning call to others and announces plans to shoot.

3. Stand behind the shooting stake and shoot four arrows if it is a one position shot or one arrow from each of four designated positions. These four positions may be fan shaped or of the walk-up type (getting closer to the target).

SCORING

1. The center circle, including the spot, scores 5 points; the outer circle scores 3.

2. An arrow cutting two rings is awarded the value of the higher circle.

3. Arrows passing through the face, but still in the target, may be pushed back and scored as a hit in the circle they penetrated.

4. Witnessed bounces or arrows passing through the target are given a 3 point value.

SAFETY AND GAME COURTESIES

Courtesy and safety are inseparable in archery. Safety practices protect the archer as well as her fellow shooters.

For self-protection:

1. Check all tackle for cracks, frayed strings, imperfect arrows.

2. Be properly equipped with glove or tab and arm guard. Wear suitable clothing that does not interfere with shooting.

3. Do not draw a bow without an arrow in it. Such a pull may cause the bow to break.

4. Make certain arrows are long enough.

Fig. 4-19. For safety purposes all archers should stand behind the shooting line until the instructor gives the signal for the group to move together toward their targets to retrieve the arrows. (Courtesy of Clifford Lewis, University of Georgia.)

For protection of others:

1. Nock the arrow only after the signal is given to shoot. Nock only in direction of target.

2. Straddle the shooting line to be sure all other archers are in line.

3. After shooting, remain behind the safety line until a signal is given for retrieving arrows.

4. Release an arrow *only* if you can see the unobstructed target and a clear area behind.

5. Always be conscious of the possible danger of bows and arrows. Treat them with respect and never leave equipment unguarded where others can use it without caution.

Terminology

Anchor — The string hand position when the archer is shooting or aiming.
Arrow rest — The shelf on the bow or bow handle that supports the arrow across the bow.
Back — Side of bow away from archer when shooting.

Belly — Inside of bow facing the archer when shooting.
Bracing the bow — Process of stringing the bow in preparation for shooting.
Cast — The ability of a bow to shoot an arrow. Refers to distance or speed that a bow delivers.
Cock feather — The feather at right angles to the nock. It is usually a different color from that of the other feathers.
Composite bow — A bow made of one or more basic materials, such as wood and plastic.
Creeping — Allowing the string hand to edge forward before or during a release.
Crest — Colorful markings on the arrow to aid in identification.
End — Six arrows shot in succession.
Fistmele — Distance between bow belly and string measured from the base of the hand to the tip of the extended thumb. Approximately 6 to 7 inches or more for recurved bows when braced.
Fletching — The 3 or 4 feathers on the arrow.
Follow-through — Holding the release position until the arrow reaches its mark.
Footed arrow — An arrow with a hardwood insert in the foreshaft to ensure greater strength.
Free style — shooting with the aid of a bow sight.
Group — A cluster of arrows that are in approximately the same place on the target.
Hand — In field archery, shooting four arrows.
Hen feathers — Two feathers on the arrow parallel to the nock, usually of the same color.

Instinctive aim — Aiming and shooting without bow sight, pre-gap, or point of aim methods. Often called "bare bow" method.

Lady Paramount — Presiding official in women's tournaments.

Limbs — Upper and lower parts of the bow, the handle being the division.

Nock — The grooves at the bow ends into which the string is slipped for bracing the bow; also the end of the arrow into which the string is fitted for nocking the arrow.

Overdraw — Unsafe act of pulling an arrow back too far so the tip passes the handle of the bow.

Overstrung — Having more than a fistmele between belly and string because the string is too short.

Petticoat — The part of the target face that extends beyond the scoring area.

Point blank range — Shooting distance at which the center of the gold and the point of aim coincide.

Point of aim — A method of aiming used by many target archers. An aiming point is sighted on with the arrow tip.

Pre-gap — A method of aiming.

Quiver — One of many types of devices for holding arrows, both on the ground and on a person.

Range — Indoor or outdoor area designated and marked for shooting.

Range finder — One of several aids to the archer in locating her aiming point.

Round — A prescribed number of hands or ends shot at specified distances.

Self — Bow or arrow made of one piece of material.

Serving — Reinforced center of the bowstring.

Tackle — Archery equipment.

Tassel — Cloth used to wipe soiled or wet arrows.

Timber! — Term used as a warning in field archery.

Timber hitch — A knot used to tie a single looped string to the lower end of the bow.

Toxophilite — An ardent student and practitioner of archery.

Trajectory — The arrow's path of flight.

Understrung — Having less than a fistmele between belly and string because the string is too long.

Selected Audio-visual Aids

Archery for Girls. (10 min., 16 mm., sound, b & w and color.) Coronet Instructional Films, 65 E. South Water St., Chicago, Ill. 60601 (Purchase.)

Beginning Archery. (35 mm. filmstrip, 4 units, 10 min. each, color.) The Athletic Institute, Rev. 1962, 805 Merchandise Mart, Chicago, Ill. 60654 (Purchase.)

Introduction to Field Archery. (12 min., 16 mm., sound, color.) Albin Films, 1710 N. La Brea Ave., Hollywood, Calif. 90028 (Rental and purchase.)

The World of Archery. American Archery Council, 100 East Ohio St., Chicago, Ill. 60611.

Suggested Readings

AAHPER: *Archery-Riding Guide*, Current edition, Division for Girls and Women's Sports, 1201 16th St., N.W., Washington, D.C. 20036.

Forbes, Thomas A.: *New Guide to Better Archery*, Harrisburg, Pa., Stackpole Co., 1960.

Haugen, Arnold O. and Metcalf Harlen G.: *Field Archery and Bowhunting*, New York, The Ronald Press Company, 1963.

Love, Albert J.: *Field Archery Technique*, Corpus Christi, Texas, Dotson Printing Co., 1956.

McKinney, Wayne C.: *Archery*, Dubuque, Iowa, William C. Brown Company, 1966.

National Field Archery Association: *Official Handbook of Field Archery*, Current edition. P.O. Box H, Palm Springs, Calif. 92262.

Niemeyer, Roy K.: *Beginning Archery*, Belmont, Calif., Wadsworth Publishing Co., 1962.

Periodicals

Archery — A Sportsman's Magazine Devoted to Hunting and Field: National Field Archery Association, P. O. Box H, Palm Springs, Calif. 92262.

Archery World: 24 South Reading Ave., Boyertown, Pa. 19512.

Suggested Study Questions

1. Explain the differences among (a) point of aim, (b) sighting, and (c) bare bow methods of aiming. What are the advantages of each?

2. What is the usual result and action of an arrow that is (a) released with a jerking motion, (b) released as the bow arm collapses, and (c) released as the string hand creeps forward?

3. Why would arrows consistently go (a) low and to the left, (b) low and to the right, (c) straight over the target?

4. Why are the anchor points different for target and field archery? Are there other differences?

CHAPTER FIVE

Courtesy of Department of Health and Physical Education, Rice University, Houston, Texas.

BADMINTON

Badminton originated from the ancient game battledore and shuttlecock played in Siam and China over 2000 years ago. A modified version of this sport, known as "Poona," caught the attention and enthusiasm of British Army officers stationed in India, who around 1870 brought the game home to England. The Duke of Beaufort gave real impetus to the game at his estate, Badminton House, in the rural hamlet of Badminton in Gloucestershire. The game spread rapidly throughout the world and reached the United States via Canada. Since 1929 it has gained thousands of enthusiastic players and spectators in this country. Numerous tournaments are sponsored by the American Badminton Association, and many individuals subscribe to "Bird Chatter," the official publication of this organization.* The game is taught and played in many of our secondary schools and colleges.

As a coeducational and family activity, badminton has no equal. It is a sport with great appeal for all ages, as well as for those of varying skill levels and degrees of physical stamina. Although the beginner can quickly learn to hit the bird back and forth across the net, it is the advanced player, who has mastered game strategy and bird placement, who receives the greatest satisfaction from the game. Since badminton requires little space and can be played outdoors or indoors on an imperfect surface, and since accident possibilities and game hazards are minimal and needed equipment is inexpensive, it is an ideal activity for schools, camps, organizations, and backyard family fun.

NATURE AND PURPOSE OF THE SPORT

Badminton can be played as a singles or doubles game with one or two players on a side. The object of this racket game is to serve and hit the shuttlecock, or bird, across a net (5 feet from the floor at its center and 5 feet and 1 inch at the sides) with such skill and accuracy that the opponent is unable to return the shot.

FACILITIES AND EQUIPMENT

Badminton rackets weigh between 4½ and 6 ounces and are approximately 26 inches long. The average handle size is 3½ to 3¾ inches. The body of the delicate racket is made of aluminum, fiberglass, plastic, or wood and strung with nylon, gut, or linen. Advanced players prefer wooden rackets strung with nylon or gut. When not in use, all such rackets should be kept in a press and hung in a dry place. A badminton cart with multiple presses is recommended for both proper storage and ease of distribution of rackets for class use.*

Shuttlecocks may have 14 to 16 goose feathers in a plastic or cork base covered with fine leather. Cork is best for skilled players. The best birds are stitched in three places to keep the 16 feather spines and quills straight. Before using the more costly birds, beginners may be taught with wool or cotton practice balls, or with fleece balls homemade of yarn or obtained commercially, or with birds made of synthetic materials and chicken feathers. Students should be taught to straighten out the feathers before hitting the bird each time and should be cautioned against damaging it by kicking or stepping on it or putting it into play with overhead strokes. All feathered birds should be kept in a humidifier at a temperature between 60 and 65° F. and a hu-

---

*For information regarding this magazine, write to the Editor, *Bird Chatter*, 2 Dolfield Rd., Owing's Mills, Md., subscription price, $1.50.

*Hale, Patricia: *Design for a Badminton Cart.* Official Tennis-Badminton Guide, 1956-1958, Division for Girls and Women's Sports, AAHPER, Washington, D.C., pp. 94-98.

midity of 70 to 75 per cent. A modified humidifier can be made by placing a small tin can filled with water on a well filled sponge in a larger can. Place a wire screen over the smaller can and scatter the birds over it; then cover both cans to retain the moisture.*

The net should be made of fine meshed cord, edged on top with 3 inch white tape. It should be kept folded and stored in a dry place when not in use.

Rubber-soled tennis shoes or sneakers are required for safe indoor play and are also recommended for outdoor use.

BASIC SKILLS

The Grip. A flexible wrist snap is imperative for efficient stroking on both the forehand and backhand. This is best accomplished on the *forehand* by grasping the handle with a handshake grip while the

---

*Bourguardez, Virginia, and Heilman, Charles: *Sports Equipment, Selection, Care and Repair*, New York, A. S. Barnes & Co., Inc., 1950, p. 214.

racket face is at right angles to the ground. The fingers are spread slightly apart, with the forefinger extended diagonally and slightly bent behind the handle. The thumb is cocked and wrapped around the inside of the handle, exerting pressure against the forefinger. The handle rests at the base of the fingers but not in the palm, with the "V" formed by the thumb and forefinger on the inside top of the handle and in line with the racket head. Swing the racket back and forth, snapping the wrist to get the feel of the necessary quick, definite movement.

The *backhand grip* is similar to the Eastern backhand grip in tennis. To gain the backhand from a forehand grip position, hold the racket by the throat with the left hand and turn the right hand to the left so that the first knuckle is on top of the racket handle. Extend the thumb diagonally up and back of the handle. The "V" line formed by the thumb and forefinger is somewhat *behind* the racket when held in front of the player (Fig. 5-3). The advanced player will notice that the backhand grip results in a slight wrist cock as the arm is brought across the body in preparation for a backhand stroke.

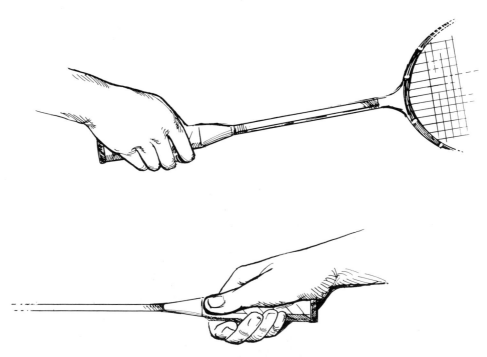

Fig. 5-1. Mastery of the correct grip is basic to developing badminton skill.

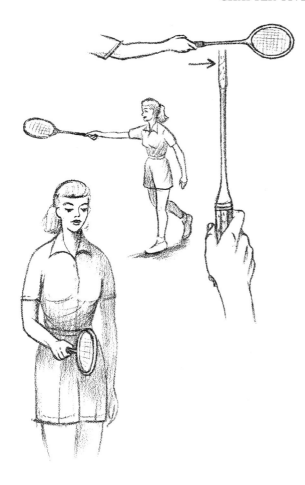

Fig. 5-2. The forehand grip.

STROKES CLASSIFIED BY MOVEMENT

The Forehand Drive. This stroke, which is similar to throwing a softball, is a flowing, free movement in which the follow-through plays an important part, It is a natural movement used when returning the bird from the right side of the body. The head of the racket should be kept higher than the wrist, and the left foot is brought forward, the body leaning slightly sideward toward the net. The backswing should start at the same time the left foot is brought forward. Simultaneous with a pivotal shift of the body weight from the rear to the forward foot, the bent elbow leads the flexed wrist into the stroking area. The wrist should be slightly ahead of the racket head and snapped at the moment of contact. If the player wants to hit the bird upward, she should swing low, then up to it, whereas to hit it downward, the forward swing is in a downward arc. The arm should be extended and relaxed and the bird hit squarely in the racket center by a quick wrist flick.

The Backhand Drive. The backhand drive is made with the right shoulder facing the net and the racket held with a backhand grip. As the bird is hit with the reverse side of the racket, the weight is shifted with the feet in a stride position from the rear to the forward foot. When the bird is played in front of the body, the thumb may be held so that it rests

Fig. 5-3. The backhand drive and grip.

Fig. 5-4. The forehand drive.

flat against the nonhitting side of the racket for more power and better control.

The Serve. The racket is held with a forehand grip. The shuttle should be struck in front of the body with the full arm stretched for a relaxed but forceful movement. With feet in stride position, the body weight shifts from the forward foot to back, then is returned to forward as the bird is hit. The wrist flick, forward arc swing and follow-through should be easy, natural movements. There is very little follow-through on a short serve. Beginners should drop the bird from the thumb and index finger, held at the extreme feather tip, and play it in front of the

forward foot. Advanced players may master the toss serve by throwing the bird slightly into the air and contacting it with a well timed forward stroke. The majority of serves in singles should be high and deep; in doubles they should be low and land just inside the service court or on a boundary line. To be a legal serve, the bird must be contacted below the waist with no part of the racket higher than the server's hand.

The *long high serve* should be used most often in singles. It is basically the same as the underhand clear shot and is used to force the opponent into the back court, thus giving the server added time to get into the best court

Fig. 5-5. The serve.

position for offensive play. For this long serve, the bird may be tossed or dropped well in front of the server. She should aim toward the ceiling, and her body should lean slightly forward as she sweeps her arm swiftly forward in a long, fast, swinging movement to contact the bird. If she chooses to drop the bird, she should do so at the end of the backswing. If the toss release is used, the bird should be thrown to the right of the forward foot as the backswing begins.

The *short serve* is best for doubles play and is used to force the receiver to hit the bird up high on the return so that the opponents can use a smash or quick kill shot to gain a point. It can also be used sometimes as a surprise or to change game pace. In this stroke, the bird should barely clear the net and be placed close to the net at either corner of the receiver's court. The bird should be stroked, rather than hit, with little follow-through. In order to deceive the receiver, the backswing should be forceful. The bird should be guided carefully so that it barely clears the net and gives the impression that it will not do so.

The *driven serve* is used most often in doubles (sometimes, too, in singles for a sur-prise) and is used to deceive the receiver into thinking that the serve will be a fault by landing in the wrong back court. Although the footwork and basic motions are the same as for other serves, the follow-through should be toward the net at chest height, and the bird should be hit hard enough to land deep in the service court and aimed to land close to the midline of the service court.

Footwork and the Ready Position. The player must learn how to move quickly over the court, carrying her weight on the balls of her feet with easy, relaxed knees and posture. The right foot should be back on the forehand drive, and the body should face the right sideline, with the left foot forward. On the stroke, body weight should shift from the back to the forward foot. On the backhand drive, this pattern is reversed. The player faces the left sideline, and body weight is shifted from the left rear foot to the right forward foot while stroking. The sweep, force and racket movement speed should all be increased and the knees more deeply bent on shots which require more force.

The player should face the net for the ready position. Her left foot should be slightly forward. The racket should be held a

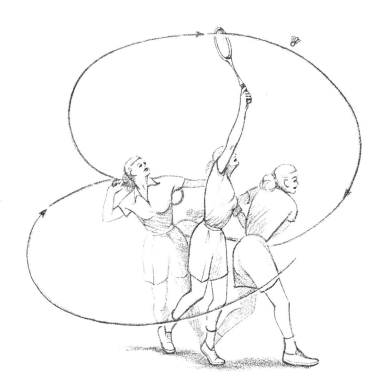

Fig. 5-6. The overhead stroke.

bit above eye level in front of her body, and its head should be pointed up and toward her opponent. Beginners should practice changing quickly from the ready position to hitting an imaginary bird forehand, backhand, above the head, and below the knees in quick, swishing movements.

The Overhead Stroke. On this shot the bird is hit above the head to the right of the body for the forehand and to the left for the backhand overhead stroke. The feet are held shoulder width apart in stride position. As the bird is contacted, body weight shifts from the rear to the forward foot. The arm is slightly bent and is extended when the bird is hit slightly in front of the body with a forceful wrist flick. The racket follow-through makes a half circle. Quick judgment, timing and accuracy are required to hit the approaching bird at least six inches in front of the body and to bring it down just over the net and well placed in the opponent's court.

The Round-the-Head Shot. Similar to the overhead stroke, this one is stronger and often more effective. The narrow stride stance and shift of weight from the rear to the forward foot are similar to those used in most shots, except that the weight should end well balanced on the left foot. Contact is made

with the bird above the shoulder and around the head on the left side by extending the bent stroking arm in order to hit the bird on the forehand side.

STROKES CLASSIFIED BY BIRD FLIGHT

The High Clear. Played either by the forehand or backhand, the high clear is a defensive stroke used to gain time, to move the opponent into the back court, or to change game pace. The bird is played just as it is in either the forehand or backhand and should land far in the back court after sailing high into the air. It is similar to the tennis lob.

The Drive. This attacking stroke should barely clear the net. It can be played with either the forehand or backhand, usually down one side, to force the opponent to switch court sides. The bird can best be controlled for this stroke at shoulder height but can be also played successfully from knee level. Variance in bird speed must be mastered in order to use this shot most effectively.

The Drop Shot. The name of this stroke best describes it, for it is a shot that causes the bird to drop sharply, close to the net, into the

Fig. 5-7. The round-the-head stroke.

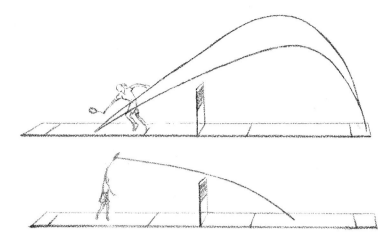

Fig. 5-8. Types of shots.

opponent's front court. Played like any other shot, it requires control and placement ability. It is used as a surprise attack to change game pace, or to fool the opponent who expects a drive or clear into the back court and has moved back for it and thus out of position. Cross court drop shots are especially effective. Overhand strokes are best for making such a shot while in the back court, and underhand strokes wisest when close to the net.

The Smash. The smash is used more in doubles than in singles. It is best played in midcourt and should be aimed directly at the opponent, to her weakest defensive body side (usually backhand for right-handed players and forehand for left-handed players), or at open court spaces. It should be a powerful, fast stroke and can be best done with a forehand. In the forehand smash the left foot should be ahead and the racket swung far back behind the head and shoulder by a flexible wrist. The bird should be hit ahead of the forward left foot and weight put into the stroke by a forceful body shift as contact is made with the bird. The term "smash" describes both the stroke and how to do it correctly.

The Net or Hairpin Shot. Played close to the net, this shot can send the bird just barely over it, diagonally across it, or far into the back court as a high clear. The bird should be hit near the net top, and the racket held face up by the extended arm as it gently taps the shuttlecock with a slight wrist action. Careful aiming, together with this restricted wrist motion, will direct the bird most effectively. The net clear is similar to the drop shot but is

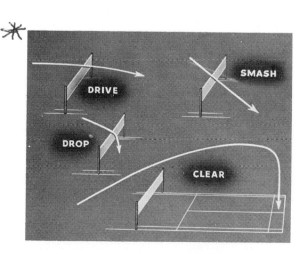

Fig. 5-9. Types of flights. (Courtesy of The Athletic Institute.)

done with a delayed, more pronounced wrist flick. This stroke is ideal for changing game pace, gaining time, wearing the opponent down, and restricting the possibility of any diagonal or outward angles to a returned shot.

✳ GAME RULES AND SCORING

A game of women's singles is <u>11 points</u>, whereas for men's singles and mixed doubles it is 15 or 21 points, as arranged. The doubles service court extends from the short service line to the long service line, and from the center line to the side boundary line. The singles service court extends from the short service line to the back boundary line, and from the center line to the side boundary line. The court service boundaries are long and narrow for singles, short and fat for doubles. After service the singles playing court remains the same, whereas the doubles playing area becomes long and wide. Points are scored only by the serving side, with loss of service known as "side out," as in volleyball.

The server serves only one bird into alternate courts (as in tennis) and begins in her right-hand court. To be good the bird must go diagonally across the net and land in the receiver's box. A serve that strikes the net but continues on into the proper court is good. In doubles only one player serves at the beginning of the game (this is called "one hand down in the first inning"), but for the rest of the game both the opposing partners alternate serves. Service in doubles always starts in the right court. In singles the service begins in the right court, but thereafter it is made in this court only when the score is even for that side, and in the left court when the score is odd for that side. The first singles player to reach 9 points when the score is 9-all may choose to play for 3 more points, or for 2 more when the score is 10-all. In doubles, when the score is tied 13-all, those first reaching 13 determine whether to finish the game at 15 or to "set" it for 5 more points. At 14-all the game may be set at 3 more points.

It is a fault (a service or hand loss for the server, or point loss for the receiver) when:

1. The bird is served above the waist or the

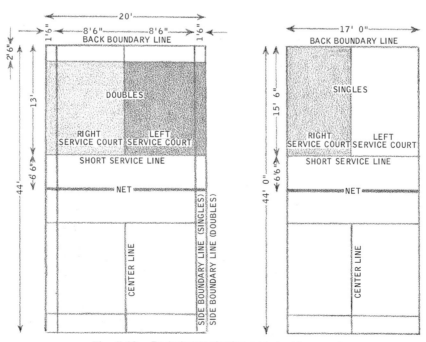

Fig. 5-10. Badminton singles and doubles courts.

racket head is higher than the hand on a serve.

2. The server or receiver fails to keep her feet within the boundaries of her service area during the serve.

3. The bird is hit into the wrong service area, out of bounds, into the net, or hits a player or any obstruction outside the court.

4. Anyone other than the intended receiver returns the bird.

5. The server feints a serve or balks her opponent.

6. A player reaches over the net to hit the bird or touches the net with any part of her body or racket.

7. A player hits the bird twice or "tosses" or "holds" it instead of stroking it correctly.

8. A player fails to return the bird, hits it twice in a row, or it is hit by one player and then her partner successively before it goes over the net.

A match consists of the best of three games. Players change ends at the start of the second game, and if needed, also at the third game. In the third game players change sides when the first player reaches 8 in a game of 15 points or 6 in a game of 11 points.

PLAYING STRATEGY

Badminton is a game of brain as well as brawn. In the pre-game warm-up, players should discover each other's weaknesses, whether they be in stroking or in inability to move quickly around the court. Then, during the game, play to that weakness. Hitting the bird *away* from the opponent or into uncovered court areas is usually the best strategy. Wearing the opponent out by running her up the court, then back, is ideal for this purpose. Since one can only score points each time she serves or is "in," the skilled player will never *beat herself* by careless mistakes such as serving incorrectly or hitting the bird into the net or out of bounds.

IN SINGLES

1. Although deep, high serves near the center line are best for singles, they should be varied in height and direction. The server's best position is about 4 feet behind the short

service line, but she should return after the serve to the middle of the court (or "home base"). The receiver's best position is in mid-court, slightly toward center.

2. Return a high serve with a drop to the opponent's forehand, or clear to her backhand, or a sparingly used smash.

3. Return a short serve with a high clear into the back court.

4. Avoid returning a net shot with a net shot unless you can do a quick diagonal one away from your opponent.

5. Anticipate returns. Hit the shuttle back to the court area your opponent is leaving.

6. Always play the bird in front of you, remembering that if it goes back over your head you are lost, and that it is easier to move forward than backward.

7. Smashes down a straight line are generally the most effective.

8. Return a smash with a drop shot away from the area from which your rival smashed.

9. Change game pace often; plan your strokes ahead.

10. Take the offensive by making accurate, well placed shots from a well prepared defensive position which moves your opponent from front to rear, side to side.

11. Deception is the key to winning. Deceive your opponent by making the same preparatory stroke for the smash, drop, and clear, then fool her by using the one for which she is least prepared.

12. Since most right-handed beginners have weak backhands and most left-handed ones have weak forehands, capitalize upon this weakness by skillful bird placement.

13. Deception is the key to gaining points. Fool your opponent by using the stroke for which she is least prepared.

IN DOUBLES — 15pt.

PLAYING POSITIONS

Four methods for playing doubles are:

1. *Side-by-side*—with each player being responsible for her half of the court.

2. *Up-and-back*—with one player at the net and her partner covering the back court.

3. *A combination*—in which the side-by-side system is used for defense and the up-and-back method for offense.

Fig. 5-11. In order to become a skilled badminton player you must master a variety of shots and the ability to place the bird where you want it to go. (Courtesy of Clifford Lewis, University of Georgia.)

4. *Rotation*—best for advanced players who circle counterclockwise in order to play the bird forehand as much as possible. As the player on the right advances to the net, the one on the left drops back, crosses into the right court, and moves into the original player's right court position, as both continue in the circle. Both players should be right-handed if the system is used.

GAME STRATEGY

1. The best defensive position is partners side-by-side near the center of the court. The best attacking formation is for one partner to smash, with the other forward and ready to "kill" a weak forecourt return.

2. Most serves should be short and low, but long, deep ones should be used occasionally.

3. Hit most shots down and away from the opponents.

4. Gain the attack and keep it by hitting the bird low so the opponents will have to hit it up and it can be smashed back at them.

5. Use hard smashes directed to the body.

6. Drive the bird occasionally down the midcourt line in the hope that both opponents go for it, or if one is left-handed and the other right-handed.

HOW TO BECOME A SKILLED BADMINTON PLAYER

1. Master a variety of shots and the ability to place the bird where you want it to go.

Learn how to change the pace of a game by the correct use of a smash, hairpin shot, or drive.

(Text continued on p. 88.)

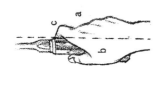

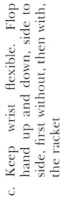

SKILL DIFFICULTIES AND THEIR CORRECTION

Difficulty	*Correction*
1. The Grip	**1.**
a. Choking the racket	a. Move hand down
b. Holding the racket too tightly, muscles too tensed	b. Relax
c. First finger up behind racket; thumb extended along handle	c. Keep fingers down. Tape fingers in proper position if you have trouble remembering
d. Failure to modify grip for the backhand	d. Review correct backhand grip
2. Hitting the Bird	**2.**
a. Missing it entirely	a. Use a wool practice ball. Suspend a bird with string and stroke it many times to get the proper timing. In wall practice, hit bird gently with racket face up 15 to 20 times. Shorten bird. Watch the bird
b. Hitting it on the racket edge	b. Hit in the correct part of the racket. Follow suggestions above
c. Stiff tennis arm swing	c. Keep wrist flexible. Flop hand up and down, side to side, first without, then with, the racket

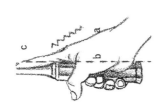

SKILL DIFFICULTIES AND THEIR CORRECTION (*Continued*)

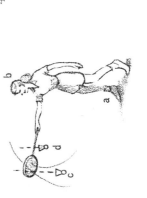

	Difficulty		*Correction*
3.	*Serving*	**3.**	
	a. Missing the bird	a.	Flex knees more and bend closer to the bird. Use wall practice with a slightly dropped shuttle. See suggestion 2a
	b. Driving it into the net	b.	Stress timing and rhythm. Learn where contact should be made with bird. Check grip to see if you are choking racket
	c. Moving the feet while serving	c.	Review serving rule
	d. Holding the bird too close to the body	d.	Ask for teacher demonstration
	e. Serving too short and high	e.	Drop bird nearer forward foot instead of too far in front
	f. Serving too low	f.	Let wrist lead racket head until bird is hit, then bring racket head up slowly for good follow-through
4.	*Footwork and Timing*	**4.**	
	a. Wrong foot forward, especially on serve	a.	Try to grasp the "feel" of the wrong and right way for feelings of naturalness
	b. Letting the bird get behind the head	b.	Always play the bird in front of you
	c. Swinging too late	c.	Practice timing with shuttle suspended with string
	d. Standing too close to the bird while stroking	d.	Ask for teacher demonstration

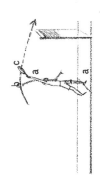

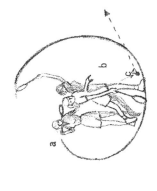

5. *Overhead Shots*

a. Driving the bird into the net

b. Weak strokes

c. Bird sails too long before dropping down

5.

a. Learn the best and poorest positions for smashing. Smash from fully extended arm with a fast wrist snap (especially when closer to the net). Have your partner throw birds far into the backcourt to get the feel of the overhand movement

b. Practice wrist snap

c. Hit bird at highest point of the reach. Practice wrist flick

6. *Underhand Shots*

a. Driving the bird out of bounds

b. Weak stroke

c. Missing the bird in game play

6.

a. Review form for the clear and drop shots. Remember the necessity for a full back-swing and snap from wrist, and correct follow-through Practice close to net, then move back

b. Practice wrist snap.

c. Remember to keep the eye on the bird at all times

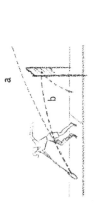
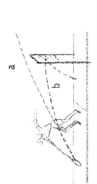

3. Practice hitting the bird against a wall line 10 feet high. Work to develop a good wrist snap, as well as quick, accurate strokes.

4. Play mixed doubles with and against skilled men players, and capitalize on what you learn from this experience.

5. Make every shot count, even in practice.

6. Hit all clears high and deep.

7. Get back quickly to the center of the court after every shot.

8. Place as many shots as you can deep and to the center of your opponent's court, for this will make a small angle for her return shot to you.

GAME COURTESIES

1. In informal play, the server should call out the score before each serve.

2. Never walk behind a person who is playing on a court.

3. Recover the server's bird promptly.

4. If you lose, be a good sport and always congratulate your opponent.

5. Never question the umpire's or your opponent's decision about a shot.

6. Learn to win and to lose gracefully.

Terminology

Ace — One point, also called "score," "point."

Alley — Used in doubles play, strips 1½ feet wide between two boundary lines.

Balk — A deceptive movement, or feint, which disconcerts an opponent before or during service.

Carry — Also a sling or throw. An illegal procedure in which the shuttle is kept in the racket too long during a stroke.

Down — Loss of serve given when serving side fails to score. In doubles, the side first serving has only one down.

Fault — A bird that falls short, hits into the net, or lands out of bounds.

Hairpin (net) stroke — A bird just barely crossing over the net and falling close to the other side, the flight resembling a hairpin.

Home position — Ideal court spot for awaiting opponent's return, usually at midcourt near center line.

Inning — Term of service. Time in which a player or side has the right to serve.

Lob — Also called a high clear or driven clear; goes over opponent's head.

Love all — The game score at the beginning of the game and after "setting."

Odd and even courts — In singles the right half court is "even" and the left half is "odd." When the server's score is love or an even number, the service is taken from the right-hand court; when it is an odd number, from the left. In doubles, the server in the right court is called the "even" player and her partner the "odd." When the "even" player is serving from the right, the score is even, when from the left, odd. The reverse is true of her partner.

Out side — the receiving side.

Playing for an opening — Getting the opponent into position for a "kill."

Rally — Rapid returns made by players. The winner of a rally usually serves, except in tournament play.

Rubber — The best of three games.

Setting — Increasing game play at a tied score, at 9-all, 10-all, 14-all. In a 15 point game when the score is tied, a player may set for 5 points, or at 3 points when tied at 14. In an 11 point game, when the score is tied at 9, one may set for 3 points, or when tied at 10, may set for 2. The one reaching the tied score first, "sets."

Side in — The side having its turn to serve.

Sling or throw — An untrue hit, usually the result of catching the feathers in the strings or drawing the racket away from the bird as it is stroked; a fault.

Toss serve — A type of serve used mostly by advanced players in which the shuttle is tossed for the serve.

Selected Audio-visual Aids

Badminton Fundamentals. (10 min., sound, b & w.) Coronet Instructional Films, 65 East South Water Street, Chicago, Ill. (Rental.)

Beginning Badminton. (Instructor's Guide and Handbooks, slide films, 4 units, color.) The Athletic Institute, 805 Merchandise Mart, Chicago 54, Ill. (Rental.)

Good Badminton. Teaching Film Custodians, 25 W. 43rd Street, New York, N.Y. (Rental.)

Let's Play Badminton, 1947. (10 min., sound, b & w.) General Sportcraft Company, 215 Fourth Avenue, New York, N.Y. (Rental.)

Tips for Better Badminton. Sports Tips and Teaching Aids, 16801 Parkside Drive, Detroit, Mich. (Purchase.)

Suggested Readings

Davidson, Kenneth, and Gustafson, Leland: *Winning Badminton*, Rev. Ed., New York, The Ronald Press Company, 1964.

Davis, Dorothy (ed.): *Selected Tennis and Badminton Articles*, 2nd ed., Washington, D.C., AAHPER, Division for Girls and Women's Sports, 1963.

Freidrich, John, and Rutledge, Abbie: *Beginning Badminton*, Belmont, California, Wadsworth Publishing Company, 1962.

Humiston, Dorothy, and Humiston, Michel: *Fundamentals of Sports for Girls and Women*, New York, The Ronald Press Company, 1965.

Varner, Margaret: *Badminton*, Dubuque, Iowa, William C. Brown Company, 1966.

Periodicals

Bird Chatter: American Badminton Association, 2 Dolfield Road, Owing's Mills, Maryland.
The Racquet: 104 E. 52nd St., New York, N.Y. 10022

Suggested Study Questions

1. Discuss the best strategy for singles and doubles play.
2. Discuss the care and repair of all badminton equipment.
3. Explain the forehand and backhand grips.
4. Describe and demonstrate four basic badminton strokes.
5. What is "setting" in scoring? When is it used?

CHAPTER SIX

Courtesy of Agnes I. Michaels, State University College, Fredonia, New York.

BOWLING

Bowling, the most popular indoor sport in the United States, attracts 30 million participants to more than 70,000 lanes each year. Although the artifacts of the Stone Age indicate that the true origin of bowling games lies in antiquity, the present sport developed from a German religious ceremony. During the 3rd and 4th centuries most German men carried a *kegel*, a small club resembling an Indian club, for use in strengthening wrists and forearms, for recreation, and for a religious ceremony. In this ceremony a man called on by the priest to prove he was leading an honorable life had to set up his kegel, called *Heide* (heathen), and knock it over with a small round stone.

The monks and laymen recognized the recreational value in bowling and continued the sport long after the religious ceremony was abolished. Martin Luther was an enthusiastic bowler in the 16th century and published a set of rules for a game of ninepins.

The ninepin game came to America with the Dutch settlers and became so popular that indoor lanes, the Knickerbocker Alleys, were built in New York in 1840. Bowling suffered a setback when the ninepins game was prohibited by the Connecticut legislature because of gambling and rowdiness. It remained for an ingenious hero to add a tenth pin to circumvent the law. The additional pin resulted in a triangular set and the birth of present-day bowling.

NATURE AND PURPOSE OF THE SPORT

The game of tenpins attracts the greatest number of bowlers, although improved equipment and playing surroundings have increased participation in duck pins, candle pins, and five pins. These games require a smaller ball, which is carried in the palm of the hand during delivery. In the late 19th century the American Bowling Congress organized and standardized rules, equipment, and alleys. In 1916 the Women's International Bowling Congress was organized and has continued to conduct national tournaments and give leadership to the sport. The American Junior Bowling Congress sponsors tournaments and helps boys and girls to receive reduced rates and free instruction. The alertness of national organizations toward meeting the needs of all ages, the emphasis given the sport by television, bringing an understanding and appreciation to millions, and the "new look" of bowling establishments are the primary reasons for increased public interest.

The object of the bowler is to roll well aimed balls down a wooden alley and knock down as many of the triangularly set ten pins at the end of the alley as possible. Ten frames constitute a game and each frame represents a player's turn. The bowler is allowed two balls each frame. When all the pins are knocked down with the first ball, a strike is scored. If all pins are knocked down on the second ball, a spare is recorded. Bonus points are added to the score for strikes and spares. (See Scoring Section.) The maximum number that can be scored in a game is 300.

The bowler stands in an approach area, walks or runs toward the alley, and delivers the ball from behind the foul line so that it rolls toward the pins. When all the pins are knocked down by the first delivery in a frame, a strike results and the second ball is not rolled. If some of the pins remain standing, a second ball is rolled. Competition can be individual, with from one to five persons on an alley, or it may be in units with as many as five on each team. A handicap scoring system allows for equitable competition among all skill levels.*

Long hours of physical conditioning and body building are not necessary for skillful bowling. Since coordination, rhythm, and

---

*For tournament competition refer to WIBC *Rules for Sanctioned Leagues.*

alertness are more important than great speed, strength, or endurance, bowling is an ideal recreational activity. As a social activity bowling allows for periods of relaxation and competition with oneself, as well as with team and league members.

FACILITIES AND EQUIPMENT

One of the appeals of the game for beginners is that it is not necessary to own a single piece of equipment to participate. An enthusiastic kegler will eventually want to own her personal shoes, ball, and equipment bag, but commercial establishments and most student unions rent shoes at a nominal fee and furnish balls.

Alley. The terms alley and lane are synonymous and include the total area where preparation, ball delivery, and contact with the pins take place. The area includes the approach, foul line, alley bed, gutters, and pit. The ball return and rack are also part of a complete lane.

The approach is a level runway extending from the seating area and scoring table to the foul line. A minimum of 15 feet is necessary for the approach. The alley bed is 63 feet long, 41 to 42 inches wide, and begins at the foul line and extends to the pit area. The alley bed is constructed of maple and pine lengths laid vertically so that the balls roll on the thickness of the boards. The harder and more durable maple is laid at the beginning of the foul line for 12 or 15 feet, then pine, then maple again on the deck area where the pins are knocked over. Many alleys have range finders to help in selecting a point of aim in spot bowling. These darts, or dots, are usually placed where the maple and pine lengths first join on the alleybed.

On the deck, 10 pin spots are marked for accuracy in setting pins. The spots are 12 inches apart from center to center, in a triangular pattern with the apex toward the bowler. The headpin is set 3 feet from the end of the alley.

The pit, at the rear of the alley, is a depressed area into which the pins are knocked and where a human or automatic pinsetter works. Automatic pinsetters are common in commercial alleys and are seen increasingly on college campuses.

On each side of the alley bed, there is a rounded and depressed gutter 9 to 9½ inches wide. This trough carries a poorly aimed ball to the pit, where it is placed manually or automatically on the ball return track, and thus returns to the ball rack next to the approach area.

Pins. Official American ten pins are hard, clear maple, 15 inches in height, 5 inches at their greatest breadth, and weigh between 2 pounds, 14 ounces, and 3 pounds, 10 ounces. Proper design and balance are assured by reputable manufacturers.

Ball. The American Bowling Congress rules that balls may not be more than 27 inches in circumference or weigh more than 16 pounds. Balls with two or three finger holes or semifingertip and fingertip grips are permissible. Most beginning women bowlers are more comfortable with a three-hole ball

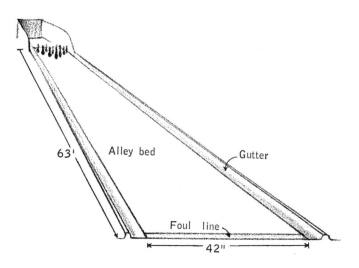

Fig. 6-1. A bowling alley.

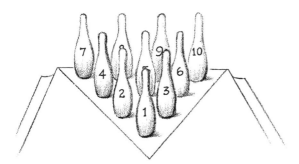

Fig. 6-2. Properly set and numbered pins.

Fig. 6-3. Selecting a proper ball.

weighing 12 to 14 pounds, while junior bowlers select smaller balls weighing around 10 pounds. Color is a personal preference and does not necessarily indicate the weight or size of the hard rubber compound balls.

Dress.   No special costume is required for recreational bowling. A comfortable full skirt and blouse are acceptable, while slacks or shorts are appropriate in some communities. Well fitting socks should be worn. Bowling shoes are essential for safety and skill development. For a right-handed bowler the left sole is leather or buckskin to allow for sliding on the approach and the right sole is rubber for braking this action. The sole materials are reversed for left-handed, or "wrong foot," bowlers. A leather-soled shoe or heavy sock on the sliding foot and a tennis shoe on the braking foot may substitute for regulation shoes during instructional periods in the gymnasium or corridors.

PURCHASE AND CARE OF EQUIPMENT

Well fitting shoes will probably be an early purchase for the frequent bowler. An investment of $5 to $15 saves rental fees and insures proper fit. Shoes require little care if they are dried after wearing, polished occasionally, and worn only in the alley so that the soles are not marred.

The advanced bowler will soon want her own custom fitted ball. A bowling instructor should aid in ball selection to evaluate overall strength, grip strength, speed of delivery, size of hand, and body weight. The well fitted ball can be comfortably gripped, swung, and released with control but without excessive strain. Custom fitted balls cost approximately $25 to $30. Cleaning the ball after each use and protecting it with a carrying bag assure long life.

BASIC SKILLS

Ball Selection and Grip.   Selecting a ball that permits a comfortable grip is basic to successful scoring. Ball choice is determined by an individual's strength and size and the location, size, and direction of the finger holes.

Most women prefer 12 to 14 pound balls. The heavier the ball the more efficiently it will knock down pins, but a lighter ball can be controlled better and delivered faster, thus resulting in better pin action.

Most women select three-hole balls, some advanced bowlers using a semifingertip, a fingertip, or a combination of a regular and a fingertip grip. Few women use a two-hole ball because of the additional finger strength needed to control the delivery.

Size and pitch of the finger and thumb holes, and span of the bowler's hand determine the proper fit of a ball. The holes must be small enough to allow the thumb, middle, and ring fingers to maintain contact with the edges of the holes toward the palm of the hand, yet loose enough for an easy release without scraping the fingers. Proper span for the conventional three-hole grip is determined by inserting the thumb about three quarters of its length into the hole drilled on the center line of the ball. If the hand is spread so the middle and ring fingers extend to the left and right of the centerline, the middle knuckles of both fingers should extend about ¼ inch past the inside edge of the holes. If the holes are bored at the usual ⅜ inch angle, a naturally balanced grip results when the thumb is inserted three quarters of its length and the fingers are inserted up to the second joint. The first and little fingers are straight and spread over the outside of the ball for control. A bowler can check the grip by asking: (1) Is my hand comfortable? (2) Do I have a feeling of control? (3) Can a pencil be slipped between my hand and the ball without changing the grip?

STANCE AND APPROACH

These two important skills are best learned as a unit, because each is dependent upon the other. Stance involves grip and how and where to stand on the approach area. The bowler determines her stance position for the four step approach by taking four regular steps and allowing several additional feet to account for increased strides and slide in an actual approach. Starting from a designated spot so that delivery will be consistent, the right-handed bowler places her feet close together with the left foot slightly forward. The feet, hips, and shoulders are facing the pins squarely. Standing position varies among the experts; some stoop forward with ball held at the waistline, while others stand erect with the ball at chest level. In either case the upper back is straight. Beginners are encouraged to stand upright, weight on the heels, bending slightly forward from the hips while holding the ball at the waistline. One hand grips the ball and the other hand, palm up, supports its weight. Each bowler should find her own comfortable, relaxed position.

The approach is a series of well coordinated movements that end in the release and delivery of the ball. Its purpose is to develop momentum and thereby gain speed and force for the delivery. Successful bowlers vary in their approaches from three to five steps, but the four step approach is the most popular. From a selected stance position the bowler follows a straight line to the foul line and point of ball release. The right-handed bowler moves the right foot forward in a slow, short, rhythmical step; the second step (left foot) is slightly longer and faster. Forward momentum increases as the right foot extends in a longer, faster third step, leading to the fastest and longest fourth step on the left foot. Forward momentum stops as

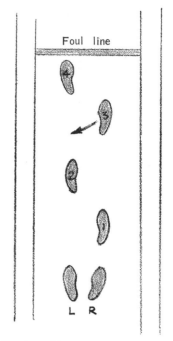

Fig. 6-4. The four step approach.

the fourth step ends in a slide. At this point, the toe of the left foot should be near the foul line and pointing to the head pin. The right foot swings behind the body for balance and for braking action of the forward movement. The approach begins from an upright position, and as the bowler picks up momentum she increases her forward leaning position. The final steps into the slide end with the left knee bent, hips tucked under the body, and the upper body straight and inclined forward.

Coordinated Approach. Preparation for delivery requires coordination of approach steps, arm swing, and body action. As the right-handed bowler takes her first step (with the right foot), the ball, held by both hands in front of the body, elbows close in, is pushed directly forward. This "pushaway" extends the arm, which remains straight throughout the swing and release. While the second step is taken (left foot), the extended right arm, gripping the ball, swings down and straight backward in a pendulum-like motion, with the ball leading the backswing. At completion of the second step the arm should be pointing straight down, alongside the leg. The ball swings back on the third step. The left arm is free to swing outward to maintain balance as

Fig. 6-5. The coordinated approach.

the body moves in a straight line toward the pins.

On the third step (right foot) the right arm and ball continue upward as the backswing carries the arm to a position parallel to the floor. As the fourth step (left foot) begins the forward slide, the left knee bends and the weight of the ball pulls the right arm downward and forward. The right arm and left foot move forward together. The ball passes the left leg and is released as the forward swing starts upward. As the arm reaches forward during the release the ball contacts the alley just beyond the foul line. The right foot swings behind the body in a natural position to maintain balance as the right arm follows through toward the pins and upward to eye level. The shoulders stay parallel to the foul line and the left foot finishes on the same board it has followed from the stance position.

DELIVERY

The beginner should carefully develop either a straight ball or a hook ball delivery. The backup and curve ball deliveries, briefly described later, should not be attempted. The straight ball delivery is well suited to the occasional bowler, for it can be controlled more consistently than the hook, particularly when bowling at spares. However, the straight ball

Fig. 6-6. The beginning bowler should develop either the straight or hook ball delivery. (Courtesy of Clifford Lewis, University of Georgia.)

has a lower percentage of strikes than the hook ball, which "mixes" the pins more effectively.

Straight Ball Delivery. The right-handed bowler stands on the right hand corner of the approach with the left foot five to ten boards from the right gutter. Throughout the coordinated approach the ball hand and arm are in line with the floor boards. As the ball is carried toward the foul line the thumb is in a 12 o'clock position, pointing toward the pins, and the fingers are under and behind the ball. As the release begins the thumb slides from the hole and the ball rolls off the fingertips beyond the foul line and six to eight boards in from the right gutter. There is no rotation of the forearm. As the ball is released the fingers impart an upward spin; then the open hand, with palm up and fingers and thumb pointing toward the pins, continues in an upward arc.

Hook Ball Delivery. The controlled hook ball has a high strike percentage because the ball hits the pins at an effective angle with a spinning motion that scatters the pins. The positioning for the approach is similar to that of a straight ball delivery. The bowler stands to the right of the center of the approach area about 10 to 15 boards from the right gutter. The right-handed bowler turns the ball hand so that the little finger is toward the floor, and the thumb is toward the body in 9 o'clock position during the swing. The "V" between thumb and forefinger points toward the 1-3 pocket. The ball is released beyond the foul line, 6 to 12 boards in from the right gutter. The thumb is released first, with the fingers following. The delayed finger release causes a right to left spin as the hand and arm follow through outward and upward toward the pins. The ball travels parallel to the right gutter toward the 3 or 6 pin, depending on the "break" of the hook. About two thirds of the way down the alley the ball angles sharply toward the pins and travels into the 1-3 pocket to the 5 pin.

Increased hooking action is accomplished in several ways:

1. Wrist hook delivery. With the hand in natural hook delivery position there is a forced rotation of the forearm in a counterclockwise direction as the ball is released from the hand.

2. Lift hook delivery. With the hand almost underneath the ball and the thumb in

Fig. 6-7. The straight ball release.

Fig. 6-8. The hook ball release.

10 or 11 o'clock position, the *fingers* are force-fully lifted upward on release, imparting a strong counterclockwise spin to the ball. Once mastered, this hook allows excellent ball control.

3. Lift and turn hook delivery. With the thumb in 10 or 11 o'clock position the fingers are forcefully lifted, with simultaneous forearm rotation. This combination delivery produces the greatest hook of the methods described.

Curve Ball Delivery. The curve is a slow, wide-sweeping ball with a counterclockwise spin, which travels in an arc toward the pins. It is difficult to control because of its wide arc and the adjustment necessary to the varying slickness of alleys. It is not recommended for beginners. The width of the ball's arch determines where the bowler stands for delivery. A right-handed bowler using a small arc stands slightly to the right of the head pin. With wide-arcing balls she may move farther to the left of the approach area, possibly to the left of the head pin. The bowler's hand is placed on the ball as in a natural hook delivery, with the thumb rotated back and to the left at a 9 o'clock position. On release the thumb leaves the ball first and the *hand* and *wrist twist* from right to left to impart spin.

Back-up Ball Delivery. This delivery is not

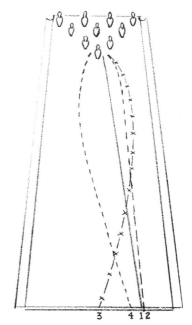

Fig. 6-11. Four types of delivery. Straight ball (1), hook ball (2), curve ball (3) and back-up ball (4).

recommended, yet it is a common delivery among women and should be corrected. This reverse ball, when delivered by a right-hander, travels toward the left, then curves to the right before striking the pins. The hand is almost directly under the ball with the thumb

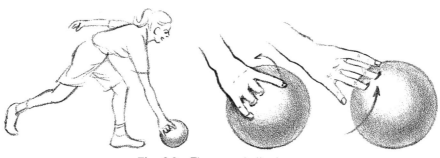

Fig. 6-9. The curve ball release.

Fig. 6-10. Back-up ball delivery.

pointing to the right of the pins (right-handed bowler). As the ball is released, a left-to-right twist causes a reverse spin.

POINT OF AIM

Point of aim refers to the place or spot where the bowler's eyes focus during the approach and delivery. There are two distinct theories of aiming and a third is gaining popularity. It remains for each bowler to experiment and select the method best suited for her delivery.

Pin Bowling. On the first ball the bowler looks at the pins and aims for the 5 pin through the 1-3 pocket (1-2 pocket for left-handers). A straight ball delivery goes directly for the pocket, whereas a hook delivery is released so that it will break into the pocket. After the first delivery the second ball is aimed at the pin or area she hopes to contact. Pin bowling is considered less accurate than spot bowling because of the distance the bowler must sight to the target. It is recommended for some beginners, as it is a natural focus point and requires less concentration.

Spot Bowling. The bowler selects one or more sports part way down the alley, between the point of release and the desired point of

contact with the pins, over which she tries to roll her ball. Most modern alleys have starting markers located 12 and 15 feet behind the foul line to aid the bowler in establishing a consistent stance position. Range markers are located on the alley bed, 7 feet beyond the foul line, and 13 feet 10 inches beyond the foul line to make spot selection easier. On a straight ball delivery the bowler attempts to release the ball between the first and second delivery dots (about 7½ boards in from the gutter) so that it will cross the second alley dart (approximately 8 inches from the gutter about 14 down the alley).

A natural hook is released halfway between the center delivery spot and the alley edge and is aimed at the dart in line with the release spot. If the alley is not marked, the bowler judges by the number of boards, measured from the alley side. The amount a ball hooks determines the varying release positions.

Line Bowling. This is a combination of pin and spot aiming methods. The line bowler draws an imaginary line from the stance position to the 1-3 pocket. She has four check points: the starting position, the slide position, the chosen spot, and the strike pocket. At any time she can select another spot and then change the other check points. This is a precision method of aiming which requires concentration and practice.

PICKING UP SPARES

The bowler who hopes to score well must be consistent in picking up spares. There are two widely accepted methods for spare bowling. The first, cross alley bowling, is based on the principle that as much of the alley width as possible should be between the delivery spot and the standing target. Therefore, when a pin or pins are on the right side of the alley, the bowler moves to the left of her regular first ball delivery spot. Conversely, when the leave is on the left, she begins to the right of the regular delivery spot. The leave and type of delivery dictate how far she moves in each direction.

The second system is based on the principle that the strike ball line can be used for leaves on the left of the alley *if* the ball is released left of the strike ball release position and the point of aim adjusted. For spare

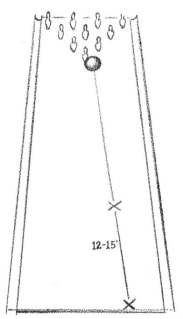

12-15'

Fig. 6-12. Spot bowling.

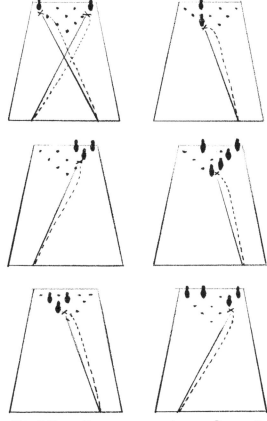

Fig. 6-13. Common spare leaves: Cross alley bowling.

leaves on the right, bowl a straight line, parallel to the alley bed toward the spare.

Speed and pin deflection are important to spare bowling. A fast ball may cause the pins to move so that they do not fall horizontally and knock down additional pins. Yet a slower ball may itself be deflected to the right or left if it does not hit a pin head-on or have sufficient momentum to carry through. The bowler should remember that some leaves are 3 feet behind the head pin, and additional thought should be given to speed and type of delivery to these pins.

GAME RULES AND SCORING

The number of pins legally knocked down in any frame, plus the pins knocked down by the first ball following a spare delivery, or the pins knocked down by the next two deliveries following a strike ball, is the total score of a frame. The score is cumulative from frame to frame for ten frames. A perfect score is 300. The player bowls two balls for each frame, unless she delivers a strike which upsets all ten pins with the first ball. When this occurs a second ball is not delivered in that frame. However, if a strike is delivered in the tenth frame, two more balls are delivered immediately. If a spare is made (all ten pins upset by the first and second balls) in the tenth frame, one more ball must be rolled at a new set of pins immediately to complete the game score.

When all pins are knocked down by the first ball in a frame, a strike is recorded by an (X) in the first small square in the upper corner of the score box of that frame. Eventually, the score in that frame will be the ten pins scored for the strike, plus the total number of pins knocked down by the next two balls.

The number of pins knocked down by the first ball (other than a strike) is recorded in the first square in the frame. When all the remaining pins are knocked over by the second roll, a spare is indicated by a diagonal line (/) in the second square of the frame. The player's score in the spare frame is a cumulative total of all pins knocked down in the preceding frames, the ten pins scored for the spare, and the pins knocked down on the next ball delivered.

When pins are left standing after both balls are rolled, an error is indicated by a straight line (−) in the score box, and only the total pins knocked down with both balls are recorded.

If, after the first ball is delivered, the head pin is down and two or more pins are left standing with at least one pin knocked down between them, a *split* is recorded by an (0). If the remaining pins are knocked down by the second ball, a spare is indicated (∅) in the score box. When pins remain standing after the second ball, only the number of pins knocked down by the two balls is scored.

If a ball is delivered to the gutter before reaching the pins, a (G) is recorded in the appropriate box.

An understanding of the foul rule is basic to accurate scoring. There are many ways in which a foul may be committed, but the commonest is permitting any part of the body to touch the foul line or go beyond it during or

Fig. 6-14. Some common fouls.

after delivery. A foul is indicated by (**F**) in the proper box.

When a foul is committed, the ball rolled shall count as a turn, but any pins knocked down or displaced are respotted and no pins are scored.

A game description and illustration of recording scores are helpful in mastering scoring techniques (see Fig. 6-15):

Frame　1 — 1. All pins are knocked down by the first ball (a strike).

Frame　2 — 1. Six pins are knocked down, head pin remains standing on first ball.

　　　　　　2. Remaining pins are knocked down by second ball. A spare is recorded and the score totaled for the first frame.

Frame　3 — 1. Eight pins fall on the first delivery, leaving pins 7 and 9. A split is recorded and total can be reached for second frame.

　　　　　　2. Second ball knocks down the remaining pins. A spare is recorded.

Frame　4 — 1. A strike is recorded. Total score recorded in frame 3.

Frame　5 — 1. Six pins are knocked down.

　　　　　　2. Three pins are knocked down by second ball. A miss is re-

corded in the score box. Total score is recorded in frames 4 and 5.

Frame　6 — 1. A strike is recorded.

Frame　7 — 1. A strike is recorded.

Frame　8 — 1. Nine pins are knocked down on the first delivery. Score is totaled in frame 6.

　　　　　　2. The second ball hits the remaining pin, but the bowler's foot crosses the foul line. A foul is recorded in the score box and the score is totaled.

Frame　9 — 1. The first ball runs into the gutter and no pins are knocked over.

　　　　　　2. The second ball knocks down all pins. A spare is scored.

Frame 10 — 1. A strike is scored. Score in frame 9 is totaled.

　　　　　　2. Next ball delivered knocks down 7 pins.

　　　　　　3. Last ball rolled knocks down 2 of the 3 remaining pins. The completed game score is recorded.

The official rules are established by the American Bowling Congress and the Women's International Bowling Congress. Basic rules follow.

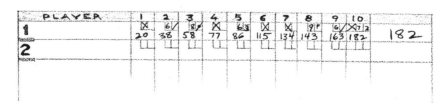

Fig. 6-15. Scoring a sample game.

Legal Pinfall. Every ball a player delivers counts unless it is ruled a dead ball.

1. Pins knocked down by another pin or pins rebounding from a side partition or rear cushion count as pins down.

2. If it is discovered after delivery that one or more pins are not properly set, though not missing, the ball and any pinfall are counted. (It is the player's responsibility to determine proper pin set prior to delivery.)

3. Pins that are knocked down by a fair ball and remain lying on the alley bed or in the gutters count as pins down. Pins that lean over and touch partitions or kickbacks also count. They are moved before the next ball is bowled.

Illegal Pinfall. The ball counts but the pins knocked down do not count when:

1. The ball leaves the alley before reaching the pins.

2. The ball rebounds from the rear cushion.

3. The pins hit any part of the pinsetter's body and rebound.

4. A standing pin falls or is knocked down by the pinsetter. It must be replaced.

5. Pins are bowled off the alley bed but rebound to standing position.

6. A foul is committed.

Dead Ball. A ball is declared dead and any pins falling are respotted for the bowler in the following instances:

1. A ball is delivered and attention is immediately called to the fact that one or more pins were missing from the setup.

2. A pinsetter interferes or moves a pin before they stop rolling or before the ball reaches them.

3. A player bowls out of turn or on the wrong alley.

4. A player is interfered with by a spectator, a bowler, a pinsetter or a moving object as the ball is delivered and before delivery is complete. The bowler may either accept the pinfall or request that the pins be respotted.

5. Pins are moved or knocked down in any manner as the ball is being delivered and before the ball reaches the pins.

6. A player's ball contacts a foreign object.

STRATEGY

Bowling, like many individual sports, requires a positive, confident attitude toward one's individual game. Mastery of bowling fundamentals can develop this confidence. Compete with yourself, always working toward your own better score and average rather than *against* your opponent's score.

In team competition (usually five on a team) place your strongest bowlers in lead-off (first) and anchor (last) position. The strong anchor bowler should be consistent and calm, for much pressure can rest on the last bowler in the last frame.

GAME COURTESIES

A knowledge of bowling etiquette assures a more enjoyable game for you and other bowlers. In brief:

1. Be alert and ready for your turn.

2. The bowler addressing the pin has the right of way. If players on adjoining alleys address the pins simultaneously, the bowler on the right has the privilege of bowling first.

3. Avoid talking and jesting with a bowler addressing pins.

4. Select one ball and use only that ball throughout the game. Rolling two balls in quick succession is dangerous if a pinsetter is in the pit.

5. Always observe the foul line.

6. Walk directly back from the foul line after delivery.

7. Control your temper. Bowling is a game to be enjoyed and should not defeat the bowler.

Terminology

Alley bed—Wooden surface between foul line and pit.

Anchor—Person who bowls last in team's lineup.

Approach—(1) Surface between the front of the lane and the foul line where the bowler stands to make a delivery. (2) Footwork and style used in delivery.

Baby split—A split leaving the 2-7 or the 3-10 pins after first ball is delivered.

Back-up ball—A reverse ball. When rolling, it curves toward the side of the bowler's body from which it was delivered. It curves right for a right handed bowler.

Bed posts—A split in which only the 7 and 10 pins remain. Often called fence or goal posts.

Big four—A split in which the 4, 6, 7, and 10 pins remain.

Blow—An error. Failure to knock down pins standing (other than a split) with the second ball.

Brooklyn—A crossover. A ball that hits the side of the head pin and rolls into the pocket opposite the side of the body from which the ball was delivered (1-2 pocket for a right-handed bowler).

Chop (cherry)—Knocking down the front pin or pins of a spare leave while leaving the back pins standing.

Cross-alley shot—A ball that crosses the center of the alley when traveling to the pins.

Dead ball—(1) A ball which hits the pins without effectively "mixing" them. (2) A ball that does not count.

Division boards—Alley area where light and dark woods meet.

Double—Two successive strikes.

Dutch 200 (Dutchman)—A 200 score attained by alternating strikes and spares for ten frames.

Fast lane—A highly polished alley that resists the working action of the ball for hooks, curves, etc.

Foul—A rule infraction; usually touching or going beyond the foul line.

Foul line—Line separating the approach and alley bed.

Frame—One of ten large scoring squares for recording total pin count; each frame represents one-tenth of a game.

Full hit—Ball that hits the center of the target pin.

Gutter ball—A delivered ball that drops into either gutter (channel on side of alley bed) before reaching the pins.

Handicap—A bonus or score adjustment used in competition to equalize opportunity between different individuals or teams.

Head pin—Number 1 pin.

Hook—A delivered ball that travels in a straight line half or two thirds the length of the alley and then curves sharply away from the side of the bowler from which it was delivered. A hook veers left for a right-handed bowler.

Inning—A frame or each bowler's turn.

Kegler—A bowler.

King pin—Number 5 pin.

Lane—The alley or alley bed.

Leave—The pin or pins standing after delivery of the first ball.

Lift—A slight upward motion imparted to the ball as it is released.

Line—A game or ten frames.

Loft—Releasing the ball above the alley bed, thus throwing it at delivery.

Mark—To make a strike or a spare.

Perfect game—Twelve successive strikes and a game total of 300.

Pit—Area behind the alley where pins fall after being hit.

Pitch—Angle at which finger holes are bored in a ball.

Pocket—The space between any two pins; usually refers to the 1-3 or 1-2 pins.

Railroad—A split. Refers to one of several kinds of splits.

Roundhouse—A wide, curving ball.

Sleeper—A pin hidden by another pin.

Show lane—Usually means an alley that responds to curve and hook deliveries.

Spare—Knocking down all remaining pins with the second ball in a frame.

Split—At least two pins are standing after the first ball; the head pin is down and at least one pin is down between or ahead of the remaining pins.

Spot—A mark or location on the alley to which the bowler aims.

Strike—All pins are knocked down by the first ball of a frame.

Strike out—Three successive strike balls in the tenth frame.

Turkey—Three successive strikes during a game.

Woolworth—A split leaving pins 5 and 10.

Selected Audio-visual Aids

America Bowls. (25 min., 16 mm., sound, b & w.) Brunswick-Balke-Collender Company, 23-33 S. Wabash Ave., Chicago, Ill. 60605 (Loan.)

Beginning Bowling. (Filmstrips and recordings.) The Sport, The Delivery, Aiming, and Scoring. The Athletic Institute, 805 Merchandise Mart, Chicago, Ill. 60654 (Sale and rental.)

Better Bowling—How It's Done. (20 min., 16 mm., color, sound.) Ebonite Company, Division of Stowe-Woodward Company, Newton, Mass. 02158 (Loan.)

Let's Go Bowling. (30 min., 16 mm., sound, b & w.) Bowling Proprietors Association of America, 111 S. Washington, Park Ridge, Ill. (Sale.)

Suggested Readings

AAHPER: *Bowling, Fencing, Golf Guide*, Current edition, Division for Girls and Women's Sports, Washington, D.C.

Audsley, Judy: *Bowling for Women*, New York, Sterling Publishing Company, 1964.

Day, Ned: *How to Bowl Better*, New York, Arco Publishing Company, 1960.

Falcaro, Joe, and Goodman, Murray: *Bowling for All*, 3rd Ed., New York, The Ronald Press, 1957.

Fraley, Oscar: *The Complete Handbook of Bowling*, Englewood Cliffs, N.J., Prentice-Hall Company, 1958.

McMahon, Junie, and Goodman, Murray: *Modern Bowling Techniques*, New York, The Ronald Press, 1958.

Periodicals

Bowling: American Bowling Congress, 1572 E. Capital Drive, Milwaukee, Wis.

Prep Pin Patter: American Junior Bowling Congress, 1913 W. 103rd St., Chicago, Ill.

Woman Bowler: Women's International Bowling Congress, 4319 W. Irving Park Road, Chicago, Ill.

Suggested Study Questions

1. What are the advantages and disadvantages of (a) straight ball delivery, (b) hook ball delivery, and (c) curve ball delivery?
2. Explain the methods of spare bowling described in this chapter. Which do you prefer? Why?
3. Explain spot bowling. Why is it considered a precision method of aiming?
4. Score a complete game, including a strike, a spare, an error, a gutter ball, a split pickup, and a tenth frame strike.
5. Explain how to check the proper fit of a three-hole bowling ball.

CHAPTER SEVEN

Courtesy of Dean Ann S. Duggan, College of Health, Physical Education and Recreation, Texas Woman's University, Denton, Texas.

FENCING

The growth of fencing as a popular international sport is a tribute to the progress of civilization. Originally the skill was used as a method of war and a device for settling personal disputes.

Through the years the weapons of fencing have reflected the purposes and types of combat of each era. The warriors of the Middle Ages used a two-handed sword for destruction and subjugation of their foes. The heavier weapons were eventually replaced by the more precise, light rapiers with sharp points and sharp edges.

After gunpowder was introduced the sword lost its value in warfare, but members of the aristocracy continued to use fencing as a method of settling personal disputes. The tragic number of injuries and deaths from combat caused nations across the world to banish the sword as a weapon. The 19th century saw fencing rise as a new and acceptable sport of skill and strategy rather than at sheer strength and brute force. Women entered into fencing when protective equipment was developed and techniques of foil fencing were refined. Fencing is the only combative activity generally acceptable for women.

Fencing gains in popularity as its inherent values are recognized and the sport becomes better known. The formation of the Amateur Fencers of America in 1891 and the Intercollegiate Fencing Association in 1894 gave necessary leadership and sponsorship to competition and league formation across the United States. Fencing clubs affiliated with the Amateur Fencers League of America are active in major cities across the nation and encourage the participation of both sexes and all age groups.

NATURE AND PURPOSE OF THE SPORT

Fencing is a game of attack and defense by two opponents who attempt to score touches on one another with a designated weapon. Women use only the foil as a weapon; men, however, fence with the saber and epée as well. The bout is conducted in a designated area—the strip—and continues until one contestant scores four valid touches, or outscores her opponent within the five minute time limit.

The foil, lightest of all fencing weapons, encourages good body mechanics through balance and posture control. Whether one is a beginner or an advanced fencer, competing with other women or with men, fencing requires quick decisions, speed of movement, energy, and endurance.

Theoretically, the foil is a pointed instrument capable of inflicting a puncture wound on the opponent's torso. The point of the foil must touch the target area, which extends from the collar to the lines of the groin in front and to a horizontal line across the top of the hipbone on the back and sides. Touches on arms, legs, hands, or mask are not valid.

To score touches a contestant must attack her opponent. A successful attack requires precision and accuracy in selecting proper distance and timing. An arm extension, a lunge, or steps and a lunge bring the attacker to striking distance.

To avoid touches the defender uses a system of parries, or blocking actions, which deflect the attack. The defender may then return an attack to score a touch.

FACILITIES AND EQUIPMENT

As is true with many activities, equipment and facility areas can be improvised. However, basic safety requirements demand some carefully selected equipment. Beginning skills may be taught indoors or outdoors on various surfaces, but ideally a separate fencing room in the physical education area should serve for instructional and recreational purposes. The gymnasium area should not be filled with wall targets, mirrors, or other fencer's equipment because of the possible danger to participants in other activites.

The ground on which combat takes place is called the field of play. The *strip*, or *piste*, is the area upon which the bout is conducted. An official strip is between 5 feet 11 inches and 6 feet 7 inches in width and 39 feet 4 inches in length and has an additional 6 feet 7 inches of level surface beyond each end. Surfacing of linoleum, rubber, cork, wood, or plastic is acceptable. The strip is divided widthwise by seven lines. At each end there is an end line, and a center line divides the strip into halves. There are two "on guard" lines, one on each side of the center line and 6 feet 7 inches from it, and there is a warning line 3 feet 3 inches in front of each end line. Each of these lines is 1 inch in width. If it is not possible to paint lines on the floor's surface because of multi-use, commercial tapes can be laid and later removed with no floor damage.

The metallic piste is made of fine metallic mesh, usually brass. Such a strip neutralizes hits made on the ground by electrical weapons. If the metallic piste is used, it must cover the entire strip and its extensions.

Mirrors, stall bars, mats, and wall targets are among the aids helpful in teaching fencing skills. Mirrors are valuable in analyzing footwork and body position and stall bars provide a device for checking body alignment. Wall targets and dummies are invaluable for warming up and in practicing accuracy while lunging.

Foil. Women fence with both the French and Italian foils; however, the French foil is more popular for instructional purposes. The total weight of the foil must be less than 17.637 ounces and the length less than 43.3 inches. The foil is composed of four major parts—*blade*, *guard*, *handle*, and *pommel*.

BLADE. The steel blade, of fine machine steel, is quadrilateral (rectangular or square cross section) and tapers from the strong half, called the *forte*, to the weaker and more flexible half, the *foible*. The blunt tip must be covered with a rubber tip or wrapped with white tape. The pliable blade measures from 32 to 35 inches from guard to tip. Electrical foils are often used in competition to facilitate scoring.

GUARD. The steel or aluminum guard is a round or oval protection of the weapon hand. The round guards are 3½ to 4 inches in diameter. The oval or "figure eight" guards cannot exceed 4⅝ inches. A thumb pad or cushion is inserted between the guard and the handle to prevent friction between the metal guard and the fencer's knuckles.

HANDLE. The handle is rectangular and curved to fit the contour of the hand. The wooden handle is wrapped with cord or covered by leather to aid in a secure grip.

POMMEL. The pommel is a threaded steel knob that screws to the tang of the blade (the threaded end) and secures all parts of the weapon together. The pommel acts as a balance to the weight of the blade.

Electrical Equipment. The difficulty of accurately judging hits led to the development of electrical scoring devices. These devices require the use of an electric foil with a special spring point mounted on the end of the blade. When the point is depressed by a direct hit, a relay is sent down a light wire which runs the length of the blade to the fencer's body cord. This automatically registers the hit on a scoring apparatus. Validity of the hit is determined by contact with a metallic (*lamé*) jacket worn by each fencer over the regular jacket. The jacket covers only the

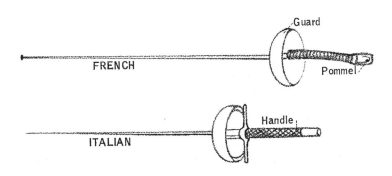

Fig. 7-1. Instructional foils.

valid target area. If a hit is made off the target an invalid hit is registered. Hits are acknowledged by a buzzer and lights on a central machine. A red or green light indicates a valid hit and the fencer who scored it. A white light indicates an invalid hit.

Martingale. The martingale or a similar strap holds the weapon near the hand so that the foil will not be knocked toward fencers or spectators in case of disarmament. It is not necessary during instructional classes.

Mask. A mask is as important to the sport of fencing as the foil itself. Prevention of injury and the fencer's confidence in safety make it essential. The mask and attached bib cover the entire front portion of the head and neck. The mask is constructed of strong wire mesh reinforced with leather or cord straps, a heavy padded cloth or canvas bib, and wire headpiece (tongue) covered with cloth which bends to adjust to a fencer's head.

Jackets and Trousers. Fencing jackets and plastrons serve as protection for the upper body. The full jacket is the most desirable protection for women, although the adjustable half jacket is more practical for group instruction. The jacket is made of heavy white material padded in front and in the upper sleeve. The shoulder seams of the jacket correspond to arm and shoulder lines. It should fully cover neck, arms, and torso and overlap the fencing breeches at the waist by at least 4 inches. Extra breast protection of padded material, plastic, or aluminum should be worn under the jacket, particularly in electrically scored events. *White trousers* which fasten below the knee, but are loose enough to allow freedom of movement, are worn by both men and women. Skirts or shorts are satisfactory for class use.

Footwear. Absorbent socks which cushion the feet and absorb perspiration are essential. Although flat leather-soled fencing shoes are desirable on regulation strips, tennis shoes or low-heeled rubber-soled shoes are practical for classwork.

Glove. A padded leather glove should be worn on the foil hand. The cuff must be long enough to overlap the jacket in order to prevent the blade from entering the sleeve. If students share gloves, they should wear a thin inner cotton glove to absorb perspiration.

CARE OF EQUIPMENT

1. Store foils in a hanging position so that blades are not damaged.

2. Foil tips should be padded with rubber tips or adhesive tape. Pommels should be secured to prevent guards and blades from wobbling.

3. The blade should have a slight bend so that when a touch is scored the tip is lower than the bend in the blade. To bend or straighten the blade, rub it between the shoe sole and floor. By friction the blade is heated and becomes more pliable. Avoid using hands to straighten a blade.

4. Replace and repair protective cushions and handles when worn. Thread or cord wrapped around the handle and glued at each end is satisfactory. Felt pads or padded leather serve as guards.

5. Before putting on a mask remove excess makeup. Always check the mask for gaps or rust spots. Wash padding and bibs frequently.

6. Store masks, jackets, and gloves in an area with maximum ventilation. Repair tears or rips immediately. Wash and fluff dry jackets regularly.

7. Gloves should be aired and cleaned with disinfectant powder. If inner glove is worn, wash frequently.

BASIC SKILLS

Grip. The handle of the foil is curved and shaped to fit the hand. Looking down on the handle, the convex portion fits into the palm of the hand as the thumb and forefinger serve as holding digits while the remaining fingers guide the fine foil action. The index finger is placed near the cushion so that the handle rests on the second joint of the finger.

Fig. 7-2. Fencing jackets.

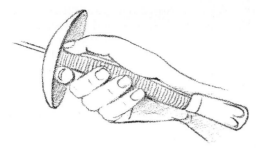

Fig. 7-3. Grip.

The thumb is placed on top of the handle, pointing toward the blade. A pinching motion is assumed. The fleshy tips of the second, third, and fourth fingers rest lightly along the concave surface and pull the handle into the palm. The wrist is straight and the pommel rests against the middle of the wrist. In this position there is a straight line from elbow to foil tip. Precision and accuracy are dependent on the coordinated grip, the thumb and index finger directing the gross action of the blade, and the other fingers controlling the direction of the foil tip.

Salute. The salute is a traditional movement of courtesy and greeting between opponents prior to crossing blades for practice, a lesson, or competition. The first position of the three-movement salute is the preparatory position. The fencers face each other with their feet at right angles and their foils extended forward and downward. The mask is held under the free arm by the back piece. On the second movement the foil is raised sharply bringing the guard to the chin, the pommel is centered in the forearm, toward the fencer, and the foil tip is directed toward the ceiling. With the third count the fencer briskly extends the foil arm at shoulder height with the point aiming at the opponent. At the completion of the salute the mask is put on, and the fencers assume the guard position.

Guard Position. The guard is the best balanced position of the body for offensive and defensive play. The fencer enters the guard position from an erect or preparatory position, knees straight and heels together at a 90 degree angle. The forward foot points toward the opponent's foot. The body is turned so that the forward shoulder and hip are toward the opponent. The front of the body is angled in the same direction as the rear foot. The foil arm is straight and extended forward and down so that the tip of the foil is held slightly off the ground. The back arm is straight, pointing downward and slightly away from the body. The hand is straight, palm up.

In assuming the crouched guard position,

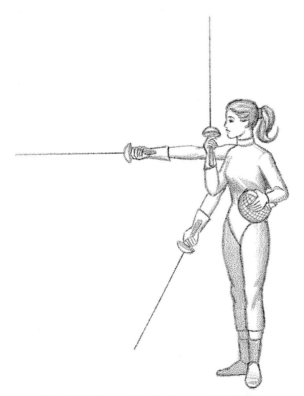

Fig. 7-4. The salute (in three movements).

Fig. 7-5. Preparatory position for guard position.

Fig. 7-6. Guard position.

move the forward foot approximately two footlengths forward. The heels remain at right angles, the knees are bent so that the kneecaps are directly over the toes of each foot. The torso is erect, as if sitting on a bench, with weight equally distributed on each foot. The back arm is bent, with the elbow at shoulder height and held in body line behind the torso. The wrist of the rear arm is relaxed, palm toward the head. The foil arm is bent and comfortably carried toward the opponent. The elbow of the foil arm is rotated toward the body line and in to a position approximately 6 to 9 inches (a hand span) from the side of the body. The foil is in a straight line with the forearm, pommel resting on the wrist as the foil tip points at opponent's eye level.

The Advance. The advance is a forward body movement used when the fencer needs to get close to her opponent for an attack. It also serves to force the opponent to retreat or to maintain a constant distance if the opponent has retreated. The advance is made from the guard position with small, even steps. (The jump advance is not recommended for beginners.) Pushing off with the toe, the forward foot leads with heel into a step of several (3 to 7) inches. The rear foot follows immediately with a step covering the same distance. The guard position is maintained and distance between the feet is constant. Weight is low, and the torso is in an erect position. The action results in a gliding motion.

The Retreat. The retreat is the reverse of the advance movement. It is a defense action which takes the fencer out of her opponent's reach, or it may be used to make the opponent advance. The rear foot moves rapidly backward, followed immediately by the front foot as the toe pushes off and the heel leads to the floor. As in the advance, small rapid steps are better than big ones. The feet do not rise far from the floor as the guard position is maintained and weight is distributed to insure rapid movement in any direction.

The Lunge and Recovery. The *lunge* is an extension of the arm and body from the guard position for the purpose of delivering an attack to the opponent. The lunge must be executed with split-second timing in sequence: (1) extend the foil arm toward opponent in line of attack (fingernails of hand up, pommel against wrist, and hand slightly higher than point), arm straight and elbow and shoulder firm; (2) straighten back leg and knee as the forward foot moves toward opponent (to a position where kneecap is over instep of forward foot); (3) simultaneous

Fig. 7-7. The lunge.

with the leg movements, straighten the rear arm, parallel to leg, with palm up to aid in balance and in preparation for recovery. The ankle of the rear foot is flexed so the foot can maintain firm floor contact.

The *recovery* to a guard position is accomplished by simultaneous movements: (1) bending rear knee as rear arm pulls to guard position, (2) pushing back with the forward toe and bringing foot to guard distance from rear foot, and (3) bending foil arm to guard position. The recovery must be a smooth, rapid movement as a slow recovery presents a weak defensive position.

ADVANCE LUNGE. The advance lunge is used when fencing out of distance and the opponent cannot be reached. It is also useful on an opponent who retreats when attacked, so that a touch necessitates extra distance. The foil arm is extended to begin the attack. It remains extended as the fencer advances and immediately lunges. Speed and determination are integral parts of the attack, but the body must be controlled and balanced at all times to avoid an easy score for the opponent.

BALLESTRA. The ballestra is a jump lunge that has its value in speed and surprise. It is similar, although quicker, than the advance lunge. The weight is shifted almost entirely to the rear foot, which hops forward as the forward foot, slightly raised, reaches ahead. The hop is short and *forward*, not upward. Both feet strike the floor at the same time, the rear foot landing approximately where the forward foot had been. Upon landing (in guard position), the right forward toe pushes, and the rear leg thrusts the body into lunge position.

LUNGE FOLLOWING FORWARD RECOVERY. A lunge followed by a forward recovery and a lunge is useful when the opponent retreats just out of reach at the moment of the initial lunge. Recover from the initial lunge by bending the rear leg and bringing it forward to guard position. (It may be necessary to defend rather than continue the attack.) Immediately lunge again or advance to a better position prior to lunging.

DEFENSES AND ATTACKS

The valid target area extends from the collar to a horizontal line which joins the top of the hip bones across the back and the groin line in front. The arms, from the shoulder

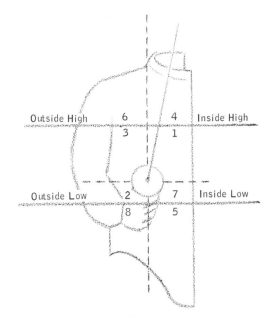

Fig. 7-8. The target area.

seam outward, and the hands, legs, bib, and mask are excluded as targets. Touches off the target area are invalid. To aid in defining attacks and parries, the target is theoretically divided into four sections or *lines of engagement.* This division results in high and low lines and inside and outside lines. The high-inside and high-outside lines are above the foil hand. The low-inside and low-outside lines are below the hand. For a right-handed fencer the inside lines are to the left of the foil; the outside lines are to the right. The reverse is true for left-handed fencers.

Engagement. While in the guard position, opponents lightly engage their blades at foible. The tip of each foil is aimed at the target and the hand holds the guard position to protect against a simple lunge.

Parries and Guard Positions. A parry is a defensive movement that blocks or deviates the attacking blade. There are eight fundamental parries, two for each line—one with hand in supination (palm upward) and the other with hand pronated (palm down). Each may be executed as (1) an *opposition parry,* in which pressure is held against the opponent's blade until a return or riposte, and (2) a *beat parry,* which deflects the opponent's blade from the line of attack. *Direct parries* are executed by moving the foil to the left or right to defend either high or low lines. *Semicircular parries* are made when moving from low to high or high to low lines. The tip of the foil travels in an arc as the parry is executed. A *circular parry* (counter) not only deviates the opponent's blade, but sweeps it into another line of attack with a circular motion of the defender's blade. The blade is carried by using only the fingers (the hand follows the blade under) and makes a small circle around the attacker's blade. It results in changing the line of engagement prior to the parry.

Parries should be looked upon as movements to guard positions and learned as movements from one guard position to another; that is, when a fencer executes a parry of sixth, she is properly moving to the guard position of sixth.

Parries are executed in an "on guard" position with the foil arm carried in guard position. The arm does not extend and bends closer to the body *only* if the opponent is fencing at closer than normal distance. Parries should deflect the blade laterally, not up and down the length of the torso.

The guard positions with the hand in supine position are recommended in foil fencing and are described (for right-handed fencers) in the logical order of presentation. A fencer can be competent with four sound parries — fourth, sixth, seventh and eighth. The other parries are rarely used.

PARRY OF FOURTH. This defends high-inside target area. The hand moves from guard position of sixth to the left, at the breast height, to the outer limits of the body to remove the threatening foil tip of the attacker. The hand is supinated, thumb up, and slightly higher than the elbow. The point of the blade remains at the opponent's eye level but slightly to the right.

PARRY OF SIXTH. The hand moves from guard position of fourth to the right to defend high-outside target. With the hand at breast height, fingers up, point at opponent's eyes, the forearm carries the weapon from pivot point of elbow so that the attacking blade can be carried by the strong part of the blade to the right of the body.

PARRY OF SEVENTH. This defends the low-inside line. The foil tip moves in a clockwise semicircle toward the opponent's knee level, hand to the left with palm facing upward.

PARRY OF EIGHTH. This defends the low-inside line. The hand moves to the right, palm up, with pommel directed past body line, and the point of the blade toward the opponent's knee level.

PARRY OF FIRST. This defends the high-inside line. The foil tip points toward the opponent's feet as the forearm is raised to a horizontal plane, elbow to the right. The hand is pronated, thumb down, fingers pointed toward the opponent.

PARRY OF THIRD. This defends the high-outside line. The foil and the pronated hand move to the right, the foil tip pointed toward the opponent's eye level.

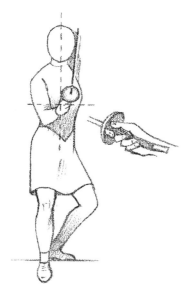

Fig. 7-9. Parry of fourth.

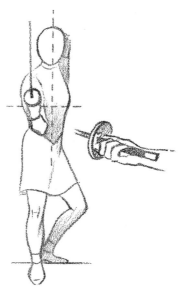

Fig. 7-10. Parry of sixth.

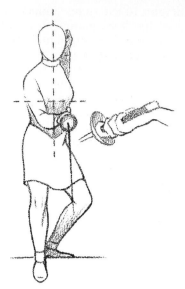

Fig. 7-11.   Parry of seventh.

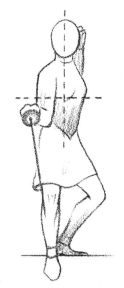

Fig. 7-12.   Parry of eighth.

Fig. 7-13.   Parry of first.

Fig. 7-14.   Parry of third.

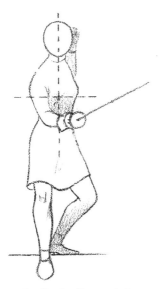

Fig. 7-15. Parry of fifth.

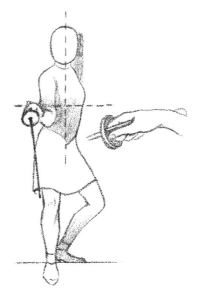

Fig. 7-16. Parry of second.

PARRY OF FIFTH. This defends the low-inside line. The pronated hand moves to the left and drops below the elbow. The point of the blade is higher than the hand.

PARRY OF SECOND. This defends the low outside line. The foil tip drops toward the opponent's knee level by a rapid, counter-clockwise, semicircular movement. The foil hand is turned to the right with the back of hand upward.

Simple Attacks. Generally, an attack is considered a forward movement of the foil,

Fig. 7-17. A successful fencing attack requires precision and accuracy in selecting proper distance and timing. (Courtesy of Clifford Lewis, University of Georgia.)

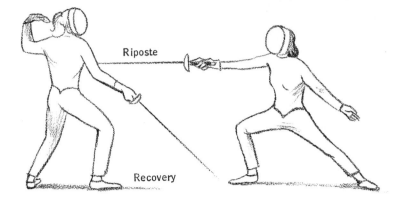

Fig. 7-18. Riposte and recovery.

with or without a lunge, toward the opponent's target. A simple attack comprises only one fast movement, such as a straight thrust, disengage, or cutover.

THE STRAIGHT THRUST. This is the simplest of all attacks. It involves a quick, smooth extension of the foil arm (shoulder high and palm up), in the line of engagement. The arm extension may be followed by a lunge if distance to the opponent requires it.

THE DISENGAGE. This is a change of line of attack made by passing the blade under the opponent's blade to an opposite line of engagement. Execution begins with an extension of the arm, shoulder high, palm up. Keeping the foil close to opponent's blade, the fingers drop the tip under the opponent's blade, circumscribing a small semicircle or a moving "V." When changing from seven to eight or eight to seven, the disengage is made over the blade, rather than under it.

THE CUTOVER. This is accomplished as the blade passes over the *point* of the opponent's dropped blade to change the line of

engagement. It is used against an opponent's lowered blade, as an opponent applies pressure with weak sections of blade against strong parts of the defender's blade, and when an opponent holds a parry too long. To execute the cutover the arm remains bent as the fingers and wrists lift the blade so that the tip circumscribes a small semicircle or inverted "V" as it crosses opponent's blade. The arm is extended immediately when the foil tip clears, and the lunge follows.

Riposte. The riposte is a return attack that follows a successful parry. The return may be a simple single thrust or compound attack. In either case, an immediate riposte has the right-of-way over a second attack by the original attacker. A *counter riposte* may be made following the parry of a riposte.

Compound Attacks. Compound, or composite, attacks are made in two or more movements by feints, attacks against the blade, or a combination of these. They include:

DOUBLE DISENGAGE (ONE-TWO ATTACK). This consists of two disengages executed in

Fig. 7-19. Lunge and parry.

rapid succession. The first disengage, with an extended arm, is made into an open line, forcing the opponent to parry. The second disengage follows immediately in the opposite direction to go on target in a newly created opening. The lunge begins with the second disengagement.

THE ONE-TWO-THREE ATTACK. An additional disengage is added to the "one-two" attack in an attempt to make an opening and a touch.

THE DOUBLE. An attack involving two disengagements in the same direction. The action consists of feinting a disengage, deceiving the counter parry, and lunging.

Attacks on the Blade. Attacks on the blade serve to create an opening in a closed line, to confuse the adversary by causing reaction to pressure on the blade and as invitations for attack.

FEINT. A feint is a false attack intended to deceive an opponent so she will close the line (parry) of attack and open a new line. A feint may take the form of a straight thrust, disengage, beat, or press, but to be deceptive it must be rapid and vigorous.

THE BEAT. A short, sharp movement executed so the middle part of the attacker's blade raps sharply against the middle or weak part of opponent's blade. The wrist and fingers control the attacking blade and cause a sharp, slapping action. It may be firm, in an attempt to open a line, or light, in anticipation of an answering beat and thus open an opposite line for a disengage attack. From an engagement in the four line the blade moves slightly to the right as the grip of the last three fingers relaxes. Quickly the fingers pull to the hand and the blade snaps sharply. The foil must remain close to the opponent's blade as a wide preparatory or follow-through movement exposes the fencer.

THE PRESS. Pressure is applied against the opponent's blade to remove it from the line. Without warning, it is executed similarly to the beat, but it is a smooth, strong action. As pressure is answered the attacker may move in the same line, or the attacker may release the pressure and cutover or disengage and attack in another line.

Attacks Taking the Blade. These attacks are developed to dominate the opponent's blade by removing the foil point from line by controlling the defending blade.

OPPOSITION. The guard of the attacking fencer is in opposition to the opponent's blade as pressure is exerted. This must be a simple attack.

BIND. A method of moving an opponent's blade from high to low line or low to high line. The action is taken against a stiff extended arm by applying the strong part of the foil blade to a weak portion of the opponent's and forcing with one's own blade and forearm. For example, when making a seventh bind from the guard position of sixth, make a small circle over the top of the defender's blade and lower blade and forearm. This action carries the blade to seventh. A slight lateral and forward motion to the right will carry the opponent's point outside the body line. This must be a rapid action, so that the opponent's blade is controlled at all times.

CROISE. The croise is an action similar to the bind; however, the blade crosses over and carries from high to low line on the *same* side. It is used when the opponent's blade is close to the target and when a bind, which brings the blade across the body, would be dangerous.

ENVELOPMENT. This is executed against a straight arm and is similar to the bind. However, it is a continuous motion carrying the opponent's blade in a complete circle and returning to original engagement.

Counter Attacks. These involve split-second timing, as they are simply arm extensions toward the fencer preparing to attack.

TIME THRUST. The time thrust is usually executed against a compound attack. It is made by an extension in opposition to the opponent's blade and constitutes a parry and a riposte in a single movement. It is most effective against an advancing opponent.

STOP THRUST. The stop thrust is executed with or without a lunge at the instant a careless opponent lifts her foot to advance. It should be used only when an opponent's blade moves out of line on a feint, when her blade leaves the defender's blade, or when the attacker's arm bends on advance.

Secondary Attacks. Secondary attacks follow immediately after the first, whether in the same line or another. They are effective when the opponent delays her riposte or when an opponent's riposte can be parried and immediately followed.

REDOUBLE. This is a second attack in a

changed line, executed immediately after the first is parried. It is successful when the defender delays or fails to riposte.

REMISE (REPLACEMENT). Without withdrawing her arm after failing to hit on the first attempt, the attacker takes a second action which places the point on the target in the same line. A touch can be attempted be replacement if the riposte is delayed or the defender loses right-of-way.

REPRISE. This is a second attack made after returning to guard position.

GAME RULES AND SCORING*

The fencers stand on the strip. They salute the director, the judge, and each other. On command from the official they cross foils over the center line, step back, and fence. The contestants fence until the director calls "Halt," indicating that a touch or foul has been seen.

If a fencer steps off the side boundary with both feet, she is penalized by the loss of 3 feet 3 inches of ground. If she steps off the end with both feet, after a warning, she loses a touch.

Fencers reverse positions on the strip after two touches are scored. There is a 5 minute time limit for a four touch bout.

Every touch, to be valid, must arrive clearly and cleanly on the target with the point.

A hit made directly or as a result of a parry

on the body other than on the target area annuls any action that follows. The bout stops.

The fencer who first extends her arm with the point threatening the target gains the *right-of-way*. The defender gains the right-of-way by a parry or evasion. If a riposte follows it must be taken without indecision or delay.

When simultaneous action results in simultaneous attacks and touches, the hits are annulled.

On a double hit (simultaneous hits with one fencer at fault) the proper touch is scored.

The beginner should study fencing techniques for a fuller understanding of technical rules.*

*Scoring.** Officiating a fencing bout requires a jury consisting of a president (director) and four judges. A scorekeeper and timekeeper assist the jury. The president stands midway between the fencers, approximately 13 feet from the strip. The judges stand on each side of both fencers. The judges to the right of the president observe touches on the fencer to the president's left. Conversely, the judges to the left observe materiality of touches on the fencer to the president's right. When only two judges are used, they are positioned to observe maximum target area. A bout conducted with electrical equipment is directed by the president. The materiality of hits is established by the electrical apparatus, but the president enforces the rules of the weapon.

---

*For complete information see A.F.L.A., *Fencing Rules and Manual.*

*See *Fencing Rules and Manual*, Amateur Fencers League of America.

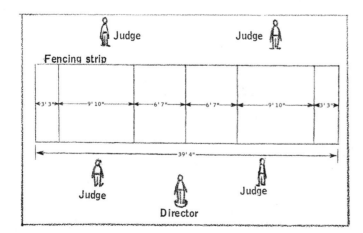

Fig. 7-20.   Regulation foil fencing strip (piste).

The winner in a women's standard fencing bout is the person who first scores four legal touches on her opponent or outscores her opponent within the 5 minute time limit. In some bouts, usually direct elimination, a winner may be required to score eight touches with a two touch advantage. In other competitions two out of three bouts, of four touches each, must be won.

Scoring of a bout is recorded by the official scorer as each touch is awarded by the director of the bout.

The most common tournament is the pool (a round robin). A sample score sheet of a five-person round robin tournament best illustrates scoring (Figure 7-21). The contestants are assigned numbers prior to competition. Thereafter, the scorer calls the participants by number. To begin the bout, the scorer calls contestants 1 and 4 to appear "on strip" for an immediate bout and contestants 2 and 3 "on deck" for the next bout. As bouts are completed, each is crossed out or checked off on the Order of Bouts.

As contestants are called, a horizontal line (——) is placed in the squares corresponding to the competitors. Reading from left to right, marks above the horizontal line indicate touches the contestant received; below the line, the W (Won) or L (lost) indicates the outcome of the bout. For example, contestant number 1 (S. Smith) received two touches from number 4 (H. Fox) and number 1 won

the bout. Contestant number 2 received four touches from number 3 and lost the bout. Number 2 failed to make a valid touch on number 5 during the bout. A similar recording is made on each participant in a bout.

At completion of the tournament, total scores, touches, and placement are recorded. Bouts won and lost are added across from *below* the horizontal line; touches received are added across the column corresponding to the participant's number, *above* the horizontal line. Touches rendered are added in the vertical column corresponding to the participant's number.

First place is awarded the fencer winning the greatest number of bouts, second place to the next greatest bout winner, and so on. When a tie for first place occurs in the finals among two or more fencers, they fence each other to determine places. If ties occur for other than first place, highest placement is given the fencer with the least number of touches received. If a tie still exists, the fencer scoring the largest number of touches receives higher placement. If a tie still remains and placement must be determined, the tied contestants fence each other.

STRATEGY

The successful bout fencer is aware of her personal resources and alert to the actions of

NAME	#	1	2	3	4	5	BOUTS		TOUCHES		PLACE
							WON	LOST	REC'VD	SCORED	
Smith, S.	1	╲	1/W	0/W	11/W	0/W	4	0	3	16	1
Brown, L.	2	1111/L	╲	1111/L	1111/L	1111/L	0	4	16	5	5
Davis, J.	3	1111/L	11/W	╲	1111/L	1/W	2	2	11	9	4
Fox, H.	4	1111/L	11/W	1/W	╲	1111/L	2	2	11	12	3
Walker, S.	5	1111/L	0/W	111/L	11/W	╲	2	2	10	9	2

ORDER of BOUTS

1 – 4	2 – 4
2 – 3	5 – 1
4 – 5	4 – 3
1 – 2	5 – 2
3 – 5	3 – 1

Figure 7-21. Scoring of a round robin tournament.

her opponent. It is important to fence your own game. Develop one or two attacks to rely and "hammer" on. Try to get opponent to fence *your way.* Several basic guides to attack and defense are helpful:

1. As the bout begins observe opponent's stance, lunge, guard position, reaction time, length of reach, and preferred attacks. Knowledge of an opponent is most important in planning bouting tactics. Much information about your opponent can be gained by watching previous bouts. Use the first minute of the bout to feel out your opponent.

2. Use simple attacks when possible. A well planned, simple attack is preferable to compound attacks. Always lunge with an extended arm. Progress from simple to complex items by building on her defensive responses to previous attacks.

3. Develop and use rapid, positive feints and false attacks for opponent's deception.

4. Recover from attacks, successful or otherwise, immediately to avoid a return.

5. Delay parries until last moment to avoid being deceived by change of line. Keep parries under control—a wide parry invites touches in an open line. There is no need to parry unless the thrust is on target.

6. The best time to attack is as your opponent prepares to attack. Be alert and move before the opponent's actual attack begins.

7. Keep footwork smooth and rapid. Keep feet and body as alert as the mind. Move about on the strip, keeping opponent guessing and your own body ready to move quickly and powerfully.

GAME COURTESIES

1. Upon arriving at the strip, salute your opponent. At the end of the bout, thank her.

2. Announce a touch on yourself at the moment it hits. Be certain it is a true touch.

3. Do *not* argue or discuss the jury's rulings.

4. Ask to speak with the president only when necessary and do so diplomatically.

5. If you disarm your opponent, pick up her weapon for her.

6. When it becomes necessary to stop for a moment when bouting, first step back and salute.

Terminology

Abstain—Declination of voting privilege when a judge was unable to see if a point was made.

Absence of the blade—Blades are not engaged.

Advance—Forward movement of the body toward opponent.

Attack—An initial attempt to hit an opponent by a thrust of the foil, usually followed by a lunge.

Attack on the blade—Beats, pressures, binds, and glides used to open a line of attack or deceive an opponent.

Balestra—Jump forward combined with the lunge when attacking.

Beat—Sharp rap against opponent's blade.

Bind—A method of removing an opponent's blade from high to low line or from low to high line. (See description p. 115.)

Call—Stamping forward foot twice to stop the bout.

Closed line—A line closed to attack due to position of foil and arm of opponent.

Compound attack—An attack consisting of two or more actions.

Compound parry—Two or more parries used in combination.

Contraction parry—A combination simple and counter parry.

Counter parry—A circular parry which carries opponent's blade to opposite line.

Counter riposte—An offensive action following the parry of a riposte.

Cutover—Disengagement made by passing over the tip of opponent's blade.

Deceive—Escaping and avoiding control of blade by opponent.

Disengage—Moving the blade from one line of engagement to an opposite line.

Engagement—Contact of two opposing blades.

Envelopment—Taking the opponent's blade and describing a circle to return to the line of engagement without losing contact.

False attack—A lunge which is intended to draw opponent's response but not intended to land on target.

Feint—An extension of foil arm as a pretense for attack.

Flèche—An attack made by running rather than lunging.

Foible—Flexible half of the blade.

Forte—Sturdy half of the blade near the guard.

Invitation—Actions that invite attack by an opponent.

Line of attack—Used to describe position of the attacking weapon.

Lunge—An extension of the arm and body from the guard position for the purpose of delivering an attack.

Measure—Distance between both fencers during the bout.

Parry—Blocking an opponent's thrust by contact with foils.

Pass—Point of foil grazes target, failing to hit properly.

Phrase—A period of continuous bouting.

Pressure—Application of pressure against an opponent's blade to draw a response and open the way for an attack.

One-two—A compound attack consisting of (1) a feint and disengage and (2) a disengage. It is used to deceive a parry.

On guard—Basic balanced body position for preparatory fencing position.

Redoublement — A second attack made when an opponent does not riposte.

Remise — A new attack initiated after first fails to hit target. The line remains unchanged and the arm remains extended in the second action.

Reprise — A new attack following a return to guard position.

Retreat — Movement to increase the distance between fencers.

Right-of-way — The right of attack gained by the fencer who first extends the foil arm, initiates an attack, or parries on an attack.

Riposte — A return or counter attack following a successful parry.

Salute — Acknowledgement to opponents and judges.

Semicircular parry — A parry from a high to low line or from low to high. The threatening blade is moved laterally.

Stop thrust — A straight thrust, with or without a lunge, made into an advancing opponent. If the hit is to be valid, it must be initiated before the final motion of the opponent's attack begins.

Thrust — An extension of the arm in a feint or an attack.

Time thrust — A counter attack made in opposition to an opponent's blade. It is usually executed against a compound attack and results in a parry and riposte simultaneously.

Touch — A valid hit on opponent's target area.

Selected Audio-visual Aids

Beginning Fencing. (Filmstrip and recording.) The Athletic Institute, 805 Merchandise Mart, Chicago, Ill. 60654

Fencing. (15 min., 16 mm., sound.) Ford Foundation TV Workshop, 447 Madison Avenue, New York, N.Y. 10022

Instructional Film on Foil Fencing (10 min., 16 mm., silent.) Castello Equipment Co., 300 East 10th St., New York, N.Y.

Techniques of Foil Fencing, 1954. (10 min., silent, b & w.) University of California, Extension Division, Educational Sales Dept., Los Angeles, Calif. 90024.

Suggested Readings

AAHPER: *Bowling-Fencing-Golf Guide.* Current edition, Division for Girls and Women's Sports, 1201 16th Street, N.W., Washington, D.C. 20036.

Amateur Fencing League of America: *Fencing Rules and Manual,* (obtained from Secretary, AFLA, 33 62nd St., West New York, New Jersey 07093.

Bower, Muriel, and Torao, Mori: *Fencing.* Dubuque, Iowa, William C. Brown Company, 1966.

Castello, Hugo, and Castello, James: *Fencing,* New York, The Ronald Press Company, 1962.

Crosnier, Roger: *Fencing with the Foil,* Cranbury, N.J., A. S. Barnes & Co., Inc., 1955.

Crosnier, Roger.: *Fencing with the Electric Foil,* A. S. Barnes & Co., Inc., 1961.

Vince, Joseph H.: *Fencing,* 2nd ed., New York, Ronald Press Co., 1962.

Periodicals

Amateur Fencing League of America: *American Fencing* (bimonthly). Write W. L. Osborn, 2709 Grand Central Terminal, New York, N.Y. 10017.

National Fencing Coaches Association of America: *The Swordmaster* (Quarterly). Write Y.M.C.A., New Britain, Conn. 06050

Suggested Study Questions

1. What is meant by right-of-way? How does a fencer secure it? Demonstrate.
2. What constitutes a legal touch? What is the target area?
3. What parries defend (a) high-inside line, and (b) low-inside line?
4. What pieces of equipment should each fencer have when bouting?
5. Describe the on guard body position. What are the advantages of such positioning?

CHAPTER EIGHT

Courtesy of Dean Anne S. Duggan, College of Health, Physical Education and Recreation,
Texas Woman's University, Denton, Texas.

GOLF

The game of golf undoubtedly grew from field hockey, the forerunner of all stick and ball games. Many authorities believe a golf type of game was played in Holland and the Low Countries centuries ago. Most agree that golf, as it is played today, originated in Scotland in the 14th century. Scottish Parliamentary action forbidding the game as a threat to the development of skill at archery, and thus of national defense, deterred the game only briefly until King James IV became a fan and golf was played openly.

Unlike many sports, golf has been a woman's game for centuries. Mary Queen of Scots was an enthusiastic and skilled golfer. Her attentive army cadet was the forerunner of the caddy of today. Appropriately the most famous course in the world is the Royal and Ancient Golf Club of St. Andrews, Scotland, founded in 1754. It remains the seat of authority for all matters pertaining to the game.

Golf crossed the Atlantic to Canada and the United States in the latter part of the 19th century. John G. Reid introduced the game to his friends in a cow pasture in Yonkers, New York, in 1885. This Scotsman, who became known as the "Father of American Golf," was instrumental in establishing the first golf club, St. Andrews of Yonkers, in 1888. Five of the private clubs in the Eastern United States joined together to form the United States Golf Association in 1894. From its beginning, the U.S.G.A. has been the ruling body for amateurs and the sponsoring body for prominent tournaments.

Early in the 20th century enthusiastic women golfers were granted playing privileges at private courses and numerous public and college courses were built. The development of equipment for consistent and accurate play and mass manufacturing brought the price of golf within the range of millions.

Today golf continues to attract many new followers. Men and women professional teachers encourage all ages to participate through their clinics, individual teaching, and examples of excellent play. At present more than 6500 courses attract 8 million participants, while driving ranges, 3 hole short courses, and instructional classes serve millions more.

NATURE AND PURPOSE OF THE GAME

Golf is a game of skill and accuracy that demands concentration and emotional control. It is played by both sexes from youth throughout life. A player sets her own pace, playing a fast and strenuous 18 holes, or a leisurely 9 holes using a mechanical cart. This vehicle enables handicapped and aged persons to participate and benefit from good fellowship and exercise in the out-of-doors.

Golf is also an excellent competitive sport, for the United States Golf Association has developed a system for computing handicaps that allows poor, average, and skilled players to compete equitably.*

The game consists of hitting a small, hard ball with selected clubs across various surface areas known as fairways, hazards, and roughs to smooth patches of grass, known as greens, and into small holes, or cups, in the greens. The object of the game is to use as few strokes as possible on each hole and over the entire course.

Although golf courses are laid out in units of 9 holes, most official courses have at least 18, and many have 27 or 36 holes. Par golf scores are based on 18 holes.

The 18 hole course is planned to balance play and avoid congestion. It is divided into the "front nine" (out) and "back nine" (in). An 18 hole course includes 5200 to 7200 yards of playing area roughly equalized between the front nine and back nine. Each hole is assigned a par value, or an arbitrary

---

*Complete information regarding the handicapping and course rating system is contained in the U.S.G.A. publication entitled "Golf Committee Manual and U.S.G.A. Golf Handicap System."

Fig. 8-1. Golf is a lifetime sport. (Courtesy of College of Health, Physical Education and Recreation, Texas Woman's University, Denton, Texas.)

standard of excellence, determined by the length and difficulty of the hole. This value allows a certain number of strokes to get to the green and two putts on the green.

An increasing number of golf clubs use the U.S.G.A. Course Rating System. The system is based on the fact that each course has peculiarities which affect its playing difficulty. Factors such as yardage, topography, prevailing winds, size of green, and hazards of each hole are considered in determining a "difficulty rating." The differential established for the course, combined with a player's individual handicap, creates an equality between players meeting on a strange course.

Course distances for par are:

Men	Women
Up to 250 yards, par 3	Up to 210 yards, par 3
251 to 470 yards, par 4	211 to 400 yards, par 4
471 to 600 yards, par 5	401 to 575 yards, par 5
601 yards and up, par 6	576 yards and up, par 6

Two, three, or four players may compete in one group. At the first tee, the order of teeing is decided by lot. Thereafter, the honor of playing first is awarded the player or team winning the preceding hole. In case of a tie, the honor is awarded the individual or side that held it at the previous tee. After the players have teed off, the person farthest away from the hole, whether on the fairway, in the rough, or on the green, shoots first. On the green the player farthest from the hole begins putting and continues until she "holes out." She may mark her ball only if her continued putting interferes with another player's line. After players "hole out," they move off the green and record their scores before going to the next teeing area.

FACILITIES AND EQUIPMENT

A golf course such as that shown in Figure 8-2 will eventually be the proving ground for all the skill and equipment of the golfer. Basic equipment includes clubs, balls, tees, and a carrying bag or rack. Other equipment may be desirable for comfort and skill improvement.

Clubs. The U.S.G.A. limits the golfer to the use of 14 clubs during a match. All 14 are not necessary for a beginning player, but even advanced players must be discriminating, for manufacturers now design and produce a variety of specialized woods such as 5, 6, 3½, and 4½ as well as a choice of several wedges. A minimum set of five clubs

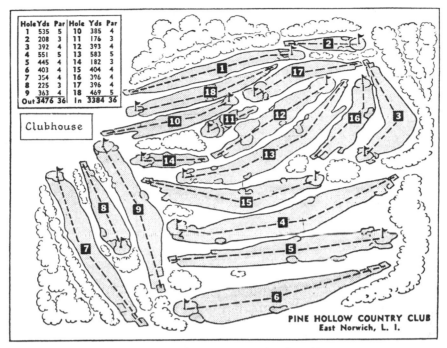

Hole	Yds	Par	Hole	Yds	Par
1	535	5	10	385	4
2	208	3	11	176	3
3	392	4	12	393	4
4	551	5	13	583	5
5	445	4	14	182	3
6	403	4	15	404	4
7	354	4	16	396	4
8	225	3	17	396	4
9	363	4	18	469	5
Out	3476	36	In	3384	36

Clubhouse

PINE HOLLOW COUNTRY CLUB
East Norwich, L. I.

Fig. 8-2. The layout of a typical 18 hole golf course.

should be available to a student on a golf course.

Clubs are generally classified into two groups: woods and irons. The designation

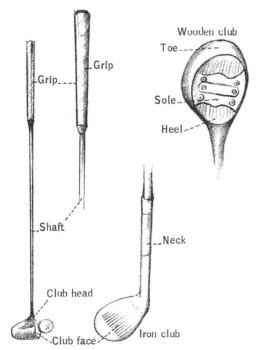

Fig. 8-3. Components of woods and irons.

originally referred to the composition of the clubheads; however, "woods" may have heads of plastic, magnesium, or laminated or persimmon wood. Essentially, iron and wood clubs have the same parts.

The main parts of the club are the grip, shaft, and clubhead. The golfer holds the club by the leather or composition grip at the top of the shaft. A cap at the top of the handle protects the upper portion of the grip and secures the wooden plug to strengthen the hollow shaft. The shaft is a tension steel tube over which the grip is placed and into which the clubhead attaches.

The clubhead is below the neck of the club where the head and shaft join. It includes the sole, or the lower part of the club that rests on the ground; the heel, or the part nearest the shaft; the toe, or outer tip of the head; and the clubface with its scored or grooved striking surface. Wooden clubs have a metal sole plate to protect the bottom as it swings across the ground. Iron clubs often have a metal flange on the back of the head to give them additional weight.

Wooden clubs are named and numbered to designate their use:

Number 1—Driver: Has the largest head

and longest shaft with a nearly vertical face. Used only for tee shots and gives a low, flat trajectory with maximum distance to the ball. For the average woman it is 41 to 42½ inches long and weighs 13 to 14 ounces.

Number 2—Brassie: Used for long shots with good lies from the fairway and from the tee. The clubface has more loft, causing a ball to go higher into the air with less forward direction than when hit with a driver.

Number 3—Spoon: Used for short tee shots and for long shots from the fairway and rough from mediocre lies. More loft to the face and often a shorter shaft than those of number 1 or 2 woods, which allows better control.

Number 4—Cleek: Used for long shots from a poor lie, as the smaller head and shallow face penetrate to the ball. It gives higher flight and less distance than 1, 2, or 3 woods.

Number 5: A popular club with women golfers, it has a small head and shallow face and is often used in preference to a number 1 or number 2 iron.

Iron clubs are informally grouped as long, medium, and short irons. This classification refers to both the length of the shaft and to the ball flight distance attained by the use of each club. A cue to the beginner; "The larger the club number, the shorter the shaft, the more loft to the face; consequently, the higher and shorter the ball flight."

The long irons include numbers 1, 2, and 3:

Number 1—Driving iron: Used for long, low, full shots from a good lie. The long shaft and straight face make it a difficult club for beginners. It is often replaced by a 3, 4 or 5 wood.

Number 2—Mid-iron: A utility club for comparatively long fairway and tee shots.

Number 3—Mid-mashie: Used for less distance than a number 2 iron, but the loft of the face allows a stroke from a relatively bad lie.

The medium irons include numbers 4, 5, and 6:

Number 4—Mashie iron: Used from the fairway and rough for medium distances, for occasional tee shots on short holes, and on "drag" strokes from the edge of the green.

Number 5—Mashie: An excellent utility club for the beginner. As the medium length club among all, it is used from the fairway and rough, for pitching a ball high to the green, for pitch and run shots to the green

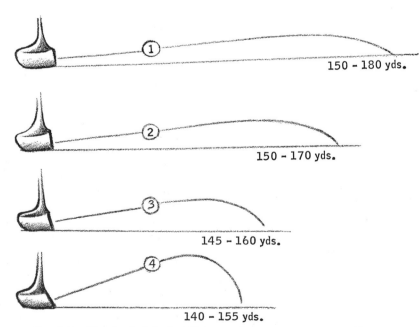

Fig. 8-4. Woods. Anticipated distances for average women golfers.

Table 8-1. *Anticipated Distances for Average Women Golfers*

Number 1 wood: 150-180 yards	Number 1 iron: 150-175 yards	Number 6 iron: 100-130 yards
Number 2 wood: 150-170 yards	Number 2 iron: 140-170 yards	Number 7 iron: 80-120 yards
Number 3 wood: 145-160 yards	Number 3 iron: 130-160 yards	Number 8 iron: 70-100 yards
Number 4 wood: 140-155 yards	Number 4 iron: 120-150 yards	Number 9 iron: 60- 90
	Number 5 iron: 110-140 yards	
	Pitching wedge .... 50-80 yards	
	Sand wedge .... 20-40 yards	
	Putter .... Distance to cup *on the green*	

when a safe approach is desired, and as a tee club on short holes.

Number 6—Spade mashie: Used from high rough, for pitch shots to the green, and

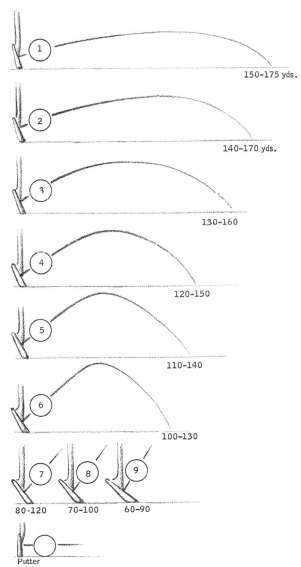

Fig. 8-5. Irons. Anticipated distances for average women golfers.

from clean lies in a sand trap when distance is needed.

The short irons include numbers 7, 8, 9, and the wedges:

Number 7—Mashie niblick: Used for short pitch shots from fairway and traps and over trees and obstacles.

Number 8—Pitching niblick: Used for quick-rising shots over hazards or as an approach from the fairway. An excellent club when obstacles prevent a follow-through.

Number 9—Niblick: The iron with the greatest loft. Used from deep rough and short approaches to the green.

Wedge: Either pitching or sand wedge. The heavy, flanged clubhead has a very slanted face and is used to loft the ball from sand, high grass, and other hazards.

The *putter* is an essential club for all golfers. In a category of its own, this short-shafted club with a straight face is used to stroke the ball over the smooth surface of the green.

Balls. Golf balls are constructed of liquid, rubber, steel, or plastic centers surrounded by tightly bound rubber yarn and encased in a balata rubber cover of dimpled design and painted white. They range in price from approximately 35¢ to $1.50. The less expensive repainted or factory-rejected balls have thick covers that decrease the chances of cutting the ball, allowing inexpensive play. The more expensive balls are designed for maximum accuracy and distance. Personal balls should be clearly marked for rapid identification.

Practice balls of plastic, cotton, felt, and woolen yarn are available for indoor and backyard use.

Tees and Tee Mats. Tees are used to elevate the balls for the first drive on each hole. Inexpensive wooden or plastic tees should be selected, as tees are often broken or lost.

If practice space is available indoors or on the lawn, mats are desirable. Heavy duty rubber mats with rubber tees, are satisfactory for tee shots, but coco mats are better for iron club practice, as they "give" with the impact of the hands and wrists and allow the clubhead to contact the ball below ground level.

Strips of close pile carpeting, or commercial indoor turfs, can serve for indoor putting surfaces.

Bag. A light fabric "Sunday" bag is ideal for the beginning golfer with limited equipment. The more durable and attractive leather or fabric bag, with shoe and ball pockets, a carry strap and handle, and a hood, is a heavy burden for the woman golfer with a full set of clubs who cannot afford regular caddy service.

Golf Carts. A number of pull carts are available for purchase or rental. The lightweight pocket bag built on a cart is ideal for the golfer with limited clubs; others prefer a sturdy collapsible cart that carries a bag and rain gear and offers such accessories as a seat and score card rack. Some courses prohibit the use of pull carts and insist on caddies or power-driven golf carts.

Costume. Shoes that offer comfort and help to maintain balance and stability while swinging are a valuable part of a golfer's equipment. Some players find rubber-soled canvas shoes satisfactory, but many insist on spikes. Spikes can be placed on flat-soled oxfords if an investment in golf shoes is inappropriate.

Jewelry should not be worn, as rings may injure the hands and the delicate mechanism of wrist watches may be ruined by the stroking impact. When in doubt about club regulations concerning dress, wear a semifull skirt and a neat, loose fitting blouse, or a manufacturer's golf dress, all of which are comfortable when walking and swinging a club. Long walking shorts or slacks are acceptable on most courses.

Accessories and Gadgets. There are many accessories for the woman golfer. Among the necessities are gloves, full or half, which aid in gripping and prevent calluses; an umbrella for the inevitable thundershowers; and a shade hat. Other useful items include stroke counters to aid the novice in keeping her score, ball markers for use on the green, and ball holders worn on the belt to eliminate bulging pockets.

Commercial gadgets designed to improve basic skills are numerous. Such items as a golf glove to correct improper grip, a plastic sleeve to prevent bending the elbow on the backswing, and an elastic band to keep the arms close and elbow down may have value, but should be prescribed by an instructor who analyzes the problems of your swing. These aids are not permitted in competitive play.

PURCHASE AND CARE OF EQUIPMENT

The most important items to successful golf are well fitted clubs and shoes. The golf professional at the course is the best consultant when buying these items.

A beginner should take special care in selecting clubs, for properly fitted clubs help to mold an efficient swing pattern. If poorly fitted, they may develop swing idiosyncrasies to fit the clubs, not the golfer.

Table 8-2. *(See Text for Explanation)*

Height of Golfer*	Shaft Length and Flex	Swingweight, Loft, Lie
5' 7" and over	42½" driver 38½" or 39" number 2 iron	Driver swingweight from C7 to C9
	Long hitters use ladies' heavy or men's light or heavy flex	Deep face driver for strong hitters; shallower face with more loft for lighter hitters
5' 3" to 5' 6"	41½" or 42" driver 37½" or 38½" number 2 iron	Driver swingweight from C3 to C6
	Medium to heavy shafts for long hitters	Medium clubface depth; 10 to 11 degree driver loft
	Light shaft for shorter hitters	
Under 5' 3"	41" driver, 36½" or 37" number 2 iron. All but strongest use light to medium shaft	Driver swingweight from B6 to C2 Shallow wood face; 12 degree driver loft

*Club length is determined by the length of a player's arms in relation to her body height. As there is some correlation between height and arm length, a general category of "height" is commonly used.

Club selection is based on length and grip of shaft, flexibility of shaft, and clubhead weight and design. A beginning golfer cannot use a full set of clubs to advantage but should buy clubs from open stock, which can be added to later. A minimal basic set of matched clubs should include a number 2 (or number 3) wood, irons 3, 5, and 7, and a putter. Early additions to the set include a driver (number 1 wood) and a 9 iron.

Table 8-2 offers *general* suggestions for beginning golfers.

Generally, the shorter hitters use lighter shafts and more shallow wood clubfaces with lighter swingweights. As the player becomes stronger specifications change.

Care of Clubs. Clubs should be wiped dry and clean after use. Occasionally wash with mild soap and water and clean the grooves on the faces with a soft brush or a wooden tee. When thoroughly dry, wooden clubheads should be waxed (paste wax) to prevent warping and cracking. A light oil should be applied to the steel shaft. Wrappings around the clubhead and grip should be checked frequently. Often a durable glue will serve; otherwise, black linen line can be applied to the head and shaft and leather stripping to the shaft. Head covers of knit, plastic, or leather protect the highly polished surface from scarring.

Little care is required to maintain irons other than drying and oiling occasionally to prevent rusting. Avoid hitting rocks or hard objects, for they nick the club, change its balance, and cause it to cut balls. Club nicks should be filed smooth when they appear on the face.

Leather grips on all clubs should be rubbed lightly with neat's-foot oil several times a year. Damaged or worn grips may be replaced at the pro shop or by the golfer with a "do-it-yourself" kit.

Golf balls should be washed before play for ease of identification. Practice balls can be "washed white" (repainted) by the golfer.

All leather equipment such as shoes and gloves should be dried slowly, away from intense heat. Gloves should be straightened and dried, out of the sun, to prevent wrinkles and cracking.

Golf carts and all metal equipment should be wiped dry after each use and oiled occasionally for better operation and to prevent rusting.

BASIC SKILLS

All skills are described in terms of a right-handed player. The skills and movements are applicable to left-handed players, but the terms *left* and *right* must be interchanged when developing or analyzing a skill.

Grip. The positioning of the hands is of initial importance, for the hands are the only connection between the body and the ball, working through the club. A sound grip serves to place the hands so that they return to their original position to contact the ball.

The same basic grip is used for all clubs except the putter. Three grips are commonly used by golfers: the overlap, the interlock, and the natural, or "baseball." Although several championship golfers use the interlocking and natural grips, for most women the overlapping (Vardon) technique assures close hands and a hinged wrist action.

To assume the overlapping grip the clubhead rests on the ground in square position, shaft pointing toward the golfer. The extended left hand is placed slightly over the top of the shaft (Fig. 8-6, *A*) as the hand grips the club across the base of the fingers (Fig. 8-6, *B*). As the hand closes around the gripping leather the shaft lies diagonally across the hand in a combination palm and finger grip. The end of the shaft extends an inch or more beyond the hand toward the body. The grip is secured by the last three fingers, with the thumb and index finger forming a "V" line. This *solid* and *closed* line points toward the chin and right shoulder. With the left hand thumb to the right of the shaft, the thumb and index finger exert a slight gripping pressure. Looking down the shaft, the golfer should see no more than three knuckle joints.

The right arm swings freely until the right hand reaches below the left to grip the club entirely in the fingers. The palm of the right hand is squarely facing the right side of the club shaft. In closing the right hand around the club, the left thumb fits snugly into the natural diagonal hollow of the right palm (under the butt of the right thumb). Overlap the little finger of the right hand by hooking it around the large knuckle of the left index finger. The next three fingers grasp the shaft as the index finger spreads to a trigger position so that there is a space between the index and second fingers. The "V" line formed by the right thumb and index finger

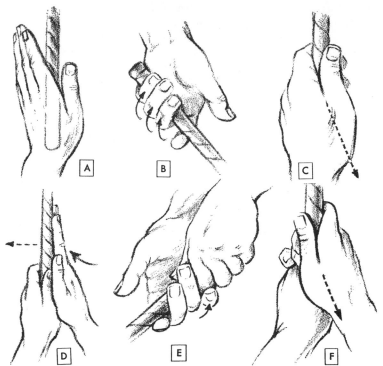

Fig. 8-6. Placing the hands for the proper grip.

Fig. 8-7. The proper hand placement on the club is of vital importance to all golfers. The design of the club grip helps the beginner establish her hand position. (Courtesy of the Los Angeles Public Schools.)

is solid and closed and points in the same direction of chin and right shoulder. With both hands close together and working as a unit, power and control are attained.

Putting Grip. The individuality of putting begins with the grip. Many golfers use the same grip as they use for other clubs; others use a baseball, crosshand, reverse overlap, or two-hand molded grip, in which both hands and thumb are molded together at the top of the shaft.

The reverse overlap grip is recommended for beginners, as the hands are placed on the club in a manner resembling the Vardon grip.

The right hand is placed a hand span from the top of the club with the thumb pointed directly down the front of the shaft toward the clubhead. The line formed by the thumb and index finger points toward the *right* shoulder. The left hand is placed above the right with the palm facing in the direction opposite from that of the palm of the right hand. The back of the left hand faces the line of the putt. The thumb is down the front of the shaft. The index finger of the left hand overlaps the little finger of the right hand. The line of the thumb and index finger of the left hand should point in the direction of the *left* shoulder.

The left hand, now firmly holding the club—more in the palm than the fingers—does most of the work. The pressure of the grip in the right hand is exerted with the thumb and index finger for control. This grip permits a hinged wrist action.

Stance and Address.   A firm, comfortable stance assures the balance necessary for a swing. In preparation for all strokes, except putting, weight is equally distributed on both feet between the balls of the feet and the heels, the toes are pointed outward, and the feet are placed comfortably apart but never more than shoulder width. The body is fairly erect, with knees flexed. The body curves as if it is sitting on a ball. With eyes on the ball, extend the left arm so that it is firm and straight. The arms hang but do not reach so as to pull the body off balance. The distance one stands from the ball depends on the length of the club used. Sole the club directly behind the ball so that the bottom is evenly placed on the turf and the face points directly along the desired line of flight.

There are three general stances which a golfer assumes for a designated stroke:

SQUARE OR PARALLEL STANCE.   The feet are parallel to, and equally distant from, the imaginary line of flight of the ball. With the knees, hips, and shoulders parallel to the flight line, this is a good beginning stance, as it gives a feeling of balanced swing motion with an equally balanced backswing and follow-through. It is the most commonly used stance for long and medium irons.

OPEN STANCE.   The left foot is drawn back from the imaginary flight line. The body is turned slightly toward the direction of ball flight. With the right hip forward a restricted body rotation in the backswing results, thus allowing the arms to stay closer to the body for a more controlled stroke. The open stance is used primarily for short irons, chipping, and pitching, when less distance and power but greater accuracy are needed. It may be used for intentional slices.

CLOSED STANCE.   The right foot is drawn back from the flight line, thus turning the body from the target and increasing backswing rotation. This stance is used for maximum power from the tee and on some fairway shots, as well as for an intentional hook shot.

Body-Ball Position.   The position of the body and the club in relation to the ball greatly affects ball flight. Basically, the longer the club the fuller the swing arc. The farther one stands from the ball, the flatter the swing; the shorter the club, the closer one stands to the ball and the more upright the swing.

When the ball is contacted as near as possible to the bottom of the swing, the more perfect will be the loft for which the clubhead was designed. To get this proper position with irons, hit *down* on the ball, which is placed an inch or two to the right of the bottom of the swing arc.

The point on the swing arc at which the ball is hit greatly affects ball spin. A forward spin, causing low ball flight and increased forward roll on the ground, results from a blow as the

Fig. 8-8.   Types of stance. A, Square stance; B, open stance; C, closed stance.

clubhead is traveling upward. A horizontal blow at the center of the swing arc results in a slight backspin, as the ball is hit below center. A definite backspin is caused if the clubhead hits the ball before the center of the swing arc is reached, for the club continues downward across the back of the ball.

Generally, tee shots and wood shots are made from a closed or square stance with the ball placed forward of center for a horizontal or upward impact of the club. The long and medium irons are most often played from a square stance off or near the center of the body. The length of the club shaft determines the golfer's relation to the ball, but the arms are easy, not forcibly reaching, and the wrists are down and firm. With shorter irons, the golfer moves closer to the ball, opens her stance, moves the feet closer together, and plays the ball off-center or right of center of the body for more loft and less roll.

Swing. An efficient swing is based on balance, rhythm, and a square clubhead position throughout. Although the total swing must be learned as a unit, the basic ingredients can be identified for analysis.

Assuming a proper stance with weight distributed and feet comfortably spread, exert a slight gripping pressure on the inside of the right foot and press the right thigh toward the center of the body. The body is inclined forward slightly at the waist; the right shoulder is slightly dropped so that the arm can reach properly and eventually bend on the backswing. The upper arms rest slightly against the sides of the body with the left arm fully extended but not stiff or tense. The hands are even with or slightly ahead of the ball.

The *backswing* is a one-piece move away from the ball. The left shoulder initiates the coordinated movement by turning down and moving under the chin. The hips rotate toward the right, with the spine and head serving as an axis. The weight shifts across the left foot to the inside of the right foot. The left knee relaxes and bends toward the right knee. The left heel is unweighted and in a full swing it *may* be raised about an inch from the ground. During the pivot the arms and shoulders pull the club backward along the flight line and upward. The shoulders turn as the upper body pivots with the hips. As the arms reach approximately waist height, the wrists cock with no deliberate

effort and the arms continue in an upward arc. The left arm and right leg remain firm, with the right elbow bent and pointing downward. The head remains stationary.

At the top of the full swing, the body is in coiled readiness with the club shaft approximately horizontal to the ground. The shoulders are turned 90 degrees; the hips 45 degrees. The palm of the right hand is under the shaft; the right elbow is pointing to the ground with the line from the right armpit to the elbow parallel to the ground.

A shift of weight back to the left foot initiates the downswing. The weight shift may be accomplished by pulling the club down sharply with the left hand or by sliding or turning the hips to the left. Beginners seem to find it easier to concentrate on a vigorous push off the right foot to the left. A proper shift allows the right elbow to move toward the body as the left hip leads the body and pulls the arms into the hitting area. Halfway through the downswing, the weight has returned to address position, the hips are square, but the shoulders are still turned 45

Fig. 8-9. To hit the ball correctly, your shoulders and arms should form a triangle, and you should maintain that triangle throughout the swing. (Courtesy of the National Golf Foundation.)

Fig. 8-10. The golf swing should be a continuous, smooth, and rhythmical movement. (Courtesy of the National Golf Foundation.)

Fig. 8-11. Keep this line in mind before you begin to guide your hands and arms down into the swing. (Courtesy of the National Golf Foundation.)

Fig. 8-12. Backswing.

Fig. 8-13.   Downswing.

degrees. The right shoulder then turns under the chin and below the left shoulder. As the arms and wrists come to the impact area the wrists uncock to strike the ball at the bottom of the swing arc. The golfer hits *against* a firm left side.

A key point in the downswing is the action of the right shoulder. At the moment of ball impact the chin is digging into the right shoulder.

The clubhead follows the line of intended flight until the right arm is fully extended in handshaking position. As weight continues to shift to the left side with the right foot pushing from the toes, the left elbow bends and the right hand takes over the club. The hips turn naturally with the turn of the arms and shoulders. At the completion of the swing the right side is fully released, the weight is on the left foot, the hands are high with the left palm under the shaft and the left elbow pointed toward the ground. The head has turned and the body is facing the target in a balanced position.

Fractional Swings. The power of a full swing is neither necessary nor desirable for

some shots and clubs. Basically, fractional swings are but segments of the full swing and are frequently used with short irons. As the swing is shortened, the club is shortened proportionately by gripping farther down on the leather.

QUARTER SWING. The hips initiate a weight shift, rather than a true rotation. The clubhead follows, going away from the ball until the arms are outside the right leg; then the wrists cock, bringing the club parallel to the ground. The downswing and follow-through carry the club to a position parallel to the ground on the left side of the body.

HALF SWING. Executed by a rotation slightly deeper than that of the quarter swing, the backswing arc continues until the cap of the grip points toward the ground. The follow-through is the same length as the backswing.

THREE-QUARTER SWING. This is executed like the full swing but less depth is taken in the ascending and descending arcs. At the top of the backswing the clubhead points to 2 o'clock; on the follow-through it points toward 10 o'clock.

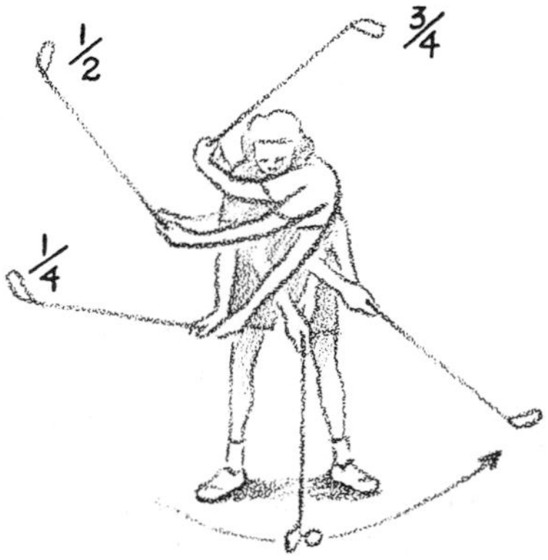

Playing Wood Shots

1. Use a square or slightly closed stance with feet 10 to 14 inches apart, depending on comfort.

2. Use a full swing for maximum power.

3. When driving from the tee, play the ball off of forward heel or toe, depending on the bottom point of the swing.

4. Play fairway shots toward the center of the body.

Playing Long and Medium Iron Shots

1. Use square stance for normal flight.

2. Stand slightly closer to irons than woods so that the swing will be more upright.

Fig. 8-14.   Fractional swings.

3. Play long irons 2 or 3 inches to right of the left foot.

4. Play medium irons from the center of the stance.

5. Hit the ball a descending blow as if trying to bury the ball. Take turf and continue through.

Playing Short Iron Shots

1. Use square to open stance with feet 6 to 10 inches apart.

2. Play the ball from the center of the stance to 2 or 3 inches to the right of center.

3. The body is close to the ball; the arms close to the body.

4. Use a fractional swing for distance desired.

Chip Shot. A chip (also called a pitch and run) is made when the ball is close to the green and there is a 5 yard unobstacled approach to the green. A chip should carry to the green and roll the rest of the way to the hole.

1. Use a number 4, 5, 6, or 7 iron; occasionally an 8 or 9 iron.

2. Keep the feet close together and the weight on the left foot as the ball is played in line with the left heel. There should be little body motion or weight transfer.

3. Grip club low on the handle, hands ahead of club to limit loft. The left hand controls as both wrists remain firm.

4. Use a short, rhythmical backswing. Stroke the ball *crisply*. The right palm faces the target throughout.

5. The follow-through is low.

Pitch Shot. The pitch carries the ball through the air in a high approach toward the green, where it stops quickly upon contact with the ground.

1. Select a wedge or 9 iron.

2. Use an open stance close to the ball with the right elbow close to the right hip.

3. Use minimum body action with a fractional swing.

4. Hit the ball several inches ahead of the bottom of the swing arc (a descending blow) to impart backspin so that it will stop when landing.

5. Follow through with clubhead pointing toward target.

Run-up Shot. The run-up is similar to the pitch and run but is taken farther from the green. The ball is hit with a 6 or 7 iron and played to travel about one-half the distance to the green in the air, hit level, firm terrain, and roll onto the green and toward the cup.

Bunker Shots. The chip shot and the blast are the fundamental strokes for getting out of a sand trap. The texture of the sand and the lie of the ball determine the shot. A chip may be used when the ball is resting on top of the sand. A number 6 or 7 iron may be used in a short approach. The club, however, must not be grounded or touch the sand on the backswing.

The explosive shot is the safest when the ball is buried or must rise over a bank.

1. Select a sand wedge or number 9 iron. Open the club face slightly (angle it backward).

2. Play the ball in line with the left (forward) heel.

3. Anchor the feet and aim an inch or two behind the ball. Take sand as a cushion to loft the ball.

4. Take a full swing; start the clubhead back at an angle outside the line of flight. Swing through the ball, cutting across the direction line, and follow through completely.

Putting. Putting is the most individualized skill of golf; its success also depends largely on the player's state of mind. Although the criterion of a good putt is its effectiveness, the following techniques may help the beginner.

1. Use the reverse overlap grip *(see Grip)*.

2. Take a square stance, with the feet 10 to 12 inches apart. Bend from the waist so that the eyes are directly over the ball. *Lock* the stance.

3. Position the ball off the instep of the left foot.

4. Keep the hands even with the ball, with the right elbow resting comfortably on the right hipbone, the left elbow barely touching the left side.

5. To execute the *wrist action putt*, the head, hips, and shoulders remain steady as the hands and wrists take a short controlled backswing. To execute an *arm action putt* or *firm wrist putt*, the head and hips are steady as the arms swing from the shoulders. The elbows remain close to the sides.

6. Two methods of striking the ball are commonly used. In both, the clubhead accel-

erates at the moment of impact. The *stroke putt* is a long, smooth stroke with backswing and follow-through of equal distance; the *tap putt* results from a swing that crisply contacts the ball and ends in a short follow-through. This is often called a "punch putt."

7. Bring the clubhead straight back, then through the ball, following through directly toward the hole.

8. Keep the putter blade close to the green throughout the stroke.

Putts account for approximately half the strokes in a round of par golf; therefore, putting deserves concentration and practice. Line up a putt by determining the distance to the hole, the slope of the green, the grain of the grass, and ultimately the course of the ball to the hole. It is helpful to pick a spot about 6 inches along the imaginary ball course and concentrate on rolling the ball over that spot.

Playing Difficult Lies

Rough.   A club is selected which will give the necessary loft to the ball. The stance is more open, the club face slightly open, and the swing upright with as full a follow-through as possible. If the ball lie is good, a 4 or 5 wood often clears heavy rough better than an iron.

Downhill Lie.   On any "uneven" lie the secret is to make contact with the ball as close as possible to the exact bottom point of the swing. Normally play the ball closer to right (rear) foot with a slightly open stance. The body weight should be equally distributed or on the left foot. Select a club with more loft, to give the ball height as it leaves the ground. Avoid shifting weight abruptly or "letting up" on the swing at impact. A smooth follow-through lessens the tendency to push or slice.

Uphill Lie.   Since the bottom of the swing falls farther to the left, play the ball left of center. Use a slight body pivot and a low trajectory club, as the height normally attained with a club is accentuated by the ground contour. Avoid the tendency to hook or pull by completing the body weight transfer on the follow-through.

Sidehill Lie.   This stroke must be made standing above or below ball level. These shots call for planned balance and anticipation of a hook or slice.

When the ball is below the stance, use a square stance, playing the ball from the center of the body. "Sit" through the legs and aim to the left to compensate for the tendency to slice. A compact three-quarter swing is helpful.

If the ball is above the feet, the ball is played slightly right of center, keep the stance slightly open and aim to the right to compensate for the hook that results from falling back on the heels.

Stroke Adjustments.   Advanced golfers can take several strokes from their game by learning to direct the ball in flight.

Intentional Hook.   To accomplish a deliberate curve of the ball from right to left, the golfer uses a closed stance with the ball almost opposite the right foot. Using a flat swing arc, the club contacts the ball from the inside to the outside. The degree of hook can be controlled by placing the right hand beneath the shaft and the left hand on top.

Intentional Slice.   A deliberate slice curves from left to right in flight because of the spin imparted to the ball. The golfer uses an open stance with the ball approximately off the center of the stance. Swing arc is almost upright, with the clubhead contacting the ball from the "outside-in." For more decided slice the right hand moves to the top of the shaft and the left hand under the shaft.

High Ball.   The beginning golfer should

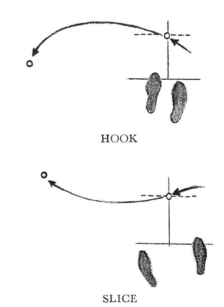

HOOK

SLICE

Fig. 8-15. Proper stance for hook shots and slice shots.

attempt to select a club with enough loft to carry the ball over obstacles or into the wind; however, advanced golfers may play the ball off the left foot and stroke the ball on the upswing with an open club face.

Low Ball. The ball is played off the right foot and hit with a closed clubface from a flat swing arc. Hit down on the ball and take turf after ball contact.

GAME RULES AND SCORING

The parent ruling body is the Royal and Ancient Golf Club of St. Andrews, Scotland. The United States Golf Association is the ruling organization for the United States and Canada.

It is advisable to carry the cross-indexed Rules book wherever you play for quick answers to questions that arise.* As the rules are numerous and appear difficult for a beginner, the following basic guides suggest conduct for the first "rounds."

1. Be able to identify one's own ball by its markings.

2. Carry only 14 clubs. The penalty in match play is loss of one hole for each excess club and loss of two strokes for each excess club per hole in stroke play.

3. At the beginning of each hole the ball should be teed between the tee markers and not more than two club lengths behind the markers.

4. An intentional swing at the ball, whether a hit or a miss, counts as a stroke.

5. Loose impediments may be removed if they hinder a stroke (except in hazards); however, no growing vegetation may be removed, broken, or bent. The penalty is two strokes in stroke play and loss of a hole in match play.

6. A ball lying near an unnatural obstacle such as a bench or hydrant may be moved no more than two club lengths, and never nearer the hole without penalty.

7. A ball in casual water (e.g., rain water or leakage) may be dropped over the shoulder, not nearer the hole, with no penalty. On the green the ball is lifted and replaced; in a hazard it is dropped in the hazard.

8. If a ball lies against an obstacle and you

*Write: U.S.G.A., 40 E. 38th St., New York, N.Y. 10016 for *The Rules of Golf*, 25¢.

term it unplayable you may (a) drop a ball near the spot from which the original was played and receive a one stroke penalty and loss of distance, (b) drop a ball no more than two club lengths from where original ball lies and receive a one stroke penalty, or (c) drop a ball anywhere behind the unplayable lie keeping that point between the player and the hole and receive a one stroke penalty.

9. A provisional ball is a second ball played when there is a possibility that the original ball is out of bounds or lost. It should be played as close to the spot of the original ball as possible.

10. If a ball goes out of bounds or is termed lost after a five minute search, a second ball must be played as near as possible to the spot from which the first ball was hit. The penalty is one stroke and loss of distance.

11. Play the ball as it lies. A ball may be lifted on the putting green only. Although U.S.G.A. does not endorse winter rules, some courses permit "preferred lies" because of the condition of the grounds.

12. When a ball rests in a hazard, the club must not be grounded in preparation for the stroke. The penalty is two strokes in stroke play and loss of hole in match play.

SCORING

Several methods of scoring are used in golf competition. Generally, competition is by stroke or match play. In *stroke play* the winner is the golfer using the least number of strokes over the designated course. In *match play*, or hole play, the victor is the player or team who wins the greatest number of holes from her opponent, regardless of the final stroke total. In match play, when opponents have the same number of strokes on a hole, they have "halved" the hole and neither scores a point. Stroke play is considered more exacting, since each stroke is of equal value; whereas in match play a loss of several strokes and the loss of a hole may be recouped by a victory of one stroke on a later hole.

The use of a scorecard is helpful in learning scoring procedures, for it usually gives the name and location of the course, entries for date, event, scorer's name, attestor and four players, course markings, and local rules on the back of the card. The inside scoring section indicates the number of yards for each hole, the total course yardage, par

Hole	Yards	Bogy	Par	Ellen	Alice	Handicap Strokes	W+/L−/HO	Hole	Yards	Bogy	Par	Ellen	Alice	Handicap Strokes	W+/L−/HO
1	325	5	4	5	5	7		10	325	5	4	4	4	8	0
2	185	3	3	4	3	15		11	185	3	3	4	3	16	+
3	325	4	4	4	5	9		12	325	4	4	4	5	10	−
4	500	5	5	5	6	1		13	500	5	5	6	6	2	0
5	375	5	4	6	7	5		14	375	5	4	6	6	6	0
6	150	3	3	3	4	17		15	150	3	3	3	4	18	−
7	450	5	5	5	6	3		16	450	5	5	5	6	4	−
8	300	4	4	5	6	11		17	300	4	4	6	4	12	+
9	300	4	4	4	4	13		18	300	4	4	5	5	14	0
Out	2910	38	36	41	46			In	2910	38	36	43	43		

SCORER... Alice

ATTEST...

Out 2910

Total 5820

HANDICAP

NET SCORE

Fig. 8-16. A completed golf scorecard. The out 9 illustrates scoring for stroke play, the back 9 illustrates scoring for match play.

for men and women, the handicap stroke ranking awarded each hole, and columns for the total score for match or stroke play.

Examples of both stroke and match scoring follow:

1. Ellen and Alice play the front nine by stroke play. Ellen has a total of 41 strokes. Alice records 46. Ellen is the winner.

2. On the back nine Ellen and Alice choose match play. During the nine holes, they halved holes 10, 13, 14 and 18. Alice won holes 11 and 17; Ellen won holes 12, 15 and 16. Although both players had 43 strokes on the last nine holes, Ellen was the victor.

The Nassau system of scoring is often used in singles or doubles stroke or match play. In a singles match (two competing) each match is worth three points. One point is given the winner of the first nine holes, one point for the winner of the second nine holes, and one point to the player with the lowest total score or winning the greatest number of holes of the 18. In doubles match play additional possible team points may be added.

Golf utilizes several handicapping systems to equalize competition among players of different abilities. The United States Golf Association gives detailed explanations for computing handicaps. Briefly, these state that the number of handicap strokes is determined by a percentage of the difference between a player's average score on a course with a

given difficulty "rating." For example, if the course rating is 70 and the player's score is 84, the handicap differential is 14. The total of the lowest ten handicap differentials, out of 25, is computed and applied to the U.S.G.A. differential chart to determine handicap strokes.

Once a handicap is established, it works as follows: Player A with a handicap of 6 is competing against Player B with a handicap of 8. In the match Player B is allowed to subtract one stroke on each of the holes numbered 1 and 2 in the scorecard column marked handicap strokes, regardless of the sequence of the holes on the course. If A had a 4 handicap and B an 8 handicap, Player B would receive a stroke on each of the holes numbered 1 through 4.

Handicapping methods such as the popular Callaway System are used for one-day amateur tournaments when not all players have established handicaps. The tournament score is computed (based on an established table) by consideration of a player's total score and her highest single hole scores.*

STRATEGY

Golf is a game of both skill and concentration. A *positive attitude* incorporating the

---

*See *Competitive Golf Events*, National Golf Foundation, Room 804, Merchandise Mart, Chicago, Ill. 60654.

following suggestions will add consistency and cut strokes from your game.

1. Plan each hole from tee to green. If a bad stroke forces readjustment of the plan, *dismiss* the error and replan.

2. Do not dwell on past strokes, good or bad. Play and concentrate on the situation at hand.

3. In competition be concerned with *your* play only, not that of your opponent. Compete with the arbitrary score of par rather than your opponent's score.

4. Avoid tension. Get accustomed to crowded courses and slow play. Do not let golfers behind unnecessarily rush you. Play at your own reasonable speed.

5. Learn the feeling of a comfortable stance. On fairway or green if you feel uncomfortable, walk away temporarily and then establish a new stance.

6. Play safe golf for low scores. Avoid gambling on difficult shots and approaches to the green. Often a safe stroke to a good playing position saves several penalty strokes resulting from a gamble.

7. Learn your clubs and their distances. Trust your clubs.

8. On long putts, putt for a *certain* second putt, rather than trying to hole the ball.

GAME COURTESIES

Since golf demands delicate coordination and concentration from players, a definite code of behavior is followed by experienced players. These courtesies are intended to prevent distraction and increase player safety.

The player should:
1. Play without undue delay.
2. Stroke from behind the markers on the tees.
3. Hold the flag for your opponent or see that the caddy does.
4. Allow the player winning the honor to tee first.
5. When a ball is lost, or players are in a slow match, invite players following to play through and allow them to get out of range before proceeding.
6. Always replace divots.
7. Elevate "dents" in the green, using the point of the tee.

8. Back out of sand traps, leveling off holes made by your club and foot tracks.
9. Admit penalty stroke.
10. Allow the player farthest away, whether on green or in field, to stroke first.
11. Call "Fore!" only if there is danger of a ball hitting a player ahead.
12. Drop the ball over one's shoulder when taking a penalty stroke.
13. Recognize course priority: single players have no standing; two, three, and four players have precedence. Any match playing a whole round is entitled to pass a match playing a shorter round.

The player should not:
1. Talk or move while a player is stroking.
2. Swing clubs while a player is stroking.
3. Hit until players ahead are out of range and have taken at least their second shots.
4. Approach the green until players ahead have putted out and are off the green.
5. Stand near the cup when another is shooting.
6. Stand in line with the one putting and the cup.
7. Concede, or ask to be conceded, a putt.
8. Take a careless stroke putt and expect to take another trial if the ball is missed.
9. Stand close enough to the rim of the cup to disturb turf.
10. Allow one's shadow to cross the line of a putt.
11. Place a golf bag in a sand trap, thus roughing up the sand for players following.
12. Place a golf bag on the green, where it may mar the surface.
13. Place a golf bag, cart, or flagstick on the near side of the green where it might stop the ball of a player following.
14. Record scores while standing on the green.
15. Practice putts or play them over if missed.
16. Invite players to play through when a ball is lost and then start shooting before they are out of range.
17. Take practice swings in the direction of the hole. (By taking them at right angles to the line of flight you eliminate possibility of being questioned by opponents.)
18. Pick up a ball for identification.
19. Press down grass or weeds to get a better stroke. This is improving the lie and is against the rules.

Terminology

Ace — Hole in one.

Addressing the ball — Placing the body and club in a position to hit the ball.

Approach shot — A shot intended to put the ball on the green.

Apron — Closely cut area adjacent to the green.

Away — Ball farthest from the hole and to be played first.

Birdie — One less than par.

Bisque — Handicaps set, but strokes to be taken on any hole designated by the recipient.

Bogey — One over par for a given hole ("blind bogey" — a phantom's score against which players may compete).

Brassie — Wooden club number 2.

Bunker — Hazard, usually artificial.

Caddie — Assistant to players: watches the ball, carries bag and clubs.

Carry — Distance the ball travels through the air.

Club — Implement used to propel the ball.

Course — Ground within playing limits.

Cup — Hole into which the ball is played.

Dead — A ball that does not roll after being hit; a ball that lies so close to the hole there is no doubt it will be sunk on the next shot.

Divot — Slice of turf cut out by club head.

Dodo — Three under par for any hole.

Dog leg — A fairway curving to left or right.

Dormie — A term indicating that a player or team is as many holes "up" as there are holes remaining to play, and therefore cannot be beaten.

Down — Number of strokes or holes one is behind an opponent.

Driver — Wooden club number 1.

Eagle — Two under par for any hole.

Face — Striking surface of club head.

Fairway — Area between a tee and the green where the grass is cut short.

Flagstick — A staff inserted in the center of the cup that indicates the position and number of the hole.

Fore! — A warning call to those ahead when a ball is traveling toward them.

Foreward press — A preliminary movement with a weight shift to the *forward* foot to prepare for a coordinated swing.

Foursome — Two players on a side.

Green — Putting surface around the hole.

Grip — Part of a club that is gripped; also method of grasping.

Halved — Tied score on a hole or complete game.

Handicap — Number of strokes conceded by a stronger to a weaker player.

Hazard — Natural or artificial obstacle other than the ordinary grass of the course.

Head — Striking portion of the club.

Heel — Part of head nearest shaft.

Hole — Cup 4½ inches in diameter into which the ball is played.

Hole out — Final stroke for a hole.

Honor — Right to play first from a tee.

Hook — A ball that curves left in flight (right-handed golfer).

Iron — Club with a steel head.

Lie — Manner and position in which a ball in play is resting; also, the angle of the club as measured from the bottom of the sole back to the shaft.

Links — The entire course.

Loft — Flight or elevation of a ball; also angle of clubface.

Match — A contest between two or more opponents or sides.

Match play — Competition based on holes won and lost.

Medal play — Competition based on total strokes per round.

Nassau — A system of scoring: one point alloted for first nine holes; one point for second nine and one point for 18 holes.

Neck — Angle between shaft and head of club.

Par — Standard score for a hole.

Penalty stroke — A stroke added to score of individual or side under certain rules.

Pivot — Body turn.

Press — Effort to hit the ball unusually hard.

Provisional ball — A ball played after the ball hit originally is assumed lost or out of bounds.

Pull — A ball hit straight but to the left of intended flight line.

Push — A ball hit straight but to the right of intended flight line.

Putt — To stroke ball with putter toward hole; also the stroke.

Rough — Rough ground and long grass on either side of fairway.

Shaft — Handle of a club.

Slice — To hit across the ball so that it curves to right in flight (right-handed golfer).

Sclaff — To scrape turf with the clubhead before contacting the ball.

Stance — Position of the feet.

Stymie — One ball lies on the green directly in line of another and the balls are more than 6 inches apart.

Tee — Elevation, of wood or plastic, upon which a ball may be placed for the first stroke on each hole.

Teeing ground — Designated area for starting every hole.

Top — To hit the ball above its center.

Trap — Hole with bed of sand, which forms a hazard.

Up — The number of holes or strokes one is ahead of opponent.

Waggle — Preliminary movements with the clubhead, forward and back, in preparation for a swing.

Whiff — To miss the ball entirely.

Winter rules — Rules that allow player to improve the lie of the ball on the fairway.

Selected Audio-visual Aids

Beginning Golf: The Game, Get Set to Swing, Building Control Into Your Swing, Getting on the Green, Putting, Courtesy and Etiquette of Golf. Filmstrips and recordings, 10 min. per unit, color.) The Athletic Institute, 804 Mercandise Mart, Chicago, Illinois 60654. (Rental and purchase.)

Building Your Golf Swing. (16 mm., color.) National Golf Foundation, 804 Merchandise Mart, Chicago, Illinois 60654. (Rental and purchase.)

Johnny Farrell Series. (16 mm., 6 units, 10 min. per unit, sound, b & w.) Ideal Pictures Inc., 58E South Water Street, Chicago, Illinois, or 233 West 32nd Street, New York, New York 10036. (Rental.)

Pitching, Pitch and Run, and Sand Shots. (16 mm., color.) National Golf Foundation, 804 Merchandise Mart, Chicago, Illinois 60654. (Rental and purchase.)

Putting. (16 mm., color.) National Golf Foundation, 804

Merchandise Mart, Chicago, Illinois 60654. (Rental and purchase.)

Rosburg, Bob: *Hear How To Improve Your Golf*. (Recording, 33⅓ rmp.) Golf Digest, Box 550, Evanston, Illinois 60200. (Purchase.)

Suggested Readings

AAHPER: *Bowling, Fencing, Golf Guide*, Current Edition, Division for Girls and Women's Sports, 1201 16th Street, N.W., Washington, D.C. 20036.

Crogen, Corinne: *Golf Fundamentals*, Palo Alto, Calif., National Press Publications, 1960.

Hogan, Ben: *Five Lessons of the Modern Fundamentals of Golf*, Cranbury, N.J., A. S. Barnes & Co., Inc., 1957.

Suggs, Louise, et al.: *Golf for Women*, Garden City, New York, Doubleday and Company, 1960.

United States Golf Association: *The Rules of Golf*, New York, N.Y., Current Edition.

Wright, Mickey: *Play Golf the Wright Way*, Garden City, New York, Doubleday and Company, 1962.

Periodicals

Golf Digest, 1236 Sherman Avenue, Evanston, Ill. 60200

Golf, 235 East 45th St., New York, N.Y. 10017.

U.S.G.A. *Golf Journal*, 40 E. 38th St., New York, N.Y., 10016.

Suggested Study Questions

1. Explain the importance of etiquette to the play and safety of golf. What considerations should you have for fellow players (a) on the tee, (b) on the fairway, (c) on the green?
2. Name all the clubs a golfer may use and discuss the proper use of each club.
3. Briefly explain the principles and techniques for playing sidehill, uphill, and downhill lies.
4. Explain scoring methods used in golf. How would you establish a handicap at the local course?
5. List ten rules a beginner must know before playing on a course.

CHAPTER NINE

Courtesy Jean Jacobs, Springfield College, Springfield, Massachusetts.

GYMNASTICS

Gymnastics is fast growing in popularity among college women. Few other physical activities provide the challenge or require the hard work and self-discipline it takes to excel in this sport. Participation in a gymnastic program can increase coordination, strength, and body flexibility, and also develop grace, rhythm, and self-reliance. It is challenging both for highly coordinated individuals and for those with average physical skills who are willing to learn intricate rhythmic patterns.

Although gymnastics was popularized by the ancient Greeks, it is mentioned frequently in ancient records found in Japan, China, Persia, and Egypt. Physical education (or gymnastics, as it was known) played a vital role in the education of every Greek youth, for it was thought that such a program would develop strength, a sense of fair play, and courage, as well as a beautiful, well-proportioned body. Girls, although not required by law to do so, also took part in this program, but not to the extent that males did.

Our first programs in school physical education in the United States, patterned upon those found in Germany, Sweden, and Denmark, were largely centered around gymnastics. By the 20th century these early programs had been greatly modified and a wide variety of informal activities had became popular. It is only in recent years that gymnastics began to appear again in school-sponsored physical education programs. Touring gymnastic teams from Denmark and Sweden have helped to increase interest in this sport in America.

The first A.A.U. gymnastic championship competition for women was held in Philadelphia in 1931. In the 1960 Olympic games in Rome most of the gymnastic medals were won by the Russian team, but this event was one of the most widely attended of all. The United States Women's Gymnastic Team for the 1968 Olympic games in Mexico City attracted more outstanding women gymnasts and spectators than ever before.

This chapter deals with gymnastic events used in international competition. Tumbling and other stunts are, of course, a part of gymnastics but are not included here since they are described in Chapter 14.

Fig. 9-1. Few other physical activities provide the challenge or require the hard work and self-discipline that it takes to excel in gymnastics. (Courtesy of Hollis Fait, University of Connecticut.)

NATURE AND PURPOSE OF THE SPORT

The primary purpose of gymnastics is the harmonious development of the body. Movements center around the big muscles, including those of the arms, chest, shoulders, legs, and abdomen. Emphasis is placed on the development of highly coordinated rhythmic skills that require alertness, courage, and precision. Since it is a self-testing activity, each student can progress at her own speed. Free calisthenics provide one with the opportunity to work out her own exercise routines made up of selected movement combinations. The major gymnastic stunts are built on basic tumbling patterns such as the head or hand stand and the techniques of chinning, balancing, and leaping over objects. The stunts may be performed on a mat, the floor, or apparatus. Activities for women include free calisthenics, the side horse vault, the balance beam, and those performed on the even and uneven parallel bars.

RULES AND SCORING

Events recommended for intramural and extramural competition are as follows:

1. *Individual events:* Floor exercise, uneven parallel bars, balance beam, side horse vault.
2. *All-around event*: To consist of the total points scored in the four individual events, both compulsory and optional.
3. *Special events:* Tumbling, trampoline.

This chapter is concerned only with the skills of the individual events. Prior to competition it is imperative that a student be familiar with the rules concerning each event. These are available in the *Official A.A.U. Gymnastics Guide* and the D.G.W.S. *Gymnastics Guide.*

Scoring. Judges award scores of 0 to 10 in tenths of a point. The only exception is in the case of the optional side horse vault. This exception is made because of the difficulty of the vault.

According to the value of the optional vault, the scoring is as follows:

1. Judges award points of 0 through 10, and the scorers deduct the number of the rating below ten.
2. The judges award points of 0 through the maximum score of 10 allowed in the evaluation of the vault.

FACILITIES AND EQUIPMENT

Desirable uniforms for women are leotards and ballet-type soft-soled shoes. The equipment should include mats, a side horse, even and uneven parallel bars, and a balance beam.

SAFETY PRECAUTIONS

Since perspiration on the hands can easily cause an accident when one is working on certain pieces of apparatus, magnesium carbonate should be rubbed on the palms to keep them dry. This chalk tends to accumulate on the apparatus and should be carefully removed, for it can quickly cause hand blisters. Beginners should master the fundamental skills before being permitted to try the more advanced exercises or apparatus activities, and all adjustable apparatus should be lowered until each student becomes a proficient performer on it. All apparatus should be well padded, with mats and ample clearance space provided so that a student leaping off or over one piece of equipment does not collide with another. Spotting or assisting another performer to do a stunt successfully is an absolute must. The spotter should know how to do the stunt that another is attempting and be able to anticipate movement errors or difficulties before they occur.

It is of utmost importance that each student be well conditioned physically before attempting any gymnastic stunt. Since good physical condition is more than having a flexible, strong body, the student should continually strive not only to keep her body strong and flexible but also work diligently toward increasing physical endurance. American women, in contrast to those in Europe who perform in competitive gymnastics, have noticeably less strength in their fingers, arms, and shoulders. Simple exercises to increase both body flexibility and strength in these areas include:

THE PUSHUP

Keeping a straight body, raise it from a prone position, supporting the weight on the hands, straightened arms, and toes (Fig. 9-2). Add 1 more additional pushup at each workout until 10 are reached. Then strive for 15, etc.

Fig. 9-2. The pushup.

THE PULLUP

With knuckles up, pull the body up to bring the chin over the top of the chinning bar (Fig. 9-3). Repeat several times, lowering the body slowly each time by fully extending the arms.

Fig. 9-4. Swinging.

THE HIGH LEG STRETCH

Used to develop body flexibility, this exercise is done by standing with your back to the wall and lifting one leg forward and up as far as possible. Have a partner grasp your ankle and raise your leg higher. Keep weight balanced on the other leg with knee locked.

THE FRONT SPLIT

Used also to develop body flexibility, this stunt is done by standing with one foot far ahead of the other. Slowly move the legs farther apart. Alternate legs and repeat. Be sure to lock the rear leg tightly with the knee down. Keep the body in an erect position.

Fig. 9-3. The pullup.

SWINGING

To develop hand and finger grip strength, hold the body in a rigid position, using either the upper or under grip on the chinning bar, swing back and forth, gaining momentum each time, then gradually decrease it (Fig. 9-4.)

Fig. 9-5. The front split.

THE SIDE SPLIT

Also for body flexibility, this stunt is done by standing with legs spread wide apart to the sides and continuing to spread them as far apart as possible. Keep the legs and body straight, the knees locked. At the farthest point of movement, bend the upper body from the waist, keeping hands well in front of the hips to force the hips down.

BASIC SKILLS

FREE EXERCISES

In competitive events, free exercises must be performed for no longer than 1½ minutes on the floor or the mat with a square area of 39.33 feet. Ballet and tumbling movements in any combination can be used. Usually, however, these exercise patterns begin with an opening sequence of tumbling, followed by the body of the routine consisting of ballet jumps, turns, spins, and balancing and agility movements, and finish with another tumbling sequence.*

*Loken, Newton C., and Willoughby, Robert J.: *Complete Book of Gymnastics*, 2nd Ed., Englewood Cliffs, N.J., Prentice-Hall, Inc., 1967.

All stunts used in free exercise competition should be mastered on a mat before they are tried on the floor. A spotter should assist the learner, and stand where she can be of most help.

Since free exercise routines are largely built on the ability to move with grace and beauty, harmonious body movement should be the starting point in learning this activity, especially if one has not had much previous experience in dance or tumbling.

In competition a performer is given from 1 to 1½ minutes (5 seconds' leeway) to perform her routine. The varied movements and floor patterns should use the entire floor space. The exercise must be accompanied by music, which should set the pace and accent and should highlight all movements. The performer is expected to demonstrate her skill in back flexion, forward flexion and extension, arm support strength, balance holds or poses, coordination and timing in tumbling stunts, and agility in springs. Tumbling and dance should both be included in the routine, but should be carefully balanced so that neither activity is dominant. All movement changes should blend naturally together. Directional turns, like all other movements, should lead harmoniously into the succeeding movement. Once the exercise

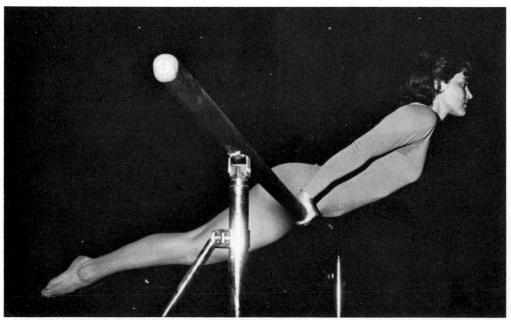

Fig. 9-6. Body balance is essential for success in gymnastic activities. (Courtesy of Hollis Fait, University of Connecticut.)

has been created, it should be practiced over and over again until it can be done beautifully.

BALLET MOVEMENTS

THE TOE STAND

Stand with an erect body, rise to toes with arms extended at the sides in a relaxed, graceful position with palms down (Fig. 9-7). Lower body to full standing position with arms at your side.

Fig. 9-7. The toe stand.

THE BALLET TOUCH

Stand in a controlled, relaxed position with right foot slightly ahead of the left. Bend and touch the forward foot with right hand. Return to original position. Repeat, using the other foot and hand.

THE PIROUETTE

This is a series of two or more full turns of the body on the ball of one foot while the body rotates. The head remains facing forward as long as possible, then is turned quickly around to face forward again, helping to give momentum to the turn.

THE BODY SWEEP

With body weight held on right knee and right hand, move the left arm forward and at the same time extend the left leg. Reach for full extension of the arm and leg (Fig. 9-8).

Fig. 9-8. The body sweep.

THE STAG LEAP

Leap high in the air, bringing the left foot up to touch the inner thigh of the other leg above the knee. Extend the left arm upward, the right out to the side (Fig. 9-9).

Fig. 9-9. The stag leap.

FLEXIBILITY AND AGILITY MOVEMENTS

THE ARABESQUE

From a standing position, move the left leg backward and out and extend right arm, keeping the fingers relaxed. Move the left arm out to the side. Stand in a balanced position (Fig. 9-10).

Fig. 9-10. The arabesque.

THE SINGLE LEG BALANCE

Standing balanced on the left leg, raise the other one to the side as high as you can, grasp its instep with the right hand and extend the leg, raising the opposite hand in a graceful position with palm up (Fig. 9-11).

Fig. 9-11. The single leg balance.

THE BALANCE STAND

Stand on the right leg. Bend forward, keeping your trunk parallel to the floor and both arms forward. Extend the left leg backward, pointing the toes, and raise it higher than the body. Keep your head up and the back arched (Fig. 9-12). This is also called a front scale.

Fig. 9-12. The balance stand.

THE NEEDLE SCALE

Stand on one leg. With arms extended forward, bend your body slowly forward and down until your palms rest on the floor and the forehead touches the front of the lower supporting leg. Then extend the other leg upward.

JUMP TO HANDSTAND

Jump upward from a standing position. Tuck the body and land on your hands, flexing elbows slightly to cushion impact. Then fully extend and lock arms, and balance the body held in full extension. Hold for three seconds, or count 1000 and 1, 1000 and 2, 1000 and 3.

THE YOGA HANDSTAND

From a handstand position, drop the hips suddenly forward and jackknife the legs backward. Bring the head forward, keeping the back stiff (Fig. 9-13). Hold for 3 seconds, or count 1000 and 1, 1000 and 2, 1000 and 3.

Fig. 9-13.   The yoga handstand.

land on your straightened arms, flex and hold weight on the arms. As you fall, extend one leg with toes pointed, keeping the other foot on the floor (Fig. 9-14).

THE SHOOT THROUGH

With your body in full extension, leaning forward on your arms flex the hips and bring the legs rapidly through the arms (Fig. 9-15). Finish in a sitting position with legs and feet together and extended, and your body tilted backward, supported by the hands held behind shoulder line.

THE FRONT WALKOVER

From a standing position, lean forward to place the hands on the floor as you do in a handstand. Bring one leg slowly off the floor and all the way over, followed by the other leg. Push with hands and return to original position. (The use of a belt or a spotter is recommended for this stunt.)

THE BACKOVER

Bend backward from the standing position until the hands touch the floor. Kick the right leg up and over, then the left one, finishing in a standing position. (A safety belt or a spotter is recommended.)

THE FORWARD DROP

Fall forward from a standing position to

Fig. 9-15.   The shoot through.

THE SUPINE ARCH-UP

From a supine floor position raise the body from the floor by moving the hands from near the hips to the shoulder area. Straighten the arms, arch the back, and keep both feet close together on the floor (Fig. 9-16).

Fig. 9-14.   The forward drop.

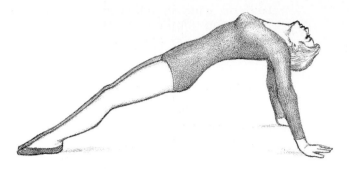

Fig. 9-16. The supine arch-up.

THE BALANCE BEAM

For competitive events the beam should be 4 inches wide, 6 inches in depth, 16 feet, 4 inches long, and 4 feet from the floor. On this board the perormers must do a variety of running and balance movements, rolls, held positions, and body turns within a two minute time limit. Each routine is judged for accuracy, control, and beauty of movement on the mount, on the beam itself, and on the dismount.

For safety purposes in this sport, mats should be placed under and around the beam, and the use of at least one spotter on each side of the beam is essential. For beginners the beam should be approximately 6 inches above the floor, then graduallly raised in height as the performer gains skill and confidence. Learning to walk and run on the beam should be the first skills mastered.

The exercises done on the beam should be rhythmical and should utilize complete body movement. The arms should be held to the side with palms down and the elbows relaxed.

MOUNTS

There are a variety of ways to get onto the beam. Regardless of the mount used, a spotter should be present to assist all beginners.

THE STRAIGHT ARM SUPPORT MOUNT

From a standing position or from a series of short running steps, jump to take off with both feet, and place both hands at shoulder width on the beam. Support the straightened body with the front of the thighs touching the beam (Fig. 9-17). Swing the body up and onto the beam.

Fig. 9-17. The straight arm support mount.

THE SQUAT MOUNT

Jump to a straight arm support position and bring legs up between the arms. The feet are placed close together on the beam, and the body is held in balance by the toes and hands (Fig. 9-18).

Fig. 9-18. The squat mount.

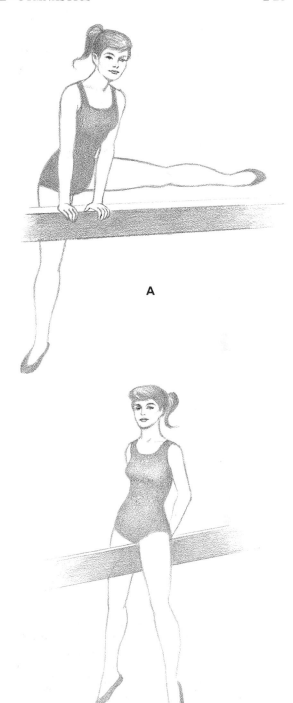

A

THE ONE KNEE MOUNT

Jump to a straight arm support position to land on the right knee on the beam and point the toes (Fig. 9-19). Keep supporting hands on the outside. Extend the left leg up and back. Keep head erect.

Fig. 9-19. The one knee mount.

B

Fig. 9-20. The crotch seat mount.

THE CROTCH SEAT MOUNT

Jump to a straight arm support, and swing the extended left leg over the beam (Fig. 9-20, *A*). Turn the body one quarter turn; sit straddling the beam, legs and feet extended, and hold on with both hands behind the body (Fig. 9-20, *B*). (This mount requires skill and arm strength and should not be attempted by beginners.)

THE SCISSORS MOUNT

Take off at an oblique angle from the beat board, placed almost parallel to the beam. With a scissoring movement bring the body up over the beam one leg at a time, and come to a sitting position.

THE HIP PULLOVER MOUNT

From a standing position, bend your knees and grasp the beam, using an undergrip. Raise first one leg, then the other (Fig. 9-21). With a fast hip-circling movement bring the body under and over the beam. Straighten the body.

Fig. 9-22. Walking the beam.

Fig. 9-21. The hip pullover mount.

POSES AND MOVEMENTS ON THE BEAM

All poses and movement skills down on the balance beam require courage, body control, and flexibility. Having one spotter on each side of the beam is recommended for beginners until they gain both confidence and skill. The beam should not be raised to its proper height until the students are beyond the novice stage in learning to perform the basic skills.

WALKING AND RUNNING THE BEAM

This should be practiced until you can move with confidence and sureness. The body should be held erect with the arms hanging naturally at the sides for balance. To add polish to walking movements, make a small knee dip with each step, letting the free foot drop slightly below the beam on each step. Keep eyes focused forward and do not look down at your feet or the beam (Fig. 9-22).

BODY TURNS ON THE BEAM

Although there are many ways of turning, the simplest is to pivot the body around to face a reverse position (Fig. 9-23). This is done by coming up to the balls of both feet held in a toe to heel position, turning the body to an acute right to left angle, and lowering the feet to the beam again. Or execute a pirouette, a half turn done on one foot. Hold the arms overhead with fingers pointed and relaxed, and rotate the body around on the supporting right foot (Fig. 9-24). On completing the turn, bring the left foot to the beam and use your arms to achieve complete body balance.

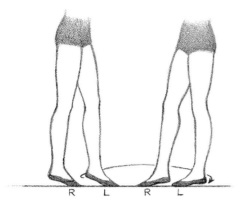

Fig. 9-23. The pivot.

Fig. 9-25. Jumping on the beam.

Fig. 9-24. The pirouette turn.

THE SWITCH STEP

From a standing position with one foot slightly in front of the other, hold your arms behind and above your head, bend your knees slightly, and then spring from the beam by straightening your legs and pushing up with your feet. Switch your feet while in the air, and as you drop your body to the beam bend your knees and make a circle with the arms. Return to a standing position. Be sure to gain good height on the upward spring and lean forward slightly as you land for better balance control.

THE FRONT SCISSORS KICK

A front scissors kick can be done following several short running steps or from a running position. If from the latter, stand with the left foot slightly in front of the right and extend the arms at the sides. With your weight on the left foot, jump by pushing off with that foot and bringing your arms down. Then bring the right leg, locked straight, forward and sharply upward while raising your arms. Quickly swing your left leg up to

JUMPS ON THE BEAM

Jumps can be made from a run or dip position. Place your right foot ahead of the left. Jump into the air by swinging your arms upward, and reverse your feet, bringing left one forward (Fig. 9-25).

make a scissors kick before coming down. Bend your knees on landing to maintain balance.

THE ONE LEG SQUAT

Slowly lower your body from an erect position into a full squat, keeping your weight on the right foot, and lift the left leg parallel to the beam. Reach your arms gracefully forward to keep your balance (Fig. 9-26).

THE KNEE SCALE

Begin from a kneeling position with left knee behind the right (Fig. 9-27). Tilt your body forward as you lift the back leg into the air. Straighten your arms and grasp the beam with one hand on each side, keeping your fingers together and down, and your head erect.

THE STRADDLE HOLD

Sit on beam with your hands gripping the beam between your extended legs. Raise your body to balance on your straight arms (Fig. 9-28).

Fig. 9-26.   The one leg squat.

Fig. 9-27.   The knee scale.

Fig. 9-28.   The straddle hold.

THE FORWARD SHOULDER ROLL

Begin from a kneeling position. Lower your head and one shoulder to the beam and hold on by gripping the fingers close together with each hand under the beam (Fig. 9-29, *A*). Move your hips slowly up and forward into a roll and finish by bringing your body into a full lying position face up (Fig. 9-29, *B, C*). Next, bring both legs down on each side, going into a crotch seat position (Fig. 9-20, *B*). The use of a spotter on each side of the beam is recommended.

THE BACK SHOULDER ROLL

Begin from a lying position with your body facing up on the beam. Lower your head to one side below the top of the beam and hold on by reaching to its underside (Fig. 9-30, *A*). Slowly do a backward roll by pulling your knees toward your chest and on over, keeping body weight supported on one shoulder (Fig. 9-30, *B*). Place your right bent knee on the top of the beam (Fig. 9-30, *C*). Then come up into a kneeling scale (Fig. 9-27). The use of two spotters is recommended for this stunt also.

A

B

C

Fig. 9-29. The forward shoulder roll.

A

B

C

Fig. 9-30. The back shoulder roll.

DISMOUNTS

THE JUMP OFF DISMOUNT

The easiest dismount is done by leaping off of the beam. Be sure to keep your movements controlled as you leap off of the beam, and to bend your knees to break the fall as you come down.

THE SIDE SEAT DISMOUNT

Seated on the beam, lean toward the right and place your right hand on the beam (Fig. 9-31, *A*). Swing the outside leg backward and lift your body up and to the side with the right hand (Fig. 9-31, *B*). Dismount and come into an erect standing position.

THE FRONT VAULT DISMOUNT

In a front rest position, support your body on your hands and fully extended arms and feet (Fig. 9-32, *A*). Kick your legs upward, and at the same time swing your body around clear of the beam (Fig. 9-32, *B*). Dismount.

Fig. 9-32. The front vault dismount.

Fig. 9-31. The side seat dismount.

THE HANDSTAND DISMOUNT

This may be used by students who have mastered the stunt (see Chapter 14). Hold the arms horizontally at the side. Then go into a handstand position, make a big circle outward as you come on around with your body fully extended, and dismount with feet held together.

Fig. 9-33. The handstand dismount.

THE VAULTS

In women's vaulting the pommels are removed from the horse, and the performer takes off from a beat board on one side of the horse, vaulting over the middle of the saddle so that the hands give momentary support to the body. In competition, excellence is judged by length of flight, vault executed, and control of body throughout.

The use of a spotter is urged until the student has progressed beyond the novice stage. Basic skills in taking off from the beat board should first be mastered.

Approach the beat board in a light run with weight on the balls of the feet. The body is straight and inclined forward and elbows are bent. A low hurdle carries the gymnast to the end of the board. The body weight lands first on the toes and then the balls of the feet. The body remains straight as it rides the quick spring upward.

THE SIDE VAULT

The most basic vault is the side or flank vault. After making a few running steps, take off from the beat board from the balls of the feet. Place hands on the horse, shoulder width apart. Shift weight to the right arm. Lift the left hand from the horse, bring feet together in a horizontal position, and move the body over the horse under this hand (Fig. 9-34). Push off from the horse with the sup-

porting hand and land with the back to the horse. As a variation, in swinging the body over, turn body downward to face toward the top of the horse. Release one hand as in the side vault and land, keeping one hand resting on the horse. This vault is called a front vault.

Fig. 9-34. The side vault.

THE SQUAT STAND VAULT

Take off and place the hands on the horse shoulder width apart. Bring the legs up between the arms in a squatting position (Fig. 9-35). Jump forward to the mat.

Fig. 9-35. The squat stand vault.

THE STRADDLE VAULT

Approach running at medium speed, spring high on the take-off and put both hands on the horse. At the same time spread the legs far apart (Fig. 9-36). Land in a standing position.

Fig. 9-36. The straddle vault.

THE STRADDLE STAND AND JUMP

Jump to straddle position, keeping legs outside the arms (Fig. 9-37). Straighten body to full standing position. Jump with both arms and body in full extension with toes pointed to land on the mat.

Fig. 9-37. The straddle stand.

THE HANDSPRING VAULT

This may be done by students who have mastered the stunt (see Chapter 14). Spring from the board and come to a handstand position, keeping arms straight and locked (Fig. 9-38). Tuck in your head and bring fully extended body over the horse to land on the mat.

Fig. 9-38. The handspring vault.

THE EVEN PARALLEL BARS

Students should learn the basic skills for parallel bar movement on the even bars before attempting the uneven bars. The use of one or two spotters is recommended. Heavy mats should cover all areas beneath and both ends of the bars. The basic movements performed on the bars are those of tumbling combined with swinging movements. The width between the bars should be adjusted for beginners.

THE STRAIGHT ARM SUPPORT

Since most stunts originate from this position, it should be learned first. With each hand grasp the top of the two bars near the end. Jump upward, straighten and lock your arms, keeping your body erect with back arched and toes pointed (Fig. 9-39). To travel up and back on the bars, shift your body weight from one hand to the other, just as you shift body weight from foot to foot in walking.

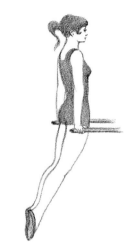

Fig. 9-39. The straight arm support.

THE RIDING SEAT

Swing your body forward on your hands and fully extended arms and then bring both legs sharply over one of the bars to come into a sitting position. Support your body with one hand held behind you and the other grasping the other bar. Extend your rear leg fully, and flex the forward one. Keep body erect, eyes focused ahead and feet pointed downward. You can do a series of these side seats by swinging your legs up and back down to a straight arm support position and then back up again.

THE STRADDLE SEAT

Jump forward and support your weight on your hands and fully extended arms. Swing both legs forward between the bars. Separate them and straddle the bars, bringing your body up into an erect sitting position, holding on to the bars with each hand behind your

Fig. 9-40. The straddle seat.

back. Raise both arms horizontally and fully extend both legs, keeping your feet pointed toward the mat (Fig. 9-40). To travel the length of the bars, lean forward, placing your hands on the bars in front of your legs, whip your legs backward and over the bars to a straight arm support position, and then go forward into another straddle position.

THE BACK ROLL TO A STRADDLE SEAT

Begin by standing facing out between the bars at the end, grasping the bars in an overgrip. In one continuous motion bring your legs up sharply, coming into an inverted hanging position, arch your back, fully extend your body, and move your face back

Fig. 9-41. The back roll to a straddle seat.

away from the mat. Then by circling around the bars go into a straddle position. Sit with your arms out to the sides with palms up, legs and feet fully extended.

THE FORWARD ROLL

From a straddle position, bend forward, placing both hands on the bars ahead and go into a forward roll. Come up over on the upper arms, and when your body starts to come down, place your hands close together behind your back to make a bridge to roll your body across, and end up in a straddle position (Fig. 9-42). The use of a spotter for this stunt is recommended.

Fig. 9-43. The single leg flank dismount.

THE DOUBLE LEG DISMOUNT

Swing your body back and forth several times from a straight arm support. On the forward part of the last swing, bring your body and both legs with feet together and toes pointed out up and over the right side of the bar (Fig. 9-44). Dismount to the mat.

Fig. 9-42. The forward roll.

THE SHOULDER BALANCE

Get into a straddle seat position and place your hands on the bars in front of your body. Lean forward, placing your upper arms on the bars, and slowly lift your legs and body into shoulder balance position. Straighten your body into full extension, arch your back, and point your feet upward.

THE SINGLE LEG FLANK DISMOUNT

Begin this dismount from a sitting position, your body facing sideward on the bars, with the right leg over the forward bar and right hand holding on to the bar, palm facing out. Rest your left leg on the rear bar in a fully extended leg and foot position and keeping your left arm and hand fully extended and slightly back. Swing your left leg and arm up around and over both bars as you push on from the front bar and dismount to the mat.

Fig. 9-44. The double leg dismount.

THE UNEVEN PARALLEL BARS

The measurements for the uneven bars are as follows: the top of the high bar should be 7 feet, 6 inches from the floor; and the distance from the floor to the low bar should be 5 feet, with a between bar width of 16½ to 18 inches.

Movements on the uneven parallel bars are predominantly swinging ones. Although there are no set combinations, the best routine movement patterns are those that enable you to go from the high bar to the low one and from it back up to the high bar. Each movement should be fluidly rhythmical and

Fig. 9-45. Moving the body gracefully from the low to the high uneven parallel bar requires skill in body control. (Courtesy of Hollis Fait, University of Connecticut.)

continuous. The three basic stages in using the bars are the mounts, the poses and movements, and the dismounts. A beat board may be used for mounting.

THE MOUNTS

THE STRAIGHT ARM SUPPORT

Face the low bar and grasp it by placing your hands over the top with your thumbs underneath. Jump, tilt your fully extended body and rest it on your thighs. Keep your arms straight, chest and head up, extend legs and toes (Fig. 9-46).

THE SHOOT OVER THE LOW BAR

Start from behind the high bar facing the low bar. Spring up and grasp the high bar, then bring both legs up and over the low bar. Finish with your seat resting on the low bar and holding on to the high bar, keeping your body fully extended (Fig. 9-47).

Fig. 9-46. The straight arm support.

Fig. 9-47. The shoot over the low bar.

THE CROSS SEAT MOUNT

Stand between the bars, grasping the low one with your right hand, the high one with left hand with fingers curled around it on the top inner side. Jump upward to support the body largely by the left hand on the high bar and the right lower arm and hand on the low bar (Fig. 9-48). Swing both legs over the low bar and come into a cross seat position, keeping legs together and toes pointed.

Fig. 9-48. The cross seat mount.

THE BACK PULLOVER MOUNT

Grasp the low bar by curling your hands and fingers around the top of it. Pull your body in toward the bar and bring legs up and around the bar, using a hip-circling movement (Fig. 9-49). Finish in a straight arm support position with your body held in full extension, keeping your feet and toes pointed downward toward the mat.

Fig. 9-49. The back pullover mount.

POSES AND MOVEMENTS

THE LOW BAR BALANCE

From a straddle position on the low bar bring your right leg up onto the bar, sup-porting your body by grasping the bar behind you with your right hand. Take hold of the high bar with the left hand, raise your left leg, and extend the foot (Fig. 9-50).

Fig. 9-50. The low bar balance.

THE CROTCH SEAT

Using a straight arm support on the inside of the low bar, raise your right leg up, over and down to the right side of the bar and come up to a crotch seat position. Hold on to the high bar with your left hand and to the low one with your right. Keep your body in an erect sitting position (Fig. 9-51).

Fig. 9-51. The crotch seat.

THE SWAN

Moving from a straight arm support position on the high bar, balance your body on your upper thighs, raise your arms and fully extend them to the sides, and arch your back (Fig. 9-52).

Fig. 9-52. The swan.

THE SWINGING HIP CIRCLE

This is done from a hanging position on the high bar, using an overgrip, with the body fully extended and facing the low bar. Swing one leg out and up and place the foot on the low bar. Push out briskly from bar and begin a backward body swing. Wrap your legs around the low bar on the forward swing and let go of the high bar to come to a sitting position on the low bar facing out.

THE THIGH REST

From a front rest position on the high bar, move your body slowly down and grasp the low bar with both hands. Raise both legs together keeping your toes pointed and come into an arched position, supporting your body with your hands and on the upper thighs (Fig. 9-53).

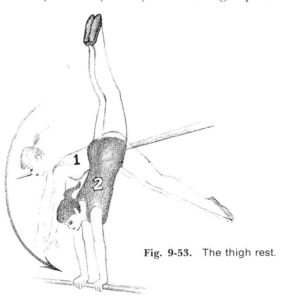

Fig. 9-53. The thigh rest.

THE LOW BAR SCALE

Hold on to the top bar with the left hand and support your body in a squat position on the right leg. Raise your body and extend your left leg behind you. Next, bring your body forward, keeping the right arm extended and your hand in a relaxed position (Fig. 9-54).

Fig. 9-54. The low bar scale

THE ARCH BACK

Hang from your knees on the high bar facing the low one. Reach backward and pull your body up above the bar. Arch your body and straighten your arms on the low bar (Fig. 9-55).

Fig. 9-55. The arch back.

THE SIDE CROSS HAND BALANCE

From a front lying position on the high bar, lean forward toward the low bar, and grasp

Fig. 9-56. The side cross hand balance.

the high bar with the left hand in an overgrip position. Bring the body slowly downward and place your right hand on the low bar. Turn your body somewhat to the left and slowly move it away from the high bar. Keep your left arm bent and the right one straight, your body arched and in full extension with both legs together and your feet pointed (Fig. 9-56).

THE DISMOUNTS

There are many dismounts that may be used. However, you should learn to do a few of them well before trying to add to these skills. Great care must be taken in dismounting, for doing so too quickly can cause jerky, uncontrolled movements and spoil your whole routine. A dismount properly done puts the finishing touch on the movements done on uneven parallel bars, giving both a last and lasting impression of a performer.

THE FRONT VAULT DISMOUNT*

This is done from a swinging position between the bars. Hold both bars in an overgrip, locking the lower arm for support. Begin by making a controlled swing between the bars, then after a forceful backswing, push vigorously out from the high bar and lift your arched body over the low bar with your feet leading (Fig. 9-57).

*Yeager, Patrick: *A Teaching Guide for Women's Gymnastics*, Georgia Southern College, 1962, p. 50.

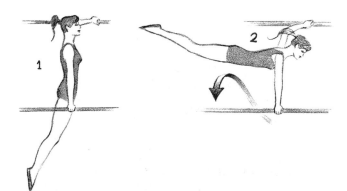

Fig. 9-57. The front vault dismount.

THE SINGLE LEG SIDE VAULT DISMOUNT

Sit in a somewhat sideward crotched position on the low bar with your left leg in front, knee flexed. Hold on to the bar with your left hand behind you in an undergrip position. Keep your right leg in full extension downward and grasp the high bar in an overgrip position. Next, swing your right leg up and over the right side of the bar, using your left arm to support your body. Release your grip on the high bar as you move your right leg over the bar and jump toward the mat with both feet (Fig. 9-58). Keep your left hand and the left side of your body close to the bar. Stretch your right arm out to full extension to the side in order to maintain balance.

Fig. 9-59. The quarter twist dismount.

Fig. 9-58. The single leg side dismount.

THE UNDERSWING DISMOUNT FROM THE HIGH BAR

Stand on the low bar grasping the higher bar with both hands. Jump into a half pike

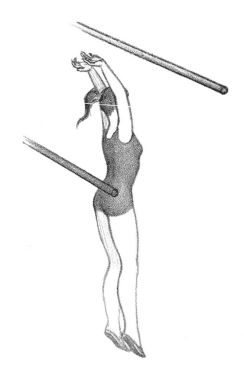

THE QUARTER TWIST DISMOUNT

From a straight arm support position on the low bar facing the high one, swing both feet slightly forward, then backward, and make a quarter turn (Fig. 9-59), and drop to the mat in a standing position, keeping your left side near the bar and holding on to it with your left hand until you have made a controlled landing.

Fig. 9-60. The underswing dismount from the high bar.

and swing both legs under and up toward the high bar. Then swing under the high bar, raising both arms above your extended body before you land on the mat behind the high bar (Fig. 9-60).

THE DOUBLE LEG DISMOUNT

Lean slightly forward from a straight arm support position between the bars. Swing both legs back and then over the low bar. Push off from the high bar and make a quarter turn with your body, coming over the low bar in a seat position to a standing dismount on the mat (Fig. 9-61).

Fig. 9-61. The double leg dismount.

performer for the take-off or at the beginning of a stunt.

Ordinary grasp — Holding on to the apparatus with the palms facing each other or the backs of the hands toward you.

Pike — A body position in which the legs are straight and the trunk is at right angles to them.

Reverse grasp — Holding on to the apparatus with backs of the hands facing each other or the palms turned toward the performer.

Scale — An arabesque in which the trunk is parallel to the floor; weight may be supported by either one foot or one knee.

Spotter — A person who helps a performer to do a routine safely.

Straddle seat — Used on the even parallel bars. The legs straddle the bars and one is placed on each bar either in front of or behind the body.

Take-off — A preliminary spring done on one or both feet.

Tuck — A position in which hips and knees are bent and knees are pulled toward the chest.

Twist — A spiral movement along and around an axis of the body.

Selected Audio-visual Aids

Gymnastics for Girls and Women. (4 slide film units.) The Athletic Institute, 805 Merchandise Mart, Chicago, Ill. 60654

Tumbling. Champions on Film Company, 303 S. Main, Ann Arbor, Mich. (Rental.)

NCAA Gymnastic Meet Films. NCAA Office, 209 Fairfax Building, Kansas City 5, Mo. (Rental.)

Skills and Techniques of Advanced Gymnastics. Nissen Corporation. 930 27th Avenue, Cedar Rapids, Iowa.

Terminology

Approach — The way the performer moves towards the apparatus to be used.

Arabesque — A body position in which one leg supports the weight and the other is raised in alignment with the trunk; arm position varies.

Beat board — A small springboard from which the performer jumps to mount a piece of apparatus.

Combined grasps — Holding on to the apparatus with one hand curled toward the performer and the other away.

Cross support — Supporting the body weight by the hands on the parallel bars by placing one hand on each bar.

Flank — A movement in which one side of the body is toward the apparatus.

Landing — Jumping from the equipment to the mat or floor and bending the knees, hips, and ankles to absorb the force of the body coming down on to the mat.

Near side of the apparatus — The approach used by the

Suggested Readings

Baley, James: *Gymnastics in the Schools*, Boston, Allyn and Bacon, 1965.

Cooper, Phyllis: *Feminine Gymnastics*, Minneapolis, Minn., Burgess Publishing Company, 1968.

Frederick, A. Bruce. *Women's Gymnastics*, Dubuque, Iowa, William C. Brown Company, 1966.

AAHPER: *Gymnastics Guide.* Current Edition, Division for Girls and Women's Sports, 1201 16th Street, N. W., Washington, D.C. 20036.

Hughes, Eric: *Gymnastics for Girls: A Competitive Approach for Teacher and Coach*, New York, The Ronald Press Company, 1963.

Loken, Newton C., and Willoughby, Robert J.: *Complete Book of Gymnastics*, 2nd Edition, Englewood Cliffs, New Jersey, Prentice-Hall, 1967.

New Gymnastic Skill Charts for Girls: Side Horse Vaulting, Uneven Parallel Bars, Balance Beam, Free Exercises — Balancing and Beginning Tumbling, Free Exercises — Acrobatics and Intermediate Tumbling,

Nissen Corporation, 930 27th Avenue, Cedar Rapids, Iowa. ($1.00 each).

Periodicals

Amateur Athletic Union Gymnastic Yearbook, 233 Broadway, New York, N.Y.

The Gymnast, J.P. Prestige, Glenwood, The Park, Sidcup, Kent, England.

The Journal of Health — Physical Education — Recreation, 1201 16th St. N.W., Washington, D.C. 20036.

The Modern Gymnast, P.O. Box 611, Santa Monica, California.

Suggested Study Questions

1. Trace the history of gymnastics from ancient times to the present.
2. Discuss the value of gymnastics in the college physical education program for women.
3. What safety precautions should a performer take in this sport in each competitive event?
4. Define the following: (a) free exercises, (b) uneven parallel bars, (c) balance beam.
5. From library research discover how the United States Team placed in the Olympic games in Rome in 1960 in Tokyo in 1964, and in Mexico City in 1968.

CHAPTER TEN

Courtesy of Jean Jacobs, Springfield College, Springfield, Massachusetts.

REBOUND TUMBLING

Since ancient times human beings have longed to fly through the air like graceful birds. Consequently, modern stunts and tumbling activities go back as far as our most primitive ancestors. In the time of the ancient kings it was the court jester who entertained royalty with his many thrilling acrobatic tricks. Ingenious entertainers devised the first crude trampoline, called "jester leaps." This was a pliable board supported at each end on heavy wooden blocks. In medieval times, the jesters learned that by jumping up and down on such a board they could gain enough height and time to do intricate flips and turns before landing back on the board, much to the delight of their spellbound audience. This crude, pliable board was the great, great, ever-so-great grandfather of the modern trampoline.

Shortly after the United States Civil War circus performers began using the flying trapeze to do a series of somersaults as they left one swinging bar to twist and turn before catching hold of a second swinging bar coming toward them. A safety net was next invented which, when placed below the daring acrobats, allowed them to do even more spectacular spinning and turning stunts while moving through midair, especially when they learned by developing perfect timing to rebound from the net back up to catch the swinging bar. Bouncing net routines then became even more daring and exciting to watch. Finally the performers devised a smaller kind of a safety net, which enabled them to bounce on and off the larger bed. As they bounced from net to net some acrobats could do a double somersault with ease. Joe E. Lewis, the famous comedian, was the first performer to accomplish a triple full twist on a small 4 by 7 foot canvas bed suspended by shockcords.*

Although rebound tumbling began in the professional entertainment world, it now has a secure place in the physical education programs for all students on all educational levels in the United States, largely because of the efforts of George Nissen. He coined the word *trampoline* for the apparatus used in this activity in honor of a Frenchman named du Trampoline, who long ago perfected the springboard and rebounding nets used by French circus aerialists for their daring stunts. During World War II rebound tumbling, or trampolining, as it is sometimes called, became a vital part of the Navy preflight training program and was used to help to orient new pilots to the sensations of the many positions in the air that they would encounter in a true flight. It was the enthusiastic response of many instructors in this Navy preflight program to the value of rebound tumbling that helped spread the popularity of this activity. Many schools now have competition in this activity in their gymnastic and intramural competitive and recreational programs.

Rebound tumbling consists of a series of stunts done singly or in a series between bounces as a person jumps up and down on a springing canvas bed.

FACILITIES AND EQUIPMENT

The trampoline consists of a canvas or nylon bed, no smaller than 5½ by 12 feet, fastened to a well padded steel frame by springs or rubber exercise cables. The frame is mounted on legs 3 feet high. Although heavy, it is portable and can be folded for ease in moving. Since it can be a dangerous apparatus for the unskilled to use, especially without supervision, it should always be kept locked up when not in use.

Although any gymnasium costume is suitable to wear when using this piece of equipment, shorts and a blouse or leotards

---

*Harris Rich: *Rebound Tumbling Teaching Guide*, The Nissen Trampoline Company, 200 A Avenue, N.W., Cedar Rapids, Iowa, p. 15.

are recommended for women. No shoes of any type should be worn on the trampoline, although socks are often worn. Many women students like to jump on it barefoot.

BASIC SKILLS

MOUNTING

Although there are several ways to get on to the trampoline, the easiest for most people is to place the hands on the frame, jump and rotate the body into a sitting position on the frame, than scoot the body toward the center in a sitting position. As you become more skilled, do a forward roll from a standing floor position up onto the bed.

THE DISMOUNT

Sit down, hang on to the frame with both hands, and slide off. Never bounce from the bed on to the floor, as the shock of its hardness in contrast to the softness of the bed can cause serious injury. As you become more skilled, you can roll or vault off the bed to come to a standing position.

THE STRAIGHT BOUNCES

Spread your feet shoulder width apart. Focus your eyes on a spot on the bed or frame

to help to maintain balance. Stand erect on the balls of the feet. Circle the arms up, out, and down, with elbows relaxed as the knees and hips flex. When the arms reach the bottom of the swing, the knees and hips extend and the heels thrust down. As the arms thrust upward again the toes extend and the body rises. To stop the bounce, bend your knees when both feet contact the mat. Work toward developing easy, rhythmical bounces and staying in the center of the bed.

BOUNCE VARIATIONS

THE TUCK

Bounce three times, then on the fourth bring both knees up to your chest briefly before your body returns to a fully extended position on to the bed.

THE JACKKNIFE

Bounce three times, then on the fourth fully extend both legs forward as you bend and reach with both hands to touch your toes before returning to the bed; keep your body fully extended.

THE JUMP AND TURN

After several preparatory bounces rise and turn in a reverse position. Repeat and turn to

Fig. 10-1. The straight bounce.

Fig. 10-2. The tuck.

Fig. 10-3. The jackknife.

Fig. 10-4. The jump and turn.

Fig. 10-5. The knee drop.

make a full circle before landing. Use both arms to swing yourself around. Keep your movements controlled and rhythmical.

THE KNEE DROP

First kneel on the bed with toes extended backward, keeping your body erect, hands at your sides, in order to get the feel of this movement, for this is the way you are to kneel after your bounce. Next, bounce three times, then drop to your knees, and by swinging your arms forward come to an erect position. Repeat.

THE SEAT DROP

In order to get the feel of this movement, first sit on the bed with both legs extended, body inclined slightly forward and hands behind the hips with fingers pointing forward. Next, bounce three times and sit so that the back of the legs and seat contact the bed simultaneously. On the upward spring push with the hands and return to an erect position.

THE BACK DROP

First lie on your back with your arms extended up and out at the sides, with hips and

Fig. 10-6. The seat drop.

Fig. 10-7. The back drop.

legs slightly flexed, in order to get the feel of this movement. Next, bounce three times, drop backward to lie down on the upper part of your back, keeping your head forward and chin in. Push with your shoulders, extend your hips and come to your former erect bouncing position. Repeat.

THE HAND-KNEE DROP

Bounce three times, then on the fourth quickly draw the hips up and back, and extend your arms forward and downward. Drop to hand-knee position, and as you bounce back up, extend your hips and knees to come into an erect bouncing position.

THE FRONT DROP

First lie down on the bed, keeping your weight over your flexed arms held close together over your chest, in order to get the feel of this movement. Next, bounce three times, then drop forward on your arms, extend your legs and your body and keep your head up. As you strike the bed, push back up with your hands and come to an erect bouncing position on the rebound.

THE FRONT TO BACK TO FEET DROP

Do several preparatory bounces before going into the front drop; then, drawing your

Fig. 10-8. The hand-knee drop.

Fig. 10-9. The front drop.

legs up, go into a back drop, and back to your feet. Repeat.

THE HAND DROP

Bounce several times, then lift and flex your hips and go into a brief handstand on the bed. On the rebound, extend your arms, legs, and body, keeping your head up.

THE HIPS SWIVEL

This stunt is a combination of a seat drop, half-twist done either to the left or right, and a seat-drop landing. Bounce three times, then on the fourth bring your arms sharply across your body and up, turn your head, and twist your body rapidly around to land sitting in the opposite direction. Repeat in order to come back to your starting point.

THE BACK FLIP—TO SEAT

Bounce three times, then on the fourth, lift your arms up quickly, grasp your knees in midair, and do a backward somersault. As your eyes are directly over the bed extend your legs, and land on your seat facing the same direction from which you started. As timing and skill develop, open the tuck more quickly and land on your feet.

Fig. 10-10. The hand drop.

Fig. 10-11. The hips swivel.

Fig. 10-12. The back flip.

Fig. 10-13. The front flip.

THE FRONT FLIP

Bounce three times, then on the fourth, bend hips and legs and tuck your head between your knees, grasping your ankles with your hands. Release the tuck quickly and extend the legs to land on your feet.

MIXED ROUTINES

1. Three bounces, knee drop, three bounces, seat drop. Repeat.

2. Three bounces, drop, three bounces, front drop. Repeat.

3. Three bounces, seat drop, three bounces, back drop. Repeat.

4. Three bounces, knee drop, three bounces, back drop. Repeat.

5. Three bounces, seat drop, front drop, back drop, to feet. Repeat.

6. Three bounces, hand drop, knee drop, hips swivel, to feet. Repeat.

7. Three bounces, front flip, back flip, to feet. Repeat.

8. Knee drop, seat drop, hips swivel, all fours, front drop-half, twist, turn-back drop. End in a standing position.

9. Back pullover or flip, feet-seat drop, hips swivel, knee drop, front somersault. End in a standing position.

10. Back flip, barani (front somersault in a pike position with a half-twist), tuck bounce, half-twist to a drop, drop to half-twist to feet, straddle leap, three fourths back layout to front drop, to full turntable, to feet.

COMPULSORY COMPETITIVE EVENTS FOR WOMEN

The following routines were required of women competing for the championship title in a recent world trampoline meet.*

1. One and a quarter back somersault to back (tuck).

2. Forward half somersault, half-twist to back.

3. Three quarters back somersault (back pullover) (tuck).

4. Back somersault (tuck).

5. Half twisting front somersault.

6. Back somersault with full twist.

8. Barani (pike).

9. Three-quarter back somersault (layout).

10. One and a quarter back somersault (body) (free).

SAFETY PRECAUTIONS

Although each student must assume responsibility for her own safety in this sport, it is imperative that at least six spotters, two at

*Loken, Newton, and Willoughby, Robert: *Complete Book of Gymnastics*, 2nd Ed., Englewood Cliffs, New Jersey, Prentice-Hall, 1967.

each side of the trampoline and one at each end, be used if you are a beginner. These assistants should keep a close watch on you as you jump up and down, and by anticipating movement difficulties be ready to push you back toward the center of the bed if you are moving too far out from it, or caution you if you are too tense (relax!) or are attempting to jump too high by using uncontrolled movements (take it easy!). You should not attempt any stunt until your instructor thinks you are ready to learn it; you should never jump on a trampoline unless a spotter is present; nor should you stay on this equipment until you become too tired (this causes the majority of accidents among beginners). Only one student at a time should be on the equipment until all advanced stunts have been learned. A safety belt may be used to help students to learn the front and back flips more quickly.

Terminology

Break — To stop or lessen the rebound on the trampoline by slightly flexing the knees.

Flex — To bend any body part such as the legs.

Jackknife — A position wherein the legs are straight and extended out, the body tucked, the hips flexed, and the fingers moved quickly to touch the toes.

Layout — A position of the body when it is held in full extension.

Pike — A position wherein the body is bent only at the hips.

Sommy — A slang term for a somersault.

Spotter — An assistant who helps the performer avoid injury.

Tassels — The bottom side of the mat.

Tuck — A body position in which the hips and knees are flexed and knees pulled to the chest.

Selected Audio-visual Aids

Beginning Tumbling, Coronet Films, 65 S. Water Street, Chicago, Ill. (Rental and purchase.)

Illustrated charts on the *Mini-Tramp; Tumbling; Balancing; Rings; Uneven Parallel Bars; and Trampoline.* Available from Physical Education Aids, Box 5117, San Mateo, California.

Intermediate Tumbling, Coronet Films, 65 S. Water Street, Chicago, Ill. (Rental and purchase.)

Loopfilms (Events for Girls and Women). *Free Calisthenics* (6 loops); *Balance Beam* (6 loops); *High-Low Bar* (6 loops); *Side-Horse* (6 loops); *Trampoline* (3 slide film units). The Athletic Institute, 805 Merchandise Mart, Chicago, Ill. 60654.

Up in the Air, Nissen Trampoline Company, 200 A Avenue, N.W., Cedar Rapids, Iowa. (Rental and purchase.) Charts on basic trampoline skills are also available from this company.

Suggested Readings

AAHPER: *Gymnastics Guide*, Current Ed., Division for Girls and Women's Sports, 1201 16th St., N.W., Washington, D.C. 20036.

Griswold, Larry: *Trampoline—Rebound Tumbling*, Cranbury, N.J., A. S. Barnes & Co., Inc., 1962.

LaDue, Frank, and Norman, Jim: *Two Seconds of Freedom*, Cedar Rapids, Iowa, Torch Press, 1960.

Loken, Newton: *Trampolining*, Ann Arbor, Mich., University of Michigan, 1958.

Loken, Newton, and Willoughby, Robert: *Complete Book of Gymnastics*, 2nd Ed., Englewood Cliffs, New Jersey, Prentice-Hall, 1967.

Norman, Randi: *Gymnastics for Girls and Women*, Dubuque, Iowa, William C. Brown Company, 1965.

Suggested Study Questions

1. Trace the development of rebound tumbling.
2. Discuss what safety precautions should be taken in this sport.
3. Describe the techniques of (a) the straight bounce, (b) the seat drop, (c) the knee drop.
4. What are the important things to remember when doing (a) hips swivel, (b) the back flip, (c) the hand drop?
5. Define the terms (a) dismounting, (b) pike, (c) spotter, (d) sommy, (e) flex, (f) break.

CHAPTER ELEVEN

Courtesy of Agnes I. Michaels, State University College, Fredonia, New York.

RECREATIONAL ACTIVITIES

Recreational activities play an important role in any well rounded physical activities program for women. All college students need opportunities to find fellowship and recreational outlets with the opposite sex. Likewise, youth seeks assistance in developing democratic leadership skills, techniques for gaining approval for positive instead of negative actions, and the know-how for fitting into, as well as contributing to, groups. Consequently, the wise leader will help each person to accept and carry out responsibilities in planning for her own fun and that of her increasing circle of friends. In co-recreational sports, both sexes can learn the vital life lessons of give and take. They broaden and deepen their values of right and wrong, good and bad, as well as develop insight into personal strengths and weaknesses.

College-age fun is more sophisticated, often less strenuous, and more skilled than that on the high school level. Since loyalty to the subgroup, such as the sorority, fraternity, or club, is intense, co-recreational sports should be played among brother and sister social groups. A well equipped lounge with easy-to-play games such as table tennis or tossing contests usually becomes a favorite, especially if refreshments can be obtained there at little cost. Work service projects, such as building a tennis court in a slum area, retreats, and weekend camps, are all popular with student groups.

Some strenuous co-recreational sports that appeal to college groups include:

Box hockey	Tobogganing
Hiking	Softball
Boating	Tether ball
Water skiing	Badminton
Skin and SCUBA	Cycling
diving	Hosteling
Swimming	Paddle tennis
Tennis	Gymnastics
Volleyball	Ping-Pong

Skating	Rowing
Skiing	Water polo

Less strenuous coeducational activities popular with these age groups are:

Fishing	Picnics
Skill games	Dancing
Outdoor cooking	Fencing
Darts	Fly and bait casting
Archery	Golf
Archery golf	Riflery
Curling	Sailing
Bowling	Trap and skeet
Croquet	shooting
Horseshoes	

ACTIVITIES

CROQUET

The game is played with a wooden ball and mallet. The object is to be the first to hit the ball through all the arches up and back the court. Simplified rules are as follows:

1. Each player alternates turns hitting the ball, starting a mallet's distance in front of the starting stake and attempting to drive the ball through the first two wickets.

2. Each player is given another hit for going through an arch, hitting another's ball, or hitting the turning stake at the opposite end of the court. Two hits are earned if the ball goes through both of the two first arches, but if through any other two arches, the player has the right of a mallet's length ahead in any direction, plus one stroke.

3. One loses a hit for playing out of turn.

4. Each ball must go through each arch in proper progression.

5. A ball driven out of bounds may be put on the boundary line where it went out.

6. One missing the ball entirely with the mallet may have a second turn.

7. If one's ball hits another, the owner may put it next to the one struck, step on it, and

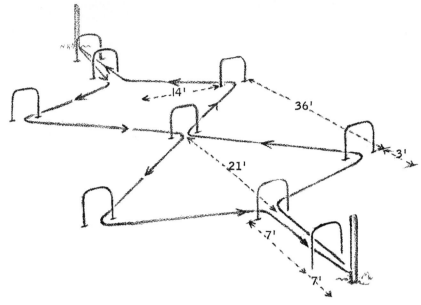

Fig. 11-1. A regulation croquet court.

hit it hard enough to send the other's far down the court or out of position; or she may measure a mallet's head distance in any direction and hit her ball from there.

PLAYGROUND GOLF

Tennis balls or beanbags can be thrown into numbered tin cans or rubber tires scattered over the area. Players take turns trying to throw the ball into these in as few tosses as possible.

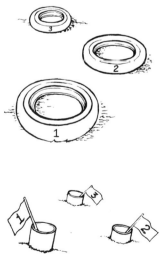

Fig. 11-2. Playground golf.

Variation: Sink numbered poles in partially buried tin cans in a widely scattered area. Hit a golf, ping-pong or jack ball into the can with a broomstick.

TETHER BALL

The game object is to hit a ball attached by a thin rope to the top of a pole so that it will wind around the pole, one person choosing to hit it always in one direction and his opponent in the other. Score one point for winding the ball around the pole. Play for 5 or 10 points. Players must take turns hitting the ball.

SHUFFLEBOARD

The players (two or four) use a cue to propel discs from the 10-off zone onto score

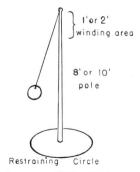

Fig. 11-3. Tether ball.

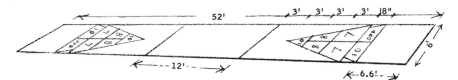

Fig. 11-4. A regulation shuffleboard court.

diagrams at the opposite end of the court in order to score, or to prevent one's opponent from scoring. Simplified rules are:

1. The red disc is shot first and then the two players alternate shooting black and red discs until all are shot from one end of the court, then the other.

2. In doubles after all discs are played at the head of the court, play starts at the foot with red leading. One red player and one black player stand at each end of the court, alternating turns, each shooting two discs.

3. A game consists of 50, 75, or 100 points.

4. After players have shot all four discs, score all within the court area but do not count those on any line.

SCOOP THROW

Equipment.   Plastic Scoop and Fun Ball.*
Game Object.   Using in turn an overhand

---

*Available from the Cosom Industries, Minneapolis, Minnesota, along with a booklet, *26 New Games for Safe Indoor and Outdoor Play.*

Overhand Throw   Underhand Throw   Sidearm Throw

Snap Throw   Overhead Catch

Underhand Catch   Cover Retrieve   Side Retrieve

Fig. 11-5. Scoop throw techniques.

throw, underhand throw, sidearm throw, snap throw, overhead catch, underhand catch, cover retrieve, and the sidearm retrieve (Fig. 11-5), couples in competing units try to be the first to score 10, 15, 25 or 30 successful throws and catches. Players return to count 1 after missing.

SCOOP GOALBALL

Equipment. One scoop for each player and one Fun Ball. The goal tender may use a Scoop, Safe-T-Bat* or both.

Playing Area. Marked as shown in Figure 11-6, with dimensions changed according to available space and age of players.

Number of Players. Five to ten on a team, with boys guarding and playing only against boys on the team, all girls against each other.

Rules

1. Line up in teams on each side of the field as in soccer, speedball, or hockey.

2. Play starts by the offensive center's flip of the ball to a teammate.

---

*Available from the Cosom Industries, Minneapolis, Minnesota, or leading sporting goods companies.

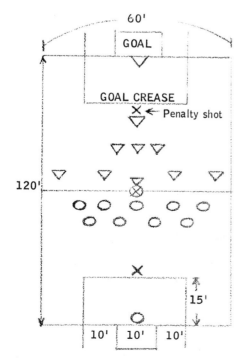

Fig. 11-6. Court dimensions — scoop goalball.

3. Players move the ball back and forth downfield by passing or intercepting passes.

4. One may take only three steps while carrying the ball in the scoop.

5. Body contact is prohibited.

6. Players cannot hold or trap the ball on the ground, play it when they are not on their feet, touch it with their hands, dribble or juggle it to themselves, or play it in their own or opponent's goal crease (except the goal tender).

7. On the offensive, the goal tender may advance as far as midfield. When tending goal, she may deflect a shot with the scoop or hand, but only when in her own zone.

8. An out-of-bounds ball is put into play by the opposing team, using a scoop throw. If the ball goes out of bounds through the goal crease, the goal tender puts it back in play.

9. On a penalty shot all except the player fouled and the goal tender stand outside the neutral area.

10. Fouls that allow the fouled team to take a penalty shot are:

    a. Slashing or hitting an opponent's scoop.

    b. Excessive, wild scoop swinging.

    c. Hitting an opponent with a scoop.

    d. Playing the ball in own or opponent's goal crease.

    e. The goal tender's leaving the penalty crease when a penalty shot is attempted at the goal.

    f. Having more players on the field than the other team.

    g. Interfering with an opponent's play by holding her scoop on her, running or falling in front of her to prevent her moving.

11. If a penalty shot is unsuccessful, the fouled team puts the ball in play at midfield at either side.

12. The ball is given to the opposing team when:

    a. It goes out of bounds.

    b. Anyone holds it in her scoop over five seconds.

    c. Anyone touches it.

    d. Anyone takes more than three steps with it.

    e. Anyone holds it on the ground or plays it while she is on the ground.

    f. It is kicked, dribbled, or juggled.

    g. The goal tender catches it in her hand.

h. Anyone enters the goal crease of the opposing team.

i. The goal tender goes over the midfield line.

13. An official game is four quarters of 10 minutes each with a 3 minute rest period between each one and a 10 minute rest between halves.

14. Each goal scores one point.

IN-LINE FUN BALL

Equipment. One scoop for each outfield or defensive player, one Fun Ball, one Safe-T-Bat.

Number of Players. Seven to ten on each team. First, second, third basemen (goalman), fielders, and a catcher.

Playing Area. A softball diamond with foul lines out from home plate (Fig. 11-8). On a regular ball diamond, the in-line baseline should run through the pitcher's box, second base, and out into center field. First, second, and third bases (or goal area) should be 35 feet apart.

Rules

1. Players must catch and throw the Fun Ball with a scoop at all times.

2. The batter places the Fun Ball on the top end of a Safe-T-Bat, shoves it upward, hits it as it comes down, and then runs toward first base. She does not have to swing at every ball, but she may never bunt one. If she hits two foul balls, or if her pop foul is caught, or if she swings three times, she is out.

3. Baserunners are forced or tagged out.

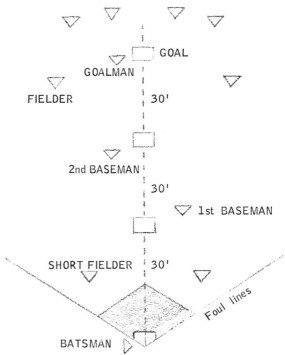

Fig. 11-8. Court dimensions — in-line fun ball.

4. A runner may not overrun first or second base. If she does, she must continue to the next base, taking a chance on being put out. Once she leaves a base, she cannot return to it. There is no leading off or stealing of bases.

5. Scoring is as in softball; nine or fewer innings may be played.

HORSESHOES

Equipment. Two pairs of matched and marked horseshoes approximately $2\frac{1}{2}$ pounds in weight, $7\frac{1}{2}$ inches in length, and 7 inches in width.

Playing Area. A court 50 feet × 10 feet is the official size for men; one 10 feet shorter, with official pitching distance for women, girls, and boys under 16 years, has 30 feet between the stakes. The pitcher's box should be 6 feet square and the bases around the stake should be filled with clay or soft dirt.

Rules and Scoring

1. An official game consists of 50 points; there are 21 points to a league game.

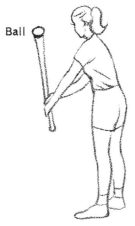

Fig. 11-7. Batting procedure for in-line fun ball.

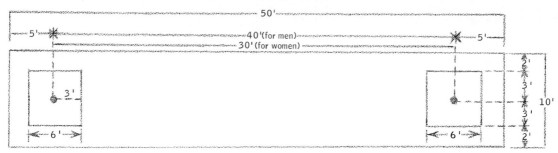

Fig. 11-9. Horseshoe court.

2. The first pitch choice is determined by the better toss (nearest the stake) of one shoe.

3. Each player pitches both shoes in turn at the same stake, then at the opposite one. The winner of each try is the one who has pitched the shoes nearest the stake. In case of a tie, the person who pitched last in that inning pitches first in the next.

4. *Scoring*   *Points*

   a. One shoe closest to the stake   5

   b. Two shoes closest to the stake (thrown by the same player)   2

   c. One ringer   3

   d. Two ringers thrown by the same player   6

   e. One ringer and one shoe thrown closest by the same player   4

   f. Two ringers are thrown by one player; one ringer is thrown by opponent   3

   g. One ringer by each player   0

   h. Two ringers by each player   0

Fig. 11-11. The forefinger hold grip.

   i. In case of a tie, the next closest shoe to the stake   1

   j. No points are awarded in the case of a tie score

5. *Fouls*

   a. Moving or placing the foot over the foul line

   b. Striking any part of the box with the shoe

   c. Striking outside the foul line, so that the shoe rebounds into the box

Fig. 11-10. The twist grip.

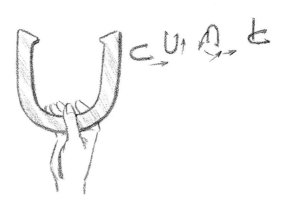

Fig. 11-12. The single flip grip.

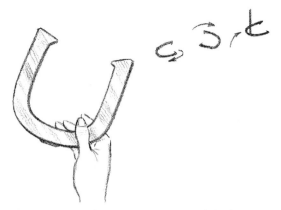

Fig. 11-13.   The three-quarter twist grip.

d. Throwing a shoe while standing outside the foul line
e. Not standing behind an opponent who is throwing a shoe
f. Touching a shoe before measurements are taken
g. Interfering in any way with an opponent who is in the act of pitching the shoe

TABLE TENNIS

As table tennis is often an instructional unit, it is given more detailed treatment than the preceding co-recreational activities.

Table tennis may be played by two (singles game) or four (doubles game). In singles, play begins with a serve and continues with the opponents alternately playing the ball until one player misses the ball, strikes it illegally, hits the ball into the net, or drives the ball over the net but not into the opponent's playing area.

Doubles play differs significantly from the singles game. In doubles, the service begins

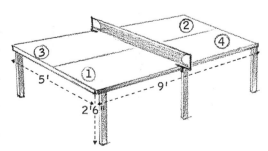

Fig. 11-14.   A regulation table tennis table showing opposite serving areas.

from the server's right-hand court and bounces in the opponent's right-hand court. After the service, partners alternate playing the ball until the rally ends and point is decided.

Scoring

A game is won by the individual or team that first gains 21 points and has at least a two point lead over the opponent. For example, if the score is tied at 20 points, play continues until one side wins two consecutive points. The winning score is 22-20, or if the score is tied at 21-21, the winner needs 23-21.

Rules basic to beginning play include:

1. The winner of a rally, coin toss, or other method of chance has option of serving or receiving, or court selection.
2. Each person serves until a total of five points is scored. The serve then passes to the opposing side.
3. When the score is tied at 20-20, service alternates between opponents after each point until game is completed.
4. At the completion of each game opponents change ends of the table for the next game of the match.
5. In doubles, the server must deliver from her right court diagonally to opponents' right court.
6. In doubles, players and partners must alternate returning the ball. That is, after the receiver returns the serve, the server's partner must return the ball, then the partner of the receiver shall play the ball and thereafter each player alternately returns the ball until the end of the rally.

Points are scored by the side making the last good rally. Unsuccessful return and loss of point occur when:

1. Ball is missed by the racket
2. Ball is hit off the table on return
3. Ball is hit into the net

Fig. 11-15.   Serve 1 to 2, 3 to 4.

4. Player hits ball into her own half court (other than on service)

5. Player's racket or clothing touches the net or net supports while ball is in play

6. Player moves the playing surface while ball is in play

7. Player puts hand on playing surface when ball is in play

Equipment

Table tennis lends itself to indoor and outdoor settings and utilizes a minimum of space and equipment.

Table and Net. The overall playing surface of official tables is 2½ feet from the floor. The playing surface may be of any material which allows an official ball an 8 to 9 inch bounce when dropped a foot above the surface. The surface should be dark and nonreflecting (dark green is desirable) with white end and side lines ½ to ¾ inch, and white center line ⅛ inch in width.

The standard net is 6 feet long and 6 inches high. It is supported by brackets outside the playing surface which pull it taut across the table, dividing the playing surface into two courts of equal size.

Racket. The racket blade should not be white, pale in color, or have a reflecting surface. Leather or composition wrapped handles assure a better grip.

Ball. Regulation celluoid balls should be purchased from reputable manufacturers who conform products to U.S.T.T.A. rules.

Space. All-purpose rooms, social-recreational areas, and gymnasiums are well suited for instructional and recreational games. Six feet of unobstructed space on each side and 12 feet on each end of the table and a ceiling

a minimum of 9½ feet above table surface is desirable. Nonreflecting finishes on all sidewalls aid in following the ball in flight.

Nonglare artificial illumination should provide 30 foot-candles of evenly distributed light on the table area. Two hundred watt frosted bulbs with a reflector shade installed over the table center are recommended.

Dress. Clothes should be selected for comfort and freedom of movement. A gymnasium costume with tennis shoes or sneakers is appropriate for use in the instructional program.

Basic Skills

Grip. The "tennis grip" is superior for firm control of the racket and better for instructional purposes than unorthodox grips. Proper grasp of the racket results in the "handshake grip" with index finger and thumb bracing opposite sides of the blade. The handle of the racket is pulled firmly into the hand against the base of second, third, and fourth fingers. Unlike the common penholder grip, the handshake grip allows maximum wrist flexibility and free movement of the racket to any position without changing the finger position.

Stance and Footwork. The principles of stance and footwork are basically the same as in other court games. The more restricted area of movement and play makes the movement pattern less difficult for beginners.

In a singles game, the right-handed player faces the net, takes a relaxed position just left of the center and 2 or 3 feet from the end of the table. The feet are placed about 12 inches apart with the left foot slightly forward. Some

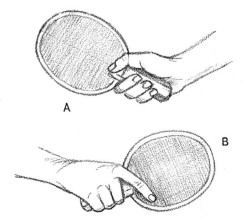

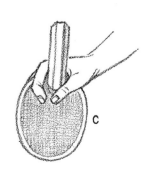

Fig. 11-16. *A*, Forehand handshake grip; *B*, backhand handshake grip; *C*, penholder grip.

Fig. 11-17. Foot position.

experts prefer the center table position, but most players reach farther and hit more accurately with their forehand strokes and play "left" to protect their backhand. Body weight is equally distributed, knees slightly flexed with weight forward on the balls of the feet. This neutral position allows rapid movement forward, backward, and to either side of the table.

At all times the racket is held in front of the body, slightly to the forehand side, in preparation for a stroking position.

Playing the forehand, the right-handed player turns to the right with the left side of the body angled toward the net. In turning, the weight rests primarily on the right (rear) foot and shifts to the left (forward) foot in completion of the stroke.

As the right-handed player reaches for a backhand stroke, her body turns left with the right side angled toward the net. The weight shifts from back to forward foot as in the forehand return.

Getting into position to return a ball often means leaving the neutral position. If steps are taken forward, backward, or to either side, the player should return immediately to her neutral position to await the next play.

Footwork in doubles play is essentially the same as in singles, as partners alternate shots and are individually responsible for getting in position for their return. The novice may experience difficulty moving away from the playing area to allow room for her partner and yet staying near enough so she can prepare for her return stroke.

The Drives

THE FOREHAND DRIVE. Assuming the proper grip, the player watches the ball and

Fig. 11-18. The forehand drive.

Fig. 11-19. The backhand drive.

places herself in position at right angles to the net. A ready position with a short backswing prepares her to contact the ball at the height of its bounce. Contact and follow-through with a swift, firm motion result in a shift of body weight (see p. 184, Stance and Footwork).

Variations in arm action and racket face cause different ball bounces. For example, a straight follow-through directed deep in the opponent's court results in a long powerful "smashing" drive with a direct bounce and an even rise; whereas a short follow-through in a downward direction puts underspin on the ball and results in a higher than normal bounce in opponent's court. Stroking the ball from left to right, or right to left, causes sidespin in flight and a bounce in the direction of the spin.

THE BACKHAND DRIVE. The backhand drive is similar to the tennis backhand. The arm extends across the body resulting in a shorter backswing than the forehand drive. Contact is made just before, or at, the height of the bounce and follow-through continues in a long arc as the player returns to a neutral position. Like the forehand drive, variations of arm and wrist action cause spins and bounces.

The Serve. The serve is the initial action and an important offensive technique in winning table tennis. Once the serve is decided (see Scoring), play begins by lofting the ball in the air, or dropping the hand from the ball and stroking it with the racket. The ball must bounce in the server's court, travel diagonally across the net and land fairly in the receiver's court.

Execution of a legal serve is often difficult for beginners. The ball must not be hidden in a cupped hand and directly stroked; finger spins are not allowed; and rubbing the ball against the racket face while imparting power is illegal. The fingers must be straight and together and the thumb free as the ball is lofted or the hand dropped. At the moment of contact, both racket and ball must be behind the end line in the server's court and within imaginary sideline extensions of the table.

The most desirable serving position is approximately a foot from the end of the table with the body facing slightly to the right (right-handed player) and left foot slightly forward. Some skilled players prefer to stand squarely facing the net and twist to left or right, serving from both sides of the body. In either case, the ball should be struck close to the playing surface with sufficient force to drive it firmly and deeply into the opponent's court.

The Half Volley. As in tennis and squash, use of the half volley is primarily defensive; however, it has merit for the skilled player as a deceptive offensive shot. The racket meets the ball just as it rises from the bounce, long

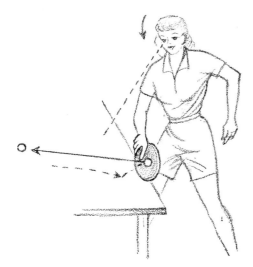

Fig. 11-20. The half volley.

before it reaches its rise height. Time does not allow for a deep backswing and contact results in a pushing stroke and a relatively weak return. A quick turn of the racket to either side adds spin to the shot.

Chop Strokes. Chops are effective offensive strokes which should be mastered on both the forehand and backhand. With the racket held at shoulder height, wrist slightly flexed, the slightly open faced racket moves forward and downward rapidly contacting the ball. Impact behind the ball from the downward movement of the racket causes an

underspin which results in a high bounce. As the stroke is completed, the arm is extended toward the front of the body.

Drop Shot. The greatest value of the drop shot is that it changes the pace of play. The stroke begins as a drive, but results in a fake as the forward stroking movement stops just before the racket hits the ball. The ball hits the stationary racket face and rebounds across the net to drop with little force and bounce.

Smash. The smash is a hard hit, fast dropping return. The stroke is similar to the drive, but it is usually hit flat, imparting no spin to the ball. It is most effective on high bouncing shots as a point winner, for the additional ball speed makes it difficult to return.

Strategy. As the player's skill increases consideration should be given to basic principles of strategy.

1. Enter every game with determination to win.
2. Warm up prior to each match.
3. Develop a sound defensive game so the ball will stay in play until the opponent's defense fails or offensive tactics win the point.
4. Observe opponent's weaknesses and play them.
5. Concentrate on the present shot, rather than the last or anticipated one.
6. Vary style, speed, and type of return to keep opponent guessing.

Fig. 11-21. The drop shot.

7. Generally, keep returns low and deep in opponent's court, unless a "change-up" for deception is timely.

8. Generally, keep the serve low.

9. Learn to serve forehand and backhand and vary the spins applied.

10. Serve to different parts of the table and avoid "telegraphing" placement with eyes or body position.

11. In doubles, get out of partner's way quickly.

12. In doubles, it is generally sound to hit toward the opponent moving out of the way.

The following novelty events increase student interest and offer pleasurable recreation.

Spin Around. Played as a regular singles game except each player must make a complete turn, or spin, after each return before playing the next shot.

Two-bat Doubles. Played as a regular doubles game except doubles partners share a single racket. Players should return the ball, place racket on the table and move out of the playing area. The second partner picks up the racket, plays the ball and places the racket on the table as the first partner moves into play.

Weak Arm Doubles or Singles. Played as a regular game of singles or doubles except all players must use their secondary hand to hold the racket, i.e., a right-handed person must use her left hand.

Elimination Table Tennis. Played as singles by a group as large as 12. One half of the group stands on each side of the table. Play begins with a serve to opponent. After playing the ball, each player places the racket on the table and moves to other end of the table. Players are eliminated when they make faulty returns. When only two competing players remain, they place racket on the table,

spin around, and pick up racket between each returning stroke.

Team Table Tennis. Played as a regular singles game with additional members on each side. Teams line up to the left side of their half court, player No. 1 serves, places the racket on the table and moves to the end of her team line. Teammate No. 2 picks up racket, returns ball, and goes to end of the line. Play continues until one team scores 21 points.

DECK TENNIS

Number of Players. Two or four.

Equipment. Official deck tennis ring or one improvised out of a heavy rubber hose or rope, and a net 2½ feet wide strung 4 feet, 8 inches high.

Singles Rules

1. The players stand on opposite sides of the net, and the player who is delivering the ring is called the server and her opponent the receiver.

2. A score is gained only from the service. If the ring is correctly caught and returned by the receiver, but missed by her opponent, no point is scored by either player, but the service changes hands. Thus points can be scored only from the service, and the server continues to serve until she fails to catch the ring in the proper manner, when the service passes to her opponent.

3. The server stands on or behind the base line in delivering her ring. The receiver also stands behind the base line until the server releases the ring. The server may not serve until her opponent is ready, and immediately after serving moves forward into the court to accept the return.

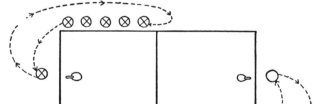

Fig. 11-22. Team table tennis.

Fig. 11-23. The server in deck tennis must not serve until her opponent is ready. Immediately after serving she should move into the court to accept the return. (Courtesy of Hollis Fait, University of Connecticut.)

4. The server must not feint or hesitate in delivering her service, or play the ring flat overhand, but must direct the ring with a minimum upward flight of 6 inches.

5. Only one hand may be used in catching the ring, but the ring may be caught between the hand and the body. If both hands are used, the player at fault loses the point of service.

6. If in delivering the ring the server throws it into the net, no point is scored or lost, but the service passes to her opponent.

7. If in the service the ring touches the top of the net and passes over, falling into "dead ground" or outside the boundaries of the court, no point is scored or lost but the service changes hands.

8. The receiver has the option of accepting any ring that touches the net in the service and passes over, if she believes that it is likely to fall into her own court. If she does not wish to do so and the ring falls within the boundaries of the court, the service is played again. After the service, a ring that passes over after touching the net is playable.

9. The ring may not be held more than 3 seconds and must be returned by the player from approximately the receiving position. This continues until one side does not make the return, or plays it on "dead ground" or outside the boundaries of the court.

10. The ring must not touch the surface of the court in play and the players' feet must not step into the "dead ground," running alongside the net or outside the court boundaries. Their feet may touch the boundary lines, but not cross them.

11. Any ring falling on "dead ground" or outside the boundaries of the court is reckoned against the player by whom it was delivered, but a ring alighting on any of the boundary lines is regarded as being in play even though it may roll out of court.

12. Each point counts 1 and the first player to score 15 points is the winner, unless before the game it was decided to play long sets. In that case, when the game has reached 14-all, it is necessary for one to secure an advantage of 2 points over her opponents, e.g., 17-15, or 18-16.

13. The players play the best of three games, changing ends at the close of each game, and if in the third game one player scores 8 points before her opponent scores (i.e., 8-0), the players change ends for the remainder of the game.

Doubles Rules

1. The game of doubles is played on principles similar to those of the singles game except that two persons stand on each side of the net and the service passes diagonally to an opponent.

2. The first service is made from the right hand court. If the service is won, the server then delivers her next ring from the left hand court, i.e., she serves alternately from each court as in lawn tennis, her partner standing in the other court.

3. After losing her service the player takes up her position in the right hand court and thus becomes the first receiver. When the service again changes hands, it is taken by the player who has been occupying the left side of the court, and in this way rings are served and received alternately by each player.

4. A ring may be caught by one hand of each partner, but must be returned by one player only, and a ring may be caught and returned by a player even though it may have

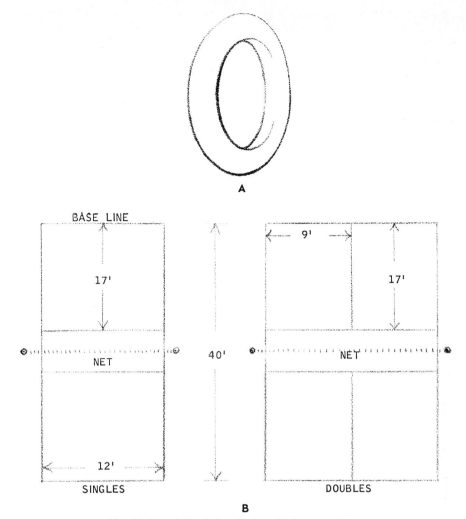

Fig. 11-24. *A*, Deck tennis ring. *B*, Court markings.

touched her partner's hand or body, providing, of course, that the ring does not touch the surface of the court before the catch is effected.

ROPE QUOITS

Played by two or four or any number, with either purchased or improvised equipment.

Rules

1. Each player shoots 4 quoits per frame, when it is her turn to shoot.

2. Opponents then shoot 4 quoits in the same manner.

3. "Ringers" count 5 points each. All other quoits remaining on the base count 1 point

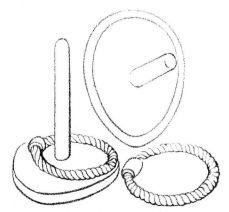

Fig. 11-25. Quoits.

each. Quoits that go off the board are lost and do not score any points.

4. A game consists of 10 frames for each player in the game.

5. The player having the highest score wins.

6. Players' feet must be behind the foul line or designated shooting point when the quoits are thrown; otherwise the shot is a foul and does not score.

7. The distance from foul line or shooting line to the rope quoit base should be as near 15 feet as possible.

8. Any number of partners may play in a game as in shuffleboard or bowling. Partners having the highest score win.

SACKET

Number of Players.   Nine or more on each team.

Equipment.   One Sacket semiflat tapered

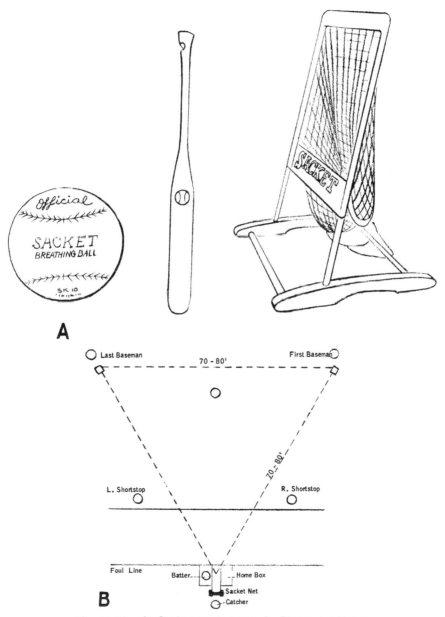

Fig. 11-26. *A,* Sacket equipment. *B,* Player positions.

handle bat, a 10 inch rubber-covered ball, and net backstop.*

This game is a form of baseball, cricket, and hockey. It is played like baseball with three bases instead of four. The net serves as automatic catcher and umpire. The ball "breathes" or compresses when hit, but regains its regular shape while in the air. A batter is retired if she throws to the base ahead of a runner, or if the ball is thrown into the net, from behind a field line 30 to 35 feet away, as she attempts to score.

BILLIARDS

Fifteen-ball. The score is decided by the actual number of pocketed balls. The numbers of the 15 balls (numbered 1 to 15) total 120; the player who first scores 61 points is the winner. A player forfeits 15 points: if the cue ball is pocketed, if a ball is not pocketed and an object ball is not driven into the cushion, if the cue ball goes off the table, if one shoots out of turn, or if one interferes with the cue ball after a stroke.

Pocket. The game is played on a pocketed table with 15 colored object balls numbered 1 to 15. The game is started by setting them up in triangular shape at the far end of the table, and the object is to knock the object balls into pockets by the use of the cue ball. On each shot the player must specify both the number of the object ball and the pocket aimed at, this being known as "calling the shot." When 14 have been pocketed they are again put in triangle formation with the apex vacant and the game proceeds until the specified number of points are scored.

Rotation. This is a game using the same table and balls as pocket billiards and is somewhat similar, except that a player must first pocket the number 1 ball, then the number 2, and so forth, in ascending order to number 15. Additional balls pocketed on a given stroke count, provided that the one aimed for is also pocketed. A game is won by the player who first scores 61 points. The cue ball must strike the object ball before touching another ball. Balls pocketed on an illegal contact are spotted.

*Available from the Sacket Sporting Goods Company, Beverly Hills, California; the Y.M.C.A. National Purchasing Service, New York City; The House of Harter, Goshen, Indiana; or from most leading sporting goods stores.

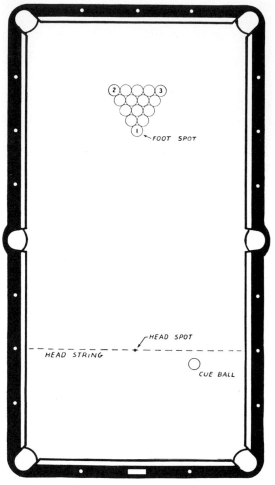

Fig. 11-27. Rotation pocket billiards. (Courtesy of the Billiard Congress of America, Chicago, Illinois.)

Three-ball. This is a game played on a pocketless table, the objective being to score caroms. Except at the start of the game and when a ball is spotted, a player may use either the dotted or the undotted white ball as a cue ball. The cue ball need hit no cushions, and there are no balklines. Only two shots may be made in the crotch.

The crotch represents a situation in which both object balls lie within a 4½ inch square at any corner. Only three caroms may be scored, unless one or both balls are forced out of the crotch. Failing to do so on the third shot, the player loses his turn. Another interpretation of crotch is the stroking of the ball and the cushion at the same time that the ball is touching the cushion.

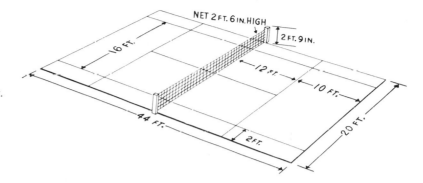

Fig. 11-28. Paddle tennis court.

PADDLE TENNIS

Paddle tennis and platform tennis are both played similarly to lawn tennis and scored like tennis. The game is played by two (singles) or four (doubles) and differs from tennis as follows:

1. One *underhand* serve is permitted for adults (two for children).
2. The entire doubles court is used for singles play after the service.

Platform paddle tennis is played on a specially constructed and enclosed platform, and rules permit the ball to be played off the side walls and backstop.

The dimensions of the adult singles court are 44 by 16 feet; the doubles, 44 by 20 feet. The senior court markings are shown in Figure 11-28. The junior singles court is 13½ by 39 feet; the doubles court is 18 by 39 feet. The top of the junior net should be 2 feet, 2 inches above the ground at the middle of the court.

ACCURACY SKISH BAIT CASTING

This game may be played by any number. The object is to land a pfluger lure or tiny tobacco sack filled with sand into a ring or circle no larger than 30 inches, using free style technique with a casting rod and reel. Ten players or fewer cast at the same time at ten different targets scattered at distances unknown to the contestants. The closest target may be no more than 45 nor less than 40 feet and the farthest no more than 80 nor less than 70 feet (65 feet indoors) from the casting area, which is 4 feet square. Each player is given two tries. Six points are awarded for a perfect first cast, 4 for a

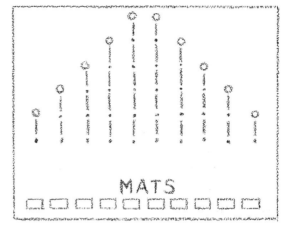

Fig. 11-29. Target area for skish.

perfect second one. If the plug falls within or on the target, a perfect cast is recorded; no score is made for a hit outside the target. A score of 100 constitutes a perfect game. The one with the highest total score for all ten targets wins.

For casting accuracy do it in three counts. Hold the rod almost horizontal. Then:

1. Raise rod to 12 o'clock position.
2. Lower to 2 o'clock position.
3. Snap your wrist, bringing the rod back down slightly above your original position (Fig. 11-30).

Practice to develop a smooth, relaxed, accurate cast. Use the rod tip for aiming and whip the line straight ahead each time. Avoid back casting too far or tensing up, for the more relaxed you are, the more successful you will be. Stand squarely, or with the left leg forward if you are a right-handed person and vice versa if you are left-handed.

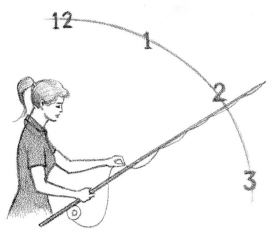

Fig. 11-30. Casting positions.

CLUB ACTIVITIES

Club activities are popular among college women and are also valuable. Each activity included in the physical education program can be used as basis for a club. The chief values of these group gatherings are to learn new skills or perfect old ones, to make new friends, to learn more about others, to be of service, and to have fun.

Types of recommended clubs include:

Archery	Hobby
Bicycling	Hosteling
Bowling	Leaders
Checker	Nature
Chess	Recreational games
Dance (square, folk,	Riding
social, acrobatic,	Rifle
tap, or ballet)	Service
First aid	Skin and SCUBA
Fly and bait casting	diving
Health	Swimming

Officers. All club officers should be elected, including the sponsor. Each officer should be energetic, popular, respected, capable of positively influencing others, and possess the ability to delegate responsibility and work democratically with others. Since all clubs are miniature democratic societies, it is here that youth can learn the vital lessons and skills necessary to perpetuate our chosen way of life.

SOCIAL RECREATION

The purpose of social recreation is to increase social contacts, to release tensions, to satisfy basic needs to "belong," to gain recognition, and to provide self-expression, the development of leadership, and experiences in democratic group participation.

Activities include:

Games—active, quiet, musical, and table games; cards, relays.

Informal drama—skits, stunts, charades, guessing games, amateur nights, radio shows.

Music—community singing, mixers, guessing games, dance bands, uke clubs, orchestras.

Dance—social, folk, square, barn dances; folk festivals, social dance contests.

Co-recreational sports—individual and team.

Arts and crafts—table decorations, costume design, metal and woodcrafts, painting and sketching.

Parties—seasonal, special.

Banquets—informal, formal.

Snow and ice sports—skating, skiing, and sleigh parties.

Teas, coke and coffee hours.

All social recreation should give each person pleasure and feelings of group worth or acceptance. These special events should be largely student planned, conducted, and evaluated with a minimum of adult guidance. Naturally, students make many mistakes while learning the necessary skills for success. The following leadership techniques for conducting social recreation activities successfully are:

1. Plan well in advance.

2. Assign or elect students to needed committees. Each group should make a list of their responsibilities and the completion dates set for each one.

3. Anticipate emergencies by drawing up alternate plans. (For example, plan for rainy as well as sunny weather.)

4. First select a theme, then games, decorations, invitations, entertainment, and refreshments to blend with it.

5. Draw up a check list of all needed supplies and equipment such as a record player or microphone, and be sure they are ready *before* the event begins.

6. Plan a well balanced program, spacing active and less active games properly.

7. Include numerous mixers and easy-to-do games.

8. Begin with preparty activities which enable all to feel welcome and that a big event is about to happen.

9. Plan a climactic ending. Do not drag out the event; make it short enough to be remembered happily.

Selected Audio-visual Aids

Table Tennis. (10 min., sound, b & w.) Teaching Films Custodians, 25 West 43rd Street, New York, N.Y. (Rental.)

Youth Hosteling. United World Films, New York City. (Rental.)

Suggested Readings

Billiard Congress of America: *Official Rule Book for All Pocket and Carom Billiard Games*, 20 N. Wacker Drive, Chicago, Ill. 60606.

Donnelly, Richard, et al.: *Active Games and Contests*, New York, The Ronald Press Company, 1958.

Mosconi, Willie: *Winning Pocket Billiards*, New York, Crown Publishers, 1965.

Vannier, Maryhelen, and Poindexter, Hally B. W.: *Individual and Team Sports for Girls and Women*, 2nd Ed., Philadelphia, W. B. Saunders Company, 1968.

Vannier, Maryhelen: *Methods and Materials in Recreation Leadership*, Rev. Ed., Belmont, California, Wadsworth Publishing Company, 1966.

Suggested Study Questions

1. What are the values of co-recreational activities in a college physical education program?
2. Describe the following games: rope quoits, skish bait casting, and deck tennis.
3. What are the values of club activities based on a definite sports interest such as archery?
4. What are the main classifications of activities that should be included in a well rounded program of recreational activities?

CHAPTER TWELVE

Courtesy of Iris Carnell, Ithaca College.

SKIING

By Iris Carnell

Skiing has become a way of life for its many devotees. From the moment the first snow-flake falls until the end of spring skiing, the skier puts her skis on the top of her car and heads for the nearest ski area.

Skiing is one of the true family sports, in which respect it is similar to camping. Both have had a tremendous surge of popularity in the last decade. It is not unusual to see a three-year-old sliding down the bunny slope or riding up the tow between his father's legs. Being able to descend a hill under control, to turn at will, and to enjoy nature at its loveliest is a thrill for all age groups. The experiences encountered in skiing are never the same: the snow conditions change hourly, every trail is different, and rarely does one traverse the same spot twice. As nature changes so does the individual: one day everything goes well and the next day nothing does, so that each skier tries to capture or recapture a moment of perfection.

The average skier spends two out of four weekends a month on the ski slopes during the winter months. When the season is over in the United States, there is always Chile, Australia, or New Zealand, where skiing is at its best during our summer months.

Ski clubs used to be organizations sponsored by high schools or colleges for their students. Now many cities and towns have one or two ski clubs, offering either family or individual membership. They may be many miles from a ski area, but they have played a tremendous part in the organization of skiing. They constitute the membership of the United States Ski Association, and through this organization they sponsor many types of programs, including preseason conditioning, ski instruction, racing, and trips, many at lowered costs to members.

The tremendous improvements in ski equipment and clothing, the ski clubs, and the many new ski areas have helped to increase the popularity and availability of skiing. In areas of the country that have very little snow, but do have temperatures below 32 degrees, snow can now be made. Many of the well established ski areas have also installed snow-making equipment to guard against snowless winters, which could be financially devastating.

In the past the rope tow was the only means of ascending a hill other than climbing it, which restricted skiing to those physically able to hold on to the rope. There were relatively few mountain areas in the country that had chair lifts to the mountain top, but now even the smallest hill is apt to have one.

NATURE AND PURPOSE OF THE SPORT

CROSS COUNTRY SKIING AND RACING

This was the earliest type of skiing and is still a mode of winter transportation in some mountainous areas. For many it is the way to enjoy the beauty and solitude of the out-of-doors. Cross country skiing demands equipment that is usually lighter than downhill equipment, and the binding must be one that allows the heel to rise from the ski so that the user can approximate the normal walking and running position.

Cross country competition is a grueling but satisfying sport. In the past, very few women competed in cross country. Recently the whole picture has changed, with a number of girls and women in the United States and other countries meeting the challenge of this, the oldest phase of skiing.

DOWNHILL SKIING AND RACING

The most popular type of skiing throughout the ski world and the one to which the ski areas cater is downhill skiing, for it is the areas' prime source of revenue. By reversing the classic theory that what goes up must come down, the developers of uphill

197

conveyances have made skiing a big business venture.

Downhill skiing is the descent of a trail or slope to the bottom or to the nearest lift. Trails and slopes are rated according to their degree of difficulty and range from novice to expert. The bunny slope is for the beginning skier.

Downhill racing is the fastest and probably most exciting kind of competition; for it has the fewest restrictions as to the path the skier must follow. Generally it follows the fall line and is often the shortest and steepest trail from the top to the bottom. The mandatory ruling regarding protective headgear for the downhill and giant slalom competitions has increased safety for the racer.

Slalom and Giant Slalom Racing

These are types of skiing associated with racing in which both sexes participate. The slalom course is one in which each skier must pass through an intricate series of gates (two flags) and demands very controlled skiing. Each slalom course is different, for it must be set according to the contours of the slope. A well set slalom course is one on which the skier is able to maintain a rhythm as she

speeds down the hill. The giant slalom is an event styled between the slalom and downhill. It has fewer gates and controls than does the slalom, but it has more controls than downhill racing.

Gates are identified by colored flags: red, blue, or yellow. A gate comprises two flags of the same color.

Jumping

Jumping is one of the specialized areas of skiing and demands specific training and specialized equipment. Jumping skis are wide and have additional grooves on the bottom: sometimes two but usually three. Jumping hills, like diving boards, are measured in meters; the higher the hill, the longer the jump. The height of a hill is frequently increased by the erection of a trestle. The jumper uses the theories of aerodynamics; the greater understanding of these principles has caused the style of jumping to change considerably over the years. The jump area, from the top to the end of the outrun, must be well conditioned, for the slightest deviation in the snow could cause the jumper much difficulty. Jumping competition is principally an event for men, though some women have competed in jumping. It is

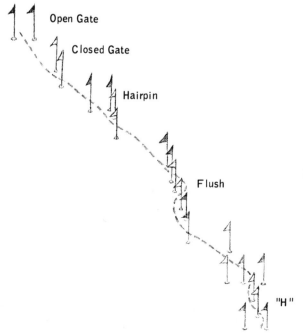

Open Gate

Closed Gate

Hairpin

Flush

"H"

Fig. 12-1. A slalom course. The skier must pass between flags of the same color.

probably the most often televised of all skiing events, and even the armchair skier recognizes a good jump.

COMPETITION IN BRIEF

All the competitive events must adhere to the rules and standards of the organization sponsoring the competition. Most of these events are sponsored by schools, ski clubs, and ski areas. The Alpine events are the downhill, slalom, and giant slalom. They are judged by elapsed time, and the skier is disqualified if she has missed a gate. The Nordic events are cross country and jumping. Cross country is judged by elapsed time, and jumping by form and distance.

The future of the United States competitive efforts lies in the breadth and depth of its junior programs. The youngsters of today are skiing at a level which would have surpassed the efforts of many of our champions of a few years ago. The extensiveness of this program is unbelievable. A recent junior race, classes C and D, drew a field of 150 boys and girls from four states, and this was just one race in one area.

FACILITIES AND EQUIPMENT

FACILITIES

The facilities for skiing consist of space for preseason conditioning, a ski slope that affords opportunities for learning and practicing, and snow, when available.

Much preseason conditioning and preparation can be done in a gymnasium, but it is preferable to learn the fundamental skills outdoors on a level grassy area and a small slope. The latest innovation is the use of plastics. Some of these resemble thousands of hair brushes fastened together to form a mat which is secured to the ground, section by section. When located on a small hill, the mat will allow the skier to slide and to turn. The mat is growing in popularity and is being used by more and more schools and colleges. It is in use for beginners and also as a training device for racers. It can be used at any temperature, summer or winter, and is resistant to wear.

The ultimate in facilities is the snow-covered slope that offers a varied terrain and

Fig. 12-2. Rope tow.

opportunities for all skill levels. In areas where natural snow is scarce, the snowmaking machines have been a boon to skiers and to the skiing industry. At present snow makers are costly and often require much maintenance. They also require temperatures below freezing to operate effectively.

Uphill conveyances are not an absolute necessity, but it would be safe to say that they are one of the major reasons for the tremendous increase in the number of skiers. Lifts give access to otherwise inaccessible areas, and they also allow the skier many more hours of downhill skiing. It is highly desirable, however, that beginning skiers climb the practice slope. The climbing serves

Fig. 12-3. T-bar.

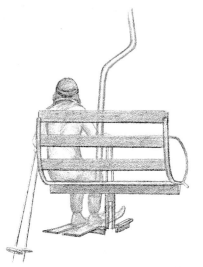

Fig. 12-4. Chair lift (double).

two purposes: it is an excellent method of conditioning, and it helps the skier to become accustomed to her equipment.

There are many types of tows and lifts: the rope tow, T-bar, J-bar, pomalift, chair lift, cable car, and gondola. The rope tow, T-bar, J-bar, and poma pull the skier up the hill. The skis remain on the snow and the skier leans against or holds on to the towing device. The chair, cable car, and gondola carry the skier and are more commonly used to reach higher altitudes.

One device that must be used in conjunction with tows and some lifts is a safety gate. The safety gate is an automatic shut-off switch that goes into operation if a skier does not get off the tow at the unloading area (it is not unusual for a skier to leave the tow before reaching the unloading area, but safety is endangered if the skier remains on the tow beyond this area). Tows and lifts are also manned by operators whose duty it is to load and unload skiers; if necessary, the tow can be stopped by a switch at top or bottom. Ski area operators are acutely conscious of any dangers in skiing, and as a result they have eliminated many hazards from the sport. Some of the safeguards are preseason slope grooming, snow packers, and the lifeguards of the ski slope—the ski patrol.

EQUIPMENT

The four important items of equipment are boots, poles, skis, and bindings.

Boots. The selection of boots must be made with the greatest care. The boot translates the movements of the body to the ski and is the single most important item of equipment.

The boot should fit the foot so that as the foot moves the boot moves. Boots are made in all sizes and widths and can be custom made. Many are double, having an inner and outer boot, and are higher and stiffer than they were in past years. The buckle boot has replaced many of the lace-type boots. It is easy to put on, easy to loosen, and a big boon to the "cold-foot clan." Plastics have also made their appearance in the boot industry, and some are replacing leather. Buckles and side hinges are also a part of the skier's vocabulary— beginners and Olympic competitors alike.

The sole is stiff and flat; ski boots are not made for walking or hiking and can be ruined by this type of use. A boot should be comfortable, but its stiffness should be retained. Leather softeners should not be applied, but a good hard wax should be used to protect the boot. Boots should be dried slowly if they get wet and should always be kept on a boot tree that maintains the shape of the sole. Boot prices range from $25 to $150.

Poles. The pole has also undergone a change. Now it is frequently used as an aid in turning and consequently a lighter pole is being manufactured. The basket is smaller and the grip is often molded so that it fits the hand. The approximate length of the pole should be from the floor to the skier's armpit. The better poles are made of aluminum that has been subjected to a hardening process to decrease breakage. The average price range is from $5 to $25.

Skis. Most modern skis are manufactured by a laminating process. Woods are combined to derive greater strength and flexibility, hickory and ash still being the most popular. Metal skis have a wood core or filler. Fiberglass skis are also available. Skis are, in general, much shorter than formerly. For the beginner a shorter ski is more maneuverable, and in some areas the very short ski (from 2½ to 5 feet) is advocated for the beginner. Most running surfaces are of plastic and many of the skis have plasticized tops. Metal edges are an absolute necessity; these may be hidden, offset, or the conventional. The amount of ski flexibility necessary is determined by the ability of the skier; a flexible ski is used by the recreational skier, whereas the racer might select a stiff ski. Different waxes can be applied to the running surface of the ski, allowing the ski to slide more easily during varying snow conditions. Each package of wax includes directions for its use and indicates the kind to use for different snow conditions.

Ski prices range from $20 to $200. Metal skis, which have had a tremendous increase in popularity, range from $70 upward. Wood skis demand more care and should be stored in a cool, dry area; they must be blocked to maintain their camber and to prevent warping.

Release Bindings. The advent of release bindings has made skiers much more safety conscious. Release bindings, erroneously called "safety bindings," are selected separately from the ski and can be purchased as a unit (a heel and toe piece of the same make) or can be purchased as separate pieces and combined. Most release bindings work on the principle of releasing the foot when there is undue stress, but each binding will release under a different degree of pressure. The skier must understand how to adjust her own binding according to her size and weight, her physical condition, and her skiing ability. Bindings should be checked regularly—they can tighten or loosen without the skier's awareness. They are excellent when correctly understood and correctly adjusted, but they are only as safe as the individual's understanding of how to use them. Since bindings are designed to release the ski from the foot, it is necessary to prevent the released ski from becoming a runaway ski. Consequently the skis are leashed to the foot by means of a retaining or Arlberg strap. The leash should be of the type that does not permit the released ski to swing freely, as this may cause danger to the body of the skier. Most ski areas require skiers to use a retaining strap because a runaway ski can be a menace on a ski slope.

Ski bindings range in price from $7 to $40; straps may be part of the binding cost or may be purchased separately. The bindings should be installed by a qualified person. This is usually done at the time of purchase.

Ski Clothing. Today's ski clothing permits freedom of action and is characterized by vibrant colors, lack of bulk, and its close-fitting stretch pants. The skier can select clothing that will prepare her for many extremes in temperatures, such as quilted down jackets, wired boots (battery operated), insulated underwear, face masks, and insulated gloves and mittens. These are all designed for colder temperatures, whereas the unlined nylon parka is designed for warmer days. Items of clothing usually consist of the following:

> Socks (one lightweight and one heavy pair)
> Turtleneck jersey
> Nylon-wool stretch pants
> Wool sweater (double knit)
> Hooded parka
> Long underwear
> Gloves or mittens
> Hat or headband

Some accessories are very necessary, others are for the additional comfort of the individual. They include:

> Goggles or sun glasses (necessary)
> Car top racks
> Ski locks

Information concerning ski equipment is published each year by the ski magazines. Local ski shops usually hire salesmen who understand ski equipment and the desirability of proper selection and adjustment as it relates to the ability of the skier.

BASIC SKILLS

Preseason Conditioning. Skiing presupposes good conditioning, as do other activities. The conditioning process may be effected by sports, gymnastics, conditioning exercises, or mountain climbing. A combination of the above plus dry skiing can be an efficient and enjoyable method, enabling the skier to be mentally and physically prepared. Dry skiing can be done indoors or outdoors. Walking, climbing, falling, getting up, edging, and turning can be practiced on grass, floor, or ski mat, allowing the beginning skier to use and begin to understand the technique of skiing and the equipment.

Pole Grip. The skier inserts her hands up through pole straps; the hands grasp the poles with the straps pressed between the palm of the hand and the pole. The pole is grasped firmly, and the little fingers of each hand do the lifting. The poles are carried approximately waist high, pole tips to the

Fig. 12-5. Gripping the poles. Insert the hand from below the strap; grasp the pole with the strap in the palm.

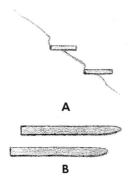

Fig. 12-7. The sidestep. *A,* Rear view of skis, showing how the inside edge is dug into the side of the hill. *B,* The position of the skis perpendicular to the fall line.

rear of the body. The poles give the skier balance and are used as an aid in turning.

Walking on the Level. The skis slide alternately across the snow, in a movement similar to walking. The poles are used in opposition to the skis (right ski, left pole). The slide may be exaggerated or lengthened by an increased flexion of the knee. This allows the skier to feel the sliding action of the ski.

Climbing

HERRINGBONE. The skis are at an angle to the fall line; the ski tips are pointing upward and outward. The skis are lifted alternately and are stepped forward and upward. The pole use is in opposition to the skis and is a pushing action from behind the body. The body leans slightly forward.

Fig. 12-6. The herringbone. The weight is on the inside edge of the ski.

SIDESTEP. The sidestep is preferred over the herringbone for steeper slopes and for beginners. The skis are parallel, at right angles to the fall line, and are edged into the hill. The skis remain in this position as they are stepped sideways up the hill. The poles should be used alternately.

Downhill Run (Straight). Initial practice for body mechanics should be executed on the level. The best first downhill experience is where the terrain offers a very gentle slope with a level approach and a level run-off. The skier slides skis forward (walking on level), then, as the skis begin to slide freely, the poles are lifted and held at waist level with pole tips behind the body. The skis are parallel and are weighted equally; one ski is advanced approximately one-half a boot length. The ankles are flexed and the knees, hips, and shoulders are relaxed and are forward of the heels. The skier reaches the bottom of the slope and allows the skis to come to a stop. To increase relaxation during the run, bounce slightly, by increasing and decreasing the flexion in the ankle and knee joints. The skis remain in contact with the snow.

DOWNHILL RUN WITH ALTERNATE SKI LIFTING. When the skier is able to execute the downhill run, an additional exercise may be practiced. As she slides down the hill, she alternately lifts each ski.

DOWNHILL RUN WITH STEPPING OFF. Stepping off is a change of direction accompanied by a transfer of weight. In turning to the right, the weight is on the left ski, the right ski is lifted (stepped) outward at a slight angle to the direction of travel. The weight is then shifted to the right ski and the left ski is closed to the newly weighted ski. To continue turning, transfer weight to left ski and repeat the above exercise. Stepping off may also be executed during the traverse by stepping up into the hill to decrease momentum.

The alternate lifting of the skis and stepping off helps to develop the ability to maintain balance while transferring the weight from one ski to the other, thereby achieving increased control of the skis.

Traverse. The traverse is used to descend a slope by pointing the skis downward and across the fall line. The skis are parallel; the uphill ski, hip, and shoulder are leading; the downhill ski is carrying the major portion of the weight; both skis are edged into the hill. The ankles are flexed and the knees are relaxed as in downhill running position. During the traverse, forward momentum may be decreased by stepping up into the hill.

Changing Direction on Flat or Hilly Terrain (Stepping Around). Starting position: skis parallel. Keep tips of skis together and using them as a pivot point, open tail of right ski to the right, close tail of left ski to the right; skis are again parallel (Fig. 12-8*A*). Continue opening and closing until skis are pointing in desired direction. This maneuver may be executed to the right or to the left. The tails of the skis may also be used as the pivot point,

and as a lead-up exercise for stepping off. Stepping around is the preferred method for the beginner who has just sidestepped up a small hill and wishes to assume the downhill running position. From the sidestep position the skier holds her position by leaning against her poles. The poles are thrust into the snow or mat below the skier, her elbows are straight, and from the pole tip through the grip on top of the pole to the skier's shoulders there is a straight line of resistance. The skier then steps her skis around to the downhill running position. She then slides between the poles (Fig. 12-8*B*).

Falling Down and Getting Up. In learning to ski, the skier will fall; therefore she should understand and practice how to fall correctly. Practice is best if it is done where the landing can be cushioned by straw or snow. The skier should attempt to fall to the rear and uphill; fall on her side, knees together, arms up and away from body, with pole tips behind body. A common error is using the hands or knees to break a fall.

To rise from this position:

1. Bring skis to a parallel position below the body, both skis pointing in the same direction.

2. Rise to a side-sitting position.

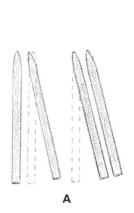

A

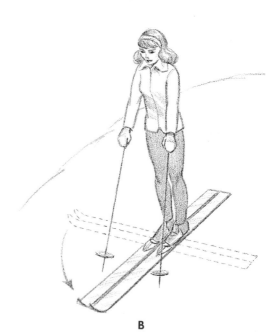

B

Fig. 12-8. See text for explanation.

A   **B**

Fig. 12-9. To get up from a fall, keep skis perpendicular to fall line.

3. Flex knees toward the chest, placing the skis at a right angle to fall line and slightly edged into the hill.

4. Remove pole straps from wrists; bring poles together and place the tips in the snow close to the hips on the uphill side of the body. If right hip is down, position right hand just above baskets of both poles.

5. Grasp pole shafts with left hand, as near to the top as possible.

6. Maintain crouched position; push with the right hand and pull with the left hand to raise the hips above and over the edged skis.

7. Straighten knees to achieve standing position.

Snowplow. The tails of the skis slide outward; the tips of the skis are almost touching. The position is a "V" with the closed end pointing in the direction of travel. The ankles are flexed, the knees are relaxed; the angle of the upper body is the same as that of the lower leg; the hips are forward of the heels. The weight is distributed equally on both skis with pressure applied to the inside edges. Poles are carried as in the downhill running position. The initial

Fig. 12-10. The snowplow. Keep knees and ankles flexed, hips in front of heels. Weight is on both skis, with inside edges pressing against snow.

practice in assuming the snowplow position is executed on level terrain, then on a gradual slope. An increase of pressure with the inside edges against the snow will decrease momentum or achieve a full stop.

Turning. The terminology used to explain turns will refer to the inside and the outside ski; the inside ski is similar to a pivot point, the outside ski is the one which passes through the greater arc. The down-up-down motion of the body accompanies each turn. The down position involves an increased flexion of the ankles and knees, the weight is forward (it is not a sitting action); if a stem is involved, it will be executed on the initial down motion. The up position is an extension of the ankles and knees simultaneously with the transfer of weight from one ski to the other. The final down is again an increased flexion near the completion of the turn. The skier then rises slightly to assume the more erect running position. During the traverse and turns, the uphill ski, hip, and shoulder are leading, the upper part of the body leans out and over the downhill ski.

Fig. 12-12. The kick turn is used to change directions on a slope.

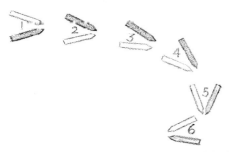

Fig. 12-11. The snowplow turn. The weight is on the dark ski. 1-2: Weight shifts to turn right. 3-4-5: Push with left heel, flatten right ski. 6: New direction, weight downhill. Maintain flexion of knees and ankles.

Snowplow Turn. The skier starts in the snowplow position, transferring the major portion of her weight to the outside ski. For example, if the left ski bears the weight, the turn will be to the right. The outside ski becomes the downhill one as the turn is completed. To turn in the opposite direction, gradually change weight to the other ski. A common error is stiffening the inside (non-weight-bearing) leg.

Kick Turn Changing Direction on Hill. The skier stands with the skis parallel and at

right angles to the fall line. The skis are edged into the hill. The upper body is rotated so that the skier is facing downhill. The poles are placed above the skis, the points angling outward (skis and poles form a tripod). The downhill ski is unweighted and made to slide forward and backward to gain momentum. The knee is straight and the foot is lifted forward and upward so that the tail of the ski is placed in the snow near the tip of the uphill ski (Fig. 12-12). Keep the tail of the ski in the snow and allow the ski to fall away from the body. Then bring the ski tip alongside the tail of the uphill ski. The weight is then transferred to that ski. Lift the other ski and swing it into a position parallel to the weighted ski. The pole will follow the ski and both will now be on the downhill side.

Stem Turn. Start in the traverse position.

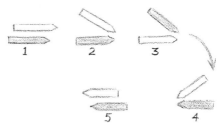

Fig. 12-13. The stem turn. The weight is on the dark ski. The skier stems (2), shifts her weight (3), and as she reaches the new direction slides in the unweighted ski (4).

Stem the uphill ski on the down motion of the body. Transfer the weight to the outside ski with an up motion. The turn will be effected by weighting and continued stemming of this ski until the new direction is reached. This is followed by a slight edging of the outside ski; at the same time, the inside ski slides into a position parallel with and slightly ahead of the outside ski. A common error is edging the inside ski.

Uphill Christy. The skier slides across the hill in a traverse position, the weight is projected forward, and the uphill edges of the front of the skis bite into the snow. The tails of the skis are unweighted and slide downhill; this forces the tips of the skis to turn uphill. The skis are parallel throughout the maneuver.

Stem Christy. The skier moves across the slope in a traverse position. With the down motion of the body, the uphill (outside) ski is stemmed. On the up motion, the weight is transferred to the stemmed ski, the edge of the inside ski is released and the ski is closed to the outside stemmed ski. The skis are now parallel and the heels are thrust to the outside to continue the turn across the fall line and into the new traverse. At this point, the body is in the down position.

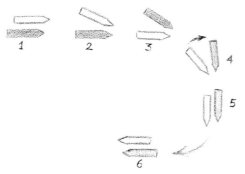

Fig. 12-14. The stem christy. Shift weight as in stem turn (3), then pull unweighted ski toward outside ski (4), bringing skis together at fall line (5). The heels are then pushed outward into the new traverse.

Parallel Christy. The skier is in a traverse and in the down position. As the weight is transferred to the outside ski with the up motion, the inside ski slides ahead of the outside ski, the edges are released, and the heels are thrust to the outside with the skis remaining parallel. The turn is completed in the same manner as in the stem christy.

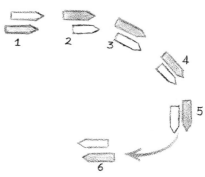

Fig. 12-15. The parallel christy. As the weight shifts (2), the inner ski is advanced slightly. The skis are flattened and the heels push to the outside (4,5). Finish as in the stem christy.

Short Swing. This consists of a rhythmical series of parallel turns without a traverse between the turns; a pole plant is usually employed in this maneuver.

Pole Planting. When the poles are used to accompany turns, they are used as a supplemental aid. Pole plants may be started early in the learning process. The pole is planted just before the up movement of the down-up-down sequence, ahead of and to the side of the lead ski. The pole is quickly withdrawn from the snow as the turn is being executed. The pole use should be rhythmical and controlled; it is not a windmill or flashing movement. A common error is the use of one pole more than the other.

SKI SAFETY AND COURTESY

Like most other sports skiing has some inherent dangers. However, most of the dangers could be avoided by the understanding and use of known safety practices, courtesy, and common sense.

Recognizing these problems, each ski area, regardless of whether it is operated by a college, township, state, or as a private enterprise, usually maintains a ski school and a ski patrol in addition to an efficient staff. The ski school offers instruction at all levels on a group or individual basis. Certified ski instructors have undergone extensive training and know the value of instruction and its relationship to enjoyment and safety in skiing. Some ski schools and ski clubs use the National Uniform Tests (progressive skill tests) to indicate the level of proficiency attained.

The ski patrol's first duty is the prevention of accidents. Should an accident occur, they are prepared to render first aid, which often includes toboggan transportation from the hill to the first aid shelter. Many ski patrols include members of the medical profession. The patrols maintain high standards and are alert to their duties. Many new ideas and new first aid equipment have emerged from this alertness.

Ski instructors, ski patrolmen, and area operators all try to give the individual pleasure in skiing. Observance of the following rules will add to this enjoyment:

1. Preseason conditioning is a necessity.
2. Ski instruction is recommended.
3. Know your equipment and keep it in good repair—this includes bindings.
4. Always ski under control; select slope or trail suited to your ability.
5. Ski only when in good physical condition.
6. Understand snow conditions; the degree of difficulty increases with certain conditions (e.g., ice or heavy wet snow).
7. If you fall, repair or smooth sitzmark.
8. Ski slopes and trails are for skiing, not walking.
9. Ski around an instructional class, not through it.
10. Schussing on a crowded slope endangers other skiers.
11. Three people are a safe minimum number when skiing cross country or on little-used trails.
12. Beginning skiers and the skier downhill from you have the right of way.
13. Be alert to the word "Track!" If on a trail, move to one side; if on a slope, stand still. Heed the cry of "Ski!" It signifies a runaway ski.
14. If unfamiliar with tows or lifts, ask the lift operator for instruction.
15. Loose-fitting clothing can become entangled in tows and lifts—be alert to this possibility (especially true on rope tows).
16. Know and regard rules and regulations of the area.
17. Be alert to the dangers of frostbite on extremely cold days or extremely windy days (usually indicated by white spots on nose, cheeks, and extremities).
18. In case of an accident, notify the ski patrolman.

Terminology

Abstem—To push out the tail of the downhill ski from parallel position.

American Ski Technique—The system that characterizes skiing in the United States; its progressions have been evolved by the Professional Ski Instructors of America (PSIA).

Base—The layer of packed snow adjacent to the ground; usually referred to in ski reports.

Camber—The arch of a ski, which permits distribution of the skier's weight along the length of the ski.

Chair lift—An uphill conveyance: a series of chairs attached to a cable; may be a single or double chair.

Corn—A type of granulated snow produced by alternate thawing and freezing during warmer weather.

Downhill ski—The ski on the downhill side of the skier.

Edging—A method of using the steel edges of the skis to control sideward movement.

Fall line—The shortest and sometimes the steepest distance between the top and bottom of the hill (the path a rolling ball would follow).

FIS—Fédération Internationale de Ski, the body that regulates skiing and competition on the international level.

Gate—Two flags through which a racer must pass; used in slalom and giant slalom courses.

Gondola—An uphill conveyance suspended on a cable.

Headgear—A hard helmet (tested according to specifications), which must be worn by racers.

Heel push—The movement of pushing the tails of the skis downhill while the fronts of the skis are edged; aids in turning.

Herringbone—A method of climbing on skis; the ski tips are turned outward and the skis are edged into the snow.

J-Bars—A series of bars shaped like J's, attached to a cable, that pull skiers uphill.

Kick turn—Changing direction on skis; a stationary turn.

Lead—The ski that is ahead of the other, usually half a boot length.

Leash—Retaining straps that affix ski to foot, used with release bindings, preferably of two contact type, wrap around.

Mogul—An accumulation of snow created by a number of skiers turning at the same spot; moguls often become 2 to 3 feet high.

NSPS—National Ski Patrol System, the national organization that promotes ski safety. Each member is trained in first aid and winter rescue operations. It is primarily a volunteer organization.

Pomalift—A platter-like disc that pulls the skier uphill; the skier straddles the disc.

Powder—A type of light, dry snow, which occurs at colder temperatures.

Rope tow—A moving rope that pulls the skier uphill. The skier grasps the rope and uses an action similar to that of water skiing.

Ruecklage—A backward leaning position.

Schuss—Skiing straight down the hill, following fall line of slope, making no turns or stops.

Sideslip—Release of the edges so that the skis slide sideward and downward. Skis are perpendicular to the fall line.

Sidestep—Method of climbing with skis perpendicular to the fall line; sidestep may be executed vertically or diagonally upward.

Sitzmark—A depression in the snow caused by a fall.

Ski-joring—A manner of skiing on the level similar to water skiing; the skier is pulled or towed by a horse, mechanized sled, or a car. Done only when there is no danger involved.

Skimobile—A small motor vehicle with skis attached. It has replaced many of the smaller functions of the Snow Cat. It is used to transport injured skiers and is also widely used as a recreational vehicle in the woods and over snow-covered fields.

Ski reports—TV, radio, or newspaper accounts of snow conditions at ski areas.

Snow bunny—A beginning skier.

Snow Cat—A type of large tractor used to pack snow, repair lift lines, transport food to mountain top restaurants, and occasionally to transport injured skiers. (Cost: approximately $10,000.)

Spring skiing—Characterized by radical changes in snow conditions because of temperature changes; enjoyed by skiers because of the milder temperatures.

Stem—An opening of the tail of the uphill ski, used for turns.

T-Bars—A series of bars shaped like upside-down T's, attached to an overhead cable, that pull skiers uphill. Each bar accommodates two skiers.

Traverse—The movement of the skier downward and across the slope.

Unweighting—The movement that characterizes the removal of weight from the ski.

Uphill ski—That ski that is on the uphill side of the skier.

Vorlage—A forward leaning position.

USSA—United States Ski Association, the national organization that promotes skiing and competition. It comprises seven divisions throughout the U.S.

Wax—A substance applied to the running surface of the skis to allow freer sliding; different waxes are applied for different snow conditions.

Weighting—The action during which the weight is applied to both skis or to one ski.

Sources of Visual Aids

AAHPER, Division for Girls and Women's Sports, 1201 Sixteenth St., N.W., Washington, D.C. 20036. *Winter Sports and Outing Activities Guide.* Published every two years. See current listing of visual aids.

Ski areas. As a means of promotion, many of the larger ski areas in the United States, Europe, Chile, New Zealand, and Australia have films on either a rental or rental-free basis. Consult ski directories in ski magazines for addresses.

Ski equipment companies. Many fine films are available through the companies that manufacture ski clothing and ski equipment. The addresses are also available through the various ski publications.

Tourist promotion and state commerce departments. Each state that has the facilities and weather for skiing and counts on skiing as one of its tourist resources has films of its ski areas. Many of these areas are located in state parks and part of the revenue derived from them goes into state funds. Information can be secured from the promotion bureau of the state—address the state tourist bureau at the state capital.

Travel agencies. Agencies that sponsor ski trips are sources of promotion films. Many of these films are sponsored by airlines or railroads. They are advertisements, but are also good sources for program material and occasionally for teaching purposes.

United States Ski Association, The Broadmoor, Colorado Springs, Colorado. This association and its divisions in each section of the country offer listings in their publications.

Suggested Readings

AAHPER: *Third National Institute on Girls Sports*, Washington, D.C., National Education Association, 1966.

Eriksen, Stein: *Come Ski with Me*, New York, W. W. Norton & Company, Inc., 1966.

Joubert, Georges, and Vuarnet, Jean: *How to Ski the New French Way*, New York, Dial Press, 1967.

Joubert, Georges, and Vuarnet, Jean: *Ski ABC*, London, Nicolas Kaye, Ltd., 1959. Distributed by Egil Stigum, 9 Downing Road, Hanover, N.H.

McCulloch, Ernie: *Learn to Ski*, New York, Universal Publishing and Distributing Corporation, 1959.

McCulloch, Ernie: *Ski the Champion's Way*, New York, Harper and Row, 1967.

Palmedo, Roland: *Ski New Horizons*, Garden City, New York, Doubleday and Co., Inc., 1961.

Polasek, Ollie: *Skiing*, Cranbury, N.J., A. S. Barnes & Co., 1960.

Schaeffler, Willy, and Bowen, Ezra: *Sports Illustrated Book of Skiing*, Philadelphia, J. B. Lippincott Co., 1960.

Ski Life Editors: *Ski Pointers by the Experts*, New York, Harper and Row, 1961.

Taylor, Clif: *Instant Skiing*, Brattleboro, Vermont, The Stephen Greene Press, 1961.

Taylor, Clif: *The Official American Ski Technique*, 2nd Ed., Salt Lake City, Utah, The Professional Ski Instructors of America, 1966.

Wallace, William: *The Young Sportsman's Guide to Skiing*, New York, Thomas Nelson and Sons, 1961.

Periodicals

Almanac and Reference Guide, Ski Magazine, Dept. No. SAS 263, P. O. Box 2080, Grand Central Station, New York, N.Y. 10017. (Published annually.)

Ski: Universal Publishing and Distributing Corporation, 800 Second Avenue, New York, N.Y. 10017.

Skier: United States Eastern Amateur Ski Association, 98 Main Street, Littleton, N.H.

Skiing: Skiing Publishing Co., 7190 W. 14th Avenue, Denver 15, Colo.

Ski View: United States Ski Association, The Broadmoor, Colorado Springs, Colo.

Sports Illustrated: 540 N. Michigan Avenue, Chicago, Ill. 60611.

Winter Sports and Outdoor Activities Guide: AAHPER, Division for Girls and Women's Sports, 1201 Sixteenth St., N.W., Washington, D.C. 20036. (Published biennially.)

Suggested Study Questions

1. In what skiing events do girls and women compete? How is each event judged?
2. A traverse is a means of crossing the slope. It precedes and follows almost every turn. Describe the position and weighting of the skis, the anatomical position of the skier, and the relative position of the poles.
3. Define the following terms: fall line, snowplow, release bindings, stem, edging, USSA.
4. What safety precautions should all skiers take?

CHAPTER THIRTEEN

Courtesy of Rice University, Houston, Texas.

SQUASH RACQUETS

The development of squash racquets is a success story of sports. Originating among the debtors in Fleet Prison in England, it is popular today in many outstanding colleges and universities and "exclusive" clubs.

Although its exact date of origin is doubtful, the parent game, called "racquets," was probably played as early as the 17th century with a small, hard rubber ball and a large, heavy bat. To this day a passageway back of Fleet Street in London is known as Racquet Court, recalling the probable site of early games.

In the middle of the 19th century the game was introduced at Harrow School in England. An outdoor game, it required a large court area. Impatient students, tired of waiting to play on the one court, devised a game playable on a smaller court either indoors or outdoors. Experimenting with balls and bat type rackets, the students developed the game as we know it, giving it its name because of the "squashy" sound made by the soft rubber ball as it rebounded from the walls.

From England the game spread to Canada and was brought to the United States in 1880 by the Reverend James P. Conover of St. Paul's School in Concord, New Hampshire. Growth of the game was slow, and confusion existed for many years over equipment and facilities. This confusion ultimately led to the popularization of squash tennis when Stephen J. Feron improvised a tennis-type ball covered with netting. With refinement and changes both squash games grew in popularity when given an enthusiastic approval by the Prince of Wales while visiting the United States.

As the popularity of the game spread, it centered in Philadelphia, New York, and other Atlantic Coast cities. Squash remained primarily a man's sport, with the greatest play in Eastern colleges and universities. Soon women college students, along with men, turned to squash as a sport for fun that did not require large team groups or arduous training. In 1928 Eleanora Sears from Boston won the first women's national tournament. Squash racquets was one of America's fastest growing sports until the 1930's, when winter activities and bowling captured sporting fancies.

NATURE AND PURPOSE OF THE GAME

Squash is a vigorous racket game played on a walled court that resembles an empty room with a high ceiling. The game may be played by two players (singles) or two teams of two persons each (doubles). The object of the game is to score points by serving and placing returns so that an opponent cannot make a legal return.

Today there are approximately 1500 courts in the United States, largely in preparatory schools, colleges, universities, Y.M.H.A.'s and Y.M.C.A.'s. Unquestionably a game for all, the appeal to beginners is the ease of learning basic skills; to the housewife and businessman, the physical workout gained by a short period of participation; and to the proficient player, the mastery of the many skills. The relatively slow growth of the sport is due to limited court facilities and the expense of new court construction.

FACILITIES AND EQUIPMENT

Court size was not standardized until 1931, and many "nonregulation" courts, handball courts, and renovated storage rooms serve enthusiastic players. The regulation singles court resembles a large rectangular box, 32 feet long, 18½ feet wide and 16 feet high. The wooden or plaster interior of the court, including the floor, is painted white or eggshell, and all lines are marked in red, 1 inch wide. Extending across the front wall and running from the floor 17 inches up the wall and set 1½ inches from the wall is a metal sheet called the tell-tale. When hit by

211

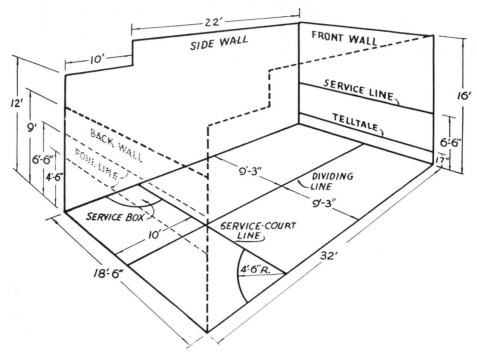

Fig. 13-1. Squash racquets court.

the ball the metal makes a resounding noise indicating an error. The top of the tell-tale is marked with a red line.

Red lines mark the out-of-bounds areas at the top of all walls. Balls hitting on or above these lines or on the ceiling are out of play. On the front wall a service line, the top of which is 6½ feet above the floor, indicates that a legal service must go above the line. On the back wall, a return line, the lower edge of which is 6½ feet from the floor, is marked across the wall.

The back of the floor is separated by a line parallel to and 10 feet from the back wall, and is equally divided into right and left courts by a line from the middle of the forward line to the middle of the back wall. The area where these lines meet is called the "T."

Two quarter circles, each with a radius of 4½ feet, mark the service boxes in the front corners, next to the walls of each receiving court.

The doubles court is 45 feet long and 25 feet wide with front and side walls 20 feet high. The front wall service line is 8 feet 2 inches, and the back wall return line is 7 feet from the floor. The forward service court line is 15 feet from the back wall. Other markings are similar to those of the single court.

Courts must be well lighted with recessed fixtures, so that no shadows fall in the court.

Equipment. Squash rackets resemble both badminton and tennis rackets in some respects. They are similar in size and shape to the badminton racket, but their weight and sturdy design approximate those of a tennis racket. The racket is made of wood, with a circular head not exceeding 9 inches in diameter. It should be no longer than 27 inches and weigh between 7 and 11 ounces. The components of head, throat, shaft, handle, and grip are the same as those of other rackets. The head is strung with gut or nylon; nylon is more durable and frays less quickly, but gut stringing offers maximum playing quality.

It is advisable to purchase a racket with professional advice, *making certain that the grip fits the hand.* Rackets should be wiped and placed in presses after each match.

The hollow black ball is 1¾ inches in diameter and weighs from 1.12 to 1.17 ounces. The official ball is manufactured by the Seamless Rubber Company. This pneumatic ball is subject to temperature changes—dead when cold and livelier as it becomes heated in play. It should *not* be chilled or heated before play. A good ball should rebound 24 to 26 inches when dropped onto a steel plate from 100 inches at 70° Fahrenheit. The doubles ball is slightly lighter and livelier.

Dress. The official gymnasium costume for squash is appropriate dress. Nonslip sneakers or tennis shoes that do not mark the floor are imperative. For tournament competition the player's attire must be white. Light colors avoid contrasts that distract an opponent.

BASIC SKILLS

Basic to all effective strokes is proper footwork and body positioning. As the player becomes more skillful, an understanding of angle shots and rebound position is necessary.

Getting Set to Hit. Preparing to stroke the ball involves moving to the proper spot and then positioning the body to hit.

Footwork within the court consists basically of short shuffle steps rather than long strides, which result in overbalancing and overrunning a desired position.

The "ideal" set position while awaiting a return is in the center of the court with the heels about an inch in front of the "T" formed by the floor service line and the court division line. The feet are comfortably spread at approximately shoulder width; the weight is equally distributed on the balls of both feet. The knees bend slightly outward as the body assumes a slight crouch while facing the front wall. Both elbows are close to the body.

When the opponent is prepared to return from behind, the player keeps her back to the opponent, turning the upper body and head slightly in the direction the opponent is favoring. Only the corner of the eye catches the opponent's movements. When an opponent is behind and to the left of a right-handed player, the racket head is across the body, held by a cocked right hand and wrist and raised slightly by the left hand (Fig. 13-2). When the opponent is behind and to the right, the racket may move to the right side, head up, for additional protection. The opponent should always be given plenty of room in which to swing her racket.

Many strokes are played off balance be-

Fig. 13-2. Ready position.

cause of the speed of the game; however, when time permits positioning for forehand or backhand strokes, place the body parallel—with feet perpendicular—to its oncoming flight.

Grip. The Continental and Eastern[*] grips are commonly used in squash. The Continental grip (for a right-handed player) is described here, for it allows forehand, backhand, and volley shots to be taken *without* changing finger or thumb position. The speed of the game makes shifting difficult.

Hold the racket by its throat in the left hand so that the racket face is perpendicular to the floor. Grasp the handle with the right hand as if picking up a hammer. The heel of the hand is slightly to the right of center and the fingers are spread slightly with the index finger well spread. The thumb is extended diagonally upward to the left of the handle.

---

[*]See p. 293 for description of the Eastern grip.

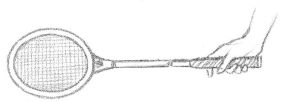

Fig. 13-3. The grip.

In this position pressure is applied by thumb, index finger, and heel of the hand (Fig. 13-3).

Forehand Stroke. The forehand is used when the ball is approaching on the right side and power and speed are desired on the return. The swing is natural and similar to a sidearm throw in softball. No *deep* backswing or follow-through is required, for much power comes from the forward motion of the arm and wrist snap.

The left side of the body is turned toward the front wall with toes and body facing the right wall. As the ball approaches, weight shifts back to the right foot, and hips and shoulders turn so that they are parallel to the right wall. The racket is brought back with the right forearm parallel to the floor; the elbow is bent and only 6 to 8 inches from the body. The right wrist is cocked so that the racket head is well up, pointing toward the ceiling. There is a pause, and then the weight shifts to the left foot, which has moved toward the ball. With right forearm and cocked wrist leading, the racket starts forward as the hips and shoulders pivot to the left (Fig. 13-4). For most strokes, except low ankle-height balls, the racket head moves parallel to the floor. For an alley shot the wrist uncocks and comes into contact with the ball nearly opposite the left knee. For a cross court shot the contact and snapping action is in front of the body with the racket angled across the court. The follow-through moves easily across the body and the player remains in a crouch anticipating the next shot.

Fig. 13-4. The forehand stroke.

Backhand Stroke. In contrast to the spaciousness of the tennis court, the confining walls of the squash court encourage less skilled players to try backhand shots. The player faces the left wall, right shoulder toward the front wall. The hips and shoulders pivot left as the weight shifts to the rear foot. The right wrist is cocked to the left and upward, holding the handle at approximately a 45 degree angle to the floor. The racket head is at about eye level. A momentary pause in the backswing is followed by a step to the left with the right foot, which moves the shoulders and hips farther around, drawing the racket farther back. The right shoulder is lowered.

As *uncoiling* begins, the hips and shoulders turn forward and the cocked wrist brings the racket forward. For a straight alley shot the ball is struck about 6 inches in front of the right foot. For a cross court shot, the ball is hit more from the center of the body. The wrist whips through for extra power as pressure is felt on the thumb. As with the forehand, the follow-through leaves the player in a crouched postion.

Serves. There are three basic serves in squash — the lob, the sidearm slice, and the overhead smash. The most consistently accurate and energy-conserving of these is the lob.

To execute the *lob* the server stands with one or both feet in the serving arc so that she is facing the front wall, yet able to watch the ball's flight into her opponent's court. Service from either side of the court is made from the right side of the body, with the body in a slight crouch and racket head pointing toward the floor and held in front of the body below waist level. The right hand and arm pull the racket slightly back; as the ball is dropped by the left hand extended in front and to the right of the body, the racket is led through by a cocked right wrist in an upward pendulum-like swing to stroke the ball (Fig. 13-5). The racket comes in contact with the ball at knee height as a slight shift of weight from rear to forward foot and a firm wrist action lift the ball to the front wall.

When serving from the right to the left court, direct the ball high and 4 or 5 feet from the left wall. The follow-through should take the racket across the body.

When serving *to* the right court lift the ball

Fig. 13-5.   The lob serve.

Fig. 13-6.   The sidearm slice serve.

high and to the right side of the wall with follow-through in the path of the ball.

An effective serve should "float" back from the front wall close to the side wall in an arc and drop almost vertically onto the back wall or in the back corner. This *nearly* vertical trajectory makes a difficult shot for the opponent.

The *sidearm slice service* is an effective change of pace and a helpful skill when playing on an improvised court with a low ceiling. With the body positioned as in the lob service, the ball is tossed by the left hand in front of the body to about shoulder height. The racket is brought back on the right side of the body by a cocked wrist, the elbow close to the body (Fig. 13-6). The racket head is at about shoulder level. As the racket strikes the ball the wrist uncocks and the strings pull sharply across the ball from right to left, imparting a spin. The ball is directed just above the service line, and the racket head follows the direction of the ball.

The *flat overhead smash serve* is similar to a flat tennis service. It requires more strength than either of the serves already described but is an effective change of pace and an offensive move against a tired opponent. The body position is almost the same from both courts; however, the serve described is for a right-handed server from the right arc to the left court.

The right foot is in the quarter circle with the left foot in front outside the service line. The body is half facing the front wall. While the left hand tosses the ball to a point high above the right shoulder, the right arm draws the racket down the right side and back. As weight shifts to the right foot the right wrist cocks and the racket is swung behind the head. At the pause at the top of the ball's flight the whole body weight shifts to the forward foot, and simultaneously the racket moves forward to hit the ball above the serving shoulder with a throwing motion. The ball is hit flat and aimed low above the center of the service line. The follow-through is in the direction of the ball.

A firm serve will send the ball directly to the rear wall, from which it will rebound as a fast, low ball into the back of the serving court. If served toward the side of the front wall, it will rebound off the side wall, bounce into the service court, and rise to the back wall, forcing the opponent to turn around to follow it. This serve has the disadvantage of keeping the server out of her "T" position for fear of being struck by a return of the "turning" player.

The technique of receiving serves is discussed farther on in the section on game strategy.

Lob.   The lob is primarily a defensive

stroke to gain time for positioning, and with good luck to force the opponent to the back court for a weak or ineffective overhead return. The preparatory motions are similar to those of forehand and backhand strokes, except that the lob is more deliberate. With a short, slow backswing the racket face is turned slightly upward to hit the ball. The ball rises high on the front wall, arcs close to the ceiling, rebounds deep in the court, and bounces nearly straight up near the back wall. When a backspin is imparted, the ball will not bounce so high, but it may "jump" from the floor bounce.

Volley. A volley is executed by hitting the ball on the fly before it takes a floor bounce. Volleys are made on both sides of the body with positioning similar to either the forehand or the backhand stroke. The stroke is made with a firm grip, wrist, and arm, the backswing is shortened, ball contact is solid, and the follow-through less pronounced. The racket is held at about shoulder height with the right shoulder and elbow down. The body is angled toward the front wall yet facing the side from which the ball is coming. When the ball comes off the side wall, the volley resembles a *block*, with little backswing or follow-through. If is often necessary to volley an overhead service.

Half Volley. A half volley requires hitting the ball *immediately* after the bounce. Often a merely defensive shot to prevent the ball from bouncing past the player, it is used by experienced players to surprise the opponent by getting the ball to the front wall sooner than expected. The firm, pendulum-like swing involves the same skills used in returning a low-bounding ball with either the forehand or backhand. The racket head is below the level of the ball on contact, to give it lift. The follow-through is in the direction of the ball flight with the racket head ending about waist level.

BASIC SHOTS

There are several basic *shots* using the *skills* described which must be mastered to command court position and play an offensive game.

Alley Shot. An alley shot is most easily played close to the wall but can be effectively played from several yards into the court. On either the forehand (right alley), or backhand (left alley), it is a hard, low drive that makes contact with the ball at its lowest point and directs it straight to the front wall several inches above the tell-tale. The body is facing the side wall with the elbow low and bent toward the body. After hitting the ball opposite the forward knee, the follow-through is in the direction of the ball with the body turning slightly to the front wall and the wrist assuming a half closed position.

The ball rebounds straight off the front wall and hangs close to the side wall before it either bounces twice on the court, or bounces once, hits the back wall, and rebounds in a low "hanging" position.

Cross Court Shot. This shot can be executed from any angle position on the court. The ball is stroked either forehand or backhand so that it strikes the front wall low and near the center. Then it will rebound from the floor to the side wall opposite the one from which it was hit. The stroke is similar to the alley shot except that the ball is met in front of the body. The ball should hit the side wall quite deep, thus passing the opponent or drawing her out of position.

Drop Shot. The effectiveness of this advanced skill rests on deception. As the name suggests, the shot drops almost *dead* to the floor after hitting the front wall. It is most effective when played from midcourt with the body concealing the stroke from the opponent.

Facing the wall in normal forehand or backhand position, a normal backswing is taken, but at the moment of contact with the ball, which has been allowed to drop almost to the floor, the swing slows and the wrist leads the pendulum-like stroke. The ball is gently lifted in an arc so that it hits the wall just above the tell-tale. The wrist leads the follow-through.

Corner Shot. This shot can be executed from many points on the court but is most effective when made from in front of the "T" not too far from the front wall. The ball should be hit low to the side wall near the corner opposite the side of the court from which the stroke was made (Fig. 13-7). The rebound goes to the front wall and off, bouncing close to the wall. The easier the hit, the lower the bounce, which makes it more difficult for the opponent to play from the "T." If a firm stroke is used, the ball will re-

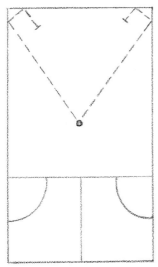

Fig. 13-7. Corner shots.

bound almost at the point from which it was hit. This may be desirable if the opponent is back and across the court or otherwise out of position.

A reverse corner, hitting the front wall first and rebounding to the side wall is equally effective.

GAME RULES AND SCORING

The object of the game of squash rackets is to serve and hit the ball so that points are scored by your own efficient play or by playing the ball so that the opponent fails to return it in a legal manner.

Serve. The server or receiver is selected by a spin of the racket. Thereafter loss of service goes with loss of point.

Each time a player receives the serve she may elect to serve from either box. She must then alternate until loss of point or until the game ends. If the server delivers from the wrong box there is no penalty, but the receiver may demand that it be played from another box *if* she does not attempt to return it.

When serving, the server must stand with at least one foot in the serving arc, not touching the lines, and serve directly to the front wall above the service line so that the ball rebounds in the opposite receiving court but not on the lines. After hitting the front wall the ball may hit the side or back walls, or

both. It *may* be volleyed by the receiver, who does not wait for a floor bounce. Two attempts at service are allowed. If the first is a fault, the second serve is taken from the same side. When both serves are faults there is a loss of point and the serve passes to opponent.

Return of Service and Subsequent Play. To make a good return of service or any play thereafter, the ball must be struck on the volley or before it has touched the floor twice. After being hit it must reach the front wall on the fly, above the tell-tale. Before or after hitting the front wall it may touch any wall, but not the ceiling.

Scoring. A game is won by the player first scoring 15 points, except that:

A. At 13-all the player who first reached the score of 13 elects one of the following:
 1. Set to 5 points, thus an 18 point game
 2. Set to 3 points, thus a 16 point game
 3. No set — game remains 15 points
B. At 14-all, provided the score has not been 13-all, the first player reaching 14 points elects:
 1. Set to 3, a game of 17 points
 2. No set

A *match* is the best three out of five games.

Hinder. It is the responsibility of each player to move on the court so that the opponent has a fair opportunity to see and play the ball. When a player fails to give this opportunity, a "let" or "hinder" is called and the point is replayed from service.

Let. When a let is called, play is stopped and the point replayed. The following constitute lets:

1. A hinder
2. A ball breaks in play
3. After the first bounce the ball rebounds on or above the 6½ foot back line.
4. A player refrains from striking the ball for fear of injuring the opponent.
5. A player is hit by a ball off the racket of her opponent which was *not* traveling directly to the front wall. (Note: In tournament play a ball traveling directly to the front wall and striking an opponent is considered loss of point for the person struck. Without a referee a let is generally accepted.)

Loss of Point.   Situations other than inaccurate returns may cause loss of a point. A ball that has hit the front wall and before being played touches a player or anything she wears or carries, results in loss of point for the player touched.

Doubles Play.   A game of doubles is played by two teams of two players each on a larger court. Play is similar to a singles game, with the major differences being in the order of service.

After a spin of the racket the two partners on a side serve in succession, the first retaining her serve until her side loses a point. On the loss of the next point, the serve passes to the opponents. The order of service is not changed during a game. On the first serve of every game the "in" side is declared "out" after it has lost only one point, as in badminton.

Each time a side becomes "in," the first server selects her service box. Thereafter service areas are alternated through both servers until the side is out or game completed.

STRATEGY

Squash is a game of skilled replacement, speed, endurance, and deception. Consistent winning rarely occurs until skillful strokes are combined with a player's ability to *think* before playing a shot.

As in all racket games the pregame warm-up gives a clue to an opponent's strengths and weaknesses. This is the time for a first analysis of her speed, court position, and strong and weak shots. Specific playing tactics depend on the opponent's strengths and weaknesses.

If the opponent is not more skilled, a beginning player will do well to attempt two key moves:

1. Try to regain the key court position in anticipation of the next play. Usually the most desirable position is the "T," or the spot in front of the intersection of the service areas.

2. Avoid placing shots within easy reach of an opponent. Try to place the ball so the opponent must move out of position for a return.

Service Strategy.   Develop a consistent lob service so that the ball rebounds deep and close to the back and side walls. The hard overhead and spin sidearm serves should be used sparingly as a change of pace.

Receiving Serves.   In anticipation of a lob service, stand inside the court several feet from the center service line and about midway from front to back. The body, crouching, faces the side wall of the service court, and the eyes look to the front wall. The racket is extended up, ready to move.

A well placed lob may be played on the fly by a volley close to the wall. If a volley is not possible, the receiver moves back to attempt play off the side wall after the rebound. Most often the receiver must move toward the back wall, place the racket against the wall, and with no backswing lift the ball to the front wall with strong wrist action. As this is a weak return, an attempt should be made to place the ball down the alley to pull the opponent out of position.

A poor lob service often hits the wall and bounces to midcourt. In anticipation the receiver backs to key court position, forcing the opponent away from the shot while the delayed stroke strategically places the ball on the opposite side of the court.

If a hard serve is executed, a volley may be appropriate. If the ball passes the receiver after hitting the side wall, she moves toward

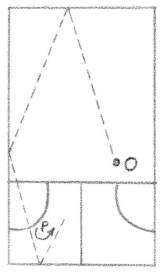

Fig. 13-8. Receiving hard serve. Opponent (O) has served. Player (P) wheels to hit ball as it rebounds from back wall.

the side wall, brings the racket across her body, and turns with the ball as it comes off the back wall. If it took a floor bounce between side and back walls, it must be stroked as it rebounds from the back wall (Fig. 13-8).

Tactical Reminders. The following tips serve as reminders for improving play:

1. Maintain top speed throughout the game so that your opponent will not sense a "let down."

2. Maintain relaxed body position, but always be ready to move.

3. Anticipate your opponent's play by awareness of her court position at all times.

4. Follow the ball with the eyes whenever it is safe to do so.

5. Regain the "T" position after each shot.

6. When your opponent seems to tire, speed up the game by volleys rather than drives; increase service speed and concentrate on placement that makes her move.

7. Unless strategy dictates another shot, hit balls low on the front wall to avoid high rebounds and time for your opponent's positioning.

8. Make each shot with a purpose, and plan to get your opponent out of the way for a clear path to the center of the court.

9. Avoid setting a pattern of play that can be anticipated. That is, do not *always* follow a drive with a corner shot or a left alley shot with a cross court shot.

10. When winning, do not change your style or speed of play.

Situation Play. The following illustrates some common situations and suggested plays *away* from an opponent.

1. With opponent (O) in key court position, the ball is hit by player (P) from the middle of the right service court (Fig. 13-9). Attempt a cross court (A) or alley (B) shot with the forehand. If play were on the left side of the court, backhand strokes would be used.

2. Opponent is in key position as player must retrieve a drop or corner shot (Fig. 13-10). Return with a corner shot (A), or an alley shot (B), if opponent starts to move up.

3. Opponent is left of center. When playing a ball to the right, attempt to shield the shot with the body, execute an alley shot, and move to the "T" (Fig. 13-11A). When

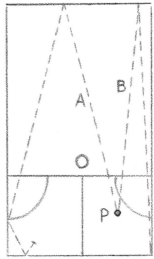

Fig. 13-9. Ball placement when opponent holds key court position.

playing from the center of the court, use an alley shot or corner shot (Fig. 13-11B).

4. The opponent is on the right side of the court moving to key position when the ball is played from deep center court. A forehand stroke down the left alley passes her (Fig. 13-12A). If opponent is moving left and back, play a corner shot or a drop shot (Fig. 13-12 B).

5. An opponent is in deep right court and

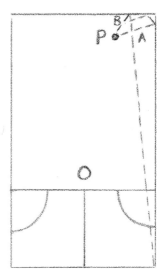

Fig. 13-10. Playing a corner slot by return of corner shot (A), or alley shot (B).

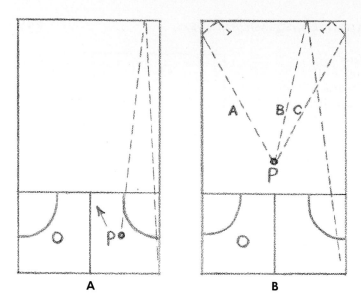

Fig. 13-11. See text for explanation.

A

B

Fig. 13-12. See text for explanation.

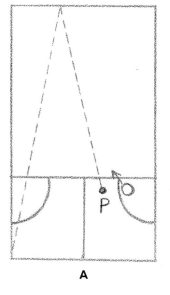

A

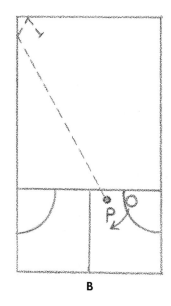

B

Fig. 13-13. Playing the ball away from an opponent moving forward.

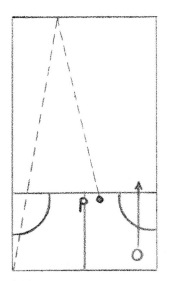

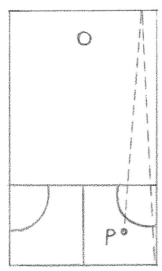

Fig. 13-14. A deep, fast shot passes an opponent left near the front wall.

moving up. A forehand drive to deep left court passes her (Fig. 13-13).

6. The opponent is left near the front wall as the ball is played deep in the court. A low, fast alley shot is usually difficult for her to return (Fig. 13-14).

Terminology

Ace—A point won by a skillful serve or shot that the opponent fails to touch in attempting to hit it.

Alley—An unmarked area comprising the space along either side wall.

Angle shot—A ball that hits the side wall and front wall and rebounds to the court. If hit very low and close to the front wall it is called a corner shot.

Arc—The two quarter circles, each with a radius of 4½ feet, marked in the forehand and backhand receiving courts between the wall and forward line. A player must place at least one foot in an arc when serving.

Backhand court—Left side of the court.

Backspin—A spin of the ball in flight caused by hitting down and under the ball with the racket face. The ball spins back in the direction of the stroke.

Balk—Interference with opponent's attempt to play the ball.

Block shot—A half volley.

Chop—A stroke that imparts backspin to the ball. The racket face strikes the lower part of the ball.

Continental grip—The most popular method of holding the squash racket. This grip requires no change in executing usual strokes.

Corner shot—A shot that hits the side wall low and close to the front wall and then hits the front wall just above the tell-tale.

Cross court shot—A shot delivered from one side of the court diagonally across to the far side of the front wall.

Drop shot—A deceptive shot. The ball is hit easily so that it strikes the front wall and "dies" close to the wall with little rebound.

Fault—Failure to execute a good service. A point is lost only when double faults are made.

Flick—A stroke using a wrist snap with little backswing, used when the ball is hit in a close corner position.

Half volley—Striking a ball *immediately* after it hits the floor.

Hinder—Unintentional interference with opponent's effort to play the ball. A let is called and the point replayed.

Kill—A hard placement shot.

Let—A situation requiring a shot to be replayed.

Out of court—A ball is out of court when it hits above the playing area on the ceiling or lights. A loss of point results.

Tell-tale—A metal strip 17 inches high extending from the front wall 1½ inches into the court. When struck with the ball it makes a resounding noise and indicates a loss of point.

Volley—Striking a ball before it touches the floor.

Suggested Readings

Debany, Walter: *Squash Racquets*, Cranbury, N.J., A. S. Barnes & Co., 1950.

Molloy, Al, Jr., and Lardner, Rex: "The ABCs of Squash Racquets," *Sports Illustrated*, January 7, 1963.

United States Squash Racquets Association: *Official Guide*, Current Edition.

Varner, Margaret, and Bramall, Norman: *Squash Racquets*, Dubuque, Iowa, William C. Brown Company, 1967.

Suggested Study Questions

1. Demonstrate three methods of serving. What are the advantages of each?
2. Why is it important to regain the "T" position after playing the ball?
3. Strategy is based upon your opponent's skill. Assuming equal skill but an opponent "out of condition," what would be your plan of winning?
4. Explain the techniques of a lob, corner shot, and volley. When are these strokes used?
5. Review safety considerations in selection of clothing, proper warm-up and court positioning.

CHAPTER FOURTEEN

Courtesy of Jean Jacobs, Springfield College. Photographed by Matt Grimaldi, 42 Kenmore Drive, Longmeadow, Massachusetts.

STUNTS AND TUMBLING

Stunts and tumbling activities may well be traced to the first child who discovered pleasure and excitement in moving his body in various positions on the ground and through space. It is believed that the Chinese developed the first basic system of gymnastics, including tumbling, for military and medical purposes as early as 2600 B.C. Artifacts of Egyptian culture dating from 2100 to 2000 B.C. indicate that balancing stunts and human pyramid building were practiced in those early times.

The Greeks and later the Romans gave emphasis and status to gymnastic activities as have no cultures before or since those eras. Women as well as men participated in running, throwing, leaping, vaulting, dancing, rope climbing, balancing, and tumbling.

With the decline of Grecian and Roman influence physical activity was de-emphasized. It was not until the Renaissance that systematic physical activity gained a following in Europe. The names of Johann Basedown, Johann Guts-Muths and Friedrich Jahn stand out as exponents of gymnastics in Germany. Adolph Spiess in Switzerland, Peter Ling of Sweden, and Franz Nachtegall of Denmark were others who were influential in developing gymnastic systems which served as patterns or were totally adopted in the United States.

Eventually United States leaders, such as Dudley Sargent and Luther Gulick, added educational emphasis to the systems brought to this country by European ethnic groups. During the past century gymnastic programs have been popular educational activities during times of national crises when indi-

Fig. 14-1. Stunts and tumbling develop agility, balance, strength, power, and flexibility. (Courtesy of the Los Angeles Public Schools.)

vidual fitness was stressed. At other times the program has been de-emphasized as too disciplined an approach to United States education. Today, with a national concern for youth and adult fitness, the value of stunts and tumbling as basic physical activities is unquestionable.

NATURE AND PURPOSE OF THE ACTIVITY

Stunts and tumbling activities are basic motor movements that involve balancing, rolling, turning, springing, and twisting. Using limited facilities and equipment, selected activities can develop many of the components of physical fitness. Although the pleasure and skill of stunts and tumbling are complete within the activities, the body control and movements developed are basic for advanced apparatus and gymnastic work.

Tumbling develops agility, balance, strength, power, and flexibility. Timing and coordination are achieved through controlled body movements; agility and flexibility result from bending, twisting, turning, and tucking.

Springing and balancing develop general muscular strength with emphasis on the legs and upper body.

Aside from the physical factors inherent in the activity, daring and courage are developed as the participant learns to control her body in more advanced movements. Decisive actions are immediate outcomes of tumbling. A lifetime safety skill, that of falling and rolling correctly, may be carried over to other sport activities.

FACILITIES AND EQUIPMENT

Little space and equipment are needed for an instructional stunt and tumbling program. Outdoors, grass or sand surfaces may be used, while indoors a gymnasium or a multipurpose or tumbling room is desirable. Many balancing stunts can be performed on bare floors or outside surfaces, but indoors, rolling and twisting should be executed on mats.

Padded horsehair or sponge rubber mats, 2 or 3 inches thick and 5 to 10 feet long, are easily handled in instructional classes. Longer mats of 60 feet are desirable for competitive

Fig. 14-2. College women as well as high school girls find stunts and tumbling both fun to do and physically challenging! (Courtesy of Clifford Lewis, University of Georgia.)

events. For cleanliness the mats should have removable washable covers, or plastic or vinyl covers, which may be sponged with disinfectant before use.

For safety there must be an adequate takeoff and clearing area at each end of the mat. When more than one row of mats is needed, they must be arranged so that there is no possibility of contact between participants. For advanced work a safety belt is desirable for spotting.

Leotards or one piece gymnasium costumes are ideal for instruction. If shorts and shirt are worn the shirt tail should be secured and elastic-leg undergarments worn. Clothing must never restrict the tumbler's movements.

BASIC SKILLS

CONDITIONERS

The following selected stunts are appropriate as conditioners and warm-up for more advanced skills. These stunts, involving one, two, or more participants, call for unique body positions or movement combinations.

INDIVIDUAL STUNTS

WALKS AND HOPS

Elephant Walk. Standing on both feet, bend forward at the waist, clasping hands and

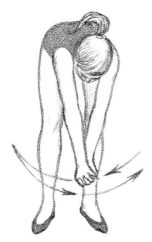

Fig. 14-3. Elephant walk.

allowing them to hang in imitation of an elephant's trunk. While maintaining a rounded back, walk with straight knees allowing the arms to swing naturally from side to side. Try to touch the floor with the hands.

Bear Walk. Standing on both feet, bend forward and place the hands on the floor. While keeping straight arms and legs, exaggerate the body sway from side to side as a lumbering bear would walk.

Fig. 14-4. Bear walk.

Lame Dog Walk. Bend forward and place hands on the floor. Lift one leg from the floor and extend it backward in line with the back. Move the body forward by pushing from the floor with the hands and the supporting foot. Repeat stunt using the other leg.

Crab Walk. From a squat position reach behind the body and place the hands flat on the floor under the shoulders. Straighten the back and support the body weight on both arms and legs. Walk backward, using the right arm and right leg simultaneously, then left arm and left leg.

Inch Worm. Lean forward in an extended position with legs and arms straight. Keep the hands stationary and walk the feet to the hands by flexing the hips and lifting the straight legs. Then keep feet stationary and walk the hands away from the feet to your original position.

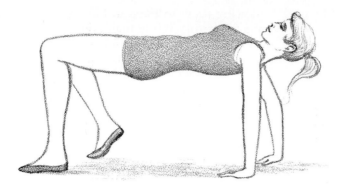

Fig. 14-5. Crab walk.

Fig. 14-6. Inch worm.

Seal Walk. Begin from a prone position resting on extended arms, hands under shoulders. The toes are pointed so that the weight is carried on top of the feet. Move the body forward by walking with the hands, dragging legs and feet.

Folded Leg Walk. While sitting on the mat, use hands to help cross legs as high as possible on opposite thighs. Fold arms across the chest or place them at the side for balance. Straighten the body to the kneeling position and walk forward on the knees.

Fig. 14-7. Seal walk.

Fig. 14-8. Folded leg walk.

Bear Dance. Assume a squat position with arms folded across the chest. Hop on the left foot while extending the right foot forward. The back remains straight. Hop on the left foot, draw the extended foot under the body and extend the left leg. Continue alternate hopping and extension.

Frog Hop. Begin in a squat position with hips low. Feet point slightly outward. Place the hands inside the feet with elbows slightly bent. Rock forward and push off with the hands. The legs hop and hands land just ahead of the feet. The forward movement must be rhythmical so that the body moves forward and arms or legs do not carry undue weight.

Fig. 14-9. Kangaroo hop.

Kangaroo Hop. With arms folded across the chest, assume a squat position with toes slightly out (Fig. 14-9). Lean forward, push with the legs and spring forward from the floor as high in the air as possible. Land on the balls of the feet and flex the ankles, knees, and hips to absorb the landing shock.

JUMPS AND BALANCES

Backward Jump. Stand on the mat with toes at the edge, heels toward the center. Jump backward as far as possible while swinging the arms forcibly down and back. Land lightly on the toes with flexed ankles and hips.

Backward Kick. Jump in place on both feet four times. On the fourth jump, kick both heels backward. Land lightly on the toes.

Jump and Slap Heels. From a standing position with hands at the side, jump into the air and lift heels outward and up to the sides. Slap the heels with the hands. Return to original position.

Balance Stand. Stand on left leg, bend the body forward to a right angle with the leg. Extend the free leg behind the body. Head is up and arms are horizontal at the sides of the body.

Half Top Spin. Begin in a standing, side stride position. Push off from the floor and swing the arms and trunk in the direction of the body turn. Land lightly on the starting spot facing the opposite direction.

Turk Stand. In a standing position, legs crossed, and weight on the outer edges of the feet, fold the arms across the chest. Sit down easily with arms and legs crossed. Rock slightly forward so that weight moves over the feet and rise to a standing position.

Cork Screw. Stand erect with feet 12 to 15 inches apart, arms comfortably at the sides. Place a handkerchief or other small object near and outside the toe of the right foot. The feet remain flat on the floor but the knees may bend as the left arm swings around the back of the right leg so that the arm and hand may reach through the legs to pick up the object (Fig. 14-10). Move the object to the left foot and reach with the right arm.

Heel Clicks. Begin from an erect standing position with the right foot slightly forward. Shift the weight to the right foot as the left leg is raised to the side. Push off from the right foot and raise this foot to meet the

Fig. 14-10. Cork screw.

extended left leg. Click the heels together and land on the right foot. Alternate push off feet.

Variations: (1) Push off from both feet, bending knees outward and clicking the heels twice before landing. (2) Push off with the rear foot and extend legs forward for heel click with legs extended in front of the body.

Dip. Kneel on a mat and place a piece of crumpled paper 12 to 14 inches from the knees in front of the body. With the hands clasped behind the back lean forward, bending the head and trunk. Grasp the paper with the teeth and pull up to starting position without losing balance. Move the paper farther from the body to increase flexibility and balance.

PREPARATIONS FOR ROLLS

Individual Squash. The body weight is supported on the hands and knees, positioned so that the upper arms and legs are at right angles to the trunk. Keeping the head high, push the arms forward and extend the legs backward at the same time so that the body falls to the mat in an extended prone position.

Log Roll. Lie across a mat on the back with the arms extended overhead and the legs straight. Roll slowly toward the end of the mat by twisting hips and shoulders in the direction of the roll. Body must move as a coordinated unit.

Egg Roll. Cross legs and kneel, facing the side of the mat. Fold arms, wrapping them across the chest, and lean forward on them. Push with arms and knees to start momentum, and roll to the side, onto the back, to the other side, and to original position.

Upswing. Kneel on the floor or mat with weight on balls of feet. The upper body is erect as the arms first swing back behind the body, then forcefully forward as the body rises and weight shifts over the balls of the feet without a break in the movements. The forward arm thrust and strong leg extension bring the body to a standing position.

STUNTS FOR TWO

Bouncing Ball. One of the partners (the "ball") assumes a squatting position, with arms clasped around the knees. Weight is on the balls of the feet.

Partner number 2 taps the "ball" on the back to make the "ball" begin a bouncing spring from the floor. The "ball" maintains a curled position with hips low and head down as the tapper continues to set the springing rhythm.

Chinese Get-up. Partners stand back to back with locked elbows. Bracing against each other's back, each partner takes small steps to "walk herself" to a sitting position with legs outstretched.

To rise, bring the legs and feet close to the buttocks, brace against the partner's back and the floor. Both partners extend their legs at the same time and come to a standing position.

Churn the Butter. Partners stand back to back with elbows locked. One partner bends forward from the hips as the other springs up and back to rest her back against that of the other (Fig. 14-12). The top partner lifts her legs at right angles to the trunk. As the partner underneath straightens, the other lowers her feet and legs and returns to standing position. Repeat, with partners alternating positions and actions.

Rocker. Partners sit on the floor facing each other. With legs together partner 1 slides her feet under the buttocks of partner 2. Number 2 places her legs outside those of number 1 and slides her feet under number 1. Pulling their bodies close together each partner grasps the other's shoulders. Number 1 rocks back and pulls number 2 forward by the shoulders while lifting her from the ground with the rocker action of the feet. Partner number 2 rocks back and pulls number 1 forward and upward. Continue in a rhythmical rocking motion.

Fig. 14-11. Couple stunts require cooperative effort and mutual confidence. (Courtesy of College of Health, Physical Education and Recreation, Texas Woman's University, Denton, Texas.)

Fig. 14-12. Churn the butter.

TUMBLING SKILLS

INDIVIDUAL STUNTS

Forward Roll. Assume a squatting position with arms about shoulder width apart, hands on the mat just in front of the toes, with fingers extended forward. With weight on the toes, tuck the chin to the chest, round the back and lean forward. As the forward lean pulls the body to the mat push with the feet and hands to increase power and momentum. As the body rolls bend the elbows to ease the back of the shoulders to the mat first (Fig. 14-13). As the weight is transferred to the shoulders take the hands from the mat and grasp the shins to keep the body in a tight tuck. The forward roll momentum continues to bring the body weight back to the feet. Straighten to a standing position.

After mastering the roll from a squat, begin from a standing position. Bend the knees and lean forward pushing with the feet. The hands and arms carry the body weight to the back of the shoulders as described above.

Fig. 14-13.   Forward roll.

Fig. 14-14.   Squat head balance.

Further skill development leads to a run toward the edge of the mat, a spring up and forward before reaching for the mat and bringing the body to a forward roll.

Backward Roll.   Start from a squat with toes toward the edge of the mat and hands near the end. Weight is supported on the hands and balls of the feet. The back is rounded and chin is tucked to the chest. Rock slightly forward to begin a coordinated movement, and then push off backward with the hands so the body rolls first to a sitting position and then to the rounded back. The chin remains tucked and the knees move closer to the chest. As the hips rise above the shoulders the hands move quickly over the shoulders, palms up and fingers leading, to contact the mat and carry the body weight across the shoulders. As the toes drop down to the mat near the head, push firmly with the hands so that the body rolls up onto both feet.

After learning the backward roll from a squat, begin from a standing position. In one continuous movement bend the knees and sit down on the mat keeping the feet as close to the body as possible. Rock back to begin the roll, execute the roll, and return to a standing position as soon as the feet touch the mat and assume the body weight.

Squat Head Balance.   Begin from a squat, with weight on toes and hands. The hands are on the mat under the shoulders with elbows inside and below the knees. The knees rest on the elbows. Lean forward and place the head on the mat 6 to 8 inches in front of the hands (Fig. 14-14). The hands and forehead form the triangular base over which the body balances as the toes lift from the mat. Descend by pushing into a forward roll or lowering the feet one at a time.

Head Balance.   The headstand may be reached from a squat head balance by pushing the knees against the elbows for the initial thrust and slowly extending the legs until they are overhead.

To reach a head balance from a squat position with feet on the floor, place the hands and forehead on the mat in a triangular base. As the fingers push to maintain balance, kick one leg up and then the other, arching the back to adjust to the balance position.

To recover, lower one leg and then the other, or tuck the chin, round the back, and end with a forward roll.

Squat Hand Balance.   This "tip-up" is similar in execution to the squat head balance, except that the head does not touch the floor. In a squatting position, the hands are between knees and the knees braced against the elbows. The head is lifted and the fingers and arms press down to maintain balance.

Head and Forearm Balance.   Place forearms and hands on the mat with thumbs almost touching. The forehead is placed between the hands to form the apex of the triangular base. The palms of the hands may be flat on the floor or clasped behind the head. Walk the hips to a near vertical position then kick one leg up and bring the other to the balance point (Fig. 14-15).

Descend as from headstand.

Handstand.   Place hands on the mat spread shoulder distance apart. The elbows are straight and the fingers are spread and pointing forward. Move shoulders over the hands and kick one leg and then the other overhead. The back is arched and the head is up, with firm extension through the hips and legs. Press with the wrists and fingers to maintain balance. Descend by lowering one leg at a time, or by bending the elbows,

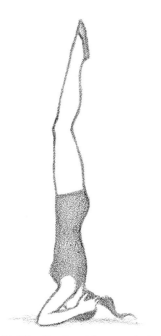

Fig. 14-15. Head and forearm balance.

lowering the head, and tucking the chin to execute a forward roll.

Dive and Forward Roll. Approach the mat with a short run and dive toward the mat with arms and hands extended. Landing on the hands to support the body, the arms bend and chin is tucked so the weight is transferred to the back of the shoulders. Proceed as in a forward roll.

Cartwheel. This movement, which makes the body resemble a moving wheel, may be done on either the left or right sides. Ideally, it should be practiced on both.

Begin with the left side of the body facing down the mat. The feet are in side stride position with arms extended upward and outward like spokes in a wheel. Rock slightly to the right to begin momentum; bend and twist slightly to the left side to prepare to place the left hand on the mat when left leg pushes off. The right leg is off the ground and extended as the left leg pushes from the ground and is lifted upward. The forward momentum shifts the weight from the left to the right hand, which is now on the mat. The elbows remain straight, the head is kept up for balance, and the knees and hips are extended. See Figure 14-16.

The legs swing over the right hand and the right leg touches down with hip and knee bent to carry the weight. The left leg follows and shares the weight.

One Arm Cartwheel. The "wheel" now has only three spokes. Beginning with the left side facing down the mat, extend the left arm and put the right arm at the side. The weight is carried on the left arm with a more rapid revolution of the legs.

Roundoff. The purpose of the roundoff is to change the forward running motion into a backward motion so that backward stunts may be performed. The roundoff may be executed either to the left or right and is logically learned after the cartwheel.

Fig. 14-16. Cartwheel.

Fig. 14-17. Roundoff.

To turn the body to the left, skip on right foot, and as weight shifts to the left foot the left arm comes to the mat about 2 feet in front of the left foot. The head is up as the right foot and leg are kicked overhead and joined by the left. The right hand is placed on the mat slightly in front of and across the left hand as the body makes a half turn overhead. The feet snap down to the mat and hands push off at the same time. The body lands with the weight on the balls of the feet, arms overhead, and facing in the opposite direction from which it began.

Neckspring. This skill is often called a kip or a snap-up. From a sitting position with the legs extended forward, roll backward, and thrust the hands straight back over the shoulders and well under the shoulders so that the thumbs are close to the ears and the fingers point forward. The weight is on the shoulders, as the legs are well over the trunk and head, and the hips are high. Quickly snap the legs forward and upward, arch the back and push vigorously with hands, head and shoulders. Bend the knees and bring the feet under the body to land. Snap the upper body forward and land in a squatting position.

Headspring. In learning this skill begin from two rolled mats, and then one, before

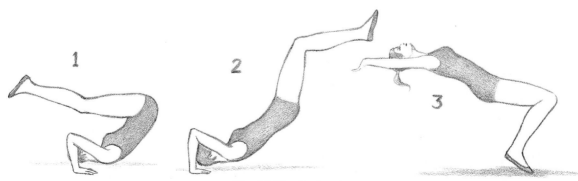

Fig. 14-18. Neckspring.

Fig. 14-19. Headspring.

working directly on a flat mat. More body spring and leg snap are needed as the body gets closer to the floor.

In a squatting position the head and hands are on the mat with the head about 6 inches in front of the hands. Both legs are lifted from the mat in a piked position and then extended, with hips and legs over the head. The legs and hips continue forward and the hips are forcibly extended as they go beyond the vertical position. Push the head and hands forcefully from the mat, arch the back, and snap the legs forward and down toward the mat. As the feet land under the body, snap the upper body upward and forward.

Front Handspring. This stunt should be learned at first over a rolled mat with a spotter or over a partner for support.

The bent arm and straight arm handsprings are similar, the major difference being that in the straight arm spring the elbows are kept firm and the shoulders push as the legs snap over. The bent arm handspring is described here.

From a run and skip on the right foot bring the left foot to the mat. Bend forward at the hips and place the hands ahead of the left foot. The right foot kicks overhead, followed by the left. Snap both legs forward and downward while pushing from the mat with the hands and forcibly extending the elbows. The head remains forward as long as possible. Arch the back so that the feet drop well under the body. Snap the upper body forward; land in a squat and then stand erect.

Handstand to Forward Roll. Assume a handstand position with head up. Hold the stand momentarily, then allow the legs to go slightly forward out of balance, bend elbows equally to lower the body, tuck chin, and flex legs toward the body. The body weight is carried on the shoulders to the rounded back and forward to standing position.

Handstand to Chest Roll. Assume a handstand position. Keep the head up and arch the back to keep balance. Gently lower the body by bending the elbows and pushing back with the hands. The weight rolls to the chest, abdomen, thighs, and extended toes. The rocker action moves completely down the body.

Backward Roll to Handstand. Movements to the head or hand balance positions are similar, with the difference lying in the balance points of the stands. The following describes the handstand.

From a sitting position begin a backward roll. As the back of the head touches the mat, forcibly snap the hips, and extend the legs upward as the hands and arms push to allow the head to pass under the body and lift. Arch the back. The hands may have to move slightly back to adjust the correct balance point.

Forward Somersault. This advanced technique should not be attempted without a tumbling belt and skilled spotters.

Begin with a run, a high skip on the left foot while bringing the right foot forward. Both arms reach forcefully overhead as the

Fig. 14-20.   Handstand to forward roll.

Fig. 14-21.   Handstand to chest roll.

Fig. 14-22.   Backward roll to handstand.

234

body springs from the balls of both feet into a near vertical hurdle. As the body rises to nearly the highest point of the hurdle the chin tucks and the arms move forward and downward to grasp the shins. The heels are close to the buttocks and the knees are pulled tightly to the chest. As the body nears a complete turn, quickly straighten from the tuck and land in a starting position on the mat.

Backward Somersault. The backward somersault is another advanced technique that requires skilled spotters. Standing on the mat with feet about shoulder width apart, the tumbler bends the knees, drops the arms to the side and back and then springs straight up from the feet while thrusting the arms upward. When the height of the jump is reached, snap the head back, tuck the knees to the chest, and grasp the shins firmly to pull the legs over the body. The body remains tucked until the ground is seen, then the tuck opens so that the body lands on the feet.

BALANCES FOR TWO

Chest Balance. Partner number 1 kneels on all fours, keeping her back flat. Partner number 2 places her arms under the chest of her partner, reaching from near to far side. With her shoulders far over the other's body, partner number 2 kicks into an inverted balance position with head up and back arched.

Fig. 14-23.   Chest balance.

Return to the floor by lowering the legs one at a time.

Angel Balance (Belly Swan). One partner lies on her back with feet and arms raised upright. She places the soles of her feet across the top of her partner's hip bone with toes angling outward. The partners grasp hands

Fig. 14-24.   Angel balance.

as the top partner leans forward and moves to an arched balance position over the base partner. When balance is reached, the hand grip is released and the top partner arches her back, raises her head and arms while supported only by the base partner's feet. The partner below lowers her arms to the mat.

When descending, partners again grasp hands as the base partner bends and lowers her legs to allow the top partner's feet to touch the mat.

Thigh Balance.   Both partners face in the same direction as the partner behind leans forward from the hips and bends the knees so that the front partner can straddle her neck in a sitting mount. The base partner keeps her knees and hips slightly flexed and leans slightly forward as the top partner places her feet on the base's thighs. Top straightens her legs as the base supports her by grasping her thighs above the knees. Top arches her back and leans forward with head and chest erect.

To dismount, top relaxes her knees and

drops forward to her feet as the base releases her hold.

Knee and Shoulder Balance.   The base partner lies on her back with knees bent and feet flat on the floor. She raises her arms diagonally upward. Top partner steps between the base's feet and places her hands backward on base's knees. As the top leans forward the base extends her arms and places her hands on the front of top's shoulders. The top partner kicks up to an inverted balance with her weight supported by the straight arms of the base and her own hands on base's knees. The back is arched and head is up.

On descending the base pushes top's shoulders back as top partner flexes hips and brings the legs to the floor.

Fig. 14-26.   Knee and shoulder balance.

Foot to Hand Balance.   The base partner lies on her back with hands beside her head, palms up; legs and feet are extended straight up. The top partner stands lightly with soles of her feet in base partner's hands while pushing downward with her hands on the bottoms of the base's feet. Simultaneously, the base lifts her arms straight up. When the feet of the top partner are secure and balanced, she releases her hands from base's

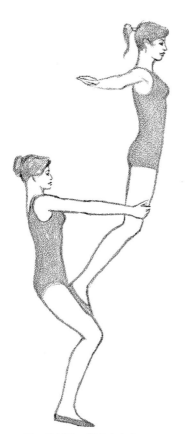

Fig. 14-25.   Thigh balance.

Fig. 14-27. Foot to hand balance.

feet. The base lowers her feet to the mat and the top partner stands erect with arms at the side for balance.

To dismount, base raises her feet for top to grasp for support. Base bends her elbows and releases grasp on top's feet. Top drops feet in wide stride landing on either side of base partner's shoulders.

PYRAMIDS

Pyramid building is often called "picture making," and the resulting pattern appeals to spectators in addition to being fun for the participants.

In pyramid building there are few rules and many opportunities for students to express individual ideas and movements. Using the basic tools of individual, partner, and group balances, many patterns can be developed, ranging from simple stunts to complex movements using apparatus.

When designing and executing pyramids remember:

1. A pyramid has symmetry and may have its high point in the center unit, on either end or elsewhere in the pattern.

2. The floor pattern may be a circle, spokes of a wheel, a rectangle, semicircle, triangle, or other basic design.

3. A pyramid requires unity and timing when building and dismounting.

4. Sturdy members should form the base while lighter persons are the tops.

5. The back arches of the base supports should be reasonably similar.

6. Where height is viewed (e.g., headstands, foot to hand balances) try to balance the heights on opposite ends or sides.

7. Pyramid members must maintain control and stability while the pyramid is held in its "finished form."

SAFETY

Safety must be considered in all tumbling activities. The student must assume some responsibility by being properly dressed,

Fig. 14-28. Pyramid building requires both individual skill and group cooperation. (Courtesy of the Los Angeles Public Schools.)

Fig. 14-29. Pyramids.

without jewelry or objects in her pockets. She must never attempt skills for which she is poorly prepared.

Always be certain the mats are properly placed and secure and a safe distance away from obstacles or other tumblers.

When attempting new skills, work with one or more trained spotters. With the assistance of the instructor learn to spot with the hands and tumbling belt to help others. Hand spotting requires the use of the hand and arm to assist a person doing a stunt, in order to prevent an injury from improper execution. Spotting with the belt requires holding a rope and lifting it, and thus the belt, for the tumbler's support.

Terminology

Arch—Hyperextension of the back with shoulders relaxed.
Balance—To maintain equilibrium while in a stationary as well as in a moving position.
Flex—To bend.
Prone—Lying full length with the face downward.
Spotter—Person assisting the performer in order to prevent injury.
Squat—In tumbling, a movement which brings knees up to the chest.
Tuck—Knees are bent and brought close to the chest.

Selected Audio-visual Aids

Beginning Tumbling and Balancing and Advanced Tumbling and Balancing. (Filmstrips.) The Athletic Institute, 805 Merchandise Mart, Chicago, Ill. 60654.

Beginning Tumbling; Intermediate Tumbling; Advanced Tumbling; Simple Stunts. (16 mm., b & w.) Coronet Instructional Films, Coronet Building, Chicago, Ill.
Headsprings in the Gym. (16 mm., b & w.) Encyclopedia Britannica, 1150 Wilmette Avenue, Wilmette, Ill.
Tumbling. (16 mm., b & w.) Champions on Film, 303 S. Main, Ann Arbor, Mich.
Tumbling for Physical Fitness. (16 mm., b & w.) Castle Films Division, 1145 Park Avenud, New York, N.Y.

Periodicals

Amateur Athletic Union Gymnastics Yearbook, 233 Broadway, New York, N.Y. 10007
The Modern Gymnast, P.O. Box 611, Santa Monica, Calif.

Suggested Readings

Armbruster, David, Irwin, Leslie, and Musker, Frank: *Basic Skills in Sports*, 4th Ed., St. Louis, The C. V. Mosby Co., 1967.
Bailey, James: *Gymnastic Activities in Schools*, Boston, Allyn & Bacon, Inc., 1965.
Pond, Charles: *Tumbling in Total Gymnastics*, Champaign, Illinois, Stipes Publishing Company, 1965.
Vannier, Maryhelen, and Fait, Hollis: *Teaching Physical Education in Secondary Schools*. 3rd Ed., Philadelphia, W. B. Saunders Company, 1968.

Suggested Study Questions

1. What is the skill progression necessary before executing a handspring?
2. Design a pyramid using 12 tumblers who can do only basic balancing stunts.
3. What stunts do you recommend for building arm strength in preparation for the headstand?
4. Describe how you and a partner could execute an angel balance.

CHAPTER FIFTEEN

Courtesy of *Surfer Magazine*, John Severson Publications, Dana Point, Calif.

SURFING

Surfing includes every kind of surf-propelled motion, but to the majority of people today it means only "stand up surfing" on a board. Modern films and television have brought the sport of surfing to the awareness of every sports-loving American. The beauty and thrill of a man riding a board on the crest of a wave from the unknown sea to the beach hold excitement and appreciation for all.

The identity of the first surfer is lost in antiquity, but there is very little doubt that early in man's history he used his body, logs, and canoe-type boats to move on the top of the water to land. The motions of animals indicate that they preceded man by many years in surfing ability. One needs only to see seals, sea lions, and penguins surfing with complete finesse to appreciate their skill. Surfing probably originated with the Polynesians off their home islands of Tahiti and Bora Bora in the Western Pacific. A group migrated eastward to the present Hawaiian Islands between 800 and 1100 A.D. and with them came the prototype of today's modern boards.

Although Europe and North Africa have beaches where the waves offer real surfing thrills, Europeans and westerners did not see the sporting possibilities as did the peoples whose lives depended upon and revolved around the water. Polynesians were riding waves with and without boards when swimming ability was still rare among Europeans. These early surfers gave ritual and meaning to the "sport of kings."

In 1777 a British explorer and sea captain, James Cook, sailed to Tahiti on his third voyage into the Southern Hemisphere. Walking along the shore he observed "a man paddling in a small canoe and looking about with such eagerness on each side." The native paddled from shore until he approached a place where the swells began to take their rise. He then "paddled before it and with great quickness 'til he found that it overtook him." Leaving Tahiti, Cook followed the same northeastern route to the Hawaiian Islands that the Polynesians had taken centuries before. He passed the island of Oahu and moored off Kauai in January, 1778. It was on this voyage that he and his crew recorded their astonishment at the sight of the large, handsome Hawaiian nobles riding the crests of the waves on their long *olos* made of wiliwili wood.

Scant mention is made of surfing for the next 50 years, although the natives continued to surf as both a sport and a religious ritual. By 1820 a few white traders, adventurers, agriculturists, and Calvinist missionaries arrived and greatly influenced the history of the island people. With the white man came disease, death, social disruption, and individual demoralization. The most obvious impact upon native culture came from missionary zeal. The natives were imbued with thoughts of guilt and sin and a sense of false modesty that resulted in restrictive clothing and long muumuus. The hula, native music, surfing, and other traditional activities were banned as pagan. The Hawaiians almost lost their art, and their national sport—surfing—entered a period of dark ages.

A brief revival of surfing began under King Kalakaua, but the real renaissance was delayed until the 20th century. Duke Kahanamouku, an Olympic gold medal winner who is well remembered for introducing the flutter kick to the crawl stroke, was largely responsible for surfing's rebirth. He led a group of young men in the pleasures of the surf at Waikiki where their play and feats attracted such dignitaries as Alexander Hume Ford and Jack London. London surfed and wrote enthusiastically about the sport. Ford remained in Hawaii and started, stimulated, and sponsored the Outrigger Canoe Club to advance the almost forgotten arts of surfing with canoes and boards.

Men and ideas change, and today one of the great appeals Hawaii holds for the tourist is its surf. Although the sport has leaped the

241

Pacific and can be seen on coasts in the United States, Peru, Australia, and even Europe, Hawaii is still the "fatherland" to the enthusiast. Hawaii's beaches are the sites of annual pilgrimages in search of the perfect surf.

NATURE AND PURPOSE OF THE SPORT

Surfing in its broadest definition includes any activity that can be performed along a beach and in breaking waves. The most fundamental skill and purest form is *body surfing*. The rider is in direct contact with the wave. The body takes different positions in riding the waves on the crests and in the hollows, as a straight-ahead ride, or simulating the action of a board on the big breakers.

Mat surfing is adventurous, enjoyable, and accessible. A rubber float, air-filled pillow-cases, or mattress covers serve as variations or substitutes for the mat. A mat can be used for glides in front of broken waves, for wild curl rides, or for crashing over the falls on large breaking waves. Mats are ridden in prone, kneeling, or standing positions, but it takes a great deal of practice to stand on a mat. Only lightweight surfers really master this technique.

Belly board surfing utilizes a small plywood or plastic board that is ridden lying on the chest and abdomen. The surfer using a *paipo board*, as they are called in Hawaii, often uses swim fins to aid in getting to the wave and catching it. *Skim boarding* is similar in that a round or oval piece of plywood is used. The board is tossed in shallow surf, and the surfer jumps aboard to ride the fast, low breakers.

Boat surfing includes canoes, dories, catamarans, and any type of boat that can be taken to the point of breaking waves far from shore and brought in to the beach on the momentum of the wave.

Board surfing is the most spectacular and thrilling skill for the true surfing enthusiast. The surfer paddles out to a point where she can manipulate her board, catch the force of the wave, and ride it prone, kneeling, or standing back to the beach.

Wake surfing is still a relatively new innovation in which the surfer is pulled initially by a power boat which creates a wake. As the wake builds the surfer releases or relaxes the tow, catches the wake, and rides it behind the boat. It is a skill which has developed for the board surfer who does not have beaches and the natural surf available.

FACILITIES AND EQUIPMENT

Surfing can require as little as a wave and a person to ride it. For board surfers almost any board suffices for paddling and getting in condition, but finding the custom board for an individual is dependent upon the surfer's size and weight and the size of the waves she will encounter. The evolution and refinement of lightweight surfboards of 30 to 35 pounds is, in large measure, responsible for the increasing number of women surfers.

Boards. Boards are made of foam with a fiberglass covering. Three major construction techniques are usually followed:

1. *Foam in skin* is one of the cheapest methods of building a board. A premolded fiberglass shell is filled with foam. These mass-produced boards are often called "popouts."

2. *Preshaped or hard shell boards* are also relatively inexpensive. A molded foam with a hard shell is produced which is then treated with fiberglass and resin.

3. *Hand-shaped custom boards* are made from an average foam blank and shaped to an individual's specifications. This method of construction is the most expensive, but generally the manufacturer uses a high quality foam and glassing material, which assures greater durability and board versatility. Such a custom design will give a choice of length, width, shape, fin, rocker, approximate weight, and glass finish, as well as color and striping.

Wetsuits. These are a must for the year-round surfer. These neoprene rubber suits trap water and heat it to body temperature. There are different designs, but most surfers presently prefer the sleeveless, short pant suit.

Helmets. Crash helmets weigh about 16 ounces and are made of a fiberglass shell and polystyrene liner. In some competitive events helmets are now required. They are worn by an increasing number of surfers in congested areas.

Fins. Swim fins are rubber flippers that are used as aids in swimming and are recom-

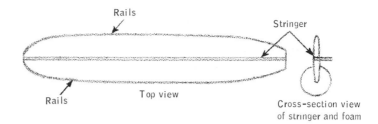

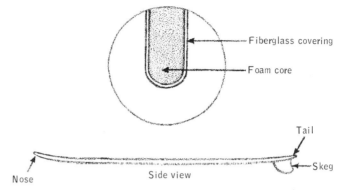

Fig. 15-1. A modern foam and fiberglass surfboard.

mended for the body surfer and the paipo board surfer.

PURCHASE AND CARE OF EQUIPMENT

The best assurance of receiving dollar value for a board, whether new or used, and one which suits the individual, is to buy from a responsible dealer or manufacturer. Inexpensive boards are rarely a bargain, for they are often poorly balanced, improperly reinforced with stringers, and more readily subject to damage because of their inferior foam and fiberglass.

In evaluating a board look for a rigid, noncompressed fiberglass covering free of all blemishes. The skeg should be well beaded where it joins the tail of the board. The built-up area between the skeg and the bottom of the board reinforces the skeg. Table 15-1 indicates suggested board dimensions for a relatively buoyant board, often called a floater.

A surfboard receives hard knocks and is bound to be damaged at one time or another. *Dings*, damaged areas, usually occur from a strong impact or when the board is hit by sharp objects. The majority of fractures and holes can be prevented by careful handling during transit, avoiding collisions with other boards, and keeping the board from rocks, pilings, and piers after wipe-outs. Small dings can await repair, but if delayed too long the foam will become discolored. If the board has a large chunk or portion ripped from it, it should be repaired by a competent craftsman

Table 15-1. *Suggested Surfboard Dimensions**

Weight of Surfer	Length of Board	Width of Board	Thickness
under 100 lbs.	8'9"	21½"	2¾"
100–120 lbs.	9'	22"	3"
120–150 lbs.	9'6"	22"	3"
150–175 lbs.	9'8" or 9'10"	23"	3½"
175–200 lbs.	10' or 10'2"	23½"	4"
200 lbs. and over	10'2" and over	24"	4"

*Dixon, Peter L., *The Complete Book of Surfing*, p. 25.

immediately. Torn or jagged areas of glass are dangerous to the surfer and to those nearby. A general rule to follow in caring for a surfboard is to "treat it like a piece of furniture—avoiding prolonged dampness and excessive heat."

Transporting a board on conventional automobiles is relatively simple when a commercially manufactured carrying top designed for two or more boards is used. Owners of panel trucks, beach buggies, and convertible automobiles should place the boards inside and pad them well to avoid damage from other boards and equipment. Be certain the surfboard is *secured* on top or within the auto, for a loose board on the highway is a hazard to all motorists.

There are several methods of carrying the board to the surf. *Never drag it.* For a short distance, lift the board to a balanced position under one arm, with the skeg in front in full view. For longer distances, carry the board on the head, safari style, or on the shoulder with one rail resting between the forearm and upper arm and the elbow cradle.

Before storing the board, wash it thoroughly to remove excess sand and salt and place it on a rack either horizontally or vertically and away from direct sunlight, excessive heat, and moisture.

BASIC SKILLS

All methods of surfing are dependent upon the principle of catching and riding waves. Surfing waves are formed either by winds blowing across the surface of the water or by the wake created by a power boat. Each wave has a character of its own which is dependent on ocean bottom, sand bars, shore reefs, or other obstructions, as well as the distance the wave travels.

BODY SURFING

Body surfing is the least expensive of all surfing methods and probably requires the keenest judgment and the most advanced swimming skills. To catch a wave requires perfect timing as well as several powerful strokes to launch the body and slide down the face of the wave. Fins are useful in obtaining the burst of speed needed to catch the wave. Individual styles vary, as in board surfing, but generally the hands and arms are used as outriggers to control the position of the body on the wave. At takeoff the chest is inflated with air for additional bouyancy. Once the wave is caught, the style of riding becomes an individual matter. Some surfers "lay in" to the wave with their backs to the wall of water and their arms out in front. On a steep curling wave some prefer to place a shoulder into the wall with one arm straight up in the air. Others prefer to leave both arms at the sides until the waves get steep and the body starts to sideslip. Only then does the outside arm drop to act as a rudder and hold the body in the wave.

BOARD SURFING

A beginning *board surfer* needs to know a little about basic oceanography, marine life, tides and currents, and the effect of weather on the sea and surf, and quite a bit more about swimming. The basic swimming requirements are the ability to swim one-half mile and stay afloat for a minimum of 15 minutes. A surfer soon decides whether to concentrate on the rare big surf or to get the most fun and excitement from the small surf. Few girls and women tackle the big surf, but many have joined the growing group of "hot doggers" who try to get the most speed and the most exciting ride from small and medium surf. It is for this growing group that these basic skills are intended.

As a beginning surfer, go where the others are and learn about the ocean bottom, the ebbs, and the dangers of a given area. Talk with surfers and learn much from their experience in the spot

Launching the Board. Before launching the board, rub paraffin wax to the top of it where the feet will contact the surface. Wax diminishes the slickness of the board when wet. For the beginner, this usually means the entire surface.

Launch the board during a calm period between waves and out of the danger of hidden obstructions and rocks. The board is placed with the nose pointing directly into the surf. A board lying broadside will be washed into the surfer or to the shore.

Paddling. Climb onto the board and

Fig. 15-2. Prone paddling position. The toes are almost even with the end of the board and the body is balanced so that the nose of the board is slightly out of the water. The arms are pulling simultaneously. (Reprinted by permission from Severson, J.: Modern Surfing Around the World. Garden City, N.Y., Doubleday & Company, Inc., 1964. Photo by John Severson.)

assume a prone position with the board *almost* level, but with the nose slightly higher than the tail. Generally, the surfer's toes are even with the end of the board, and the body is centered for balance. If the weight is too far to the rear, the board will not glide, or if it is too far forward, the nose will sink and cause too much drag in the water. The chin is up with eyes focused on the incoming surf. The back is arched just enough to raise the chest and shoulders above the board, and the body weight is resting on the short ribs, stomach, and thighs. Both hands are placed in the water at the same time and as far forward as possible. The fingers are close together and the arms pull straight downward and to the rear. *The arms should be as straight as possible.* Alternating overarm paddling will follow when the body is adjusted to a balanced board position. Paddling in this prone position has advantages in the big surf, for the body offers less wind resistance and allows a faster, smoother change to a standing position.

To turn the board while in a prone position, drag the arms and toes on the side on which the turn is desired. Shifting the weight of the legs to the side to which the surfer wants to turn is accomplished by raising the leg on the opposite side slightly and crossing it over to the other side. If a substantial wave is encountered while paddling out, hold the rails and raise the upper body from the board to allow a portion of the wave to pass between the body and board.

Paddling on the knees requires a little more balance but is used by many as a variation and to avoid full water contact in cold water. In the resting phase, the body is sitting on the heels. It rocks forward and weight shifts forward as the hands dig in. The body then rocks back to add momentum to the backward arm pull. Some surfers seem to get more power and drive from this kneeling position.

The sit paddle position is comfortable and casual but not very powerful. It is used pri-

Fig. 15-3. Knee paddling position. The body is balanced sitting on the feet. The upper body rocks forward, the arms catch the water, and the body pulls back to the original position. (Reprinted by permission from Severson, J.: Modern Surfing Around the World. Garden City, N.Y., Doubleday & Company, Inc., 1964. Photo by John Severson.)

marily to correct board positions while waiting for swells at the take-off point.

No matter what style of paddling is used, paddle around the surf going out in order to stay out of the lanes of the oncoming surfers. If it is necessary to paddle through white water, point the nose directly into it. If the waves are small, hold on to the rails, lean back, and pull the nose of the board up so it glides over the white water. If the white water is over several feet high, paddle directly into the surf and just before the wave hits, grasp the rails and roll over into a *turtle* position with the board upside down on top of the body. After the wave subsides, roll the board over, climb on, and paddle once again.

Positioning to Catch a Wave. Beginners should catch their first waves in broken surf or white water, and only as skill develops should they attempt an unbroken wave. Once confidence and skill have grown, the surfer paddles seaward (outside) of the breaking point. While awaiting a wave and resting from the paddling, the surfer keeps the board parallel to the shoreline and may rest in a sit-straddle position. The position is comfortable and affords a good view of the incoming surf. When an incoming swell approaches, the surfer shifts back until she is

sitting near the tailblock, and the bow is tilted up about 30 degrees. To turn the nose from the oncoming wave, the feet begin a rotary gyration from the knees down. If the board is to move clockwise, both feet move counterclockwise, alternating, so that when the right foot is swinging from front to back, the left is swinging from back to front and contrariwise.

Catching a Wave. Face the nose toward the shore, return to a kneeling or prone position and begin paddling in front of the slope of the wave as the white water reaches the back of the board. Paddle strongly toward shore. As momentum is gained, the wave moves beneath the surfer and paddling becomes a drag rather than a pull. Add another stroke or two to be certain of having sufficient momentum to glide down the face of the wave and not slip over the back of the wave as it passes by. Ride several waves in either prone or kneeling position to get the feeling of the takeoff and slide before attempting to stand.

The surfer is not yet standing as she moves down the front of the wave, but she quickly arches her back and moves her weight to the rear of the board to keep from nosing, or pearling, into the water. As soon as she *feels* the wave is caught, she stands up quickly but

Fig. 15-4. Three phases of the take off. The surfer in the center is just pushing up, and he still maintains contact on the rails. The surfer on the right has just released the board with his hands. The surfer on the left is balanced in the stand and is preparing to move down the face of the wave. (Reprinted by permission from Severson, J.: Modern Surfing Around the World. Garden City, N.Y., Doubleday & Company, Inc., 1964. Photo by John Severson.)

cautiously by pushing with the hands beneath the chest. The hands stay in contact with the board until the feet are placed and balance feels correct. The faster a surfer can stand, the less chance of a mishap at this early stage. One foot is placed in front of the other, preferably the left foot forward unless it feels unnatural. In a basic stand up position, the feet are spread about a foot and a half apart. The forward foot is placed with toes pointing forward at about a 45 degree angle; the trailing foot is almost at right angles to the center of the board.

Turns. The standing position described is adequate for the first *straight-off* rides toward shore, but the ultimate goal is a fast, controlled ride across the face or wall of the wave, as nearly parallel to the shore as possible and just ahead of the breaking part of the wave. This requires control, and control means the ability to turn, to cut back, and to use the riding forward position. There are as many styles of maneuvering the board as there are surfers, but all are derived from the same basic patterns. The principle of a turn is to create friction along one side of the board and to cause one edge to slide faster. The two basic turns are the standing (foot and heel pressure) and the leaning turns.

In the *standing turn* the forward foot is considered the main balance foot, and the trailing foot is both a balance and a turning foot. The knees are held easy. A right turn is made by applying pressure with the trail foot on the right rear of the board. Similarly, a left turn is made by shifting the trail foot to the left rear of the board and pushing downward. The body may lean slightly in the direction of the turn.

The second basic turn, the *leaning turn*, is slower and more rhythmical and a bit more difficult than the rear foot turn. With the feet in normal riding position and with the forward toes pointing about 45 degrees from the center line of the board, the body weight is shifted toward the rail on the side toward the desired turn. The upper body leans beyond the rails and over the water as the arms and the speed of the board counterbalance the leaning movement of the body.

Fig. 15-5.   A forward standing position. The surfer has just risen to a balanced standing position. Notice the forward position on the board and the position of the feet in preparation for a slide to the right. (Reprinted by permission from Severson, J.: Modern Surfing Around the World. Garden City, N.Y., Doubleday & Company, Inc., 1964. Photo by Bev Morgan.)

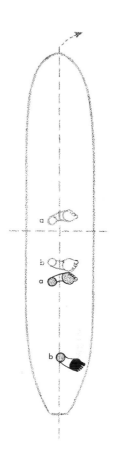

Fig. 15-6. Pressure turn to the right. The broken lines illustrate positioning in a normal stance for a straight-on ride. The weight is equally distributed between the two feet and spread over the entire foot. The right foot slides backward quickly and the forward foot (a) shifts to a new position back of the center of the board. Pressure is applied by the b foot, with the greatest pressure applied through the ball of the foot. The board turns right. (Modified from diagrams by R. D. Smith. In Klein, H. A.: Surfing. Philadelphia, J. B. Lippincott Co., 1965.)

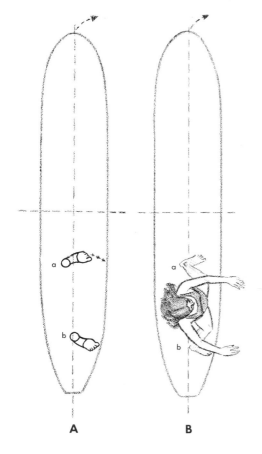

A   **B**

Fig. 15-7. The twist turn. *A* illustrates the run effect caused by the twist of the forward foot (a). Such action results in a swift pivot. *B* demonstrates the twist of the body in a clockwise direction –the same direction as the intended turn. The twist of the body generates additional force which is applied to the board through the forward foot. (Modified from diagrams by R. D. Smith. *In* Klein, H. A.: Surfing. Philadelphia, J. B. Lippincott Co., 1965.)

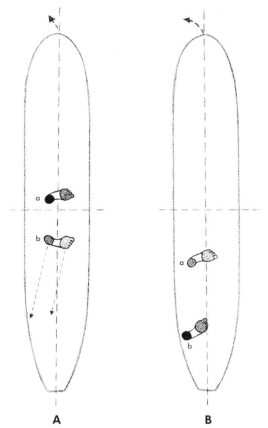

A   **B**

Fig. 15-8. Tail down turn in the direction of the heels. *A* shows the weight of the lead foot (a) primarily on the heel to allow the trailing foot (b) to slide back quickly. *B* shows the foot positioning and primary pressure points during the turn in the direction of the heels. Note that the greatest pressure is on the heel of the trailing foot (b). (Modified from diagrams by R. D. Smith. *In* Klein, H. A.: Surfing. Philadelphia, J. B. Lippincott Co., 1965.)

Falls and Pull-outs. Falls are an inevitable part of surfing and, properly executed, should be a basic skill. Try to anticipate falls and go alongside the board, grabbing it as soon as possible. A loose board is dangerous, as it may hit another board or surfer. Having the board also eliminates long and unnecessary swims. If the wave is sizeable, the surfer should try to dive to the inside, toward the wave and away from the direction of the board. Again, grasp the board as soon as possible.

Pull-outs are techniques for steering the board over and through the back of the wave and thus ending the ride. Basically, a pull-out parts the surfer from the wave.

Many beginners riding white water prefer to *prone out* or ride the wave out in a prone position. Sooner or later the ride must be stopped, and for beginners in a prone position it seems easy to slide the body backward quickly, rise to a sitting position while holding the rails and drag the feet in the water. This is similar in principle to the stall-out to be described. Beginners in a standing position simply step back and stall the board out of the wave.

The most common pull-out is one in which the surfer merely turns over the back of the wave or turns herself *out* of the wave. This pull-out is most often used as the wave is dying out, and the surfer immediately returns to a paddling position.

To accomplish a *kick-out* or a turn over the top of a wave, apply pressure through the trail foot on the rear of the board to the right side, if going right; to the left, if sliding left. The surfer actually falls back into the wave and kicks the board over the back as she does so.

Leap off and catch is a simple pull-out that should be learned in the early days of surfing. At the end of the ride the surfer falls or slides off and inside the board. She wraps the outside arm around the nose of the board and as the surfer falls into the face of the wave she pulls the nose of the board. The white water pushes the tail of the board around, and the surfer draws the nose through the surf and is ready to climb on and paddle out once again.

Trimming the surfboard allows it to slide efficiently. Use the front foot as a guide as the board comes up through the wave. To *accelerate* the board, step foot over foot toward the nose. This skill is known as *walking the board.* If the wave is breaking or the board is headed for a pearl (nose dive), the surfer must step back foot over foot (back pedal) until control is regained.

When it is desirable to slow the board, perhaps while waiting for a wave to build in front, or to let a wave go by, the board can be stalled. *Stalling* is achieved by applying weight to the board with the trail foot. The tail sinks and the nose of the board rises. Too much weight on the trail foot may stall the surfer right out of the wave.

Advanced Skills. An ardent surfer soon discovers that there are numerous tricks and stunts that can be accomplished on the board.

Nearly all stunts involve a forward riding style. Some of the main feats are standing and riding backward, balancing on one leg, riding with the toes of one or both feet curled over, standing on the hands or the head, or riding tandem.

GAME RULES AND SCORING

Surfing competition is as old as the sport. History tells us that surfing was fiercely competitive for sport and gain among the Hawaiian nobility, and fortunes often rode on the crest of a wave.

Competitive events are numerous, with the west coast of California leading in number but Hawaiian events still leading in prestige. Several international surfing championships are held throughout the world in France, South Africa, and Peru, but the International Surfing Championship at Makaha Beach, Hawaii, is still considered the most exciting.

Rules vary from area to area. The United States Surfing Association has tried to develop standards, but only west coast association events follow those outlined. There is still no universal definition of good or bad surfing style. Unofficial events are held on most beaches to determine the best wave rider, best hot dogger, most stylish, and most aggressive surfer.

Although some meets are specialized and limited to single or several events, such as body surfing or tandem surfing, a major surfing contest includes senior men's events (over 35 years), men's events (16 years and up), senior women's events (16 years and up), tandem events (men with women partners), novice tandem events (for tandem teams who have not placed in competition), boys' events (15 years and under), team paddling events, dory races, and singles paddling.

Surfers are required to ride a certain number of waves in a designated time period. Generally, there are five or six surfers in a heat of approximately 15 minutes. They must ride a minimum of four waves and no more than six in the allotted time. Judges score each rider on each wave on a 10 point score similar to diving and synchronized swimming events.

Because of a lack of standardization, judges will vary in their weightings and personal emphasis. However, they consider the difficulty of the wave, the distance the wave is ridden, the skill and style of the rider, and his sportsmanship. There are usually five judges and three official score keepers in any major U.S.S.A. meet.

SAFETY

Safety and courtesy are as fundamental and necessary to surfing as the board itself.

RULES OF THE ROAD FOR ALL SURFERS

1. Surf at your own level of skill.
2. When paddling out, be certain to paddle around the break, avoiding surfing lanes and riders.
3. Avoid surfing in swimming areas.
4. The right of way belongs to the person in the curl or tube inside the wave. Avoid dropping into the wave if it might interrupt or spoil another's ride.
5. Know who is on the wave with you. Anticipate dangerous situations and avoid creating them.
6. Know your board and keep it in good repair.
7. Avoid losing control of the board while riding and after a fall. Whenever possible try to hold on to it.
8. Perform sensible maneuvers and be courteous at all times.

A *beginning surfer* should consider the following personal safety hints:

1. Before surfing a spot, know something about the beach, the bottom, and the waves.
2. Learn to make safe wipe-outs and plan a safe course of action. If the wave is not too large, try to anticipate a wipe-out, straighten off, and perhaps even drop to the stomach and prone the wave out. If possible, stay with the board.
3. If staying with the board is impossible or dangerous, get away from it by going into the wave, away from the shore and the board.
4. In a wipe-out relax and do not panic. Avoid fighting the wave and conserve oxygen until you feel the wave subside, then be sure to *swim for the surface.*

Terminology

Surfers have a language all their own, and it is important to many beginners as the basic skills.

Angling — Riding (sliding) across the face of a wave either to the left or right.

Arch — A backbend used by a surfer primarily in making turns.

Backing out — Pulling back rather than continuing into a wave.

Backpedal — Walking foot over foot backward to the rear of the board.

Backwash — A rush of water seaward after a wave has run up the beach.

Baggies — Large, boxer-type trunks worn by surfers.

Bailing out — A planned dive or jump from the surfboard to avoid a wipe-out.

Big gun — A big, long board designed especially to ride large waves.

Blown out — There are two meanings: (1) Surf that has been wind-whipped and choppy so that it is unridable. (2) A surfer who has been caught by the wind and blown off the top of the wave and down the back side.

Bottom-turn — A swinging turn made at the bottom or below the crest of the wave.

Choppy — Ruffled water surface caused by winds. It creates a bumpy and difficult surface.

Classic — Perfect surfing form or a perfect day for surfing.

Clean up — A wave that breaks outside the surfers, causing them to lose their boards.

Climbing — Angling up the face of the wave toward the crest.

Close-out — A wave or a series of waves that break all the way across the normal surfing area. Usually considered too big to ride.

Crest — The highest portion of a wave just before it breaks.

Curl — The part of the wave that is spilling over and breaking back.

Cut-out — To pull out of the wave. Same as pull-out or kick-out.

Deck — The top surface of the board.

Ding — A break or hole in the surface of the surfboard.

Drop — The first downward slide after taking off in a wave.

Drop-in — A term used in speaking of the big surf which means sliding down the face of the wave immediately after it is caught.

Face — The unbroken front of a wave.

Fiberglass — A woven glass fabric or glass cloth used in surfboard construction.

Fin — Skeg.

Fins — Rubber fins or flippers used as an aid in swimming or body surfing.

Glassy — A smooth water surface or wave, with the absence of winds.

Goofy-foot — A surfer who rides with his right foot forward.

Grabbing the rail — A technique for pulling out, accomplished by grabbing the rail on the side away from the wave and pulling the board into the wave to keep from begin knocked off and to continue in the curl or on the unbroken wave ahead.

Hanging five (or ten) — Placing five or ten toes over the nose of the board.

Head dip — A riding style in which the head is lowered so that it touches the wave or white water.

Heavies — Big surf.

Hook — The curling part of the wave.

Hot dogging — Performance on a board showing a great deal of ability, usually demonstrating fancy turns, walking to the nose, etc.

Humping — Medium to large waves rising suddenly just before breaking.

In shore — A place in the water off the beach and inside the break.

Inside — Refers to the position of being shoreward from the normal breaking point of the waves or, when surfing, completely within the curling part of the wave or inside the tunnel.

Kick-out — A final effort to keep from losing the board, which involves flipping the board over the back or through the back of the wave as the surfer falls off the tail of the board into the wave.

Left slide — A ride in which the surfer slides or glides to his left.

Locked in — A position in which the surfer and the board are firmly set in the curling portion of the wave, with the water holding the tail of the board. It is impossible to pull out in this position.

Outside — Reference to a point seaward of the normal breaking position of the waves.

Paraffin — Wax applied to the deck of surfboards to reduce the slickness.

Peak — The highest point of the wave.

Pearl or pearling — The nose of the surfboard drops beneath the surface and continues downward.

Polyurethane — Most common type of plastic foam used in the construction of surfboards.

Pop-outs — Mass-produced surfboards, generally of low quality.

Pull-out — Ending the ride of a wave by steering the board over or through the back of a wave.

Rails — Rounded sides of the surfboard.

Resin — Liquid plastic used to laminate fiberglass to foam of surfboards.

Right slide — Riding or sliding a wave to the surface right.

Rocker — The lengthwise curve of a surfboard.

Shooting the tube or curl — Riding through the curl or the tube part of the wave.

Shore break — Waves that break very close to the beach. Generally, surf that is not breaking well for riding.

Shoulder turn — A board turned where the shoulders are rotated in the direction of the turn.

Shuffle — A sliding or shuffling maneuver of moving the feet toward the nose of the board without crossing foot over foot.

Skeg — The rudder or fin of the board.

Slide — To ride the wave either left or right, somewhat paralleling the shore.

Soup — White water or the foamy part of a broken wave.

Spinner — A 360 degree turn made by a standing surfer.

Stall — Slowing the board so that the breaker can catch up with the surfer.

Stringers — Wood strips running the length of the board used for strength in design.

Tail — The stern or rear of the surfboard.

Tandem—Two people riding one board, usually a man and a woman.

Trimming—Steering the board so that it planes almost parallel with the line of the wave. Trimming gives the most possible speed and stability out of the wave.

Walk the nose—Moving foot over foot toward the nose of the board.

Wetsuit—A neoprene rubber suit designed to trap water between the suit and the body. The body temperature warms the water and keeps the surfer warm.

Wipe-out—Being knocked from, blown, or pushed off the board by a breaking wave.

Selected Audio-visual Aids

Commercial motion pictures with surfing emphasis:

The Big Surf, Universal Productions, 1966.

King of the Wild Waves (Borde Sonney), released by Paramount Pictures, 1964.

The Surfers, Robert Springer Productions, 1967.

Short productions:

Let's Get Wet (1967). (16 mm., color, 26 min., sound.) Johnson Motors. (Free loan.)

Riding the Big Surf (1959). (16 mm., color, 11 min., sound). Cine Pic, 1847 Fort St., Honolulu, Hawaii. (Rental and purchase.)

Surf Riders (1961). (16 mm., 9 min., b & w., sound.) United World Films, Inc., 1445 Park Avenue, New York, New York, 10027. (Rental and purchase.)

Suggested Readings

Bloomfield, John: *Know-how in the Surf*, Rutland, Vermont, Charles E. Tuttle Company, 1965.

Dixon, Peter L.: *The Complete Book of Surfing*, New York, Coward-McCann, Inc., 1965.

Klein, H. Arthur: *Surfing*, Philadelphia, J. B. Lippincott Company, 1965.

Kuhns, Grant: *On Surfing*, Rutland, Vermont, Charles E. Tuttle Company, 1963.

Patterson, O. B.: *Surf-Riding: Its Thrills and Techniques*, Rutland, Vermont, Charles E. Tuttle Company, 1960.

Severson, John: *Modern Surfing Around the World*, Garden City, New York, Doubleday and Company, 1964.

Periodicals

Surf Guide, Box 1278, Santa Monica, California 90406 (monthly).

Surfing Magazine, 5959 Hollywood Blvd., Los Angeles, California 90028.

Suggested Study Questions

1. Plan a conditioning program for the beginning surfer. What dry land activities will you suggest?
2. Define "pearling" and "stalling-out." Explain what causes each. How can you prevent it?
3. What is the *principle* of turning the board? Explain one method of turning to the right.
4. How does a surfer make the board travel faster? How does she slow it?
5. Why is surfing called the "sport of kings"?

CHAPTER SIXTEEN

Courtesy of Agnes I. Michaels, State University College, Fredonia, New York.

SWIMMING AND DIVING

It is difficult to know when and how man first learned to swim. Perhaps he swam in search of food, to survive a pursuer, to fulfill a religious rite, or totally as the result of an accident that threw him into water. Progression of man's skill in water has been slow because of his structural handicaps. A beginning swimmer quickly realizes that the eyes, ears, nose, and mouth are not ideally placed for natural efficiency in the water.

Pictures on the walls of caves in the Libyan Desert indicate man's ability to swim as early as 9000 B.C. Throughout history there is mention of "bathing" for hygienic, military, or pleasurable purposes, and there is written evidence that swimming instruction was given to select groups in Egypt around 2160 B.C.

The art and skill of swimming as it is practiced today may be traced to Nicolaus Wynman, a German professor of languages, who wrote the *Art of Swimming* in 1538. His description of the breaststroke served as a basis for technique until the desire for speed

resulted in adaptations of the sidestroke, side overarm, and trudgen.

It is believed that the ancient Indians of the Western Hemisphere were capable swimmers, and some experts attribute the overarm stroke to their technique. Swimming was vigorously pursued in early America, and a swimming school flourished in Boston as early as 1827.

Great progress has been made in stroke development in less than 100 years. The Australian crawl, American crawl, inverted breaststroke, backstroke, butterfly breaststroke, butterfly (with the dolphin, or fishtail, kick), and a refinement of the trudgen have expanded the interest, skill, and recreational value of this sport. Development of scientific equipment and underwater skills have revealed an underwater world for study and pleasure.

Diving combines the skills of tumbling and swimming into a form of aerial acrobatics. It is a newcomer to the sports field, the first

Fig. 16-1. All students should learn how to swim for pleasure and personal safety! (Courtesy of College of Health, Physical Education and Recreation, Texas Woman's University, Denton, Texas.)

255

diving competition having been held in England in 1905, but today has developed into an exciting activity for millions.

THE NATURE AND PURPOSE OF SWIMMING AND DIVING

Swimming serves us today as it has for centuries, that is, for survival, food, and pleasure. As a healthful and beneficial form of exercise, it attracts more participants of all ages than any other sport. Swimming skills are basic to all aquatic activities, from fishing, canoeing, boating, water skiing, diving, synchronized swimming, to skin and SCUBA* diving, and surfing. The age-old struggle for self-preservation and survival is a strong motivating factor in our space age.

Regardless of one's motive for swimming, the principles basic to a coordinated stroke are the same. The body on its front, side, or back is propelled through water by movements of the arms and legs. Skill development is complicated by the different body position from a normal position for action

---

*SCUBA is the abbreviation for "self-contained underwater breathing apparatus."

and by the human being's inability to breathe under water. Effective stroke development is dependent on learning to inhale above the surface and to exhale below the water's surface.

Diving serves to get the swimmer into the water in the most efficient way. Fancy diving is primarily a spectacular and skillful sport.

FACILITIES AND EQUIPMENT

The Swimming Area. Although swimming can be pleasurable in many bodies of water, a sound instructional program should be conducted in a well controlled, sanitary swimming area. Instructors training competitive swimmers and divers should work in 75 or 60 foot areas with 1 meter and 3 meter diving boards at least 14 feet long and 20 inches wide, covered with coco matting or nonslip materials.

Accessories. Many instructors prefer to teach without any artificial aids; others like the feeling of security and isolated practice offered by swimming jackets, kickboards, leg floats, and shoe fins. All swimming areas should have minimum equipment for the

Fig. 16-2. A modern swimming pool is designed for instruction, recreation, and competition. (Courtesy Department of Health and Physical Education for Women, Miami University, Oxford, Ohio.)

safety of swimmers. A swimming area should have ring buoys, bamboo poles, shallow water markers, canoes, boats, and other equipment. Properly selected music is helpful in developing relaxation, coordination, and stroke rhythm.

Costume. Women should wear suits that do not interfere with body movements. Competitive swimmers seem to prefer the one-piece nylon or durene speed suits. Caps not only protect the swimmer's hair and prevent annoyance, but also preserve the natural hair oil and keep hair out of the pool and filtration system. Bobby pins and clips should be removed. Slides or clogs may be used when walking to and from the swimming area.

Regulations Concerning Pool Use. Students and teachers should establish basic safety and sanitary rules for every swimming area. These should include the following:

1. Soap shower without suit before swimming.
2. Remove all jewelry and accessories.
3. Expectorate only in designated receptacles.
4. Refrain from chewing gum and candy.
5. Refrain from wearing street clothes and shoes on pool deck.
6. Refrain from running and "horseplay" on pool deck; also in the pool unless with instructor's permission.
7. Persons with ear and eye infections, cuts and abrasions, and athlete's foot should not be permitted in pool.

BASIC SKILLS

Whatever the age of a beginning swimmer, there are certain steps of skill development to be mastered.

Water Adjustment and Beginning Skills. The beginner wades into waist deep water, splashing her wrists, body, and arms to lessen the shock and to become accustomed to a new environment. Dunk to chin depth and jump up and down cautiously. Standing with feet apart for balance, inhale and hold breath for five or six counts; exhale. Move to shoulder depth, bending forward to submerge the face, repeat breath holding. Lengthening the time of breath holding, repeat until you feel the confidence and ability to submerge the

entire head. Open the eyes under water and count toes, fingers, or objects on the pool floor.

JELLYFISH FLOAT. In waist deep water bend from the hips, submerge the face, and slowly reach for the ankles. As the feet rise from the bottom, grasp the ankles, hold for three counts, then slowly release. Extend the legs and recover to standing position.

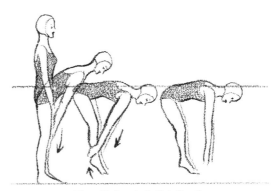

Fig. 16-3. Jellyfish float.

TURTLE FLOAT. Begin as in jellyfish float, raising knees to chest, arms encircling knees. Allow the water to move the body, then extend legs and recover.

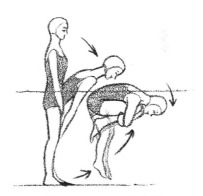

Fig. 16-4. Turtle float.

PRONE FLOAT. Assume a turtle float and go to full extension, gently pushing arms forward and legs back. Hold the float 10 counts and recover by bringing knees to chest and extending legs toward bottom. The head rises and arms press downward and back as the body becomes vertical.

Fig. 16-5. Prone float.

PRONE GLIDE. Place one foot against the side of pool, bend forward at hips, take a breath, and put face in the water. Gently push against side of the pool and glide forward. Recover to standing position.

BACK FLOAT. Submerge with shoulders below the surface, in waist deep water. Raise arms to the sides, palms up. With partner supporting the back of the head with one hand, push off gently. Lift the hips and extend arms, palms up. The head is back and the ears are in the water.

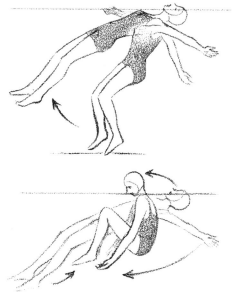

Fig. 16-6. Back float.

A partner aids in recovery until the beginner can return to standing position by dropping the chin forward and bringing the knees toward the chest as the hands scoop down and forward.

BACK GLIDE. Hold the pool bracket with both hands, facing the wall. With head back, ears in the water, draw both feet against the side. (In shallow water push from the bottom.) Remove hands from the side and firmly straighten the legs, pushing away. Hands should be close to the side for balance, and the legs close together. Recover as in a back float.

KICK GLIDE IN PRONE POSITION. With the body in a prone position, the legs move up and down alternately from the hips in a thrashing action with loose knees and relaxed ankles.

KICK GLIDE IN BACK (SUPINE) POSITION. From a back glide flatten the back and tuck the chin, look toward the toes. A flutter kick from the hips, with relaxed knees and emphasis on the "up kick," moves the body forward.

Arm Movements on the Back. FINNING. To combine arm movements with back glide and kick, start with the arms straight and hands at the side. Elbows bend as hands simultaneously move up the body about a foot. With fingers pointing away and heel of hand near hips, the hands thrust out and down with a wrist flip to original position.

WINGING. In a back glide, hands and arms work together. Begin with arms straight and hands at side. Hands move up, elbows bend and follow the line of the body until fingertips are at waist level. Arms extend to side (45 degree angle) and pull to original position. When combined with a resting phase, this is an excellent lead-up for elementary back stroke.

SCULLING. From a back glide, palms near the legs, paired arm action begins by turning hands (rotating wrists) so that thumbs are down and backs of hands are toward legs. Press the hands out and slightly down for about 8 inches. Turn thumbs up, and move each hand back to the legs with palms facing body. Keep wrists flexible and arms firm.

Arm Stroke in Prone Position. Take a prone position, face in water, arms extended. Pull the left arm below the surface straight toward bottom of pool. The elbow bends and

Fig. 16-7. Human stroke.

shoulder relaxes so that the left hand touches the midline of the abdomen. As the left hand extends toward the chin and moves underwater toward its beginning position, the cupped right hand and arm begin a similar pattern.

Combined Elementary Movement. THE BACK. Combine simple flutter kick with finning, winging, or sculling while breathing naturally through the mouth.

THE FRONT. Combined leg and arm movements result in the human stroke, or dog paddle. The head is held above the surface with hips below the surface and back arched. The arms reach and pull alternately, recovering below the surface (see "Arm Stroke in Prone Position"). The kick is the elementary flutter with a pronounced knee bend. As the left arm pulls, the right leg bends downward and kicks. Legs alternate with two beats for each arm cycle. Later, three leg beats to a single arm stroke can be developed in preparation for the crawl.

There will be greater stroke efficiency when the face is in the water and raised only for inhalation. Develop a pattern of inhaling from the side and exhaling breath in the water. If the right side is the most comfortable, turn the head to the right, lifting it slightly for a breath as the right hand pulls through and the left arm recovers. As the right arm begins recovery the face turns into the water and exhalation begins.

Changing Body Positions and Directions. Confidence and control are gained by the beginner who can move on the front and back and change positions easily.

TURNING FROM FRONT TO BACK. From an extended glide position with both arms overhead, bring the right arm down and across the body and roll left as the head turns left.

TURNING FROM BACK TO FRONT. Head and shoulders remain low and horizontal with arms at side. As right arm and right leg reach across the body, both arms extend to an overhead prone position.

TURNING RIGHT, LEFT, OR AROUND. Stop swimming action and allow the body to drop to a near vertical position. Extend hands and pull in the direction of desired change. Return to front or back position and resume stroke.

Treading Water. This is a support skill that has value for personal safety. Combine a scissors, frog, or breaststroke kick with a sculling or finning hand and arm action. Treading is done in a vertical position and requires individualized adaptations.

STROKE SKILLS

Elementary Backstroke. This resting stroke enables one to cover long distances without undue exertion. Since it is easily mastered by beginners, it should be learned after the horizontal float. The body is on the back with head up, chin slightly tucked, ears in the

Fig. 16-8. Elementary backstroke.

water. The legs are extended and straight with arms at the sides, palms downward.

ARMS.   The hands begin the stroke as they move up along the side, thumbs close to the body, elbows bent and shoulders back. As the fingers reach toward the armpits, the wrists rotate and the fingers lead the arms upward and outward to a "V" position. The arms pull firmly back to the starting position in the power phase and then rest as the body glides through the water.

LEGS.   Powered leg action begins as the fingers reach the top of the ribs. With heels together, the legs draw toward the body with soles of the feet toward the bottom of the pool. The knees bend and move away from the body. Heels separate and ankles flex, turning the toes outward, as knees remain bent. The legs then sweep outward and together, pressing the sole of the foot against the water. Squeeze thighs together as legs return to starting position.

The whip kick, described in the breast-stroke and inverted breaststroke, is a more efficient kick. Beginners often find it difficult to master.

BREATHING.   Breathing is regular, with inhalation during the recovery and exhalation as the body moves.

COORDINATION.   The stroke can be phrased in four flowing counts: (1) Arms begin action; (2) legs move up and knees extend as arms move outward; (3) legs spread and whip together as arms complete pull; (4) glide in initial position.

Crawl Stroke.   The American crawl is an efficient and graceful speed stroke using the flutter kick and overhand arm action with rhythmical breathing. The body is in an extended prone position with the face submerged so that the surface of the water is just below the hairline. The chin is slightly up and away from the neck.

ARMS.   With both arms extended overhead, above the shoulders, the left arm pulls firmly, with a bent elbow, to press the water down and back. The left arm, hand slightly cupped, "catches" the water and increases power as the pull progresses. The water is pushed with the palm of the hand and the underside of the forearm as the pull arcs toward the body. The left arm begins recovery as the elbow bends and shoulder action lifts the elbow and relaxed hand clear of the water. The forearm is relaxed and

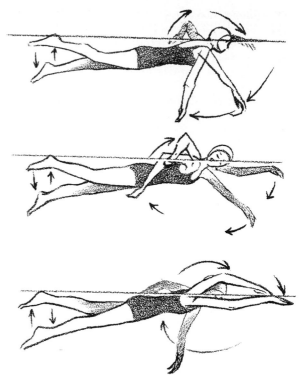

Fig. 16-9.   Crawl stroke.

forward as the fingers enter the water directly in front of the shoulder and begin a new pull with the slightly cupped hand.

The right arm begins identical action as the left begins its recovery forward. The hands enter the water at natural arms' length.

LEGS.   The kick begins with slightly "pigeon-toed" leg extension. Right leg bends slightly at the knee as it drops downward from the hip. As the right leg snaps back to extended position, the left leg drops. The action is primarily from the hips with relaxed knee and ankle action. Legs pass close together as they penetrate 12 to 16 inches into the water and rise almost to the surface.

BREATHING.   Turn the head to inhale as the arm opposite the breathing side is set and forward for support. A quick "bite of air" is taken, the head turns back into the water and exhalation begins. It continues as the head turns for a breath when the "breathing arm" pulls by the shoulder and the support arm is forward.

COORDINATION.   The complete rhythmical stroke is a coordinated movement of 6 evenly measured leg beats to a complete cycle of both arms with a breathing ratio of one inhalation and exhalation.*

Sidestroke. A sidestroke is a restful, powerful stroke that is a necessity in executing lifesaving skills. Its mastery makes the overarm side and trudgen strokes relatively easy. The sidestroke should be learned on both sides with conventional and inverted kicks. The following description is for the right side.

Ready position is reclining on the right side, body straight, feet together and legs extended. The left arm is resting on the front of the thigh of the left leg, right arm is extended in the water, palm down, The head is supported comfortably by the water and right shoulder.

ARMS. The right arm begins a downward pull toward a line directly beneath the head.

*Some competitive swimmers use an 8 beat kick; some a 4 beat synchronized cycle; breathing may be every two or three complete strokes.

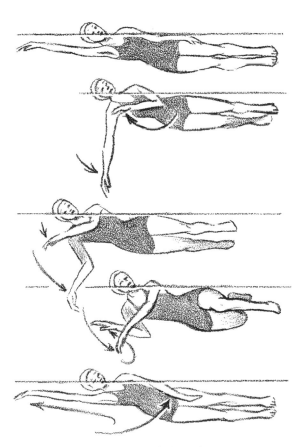

Fig. 16-10. Sidestroke.

The left arm, elbow bent, glides across in front of the body toward the right armpit. The right elbow bends and the hand is brought in toward the lower shoulder, fingers leading. Right arm slides forward beneath the surface, palm down, as the left hand "catches" and presses toward the feet and starting position.

LEGS. The legs execute a scissors kick. From an extended position the knees flex, drawing the heels backward in line with the back. Legs remain close together. The toes lead in a lateral leg extension as the top (left) leg reaches to the front of the body and lower leg behind. The top foot flexes and the lower foot remains extended. The legs, still flexed, begin driving backward and together with the sole of the top foot and the instep of lower foot pressing the water, then meeting, stopping, and remaining extended during the glide.

In the inverted scissors kick the top leg goes to the back of the body and the bottom leg moves forward. It serves as a change of pace and an excellent lifesaving skill for carrying a victim.

BREATHING. Breathing is natural, as the head is out of the water. Most swimmers prefer to inhale during the power phase and exhale during the glide.

COORDINATION. The lower arm pull downward is the initial movement. Immediately, the top arm begins moving forward and the legs bend. As the lower arm completes a power phase and the top arm prepares for power delivery, the legs separate and drive as the arms return to starting position.

Ride the glide.

Single Overarm or Side Overarm. The side overarm is a comparatively simple stroke following mastery of the sidestroke. The basic timing is the same in both strokes except for the recovery by the top arm above the surface.

ARMS. From the sidestroke position the lower arm begins a pull to shoulder level. As it starts upward, the top arm, with elbow relaxed, recovers over the water and the fingers enter slightly in front and above the forehead. The stroke continues as in the sidestroke.

LEGS. Scissors kick.

BREATHING. Same as with sidestroke.

COORDINATION. The coordinated stroke is similar to the sidestroke.

Fig. 16-11.   Side overarm stroke.

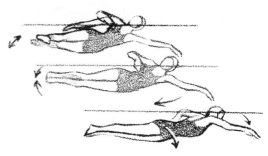

Fig. 16-12.   Trudgen.

Trudgen.   This is an excellent stroke for distance, as it is fast, steady, and not so tiring as the crawl to the average swimmer.

ARMS.   Overhand (crawl) stroke.

LEGS.   Single scissors kick.

BREATHING.   Similar to crawl stroke on selected side.

COORDINATION.   Beginning from a prone glide position, face down, the left arm begins a pull. Legs trail motionless. As the left arm begins recovery, the right arm pulls and the legs draw to a modified scissors position. With the left arm forward for support, the body rolls slightly right, mouth clears the water for inhalation and re-enters the water as the right arm recovers and the scissors kick is delivered. The body has rolled back onto the face and exhalation continues as the arm cycle is completed.

Trudgen Crawl.   This is an efficient stroke using hand-over-hand arm strokes and scissors and flutter kicks. While executing a trudgen, simply add three or four flutter kicks between scissors kicks instead of allowing the legs to trail. When learned from a crawl, roll to the breathing side and add a scissors kick as inhalation occurs.

Backstroke.   This is the fastest stroke executed on the back. In most respects it is a

Fig. 16-13.   Backstroke.

graceful and rhythmical inverted American crawl.

ARMS. The arm pull may be deep or shallow with a bent or straight arm recovery. The shallow pull, straight recovery is described below. On the back with chin tucked, hips slightly dropped, and eyes focused where toes will kick the surface, extend both arms to a "V" position overhead. The right arm pulls directly toward the right side with palm leading a cupped hand traveling 2 or 3 inches below the surface. As the recovery begins, the hand rotates so that the palm is away from the body as the little finger leads a straight arm upward and slightly sideward. Wrists are relaxed as the fingers reach toward the water to begin a new cycle. The left arm works alternately and begins its power phase as the right arm recovers.

LEGS. The inverted flutter kick is used. With legs extended, one knee bends and the foot drops 12 to 16 inches toward the bottom. A hip lift forces the leg upward, toes extended so that instep presses against the water. The toes break the water as the knee remains below. As one leg begins upward pressure the other drops in alternating action. Six or 8 "pigeon-toed" kicks are done with each arm cycle.

BREATHING. As the head is out of the water, inhalation time is optional.

COORDINATION. As one arm begins a pull, the opposite leg begins a kick lift. A rhythm of 6 to 8 beats is set for each completed arm cycle.

Breaststroke. The breaststroke was the first competitive stroke and has been refined more than any single stroke. It is basic to the fast and powerful butterfly. The orthodox breaststroke is a smooth, graceful movement done from a prone position. The body is in extension with arms beyond the head several inches below the water with thumbs together and palms down. Legs are straight and together.

ARMS. Arm action begins as palms turn outward, thumbs down and pull begins downward and backward until arms approach shoulder level. Elbows bend and the hands lead inward toward the chest, with elbows coming close to the sides. As the fingers meet beneath the chin with palms down, arms extend forward to starting position.

Fig. 16-14. Breaststroke.

LEGS. Leg action begins from extension, knees draw toward the body, dropping slightly and separating easily. Feet flex outward and reach away from the body. The power and drive is accomplished by a whipping sweep out and backward with ankles and feet leading to an extension for riding the glide.

BREATHING. As the arms press back against the water on the first movement there is a natural lift to the upper body that allows for a quick bite of air before submerging the face.

COORDINATION. Coordination and timing are often difficult. Using a four count pattern the following occurs:

Count 1: Arms begin press; head rises for breath.

Count 2: Arms move toward chest as legs draw toward body; face submerges.

Count 3: Arms slide forward and legs whip outward and backward.

Count 4: Glide in extended position.

Inverted Breaststroke. This is a resting stroke similar to the elementary backstroke. The body is flat on the back with legs straight and arms extended beyond the head, thumbs touching.

ARMS. Slightly cupped palms turn away from each other and pull out, down, and in to the sides. With arms still several inches below the water the elbows bend outward, allowing the palms-down hands to follow the body toward the armpits, where the hands turn over and fingers lead past the shoulders and under the head to initial position.

LEGS. Knees bend and separate slightly as heels drop toward the bottom. Toes point sideward and back. The legs extend and whip out and together.

BREATHING. Inhale as arms pull toward the body and exhale as legs kick and arms recover.

COORDINATION. Arms come to the sides before legs prepare for the kick. As the arms recover along the body, the legs recover and drive together. The arms then extend to glide position.

Butterfly Stroke. For this stroke both arms must be brought forward simultaneously over the water and brought backward simultaneously. All movements of the legs and feet must be executed simultaneously. Simultaneous up and down movements of the legs and feet in the vertical phase (dolphin kick) are permitted.

ARMS. Arms are extended upward from the shoulders and underwater several inches apart. Palms are cupped and the face is downward. Simultaneous arm movement is down and outside the body to shoulder level, where the palms turn and press backward toward the thighs. Arms lift out of the water, upper arm first, with relaxed elbows. The hands circle outward and forward until they slide into the water in front of the shoulders.

LEGS. Although the breaststroke kick may be used with slight modification in timing, speed can be increased by the dolphin (fishtail) kick. The dolphin involves a vertical

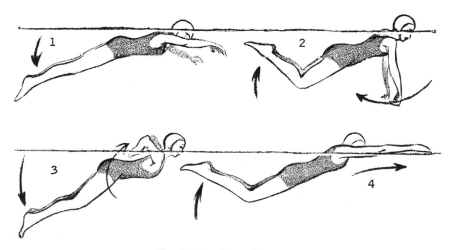

Fig. 16-15.   Butterfly stroke.

movement of both legs together. It is similar to the flutter kick, except that the legs are extended in prone position with heels, toes, and knees together and the feet are drawn toward the body by bending the knees. Hips and ankles flex, but concentration should center on the knees. The knees bend about 30 degrees and heels come just below the surface of the water before the top of the feet press back and knees straighten. The upward undulation begins as the legs lift to begin another sequence.

BREATHING. Exhale during the last phase of arm power and inhale as the hands leave the water on recovery. The head is pushed forward, rather than lifted, to keep from raising the torso out of the water. Competitive swimmers often prefer a two or three cycle stroke for each breath.

COORDINATION. A properly executed stroke has two kicks to an arm cycle. In four counts (begin with arms extended, legs beginning to bend):

Count 1: Arms pull downward; legs push downward and straighten; exhalation begins.

Count 2: Hands continue backward pull and start upward; legs bend upward; inhale.

Count 3: Arms recover; legs push downward and straighten.

Count 4: Hands placed in water; legs bent upward.

Turns. In swimming a closed course in a pool, efficient turns are valuable to the recreational swimmer and essential to the competitive swimmer. There are three types of turns used by the sprint and distance freestyle swimmer.

LATERAL OR CLOSED TURN. On the closed turn, the head is held under the water. As the lead hand touches the wall below the water surface, the elbow bends to allow the body to move toward the wall. The knees are together, the legs tuck tightly as the body pivots, and the head and shoulders move away from the wall toward the free hand that is sculling to speed the turn. The wall hand is removed and tucked closely to the body as the pivot is completed. The legs and feet extend with a thrust and push the body, head still submerged, in a glide, away and upward.

OPEN TURN. The open or spin turn is used for distance, middle distance, and for the last turn of a sprint, if air is needed. The head is out of the water. The turn is executed as a closed turn except that as the head turns away from the arm at the wall, the head *turns,* not lifted, so that the face is to the side, lifting the entire body just enough for the mouth to clear the water for a breath. The face is turned just as in breathing for the crawl stroke; the air is taken *as* the turn is executed. When the body has completed the turn, the face is still on the side. The body is submerged with a downward plunge; simultaneously the arm is drawn away from the wall and tucked close to the body. Both arms then thrust forward beneath the water as the legs drive from the wall.

SOMERSAULT TURN. The somersault turn is faster than the previously described methods because the body momentum is not lost in the turn. It should be used in all competitive crawl events, if possible, but certainly in the sprint events. As the swimmer approaches the wall, she lowers the head and dives at the wall, with the lead arm in front of the head. Her head is tucked toward the armpit on the turning side of the body. As the diagonal (rather than vertical) "flip" begins, the body is almost standing on its head with hips high. The knees and heels are tucked tightly toward the hips. This vigorous action somersaults the body and throws the legs beneath the surface with the feet against the wall. Toward the completion of the somersault, the body completes the twist to face downward as the legs thrust into the push-off.

LATERAL SOMERSAULT TURN. This is used by a few swimmers whose equilibrium is disturbed by a full somersault. Beginning as in a regular somersault, with the body in a tuck position, the head and shoulders are turned laterally in the direction of the turn. The head and shoulders lift to raise the body to the surface.

BACKSTROKE TUMBLE TURN. The swimmer is on her back driving to the wall, with the lead hand 6 to 10 inches below the water surface. A quick breath precedes lowering the head. The elbow bends to allow the head to come close to the wall. The body is brought into a close tuck position, which throws the knees over the shoulder of the contact arm. The body is flat on its back and is half turned around as the knees come over the shoulder. The spin is completed as the wall hand pushes away; the free hand sculls and the feet are planted on the wall, prepared to push. The arms, with elbows flexed, palms up, and close to the ears over each shoulder, are poised for the thrust. The vigorous drive of the legs is simultaneous with the arm extension as the body drives to the surface.

BREASTSTROKE TURN. The kick drives the paired arms to the wall with the hands 4 to 8 inches apart. The head is lowered just before the hands contact the wall, with the palms flat and the fingers turned slightly above the surface. Simultaneously, the legs tuck, the elbows bend, and the body rises. The head *may* lift for a quick breath of air. Immediately, the body spins, and the feet set against the wall for the push-off. Hands join under the chin and the arms thrust forward as the body is directed slightly upward so that the head breaks the surface before starting the second arm pull.

BUTTERFLY TURN. In the approach the dolphin kick is timed so that as the arms recover they lunge into the wall above the surface. The head remains lowered. The mechanics of turning are the same as those previously described. After the touch is made with both hands, one hand is removed to assist in turning the hips around by a finning action. In a sprint, the push-off is shallow, so that the body rises quickly near the surface on the initial armstroke.

Underwater Swimming. Underwater skills are increasingly necessary for skin and SCUBA diving. Many strokes can be used but a modified breaststroke seems superior.

ARMS. Arms pull all the way to the sides with little or no downward pressure.

LEGS. The kick is identical with that of the breaststroke. Flutter or scissors kick may be used.

BREATHING. Take several deep breaths at the surface, then a normal breath before submerging. Hold the breath as long as there is no tension in the chest, then release it slowly.

COORDINATION. The timing may be identical with breaststroke or with simultaneous arm and leg action.

DIVING SKILLS

Diving is an exciting skill, which should develop with swimming. Before actually diving from the deck or float, students should learn to jump into water of various depths. While in the water, a beginner should push off in a prone glide and direct the body below the surface by dropping the head and arms. When the head and hands are turned upward the body rises to the surface. Next, standing in waist deep water with arms overhead, thumbs locked together, the swimmer takes a breath, bends forward at the hips and pushes up and forward into the water.

Surface Dives. Generally, surface dives are easily learned since the swimmer is in the water and does not need additional courage for a ledge or board entry. Considerable skill must be developed in the use of hands, arms, and head.

To begin a head-first surface dive with a tuck, the body is in prone position on the surface. Take a deep breath and duck the head sharply. As the arms pull back toward the shoulders the body is drawn into a flexed position with knees and hips bent. The arms continue a pull through to the thighs. Immediately the hips and knees straighten above the surface. The weight of the legs above helps the body to glide toward the bottom as palms turn toward the head and scoop downward.

The head-first surface dive with a pike is similar to the previous dive except that there is no bend in the knees. As the dive begins the body bends into a jackknife position. The hips straighten and the legs are extended. The feet are together and the toes are pointed to complete the dive.

The foot-first surface dive begins with the body in a vertical position, arms at sides, palms in. Palms turn toward the bottom and with a kick force the upper body out of the water. As the body sinks, legs come together and toes point as the arms turn, palms away, and begin pressure upward against the water and the head goes below the surface. In a completed dive the body and extended arms are submerged.

Elementary Diving. Diving from the pool deck should follow surface dives. The following progression leads to a standing dive:

SITTING DIVE. Sit on pool or float edge with feet braced against the side. Place extended arms overhead, upper arms by ears, thumbs locked together, palms down. Bend between spread knees, take a breath through

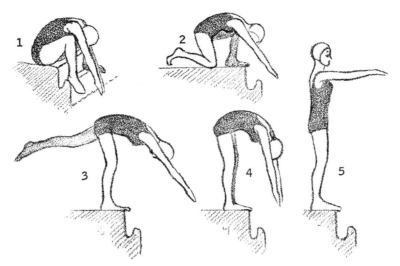

Fig. 16-16. Diving progression.

the mouth and as the body falls forward gently push with the legs. Bring legs together and straighten and extend toes.

KNEELING DIVE. Place one knee close to the edge of the pool and toes of the other foot over the edge. With arms above head roll forward toward the water. The head remains down and between the arms, and the eyes are fixed on the entering spot. Alternate knees.

STANDING ONE LEG DIVE. Standing on one leg with toes over the edge, bend the other leg behind the body for balance. With the arms over head and the head down, the upper body bends forward and the balance leg lifts, aiming the body downward. Roll into the water bringing the stationary leg up to meet the other.

STANDING SEMICROUCH DIVE. Stand on both legs with toes over the edge. Knees are easily bent, arms extended. Bend forward at the hips and push up and into the water.

STANDING STATIONARY DIVE. Stand erect with toes over pool edge, legs together, and arms at sides. Raise arms forward to shoulder height, bending knees. Lift the heels and push up and slightly out. Drop the head and shoulders between the arms before entering the water. After this has been mastered, begin in an erect position and swing arms upward as the legs push. Extend legs and toes.

Springboard Diving. Instruction begins on the 1 meter board. Many teachers like students to progress through a series of jump dives prior to "headers." Foot-first practice should precede each new dive. Beginning dives are done from a standing position at the take-off end of the board and later with an approach and hurdle.

The Front Jump. Standing several inches from the take-off end, jump up and down and push (riding the spring) with the balls of the feet as the arms reach forward and upward. To keep the body from falling forward, press the head and shoulders back against the arm pull. At first let the arms stay extended overhead for the feeling of lift; later bring arms down alongside the body before entering the water feet first.

Standing Front Header. Preparation for the take-off is the same as for the foot-first entry. Allow the body to follow arms upward, then turn over and enter the water with legs together and extended, and toes pointed.

Running Front Dive. All running dives have an approach that includes the stance, walk, hurdle, and takeoff. A beginner determines where to begin her approach by placing her heels on the takeoff end of the board and mimetically taking desired steps and a hurdle. Once the spot is determined, begin each dive there unless the approach pattern is changed.

STANCE. Stand erect with chest and chin up and eyes focused toward the end of the board at the desired height of the dive. Arms are firmly by the side, palms in, feet together and parallel.

WALK AND RUN. A minimum of three

Fig. 16-17 Running dive.

steps must be taken in the approach, and many divers prefer four. The steps are natural, increasing in momentum. The arms move slightly forward with the first step, slightly backward on the second step, and then forward with the third step. Eyes look straight ahead and head is up.

HURDLE. As the leg and knee lift for the hurdle, the arms move strongly forward and upward, pulling the diver off the board. Both feet then come down together on the end of the board and the arms move downward toward the hips to add weight to bend the board. As the board rebounds, legs and ankles straighten, arms lift upward and chin and chest rise. The eyes are focused on an object at the end of the pool.

ACTION POSITION IN THE AIR. The diver

Fig. 16-18. A diver must develop complete control of her body as it moves through space. (Courtesy of College of Health, Physical Education and Recreation, Texas Woman's University, Denton, Texas.)

leaves the board in an upward and slightly outward direction with arms reaching overhead, legs straight, and toes extended. The back arches very slightly.

ENTRY.   The point of entry is in front of the board, directly beneath the body and descending downward toward the pool bottom. In a header, the fingertips touch the water first; the body follows in a straight line at right angles to the water surface. On a foot-first entry the body is erect and extended with arms at the sides.

Fancy Dives.   There are five groups of dives as categorized by the Amateur Athletic Union and the Division for Girls and Women's Sports: forward, back, reverse (gainer), inward (cutaway), and twist. The handstand group is not given official competitive status. Selected dives from the five groups will be described.

FORWARD GROUP—Swan, Jackknife, Forward Somersault, Forward One and a Half Somersault.

Swan Dive.   In competitive events the running front and swan are considered the same. The difference is in the arm movements. As the diver leaves the board her hands are lifted from the hips and spread straight from the shoulders with a slight backward angle. At the peak of the dive the body rotates and the head slowly drops between the arms as they close for entry.

Front Jackknife.   The diver climbs with hands extended. At the end of the reach, the arms reach down as legs and toes are pressed forward with hips higher than the head. Hands contact the feet and the body remains piked for an instant before the legs lift slowly for a vertical entry with head between the arms.

Forward Somersault.   This may be done in a tuck, pike, or layout position. In a tuck the

Fig. 16-19.   Swan dive.

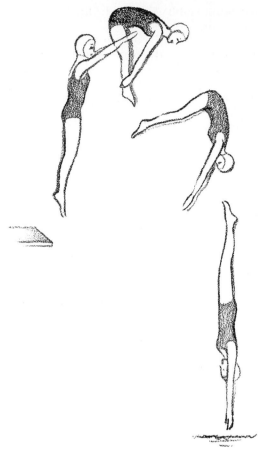

Fig. 16-20. Front jackknife.

as heels are extended over the end of the board. To lift from the board, lower the arms to the side and lower the heels simultaneously. Then raise the arms in front of the face and upward above the head.

The diver leaves the board straight upward with arms extended. At height of the upward momentum, the head stretches backward, the back arches and the eyes focus on the water. For a swan, the arms move out at shoulder level and come together as they pass the end of the board on descent.

Back Somersault. The back somersault can be done in pike or tuck position. From take-off position, rise and lift the arms forcibly. Immediately lift the knees to the chest in a tuck or bend at the hips for a pike. Pull the head backward and continue backward motion until the body falls in line for a vertical descent. Straighten legs and point toes downward as arms straighten by the thighs.

knees are close to the body, in pike position the body is bent at the hips with legs straight, and in the layout the body remains straight and in the same plane throughout the dive.

In a tuck or pike the somersault is made by bringing the heels backward and upward as the head and chest pull to the knees. In a tuck the knees bend and heels come to the buttocks with arms below the knees. In a pike the hands are placed at shin level. Before the body reaches a vertical position the legs extend and feet begin entry.

Forward One and a Half Somersault. This is like a forward somersault with additional rotation for a head entry.

BACK GROUP—Back Dive and Back Somersault.

Back Dive. This is a standing rather than a running dive. Standing at the end of the board, eyes focused on the back wall, raise arms to shoulder height in front of the body. Toes and balls of the feet carry body weight

Fig. 16-21. Forward somersault in pike position.

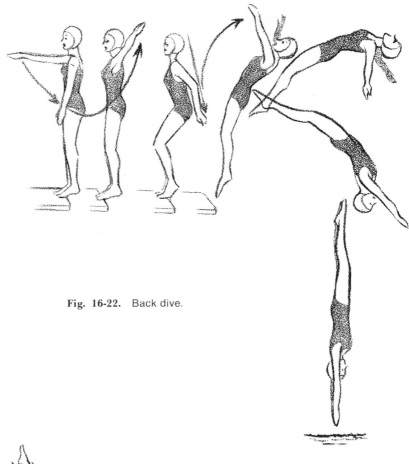

Fig. 16-22. Back dive.

Fig. 16-23. Back somersault in tuck position.

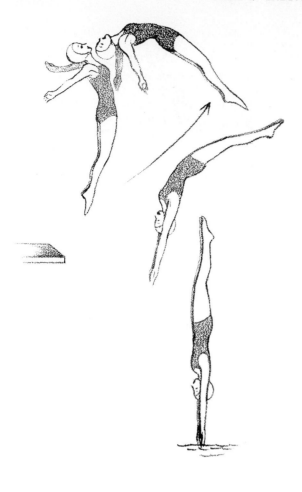

Fig. 16-24. Half gainer.

Fig. 16-25. Back jackknife.

REVERSE GROUP—Half Gainer.

Half Gainer (Islander). A beautiful dive that requires excellent hurdle and take-off control. Simply, it is a backward dive from a forward take-off. At the end of the lift with arms in spread position, the head, arms, and shoulders pull backward and the chest, hips, and legs are lifted in a stretched position. As the body reaches a horizontal position the legs remain lifted and relatively stationary as arms, shoulders, and head continue rotation downward. The arms are brought close to the head at board level and lead a vertical entry.

INWARD GROUP—Back Jackknife.

Back Jackknife. Begin as if a back dive. Lift from the board, forcing hips upward, and bring hands down to touch the instep in pike position. Raise hips and legs and lower the head between the arms for head-first entry.

TWIST GROUP—Front Dive with Half Twist and Front Dive with Full Twist.

Half Twist. Take off as in a front header

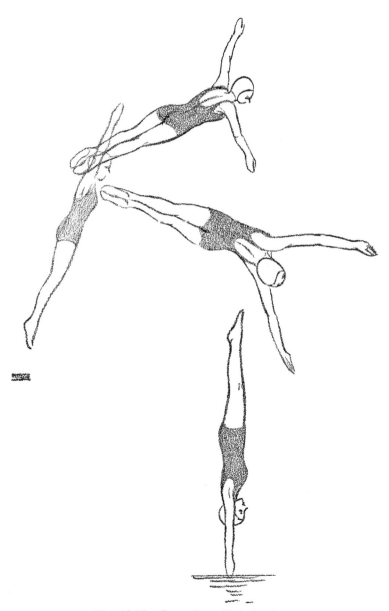

Fig. 16-26. Front dive with half twist.

with arms reaching up and out from the shoulders. At the peak of the reach, if the twist is made to the right, lower the right shoulder and direct the right arm toward a spot of entry in the water. The head turns and the eyes focus on the lowered right arm. Entry into the water is straight, with the back toward the board.

Full Twist. Rise from the board in a swan position. If twisting to the right, thrust the left arm across the hip and downward. Raise the right arm above the head as legs bear upward during rise and descent. A half twist is completed while rising and continues as the head turns forcibly to the right and the left arm extends by the head with the right arm upon entry.

In a piked dive with a twist, the twist must not start until there is a marked pike.

GAME RULES AND SCORING*

A swimming meet may require as many as 20 officials for proper administration. Officials include a referee, a diving referee, a clerk, one official scorer, three to five finish judges, three or five judges of diving, timekeepers, a starter, an announcer, and a turn and lane inspector.

Dual, triangular, and group meets are conducted in which no contestant is allowed to participate in more than three different events. General rules for competitive racing are as follows:

1. No swimmer may swim more than one distance of a relay.

2. No contestant may wear or use any device to aid her speed or buoyancy during competition.

3. In all races, except the backstroke, the contestants start on their starting marks. The surface for the takeoff is flat and parallel to the surface of the water and not more than 30 inches above the water level. In backstroke competition the swimmer starts in the water with both hands in contact with the starting mark until the starting signal is given.

4. A contestant leaving her mark before the official start is charged with a false start. Two false starts disqualify a swimmer for that

event; in relay races her team is disqualified for that race.

5. Swimmers must keep a straight course. If a swimmer touches another swimmer or impedes her progress she is subject to disqualification.

6. A swimmer failing to execute the stroke properly or make legal touches on the turns and at the finish is disqualified in the event. A hand touch on the freestyle turn is not required. On the backstroke turn she must touch the end of the pool before starting the body roll.

On breaststroke and butterfly stroke a contestant is disqualified if she (a) fails to touch with both hands simultaneously; (b) anticipates the turn by extending one hand out for the turn or by engaging the water with the instep of one foot and the sole of the other (partial scissors); or (c) pushes off in a position other than the breast.

7. A swimmer finishes a race when she touches the finish mark or passes under a marker. In the breaststroke and butterfly stroke both hands must touch simultaneously. The freestyle and backstroke touches may be with one hand.

8. In relays a team is disqualified if a swimmer leaves her starting mark before the incoming swimmer touches the end of the pool. She may continue, however, if she returns and touches the pool edge.

General rules for diving:

1. A written record of the required and voluntary dives and of the manner of takeoff selected must be presented before the meet begins. Only dives mentioned in the approved table or agreed upon by the officials may be executed.

2. A diver has one attempt to execute each dive unless the referee rules that the circumstances warrant another attempt.

3. Dives are executed and judged on (a) starting position, approach, and takeoff (all springboard dives with forward takeoff may be performed either standing or running at the option of the diver), (b) height, (c) position in the air, and (d) entry.

SCORING

The Division for Girls and Women's Sports recommends the following competitive events:

---

*For complete rules see D.G.W.S., *Aquatics Guide*, current edition.

75-foot Pools

Team Events

1. 75 or 150 yard medley relay
   Order of strokes: Backstroke, breast-stroke, freestyle

or

2. 100 or 200 yard medley relay
   Order of strokes: Backstroke, breast-stroke, butterfly stroke, freestyle
3. 100 or 200 yard freestyle relay

Individual Events

1. Freestyle, backstroke, breaststroke, butterfly stroke (25 yards, 50 yards, 100 yards, 200 yards)
2. 75 yard individual medley
   Order of strokes: Breaststroke, back-stroke, freestyle

or

3. 100 yard individual medley
   Order of strokes: Butterfly stroke, backstroke, breaststroke, freestyle

60-foot Pools

Team Events

1. 60 or 120 yard medley relay
   Order of strokes: Backstroke, breast-stroke, freestyle

or

2. 80 or 160 yard medley relay
   Order of strokes: Backstroke, breast-stroke, butterfly stroke, freestyle
3. 80 or 160 yard freestyle relay

Individual Events

1. Freestyle, backstroke, breaststroke, butterfly stroke (20 yards, 40 yards, 100 yards, 200-220 yards)
2. 60 yard individual medley
   Order of strokes: Breaststroke, back-stroke, freestyle

or

3. 80 yard individual medley
   Order of strokes: Butterfly stroke, backstroke, breaststroke, freestyle

Places in a swimming meet are determined by the point total of each team. Places in *racing* events are decided by the fastest times. Places in each event are scored on an assigned

value for team relays or individual events. These values vary with the type of meet. Places in meets shall be scored as follows:*

Dual Meets
a. Relays:
   First place . . . . 7 points
   Second place . . . . 0 points
b. All other events:
   First place . . . . 5 points
   Second place . . . . 3 points
   Third place . . . . 1 point

Triangular Meets
a. Relays:
   First place . . . . 8 points
   Second place . . . . 4 points
   Third place . . . . 0 points
b. All other events:
   First place . . . . 6 points
   Second place . . . . 4 points
   Third place . . . . 3 points
   Fourth place . . . . 2 points
   Fifth place . . . . 1 point
   Sixth place . . . . 0 points

Group Meets
Scoring depends upon the number of lanes used in the finals.
   If four lanes are used—
      Relays are scored: 10-6-4-2
      All other events: 5-3-2-1
   If five lanes are used—
      Relays are scored: 12-8-6-4-2
      All other events: 6-4-3-2-1
   If six lanes are used—
      Relays are scored: 14-10-8-6-4-2
      All other events: 7-5-4-3-2-1

In the event that two tie for first place, the first and second place awards shall be added and half the sum shall be awarded to each contestant in the tie; there shall be no second place. If three tie for first place, the first, second, and third places shall be added and one third of the sum shall be awarded to each contestant in the tie; there shall be no second or third place. The same is true for those tying for second place, third place, and whatever other places there may be.

The team having the greatest number of points shall be declared the winner of the swimming meet.

---

*D.G.W.S.: *Aquatic Guide*, 1967-1969, pp. 134-135.

Diving Events. Diving competition is based on the execution of compulsory and voluntary dives, each one being evaluated by three to five judges on a point scale of 0 to 10. When five judges are used, the highest and lowest scores are cancelled before computing the single dive score. The total score of each dive is multiplied by the assigned difficulty rating of the dive. Each dive score total is then tabulated to give a diver's total for the event.

The winner is the contestant earning the greatest point total. If two or more divers obtain the same number of points, a tie is declared. When determining a team total, points are awarded for diving as for all other individual events in the meet.

Terminology

Aquatics—Water activities of all kinds: swimming, diving, skiing, skin and SCUBA diving, water games, synchronized swimming, boating, sailing, and surfing.

Beat—A phase of the flutter kick, a thrust of the leg. "Six beat kick" refers to six thrusting movements of the legs to one complete cycle of both arms.

Bobbing—Process of raising the head from beneath the surface and then submerging again in a rhythmical pattern.

Buoyancy—Property and tendency of the body that makes floating possible.

Catch—Applying pressure to the water with the hand just before the power phase.

Coordination—Proper movements controlled accurately as to direction, force, and timing to produce efficient action.

Cycle—Complete movement of both arms and legs in executing a total stroke.

Dive—A descent into the water.

Entry—The movement of the entire body or a part of the body (usually arms) into the water.

Extension—To reach or stretch out a selected part or the entire body.

Flexion—Bending of the body at a joint.

Float—To sustain the body position with little or no movement.

Medley—A combination of strokes or distances in individual or relay events.

Natatorium—An enclosure containing a pool.

Recovery—The phase of arm or leg action which is without propelling force. It follows the power phase.

SCUBA—Self-Contained Underwater Breathing Apparatus

Stroke—A complete pattern of arm and leg movements which propels the body through the water.

Surfing—*Body* surfing uses the waves to carry the extended body to the shore. *Board* surfing consists of riding the waves on a long board in a sitting, kneeling, or standing position.

Turn—A reversal of direction at the end of the pool or course.

Selected Audio-visual Aids

Beginning Diving, 1957. (3 filmstrips.) The Athletic Institute, 805 Merchandise Mart, Chicago, Ill. 60654 (Purchase and rental.)

Beginning Swimming, 1957. (4 filmstrips.) The Athletic Institute, 805 Merchandise Mart, Chicago, Ill. 60654 (Purchase and rental.)

Diving, 1954. (9 loop films, 16 mm., b & w.) AAHPER, 1201 16th St. N.W., Washington, D.C. 20036.

Diving Skills Learned on the Trampoline, 1964. (14 min., 16 mm., b & w.) H. Billingsley, 1504 Matlock Rd., Bloomington, Ind. 47405.

Dolphin Kick, 1956. (8 min., 16 mm., b & w, sound.) Coronet Films, Coronet Bldg., Chicago, Ill. (Purchase.)

Fancy Diving, 1954. (9 loop films, 16 mm., b & w, silent.) AAHPER, 1201 16th St. N.W., Washington, D.C. 20036 (Purchase.)

Learning to Swim Series. (Crawl—12 min; breaststroke—12 min., backstroke—8 min., 16 mm., b & w.) International Film Bureau, 57 E. Jackson Blvd., Chicago, Ill. 60604, or 20 W. 55th St., New York, N.Y. 10017 (Rental.)

Sprint Crawl, 1966. (16 mm., color, 15 min., sound.) Ryan Films Inc., Box 4051, Hamden, Conn. 06514.

Starts and Turns, 1965. (16 mm., b & w, 14 min., sound.) National Association of Engine and Boat Manufacturers, 420 Lexington Ave., N.Y., N.Y. 10017.

Swimming—Dolphin, Butterfly, Breaststroke, 1955. (16 mm., b & w, sound.) State University of Iowa, Bureau of Audio Visual Instruction, Iowa City, Iowa.

Suggested Readings

AAHPER: *Official Aquatics Guide*, Current Ed., Division for Girls and Women's Sports, 1201 16th St., N.W., Washington, D.C. 20036.

American National Red Cross: Life Saving and Water Safety, 2nd Ed., Philadelphia, P. Blakiston's Sons & Co., 1937.

Armbruster, David A., Sr., Allen, Robert H., and Billingsley, Hobart; *Swimming and Diving*, 4th Ed., St. Louis, The C. V. Mosby Co., 1963.

Billingsley, Hobbie: *Diving Illustrated*, New York, The Ronald Press Company, 1965.

Fairbanks, Anne Ross: *Teaching Springboard Diving*, Englewood Cliffs, N.J., Prentice-Hall, Inc., 1963.

Gabrielson, M. A., Spears, Betty, and Gabrielson, B. W.: *Aquatics Handbook*, Englewood Cliffs, N.J., Prentice-Hall, Inc., 1960.

Periodicals

Skin Diver (monthly), 5959 Hollywood Blvd., Los Angeles, Calif.

Swimming Pool Age—Beach and Pool, Hoffman-Harris, 425 Fourth Ave., New York, N.Y.

Suggested Study Questions

1. Define the power and recovery phases of a stroke. Describe any stroke and define the specific phases.
2. Describe the coordination for the sidestroke.
3. What is meant by the term aquatics? Elaborate on the activities included.
4. What is an individual medley?
5. Describe the body position for a front running dive during the approach, the takeoff and the entry into the water.
6. What safety precautions must be taken in the pool area? What hygienic procedures should be followed before entering the pool?

CHAPTER SEVENTEEN

Courtesy of Agnes I. Michaels, State University College, Fredonia, New York.

SYNCHRONIZED SWIMMING

Today recreational or competitive synchronized swimming is more popular in the United States than in any other nation, although it is not truly of American origin. For many years Germany has had floating competitive formations; England, group swimming; and Canada, individual competition in "Ornamental Swimming."

The origin of the term synchronized swimming is credited to Norman Ross, who used it when announcing a water show prepared by Katherine Curtis for the 1933 Chicago World's Fair. Prior to this time group presentations were largely floating formations with minimal swimming or sculling to move from one formation to the next. These presentations were termed water ballet or rhythmical swimming and were executed with muscial background or accompaniment.

The growth in the popularity of synchronized swimming has resulted in the formation of the Association of Synchronized Swimming for College Women and the International Academy of Aquatic Art. For several years the Amateur Athletic Union has sponsored competitive events and has been instrumental, in cooperation with Fédération Internationale de Natation Amateur, in encouraging synchronized exhibitions at the Olympic games, such as the exhibition in Tokyo in the 1964 Olympics. Every four years the Pan-American Games include synchronized swimming in their schedule of events.

NATURE AND PURPOSE OF THE SPORT

Synchronized swimming is both a sport and an art form of rhythmical water activity that is performed in a definite pattern and syn-

Fig. 17-1. Synchronized swimming is both a sport and an art form. (Courtesy of Clifford Lewis, University of Georgia.)

chronized with a prescribed accompaniment.

Synchronization implies movements of individual swimmers synchronized with vocal, percussive, instrumental, or other accompaniment. When more than one swimmer participates, her movements are synchronized with those of other swimmers—either in unison or in a planned order. Basic swimming strokes, modified strokes, and water stunts are the basic techniques the swimmer uses in conjunction with accompaniment.

When synchronized swimming became competitive, routines were developed using required figures of a specified level of difficulty. Deck work, costuming, and lighting became important for establishing mood. Moving beyond competitive limitations, other groups allow freedom of interpretation and design, using creative and expressive movements beyond the conventional figures. In all cases, synchronized swimming as taught in schools and colleges is creative, skillful, imaginative, and pleasurable.

FACILITIES AND EQUIPMENT

The swimming area should be at least 60 by 20 feet, with water at least 8 feet deep in half of the area. This depth is necessary to allow for proper descent in executing stunts. Clear water and a light pool bottom and sides with sufficient overhead light are necessary for viewing by participants, spectators, and judges.

Materials and equipment for accompaniment are imperative. A record player, percussive instruments, or choral groups usually serve. An underwater speaker system and underwater lights are desirable.

Personal equipment includes a comfortable suit, swimming cap, and a nose clip. This simple clip squeezes the nostrils together and prevents water from entering the nose and sinuses as one executes stunts.

Costumes are important for colorful production. Their nature is dictated by the composition and the funds available.

BASIC SKILLS

Swimming strokes and techniques termed "stunts" are the basic skills of synchronized work. Five strokes, often modified, provide the methods of moving from place to place in a manner in keeping with the atmosphere of the composition. A swimmer should develop strong standard strokes of crawl, backstroke, elementary backstroke, sidestroke, and breaststroke. The inverted breaststroke may also be helpful. (See Chapter 16 for descriptions of the standard strokes.)

Basic Stroke Modification. All strokes must be adapted so that:

1. The face is above the water to observe other swimmers and hear the accompaniment if there are no underwater speakers.
2. The arms are carried higher for effect.
3. The legs kick deeper. They are lowered by raising the head and arms in order to prevent a splash of the kick at water level.
4. Only the head and arms are visible above the water. The arm action is frequently seen and must be timed, directed and positioned in keeping with that of others.
5. Breathing can be timed and conditioned for the stroke and in preparation for a stunt.

FRONT CRAWL MODIFICATION:

1. Lower the legs slightly. A 6 or 8 beat kick is generally used.
2. Raise the head so that the chin is in the water. Eyes focus straight ahead.
3. Arm pull is straight down under the shoulder to a vertical position.
4. The arm lifts high on recovery. The elbow lifts until the entire arm is out of the water. The forearm then moves forward and fingertips enter the water.

BACKSTROKE MODIFICATION:

1. Drop hips slightly so that they are lower than the head.
2. Head is above the water with chin tucked.
3. The legs are lowered so that the 6 to 8 beat kick is below the surface.
4. Hands catch from a 5 o'clock to a 1 o'clock position with the arm pull parallel to the water surface directly to the thigh.
5. Arm recovery is in an arc above the water. A straight arm (fingers leading) or bent arm (elbow leading initially) may be used, depending on the desired effect.

SIDESTROKE MODIFICATION:

1. Drop legs slightly.
2. The head is up and out of the water rather than resting on the extended arm.

BREASTSTROKE MODIFICATION:

1. Face remains above the water with chin slightly submerged.
2. Arm pull *may be* less pronounced and shorter than in the standard stroke. In a modified pull the arms move in a small circle; the elbows bend toward the bottom of the pool as hands begin recovery under the chin.

ELEMENTARY BACKSTROKE MODIFICATION:

1. Hips are lowered to a position beneath the shoulders.
2. Head is raised and the chin is tucked as the body remains extended.

Stroke Variations. By varying the stroke the pattern may become more interesting and more in keeping with the accompaniment. Such variations include accenting parts of the recovery (e.g., extending the top arm in the sidestroke and holding it above the water before entry), changing arm actions above the water (e.g., in the front crawl, recovering forward, withdrawing the arm and finally entering the water), or a change in the action of the stroke itself (e.g., a two-arm overwater recovery in the inverted breaststroke).

Combined and Hybrid Strokes. Combined stroking refers to complete strokes performed in a series; for example, a front crawl, followed by a backstroke, and then a breaststroke.

Hybrid strokes combine parts of two or more standard or modified strokes to set a pattern, rhythm, or effect; for example, begin with a backstroke left, turn to a sidestroke left, turn to a backstroke right, and roll to a sidestroke right.

Duo Skills. Once the modified standard strokes and selected combined and hybrid forms are learned, swimmers begin working in pairs to accompaniment. They may be attached or unattached. Unattached pairs swim in vertical, horizontal, or staggered lines. *Tandem* swimmers are directly behind one another doing identical or complementary actions. They may be attached at the neck, under the arms, or at the waist.

Floating Formations. Swimmers maintain

Fig. 17-2 A floating formation.

these so-called "floating" formations by sculling or other hand motions. Groups of from 2 to 16 or more swimmers make a colorful presentation, whether in a stationary pattern or one moved by other swimmers.

Fundamental Positions Basic to Stunt Execution. These positions are defined, for they represent basic starting positions for stunt execution.

LAYOUT POSITION (SUPINE POSITION). Contract the abdominal muscles so that the small of the back is as flat as possible. Keep the back of the head in a straight line with the spine. Toe tips, ankle bones, hip bone, shoulders, and ears are in a straight line. Hands begin in a flat sculling position.

VERTICAL BODY POSITION. The body alignment is the same as in layout position except that the body is vertical in the water. This position is used for stunts that involve a lift or descent from the pool in a straight line.

BACK LAYOUT POSITION. Similar to the layout position, with head lifted slightly forward, chin in, shoulders back and relaxed.

Fig. 17-3. Body spacing variation adds to the effectiveness of a synchronized swimming routine. (Courtesy of College of Health, Physical Education and Recreation, Texas Woman's University, Denton, Texas.)

Thighs and feet are close to the surface of the water.

FRONT LAYOUT POSITION (PRONE). Lying on the face, contract the abdominal muscles. The body is slightly arched, head above the surface, and heels at the surface. Arms and hands are under the body near the sides, in basic sculling position.

PIKE POSITION. The body bends sharply at the hips, legs extended with toes pointed sharply. To tighten the pike the head moves close to the knees, and hands to the ankles.

TUCK POSITION. The knees bend as the thighs pull into the chest. Toes are extended and the heels press against the buttocks. The head is positioned close to the knees and the back is rounded.

Sculling. This movement is basic to skill development in synchronized swimming. It is estimated that there are nine types of sculling, all using either a flexion or hyperextension of the wrists and a small outward push and inward pull of the hands beneath the surface.

To control the body in a floating formation or in a back layout position in preparation for a stunt, the arms are close to the body, and the hands are near the surface with fingers and wrists level during the *flat* scull.

The *standard scull* moves the body toward the head when in a layout position (supine). The arms are at the sides with elbows close to the body; hands are at the hips. Paired arm action begins so that palms turn down and out and press outward through arm action. The thumbs turn up, then whip the palms toward the feet and back to starting position.

Sculling feet-first with the *arms at the side* is accomplished by turning the palms out and pulling against the water in a small semicircle away from the feet and toward the head. The wrists relax to complete the circle and return to original position.

When sculling with the *arms and hands overhead* so that the body moves *toward the feet*, the palms are turned away from the body and pressure is applied outward and downward. The hands move no more than the width of the shoulders. The palms face each other and the thumbs touch on the recovery. This is often called *propeller sculling.*

For *reverse sculling* the hands are lifted behind the head with the same hand position described for sculling feet-first. At the beginning of the outward pull, the back of the wrists touch. At the end of the inward movement the fingertips are facing. The body moves toward the head.

Fig. 17-4.   Sculling is basic to skill development and movement control. (Courtesy of College of Health, Physical Education and Recreation, Texas Woman's University, Denton, Texas.)

To scull so that the body moves *sideward*, one arm pulls in the desired direction as the other pushes.

To *circle* around the head or feet, one hand pulls or pushes near the pivotal point to maintain position as the other pulls or pushes with larger sweeping sculling motion.

Surface Dives.   A review of surface dive execution, particularly the foot-first entry, will be helpful at this point (see Chapter 16, p. 266).

Simple Stunts.   A stunt may be performed above, on, or below the water level. There is difference of opinion concerning the difficulty of learning and executing these stunts. The following progression is suggested:

TUB.   Begin from a back layout position with a flat scull. The knees are drawn to the chest so that the hips sink and the swimmer is sitting in the water, with extended toes and lower legs remaining near the surface of the water. Sculling motion of the hands turns the body in a circle.

BACK TUCK SOMERSAULT.   Begin from a back layout position. Draw the knees to the chest; legs remain together and toes are pointed as the hips sink. The body drops

backward as the arms press down, back, up, and forward in a circle. The body remains tucked until the somersault is completed and legs then straighten to starting position.

FRONT TUCK SOMERSAULT.   Begin from a front layout position. The knees are bent and pulled toward the chest as the head is dropped forward toward the bottom of the pool. Palms turn out and arms press outward, backward, and upward, and then downward

Fig. 17-5.   Tub.

and forward. After a complete turn the body returns to starting position.

A somerault in a *pike* position is executed in a similar way, but the body is bent only at the hips. Legs remain together, knees extended and toes pointed.

CORKSCREW. Begin in a front layout position with one arm at the surface extended in front of the head and the other arm at the side. The body rolls around the extended arm by turning the head and body in the direction of the turn and away from the extended arm. The side arm sculls for additional pull.

PORPOISE. This is similar to a surface dive in a pike position. From a front layout the trunk bends at the hips as the head moves forward and downward. The arms (positioned at sides or forward) scoop sideward and downward. As the hips are brought over the head the back straightens and the legs are brought up perpendicular to the water surface. The hands sweep forward to maintain this position. The hands then pull the body below the water in this vertical position. Once under the water the recovery begins by lifting the head, arching the back, and pulling in the direction of the surface.

FLYING PORPOISE. The figure begins with a vertical foot-first surface dive to the bottom of the pool. Flexed knees and ankles push the body to the surface. When the upper half of the body is above the water, the body assumes a pike position to execute a porpoise. Once started, there is no break in the movements.

Side and back porpoises, after the body "flies" from the water, are variations.

Fig. 17-7. An underwater view of a bent knee dolphin. (Courtesy of Miss Dorothy Shields, Department of Required Physical Education, University of Flordia, Gainesville.)

DOLPHIN. Begin in a back layout position. The shoulders and upper back arch as the arms extend and execute a scooping movement outward and upward to pull the body gracefully downward. The body describes a large circle as the arms continue the pulling action (down, around, and up) to return the extended body to original position.

FLYING DOLPHIN. From a vertical foot-first surface dive the body lifts halfway out of the water. Execute a dolphin from the top of the lift.

SHARK. Begin with the body in a side layout position. The body arches and the top arm extends overhead in a continuing arc. (The top arm position may vary for effect.) The lower hand and arm execute a shallow arm pull and with small scooping movements pull the arched body, with locked knees and extended toes, in a wide circle.

MARLIN. Begin on the back with arms extended from the shoulders, palms up. To turn left, the right knee bends to the chest

Fig. 17-6. Dolphin.

and the left arm moves above the head. The body rolls left as the right arm lowers to the thigh to assist the roll. When on the chest, keep head up and again extend arms from the shoulders. Continue rolling in the same direction by pushing downward with the right arm. The arms are at shoulder level at the end of the roll. Return leg to extended position. The stunt may be executed with both legs straight; but in either case, at completion of the roll, the feet remain on the pivotal spot and the body has moved horizontally 90 degrees.

BALLET LEGS. To execute a single ballet leg the body is in layout position. The hands execute a flat scull. One leg remains extended at the surface as one knee bends toward the chest, then rises to a vertical position with knee and toe firmly extended. The leg bends back to the chest and is extended to starting position. Legs should be alternated to develop equal skill.

Fig. 17-8. An underwater view of the execution of the bent knee foot first dolphin. The swimmer is ascending. (Courtesy of Miss Dorothy Shields, Department of Required Physical Education, University of Florida, Gainesville.)

Fig. 17-9. Ballet leg.

Fig. 17-10. An underwater view of a single ballet leg roll. (Courtesy of Miss Dorothy Shields, Department of Required Physical Education, University of Florida, Gainesville.)

A *double ballet leg* is accomplished by simultaneous (paired) leg movements. With the additional body weight over the hips sculling becomes more vigorous.

CATALINA. Begin from a back layout position. Assume a right ballet leg position. Drop the head and turn under the left arm, maintaining the ballet leg as the body reaches a vertical position, with head down. Arch the body and raise the left leg from the surface to meet the right leg. Submerge and recover.

Fig. 17-12. Submarine.

OYSTER. From a back layout position the arms swing down and then up over the head as the hips flex and the body pikes sharply. The hands are near the ankles as the hips lead to a submerged position.

KIP. In a back layout position the knees are drawn sharply to the chin. From this tucked position roll backward by pulling the head down and under the hips while pressing down with the hands. Once the torso is vertical in the water, legs and head extend. Completely submerge, vertically, and recover as in a dolphin.

Variations include a split or scissors with extended legs before submerging.

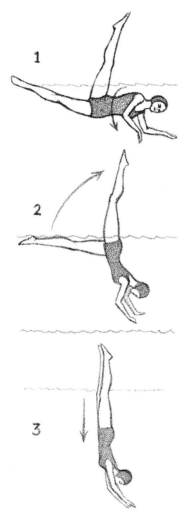

Fig. 17-11. Catalina.

SUBMARINE. Begin from a back layout position. One leg extends vertically as the hands move back and forcefully press toward the surface and sideward to pull the body directly down. A portion of the leg may remain above the water or it may submerge completely. Rise to the surface by pressing downward with the palms of the hands.

Fig. 17-13. Execution of a hybrid oyster. This is a routine stunt and is considered by many to be much prettier than a simple oyster. It is frequently used as a transitional stunt. (Courtesy of Miss Dorothy Shields, Department of Required Physical Education. University of Florida, Gainesville.)

Fig. 17-14. Kip.

SOMER-SUB. From an extended prone position, begin a pike somersault. When the legs are parallel to water surface the back is toward the bottom of the pool and the face is toward the surface. Extend one leg in a vertical position, the other forward and parallel

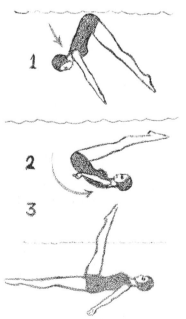

Fig. 17-15. Somer-sub.

to the water surface. Rise to the surface with vertical leg leading. Once on the surface, bend the knee of the vertical leg, draw it to the chest, and then lower it to join the extended leg.

GAMES RULES AND SCORING*

Competition in synchronized swimming is generally conducted under rules established by the Amateur Athletic Union or the Fédération Internationale de Natation Amateur.† The Division for Girls and Women's Sports recommends the use of Official A.A.U. Synchronized Swimming Rules by schools and colleges. The events in A.A.U. are solo, duet, and teams of four to eight.

The Association of Synchronized Swimming for College Women sponsors annual meetings with representatives from over 50 colleges participating in workshops and discussions. Individual and group demonstrations are included in the activities.

At the present time most competition in the United States is conducted under A.A.U. rules. Awards are presented to solo, duet, and team entries. The productions are limited in time (usually 5 minutes) and include required and optional stunts of specified difficulty. Individuals are required to participate in stunt competition (three compulsory and three optional) and their scores are added to the routine score. The A.A.U. publishes a stunt difficulty rating scale.

In solo, duet, and team competition, judging is based on execution and style. Execution includes the performance of strokes, stunts, and figures from the standpoint of perfection. Style includes: (1) synchronization—both with others and with the accompaniment; (2) construction—structure of the routine, interpretation, fluidity, and pool utilization; (3) variety, difficulty, and originality, that is, diversity and creativity in the routine.

The three to five judges score on execution, and then on style, using a one-half point scale from 0 to 10. In judging *style* in solo competition and dual and team competition, the weighting is as follows:

*See the A.A.U. *Official Synchronized Swimming Handbook.*

†The organization managing and controlling all contests in swimming and diving held at the Olympic Games.

	Synchronization	Construction	Variety
Solo	2 points	4 points	4 points
Duet and team	4 points	3 points	3 points

COMPOSING A SYNCHRONIZED SWIMMING ROUTINE

Development of a routine requires an understanding of synchronized water skills, timing of the skill execution, rhythm of the accompaniment, lighting, costuming, and general design of the entire production. The following suggestions offer two approaches for the beginning composer.*

1. Routine to be based on an accompaniment, such as a song, instrumental recording, poem, or chant.
  A. Listen to and analyze the accompaniment.
    1. Learn the basic rhythm and underlying beat.
    2. Analyze for themes and phrases.
    3. Identify the climax.
  B. Identify the types of water movements

---

*Adapted from Betty Spears, *Beginning Synchronized Swimming*. Minneapolis, Minn., Burgess Publishing Company, 1959.

that best express the rhythms of the music. Experiment with the strokes, hybrids, and stunts, as well as with original movements.
  C. Begin to structure the routine by considering:
    1. Entrance
    2. Basic stroke
    3. Climax
    4. Exit
  D. Plan a tentative "space pattern" with the techniques mentioned above.
  E. Try the routine in the water, continue to polish and develop.
  F. Continue to refine the routine, checking expression of mood, timing, tempo, and quality of performance.
  G. Learn and perform the routine. When possible add lighting and costuming for effect.

When developing a routine based on an idea or water action, the accompaniment often must be developed from the routine. Bear in mind:

1. The basic idea to be expressed.
2. The types of water movements, as well as entrances and exits that best express the idea.
3. The basic rhythmic patterns of these

Fig. 17-16. Costuming, carefully planned accompaniment, lighting, and exact timing of skill execution can add much to the effectiveness of a synchronized swimming routine. (Courtesy of Clifford Lewis, University of Georgia.)

movements. What is the accent? Is the same meter used throughout?

At this point tentatively structure the routine and then analyze it to see how to construct accompaniment.

1. Use basic meters.
2. Combine these into phrases.
3. Outline the routine for use in composing the accompaniment.

Work with the composer, sharing the basic rhythmic idea and water actions, until a composition is developed. Refine accompaniment and water skills; add lighting and costuming and perform.

Terminology

An extensive glossary is not appropriate, as basic terms are defined in the chapter content. Several terms deserve emphasis and a few musical terms warrant definition.

Accent — In music, the beat of a measure that is regularly emphasized.

Aquatic art — The integration of swimming stunts, strokes, and floating figures with other art forms, such as music and dance, in order to create compositions.

Combined strokes — Two or more complete strokes performed in a series.

Hybrid strokes — Combination of two or more parts of standard strokes to set a pattern, rhythm, or effect.

Measure — A unit of music that divides the basic rhythm at regular intervals.

Modified strokes — An adaptation of standard strokes for synchronized use.

Phrase — In music, usually a grouping of four measures. There is a natural break in the rhythm at the end of a phrase.

Rhythm — Musically, the pattern the notes make, including the accents, rests, and time spacing. Also, a sense of understanding the relationship of the underlying musical beat with a movement.

Sculling — Use of the hands in propelling the body through the water.

Section — A portion of a musical selection composed of a group of phrases.

Synchronized swimming — Coordination of movements of a swimmer to musical accompaniment; when there are two or more swimmers, their movements must be coordinated with each other.

Selected Audio-visual Aids

Champions on Film — Synchronized Swimming, 1956. (2 sets, 16 mm. loops, b & w.) Basic Figures and Advanced Figures. Champions on Film, 1643 S. State Street, Ann Arbor, Mich. (Purchase.)

Fundamentals of Creative Swimming, 1961. (24 min., b & w and color, sound.) Part I: Strokes and Stroking Skills; Part II: Body Positions and Figures. Colburn Film Distributors, Inc., P.O. Box 470, 668 N. Western Avenue, Lake Forest, Ill.

Synchronized Swimming, 1957. (2 sets, 16 mm. loops, b & w.) American Association for Health, Phsyical Education, and Recreation, 1201 16th Street, N.W., Washington, D.C. 20036 (Purchase.)

This is Synchronized Swimming, 1958. (3 reels, 16 mm., color, sound; basic and intermediate reels: 12 min. each; advanced reel: 16 min.) Jole and Co., 1027 Camino Ricardo, San Jose, Calif. 95126.

Suggested Readings

Amateur Athletic Union, *Official Synchronized Swimming Handbook*. Current ed. 231 W. 58th St. New York, N.Y. 10019.

Gundling, Beulah: *Exploring Aquatic Art*. Revised ed. International Academy of Aquatic Art, 403 Iowa Theatre Bldg., Cedar Rapids, Iowa 52401, 1966.

Official Aquatics Guide, AAHPER, Division for Girls and Women's Sports, 1201 16th St., N.W., Washington, D.C. 20036.

Seller, Peg, and Gundling, Beulah: *Aquatic Art*, Adcraft, 120 First Street, S.E., Cedar Rapids, Iowa, 1957.

Spears, Betty: *Fundamentals of Synchronized Swimming*. 3rd ed. Minneapolis, Minn., Burgess Publishing Company, 1966.

Vickers, Betty J.: *Teaching Synchronized Swimming*, Englewood Cliffs, New Jersey, Prentice Hall, Inc., 1965.

Yates, Fern, and Anderson, Theresa: *Synchronized Swimming*, 2nd Ed., New York, The Ronald Press Company, 1958.

Periodicals

Aquatic Artist (monthly), Official Publication of the International Academy of Aquatic Art, 403 Iowa Theatre Bldg., Cedar Rapids, Iowa.

Synchro-Info, Dawn Bean, 1911 Prince Albert Drive, Riverside, Calif.

Suggested Study Questions

1. What are the differences between combined strokes and hybrid strokes?
2. Why is "water ballet" an inappropriate term for synchronized swimming? What is synchronized swimming?
3. What stunts begin from a back position and go immediately to a tuck?
4. Describe the execution of a flying dolphin.
5. What modifications are made of the standard crawl for use in synchronized work?

CHAPTER EIGHTEEN

Courtesy of Dean Anne Schley Duggan, College of Health, Physical Education and Recreation, Texas Woman's University, Denton, Texas.

TENNIS

Although the French are often credited with originating tennis, actually it evolved from a game played by the ancient Greeks and Romans that is similar to modern handball. The English popularized an Irish version of the sport and played it on a court bounded at the sides by two parallel nets staked down at the center so that each was shaped like an hourglass. At first a hard leather, hair-stuffed ball was batted between partners back and forth across a rope by their bare hands; several years later by a gloved fist, then with a glove protected by leather thongs wrapped around it. Later, a parchment tambourine was used to swat a linen ball, then a crude short-handled paddle was devised, and finally a racket and ball similar to those of today were used. It is believed that the word "tennis" is from the French "tenez," meaning "hold" or "take."

Early scoring was complicated with 15 "chases" given for 1 point, from which arose the 15, 30, 40 game method of scoring. "Love," or nothing, which is symbolized by a zero or egg-shaped O, is from the French word "l'oeuf" for "the egg," pronounced by the English as "love."

King Louis X of France is responsible for the fact that tennis is called "The Sport of Kings." He jealously guarded the game for members of his court and banned the game for the masses when he found them playing it. In spite of the ban, the game became an activity for the "masses as well as the classes" and spread rapidly into England. It was during this period that a mesh net replaced the rope and the crude racket, the tambourine.

The popularity of tennis swept out from England into the world. Major Walter C. Wingfield, a British army officer, did much to give the game impetus at home and in the colonies. Mary Outerbridge, a United States visitor in Bermuda, was intrigued with the sport and returned to the United States in 1874 well supplied with rackets and balls. Although delayed several hours by customs officers while they debated whether to permit her to bring such strange gadgets into the country, she not only succeeded in doing so, but with her brother successfully introduced the game to Americans. Largely due to their efforts and their following among enthusiastic fans, the official governing body of this sport, The United States Lawn Tennis Association, was founded in 1881. By 1900 the Davis Cup Matches for international competition among men were established, followed shortly afterwards by the Wightman Cup Matches for women in the United States and England.

NATURE AND PURPOSE OF THE GAME

Tennis is a game played with racket and ball on an indoor or outdoor court by two or four players. In both singles and doubles play the object of the game is to score points while preventing opponents from scoring. Points are scored by effective service and ball placement, which cause opponents to miss the ball, or to drive it into the net or out of the court area. The skill of the game lies in mastering serving techniques, offensive and defensive strokes and footwork, and game strategy. In competition a player strives to win points, games, sets, and ultimately a match.

The singles game is played on a 27 by 78 foot court. The area is divided by a net strung tautly across the court parallel to the base lines. The top of the net is 3 feet, 6 inches at each net post, tapering to 3 feet in the center of the court. Each half of the court is divided into a back and fore court. The fore court is further divided into the right and left serving or receiving areas. The doubles court is 4½ feet wider on each side. In a doubles game the additional "alley" area becomes valid playing space only *after* the service.

Play begins as the server delivers from behind the baseline and to the right of the

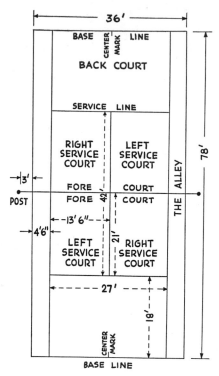

Fig. 18-1. Official tennis court.

center of the court. Serving from the right, she serves to her opponent's right court. Play between opponents continues until the winner of the point is determined. The server then moves to the left of center and behind the base line to serve and begin play for the second point. Serving positions are alternated until the game winner is determined.

FACILITIES AND EQUIPMENT

The *court* used out of doors has a surface of grass, clay, concrete, crushed stone, asphalt, or other composition materials. Indoor play is on a wooden floor or on canvas covering. Markings on concrete and asphalt courts are painted in white or bright yellow. Dry or white lime is usually used to mark grass or clay courts, although cotton and plastic tapes stapled securely in the ground are favored in some sections of the country, especially for camp use.

The *net* may be made of steel or other metal, and of hemp or cotton cord twine. Although tarred nets are more expensive, they are almost a must for outdoor use and should be strung on a weather-resistant cable. The official net height is 3 feet 6 inches at the net posts and 3 feet at the court center. The net is held down at the center by a strap not more than two inches wide. The band covering the cord or metal cable should not be more than 2½ inches in depth at each side. The net for singles should be 33 feet long, for doubles 42 feet, and should touch the ground along its entire length and come flush to the net posts at all points.

The recommended *costume* for this sport is a white tennis dress, sneakers, a white or colored blazer, and white wool socks. White shorts and blouse are acceptable on most courts.

Other necessary personal equipment includes balls and a racket with a well fitting cover and press. The racket frames are made of wood, steel, aluminum, plastic, or fiberglass, and strung with steel, aluminum, plastic, silk, nylon, or gut. A maximum of 18 main strings crossed by 20 evenly spaced, lateral strings is standard and meets the specifications of the United States Lawn Tennis Association. Quality rackets have handles made of basswood or Malacca, covered with fine leather, whereas cheaper ones have "leather" grips made of rubber, plastic, or imitation leather. The racket should weigh between 12 and 13½ ounces with a grip of 4½ to 4⅝ inches for women, and weigh between 11 and 13 ounces with a grip of 4 to 4½ inches for those between 9 and 12 years. Above all, the racket should not seem too heavy when swung vigorously back and forth for several minutes, and the grip should be small enough so that the hand fits comfortably around the handle.

Good balls are a must for all players, regardless of skill. Balls are manufactured under specifications of the United States Lawn Tennis Association, which requires that balls have a uniform outer surface, be more than 2½ inches and less than 2⅝ inches in diameter, and weigh more than 2 ounces but less than 2 1/16 ounces. Those meeting such specifications are packed and sealed in air-tight containers and bear the mark of United States Lawn Tennis Association approval. "Seconds" are not always marked, although some companies indicate that they are slightly defective by stamping out the letters USLTA. These cheaper balls are usually available at sporting goods shops on request and are suggested for beginners with a limited budget.

A backboard is the best opponent a player can have because it usually returns the balls. The best backboards are made of heavy beaverboard or pressboard in regulation half tennis court size, painted green with a white line 3½ feet above the ground. They should be located at one end of each court. A line 39 feet from the backboard and parallel to it should be painted on the area to indicate a court base line. Additional lines, 12 and 25 feet away, enable students to station themselves quickly for short and long rallying distances.

CARE AND REPAIR OF EQUIPMENT

BALLS

1. Brush dirt from balls before putting them back into the can.
2. Dry balls thoroughly before using them again.
3. Store at normal room temperature; avoid extremes of heat or cold.

RACKETS

Wood

1. Wipe the racket off with a dry cloth before putting it in a waterproof cover.
2. Put it squarely in a press and tighten the four screws evenly.
3. Hang the racket in a storage room of even temperature, not to exceed 75° or 60 per cent humidity.
4. Apply a thin coat of shellac over the strings at the end of the season, and a thin coat of wax over the entire frame.
5. Have broken strings repaired at a local sporting goods shop or by the manufacturer.

Metal

1. Occasionally wipe off the racket with a good cleanser that has a wax base to prevent rusting.
2. Although broken shafts and heads can be welded in local machine shops inexpensively, this can often be done better by the manufacturer.

Fiberglass and Plastic

1. Wipe off carefully before storing.
2. A press or cover is not necessary for these rackets.
3. Return to the manufacturer for re stringing or other repairs.

BASIC SKILLS

Footwork. The ability to get around the court quickly, moving forward or back, to either side, as well as to shift body weight and position, is the prerequisite to successful play. The knees should be kept relaxed and slightly bent, with body weight carried forward. Players should shift their weight to the forward foot (usually the one opposite the hand holding the racket), *move into* each stroke with full power, and move quickly around the court in order to play the ball in *front of the body*.

Jump rope drills are ideal for learning to push off from the balls of the feet as you start each movement, as well as for general warm-up purposes. Suggested patterns include:

1. Skip in place 25 times on both feet, 10 hopping from the left foot, 10 from the right.
2. Skip forward 10 times, 10 backward, 10 to the left, 10 to the right.
3. Skip on both feet in place facing forward, turn to the left and hop twice, return to place, hop twice turned to the right, return to place.
4. Move forward with fast running steps, skip backward, round in a circle, to both sides, changing directions suddenly upon command.
5. Repeat all four patterns mimetically swinging a racket without skipping the rope, then with an actual racket.

The Grip. Three standard grips are the Eastern, Western, and a modification of the two, or the Continental. Although there are certain values in all three, the one most commonly and most successfully used is the Eastern, for it permits easy free ball stroking.

THE EASTERN GRIP. Shake hands with a racket held perpendicular to the ground,

Fig. 18-2. Mastery of the correct tennis racket grip is essential for all beginners. (Courtesy of Clifford Lewis, University of Georgia.)

holding the first two fingers directly behind and well around the handle, with the heel of the hand at the end and the index finger spread slightly apart, thumb extended.

The Serve. A correct serve results from a combination of the correct stance, ball toss, swing, and footwork. In movement it is similar to the overhand baseball throw. The student stands sideways to the base line with feet spread comfortably apart, weight equally distributed, and the forward shoulder pointed in the direction the ball is to go. The racket is held in the *Continental grip* (similar to the Eastern backhand with the racket

Fig. 18-3. The Eastern grip.

Fig. 18-4. The serve.

shifted from one-sixteenth to one-eighth of a turn toward the forehand grip). The higher the point of contact with the ball, the better the serve is likely to be. The ball should therefore be thrown straight up into the air as high as the fully extended arm and racket can reach, above the head, and over the forward foot, and be hit at its maximum height when practically motionless, just before it comes back down toward the ground. As the ball is tossed into the air, the weight shifts to the rear foot. When the ball starts down, the racket is swung back behind the head and the whole body weight shifts to the forward foot as contact is made with the ball above the serving shoulder. On the natural follow-through the racket is brought down and across the body. The amount of spin put into the ball is determined by the angle of the racket and is largely a matter of individual experimentation and discovery. Although this spin-type serve is often difficult to learn, it has so many advantages to the player who masters it that it is especially recommended to those students who are highly coordinated.

The straight, or flat, serve, in which the same footwork, ball toss, and arm motion patterns are used as in the foregoing spin, or slice, serve, is best for those beginners who have average coordination or below. In this serve, the *Western grip* is suggested: That is, hold the racket as though it were a hammer being used to drive a nail into a board above one's head in front of the body. To get this grip, place the racket flat on the

Fig. 18-5. On the serve, the ball should be tossed high into the air. (Courtesy of College of Health, Physical Education and Recreation, Texas Woman's University, Denton, Texas.)

ball with a fully extended arm and racket, holding the elbow well out and away from the body. Shift the entire body weight forward as the ball is hit.

The wrist should be kept firm and one should *move into the stroke*, hitting the ball in the center or "sweet part" of the racket so that it travels swiftly in a straight line and barely clears the net. The follow-through should also be in a straight line pattern, and will be if the ball is hit at an imaginary 9 o'clock position and the racket swept on through to 3 o'clock without the racket head's dropping lower than the wrist.

The Backhand Drive. Although similar to the forehand stroke, the backhand drive is often more difficult for right-handed players to master, whereas many left-handed ones will develop a backhand superior to their forehand. Hold the racket in the Eastern grip, modified by moving it one-quarter turn forward, and hold the thumb behind the handle for additional support. Stand facing sideways, feet in a forward and back stride, knees relaxed, and bend forward at the waist so that the racket arm can swing freely back and then across the body at waist height. Hold the racket head perpendicular to the ground, contact the ball, shift body weight forward, and follow through in a straight line pattern.

The _Volley_. Used primarily at the net and in the fore court, a volleyed ball is hit either forehand or backhand before it bounces. The best grip is that used for the serve (the Continental), with the hand holding the racket moved up about three inches from the end in a shortened grip. The stroke is a short,

ground, reach, and pick it up without changing hand or racket position.

The _Forehand_ Drive. Used most often in game play, this stroke is usually the most easily mastered. Stand sideways to the net, feet in a forward-back position, hold the racket in the handshake grip, and hit the

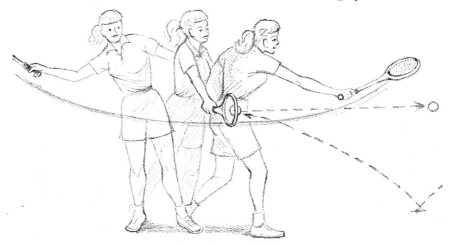

Fig. 18-6. The forehand drive.

Fig. 18-7. The backhand drive.

sharp, chopping motion that causes the ball to spin. The ball should be well above the top of the net when volleyed, and the stroke used as an aggressive, sudden attack. The footwork and stroking fundamentals are the same as for the forehand and backhand, but the swing is shorter and the ball rebounds off the racket face more than it is stroked.

The *half volley*, in which the ball is "picked up" just as it bounces, is hit like the regular volley and is used to return a ball when in a tight spot at an unfavorable court position.

The Smash. Similar to the serve, this stroke can be a forceful attacking shot of great speed. It is done using the same grip, footwork, and timing as the serve and is

Fig. 18-8. On the backhand drive, the follow-through should be in a straight line pattern. (Courtesy of Clifford Lewis, University of Georgia.)

Fig. 18-9. The volley.

ening and slowing down the backswing and lifting the ball with a forward upswing and follow-through as the racket, with the face tilted back, makes contact with the ball. This often effective, but delicate, stroke can send an aimed high and flatly hit ball into an unguarded area, and thus often becomes a sure point winner.

The Chop. The chop stroke is more defensive than offensive and is used to break up a strong drive or service. For both forehand and backhand chops the racket is held in a grip halfway between the Eastern forehand and the backhand. A short backswing precedes a descending blow on the back of the ball with an open racket face. The downward and forward follow-through completes the action, which results in a ball that bounces short and low in the opponent's court.

The Drop. The drop shot serves as a change of pace or a deceptive stroke intended to place the ball just over the net and catch the opponent deep in the back court. Use a grip similar to that used for the chop stroke. The body faces the net more squarely than for a drive, and a short backswing leads the racket to the ball. The racket strokes the ball lightly so that it barely clears the net in the intended direction. The follow-through should be very short.

most effective when used on a high, weak return at the net or in midcourt. The player watches and waits, relaxed, until the ball drops toward the court. Contact is powerful with a firm follow-through.

The Lob. The purpose of the lob is to move the opponent around the court or send the ball over her head. It is a defensive time-gainer and should be placed strategically on the court. Played either on the forehand or backhand side, it is done by short-

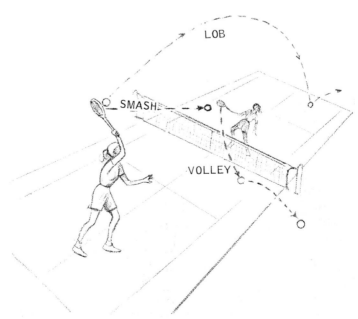

Fig. 18-10. Types of strokes.

TIPS FOR DEVELOPING SKILL IN TENNIS

1. Work on learning to do the basic strokes until you can hit the ball where you want it to go. Wall practice is one of the best ways to develop this skill.

2. Make all strokes smooth and rhythmical rather than trying to "kill" the ball, for it is not how hard you hit the ball that counts, but rather *where* you place it on the court.

3. Watch the ball when it leaves your opponent's racket, and continue doing so as you get into the best position to hit it back across the net.

4. Learn to hit the ball on the half volley as it rises from the court, thus giving your opponent less time to anticipate what you are going to do.

5. Correct your weakness. If it is your backhand (and likely it is if you are right handed) or if it is your forehand (probably so, if you are left handed), analyze *why* you are not hitting the ball correctly, and then correct your movements.

6. Remember that practice does not make perfect *unless* one is practicing perfectly. Rather, practice makes permanent, and it is harder to "unlearn" a skill than to learn it correctly.

7. Work hard to develop good footwork (rope skipping is recommended) and a strong wrist (hitting the ball up and down on the court, while standing in place or kneeling, 100 or more times daily is recommended).

8. Learn the American twist serve, and how to smash it successfully.

9. Learn to put a spin on the ball, which will make it bounce in a direction unexpected by your opponent. See Table 18-1.

GAME RULES AND SCORING

Game Scoring. The point progress of a game is 15, 30, 40 and game. (Throughout this discussion *a point* should be understood to mean one of these scoring units.) When the score is tied 40-40 the score is called deuce and the tie must be broken and the game won by winning two consecutive points. If the server wins the first point after deuce it is called *advantage in*, short for advantage in favor of the server. If the receiver wins the first point it is called *advantage out*. Players speak of it as "ad out" and "ad there." When a player has no score, it is referred to as "love." The server's score is called first during a game, whether officiated by tournament officials or by the players themselves. For example, the server's score would be love-30 if she has lost the first two game points, or 40-30 if she gains the next three. Singles and doubles are scored in the same way.

SET AND MATCH. A set is won by the player or team who first wins six games, providing they have at least a two-game lead over the opponents. A set can be won at 6-0, 6-1, 6-2, 6-3, and 6-4. It cannot be won at 6-5, but may terminate at 7-5, or in the case of a hard

Table 18-1. *Analytical Chart of Spins*

Kind of Spin	How to Impart to Ball	Action of Ball on Bounce	How to Play
1. Topspin	Stroke forward and upward	Ball rotates away from striker in flight; as ball hits court it will dive down	1. Impart the opposite spin, which is underspin 2. Half volley
2. Underspin	Stroke forward and downward	Ball rotates toward striker in flight; as it hits court it will "bite" and bounce higher than normal	1. Impart the opposite spin, which is topspin 2. Drop shot 3. Half volley
3. Sidespin to left	Stroke across ball from right to left	Ball rotates about its oblique axis from right to left in flight; as ball hits court it will hop right on opponent's court	Aim ball to side of court— the side from which opponent's racket started in its stroking
4. Sidespin to right	Stroke across ball from left to right	Ball rotates as above, only left to right—hops left on opponent's court	Same as above, only aim left of opponent

won battle may go to as many as 15-13 games or even more. A *match* is made up of the winner of two out of three sets for women and for mixed doubles. (Men's competition requires the best three out of five sets.)

GENERAL RULES

Service. Each server serves a complete game. The first serve of the game must be from the right half of the court behind the base line. She has two chances to send the ball over the net diagonally into her opponent's service court. If the first ball is good, a second is not used. The next serve is made from the left, and so on until the game is completed. A double service fault (such as hitting the first ball into the net and the second out of bounds) causes a loss of point. The ball must land in the opponent's service court before it can be hit by the receiver, who must wait until it bounces before returning it. After the service the ball may be hit before it bounces, throughout the game.

The serve is a fault if the server:

a. does not take the proper position before serving.

b. commits a foot fault.

c. misses the ball but hits it slightly with the racket. The server may toss and catch the ball on an attempted serve without penalty if her racket does not touch it.

d. fails to hit the ball into the correct service court.

e. hits any permanent structure with the served ball other than the net, strap, or hand.

f. hits her partner or anything she wears or carries with the served ball.

(The penalty for any one of the above is a single fault, and is a double fault and loss of point if such an error happens on both serves.)

FOOT FAULT. It is a foot fault on the serve:

a. for the server to change her position by walking or running.

b. to step on or over the back line as the ball is hit.

The Let. The ball is considered to be a "let" when:

a. a served ball touches the net, strap, or band, and is otherwise good.

b. because of circumstances beyond a player's control of interference, she is unable to play the ball.

c. it is delivered before the receiver is ready. (Call "ready?" before each serve.)

Loss of Point. The player loses a point if:

a. she does not return the ball to her opponent's court on the volley or first bounce after service.

b. she or her clothing touches the net on any play.

c. she reaches over the net to play a ball unless it has bounced back over the net because of a spin or a strong wind.

d. she throws her racket at the ball.

e. she hits the ball more than once.

f. she misses the ball or hits it out of bounds or into the net.

g. she plays a served ball before it bounces.

Good Returns. A ball is considered good if:

a. it lands on any line.

b. it touches the top of a net post or the net and falls into the proper court.

c. a player reaches outside the net posts to play a ball and returns it successfully.

d. the player's racket on the follow-through goes over the net but does not touch it.

Changing Sides. Players should change after the first, third, and every following alternate game of each set, and at the end of each set, so that each side will compete under the same sun, wind, court, and spectator conditions. If the total number of games won in the set is even, however, courts should not be changed until the end of the first game of the next set.

DOUBLES RULES

Service

1. The players on one side take turns serving. The order of serving should be determined before the beginning of each set. One of the alternating serving pair should serve games 1, 3, 5, 7, and so on, while those of the opposite side should alternate serving the even-numbered games.

2. The order of serving must be consistent throughout the set, but may change at the beginning of a new set.

3. During the serve, the server's partner may stand anywhere on her half of the court.

4. When one serves out of turn, the proper server must serve as soon as the error is discovered, but all points already earned should be counted. If a complete game is played before the error is known, the game counts, and the service order should remain as altered.

Receiving

1. Before each set begins, the couple receiving in the first game should determine which one will receive first; that player should continue to receive first in all odd-numbered games of the set. The opponents should also decide which one will receive first in the second game; such a person should receive first in all even-numbered games.

2. When a player receives out of turn, she should stay in that position until the game then being played is over. The partners should then return to their original receiving order.

GAME STRATEGY

The attacking style is usually played at the net with the defensive players moving back to base line positions. Although most players "beat themselves" through their own errors, this may be avoided by carefully analyzing all mistakes made and not repeating them. Consistent, steady play is more fruitful than taking unwise chances, or trying to "kill" as many shots as possible. Beginners especially should learn (a) to hit the ball *away* from their opponents, (b) to *anticipate* where the returned ball will land on the court and *be ready* to receive it, and (c) to *outsmart their opponents* by placing returned shots to their weakness (this may be one of the doubles partners, the backhand of one, or the inability of both to move quickly around the court). Other aspects of general strategy include:

1. Return to the center line at fore or back court position after each stroke.

2. Conserve strength by letting impossible shots go past and only going after those you can get.

3. Take your time and get into proper position before hitting the ball and *play it in front of your forward foot.*

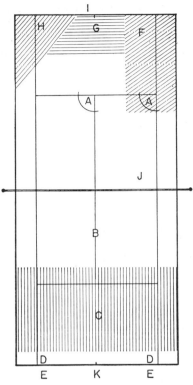

Fig. 18-11. Strategic court positions and placements. A, Placement of serve to weakness (opponent's backhand). B, Center net position when ball has been played to center of opponent's court. C, Avoid standing in shaded zone; play in front or behind it. D, Position in receiving a slow serve. E, Position in receiving a fast serve. F, G, and H, Where to place the lob. I, Position in serving to right service court. J, Partner's net position when I is serving to right service court. K, Back court on guard position. (From Fait et al.: A Manual of Physical Education Activities. 2nd ed.)

4. It is not how *hard* you hit the ball, but *where* you hit it.

5. Always win your own serve and vary its speed and placement.

6. Hit the ball *away* from your opponent, trying to make her move around the court, from back to front to base line.

7. A deep cross court shot is usually much more effective than a base line drive.

8. Disguise your intended return as long as possible.

9. Play against opponents who are more skillful than you are, but remember to profit from what you have learned from each of these experiences.

10. Direct most serves to your opponent's backhand if this is her weakest stroke (this is

often not true of left-handed players). Remember that the flat serve is most successfully placed when it lands in the backhand corner of the forehand court and also that the American twist serve is placed best when it lands in the backhand corner of the backhand court.

11. Vary the pace, spin, depth, and direction of your strokes in order to keep your opponent guessing and on the defensive. Master the art of anticipating what your opponent is going to do.

DOUBLES STRATEGY

Teamwork is necessary for success in doubles. Although advanced players prefer to play side by side, beginners should learn the up and back method, the side by side, and a fast shift to either one. Since the most advantageous court spot is at the net, this position should be gained and held as long as possible. Other suggestions include:

1. Keep the ball in the opponents' back court as much as possible.
2. Make the opponents hit the ball up to you on their returns by placing it at their feet.
3. Play the ball so that it lands halfway along the base line until an open spot appears, then shoot quickly for this hole.
4. The server should come to the net after most serves if both partners are especially good net players.
5. Smash, volley, and lob as often as possible and keep sending the ball back into the far court.
6. Keep your opponents guessing and on the move by playing to their weakness and using a variety of shots.
7. Make your opponent hit the ball up so you can hit it down on the return.
8. Keep attacking and moving in.

9. When all four players are at the net, drive the ball hard to the closest player; when both players are equal distance from the net, hit the ball so that it lands low down the center of the court or is hit to the weaker opponent.
10. Remember that in doubles most points are won from the net position.

Key phrases in learning strategy are (a) play through *your strength* to your opponent's *weaknesses*, (b) anticipate, (c) keep your opponent moving, (d) change the pace, and (e) always change a losing game.

GAME COURTESIES

1. Play to win every game, but do not make excuses or show poor sportsmanship should you lose.
2. Do not return the first ball on the serve if it is a fault.
3. When both you and your opponent are in doubt of the score or about a line decision, play the point over.
4. Do not serve until your opponent is ready.
5. Always have two balls in your hand before you start to serve.
6. As a spectator, do not applaud until a point has been made, and never walk behind or on a court on which a game is in progress. Do not applaud a fault.
7. Do not have temper tantrums or show that you are upset about your own mistakes or an umpire's decision.
8. Win graciously.
9. Be courteous to the others playing on adjoining courts.
10. Be sure to shake hands after a game in tournament play.
11. Play honestly whether or not an umpire is present.

SKILL DIFFICULTIES AND THEIR CORRECTION

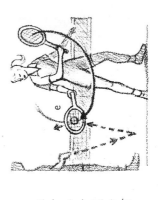

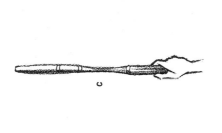

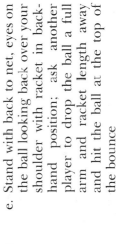

Difficulty	*Correction*
1. The Forehand and Backhand Drives	
Grip	
a. Forefinger extended	a. Curl all fingers around the racket
b. Too tight and tense a grip	b. Say "relax" to yourself repeatedly
c. Racket face tilted back or forward too far	c. Regrasp the racket several times and check the face position
d. Awkward, incomplete swing; swinging the racket too close to the body	d. Ask your instructor to place her hand over yours, and do the stroke together until you get the "feel" of the stroke
e. Body gets in the way for the backhand stroke	e. Stand with back to net, eyes on the ball looking back over your shoulder with racket in backhand position; ask another player to drop the ball a full arm and racket length away and hit the ball at the top of the bounce

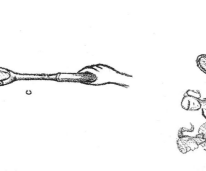

SKILL DIFFICULTIES AND THEIR CORRECTION (*Continued*)

Difficulty	*Correction*
Footwork	
f. Wrong foot forward	f. Practice putting weight on the left foot as you reach for the ball with the right hand (or vice versa if you are left handed); get the feel of the better balance this opposition in movement gives you
g. Weight shifted at wrong time	g. Ask your instructor to demonstrate weight shift; imitate her until you get the feel of the movement
The Swing	
h. Unrhythmical movements, "punching at" the ball	h. Copy your instructor's stroke first without, then with, a racket; use a full swing each time the ball is hit

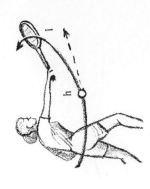

i. Swinging racket up or down too far instead of in a straight line in a faulty follow-through; turning the racket face too far forward or back

i. Remember to start from 9 o'clock position and end at 3 o'clock

j. Improper timing

j. Start backswing sooner. Start forward swing before the ball bounces in front of the body.

2. The Serve

a. Incorrect grip

a. Remember to move fingers slightly toward inside of racket for serve

b. Incorrect wrist action

b. Keep wrist flexible; remember the similarity to the overhand softball throw ("throw the racket at the ball")

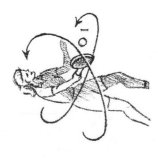

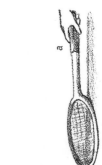

SKILL DIFFICULTIES AND THEIR CORRECTION (*Continued*)

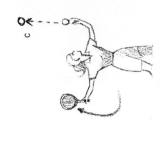

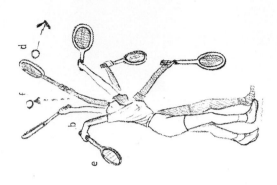

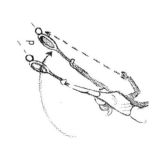

Difficulty	*Correction*
c. Ball toss too far in front of, or behind; too far left or right; too low, or too high	c. Practice correct ball toss, stressing correct height in relationship to body position; toss and catch several balls correctly without using the racket; toss and hit several balls as teacher observes and gives corrective suggestions
d. Hitting the ball with the wood of the racket; failure to connect ball with the racket	d. Practice hitting the ball on the "sweet part"; observe and correct timing of ball toss and swing
e. Incorrect backswing; serving too early or too late; too far back of head; too far right; too far left	e. Work on individual part of the serve until you get the feel of correct timing of swing to the ball toss

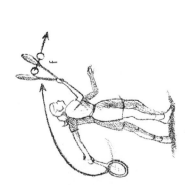

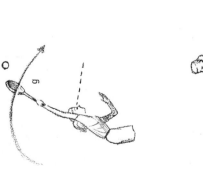

f. Toss ball higher, hit it avove the head instead of at eye level

g. *Watch the ball*; repeat ball bounce drills; work against the backboard

a. Assume a relaxed, easy body position with knees slightly bent

f. Hitting the ball into the net

g. Missing the ball entire y

3. *The Volley*

a. Being too tense

too close

307

SKILL DIFFICULTIES AND THEIR CORRECTION (*Continued*)

Difficulty	*Correction*
b. Standing too near or too far from the net	b. Ask your instructor to show you the correct court area from which the volley can best be played
c. Dropping the head of the racket	c. Do the stroke in slow motion several times; be sure you understand what this mistake causes the ball to do
d. Wobbly wrist action	d. Tighten grip slightly before stroking the ball
e. Missing the ball entirely	e. *Watch the ball!*

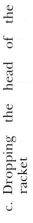

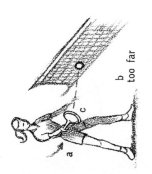

Terminology

Ace—A skillfully placed serve that the receiver cannot return and usually cannot touch with her racket.

Ad—An abbreviation for advantage in favor of the server.

All—Tie score, such as 15-all.

Break a serve—Winning a game served by an opponent.

Chop stroke—A sharp hack-like stroke that causes the ball to backspin and bounce low.

Deuce—Even score when each side has won three or more points.

Drop shot—A deceptive shot that barely clears the net.

Fault—A served ball that goes out of bounds, or not into the proper service court.

Foot fault—Moving the feet, failure to keep contact with the ground, or stepping over the base line while serving.

Half volley—Stroke made by hitting the ball just after it hits the court.

Lob—Upward ball flight sending it far over the head of an opponent.

Love—Nothing; no score.

Match point—A point that, when won, wins the match for a player.

Slice stroke—Similar to the chop, this aggressive stroke is used to hit the ball downward and off to one side.

Smash—Hitting a high ball down with great force.

Volley—Playing the ball before it bounces.

Wide—A shot that lands beyond the side line.

Selected Audio-visual Aids

Beginning Tennis Series. (6 slide films, 35 mm., sound, color.) Athletic Institute, 805 Merchandise Mart, Chicago, Illinois 60654. (Purchase and rental.)

Don Budge Instructional Films: Tennis for Beginners, Tennis for Everybody, Slow Motion Long Films for Tennis Instruction. United States Lawn Tennis Association, 120 Broadway, New York, New York. (Purchase and rental.)

Tennis Class Organization. (16 mm., 25 min., sound, color.) T. N. Rogers Productions, 5951 Stafford Avenue, Huntington Park, California. (Rental.)

Tennis Tactics. (11 min., sound, b & w.) Association Films. Chicago, Dallas, and San Francisco, (Rental.)

Tennis Techniques, (16 mm., 12 min., sound, color.) T. N. Rogers Productions, 5951 Stafford Avenue, Huntington Park, California. (Purchase.)

Suggested Readings

Gould, Dick: *Tennis, Anyone?* Palo Alto, California, The National Press, 1965.

Heldman, Gladys, ed.: *The Book of Tennis,* New York, World Tennis Magazine, 1965.

Johnson, Joan, and Xanthos, Paul: *Tennis,* Dubuque, Iowa, William C. Brown Company, 1967.

Kenfield, John: *Teaching and Coaching Tennis,* Dubuque, Iowa, William C. Brown Company, 1964.

Laver, Rod: *How to Play Championship Tennis,* New York, The Macmillan Co., 1965.

Murphy, Bill, and Murphy, Chet: *Tennis Handbook,* New York, The Ronald Press Company, 1962.

Selected Tennis and Badminton Articles, 2nd Ed., AAHPER, Division for Girls' and Women's Sports, Washington, D.C. 20036.

Tennis and Badminton Guide, AAHPER, D.G.W.S., Washington, D.C.

Tennis Clinic Kit: How to Organize and Conduct a Tennis Clinic, How to Improve Your Tennis, Tennis Instructor's Guide, Rules of Lawn Tennis, Your Guide to Good Courtmanship, Tennis Lessons for Young Players. A Tennis Program for Elementary and Secondary Schools, United States Lawn Tennis Association, 120 Broadway, New York, New York.

Unit on Tennis: The Serve, Return Service, Forehand Drive, Net Attack, Doubles, Practice and Training for Match Play, United States Lawn Tennis Association, 120 Broadway, New York, New York.

Periodicals

Sports Illustrated, 540 North Michigan Avenue, Chicago, Illinois.

Tennis, U.S.A., United States Lawn Tennis Association, 51 E. 42nd Street, New York, N.Y. 10017.

World Tennis, Box 3, Gracie Station, New York, New York.

Suggested Study Questions

1. Define the following terms: love, ad in, ad out, deuce, backhand, serve.
2. What is the best strategy to use for playing singles; for playing doubles?
3. Demonstrate the correct footwork for the serve, forehand drive, backhand drive, volley, and lob.
4. When is a ball a "let" ball?
5. What is the best method of caring for and repairing tennis equipment?

CHAPTER NINETEEN

Courtesy of Rice University, Houston, Texas.

TRACK AND FIELD

Track and field includes activities as old as basic human movements. The competitive events of today undoubtedly grew from the first men who gained pleasure from running, leaping over streams and fallen trees, and throwing rocks and spears. These survival skills turned to sport as man became less dependent on them for existence.

During the Golden Age of Greece, the pattern for modern track and field events developed. In the Olympic Festival of 776 B.C. men participated in broad jumping and discus and javelin throwing in much the same form as in the Olympic Games of today. Although women were barred as competitors and spectators at the Olympiad, they engaged in a special festival, the Herea, in which they competed in foot races in specified age groups.

Competitive track was not popular until brief enthusiasm for it grew in England in the middle of the nineteenth century. The real emphasis came with the opening of the modern Olympic Games in 1896. At this time, women were not included as participants in track and field events, and it was not until after World War I that international interest was aroused for competition between women. Lacking permission to compete in the Olympics, five countries sent 111 athletes to an international track and field meet for women in 1921. With this added pressure, the governing body of the Olympics reconsidered allowing women to enter, and in 1928 six events were open to them in track and field competition. Expansion of interest and participation continued, and in the 1964 Tokyo Olympic Games women participated in 12 events, including the challenging pentathlon.

American men have long been enthusiastic competitors and have dominated track and field events. American women, however, have neither responded so well nor been so successful in competition. Interest in track and field events for women is growing each year on the local, state, national, and interna-

tional level. The American woman has not yet attained the proficiency of European and Asian women, but her progress and improvement are far more spectacular than those of the American male.

NATURE AND PURPOSE OF THE SPORT

Track and field events are divided into the three major groups: running, jumping, and throwing. Many forms of competition use a combination of these skills. Performance is individual but a group may combine and participate in selected team events. Track competition recognizes individual skills as well as team scores. The variety of events assures everyone an activity in which she can develop speed, skill, agility, and endurance. Although many people do not look to track and field for social or recreational values found in other sports, skills developed in this area can be of lifelong benefit and are important lead-ups to the many other sports involving running, jumping, and throwing.

Women participate in events modified and designed for their age and ability levels. The track events for high school and college age include dashes, runs, relays, and hurdles. Field events are the running high jump, broad (long) jumps, the shot put, basketball, soccerball,* baseball,* softball, the discus throw, and the javelin throw.

FACILITIES AND EQUIPMENT

Track Area. The track is an oval, usually ¼ mile in length with curves having a radius of 80 to 110 feet. The outdoor track has a hard, level subsurface covered with cinders or composition materials. It must be smooth and properly graded for drainage. The in-

---

*Events to be discontinued in 1970.

311

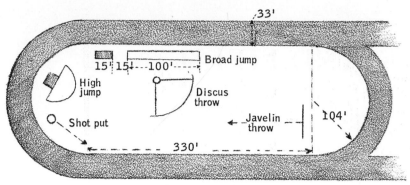

Fig. 19-1. Quarter mile track.

door track is wood, clay, or dirt. In both cases one side is known as the straightaway and is measured for dash events. It should be a minimum of 22 feet wide to allow for six lanes of 42-inch hurdles. The curves and back side should be 18 feet, allowing a minimum of 3 feet for each of six lanes.

Field Area. Field events are generally held inside the running track. When properly placed and conducted, there are no safety hazards. The following markings are necessary:

1. Shot put — a circle 7 feet in diameter with a white stop board 4 feet long 4½ inches wide and 4 inches high.

2. Discus — a circle 8 feet 2½ inches in diameter (made of wood, steel, or iron and sunk into the ground).

3. Baseball, softball, soccerball, and basketball throw — a line 10 feet long and 2 inches wide.

4. Javelin throw — two parallel lines 13 feet 1½ inches apart, leading to a scratch line arc drawn from a point so that the radius is 26 feet 3 inches. The arc is wood or metal, 2¾ inches in width, painted white, and sunk flush with the ground. The radii extend for 295 feet to form the sector lines.

5. Broad jumping events — a pit at least 15 by 9 feet filled with sawdust or sawdust and sand to aid drainage. A takeoff board must be 4 feet long and 8 inches wide, 4 inches high, and sunk flush with the ground. It is painted white.

6. High jump — a pit at least 13 feet 1½ inches in length and 16 feet 4 inches in width and built up no more than 18 nor less than 12 inches above the ground. Standards and a

crossbar 13 feet 1½ inches long complete basic equipment. The crossbar may be made of wood, metal, fiberglass, bamboo, or other resilient material.

Equipment. For competition the following are essentials: pistol, cartridges, whistle, steel measuring tapes, stop watches, wool yarn, marking sticks, rakes, and shovels.

Equipment for specific events includes: starting blocks, batons, 2½-foot hurdles; beat board or raised take-off board; high jump standards and bar; shots—6 pounds for elementary school girls, 8 pounds for high school girls and 4 kilograms (8 lb. 13 oz.) for women of college age; discus measuring between 7³/₃₂ and 7⁵/₃₂ inches in diameter and weighing 2 pounds 3¼ ounces; javelin of metal or solid wood with a metal point weighing no less than 1 pound 5.2 ounces and measuring no less than 7 feet 2½ inches; official baseballs, softballs, soccerballs, and basketballs.

Costume. There is great variation in dress, and competitors should be governed in their selection by safety, comfort, and attractiveness. Shirts should have sleeves of some sort and a tail that does not fly out or drag over the bar when jumping. Shorts should fit the leg snugly and comfortably. Elastic in the undergarment or outer shorts is desirable. Tennis shoes and sneakers are satisfactory for classwork and may be used in competitive meets, provided all persons wear a similar type of shoes. Spikes are unquestionably valuable and may be used for interscholastic and intercollegiate competition. Thin white socks or pushers (half-socks) may be worn with track and field shoes. A warm-up suit should be worn before and after all events.

BASIC SKILLS

Warm-up and Conditioning Activities.
Warm-up activities should be designed to increase flexibility of all parts of the body. An organized program of conditioning should increase strength and endurance in all events. Jogging is an excellent way to begin. Jog high on the toes, feet straight, at a tempo slightly faster than a walk. Swing arms freely and increase jogging pace. Light calisthenic exercises that stretch and relax the muscles are beneficial in preparing the body for increased movement and preventing strains and pulls. Bicycling, leg stretches, reaches, and torso bends should be included in the warm-up. The 5 to 10 minute period should terminate in a series of one or more wind sprints. Begin on a 40 or 50 yard course in a jog and increase speed until full effort is being given at the end of the course. Walk or jog back to the starting point and repeat the run. Sprints are usually run in series of three.

RUNNING EVENTS

Some skills are basic to all or part of every dash, run, or relay.

The Start. The runner begins from starting blocks or holes dug for the feet to aid in drive and speed at the takeoff. There are three general starting positions—the bunched start, the medium, or medium elongated, position, and the elongated start. In the bunched start the toe of the rear foot is opposite the front heel. In the more common medium start the knee of the rear leg is slightly ahead of the toes of the forward foot (this position is sometimes described as the

feet placement

knee of the rear leg opposite the instep of the front foot). In the elongated position the knee of the rear leg is opposite the back of the heel of the forward foot. Experience has shown that a slightly modified medium start is the one women use most often.

Block position is determined in the following manner: The front block is placed as close to the starting line as is comfortable for the runner. This is generally about 2 hand spans from the line, allowing for minor adjustments. The back block is placed according to the type of start to be used by the runner. The runner sets her foot in the front block and adjusts the rear block prior to the start. Minor adjustments may be made if the feet seem too close or too far apart. At the official's signal "on your mark" the runner backs into the blocks and places the stronger leg (usually the left) in the front block with her toe on the ground and ball of the foot pushing. The rear foot touches the block and the knee drops to the ground. The hands are shoulder width apart. The thumb and index finger are placed parallel to the starting line as the other fingers extend to the ground, forming a firm, triangular base beneath the shoulders and extended arms. Body weight is on the thumb and fingers, the rear knee, and the foot of the forward left leg. The eyes look down the track 8 to 10 yards.

On the signal "get set" the hips are raised. Weight moves forward, and the back knee is raised approximately 4 inches from the ground. Weight is carried primarily on the hands and forward foot. If using a bunch start with feet close together, the hips rise more than in the other starts. The hips are at least level with the back. The position is held for 2 seconds.

Fig. 19-2. The start.

Fig. 19-3. The angle of the body as the runner steps from the blocks.

The gunshot is the signal for both legs to drive. The back leg immediately leaves the block as the knee comes forward with foot low to the ground. The front leg pushes forcefully against the block, and arms and hands begin a powerful thrust as the body pulls out at a 45 degree angle (see Figure 19-3). The arm, in opposition to the leg moving forward (right arm as left leg moves out), reaches forward forcefully as if trying to grasp something.

As the body is thrust forward, not upward, the back foot lands about 18 to 20 inches in front of the starting line. Succeeding strides should be about 3/4 of an inch longer than the one before until full stride is reached. The arms work in opposition — the left one swings upward as the right foot swings through. Shoulders move forward and slightly up as the head and chest rise with the first strides until the runner is at proper sprinting angle in six or seven steps.

The standing start is used by the second, third, and fourth runners in a relay and in long distance runs. The runner leans slightly

Fig. 19-4. The standing start.

forward with feet comfortably spread, arms in opposition to legs. The initial push is from the forward leg as the back leg steps out; arms continue coordinated opposition movements.

Sprinting. A common misconception is that a short, choppy stride is more effective than a longer stride for sprinting. A sprinter should try to reach her full stride as quickly as possible and hold it throughout the race. At full stride the body is angled about 20 or 25 degrees to benefit from the pushing power of the kick. On each stride the rear leg just completing the drive is brought forward with the heel under the hip as the knee is lifted fairly high in front to take advantage of the back leg drive. Weight lands on the ball of the foot, knee straightens, and pressure is applied through the foot as heels almost touch the ground. The arms held close to the sides, with elbows bent at right angles, swing directly front and back; the hands swing to shoulder level.

Breathing should be as normal as possible. Take a breath on "go" and at least two or three while running if natural breathing is too tiring.

Regular running form should be continued until the torso crosses the finish line; then the runner gradually diminishes her speed. It is not advisable to jump, lunge, throw the head back, or raise the arms to throw the chest out when crossing the finish line.

Middle and Long Distance Running. In middle distance races, such as the 220 or 440, a runner finds that when trying to run full power she suffers muscle fatigue. She must learn to "float" or coast for part of the distance. She applies full power for the first third, floats for the middle third, and reapplies power to finish.

In 1/2 mile races (or longer where sanctioned), when a given speed must be maintained over the distance, the knee lift is not so great. The runner is more erect, takes shorter strides and uses more of her foot.

Relays. Relay races are of two types — pursuit and shuttle. In both types each member of a team of four girls runs a specified distance, each then being relieved by another at some designated point.

All the techniques of starting and sprinting apply in the short distance relays. A shuttle relay involves a team traveling over and back across the same ground touching right

Fig. 19-5. Starting with the baton.

shoulder, hand, or passing a baton for the exchange. In the more popular pursuit relay an awaiting runner is followed by her teammate and contact is made as both run to continue the course in the same direction. Generally, the most advantageous placement of runners is to begin with the second fastest, then the slowest, and the next slowest third. The fastest runner is the last, or *anchor.*

In pursuit relays the baton is passed in a nonvisual or blind exchange, or a visual or sight exchange. The visual exchange is the safest but also the slowest method. The condition of the incoming runner determines the type of pass. If she has come only a short distance and is not too tired to control the placement of the baton, a blind exchange is made. Use a sight exchange if the runner is obviously too fatigued to control the baton. This is the most popular pass for beginners.

The first runner starts from a crouched position with the baton grasped back of center by the three last fingers of the left hand. The thumb and index finger are arched behind the starting line.

The baton transfer must be completed within a 22 yard zone or the team suffers disqualification.*

The waiting runner stands to the left of the lane inside the restraining line of the 22 yard zone. With weight on the balls of her feet in standing start position, she turns her head to look at the oncoming runner. When the oncoming runner reaches a predetermined mark, usually six or seven strides from the restraining line, the waiting runner begins to sprint. The passer must have sufficient reserve speed to overtake the runner and place the baton. *Blind exchanges* with the right hand are made as follows:

BASKET PASS. The receiving runner places fingertips on hips, elbow out at the side. The baton is placed in the open palm by a downward motion. This pass loses an arm's distance in the exchange and is dangerous for beginners, as the elbow often blocks the opening or the thumb blocks the baton placement.

INVERTED BASKET PASS. The receiver's

*D.G.W.S. rules; international competition allows 20 meters for some events.

Fig. 19-6. Basket pass.

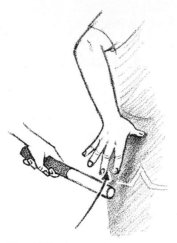

Fig. 19-7.   Inverted basket pass.

thumb is on the hip, palm open, fingers spread out and down. The baton is placed in the palm by an upward swing. It has some of the dangers of the basket pass.

UNDERARM EXTENSION PALM UP PASS. The arm of the receiver is extended to the rear in an underarm fashion with palm up. The baton is placed by a downward motion.

Fig. 19-8.   Underarm extension palm up pass.

UNDERARM EXTENSION PALM BACKWARD PASS.   The arm and hand extend to the rear with thumb and fingers spread so that the

Fig. 19-9.   Underarm extension palm backward pass.

palm is toward the oncoming runner. The baton is placed in the "V" of thumb and forefinger on upward swing. This is a safe pass, once the receiver learns to keep her arm from wavering when receiving. It is often called the "natural" pass and is probably the most commonly used today.

Visual exchanges with the receiver facing the approaching runner are as follows:

OVERARM EXTENSION PALM UP PASS.   Arm of the receiver is palm up reaching back as the runner places the baton with a downward swing.

OVERARM EXTENSION PALM OUTWARD. The receiving thumb and fingers are extended with palm out to receive the baton passed perpendicular to the ground.

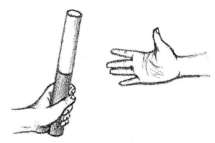

Fig. 19-10.   Overarm extension palm outward pass.

UNDERARM EXTENSION PALM BACKWARD PASS.   Executed like the blind underarm extension.   This is an excellent pass for beginners, as the movements are simple and familiar.

The baton must be actually passed, not thrown or dropped. If it is dropped, it must be picked up by the same runner and then passed. After grasping the baton securely, the runner transfers it to her left hand if she is to pass to another runner. After the pass has been completed, the runner finishing her "leg" should jog straight ahead. She then leaves the track as soon as possible.

Baton passing is more difficult in shuttle relays, and beginners should use a hand or shoulder touch in preference to a baton. When using a baton, the right hand of the receiver should be raised above the shoulder, palm upward and forward. The incoming runner slaps the baton across the palm of the receiver between the thumb and forefinger.

Fig. 19-11. Overarm extension palm up pass.

Hurdling. The techniques of the start, sprint, and finish as previously described also apply to hurdles. Hurdling is divided into the phases of start, approach, hurdle stride, and sprint between hurdles.

START. The start is the same as that described for dashes, except that some runners find it necessary to reverse the position of the feet so that the forward foot at the start is the takeoff foot in clearing the hurdles. Usually the foot that is back at the start is the one that leads over the hurdle.

APPROACH. A runner defines her strongest leg as the takeoff leg. The first hurdle is 39 feet 4½ inches or 13 or 16 meters from the starting line. The runner counts her strides to the takeoff point in front of the hurdle. If she uses seven strides, her takeoff leg is placed on the rear starting block; if eight strides, the takeoff leg is on the front block with the lead leg behind. Timing and consistent starts are important. If adjustments must be made they should be at the block rather than at the hurdle. Watch the hurdle bar rather than predetermined marks on the track.

In all hurdle events, including the shuttle hurdle relay, the hurdle height is 2 feet 6 inches, with 26 feet 3 inches or 8.5 or 19 meters between each hurdle. The distance from the start to the first hurdle, distance between hurdles and distance from the last hurdle to the finish varies with the total distance of the race.

HURDLE STRIDE. When the takeoff leg is 5 or 6 feet from the hurdle, the lead leg is brought straight forward with a high knee lift. The toe is pointing upward with slight flexion in the lead leg. The body leans forward with shoulders kept square. The lead arm swings in opposition to the lead leg and extends with the body thrust.

Correct hurdling form duplicates, as nearly as possible, the basic movements of sprinting action. The takeoff leg should push the center of gravity forward and upward for the body to clear the barrier. The leg extends fully so the hurdler "runs over" rather than jumps up and down. The head of the skillful hurdler remains at the same level, that is, does not bob, when she is sprinting or hurdling. As the leg rises to a position parallel to the ground, the knee rotates so that the toes

Fig. 19-12. Hurdle stride.

are pointing away from the body with the knee and ankle flexed. The knee is higher than the toes, and the toes are higher than the ankle.

SPRINT. The lead leg comes to the track on the ball of the foot with toes pointing straight ahead and close to the barrier so that a sprint push can begin. The ball of the foot is beneath or behind the body to insure a balanced landing. Assume a sprint position and stride toward the next hurdle. The distance between hurdles is measured so that an odd number of strides (usually three) is taken and the takeoff and lead legs are the same for each barrier.

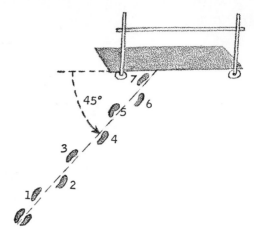

Fig. 19-13.   Running high jump—the approach.

FIELD EVENTS

The field events include all jumping and throwing skills.

Running High Jump. The jump is preceded by a running approach, which develops momentum to get across the bar. To determine the spot to begin the approach, go to the front of the bar and turn the takeoff side to the bar. A girl who kicks a ball with the right foot usually uses the left as the takeoff foot. Extend the left arm and step away from the bar so that the knuckles of the left hand are touching the bar. This is the takeoff spot. Turn and angle off at approximately 45

degrees, taking a seven stride run. From this mark, turn around and begin on your right foot angling to the bar for a seven step approach.

THE JUMP. The western roll and straddle roll have replaced the "scissors" form of clearing the bar in a sitting position with legs scissoring.

TAKEOFF. As the jumper approaches the bar with a relaxed, springy stride, her left shoulder is toward the bar. From the longer final stride and a wide takeoff base, she leans slightly backward to achieve a vertical takeoff.

Fig. 19-14.   Western roll.

Fig. 19-15. Straddle roll.

With the eyes above the center of the crossbar she kicks the right leg forward and upward moving the body directly over the left foot. Upward drive is helped by forcefully lifting both arms, with emphasis on the left to correspond with right leg swing-up. The takeoff foot pushes off the toes when the kick-up leg is between the waist and the chest.

WESTERN ROLL. The takeoff leg (left) tucks by the side of the right leg with toes almost touching behind the right knee as they pass over the bar. Crossing the bar, the body is on its side, thighs close together. The action of thrusting the left arm and head downward raises the left hip an inch or more over the bar. Once over the bar, the left leg touches the ground first, with the hands following quickly. As the body turns after passing over the bar the right leg is extended behind.

STRADDLE ROLL. The straddle roll is considered easier by many jumpers and more effective for height. With a similar approach and takeoff the right (lead) leg swings up, and as the left foot leaves the ground the layout begins. The toes of the left leg turn out, and the knee twists out and up. The body is facing down as it passes the bar with right arm and head clearing the bar first. The left arm and shoulder are up and back from the bar until the body is over the bar. The head turns to the left to aid in the roll as the body clears the bar. The body will roll so that the landing is on the jumper's back and seat. If the roll is not full, the landing is on the right leg and both hands, followed by a roll to the right shoulder. This should be considered when learning or jumping at low heights.

Long Jump (Running Broad Jump). The total jump includes an approach, takeoff, flight, and landing.

APPROACH. For the approach the runner finds her starting position by standing on the takeoff board with both feet and stepping out with the foot opposite the desired takeoff foot. Run 16 to 20 full strides (approximately 85 to 110 feet) while someone counts the third or fourth, seventh or ninth, and sixteenth to twentieth strides. Selection of checkpoints depends upon the runner's choice, but mark the last stride as the starting

Fig. 19-16. Running broad jump.

point. Use these checkpoints to standardize the stride and determine speed and takeoff position. Begin the approach on the takeoff foot, and sprint forward. The run should provide optimum, not maximum, speed the last three strides before takeoff. The last three strides are used for gathering force and power for the jump; the last stride is shortened before hitting the takeoff board with the heel first.

TAKE-OFF.   The takeoff begins from a heel first or flat-footed position on the board. The leg straightens and the body rocks over the foot as the toe and ankle aid the drive of the takeoff leg. The first movements after the takeoff are concerned with gaining maximum height in the jump. The eyes should look above the horizon.

FLIGHT.   There are two basic methods of flight—the *tuck jump* and the *hitch kick*. The tuck jump is an easier technique for beginners, but some feel there is more power in the more difficult hitch kick. In executing the hitch kick the lead leg is forward; it then straightens and swings down and back as the takeoff leg kicks forward and upward. The original lead leg kicks forward, and the legs are extended and brought together for landing. The arms work in opposition to leg action and are thrust forward vigorously on landing.

The takeoff is the same for the tuck (also called sailing jump, or float). The lead leg swings upward and the takeoff leg kicks forward as both knees come toward the body. The body appears to be sitting in the air with legs extended.

LANDING.   In preparation for landing, the legs and heels are extended. At the moment the heels touch the ground, the lowest point of the buttocks is but a fraction above the level of the extended heels. As the heels contact, the head and shoulders thrust forward and downward and the chin is pulled between the knees. The arms are thrust forward simultaneously and the knees bend quickly and fully, allowing the body to fall forward.

Standing Broad Jump.   The jumper stands with both feet on the takeoff board. With toes over the edge, the body rocks forward and back. The takeoff is made by simultaneous drive and spring from both legs as the arms swing upward, lifting the body. At the height of the jump the arms are forward, the heels are near hip height and the upper part of the body is leaning forward. The legs swing forward as the arms remain extended to assure a forward or sideward fall.

THROWING EVENTS

Basketball and Soccerball Throws.   In addition to being independent field events, these throws are used to lead up to the discus throw. A running approach may be used prior to delivery. (For specific techniques refer to running approaches in the section on the javelin.) The hurler stands with feet apart and left shoulder toward the throwing line. The official ball is held by the right hand and supported by the wrist and fingers. As the body bends to the right over a bent right knee, the left leg and arm extend. Hips lead through and weight transfers to the forward left foot before the right arm whips through in a sidearm delivery with a wrist and finger snap. A reverse follows.

Baseball and Softball Throws.   These throws are generally preceded by a run ending in a hop-step. (Refer to running approaches for the javelin throw.) The preferred overarm throw begins with facing the throwing line with the left foot slightly in front. Both hands grasp the ball at chest or chin level. The hands pass overhead as the left leg lifts. The body leans backward, rotating slightly to the right. The right knee flexes as the bent right arm comes back to a position parallel to the ground. The left arm is up for balance. The body braces against a firm left leg and the right arm follows with a whip-like motion and a flick of the wrist and fingers. These throws are often used to lead up to the javelin throw.

Shot Put.   The shot put is classified as a throwing event, but beginners should remember that it actually involves a pushing or thrusting action rather than throwing action. The following description is for a right-handed delivery. Grip the shot near the base of comfortably spread fingers with the hand behind the shot. The shot *must not* rest in the palm of the hand. As control and strength of the hand increase, the shot is held by the first three fingers with the thumb and little finger curled under and around the sides. The shot is tucked against the neck, close to the jawbone and slightly in front of

Fig. 19-17.   The shot put.

The weight is transferred to the left foot as the torso and hips push through and the shot is brought forward. The shot must not advance in front of the body before the hips rotate. The push-off is made from the right toes, but the foot stays in contact with the ground until the shot is released. (The body push comes from both legs and the hips, *not* the shoulders.)

As the body faces front, the right arm extends firmly and smoothly and pushes upward and forward at approximately a 45 degree angle. The shot is released with a wrist snap and finger push. At the moment of release the weight is over the left foot and the left arm remains at shoulder level.

After the shot is released the right foot replaces the left in the follow-through, and the left arm pulls back to aid in the reverse. This reverse action helps to stop forward momentum so the putter does not step on or over the toe board or circle.

Discus.   The right-handed thrower places the discus on the palm of the right hand and hooks the end joint of the first three fingers over the rim. The thumb and little fingers are spread across the back, covering the discus with as much of the hand as possible. To aid in support, the back edge of the discus rests against the wrist.

Beginners should master the *standing throw* before attempting a turn. Place the left side of the body toward the direction of the throw, and spread feet comfortably. Several preliminary swings are executed to gain rhythm and momentum prior to the release. In preparation, the right arm, slightly flexed, is in front of the body, and the right hand is holding the discus with support by the palm

the shoulder. The hand is behind and under the shot, and the right elbow is bent, pointing sideward and away from the body.

Stand at the back of the ring with the left shoulder pointed in the direction of the put and the left arm extended forward and upward for balance. The body is facing backward and is supported by a bent right leg. The feet are comfortably spread with both feet angled toward the rear of the circle. The left leg lifts and may swing forward and kick backward (to front of ring) several times in anticipation of forward momentum. As the left leg kicks backward close to the ground for the last time, a quick gliding hop of the right leg is immediately followed by a pivot of the right foot; and as the right leg, still bearing the body weight, straightens, the hips and trunk rotate toward the left.

Fig. 19-18.   The discus throw.

of the left hand. The right arm extends and swings backward at waist level as far as possible. The discus is no longer supported by the left hand but remains in the fingers of the right hand through the force and momentum of the swing. The left arm is bent and in front of the body at chest level. As the backswing begins, the knees are bent and relaxed, the weight shifts to the right foot, and the hips and shoulders rotate to the right.

The return forward movement of the body is initiated by the right foot, leg thrust, and hip rotation. The arm and discus follow the rotation of the trunk and the shift of weight to the left foot.

After a limited number of purposeful preliminary swings the discus is released at approximately a 40 degree angle by a vigorous armswing and snap of the forearm, wrist, and fingers. The discus leaves the index finger last so that a clockwise spin is imparted.

At the moment of release the body weight is over the left leg and the head and chest are raised. The throwing arm continues upward and across the body at eye level and ends in a "salute" position by the head. In a vigorous throw the hurler may be carried into a half turn so that her right foot ends where the left was at the start.

THROW WITH A TURN. To gain more power the throw is preceded by a turn. The turn must be smooth and rapid throughout the gliding action. Both knees are flexed and the body is slightly bent as it faces the rear of the circle. Both feet point to the rear of the circle with the right slightly forward of the left in a stride stance position. The turn begins as the arm swings back from the last preliminary swing. The weight shifts to the left foot, and the body pivots over and around the left foot. The right foot, without breaking momentum, steps in front of the left in continuing the turn. The hurler has now completed a full turn and is again facing the back of the circle. From this point, with body weight on the right leg, the hips initiate action, and the turn continues with the throwing arm trailing as the left leg steps through. The arm follows the body turn, and action terminates in the release as described above. The right leg steps forward and extends in a reverse to stop the forward momentum of the thrower.

Javelin Throw. The techniques of the javelin throw are similar to an overarm ball throw and should be familiar movements to the beginning javelin thrower. The throw may be taken with or without a run, but the beginner should practice it from a standstill before coordinating all movements for a running delivery.

GRIP. The most common grip used by women is the *American grip*. It is quite natural and somewhat similar to the tennis handshake with the arm extended. The thumb and index finger grasp the rear edge of the 5⅞ inch cord binding near the middle of the shaft, and the other three fingers close around the binding. The javelin rests across the palm diagonally from between the thumb and index finger to the base of the palm. The grip is relaxed and the wrist flexible.

Fig. 19-19.   The American grip.

CARRY. The carry is an important phase in the preparation for delivery. The most natural and frequently used carry is the *Finnish carry*. In executing this carry the elbow is bent and pointing downward and the hand is over the shoulder and carried about eye level. The palm is up, and the tip of the javelin is pointing slightly downward toward the front as the arm moves smoothly and easily with the run.

In the *over the shoulder carry* the elbow is bent and pointing forward to the throwing line, and the point of the javelin is raised upward.

Over-shoulder   Finnish front
Fig. 19-20.   Javelin carries.

APPROACH RUN. The purpose of the approach run in any throwing event is to develop momentum and thereby gain speed and force for the throw. To measure the distance and establish a pattern for the run, measure the distance of the run as if preparing for the running broad jump. Begin at the throwing line and run approximately 90 feet, marking two checkpoints—one at the beginning of the run and one about 30 feet from the throwing line. The second checkpoint should be six strides from the throwing line where the cross-step begins prior to the throw.

The run begins from a standing position in which both feet are together. The runner steps out on her left foot and starts running slowly. She accelerates until she hits the second checkpoint with her left foot (at this point she should be running at optimum speed). She then begins the preparation for the throw and reverse by one of the following methods:

FINNISH CROSS-STEP. This technique of preparing for the throw is considered superior to the two other techniques that follow. Most throwers prefer this technique, but some find the hop-step more satisfactory and less difficult.

The cross-step begins after the left foot hits the checkpoint.

1. The right foot strikes the ground with toes pointing straight ahead in the direction of the throw. The body begins to lean backward, and the throwing arm begins to straighten backward. The shoulders remain parallel to the throwing line.

2. The left foot steps forward and slightly into the path of the right foot with toes pointing toward the throwing line. The body turns slightly, placing the left side toward the line, as the right arm extends farther back. The tip of the javelin remains at eye level.

3. The right foot and leg cross the left with the body turned slightly and the left shoulder angled toward the direction of delivery.

4. The left foot steps forward with the toes angled slightly to the right and toward the delivery line. As the left foot is moving into this step, the body whips into the throw, and the arm moves forcefully overhead to release the javelin at approximately a 45 degree angle.

5. The throw is completed and the right foot steps left to reverse the forward action and prevent fouling.

In practicing the cross-step, the rhythm of the steps is important. Diagrammed it is:1 . . . 2-3 . . . 4 . . . 5.

REAR CROSS-STEP. After the left foot reaches the checkpoint, the right foot moves forward, the left foot moves into the path, turning left side toward line. The right foot moves up and *behind* the left, and the left foot moves forward and to the right. After the throw the right foot reverses.

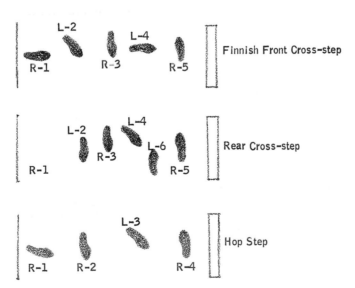

Fig. 19-21. Approach runs.

HOP-STEP. After the left foot hits the checkpoint, the right one moves forward, going right. On the second count the right foot hops with foot parallel to the line. On count three the left foot moves forward and the throw and reverse follow.

THE THROW. As mentioned previously, the throw is similar to an overarm ball throw for distance. The throw begins as the body is pushed upward and forward by leg thrust and torso and hip action. The extended arm bends slightly as it moves upward and forward. The head is up, eyes are focused on the line of flight, and the left arm is extended for balance. The javelin rests on the palm. The forward thrust is given by the arm, shoulder, and body until the instant of the whip-like release when the wrist snaps forcefully. "The height of the javelin throw is more dependent upon the backward angle of the trunk than it is upon getting the point high."*

GAME RULES AND SCORING

There are numerous rules governing track and field events. The D.G.W.S. *Track and Field Guide* should be consulted for detailed rules and recommended events for all age groups.

DASH, RELAY, AND HURDLE EVENTS

1. At the start, runners may not touch on or over the starting line before the gun is fired. Two false starts disqualify a runner.
2. Each runner must stay in her own lane during the entire race on a straightaway track.
3. She finishes the race when any part of her *torso* has reached the finish line.
4. When hurdling, the individual must pass over the hurdle. She is disqualified if any part of her body passes to the side. Knocking down hurdles does not disqualify the runner.
5. Relays are run by four different girls running their prescribed distance.
6. In pursuit relays, the baton must be passed in the 22 yard zone. If the baton is dropped, it must be picked up by the same runner and then passed.

---

*Scott, Phebe, and Crafts, Virginia: *Track and Field for Girls and Women.* New York, Appleton-Century-Crofts, Inc., 1964, p. 149.

7. The events are timed from the pistol flash to the moment the finish line is crossed.

JUMPING EVENTS

All the jumping events allow three trials and the running jumps permit unlimited approaches. (The seven best competitors have three additional trials.)

RUNNING BROAD JUMP

1. Using as long a run as she desires, the runner uses only one foot to leave the takeoff board.
2. The scratch line is the edge of the takeoff board nearest the jumping pit. If the jumper touches the ground in front, the jump is a foul.

STANDING BROAD JUMP

1. The jumper may curl her toes over the end of the board. Part of both feet must remain in contact with the takeoff board until the jump is made.
2. If the jumper touches the ground in front of the scratch line with any part of her body, the jump is a foul and not measured.
3. As in the running broad jump, measurement of the jump is made at right angles from the scratch line to the nearest break in the sand made by any part of the body of the jumper.

RUNNING HIGH JUMP

1. The jumper may take an unlimited approach, but she may use only one foot on takeoff.
2. Three trials at each height are allowed. Three successive failures at one height disqualifies the jumper.
3. Displacing the bar, passing under it, crossing the line of the bar extended, or leaving the ground are trials.
4. The measurement is taken from the ground to the lowest part of the upper side of the bar. The last jump cleared is recorded as the jumper's best effort.

THROWING EVENTS

In all throwing events the competitor has three throws and the seven best competitors have three more.

SHOT PUT AND DISCUS

1. No part of the person may touch the stop-board, circle, or ground outside the circle before the distance has been marked.

2. Valid puts must fall within the sector lines.

3. The put must be made with one hand on a line with, and in front of, the shoulder.

4. Both shot and discus throwers leave the ring from the rear after the throw is marked.

5. The discus may be thrown with or without a body turn.

6. Valid discus throws must fall within a 60 degree sector extending from the center of the circle.

7. Measurement of the throws is made from the nearest mark of the object to the inside circumference of the circle (on a line from the mark to the center of the circle).

JAVELIN THROW

1. The javelin may be thrown from a standing position or a run, but only one hand (little finger nearest to the point) may grip during the approach and throw.

2. The throw must be made behind the scratch line arc of a circle drawn with a radius of 26 feet 3 inches. The runway is 13 feet 1½ inches wide, terminating at the arc.

3. A valid throw must fall within the sector formed by extending the radii through the ends of the arc for 295 feet.

4. Touching on or over the arc or runway lines is a foul but counts as a trial.

5. The point of the javelin must hit the ground first, but the javelin does not have to stick in the ground.

6. Measurement is taken at the inner edge of the circumference of the arc (made on a line from the nearest mark made by javelin point to the center of the arc circle).

BALL THROWS

1. The throws may be made with or without a run.

2. Throws are made from behind a scratch line 10 feet long and 2 inches wide.

3. Stepping on or over the line before the throw has been marked is a foul.

4. The delivery must be made with one hand.

5. Measurement is taken from the nearest mark to the inside edge of the center of the scratch line.

SCORING

Track and field officials include a referee, inspectors, judges, field judges, timekeepers, a starter, a course clerk, a scorer, and numerous other persons. Many persons are responsible for an efficient meet. The judges and timekeepers are directly responsible for determining the correct times and winners of the running events and distances for the field events. A point award system is suggested, which will make it possible to recognize any number of place-standings in the competition.*

If there is a tie for any place, unless specifically covered in the rules, as for the running high jump, points are equally divided among the tying competitors. Team scores are the total of individual and relay event points.

COURTESY AND SAFETY

Courteous competition is safe competition when facilities are well laid out and equipment is properly maintained. There are no hidden dangers for the girl who is properly conditioned, warms up, and practices and competes under supervision.

The area used for each event should be clearly marked and only participants and officials allowed in the location. Events must be spaced and conducted so that there is no danger to others competing. Competitors must *never* casually throw their equipment, or practice throwing events out of their area.

Minor injuries can be kept minimal by having the running surface smooth and dry, pits soft and smooth, and jumping standards and poles in perfect condition.

All equipment should be of excellent quality and the recommended size and weight for the girl's age.

---

*See D.G.W.S. *Official Track and Field Guide.*

Terminology

Anchor — Final, or fourth, runner in a relay.

Barrier — A hurdle.

Baton — A tube-like object made of wood, metal, plastic, or cardboard which is passed from one runner to the next in a relay.

Beat board — An elevated takeoff board used for the standing broad jump. It is generally used indoors.

Blind pass — A relay exchange accomplished without looking back at the passer.

Break — Making a movement from a set position before the gun sounds.

Break in the pit — Mark made in the pit by the jumper.

Checkpoint — A visual mark used by a competitor to insure accuracy in stride.

Course — The path of the runner.

Curb — Inside border of the track.

Dash — A short distance race run at top speed the entire distance.

Dead heat — A race in which two or more runners cross the finish line at the same moment. It results in a tie.

Exchange zone — An area the width of one lane and 22 yards long in which the baton must be passed in a relay race.

False start — The forward movement of any part of the competitor's body after the command "Set" and prior to the firing of the gun.

Finish yarn (or tape) — A cord stretched across the track above the finish line to aid the judges in determining the first runner across the line.

Foul throw — A throw counted as a trial but not measured because of some violation of the field event rule.

Heat — A preliminary round of a race. The winners of heats participate in the semifinals or finals of the race.

Inside lane — The lane on the inside or curb of the track. Often referred to as the pole position.

Jog — Easy, slow, short-stride running action.

Kick — Increased speed and power exerted at the end of a race.

Lane — The path marked on the track for a race which defines where the runner must stay during the race or for a portion of the race.

Lap — One complete circle of the track.

Lead-off runner — The first runner on a relay team.

Medley relay — A relay in which runners run different distances.

Pace — The rate of speed at which the runner selects to run after considering the distance and her available energy.

Pit — Area where the jumper lands. It is usually filled with sand, sawdust, or foam rubber.

Preliminaries — A series of heats in running events and trials in field events which eliminate less expert participants.

Pursuit relay — A relay in which all runners run in the same direction.

Recall — Bringing the runners back after a false start.

Reverse — The interchange of feet after release in a throwing event. Also called recovery because it serves to maintain balance.

Runway — The approach to the scratch line or takeoff board in field events.

Scratch line — The line which may not be crossed on takeoff in the standing broad jump or when exe-

cuting the basketball, soccerball, softball, or baseball throws.

Sector lines — The boundary line within which the discus, shot, and javelin must land to be a fair throw.

Shuttle relay — Relay run with half of each team at opposite ends. Alternate runners travel back and forth over the same course.

Staggered start — The placement of runners in a step-like position at the start of a race to be run around a curve so that all competitors will run an equal distance.

Straightaway — Straight area of track between curves.

Takeoff board — Board set flush in the ground for the long jump.

Takeoff foot — The foot that leaves the ground last and drives the jumper.

Toe board — Curved piece of wood used as a foul line for the shot put.

Trailing leg — Takeoff leg or the rear leg in hurdling.

Trial — An attempt in a field event.

Wind sprint — An all-out effort of speed and power over a short prescribed course (usually 50 yards) followed by a brief rest before repeating the sprint.

Selected Audio-visual Aids

Beginning Track and Field, 1956. (9 filmstrips.) The Athletic Institute, 805 Merchandise Mart, Chicago Ill. 60654. (Purchase.)

Track and Field Events for Women. (still prints.) Dean — Brunson Studio, 139 N. Main St., Logan, Utah. (Purchase.)

Track and Field for Girls and Women. (3 reels 16 mm.; color, sound.) Teaching Aids Service, Inc., 31 Union Square West, New York, N.Y. (Purchase or rental.)

Suggested Readings

AAHPER: *Official Track and Field Guide*, Current Edition, Division for Girls and Women's Sports, 1201 16th St. N.W., Washington, D.C. 20036.

Brensnahan, George T., Tuttle, W.W., and Cretzmeyer, Francis X.: *Track and Field Athletics*, 5th Ed., St. Louis, The C.V. Mosby Co., 1960.

Foreman, Ken, and Husted, Virginia: *Track and Field Techniques for Girls and Women*, Dubuque, Iowa, William C. Brown Company, 1965.

Kinzle, Donn: *Practical Track Athletics*, New York, The Ronald Press Company, 1957.

Miller, Kenneth: *Track and Field for Girls.* New York, The Ronald Press Company, 1964.

Pallett, George: *Women's Athletics*, New Rochelle, New York, Sport Shelf, P.O. Box 634, 1959.

Scott, Phebe M., and Crafts, Virginia R.: *Track and Field for Girls and Women*, New York, Appleton-Century-Crofts, Inc., 1964.

Periodical

Women's Track and Field World, P.O. Box 371, Claremont, Calif. 91711 (monthly).

Suggested Study Questions

1. Explain the differences between the straddle roll and the western roll. Which do you prefer? Why?
2. Analyze the throwing events. What are some movements common to each of these events? From the standpoint of body mechanics, can you explain why these movements are necessary?
3. Describe one visual and one blind baton passing technique. What are the advantages of each? the disadvantages?
4. Describe the track layout for a 70 yard hurdle event. How many hurdles will you face? How will you run the race?

CHAPTER TWENTY

Elizabeth Allan of Winter Park, Fla., holds the world women's water ski jumping record of 106 feet and is the current world women's slalom champion. She is shown going around a slalom buoy during a Dixie Championships meet at Cypress Gardens, Fla. (Courtesy of Thomas C. Hardman, Editor and Publisher, *The Water Skier.*)

WATER SKIING

By Aimeé Loftin

Water skiing has become a popular sport for people of all ages, for skimming along the top of the water at brisk speeds is a most exhilarating experience. Even though water skiing can become technical, most people succeed in riding the skis the first day they try. It is an easy but safe sport that seldom ceases to challenge, because new techniques and skills are always ahead. From the basic techniques presented here, a person can go on to learn an infinite number of tricks, slalom skiing, and jumping. These skills can be pursued just for the fun of it or they can be matched against the skills of others in tournaments. With sufficient skill and practice it is possible to become a professional who either performs extensively for others, or teaches water skiing as a means of livelihood.

FACILITIES AND EQUIPMENT

Conventional Skis. Wood skis 5 feet 6 inches long, and 6½ inches wide, are recommended for most people. However, skis are made in varying lengths and by trial and error an individual may find the size skis she prefers. Skis can be straight or have a tapered heel. One or two wood fins, preferably one, near the back on the underside gives stability and prevents sliding on sharp turns.

Single Ski. The single ski or slalom ski is usually slightly longer than conventional skis. This ski has a regular binding for one foot and a second or back binding. The back binding does not have the heel piece to facilitate slipping the foot in and out. The fin for the single ski is much deeper than those

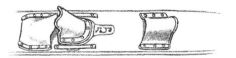

Fig. 20-1. Slalom ski bindings.

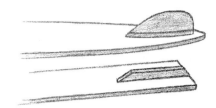

Fig. 20-2. Fins. The fin on the slalom ski (above) is much deeper than that of the conventional ski (below).

found on conventional skis. This fin is made of metal instead of wood.

Towline and Handles. Manila or braided polyethylene rope ¼ inch in diameter is recommended for the towline. The overall length of the towline should be the standard 75 feet. There are three types of handles used. The single handle is about 1½ inches thick and a foot long; the trick handle is about 18 inches long. The double handles are about 6 inches in length and provide more control over slack in the tow rope. Usually the towline and handle are made in separate units with a snap ring, which facilitates changing to the handle preferred.

Life Jackets and Belts. Skiers should wear a life jacket or belt whenever skiing. The poor swimmer should wear the full or standard Coast Guard approved jacket. A more experienced swimmer can use the belt. These flotation devices are not a substitute for the ability to swim or float until picked up by a boat, but merely to make the task easier.

Tow Boat. The boat used for skiing can be either inboard or outboard. It should have a sufficient power (60 to 160 h.p. inboard, or 40 to 100 h.p. outboard) to carry two people and to pull two skiers. It should be equipped with a towline bridle or pylon, rearview mirror, boarding ladder, approved life preservers, and an aquameter.

Dock or Float. There should be either a stationary or floating dock 8 to 16 inches above the water. The pier or dock should be at least 18 feet long and parallel to the shore to facilitate dock landing. If a stationary dock is prohibited by law, then a float at least 10 feet square should be securely anchored in a convenient place. The dock or float enables skiers to land and take off without necessarily getting into the water and provides a place to rest between rides.

CARE OF EQUIPMENT

Most skis are finished with enamel or spar varnish. Many prefer spar varnish because the smoother finish tends to give a faster ride. Regardless of the finish, the skis should be kept waxed with paraffin. Waxing helps to reduce wear and surface friction. Skis should not be left out in the sun for long periods of time.

It is recommended that skis be completely refinished after a season of skiing to prolong their life. The skis should be completely dried out before starting to refinish. The old finish should be completely removed by following the instructions of the manufacturer for enamel or varnish remover. The skis should then be sanded, and any nicks or gouges should be filled with plastic wood. Several coats of varnish should be applied, with a light sanding between each coat. The skis should then be stored in a warm, dry place in an upright position.

If the skis become damaged during the season, repair should be made at that time rather than waiting until the end of the season. Allow the ski to dry out completely and repair by sanding or filling with plastic wood and refinishing the damaged area. Failure to do so may result in discoloration and rotting of the wood.

The bindings on skis do not require much care. If used in salt water, the skis, and particularly the bindings, should be rinsed with clear water after each use. If the bindings become cracked, they can be repaired by spraying several coats of liquid neoprene on them. The life of the skis can be prolonged if all the metal parts are kept waxed. The screws on the bindings should be checked frequently to prevent any from working loose and either tearing the binding or pulling away from the skis.

All equipment used in skiing should be checked regularly to see that any loose or worn parts are repaired. This inspection should include belts, skis, towline, tow handles, and all the equipment on the boat. Any malfunction of one of these may cause a serious injury.

BASIC SKILLS

Dry Land Skiing. Wet the bindings to facilitate slipping the feet into the skis and place them parallel, 8 to 10 inches apart, on the beach. Insert one foot at a time into the binding. Slide the foot in as far forward as it will go and then slip the heel piece up. Adjust the bindings so that each fits snugly and tighten the adjustment. Holding the handle, sit down on the back of the skis with the back straight, knees bent close to the chest, arms outside of the knees and slightly flexed (Fig. 20-3). Have someone pull the towline until you are in a standing position with the knees flexed, arms and back straight. Throughout this practice keep the back straight and push up with the legs. Do not pull back on the tow handle. Repeat this several times until the feeling of being lifted is achieved.

Deep Water Start. After land practice the skier is ready for a water start. Adjust the bindings to the correct size before going into the water. Put on a life jacket or belt and go to about shoulder-deep water, holding a ski under each arm so that they are floating parallel in the water. Let go of one ski and let it float near by. Use both hands and push the ski down into the water. Take a deep breath, bend the knee toward the chest, duck the

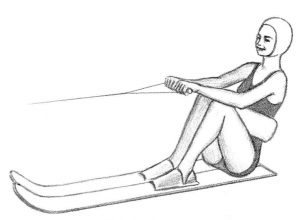

Fig. 20-3. Dry land practice.

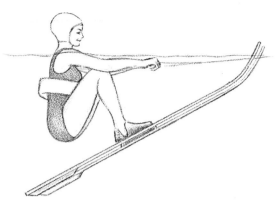

Fig. 20-4. Starting in water. Position before the pull.

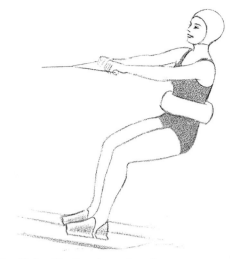

Fig. 20-6. Starting in water. Come to a standing position slowly.

head into the water, and slip the ski on as was done during the land practice. Repeat with the other ski. Keep both skis under the body and assume the same land practice sitting position with the knees bent and back straight. Use both arms to paddle if necessary until a balanced position is achieved. The tow boat will then bring the line to you. Do not reach for the line, as this will tend to cause you to lose your balanced position. As soon as you have the line, flip it over your head, and let it slip through a circle made by the thumb and first finger. When the handle reaches you, grasp it and bring both ski tips up and out of the water about 8 inches with the line between the skis (Fig. 20-4). Shout "in gear," and as the line becomes taut sit in the water with knees bent, back straight, towline between skis, and arms outside of the knees and slightly flexed. When in balance shout

"hit it," and the boat will accelerate to 18 to 20 miles per hour, depending on the weight of the skier. Keep the skis parallel and pointed straight ahead (Fig. 20-5). Do not try to hurry to a standing position. Wait until the skis are planing and then straighten slowly by pushing up with the legs (Figs. 20-6, 20-7).

Riding inside the Wake. When the skis are planing, assume an erect position with the knees flexed, the back and arms straight. Follow the boat in the center of the wake. This is the area directly behind the boat

Fig. 20-5. Starting in water. The pull begins.

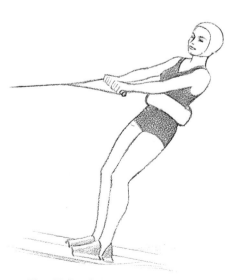

Fig. 20-7. Correct riding position.

between the swells of turbulent water. Remain inside the wake until balance is assured.

To turn to the right the body leans in that direction with the right knee flexed and pushes from both ankles. To turn left, reverse the procedure. A slight amount of pressure is all that is necessary. Practice leaning and turning back and forth inside the wake. During these turns the skier may experience some slack in the towline. When this occurs, lower the towline and pull back toward the body. If necessary, pull toward one hip and release the handle with one hand. Maintain pressure on the line, and as the boat and skier regain the same speed, return to the normal straightahead position. Never lift the line to remove slack.

Crossing the Wake. A sharper turn is necessary to enable the skier to cross the wake. If the skier wants to cross the wake to the right, turn inside the wake toward the left, then lean sharply to the right and flex the right knee. This lean should be from the ankles. Cross the wake at as close to a right angle as possible. Allow the knees to flex as the skis pass over the turbulent water. Once outside the wake do not lean as much as was necessary to cross the wake. When the pressure is removed, the skier will be pulled by the towline straight ahead once again. To return to the center of the wake, ski about 15 to 20 feet to the right of the boat and lean sharply to the left. Flex the knees when crossing the hump in the water. Attempt to keep the turn as smooth as possible to avoid excessive slack in the towline. Should slack occur, pull the line down and to one side of the body.

Landing. At any time the skier wants to stop, she simply lets go of the towline. As momentum is lost the skier will sink slowly into the water. The arms should be extended to the side at shoulder height to aid in keeping balance.

To land near the dock or float the skier should always come in parallel to the objective. Skiing at about 15 to 20 miles per hour, the skier will plane 20 to 25 yards before sinking into the water. On the first attempts at landing at a specific spot, stay inside the wake and practice judging the length of the plane. Once this has been learned, the skier can cross the wake and release the line at the end of the "whip off." To do the "whip

off" the skier crosses the wake and releases the line. If the skier approaches the landing spot too fast, she should squat down and let her cupped hands drag in the water to slow herself down. If the glide appears much too long, the skier should sit down in the water to avoid hitting the dock or float.

Sitting Dock Start. Place feet in the binding as described in the preliminary land practice. Sit down to one side of the skis and swing them over the edge of the pier. Face the back of the boat, even though this might mean sitting sideways on the dock. The position of the body on the edge of the dock is with knees bent and 8 to 10 inches of the ski tips up and out of the water. The back should be straight and slanted away from the boat, and arms slightly flexed toward the chest. Because the boat must be moving to have sufficient momentum to pull the skier at planing speed sooner than was necessary with the water start, have about 4 feet of towline coiled on the dock to one side. When ready, shout "in gear." When the rope straightens out and the coil starts to unwind, shout "hit it." As the boat accelerates there will be a strong pull on the towline. The skier must keep the back straight and the knees flexed. The pull of the

Fig. 20-8. Starting from dock.

boat will straighten the arms. Keep the flexed knee position until balance is assured. Some skiers may prefer to hold the coil in one hand. If the coil of line is held, it should be dropped as the line becomes taut and just before the "hit it" signal is given.

Single or Mono Skiing. Start with two skis from a water or dock start. Once planing, try placing all the weight first on one foot and then on the other. Determine whether the right or left foot feels more secure. If there seems to be little difference in the feeling on either foot, practice balancing on the left foot. It is contended by some professionals that having the right foot back when running the slalom is a stronger position, and that this should be the encouraged position for beginners. Slowly put all the weight on the preferred leg and lift the other ski out of the water. Be sure to lift the toe of the ski up and out of the water so that it does not catch and cause you to fall. Repeat several times, holding the lifted ski position. The single ski will tend to wobble in the water more than when riding two skis, because it is more sensitive to changes in ankle position. Do not overcorrect this by moving the ankle too radically. After riding in balance on one ski, drop the other ski by lifting the heel out of the binding. Keep the ski tip up and let the ski slide off the foot. Bring the free leg high enough to clear the spray and either press the foot against the calf of the other leg or move it back and forth to aid in attaining balance. Do not drag the free foot in the water. A novice will tend to put some weight down on that foot and a fall will result. Once a balanced position is achieved, slowly place the free foot in the back binding. The body is held in an erect position with a moderate lean backward and with knees slightly flexed.

To turn the single ski, push down with the rear foot and lean from the ankles in the direction of the turn. The body is held erect during the turn. To increase the sharpness of the turn, lean farther back and into the direction of the turn while pressing down with the rear foot. Crossing the wake on a single ski is accomplished in the same manner as on two skis. To cross to the right, swing as far left as possible inside the wake, lean to the right and push with the rear foot. Keep the arms and back straight and cross the wake in as close to a right angle as possible. Flex the knees to help to absorb the shock when

Fig. 20-9. Single ski riding position.

crossing the turbulent water of the wake. If there is slack in the line, pull the tow bar down and to one side of the body, releasing one hand from the tow bar. If double handles are used and slack occurs, pull the arms out to either side of the body at waist height. To return inside the wake, swing out to the right, lean from the ankles to the left, and push with the rear foot.

Single Ski Water Start. There are two basic methods used in the single ski water start. A small, light person will probably use both feet on the ski, whereas a heavier person will prefer dragging the free foot to get the added lift of a second surface pushing on the water. There will be a great deal more pull on the tow bar than the skier felt during a water start on two skis. Some prefer to use a baseball grip on the handle, that is, with one palm up and the other palm down.

Put on the single ski in at least 5 feet of water. Place both feet in the bindings and bend the knees as close to the chest as possible (Fig. 20-10). This will reduce the angle of the ski in the water to one that is as close as possible to parallel with the surface. Put the towline to the left side of the ski if the right foot is in the back binding, or to the right if the left foot is back. When in balance shout "in gear," and when the slack is out, shout "hit it." The skier should stay in the crouch position until the ski is planing and then,

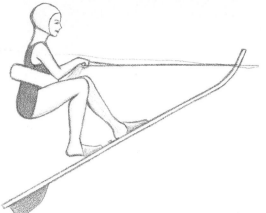

Fig. 20-10.   Single ski start: First method.

standing position, keeping the weight well back. When a balanced position has been achieved, slowly place the free foot in the back binding.

Single Ski Dock Start.   Sit on the edge of the dock and swing the ski out into the water. Put the free foot in the back binding and lift the ski tip up 6 to 8 inches above the water. The skier should keep the back straight and arms and knees flexed. The whole body should be tilted back away from the line of pull (Fig. 20-12). Hold, or coil on the dock about 5 feet of line. Give the "in gear" signal, and as the coil starts out shout "hit it." Keep the knees flexed and the weight well back during the start.

keeping the weight well back, push up to a standing position.

The second method of the single ski water start is similar to the one just described. Place one foot in the binding and bend the knee as close as possible to the chest. The free leg drags in the water with the lower part parallel with and close to the ski (Fig. 20-11). The towline is on the opposite side of the ski from the free leg. When in balance shout "in gear," and as the slack is taken out shout "hit it." As the boat starts, push down against the water with the free leg. Do not let the knee relax, and keep the toes pointed. The free leg tends to act as a rudder and will assist in maintaining an upright position in the water. When the ski is planing, push up to a

Fig. 20-12.   Single ski dock start.

SAUCER RIDING

Riding a saucer is closely related to water skiing and is a good introduction to trick riding. Riding a saucer has almost as many variations as riding skis. Saucers are round disks 3 to 4 feet in diameter. Some have fins, but most have a smooth underside.

Water starts are almost always used in saucer riding. Lie on the saucer and grasp the tow bar and front edge of the saucer at the same time. Shout "in gear" and have the boat pull out the slack from the line. As the line tightens shout "hit it." The boat will accelerate to between 8 and 12 miles per hour,

Fig. 20-11.   Single ski start: Second method.

depending on the weight of the person riding. When planing, slide the knees up to the middle of the saucer and kneel on it. Release the front of the disk so that an erect position can be achieved. Keeping the back as straight as possible, place one hand next to the knee and then bring the same foot up and onto the saucer. The same hand and foot must be used or the saucer will dip into the water, causing a fall. Change hands on the tow handle and repeat this procedure to get the other foot up. Push from the legs to get to the standing position. Care must be taken to place the feet in the center of the saucer, shoulder width apart. If the feet are too far forward from this center of the disk, the front digs into the water and a fall will result. If the feet are too far back from this center, the saucer will bounce up and down, resulting in a loss of balance and a fall. Should a fall occur, it is advisable to stay under the water a few seconds and come to the top slowly to avoid hitting the saucer with the head.

Saucer Turns. The saucer is most often ridden right behind the boat. Because the saucer does not have fins, changing direction is more difficult than on skis but can be accomplished by leaning slightly to one side and flexing the knee in the direction of the turn. The saucer will then move in the direction of the lean.

Turns of 180 and 360 degrees are accomplished by releasing the tow bar with one hand, pivoting away from the boat, and swinging the free arm around in the direction of the turn. As the body turns, rotate the arm holding the tow bar down and behind the body so that it can be easily grasped behind the back as the turn is completed. The hand holding the bar will start with the palm down but will have the palm up as the 180 degree turn is completed and the rider is facing backward. To make a 360 degree turn, the rider should start as described above but, instead of stopping at 180 degrees, change hands on the tow bar behind the back and swing the free arm around to complete the turn. The rider will fall if her body does not lean away from the boat throughout the entire turn.

SKIER'S SIGNALS

A series of signals are used to notify the boat driver how and where the skier wants

the boat driven. These signals should be understood by both skier and driver before leaving the dock. As already described, there are two verbal signals given at the time of the start: "in gear," which notifies the driver to take slack out of the towline, and "hit it," which means to accelerate the boat fast enough to get the skier planing. Some of the other signals are as follows:

Slower—Fist with thumb down

Fig. 20-13.   Signal: "Slower."

Faster—Fist with thumb up

Turn—A sweeping circular motion in the direction of the desired turn

Return to dock—Point to the dock

Fig. 20-14.   Signal: "Return to dock."

Speed all right—Circle with thumb and first finger, other fingers extended

Fig. 20-15.   Signal: "Speed all right."

Stop—Palm ahead with fingers together

Fig. 20-16. Signal: "Stop."

Should the skier fall, she should signal with both arms upraised and the fingers touching above the head. This notifies the driver that the skier is all right.

Fig. 20-17. Signal: "Skier not hurt."

SAFETY AND COURTESY

There are some fundamental safety procedures that should be followed to make water skiing a safe and enjoyable sport. It is strongly recommended that all skiers, regardless of swimming ability, wear a belt or a jacket. It is possible to fall in such a manner that all breath will be knocked out. Should this happen, the belt or jacket will be of considerable help while regaining normal breathing. If a fall cannot be avoided, the skier should first throw the tow handle away. This avoids any entanglement in the line, which might cause serious injury. The fall, if possible, should be backward so that the skier tends to sit in the water. Contrary to what some might believe, a head dive into the water should be avoided. If the skier cannot

help falling forward, the hands should be brought up over the face and, if possible, the knees brought up to the chest. The "ball" position will minimize the possibility of injury. Other courtesies and safety precautions that should be followed while skiing are as follows:

Safety check all equipment before using.
Learn skills in progression.
Always have an observer in the boat.
Ski at a speed that is reasonable for the type of skiing being attempted.
Ski only in areas that are free of submerged rocks or other hazards.
Avoid swimming areas.
Avoid skiing near other boats that are under way or anchored.
Land parallel to dock or beach.
If a coil of rope is held during a dock start, it should be dropped as the slack in the line is taken out.

BOAT HANDLING

Correct boat handling is essential to insure a safe and enjoyable ride. The driver should always have an observer in the boat to watch the skier. This enables the driver to concentrate on correct handling of the craft.

When starting a skier, the boat should, if possible, be headed out toward open water. It is easier on the skier if the start is made so that the pull up out of the water is straight ahead. A turn by the boat in a start will often cause the novice to fall. Starts made with the wind blowing the boat and skier sideways are more difficult than one made into the wind.

For water starts the skier should have the towline out the full length. On the signal "in gear" let the boat idle forward to eliminate all the slack. The driver should never accelerate until the skier gives the "hit it" signal. Do not change speed in an effort to help the skier. Once the skier is planing, the speed can be reduced to the one desired by the skier. When a novice is being pulled, sharp turns should be avoided. If necessary, the observer can signal the skier of an impending turn so that she will not be on the same side of the wake as the direction of the turn. If this occurs, a great deal of slack will come into the

Fig. 20-18. Picking up skier. The boat maneuvers so that the towline comes to the skier.

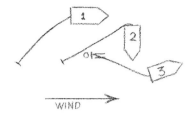

line; when the boat speed snaps the line taut, it often results in pulling the handle out of the skier's hands.

Dock starts require that the driver pay particular attention to the signals given by the skier. The boat should be out from the dock about 40 to 50 feet and headed away from the skier. At the "in gear" signal, the boat should idle forward to take up the slack and yet have some forward momentum when the "hit it" signal is given. A smooth, straight start is essential if the beginner is to succeed in the dock start.

Picking up a skier after a fall requires that the driver be in absolute control of the boat. Misjudgment may result in a serious injury. The propeller on an outboard motor can mangle an arm or leg. The boat should return to the fallen skier as soon as possible. Approach from behind the skier at least 6 feet to the side. When about 6 feet ahead of her, turn sharply to pass in front of her. When the stern of the boat is well past the skier, return to the direction of the approach. This maneuver will cause the towline to come to the skier (Fig. 20-18).

The skier should then flip the line over her head and let it slip through the hands until the handle reaches her. At this point the motor should be put into neutral and idle until the signals for the start are given. This entire procedure should be done with the wind pushing the boat away from the skier, never toward her. Unless the wind interferes,

Fig. 20-19. Dicksie Ann Hoyt of Fair Haven, N.J., former women's national and Masters' water ski champion, completes a front to back toehold turn on a single trick ski. (Courtesy Thomas C. Hardman, Editor and Publisher, *The Water Skier.*)

Fig. 20-20. The current national women's jumping champion, Barbara Cooper Newsom of Austin, Texas, was the first woman water skier to jump over 100 feet back in 1964. (Courtesy Thomas C. Hardman, Editor and Publisher, *The Water Skier.*)

the circle around the skier should be done on the driver's side of the boat.

Terminology

Aquameter — Device attached to the boat to give the actual speed. This is a trade name in common use instead of speedometer.

Back binding — A second binding on the single ski behind the main binding. This is usually only a toe piece.

Binding — The device on a double or single ski consisting of a toe and heel piece used to hold the foot securely in place. This piece is adjustable to fit all sizes of feet.

Bridle — A device used on the boat to attach the towline. This term is also used to designate the two pieces of rope that connect the single line to each end of the tow handle.

Buoy — An anchored floating marker used as a guide to the skier or driver.

Cut — Used to designate the sharp turn by the skier when crossing the wake. This term is also used to indicate turning off the boat's motor.

Deep water start — A start when the depth of the water is at least as deep as the skier's shoulder. This may be done on one or two skis.

Double handles — Two tow grips connected to the towline by 5 feet of rope. Used primarily in slalom skiing.

Fin — Wood or metal attached to the underneath side of the skis to aid in turning and to prevent side slipping. These devices vary in size and design.

Hit it! — Signal given to have the boat accelerate to skiing speed.

In gear — Signal given to have the boat put into gear so that it moves forward slowly until slack is taken from the towline.

Pylon — A device on the boat used to attach the towline.

Single handle — A grip, 12 to 18 inches long, and about 1 inch in diameter, connected to the towline. Also referred to as the conventional grip or tow bar.

Tow bar — The handle or grip connected to the towline.

Towline — The rope connected to the boat. The standard length, including the attached handle, is 75 feet.

Trick handle — A device attached to the tow handle to facilitate holding on with the foot while skiing.

Trick riding — Various maneuvers performed on one or two skis without fins. Each trick has a point value that is figured in determining the winner of this event in competition.

Wake — The turbulent water created by the movement of the boat. This rough water is found on either side of the path of the boat.

Whip off — To cut across the wake to gain speed before releasing the towline to land at the dock or on the beach.

Selected Audio-visual Aids

Greatest Show on Water. (13 min., color; 8 or 13 min., b & w, 16 mm., sound.) Mercury dealers.

Ski Jump Thrills — From the 1960 National Water Ski Championships. (15 min., 16 mm., color, sound.) Johnson Motor dealers.

Ski Jump Thrills — From the 1961 National Water Ski Championships. (12 min., 16 mm., color, sound.) Johnson Motor dealers.

Ski Tricks. (14 min., color.) Evinrude Motors.

The Greatest Show on Water. (27 min., 16 mm., color, sound.) Johnson Motor dealers.

Water Ski Fun. (13½ min., 16 mm., color, sound.) Mercury dealers.

Water Ski Tips. (15 min., color.) Evinrude Motors.

Water Skiing. (21 min., 16 mm., color, sound.) Johnson Motor dealers.

Suggested Readings

Andresen, John H.: *Skiing on Water*, New York, The Ronald Press Company, 1960.

Bartlett, Tommy: *Guide to Water Skiing*, Philadelphia, Chilton Company, 1959.

Pearsall, William H.: *Young Sportsman Guide to Water Skiing*, New York, Thomas Nelson & Sons, 1961.

Prince, Walter N.: *Water Skiing for All*, New York, John deGraff, Inc., 1960.

Scharff, Robert: *Complete Book of Water Skiing*, New York, G. P. Putnam's Sons, 1959.

Pope, Dick, Sr.: *Water Skiing*, Englewood Cliffs, New Jersey, Prentice-Hall, Inc., 1958.

Periodical

The Water Skier, American Water Ski Association, 7th Street and Avenue G, S.W., Winter Haven, Florida.

Suggested Study Questions

1. What equipment is needed for water skiing and how should it be taken care of in order to obtain the most good out of it?
2. Review the things the skier should do before the deep water start.
3. What is the best way to cross over the wake?
4. What should the skier remember when making a sitting dock start?
5. Discuss the sport of saucer riding, turns, and signals.

3

TEAM SPORTS

"Sport, which keeps the flag
of idealism flying,
is perhaps the most saving grace
in the world at this moment,
with its spirit of rules kept,
and regard for the adversary."

—*John Galsworthy*

CHAPTER TWENTY-ONE

Courtesy of Agnes I. Michaels, State University College, Fredonia, New York.

BASKETBALL

Basketball is truly the "All-American game." Created by Dr. James Naismith to fulfill a class assignment, basketball has grown into the most popular participating and spectator team sport in the country. The game as originally played in Y.M.C.A. class at Springfield, Massachusetts, was a simple, 13 rule, indoor winter sport that served the same team purposes as football during the fall and baseball in the spring. Originally, a large number of men composed two teams and were allowed to bat, pass, and throw in an attempt to get the ball into peach basket goals nailed to each end of the gymnasium balcony.

Although women were not in Dr. Naismith's original plans, they quickly saw the value of the game. A short two weeks after the game was introduced, a group of women teachers asked to play. The game spread rapidly, but misinterpretations and misunderstandings of the rules led to confusion across the nation. A rule misinterpretation by Miss Clara Baer in 1893 at Newcomb College in New Orleans ultimately developed the three division court game. The first rules committee met in 1899 and accepted the three court game. The first basketball guide for women was edited by Senda Berenson and eliminated snatching and batting of the ball, limited the dribble to three floor contacts, and ruled a foul for holding the ball more than three seconds. It was not until 1936 that the two division game with three forwards in one half of the court and three guards in the other was recognized by the basketball rules committee. This basic pattern remained official for more than a quarter of a century.

Throughout the years the sport has had a history of multiple and differing rules. In 1899 some players and teachers refused to accept the modification of the men's rules. Today a limited number of teams play modified boys' rules rather than rules designed for women. A limited number of state high school athletic associations have independent rules, but the differences between their rules and those of the A.A.U. and D.G.W.S. are fewer each year.

Since 1905 there has been an active and permanent basketball committee that plans and revises rules. Recently, in an attempt to bring A.A.U. and D.G.W.S. rules into agreement, a rule was changed to allow roving players. This change made basketball more physically demanding and strategically challenging and created more opportunity for general skill development among all players. This committee remains the most active in team sports in the Division for Girls and Women's Sports of the American Association for Health, Physical Education, and Recreation in its effort to revise and introduce rules to make the game more interesting and to protect the health and safety of players.

NATURE AND PURPOSE OF THE GAME

Basketball is played by two teams of six players each on a rectangular court no larger than 94 by 50 feet (Fig. 21-1). The court is divided into two equal areas so that each team has a front court, where its own basket is located, and a back court, which has the basket it defends (the opponents' basket). Each team tries to get the ball and move it by passing, throwing, batting, bouncing, rolling, or handing it to a player who may shoot it into her basket and score a goal. The team not in possession of the ball tries to keep the opposing team from scoring as it tries to intercept, tie, or otherwise gain the ball and eventually make a scoring effort. The score of a team is the total of its field goals and free throws.

FACILITIES AND EQUIPMENT

The Court. Basketball is played in and out of doors with leather and rubber balls in

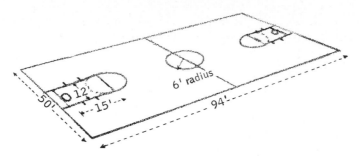

Fig. 21-1.   Basketball court. (Official D.G.W.S. specifications.)

many informal settings; however, an official game is played on a rectangular court at least 74 feet long and 42 feet wide and no larger than 94 by 50 feet. There should be at least 22 feet of overhead clearance. The outer court boundary line and center division line across the court width are 2 inches wide. Where possible, the boundaries should be 10 feet from any outside obstruction. A center restraining circle with a radius of 6 feet is marked by a line 2 inches wide in the center of the court.

The free throw line, 2 inches wide, is marked from a spot 15 feet from the center of the face of the backboard and extends 6 feet in either direction, parallel to the end line. A free throw circle 6 feet in radius is drawn from the center of the free throw line. The half of the circle within the free throw lane is marked in dotted lines. Lines 2 inches wide from the free throw line to the end line enclose the 12 foot wide free throw lane. Three lines 8 inches long and 2 inches wide are placed perpendicular to each of the lane lines at distances of 7, 10, and 13 feet from the end line of the court (3, 6, and 9 feet from the face of the backboard).

Backboards. Rectangular or fan-shaped boards are made of plate glass, wood, metal, or other flat rigid material. The white or transparent boards, with white marking, hang 4 feet inside the court parallel to the endline.

Orange colored metal basket rings with nets attached hang in the center of the board with the rim 10 feet above the floor.

Ball. The leather or composition covered round ball is between 29½ and 30¼ inches in circumference, weighs between 20 and 22 ounces, and bounces between 49 and 54 inches when dropped from a height of 6 feet. Balls of reputable manufacturers meet of-

ficial specifications. Each team of six should have at least two balls for practice.

Costume. The official gymnasium costume is satisfactory for most game situations. Attractive shorts and shirts which allow freedom are desirable for interscholastic and intercollegiate games. Footwear is an important safety feature. Each player should wear one or two pairs of light socks that cushion the feet and prevent blisters. Basketball shoes with cupped soles are generally preferred over the tennis-type shoe.

In competitive games each player should wear a solid color number on her uniform. Slipover pinnies are suitable with back numbers at least 6 inches high and front numerals 4 inches high. Both must be at least ¾ inches wide. The single digits 1 and 2 should not be used. Combinations of two digits from 0 to 5 should be used.

BASIC SKILLS

Footwork, body balance, and ball handling are the foundation skills of basketball. A review of basic sports skills is helpful in preparation for game play.

Stance. A player preparing to move or receive a pass is in a slightly crouched position with the knees bent and head and chin up; shoulders are slightly forward. The arms are relaxed and elbows bent with fingers spread comfortably at waist level. One foot is slightly ahead of the other so that the body is comfortable. Weight is distributed on the balls of the feet.

Running. In running, the body leans forward as the knees rise to medium height. The arm action is natural and relaxed, and the arms swing forward to near shoulder height, poised to receive or intercept the ball.

Jumping. Development of leg force for high and accurate jumping is necessary for playing rebounds, tie balls, tipping, and shooting. Under the current rules one of the best offensive shots is executed from an extended jump position while the body is in the air.

Jumps may be made from one or both feet or from a skip step. With a push from the toes over flexed knees, the body "stretches out" high off the floor. The landing is on the balls of the feet and the knees are flexed.

Catching. The type of catch used depends on the position of the ball, the position of opposing players, and the anticipated move to follow. In preparation the arms are relaxed, the elbows are away from the body, and the hands are at waist level. The fingers are relaxed and spread upward in the direction of the ball. With the receiver facing the oncoming ball, she steps forward to meet the ball with arms extended, elbows in, and hands extended. As the ball reaches the fingertips it is cushioned into the fingers as the arms pull back slightly to "give" to ball momentum. The ball is caught by the fingers, thumb, and heel of the thumb, *not the palm.*

The hands are on the sides and to the back of the ball for all catches. When catching a high pass (above the waist), the thumbs point toward each other with fingers pointing upward. On a low pass (below the waist) the fingers point downward, little fingers pointing toward an imaginary spot to the rear and bottom of the ball; thumbs are directed to the back and top of the ball.

Passing. A skillful basketball game hinges on effective passing to maintain possession of the ball. There are numerous ways of passing. The type used by a player depends upon the position of the body and hands of the passer and intended receiver.

CHEST PASS. The two-handed chest pass is the most widely used because it can be caught at chest height and lead to a speedy and accurate shot or return pass. The body may be almost erect or crouched, with the ball at chest level close to the body. Both hands hold the ball with fingers spread from the rear to the side, and pointing slightly upward. Thumbs are behind the ball with palms near, but not touching. Elbows are flexed and close to the body. The arms push forward from the shoulders as the elbows extend and the wrists snap as the ball is released in a straight line. As the ball leaves the hands, the thumbs give a simultaneous push and the palms turn toward the line of ball flight. The hands rotate inward on the follow-through as thumbs point downward and fingers extend in the direction of the pass. If it is not a deceptive pass, body weight should be transferred to the forward foot to give additional power.

TWO-HAND UNDERHAND PASS. The "flip" pass is not popular among girls except as a hand-off to a forward in a pivot play, or as a short pass when unguarded in front.

The pass may be made off the front of the body or from either hip. In any case, the cupped hands grasp the ball with fingers behind and on the side pointing downward;

Fig. 21-2.   Catching.

Figs. 21-3 and 21-4. Catching and passing skills are fundamental to the game of basketball. (College of Health, Physical Education and Recreation, Texas Woman's University, Denton, Texas.)

Fig. 21-5. Chest pass.

TWO-HAND SHOULDER PASS. The two-hand shoulder, or sidearm, pass is useful at the completion of a pivot, or as a deceptive pass when the ball moves one direction and the body another. The pass may be made from either shoulder. The ball is held in both hands so the fingers and thumbs point upward and back and cover the sides and rear of the ball. The elbows are flexed so that the right arm is close to the side and the left is across the front of the body. Feet are in forward or side stride position with the body rotated to the right from the hips and waist. The arms extend and wrists snap in a rapid movement as the weight shifts to the left leg. The body follows the ball as the arms and the hands extend and rotate inward as in the chest pass.

thumbs are on top pointing toward line of flight. When passed off the front of the body, the elbows are flexed and point away from the body more than in the chest pass. Feet are in side stride position. The arms extend forward as the elbows straighten, and wrists snap upward as the ball is released at waist height. The arms follow through low, with thumbs pointing up and fingers toward the path of the ball.

When the ball is passed off either hip, body position varies slightly. To pass from the right hip the body is in forward stride position with the left foot forward. The hands draw the ball to the right hip so that the right elbow is bent, pointing outward from the body, and the left elbow is across the body with the back of the left hand resting on the hip. The ball moves forward with an arm extension and wrist snap as the body weight transfers to the forward left foot. The release and follow-through are the same as the "flip" from the middle of the body.

Fig. 21-7. Two-hand shoulder pass.

Fig. 21-6. Two-hand underhand pass.

TWO-HAND OVERHEAD PASS. This is a successful pass for skillful, tall players who are closely guarded or for any player who wants to release the ball quickly after catching a high pass. The ball is raised above the head, with the fingers at side and rear and thumbs beneath the ball. The elbows are slightly bent and the wrists flexed. The body inclines forward and the weight shifts forward as the arms extend and wrists and fingers snap to add thrust to arm and shoulder power. The ball is released at a point in front of the body about head level as the hands follow the ball to eye level and turn inward, palms down and thumbs toward one another.

Fig. 21-8.   Two-hand overhead pass.

ONE-HAND SHOULDER PASS.   The pass is much like an overarm softball throw and is effective as a well controlled long or medium distance pass. To execute the pass the feet are comfortably spread and body weight equally distributed. The right hand is spread behind the ball so that it is supported by the fingers and thumbs. It is brought back to the right shoulder by bending the elbow back and away from the body. The left hand comes across the body to serve as a steadying guide as the body rotates to the right. As the body weight shifts to the left foot, the left hand leaves the ball. The right arm brings the ball forward, passing close to the ear. The right elbow extends and the wrist snaps as the fingers thrust forward and pass under the ball, causing a slight reverse spin. The throwing hand and arm follow through in the direction of the ball and end with palm down and fingers extended forward.

ONE-HAND UNDERHAND PASS.   The underhand pass is effective from both sides of the body as a short, deceptive pass and a "feeder" to a forward cutting to the basket. The pass resembles the underarm softball pitch. In executing a pass from the right side, the left foot is forward and body is comfortably crouched. The right hand is spread over the back of the ball and the right wrist and lower arm support the ball. The right elbow bends and leads the arm and ball past the hip as the left hand is placed on the ball as a guide. As the right arm starts forward the left hand moves away. The arm swings by the body and parallel to it, the arm extends, and weight transfers to the forward foot. The ball is released at waist height as the fingertips, hand (palm up), and arm follow the ball flight.

Fig. 21-10.   One-hand shoulder pass.

BOUNCE PASSES.   .One- and two-hand bounce passes are used for short passes in the scoring area, or any other place on the court when an opponent is between the passer and receiver. They are often used on plays from out of bounds.

For the one-hand bounce pass the preliminary movements are similar to those of the shoulder or push pass, except that the ball is brought between the shoulder and waist on the right side of the body. The left hand may balance the ball as the right hand is behind and toward the top with fingers extending upward. The right elbow is flexed and close to the side. The ball is pushed to the floor so that it bounces and rises to a level at

Fig. 21-9.   One-hand underhand pass.

which the receiver can get it easily. The arm follows through toward the floor with palms down. If a waist level rebound is desired the ball should bounce 3 or 4 feet from the receiver. If a lower rebound is necessary, bounce farther from the receiver.

The two-hand bounce is executed much like the two-hand chest pass except that the action begins about waist height. The fingers are spread to the sides with the thumbs behind the ball. The elbows are close to the sides as the ball is pushed toward the floor with a firm arm extension out toward a point on the floor. The arms rotate outward as the wrists and fingers thrust the ball away at waist level. At certain times a spin is valuable with the bounce pass. On a long pass or when the ball must rebound close to the receiver with considerable momentum, top spin can be added by cocking the wrists back and then uncocking them vigorously on the release. The ball leaves the small fingers first and the index fingers last. The hands follow through so that the fingers point toward the floor.

Backspin is used on short, relatively fast passes where a rebound up and away from the receiver is desired. The ball is released by a vigorous cocking action of the wrists toward the passer's body. The fingers release the ball after pulling upward and backward and the thumbs complete the action by pushing the ball down and forward. As the ball leaves the hands of the passer it is spinning toward her; the palms of the hands follow through, facing the spot where the ball strikes the floor.

Side spins are applied when it is necessary for the ball to bounce right or left on the rebound. To spin the ball so that it bounces to the receiver's right side, bring the left hand to the right (under the ball) while pulling the right hand forcefully to the left (on top of the ball). At the moment of release, the ball is spinning in a counterclockwise direction. As the ball hits the floor it "jumps" to the passer's left. A reverse hand action results in a clockwise spin and a bounce to the left of the receiver.

SHOVE PASS. This advanced pass is also called the push-shove, or pass-volley and is an effective way of clearing the ball from under the basket or controlling a rebound or pass without really gaining possession of or "holding" the ball. As the ball comes toward the receiver, she pushes the ball toward a teammate by using one or both hands. The

hands and fingers are firm and extended, elbows flexed. The wrists are flexed as the hands meet the ball. The arms extend and the wrists snap, giving direction to the ball. The palms and firm arms follow through in the direction of the pass.

HOOK PASS. The hook pass is an advanced technique used effectively to return a ball to an inside court position when the player is held along the sidelines. For a right-hand hook pass, the body is in forward stride position, left foot forward. Initially the ball is held firmly by both hands at waist level. The body turns so that the left shoulder is toward the receiver as the left hand moves toward the left side, leaving the right hand (fingers spread and pointing upward) and right forearm supporting the ball.

When a passer is standing or jumping upward, her right arm is raised sideward, so that it crosses the right shoulder and passes overhead, where the ball is released by a forceful wrist and finger snap. The left arm remains extended for balance while the right hand pulls under the ball as it rolls off the fingertips. The hand (palm down) and fingers follow the path of the ball as far as possible.

Fig. 21-11. Hook pass.

JUMP PASS. This advanced pass technique is executed from an extended jump position while the body is in the air. Following receipt

Fig. 21-12. The jump pass.

of a pass, dribble, or rebound, the jump may be made from a stationary position in which the player is standing on both feet or by stepping forward and jumping from one leg with the other following. The ball is held in position for either a two-hand overhead or one-hand push pass. If taking off from both legs simultaneously, the knees bend deeply and both legs thrust the body directly up from the floor. If the jump follows a bounce or dribble, one leg thrusts upward forcefully and the other immediately comes alongside. As the player leaves the floor, the ball is brought in front of the body and raised high and directly overhead for a two-hand overhead pass or high overhead and slightly toward the shoulder side for the one-hand push pass. To avoid contact with an opponent, the jump must be directly upward rather than forward. The player must jump as high as possible, for the greater the height the less opportunity for interception or blocking of the pass by an opponent. At the height of the jump, when the passer is motionless for a brief instant before returning to the floor, she releases the ball in the direction of the intended receiver.

Evading and Maneuvering Techniques. There are many skills involving ball handling and body control that are important to all offensive and defensive playing positions.

DRIBBLE. Dribbling is the skill of imparting impetus to the ball one or more times,

causing it to rebound from the floor while controlling and maintaining possession of it. The first impetus may be given with one or both hands, but thereafter contact must be with only one hand until the ball is passed or the dribbler touches the ball with both hands to complete the dribble.

Players should remember that accurate passing is a faster way of moving the ball and that the dribble is generally used to: (a) get somewhere with the ball (often for an opportune shot at the basket); (b) allow time to establish and execute a play pattern; and (c) avoid losing possession of the ball. When executing the dribble the ball is pushed to the floor by wrist and finger action at an angle determined by the distance the player will cover. Players should develop the ability to dribble with either hand, as well as the skill of changing hands during a dribble series.

JUMPING FOR JUMP BALL. The player crouches in a forward stride position with both feet on the floor. A player may choose to place either shoulder toward her opponent and reach with the arm and hand across the body or with the one closest to her opponent. The weight is forward on the toes and the body weight is down through flexed hips and knees. The first push-off comes from the rear foot (right when players have left shoulders together); the final push-off comes from an extension of ankles, knees, and hips. Simultaneously, the arms swing forward and upward with the tapping hand extended, fingers cupped, wrist flexed. The tap is timed so that the ball is touched and directed to a teammate or open area at the height of the jump.

Fig. 21-13. Jumping for jump ball.

Fig. 21-14. A tie ball is put into play by a jump between two opposing players. (Courtesy of Clifford Lewis, University of Georgia.)

STOPS. There are two common methods of stopping body momentum—the two-step stop and jump stop. The two-step stop is considered the superior, as it leaves the player in a stance suitable for passing, shooting, or bouncing and dribbling. It is a lead-up for footwork in the lay-up shot. The two-step stop is simply described as a half skip coming to a sudden stop. The player hops off her right foot, grasps the ball, lands on her right foot, and steps forward on the left foot. At the end of the stop the feet are in a running stride position, 12 to 15 inches apart. The body weight is low and the rear foot serves as the pivot foot. Players should be able to use either foot as the hopping foot. If the skills are mastered as simple stops then they become foundation skills for shooting left- and right-hand lay-ups.

In the jump stop both feet touch the floor simultaneously and either foot may be used as the pivot foot. The player anticipates the ball, pushes off the floor to catch the ball, and then brings the feet down together.

PIVOTING. Pivots are used when a player has possession of the ball and wants to change or reverse body direction to elude an opponent. Throughout the pivot, one foot must remain in contact with the floor. Whether the pivot is made from a forward or side stride position, the knees are relaxed and the body weight is low. The ball is kept close to the body as the pivot is made. It may be a movement of only a few inches, or it may be a full turn.

The body weight is on the ball of the stationary foot as the free foot pushes off. In a side stride position the body backs away or moves forward with *either* foot remaining on the floor. In a forward stride position, if the left foot is forward, the body turns left and backward or the left leg crosses forward and in front of the right pivot foot.

THE REVERSE TURN. This is used when the player is in forward stride position and confronted by an opponent. The knees are bent and the body crouched. The body turns, as if to a command of "to the rear, march," in the direction of the rear foot and away from the forward foot. The body spins on the balls of both feet as the toes of the front foot push off. The "new" rear foot may be lifted into a step after the turn is completed.

FEINTS. Feints, or fakes, are movements of the ball, body, or eyes designed to mislead an opponent and draw her out of position. They may be used effectively by both offensive and defensive players. Usually it is a movement contrary to the intended final movement of the player. Feints are done very quickly from either a stationary position or while moving. Feints (fakes) include:

1. *Ball fake.* Accomplished by moving the ball in one direction and shooting, passing, bouncing, or dribbling in another.

2. *Foot fake.* Placing the foot in one direction and then moving the body or ball in another. This is used by offensive and defensive players.

3. *Eye feint.* Looking one way and passing another.

4. *Head fake.* The head and upper part of the body make a movement in one direction and then suddenly turn and bounce, dribble, pass, or shoot in another.

5. *Arm fake.* Thrusting the arm upward or sideward to raise the opponent's defense and then passing below the defense.

Cutting. These are techniques designed to get a player free so she may receive a pass or shoot. The techniques include changing running pace, stopping, pivoting, body fakes, and combinations of these skills. To be effective the player must "break" smoothly and rapidly and avoid a set pattern of movements. Beginning players should concentrate on:

1. Cutting in front of guards.

2. Cutting toward player with the ball in anticipation of a pass.

3. Recutting if she does not receive the ball on first cut.

4. Being aware of position of her teammates and adjusting her cuts to those of her teammates.

5. Varying type, length, and speed of cuts.

Goal Shooting. Shooting incorporates all the skills of stance, body balance, finger control, and follow-through. The type of shot a player makes depends upon her position on the court. Figure 21-15 gives an indication of when a player should use a rim shot or a bank or angle shot off the backboard.

Two-Hand Chest Shot. This is used from a set position anywhere in the offensive court when the forward is not too closely threatened by a defender. The feet may be in forward or side stride position. The body is relaxed in a semicrouch, weight equally distributed, and eyes focused on the rim where the shooter will generally aim. The ball is in front of the body at chest level (lower for a very long shot) and is grasped by the fingers behind and to the sides. Fingers point upward and thumbs toward each other. The relaxed shoulders help to keep the elbows comfortably close to the body. The force of the shot begins as the knees flex and the wrists "cock," allowing the ball to drop *down* toward the shooter. As the arms extend the ball upward in front of the chest, the body extends upward and forward; the wrists straighten as the fingers direct the ball in an upward arc. The palms of the hands follow through to face the basket, and the fingers maintain extension as the shooter moves forward for a possible rebound.

Fig. 21-16. Two hand chest shot.

Two-Hand Overhead Shot. This is used for a short or medium distance set shot. Proper execution requires strong arm and finger action. The body is erect, head up, and eyes on the target. The knees flex slightly as

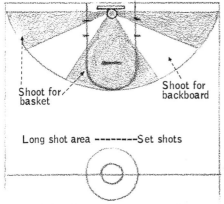

Shoot for basket

Shoot for backboard

Long shot area --------Set shots

Fig. 21-15. Goal shooting.

Fig. 21-17.   Two-hand overhead shot.

the ball is raised overhead by easily bent elbows and held by the thumbs behind and underneath, with the fingers pointing outward on the sides and rear half of the ball. The arms and knees extend as the body weight shifts to the toes. The wrists extend and the fingers and thumbs drive the ball toward the basket.

ONE-HAND SHOULDER (PUSH) SHOT.   This shot can be used effectively when the shooter is closely guarded in a set position, or following a bounce or dribble. The shot may be taken without leaving the ground, but if the player rises from the ground the shot is similar to the lay-up in hand position and take-

off. The right handed player may take off on either the right or the left foot, with the guiding left hand leaving the ball. As the body rises away from the defender the right arm extends upward and forward. The ball is released well above the shoulder with a finger push at the height of the jump.

LAY-UP SHOT.   Often called an angle or under the basket shot, it is made from a position close to the basket, from the front or either side. An angle shot from the side is banked off the backboard. Players should develop lay-ups from both sides. Shooting from the right of the basket should be done with the right arm from a left-foot take-off; the opposite should be done in shooting from the left. A lay-up from the right may be analyzed as follows: a player moving in from the right cuts for the basket, receives the ball and may bounce, dribble, or move directly to the shot. The ball is carried with the left hand to the front and underneath, and the right hand on top and slightly behind. Both hands carry the ball to shoulder or head height as the left foot pushes off. The right knee rises to lift the body, the guiding hand leaves the ball as the right arm and wrist straighten and direct the ball to the backboard. The ball is *placed* rather than thrown. The palm of the right hand follows in the direction of the backboard as the fingertips "guide" the ball. The player turns as she lands from the jump so that she partially faces the court, ready to play for a rebound.

When playing a lay-up shot from the front of the basket, use either hand to lay the ball over the rim.

TWO-HAND SPIN SHOT.   The two-hand spin shot is a shot for the highly skilled player that is used as a "change of pace" when the person in possession of the ball or no other forward is in a position for a safer shot. The ball is held below the waist near the body with the fingers pointing downward and thumbs on top pointing forward. The ball is carried to the side and directed to the basket by a forward and upward motion of the arms as the elbows extend, the wrists snap, and the body turns. The wrist and finger action upward causes the ball to spin toward the shooter. The palms and fingers follow through upward with palms facing. This shot is easily guarded and is used only when a player, committed to a shot such as the lay-up, makes a final attempt to score.

Fig. 21-18.   One-hand shoulder (push) shot.

Fig. 21-19. Lay-up shot.

Hook Shot. This shot is executed from both the right and left sides when the shooter is facing away from the basket and is closely guarded from the rear, or when the shooter

Fig. 21-20. Hook shot.

is moving away from the basket. The ball is held by the fingers and supported by the heel of the right hand. The shot is preceded by a forward or sideward step (left quarter-turn) and is immediately followed by a left shoulder turn toward the basket. Simultaneously, the right arm swings upward in an overhead arc and toward and above the left shoulder. The fingertips and wrists guide the arcing ball over the rim (if shot is from the front) or to the backboard. On the follow-through, the hand pulls under the ball, palm down, and fingers extend toward the target.

Jump Shot. The jump shot is most effective from within a 15 foot radius of the basket. It is the most effective way to rise above a threatening opponent to execute a shot. The mechanics of body action are the same as for the jump pass. The ball is held in position for a two-hand overhead or one-hand push shot. The release of the two-hand shot is from a high overhead position and the one-hand shot from overhead and slightly to the shoulder side of the shooting arm. The release of either shot is at the height of the jump. The jump must be directly upward to avoid contact with an opponent.

A *turning jump shot* can be used when a

Fig. 21-21. Executing a jump shot. (College of Health, Physical Education and Recreation, Texas Woman's University, Denton, Texas.)

Fig. 21-22. Foul shooting.

player has her back or side to the basket. For example, as a right-handed shooter leaves the floor she turns to her left while in the air and is facing the basket as she releases the ball at the height of her jump. As a variation she may step or dribble left, jump, and turn in the air prior to her shot.

TIP-IN. The tip-in is an advanced offensive skill that is most often used on a rebound and is occasionally used to control a misdirected goal shot by a teammate. The player jumps to meet the ball just before the height of her full jump is reached. She controls it momentarily and then shoots or pushes the ball to the basket at the top of her jump *before* returning to the floor. This skill requires excellent timing and a strong and agile hand and arm.

FOUL SHOOTING. Several types of shots are successfully used in the attempt for a free throw. It is generally agreed that a player is more successful using her *best* personal shot. This will frequently be a one-hand shoulder shot and occasionally a two-hand chest or overhead shot. For the player who rarely

plays a court position that requires extensive shooting, a two-hand underhand loop shot may be appropriate. Whatever the shooting technique, the player taking a free throw stands directly in front of the basket with toes behind and near the foul line.

To execute an underhand loop shot the feet are spread and toe out from the body to insure balance. A side stride offers the best balanced position. The fingers are spread over the sides of the ball pointing downward, and the thumbs are on top and forward. The arms hang comfortably down as the eyes focus on the forward rim of the basket. The body remains erect as it sinks with a knee bend and the heels rise from the floor.

The force of the throw begins as the body straightens naturally, and the arms and hands extend upward and forward toward the basket. The hands release the ball at the closest point to the basket without applying a deliberate spin. At the completion of the shot the weight is forward and the body is balanced and erect. The arms and hands are outstretched to the basket.

GAME RULES AND SCORING

The official *Basketball Guide*, published by the Division for Girls and Women's Sports of the American Association for Health, Physical Education, and Recreation, should be consulted for complete rules.

Playing Time. Basketball is played in four quarters of 8 minutes each. There is a 2 minute interval between the first and second quarters and the third and fourth quarters. There is a 10 minute interval at the half. If the score is tied at the end of the regular game time, overtime periods are added (see Scoring section).

During the game, time-out is taken for:

1. A player or coach requesting it for her team, when her team is in possession of the ball or the ball is dead. Five 1 minute periods are allowed for each team, and an additional one is allowed for each overtime period.
2. Fouls.
3. Jump balls.
4. Substitutions.
5. Injuries.
6. Suspension of play or at any time at the discretion of the referee or umpire.

Time-in begins:

1. When the ball touches a player on the court from a throw-in from out of bounds.
2. When the ball is tapped by either player on a jump ball.
3. When a player on the court touches a missed free throw that has touched the ring of the basket.

Conduct of the Game. A team may have four of its six players in one half of the court at one time. In practice this allows two roving players—a forward, or front-court player, and a guard, or back-court player—to cross the division line into the opposite court. The two players designated to cover the entire court may change with teammates at any time as long as no more than four players are in one half the court at any time.

Play begins with a jump ball in the center circle between any two opposing players. The same procedure is followed at the beginning of each quarter and overtime period. The visiting team has the choice of baskets. If both teams are "home," the winner of the toss of a coin has the choice of baskets.

Whenever a field goal is scored, the ball is put in play by a member of the opposing team at any point behind the end line where the goal was scored. Teams exchange goals at the half.

Time-in begins as the ball is tapped. From the toss, both opposing players attempt to tap the ball to a teammate. During the toss all other players must remain outside the 6 foot restraining circle. The *Thirty Second Clock Rule* is official in A.A.U. tournament play and may be used in D.G.W.S. play when mutually agreed upon by the teams involved. The rule states that when a team gains possession of the ball, a try for goal must be made within 30 seconds. If the ball goes out of bounds during the 30 second period, a new 30 second period shall begin as play resumes. The touching of the ball by an opponent, without gaining control of the ball, does not start a new 30 second period. Failure to try for goal in the allotted time results in a violation for the offending team.

Throughout play, in handling the ball, a player may:*

1. Throw, bat, bounce, hand or roll the ball to another player, or throw for goal from her front court.
2. Catch, retain, or throw the ball with one or both hands.
3. Take or tap the ball from an opponent.
4. Advance the ball by means of a dribble or an air dribble, taking any number of steps between the release and the recovery of the ball.
5. Hold the ball for 5 seconds in bounds if closely guarded, 5 seconds out of bounds, and 10 seconds on a free throw.
6. Touch the ball to the floor while retaining possession of it. This shall not be considered a bounce or part of a limited dribble.
7. Use two steps after receiving the ball in the air, on the run, or on the completion of a dribble.
8. Catch the ball while both feet are off the floor, land on both feet simultaneously, and take a second step on either foot.
9. Catch the ball while both feet are off the floor, land on one foot, and take a second step on either foot or on both feet simultaneously.
10. Use either foot as a pivot foot after catching the ball while standing still.
11. Use either foot as a pivot foot after coming to a stop on the first step.
12. Use the rear foot as the pivot foot after a two-step when catching the ball in the air, or at the end of a run, dribble, or air dribble. If

---

*D.G.W.S. *Basketball Guide*, 1968-1969, pp. 134-135.

one foot is in advance of the other, only the rear foot may be used.

13. Lift the pivot foot when releasing the ball for a pass, trying for a goal or dribbling. The ball must leave the hands before the pivot foot again touches the floor.

14. Jump while holding the ball, provided it is released before landing from the jump.

15. Continue to play a ball which happens to touch an official on the playing court.

During play, tie balls, violations, fouls, and out-of-bounds balls occur.

A *tie ball* is called when two opposing players place one or both hands on the ball simultaneously or when a player places one or both hands firmly on the ball held by an opponent. A tie ball is put into play by a jump between the two opposing players in the nearest restraining circle.

A *violation* is a minor offense, such as failure to jump correctly on tie balls; intentionally kicking or striking the ball with the fist; illegally throwing at the basket; traveling; causing the ball to go out of bounds; or holding the ball longer than 5 seconds in bounds when closely guarded, 5 seconds out of bounds, or 10 seconds on a free throw. It is also a violation if a forward without the ball remains more than 3 seconds in the free-throw lane when the ball is in possession of her team in the front half of the court.

Violations result in the opposing team's being awarded the ball out of bounds over the side or end line. Double violations require a jump ball between opponents.

A ball is awarded to a player *out of bounds*:

1. When an opponent causes the ball to go out of bounds.

2. When the opposing team scores a field goal or free-throw.

3. When an opponent commits a violation.

4. When the ball was in possession of a team when the game was stopped; that team returns the ball to play.

Fouls are rule infringements that result in a penalty for the fouling individual or team, and one or more unguarded free-throw attempts for the team fouled. Multiple fouls occur when more than one player from the same team or two or more opponents foul at the same time. A double foul is called when players of both teams foul simultaneously. Individual fouls are charged against an individual player responsible for personal contact by blocking an opponent's progress; charging

an opponent with the body or ball; pushing or tagging an opponent; holding; tripping; hacking; blocking the progress of an opponent by holding both arms fully extended horizontally; threatening the eyes of an opponent; pulling or spinning an opponent into an off-balance position while attempting to take the ball; being unnecessarily rough; delaying the game; or using unsportsmanlike tactics.

A player must leave the game when she commits five fouls or a single disqualifying foul. Fouls charged to a team occur in the conduct of the game by the team, coaches, or spectators.

One free-throw is awarded unless the player fouled was in the act of shooting for goal. If the player fouled was shooting and the goal was made in spite of the foul, the goal is scored and one free-throw is awarded. If the goal attempt was unsuccessful, two free-throws are awarded. If the player shooting is fouled by two opponents simultaneously, the goal, if made, shall count and two free-throws are awarded. If the goal is missed, three free-throws are awarded. If one free-throw is awarded and the unguarded throw is made, the ball is put into play from out of bounds behind the end line by an opponent of the player making the free-throw. If the throw is missed and the ball touches the ring, the ball is in play. (If the ring is not touched, a violation is ruled.) If two or more free-throws are awarded, the ball is dead after all but the last one when procedure of the single foul is followed.

When two minutes or less remain in the fourth quarter, and during all overtime periods, any foul results in two free-throws. If the player fouled scored a field goal, however, only one free throw is awarded. If a player is fouled by two opponents simultaneously during this period, each opponent is charged with a foul and a maximum of three free-throws is awarded.

Players and Substitutes. Each team consists of six players. There may be any number of substitutes who may reenter the game any number of times unless disqualified. Substitutes must report to the scorer before entering the court and be recognized by an official before going in (except between quarters and halves). When the team has no eligible substitutes and one player is disqualified, the team may continue to play with five players. If the team loses two or more players, either by injury or disqualification, the game is defaulted to the opponents.

SCORING

The score of a team is the total of its field goals and free throws. Each field goal counts 2 points and each free-throw 1 point. The team with the largest score at the end of the official playing time is declared the winner. If the score is tied at the end of the playing time, the game continues for one or more extra periods of 3 minutes each with an intermission of 2 minutes before each extra period.

When a game is discontinued the score is recorded as 0-0. A defaulted game score remains unchanged if the defaulting team had the lesser score. If the defaulting team was leading, the score is recorded as 2-0. If a default occurs before play begins, the score is 2-0.

Scorers keep official records of names and numbers of players and substitutes, individual scoring, individual and team fouls, and time-out periods. A sample score sheet for one competing team illustrates the scoring method (Fig. 21-23).

1. Names and numbers of all team members are entered in the proper spaces before the start of the game. A "C" indicates the team captain.

2. The starting line-up is indicated by tally marks in the column headed "Times in Game." When a substitute enters the game, a mark is placed in the times-in-game column and the tally of the player leaving the game is marked out.

3. Score a field goal in the proper column beside the scoring player's name by making a figure 2. When the player is awarded a free-throw, draw a circle. If two free-throws are awarded for one foul, connect the two circles by a line. When free-throws are made, mark an (X) in the circle.

4. If a player makes a goal for the opposing team, record it below the players of the team for whom the goal is to be scored.

5. Keep the running score by marking through one point for each free-throw and two points for a field goal.

6. Mark individual and team fouls in the space provided.

7. Record team time-outs in the appropriate space.

GAME STRATEGY

Basketball is a game of offensive and defensive tactics with the ultimate team objective of scoring goals and preventing oppo-

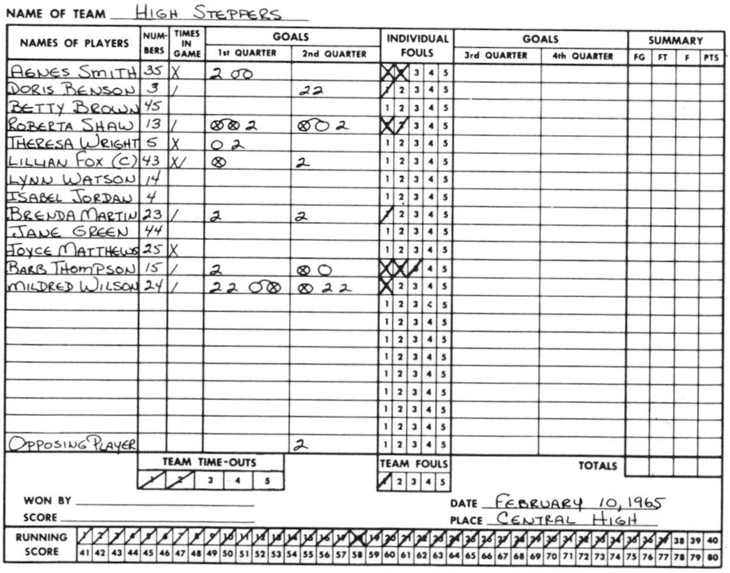

Fig. 21-23. Official score sheet for one team. (Adapted from D.G.W.S. *Basketball Guide*, 1968-69. *Official Rules*, p. 126.)

nents from scoring. The team in possession of the ball is the offensive team. The system of play used by both the offensive and defensive teams is dependent on the style of play and the skill of the opponents. The addition of the roving players requires more knowledge of full-court play and more team strategy, involving four offensive and defensive players.

DEFENSIVE PLAY

Every player on a team becomes a defensive player when a member of the opposing team gains possession of the ball. Forwards strive for interception of passes, bounces, and dribbles. In their front court this is done by aggressive guarding or by setting up a blockade to keep the ball from passing the division line. For a real "press" to gain possession of the ball, the roving players will have to assist, rather than pulling to their own back court to their guard positions.

Guards must concentrate on defending the goal and must stay between the goal and the ball to prevent a forward from penetrating to a position of a "sure shot." When forwards are outside the scoring zone (an area where there is general effectiveness within 15 to 18 feet of the basket), the guards may stay several feet away and toward the goal in anticipation of a pass, break, bounce, or dribble. Shooting accuracy is lessened in this outside area and chances for interception are greater. If the forwards attempt a shot, there is usually indication and time for the guard to move in to the ball.

Defensive Team Play. There are two basic types of defensive play: (1) player to player, and (2) zone; and there are variations and combinations of both forms. The skill and endurance of guards, their ability to work together, the type of offensive game played, and the skill of the opponents are the major factors that determine the system used.

When *player-to-player defense* is used, each guard is responsible for her own particular forward. No matter where the forward moves in the court, the guard is responsible for defending against her actions and shots. A team will find this its most reliable defense only if all guards are unusually quick and agile and there are no unusually tall players who should be utilized under the basket. A defense is most effective when opponents are

forced to shoot primarily from farther than 15 to 18 feet from the basket and are allowed few attempts to break to the basket. This is not the best method of defense in many situations, however, for guards cannot use their height to best advantage while playing under the basket. It can also be a very tiring pattern of play, since players are moving at all times. Close guarding also makes possible more body contact and fouling, and it also increases the difficulty of guarding a forward who evades her original guard. Psychologically, there seems to be less feeling of team play when a player-to-player defense is used.

This system of defense can be very effective as a change of pace when used for a short period of time to force the offense to change its style of play. Even in zone systems, defensive players may play man to man until roving players move into position. Roving players may play man to man as they come down court until they reach guarding positions in the zone. They may move directly to guarding positions and let the opposing rovers bring the ball down free.

Whenever the player-to-player pattern is used, players must rely on individual skills of guarding and their ability to scissor or switch when a forward maneuvers free, evading her guard. Guards return to cover their own forwards when the ball crosses the center line or when it moves out of the dangerous scoring area.

When a *zone defense* is used, each guard is assigned an area around the opponent's basket and has the responsibility of guarding any offensive play entering the area. In zone guarding, only the player with the ball is actively guarded; the other defensive players guard spaces and attempt to block passes, intercept passes, and block the moves of the other offensive players. The team shifts as a unit as the ball moves, rather than as individual forwards move. With four players to guard against a four person offense, several basic patterns can be used:

THE 2-2 ZONE. This is often called the box. It serves as a strong defense against outside shooting and a high post player but often leaves the center of the keyhole open. The initial position places the two guards deep and on either side of the basket; two guards are directly in front of them near the free-throw line (Figure 21-24). As the offense brings the ball in, the player closest covers it.

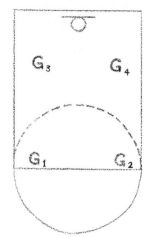

Fig. 21-24. Basic 2-2 zone.

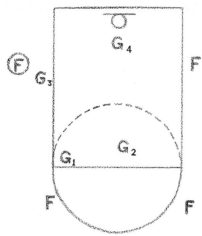

Fig. 21-26. Deep zone overloaded to the defense's right side.

The three other guards pull to a triangular formation (2-1) behind the out guard. One player remains deep to protect the basket under any conditions (Figure 21-25). When the ball goes to the corner of the court, a deep guard moves to cover as the others reform a 2-2 defense with one player close to the basket (Figure 21-26). If the ball goes to a high post player, normal guarding position follows. When the ball is passed to a low post player, the two back guards should attempt to intercept; but if the interception fails, they should double-team the post in anticipation of a shot and remain alert and ready to move should the ball be passed to another player moving in for a shot.

DIAMOND ZONE (1-2-1 ZONE). One guard is placed in front of the basket, two are placed on either side of the keyhole and near the foul-shooting line and another is placed at the edge of the circle (Figure 21-27). The guard nearest the ball moves to cover as the others move to a 2-1 formation behind her (Figure 21-28).

If two offensive players move into an area normally covered by only one guard (deep toward the basket or out toward the circle), one of the middle guards must shift to cover the play temporarily.

TRIANGLE WITH CHASER. The original formation of this defense is similar to the 1-2-1 zone. The major difference lies in the

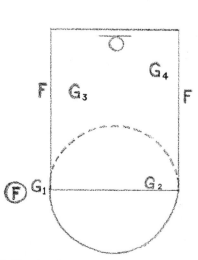

Fig. 21-25. 1-2-1 zone (from 2-2) to ball side with chaser.

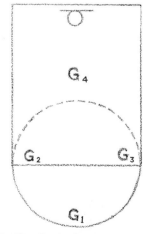

Fig. 21-27. Basic diamond zone (1-2-1)

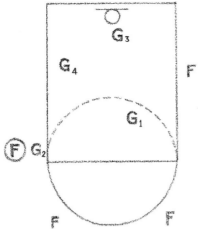

Fig. 21-28.   1-2-1 zone shifted to ball side.

shifting method. The zone is triangular, with the guard toward the circle playing either "chaser" or player to player while her teammates use the triangular shift. This formation is most effective when the chaser plays against the offensive team's strong outside shooter or the strongest offensive player. Covering this "playmaker" effectively, the chaser prevents her from getting the ball and setting up the offense. This is effective only if the chaser is fast and does not tire easily.

If the chaser's offensive player moves past her, a guard must move in and cover as the chaser joins the other two guards to set up a 2-1 pattern until the ball passes back out.

This formation is weak against several good outside shooters but is a strong and waiting defense against a post player or a forward cutting to the center.

OFFENSIVE PLAY

At the beginning of a game the offensive team "feels out" the defense's strengths and weaknesses and determines the type of defense pattern they are using. Generally, when player-to-player defense is used by the opponent, the offensive team players attempt to elude their defense quickly and make a direct attack on the goal. Fast break tactics and screens are particularly effective. Forwards should also spread to prevent an umbrella grouping of the guards and pass rapidly so that there is only one defensive player between the passer and receiver.

The zone defense is penetrated best by playing away from the scoring area in an attempt to pull the guards out by drawing the attention to one side or the front of the court, and then moving the ball to an open area and shooting. If the defense is tight near the basket, long shots should be used to draw defensive players out; then the ball should be passed quickly, and a player should cut through and in with it. If the defense is out, rapid passes should be used, and the player with the ball should cut toward the basket. An effective tactic is overloading a zone to one side with two or three offensive players and then passing off to a player cutting in on the weak side. A basic tactic in beating the zone is to pass the ball faster than the guards can move to protect their zones. An offense with an effective standing or running screen combined with a long shot will probably cause the opposing team to shift to a player-to-player defense. A team must keep a flexible offense so that it can change as the defense changes its patterns and player positions. However, flexibility does not necessarily mean that a team always adapts its game to the defense pattern; the offense should attempt to make the defense play *its* type of game.

The offensive movements begin as soon as the team gains possession of the ball. When recovering from their back court, roving and stationary defensive players combine to work the ball quickly into the front court. When possible, a fast break is an effective method of bringing the ball to the front court. A stationary defensive player rebounds and passes to a rover to the side of the key. This rover immediately passes to the other roving player, who is breaking rapidly near the center of the court. If the passes are successful, three offensive players end up near the basket and are opposed by only two guards.

If players lack competitive speed, are tired, or are prevented from making a fast break, the stationary defensive and roving players combine in a series of passes and cuts that work the ball (preferably up the sidelines) to the front court as quickly as possible. In crossing the center line, the rovers may either come straight up the court or crisscross to opposite sides. Once across the line, the rovers may move toward the end line, cut across the lane for a middle position, or move in and out to work the ball to the stationary offensive players. In all cases, once into the front court, dribbling should be kept at a minimum and the ball should be passed accurately and rapidly.

Stationary offensive players usually begin their movement pattern after the roving players cross the line. Against the zone, the patterns of the stationary forwards should include the following:

1. Cut behind the deep guards in the zone to the opposite side.
2. Cut diagonally in front of the deep guards to the opposite side.
3. Go straight out to meet rovers.
4. Cut diagonally to center of free-throw line to the front of and between the two front defensive players.
5. Use any combination of the above in which one stationary forward does one type of movement pattern and the other forward does a different one.

In a fast break situation the stationary offensive players pull a medium distance from the basket, then hold until one of the guards is forced to meet the oncoming free rover. The free stationary forward then cuts toward the basket to receive the pass and shoot. She must be aware that a second pass may be necessary if the remaining guard leaves her forward to cover the shot.

A team should encourage the front-court players to develop *screen* plays against all types of defense. In a screen play, a player passes to her teammate and moves to a position where her body protects the teammate's possession of the ball from the defending player. In a *moving screen*, the protecting teammate moves alongside of the player who dribbles unguarded. The stationary screen usually protects a player shooting near the goal. A player pivots and passes to a teammate behind her, then remains in a protective position in front of her until she shoots.

An offensive team gains confidence if it has a few simple plays as a basis for a plan of attack when it gains possession of the ball. These plays should not be confusing, with numerous maneuvers or difficult ball handling skills, but should be simple weave, hand-off, or cutting patterns.

DUTIES AND SPECIFIC SKILLS OF PLAYERS

All players should be skilled in ball handling, passing, maneuvering, and guarding.

Offensive players should have:

1. Several consistent shots for scoring, particularly an accurate lay-up from in front and both sides of the basket and a good set and jump shot.
2. Ability to move in and recover rebounds.
3. Ability to maneuver against player-to-player and zone defense.
4. Ability to vary style and speed of play, avoiding "set plays."
5. Ability to "feel out" style and weaknesses of a single guard and of total defense.
6. Ability to pass to a spot so a moving player receives the ball.
7. Ability to regain composure and shoot quickly under pressure.
8. Ability to handle ball accurately in tight situations.

Defensive players should have:

1. Ability to "feel out" strengths and weaknesses of opposing forwards, and to look for patterns of movement repeated frequently.
2. Ability to anticipate movements of the opposing forwards without being drawn out by feints.
3. Alertness to signals used by opponent.
4. Ability to cover a teammate's position, if necessary.
5. Ability to play the ball rather than an opponent in zone defense and move with the player in player-to-player situations.
6. Ability to tie the ball without fouling or being pulled out of position.
7. Ability to change defensive team pattern and individual guarding style when the situation requires it.
8. Ability to rebound and change to offensive play.

Terminology

Air dribble—Playing the ball so that one person sends the ball into the air and gains possession of it again before it is touched by another player or hits the floor.

Back court—The half of the court that contains the opponent's basket.

Balanced court—Placement of players so that three members of each team are in each half of the court.

Blocking—Personal contact that impedes the progress of an opponent with or without the ball.

Charging—A foul committed by the player in possession of the ball or who has just thrown or shot the ball, consisting of moving the ball or her body to make contact with an opponent.

Closely guarded—Guarding within 3 feet of the player with the ball.

Dead ball—A ball that is temporarily out of play.

Defensive player—A player whose team does not possess the ball.

Dribbling—The skill of imparting impetus to the ball one or more times, causing it to rebound from the floor while controlling and maintaining possession of it. The first impetus may be given with one or both hands, but thereafter contact must be with only one hand until the ball is passed or the dribbler touches the ball with both hands to complete the dribble.

Foul—A rule infraction by a team or an individual that results in one or more free throws for the opponent.

Free throw—An unguarded shot taken from behind the free-throw line. It is awarded to a player as the result of an opponent's foul.

Front court—That half of the court in which a team's own basket is located.

Goal—A ball that legally scores by passing through the basket from above with the impetus given by a player legally in the half court where the goal was made.

Goal tending—A player interfering with the ball or basket when the ball is on a downward flight to the basket, on the rim, or en route through the basket.

Holding the ball—A violation for possession of the ball for more than 5 seconds in the court when closely guarded, 5 seconds out of bounds, or 10 seconds in taking a foul shot.

Jump ball—A ball tossed between opponents in one of the three restraining circles. Players attempt to tap the ball to their respective teammates.

Offensive player—A player whose team has possession of the ball.

Pivoting—Moving the body around in a circle, or part of a circle, while one foot remains in contact with the floor.

Roving player—A player who crosses the division line into the opposite court to become her team's third or fourth player in the court.

Tie ball—Opposing players simultaneously gain possession of the ball, with one or two hands; or one player places one or both hands securely on a ball already held by an opponent.

Traveling—Illegal progression, such as jumping or walking while maintaining possession of the ball.

Unbalanced court—Positioning of players so that four members of one or both teams are on one half of the court.

Violation—An infraction which results in a throw-in from out of bounds by the opposing team. When both teams have simultaneous violations, play is resumed by a jump ball.

Selected Audio-visual Aids

Basic Skills and Drills, 1963. (16 mm., 27 min., sound, b & w.) Dr. Alta Gaynor, Department of Physical Education for Women, Marshall University, Huntington, West Virginia. (Purchase and rental.)

Basketball for Girls, 1964. (8 units, filmstrips 6 min. per strip, sound, color.) Athletic Institute, 805 Merchandise Mart, Chicago, Illinois 60654. (Purchase and rental.)

Basketball Fundamentals, 1964 (14 min., sound, b & w.) Coronet Instructional Films, Sales Dept., 65 E. South Water St., Chicago, Ill. 60601 (Purchase and rental.)

Basketball—Individual Skills. (Men's film.) (16 mm., 10 min., sound, b & w.) University of California, Berkeley, California. (Available through local Coca Cola distributor, free loan.)

Suggested Readings

AAHPER: *Basketball Guide*, Current Ed., Division for Girls and Women's Sports, 1201 16th St. N.W., Washington, D.C. 20036.

Bell, Mary M.: *Women's Basketball*, Dubuque, Iowa, William C. Brown Company, 1964.

Neal, Patsy: *Basketball Techniques for Women*. New York, The Ronald Press Company, 1966.

Schaafsma, Frances: *Women's Basketball*, Dubuque, Iowa, William C. Brown Company, 1966.

Wooden, John R.; *Practical Modern Basketball*, New York, Ronald Press Co., 1966.

Suggested Study Questions

1. Why is so much emphasis placed on mastery of the jump shot for advanced players? Explain the techniques of your jump shot.
2. Explain the fouls of blocking and charging. What are the penalties for such fouls?
3. How may a ball be tied? What procedure puts it back in play?
4. Explain player-to-player defense. How does the box zone defense operate?
5. Design two simple offensive plays from (a) the end line of the back court, and (b) the side line of the front court.

CHAPTER TWENTY-TWO

Courtesy of College of Health, Physical Education and Recreation, Texas Woman's University, Denton, Texas.

FIELD HOCKEY

Hockey is one of our oldest team games. Early Greek art and Egyptian hieroglyphics show figures playing the sport with sticks similar to those used today. The word "hockey" comes from the French "hoguet." The game has been called "hurley" in Ireland, "shinty" in Scotland, and "bandy" in Wales. Originally it was an activity for men, but in the United States it is now played almost exclusively by girls and women.

Field hockey was brought to the United States from England in 1901 and introduced to the college women at Vassar, Bryn Mawr, Smith, Wellesley, and Mount Holyoke by Constance Applebee. "The Apple," as she is affectionately known throughout the country by her many admirers, still advises and coaches. It is largely through her efforts that hockey has been so enthusiastically received and has grown in popularity in America. In 1922 the United States Field Hockey Association was organized to promote the best interests of the game. Girls and women who

enjoy playing may join the local hockey clubs that form this association. Since 1927, when the International Federation of Women's Hockey Associations was formed, teams from England, Scotland, Wales, Australia, New Zealand, South Africa, and the United States have enjoyed competing against each other. Every four years an international conference is held in one of the member countries for international exchange, competition, and meetings. An All-American team, composed of outstanding players from sectional and national tournaments, plays throughout this country demonstrating games and taking part in hockey clinics.

In 1963 more than 20 countries participated in the Eighth Triennial Conference of the International Federation of Women's Hockey Associations held at Goucher College in Maryland. Following the conference, teams toured the United States playing local groups to further hockey and international relations.

Fig. 22-1. Hockey is a team game which requires movement skill, group cooperation, and physical stamina. (Courtesy of College of Health, Physical Education and Recreation, Texas Woman's University, Denton, Texas.)

NATURE AND PURPOSE OF THE GAME

Hockey is a vigorous field sport in which two teams of 11 players each try to score goals by using a wooden stick to direct a hard ball. Players move the ball by dribbling and passing.

For a goal to count, at least one member of the attacking team must contact the ball within the defenders' striking circle. Goals count one point and are scored only if the whole ball passes over the goal line into the goal cage.

Players. A hockey team is composed of five forwards (a center forward, two inners, and two wings), and six defensive players (three halfbacks, two fullbacks, and a goalkeeper). "Right" or "left" precedes the position names of inners, wings, and backs; halfbacks are called "right," "left," or "center," e.g., right wing or center halfback. Every player must carry a stick during the game and use it to move the ball (except the goalkeeper, who does not have to *use* the stick although she holds it). The ball may be stopped with the stick or the hand, but the goalkeeper is the only player who may advance the ball with her body, legs, or hands.

The Game. An official game is played in two 30 minute halves with a maximum of 10 minutes of halftime. Time-outs may be called by an umpire and are taken for injury, damaged equipment, or game interference. Games for less experienced players are usually shortened to 25 or 15 minute halves. The ball is put into play with a center bully at the beginning of each half and after a goal has been scored. At the end of playing time the team with the larger score is declared winner.

FACILITIES AND EQUIPMENT

The following items represent a minimum list of necessary equipment and facilities

Fig. 22-2. "Penalty corner." The ball is returned to play by the left wing. (Courtesy of Carole L. Mushier, University of Southern California.)

which should be available. They are discussed in more detail later.

1. A well marked, turfed, and smooth field.
2. A stick for each player.
3. At least one ball for every 8 to 10 players.
4. Shin guards for each person.
5. Two pairs of goalie pads and kickers.
6. Distinguishing team pinnies.
7. Whistles, official rule guide, score book.
8. First aid kit.
9. Protective glasses guards.

Field. The playing field is a turf-covered rectangle 90 to 100 yards long by 50 to 60 yards wide. (The turf should be as smooth as possible, with all lines clearly marked with 2 inch white lines.) At the center of each goal line is a goal 4 yards wide. Two 7 foot goal posts, 4 yards apart and joined by a crossbar 7 feet from the ground, mark the goal mouth. Six feet behind the goal line are two 6 foot posts. The sides, back, and top are enclosed by netting or wire mesh.

The field is divided into two equal halves by a center line parallel to the goal lines. Two lines at either end of the field, at right angles to the side line and extending onto the field 7 yards indicate the 25 yard lines. Parallel to, and 5 yards in from each side line, is a broken 5 yard line. The space between the 5 yard and side lines is called the alley. At each end of the field is a striking circle. The "circle" is actually two quarter circles, measured 15 yards from the corresponding goal post and joined in front of the goal by a 4 yard line parallel to the goal line.

On both sides of the goal cage and 10 yards from either goal is a line 12 inches long running from the goal line into the field. This line is used in administering *penalty corners.*

On the side line and 5 yards from each corner of the field is a line 12 inches long running from the side line, parallel to the end line, into the alley. This line and the line where the inside alley line bisects the end line are marks for long corners.

Stick. The hockey stick has two major parts—a shaft-like handle and a curved head. The left side of the head is the flat, hitting surface; the right side is rounded. Only the flat side may be used to contact the ball. There are no left-handed hockey sticks; right-handed and left-handed players use the same stick and grip.

Hockey sticks vary in weight, height, and hand grip and should be selected to fit the individual player. As in other sports equipment, hockey sticks vary in quality. The head is made of ash or mulberry and the grain of the wood should follow the curve of the blade. The handle, or shaft, is cane with rubber or cork insertions, bound with string and encased in a rubber grip.

Selection of a stick depends on the player's height, arm length, playing position, and preference. To determine the length of stick needed, stand erect, hold the stick with both hands at the top of the shaft as if preparing for a drive. The blade should just clear the ground. Weight and size of blade should also be considered. The usual stick length is 36 or 37 inches; weight, 18 or 19 ounces. Forward line players may prefer lighter sticks with thinner blades; backfield players may choose sticks with heavier heads.

Balls. Official hockey balls are made of cork and string, covered with leather or plastic and painted white. Plastic covered

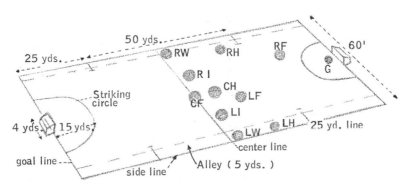

Fig. 22-3. Hockey field, as specified by the USFHA. Players are positioned for center bully.

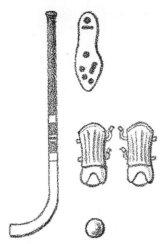

Fig. 22-4. Hockey equipment.

balls are usually "livelier." The ball must weigh between 5½ and 5¾ ounces. The circumference is not less than 8¾ nor more than 9¼ inches. Less expensive composition cork balls are often used in practice.

Costume. The players' gymnasium costume is satisfactory for instructional purposes, but for school or club games a tunic is recommended. Freedom of motion and appropriateness are the chief determining factors. Socks and rubber-soled shoes are essential. Rubber cleated shoes are helpful on wet or muddy fields. Shin guards should be worn to protect the lower legs.

The goalkeeper wears white hockey leg pads and heavy shoes. The leg pads are much larger than shin guards, extending from the thigh over the instep. They should be buckled to the outside of the player's legs. If pads extend only to the ankles, kickers should be worn. Cleated, square-toed, padded shoes protect the goalkeeper when she is kicking the ball. Squares of sponge rubber inserted over the instep increase protection for the foot.

CARE OF EQUIPMENT

Many players will want their personal equipment and should care for it to insure long life.

Stick. During the season the stick should be carefully wiped and stored. After each session all dirt is removed and rough places are sanded smooth; if splinters appear, tape lightly after sandpapering. A dry ash stick is treated with linseed oil, the excess removed, and wax applied for protection against moisture. A mulberry stick is treated with oil only. If worn, rubber grips will need to be replaced and the decorative stringing holding the grip in place retied. Sticks should be stored in a cool, dry place.

Ball. Match balls probably will need repainting after each match. Practice balls, depending on amount of use, should be repainted two or three times during the season. A ball rack makes painting easier and holds freshly painted balls. Plastic covered balls can be easily washed but should not be painted.

Shin Guards. Straps and rubber pieces should be kept in repair. Buckling skin guards in pairs after use is a time saver.

Goalkeeping Equipment. Goal pads should be brushed, the straps checked and buckled in pairs, and then stored in a dry, well ventilated place. Soiled pads and kickers should be scrubbed by a brush with soap and water, dried, and white shoe polish applied.

Goal shoes collect mud and often require scraping. Neat's-foot oil is used to protect the leather.

BASIC SKILLS

Development of hockey skills is extremely important for enjoyment of the game. For clarity, an explanation of skills is divided into three main categories: (1) controlling and advancing the ball, (2) fielding and tackling, and (3) play for specific situations. Basic to all skills is footwork.

Footwork. Agility, speed, and control of one's body while handling the stick is necessary for putting the body in the best position for playing the ball. As a situation in play changes and different strokes are needed the player must "get her feet around" so that they are always in proper relationship to the ball. A beginning player will do well to develop small, sure steps, particularly when running at top speed, in order to be ready for quick changes in direction. The eyes must be on the ball constantly and the feet ready to move. Poor footwork results in inaccurate strokes and fouls.

CONTROLLING AND ADVANCING THE BALL

Holding the Stick. Place the head of the stick on the ground, toe pointing forward and the top of the handle against the front of the leg. Place the left hand at the top of the stick and grip easily. Raise the stick to a vertical position, toe pointing upward. The right hand is placed directly below the left, fingers curled around the handle. A "V" formed by the thumb and index finger of each hand is in line with the toe of the stick. Lower the stick to a perpendicular position, so that the head is slightly to the right and in front of the right foot. The flat hitting surface is facing forward. The left forearm is straight and in line with the stick, and hands and wrists are relaxed. This is the basic grip position. The left hand seldom changes this position, but for some strokes, the right hand moves farther down the stick.

Carrying the Stick. The stick is carried in a comfortable position for running and in such a way that it may quickly be used for play. Beginners should be encouraged to carry the stick with two hands, maintaining a dribble grip, with the toe of the stick toward the ground.

When quite a distance from the ball, more advanced players may find it easier to run with the stick parallel to the ground with toe facing up. The elbows are easy and flexed. The left hand is at the top of the handle, and the right is 6 to 8 inches down, holding the stick in front of the body and parallel to the ground. The stick should swing easily with the running motion. Other advanced players may prefer a one-hand grip in anticipation of the immediate play of the ball. The stick is held by the left hand at the top, and the blade of the stick is carried close to the ground, facing in the direction of the oncoming ball.

Dribble. The dribble is a series of short taps on the ball that enables a player to advance the ball while running. Players use a "close" dribble when near opponents or expecting to pass or shoot momentarily. A "loose" dribble allows additional speed when the field is clear and there is no threat of an interception or tackle.

The left hand is at the top of the handle with the back of the hand facing forward. The right hand is placed 3 to 4 inches down the stick with palm forward. The stick is gripped firmly with thumbs circling. The arms are away from the body and firmly extended. The left elbow points diagonally forward. The player should have the feeling of reaching for the ball with the stick nearly perpendicular and slightly to the right of the right foot. The body faces forward. The left shoulder should be slightly ahead of the right in good upright running position. A free wrist motion is used to execute short suc-

Fig. 22-5. Carrying the stick.

Fig. 22-6. Dribble.

Fig. 22-7. "The bully." (Courtesy of Carole L. Mushier, University of Southern California.)

cessive taps. The action is a push with the right hand and a pull with the left.

In a controlled dribble the ball is never more than 6 to 8 inches away from the stick. The loose dribble in the clear field allows the player to hit the ball harder and farther ahead of the stick. This series of "passes to oneself" must be well timed and used sparingly to avoid interception.

Drive. Drives are powerful strokes used

Fig. 22-8. The drive.

for passing, clearing, and goal shooting. The body is in an upright position whether standing or running (avoid crouching), with the hands close together near the top of the stick. With the stick perpendicular to the ground, the right elbow bends close to the body and points toward the back of the player as the right arm pulls the stick back in a short backswing. The left arm remains close to the body, and both wrists cock as the arms swing back. At the moment of impact both arms are straight and the wrists uncock with a snap as the ball is hit. The body weight moves through for added power as the left arm pulls the stick forward in a low follow-through. As the stick swings in a pendulum-like motion in line with the intended path of the ball, the wrists remain firm to prevent swinging the stick above the shoulders. The force is applied by shoulders, arms, wrists, and body weight.

Straight Drive. A stationary straight drive is used for free hits and corner hits. This drive must also be perfected when running at full speed. Lead with either foot. The feet should be 1½ to 2 feet apart and the body turned sideways to the direction of the intended hit. The ball should be slightly nearer the forward foot, about 18 inches from the toe.

On a straight drive when force is necessary, it is important to have the left side of the body pointed toward the path the ball will take. The ball is in front of the forward foot to assure the force of body weight into the ball. Be certain to follow through rather than pull back on the stroke.

Drive to the Left. The ball is played in front of the body and feet, slightly nearer the left foot. The stick swings back in a straight line from the ball as weight shifts to the right foot. As the pendulum arc swings forward the body weight shifts, arms and firm wrists extend, and the extended arms carry the stick in a low follow-through in the direction of the drive.

Drive to the Right. The ball is to the right of the body and farther behind the feet than in the basic drive position. With the right foot forward, the shoulders and hips point to the right as the left shoulder moves toward the direction of the pass. The stroke moves down and through to the right as the left foot steps forward and the body weight shifts. Many players gain extra power by using a one-

Fig. 22-9. Drive to the right.

movement circular swing to the right without a shift of feet or change of body direction. The wrists cock sharply and then uncock firmly as the ball is hit to the right. The arms follow through in the direction of the hit as the body continues in a forward path.

Chop Drive. This drive is done quickly with hands in dribble grip position after fielding the ball or from a dribble. The stick moves away from the ball only a few inches as the wrists cock. On contact the wrists snap firmly and the follow-through is short, yet definite, in the direction of the drive. It is a fast and often powerful drive, and the player must hit the ball squarely on the face of the blade to avoid lofting.

Push Pass. The push pass is used for short, accurate passes or for a scoring attempt when there is no time to execute a backswing and a drive. The right hand moves down the stick, slightly farther than for dribble position. With the body in a slight crouched position and weight on the forward foot, both arms move forward, sweeping the stick along the ground. Immediately before power is applied, the blade is directly behind the ball and the top of the stick slightly ahead of the blade. With the arms extended to the limit of their reach, the right hand pushes sharply forward simultaneously with a slight pull back with the left. The follow-through continues in the direction of the pass until the stick is *almost* parallel to the ground with left

Fig. 22-10. Push pass.

forearm and stick in a straight line, right arm extended and toe of the stick facing up.

Flick.   Accurate and hard to intercept, the flick is used in passing to a marked teammate and in shooting at close range. It is a difficult shot to intercept, for it travels off the ground and the stroke itself disguises the path of the ball. The grip and body position are similar to those of the push pass. The body is in a semicrouched position, and weight is distributed between the toe of the rear foot and the entire forward foot. The ball is positioned to the right and ahead of the forward foot with the face of the stick in contact with the right side of the ball. There is no backswing in preparation for the stroke.

With simultaneous movements the stick face moves behind the ball as the left hand pulls the stick handle to the body and the right hand pushes the blade under the ball. Wrists snap and the body pushes forward forcefully from the back foot. (Additional body crouch will give more power to the stroke.) As the ball is raised from the ground, the left arm twists quickly to the left, and the blade turns slightly toward the ground at the completion of the stroke. Emphasis is placed on a low body position and a low follow-through.

Scoop.   The scoop is used for short passes, an occasional goal shot, and to evade an opponent's tackle. It is executed from a dribble grip with the ball in front of the player.

Place the blade behind and under the ball, scoop up, and shove the stick forward by pulling upward and forward with the right hand while using the left hand to stabilize the movement of the right. The stroke must be smooth and gentle to avoid scooping under the ball. The stick is about knee high at the completion of the stroke, and the body weight is over the forward foot. When avoiding a tackle, the most effective scoop is to the dribbler's left over the attacker's stick side.

Fig. 22-11. Flick.

Fig. 22-12. Scoop.

Jab. The jab, or job, is a one-handed spoil stroke used when maximum reach is needed. *Either hand* may be at the top of the stick and the jab is made from either side of the opponent. To avoid obstruction, hold the stick in the left hand (right shoulder back) on the opponent's non-stick side, use the right hand on her stick side.

In preparation for the stroke, grasp the end of the stick with one hand, wrist on top. Lay the blade of the stick back, and as an attempt is made at the ball, bend the body forward and take a long stride. Extend the stick arm close to the ground as far as possible. The edge, heel, or toe of the stick jabs at the ball when it is off the opponent's stick. This "last resort" stroke must be timed perfectly or several jabs may be needed to contact the ball and the danger of fouling increases. The jab must be followed by another play immediately in order to gain control of the ball.

FIELDING AND TACKLING

Fielding is the skill of gaining control of the ball so that it may be dribbled or passed or a goal shot executed. The stick is held with the left hand at the top and the wrist over the top end of the stick. The left elbow is bent up and out and the forearm is in line with the stick. The right hand, palm facing forward, is spread in dribble position. The body is in-clined forward, weight over the forward foot and head over the stick. Closely watching the approaching ball, point the toe of the stick toward the ball to line up its path of travel. Prior to contact, the stick is lowered to a perpendicular position, and the blade grazes the ground as the flat surface moves directly behind the oncoming ball in an easy, gathering motion. The left hand remains firm while the right is relaxed enough to give with the stick on contact. Allow the hands and handle to move ahead of the ball. There should not be a rebound of more than 6 or 8 inches for control of the ball. If the ball is very hard and fast, allow the blade to give more in order to avoid rebound. If the ball is bouncing, follow it carefully with the eyes while maintaining an easy grip and relaxed arms to field it off the ground if necessary. A high ball should be stopped with the hand when possible, but if a bouncing or high rebounding ball is played with the stick, it may be necessary to jump from the ground with the stick at waist or chest level to avoid "sticks" in making contact with the ball. *Place the ball after fielding it with the stick, and prepare for the next stroke.

Stopping the Ball. The ball may be *stopped* with the stick or hand. When using the hand, catch the ball or stop it with an open hand so that it rebounds or is dropped as nearly perpendicular as possible. A slight forward motion of a falling ball due to a player's forward momentum is not considered a foul.

Fig. 22-13. Stopping the ball.

A foul will be called if it rebounds to the player's advantage or if the player made an effort to place the ball with her hand.

Stopping a ball "dead" with the stick is simi-lar to fielding. On the rare occasions when a ball should be stopped still, allow more give with the stick.

Tackles. Tackles are used when a player wants to get possession of the ball from an opponent or force her to rush a pass. An approach may be made from the front or from the right or left side of an opponent. Tackles should be made when the ball is off the opponent's stick.

STRAIGHT TACKLE. The tackle is made on an opponent approaching from the front. With the stick held in dribble position, move forward to meet the opponent stick to stick. Face the opponent and keep slightly to her stick side. Keep eyes on the ball and opponent's stick while maintaining controlled balance, and be ready to move in any direction. Unexpectedly place the stick in the path of the oncoming ball. Trap the ball with a firm stick and solid body position. This should cause the opponent to overrun the ball.

LEFT HAND LUNGE. The tackler is on the

Fig. 22-14. "Left wing moving toward a free ball." (Courtesy of Carole L. Mushier, University of Southern California.)

Fig. 22-15. Left-hand lunge.

opponent's stick side running in the same direction. While running with the opponent the stick is in carrying position. To attempt a lunge, the tackler must be close enough to reach the ball with one stride and a long reach. (If she is able to get closer she should use a safer two-hand tackle.) The tackler pulls the stick to her right side, and at the moment her opponent taps the ball, the tackler reaches left with both hands (until the right hand can reach no farther), then firmly extends the left arm and lunges with weight on the left leg. The stick head is "thrown down" just in front of the ball so that it traps the ball on the stick. The tackler quickly turns to her left (as opponent overruns the play), places her right hand on the stick, and gains possession of the ball. Hitting the stick of an

opponent is a foul and players should avoid slashing or chopping at the ball or an opponent's stick.

CIRCULAR TACKLE. This is used by a tackler approaching from the opponent's left side. Both players are running in the same direction or the tackler is coming diagonally from the left of the dribbler. With stick held in dribble position the tackler must move a stride or two ahead of her opponent. As the tackler circles in front she must avoid touching her opponent or in any way obstructing her movement. She must time her tackle to contact the ball when it is off her opponent's stick. The right shoulder is pulled back and the left arm and shoulder lead to contact the ball and move it with short quick taps in a small circle. At the same time the player's feet move in a larger circle and her body leans toward the ball.

Dodges.   These techniques are used by the player with the ball to avoid a tackler approaching head on. The elements of surprise and speed are important in effective dodges. There are times, such as in avoiding a fast opponent with an effective left-hand lunge or circular tackle, when it may be wise to pass to a teammate rather than to attempt a dodge. At other times, a pass ahead of several feet and a sudden burst of speed will avert an opponent who has committed herself to a tackle.

Prior to executing a dodge, it is important that a normal dribble be used so that the op-

Fig. 22-16.   Circular tackle.

ponent is not aware of the action to follow. With increased speed, a player will learn to fake one dodge and execute another.

RIGHT DODGE.   As the tackler approaches, the ball is passed to the tackler's non-stick side with a short pass so that it rolls by her left toe and behind her. The dodger runs past the stick side of her opponent, controls the ball, and continues play. Often called "push right, run left," this dodge must be perfectly timed so that the opponent is out of ball reach but not so far from the play that she has time to change directions.

LEFT DODGE.   The ball is kept in normal dribbling position in front of the right foot. Just before the player expects to be tackled she quickly pulls the ball about 6 inches to her left as her feet move left with small, quick steps. (Move the ball only far enough to avoid the tackler's reach.) Immediately she continues her dribble forward with increased acceleration. This dodge is often referred to as an "L" because of the pattern of the ball path.

REVERSE STICK DODGE.   Although not frequently used, the reverse stick dodge can be most effective when a player is about to be tackled with a left-hand lunge. As the opponent begins her lunge, the dribbler reverses her stick by wrist and lower arm roll and immediately pulls the ball back diagonally right. She then either continues to dribble or passes.

SCOOP.   As in the scoop stroke, the ball is lifted and pushed forward. When the tackling player extends her stick for the ball, the dodger scoops over the opponent's stick and continues dribbling.

TRIANGULAR PASS.   This is an effective dodge as well as a fundamental play. The dribbler passes diagonally to her left or right to a teammate as the tackler approaches. The initial dribbler runs past and behind the tackler and receives a return pass from her teammate.

PLAY FOR SPECIFIC SITUATIONS

The Bully.   This is used by two opposing players in the center of the field to start the

Fig. 22-17.   "Preparing for the bully." (Courtesy of Carol L. Mushier, University of Southern California.)

game at the beginning of each half and after each goal. It is used to restart the game after a penalty bully, after simultaneous fouls by two opponents, and at the 25 yard line after the ball has gone over the end line off an attacker's stick or off two opponents' sticks simultaneously.* The players taking the bully stand facing each other and opposite side lines. The players' feet are apart, knees bent, and weight forward. Their heads are over the ball. The left hand is near the top of the handle, the right hand well down the handle for strength. The right hand *may* be turned slightly to the right, fingers pointing upward, to deceive opponents as to the stroke that will follow the bully. Each player taps the heel of the stick on the ground, then her opponent's stick. Do this three times. Sticks are tapped on the ground on either side of the ball and they tap each other above the ball. After the third tap of the sticks either player may play the ball. Players bullying may not move their feet until the bully is completed. All other players must be at least 5 yards away until the bully is completed.

Offensive plays should be planned following the bully. The following suggestions initiate an offense after hitting sticks for the third time:

1. Pull the ball toward the center of the body while moving the feet back with the pull. The ball is passed right or left. (Be careful not to obstruct with the right shoulder on the pass to left inner.)
2. Reverse the toe of the stick and tap the ball back to a defensive player backing up the bully.
3. Pass the ball between opponent's stick and right foot to the right inner. The ball may also be passed between opponent's legs, but this may result in an obstruction by the opponent. Such a ball travels parallel to the 50 yard line and does not encourage rapid downfield movement by the inner.

Penalty Bully. A penalty bully is awarded when a defense player in the circle:

1. Fouls while preventing a sure goal from being made.
2. Commits a willful breach of a rule.
3. Repeatedly fouls.

---

*An experimental rule change calls for a free hit for the defense (See Summary of Game Rules).

The bully is taken 5 yards in from the center of the goal by the defense player who fouled and any selected member of the attacking team. All other players, including the goalkeeper when she is not participating in the bully, must stand beyond the 25 yard line and stay out of play until the bully is completed. If the goalkeeper is bullying, she may not remove her pads or use her kicking or rebound privileges.

The two players taking the penalty bully continue play until one of the following situations occurs:

1. A goal is awarded and the play restarted on the center line, when
   a. the ball goes between the goalposts off the stick of either player, or
   b. the defender fouls.
2. The bully is over and play restarted on the center of the 25 yard line, when
   a. the attacker fouls,
   b. the attacker sends the ball over the goal line but not between the goal posts, or
   c. the defender sends the ball outside the circle, into the field of play.
3. The penalty bully is taken again, when
   a. the ball goes over the goal line but not between the goal posts, off the stick of the defender,
   b. there is a double foul or improper bully,
   c. any other player interferes, or
   d. the ball goes over the goal line but not between the goal posts, off the sticks of both players.

Corner. Two formations of corners are awarded to give an advantage to the attacking team.

LONG CORNER. This is often called only *corner.* It is awarded an attack player on a spot 5 yards from the corner of the field on the side or goal line when a member of the defending team, within the 25 yard line, unintentionally hits or deflects the ball over the goal line but not between the posts. The ball is played on the side of the goal where the ball went out.

PENALTY CORNER. A "short" corner is awarded an attack player at a spot 10 yards from the goal post on the goal line when the defense fouls in the circle, when the ball goes over the goal line off the person of the

Fig. 22-18. Roll-in.

defense or when the defense *intentionally* directs the ball out of play over the goal line, but not between the posts.

CORNER FORMATION. The wing usually takes the hit. On a long corner, play must be on the side line or goal line on the side of the goal where the ball went out. On a penalty corner the attacking team selects the side of the goal for the hit. The attacking forwards must be at least 5 yards from the ball and outside the circle until the hit. The four forwards line up with feet and sticks near the outside of the circle poised to move. Halfbacks back up the forwards.

Six defensive players must stand with feet and sticks behind their own goal line and at least 5 yards from the ball until the hit. Usually these players are the goalkeeper, two backs, and three halfbacks. The forwards of the defending team must remain beyond the 25 yard line until the ball is touched by a player other than the wing taking the corner, or until the ball has come out of the striking circle.

The wing attempts to hit a firm ball, with no bounce, to a forward, who controls the ball and makes a quick goal shot. The ball may be deflected or passed, but a goal must not be attempted until the ball has been controlled on the ground by an attack player or has touched the stick or person of a defender.

Free Hit. For a foul occurring outside the striking circles the free hit is taken on the spot of the foul. When the attack fouls in the circle, the defense may take the hit anywhere in the circle.

The ball is played by the defensive player in whose area it lies. In the circle, it is usually taken by a back at the circle edge. All other players must be 5 yards away.

The ball must be motionless and must be hit or pushed along the ground (flick and scoop strokes are illegal). It may not be played again by the hitter until touched by another player. A free hit should be taken quickly to gain advantage before the defense is set.

Roll-in. This method is used to put the ball in play after it has gone out of bounds over the side line, unless put out by two opposing players simultaneously. Usually taken by a wing halfback, the ball is rolled by the player outside the field to a teammate on the field. All players must be on the field of play and inside the 5 yard line bounding the inside of the alley until the ball is released. The player making the roll-in must have feet and stick outside the field and her stick in one hand. The left halfback should roll the ball with her right hand; the right halfback with her left hand.

The player crouches in a forward stride position, getting low to the ground, and uses an underhand swing. She must roll the ball, *not* bounce or throw, so that it touches the ground within 1 yard of the point where it left the field. She immediately re-enters the field but may not play the ball until it is touched by another player.

GAME RULES*

An official game is played in two 30 minute halves with a minimum of 5 and a maximum of 10 minutes between halves. Two score-

---

*For complete rules see the current *Field Hockey-Lacrosse Guide*, published by D.G.W.S.

keepers, two timers and two umpires conduct the game.

The game begins with a bully in the center of the field. Thereafter, each team attempts to move the ball with their sticks to the opponents' striking circle, where an attacking team member can shoot the ball into the goal cage for a score of 1 point.

During play the ball may be sent out of bounds, and fouls and rule infractions may occur. The following simplified rules may prove helpful.

SUMMARY OF GAME RULES

OUT OF BOUNDS

If a ball goes:	*The ball is put in play by:*
1. Over the side line off stick of player or players on same team	1. Roll-in for opponents
2. Over side line off sticks of two opponents simultaneously	2. Bully on 5 yard line
3. Over side line off body of player	3. Free hit for opponents
4. Over end line off stick of attack*	4. Twenty-five yard line bully
5. Over end line off sticks of two opponents simultaneously*	5. Twenty-five yard line bully
6. Over end line unintentionally off stick of defense	6. Corner
7. Over end line intentionally off stick of defense	7. Penalty corner
8. Over end line unintentionally off stick of defense beyond 25 yard line*	8. Twenty-five yard line bully
9. Over end line off body of defense	9. Penalty corner
10. Over end line off body of attack	10. Free hit for opponents

*An experimental rule change calls for a free hit for the defending team from a point 15 yards from the end line and directly opposite the place where the ball crossed the line.

FOULS

1. *Sticks:* Raising any part of the stick above shoulder level while playing the ball.

2. *Dangerous hitting:* Undercutting the ball so that it goes into the air in a manner dangerous to an opponent, or hitting the ball directly into an opponent.

3. *Advancing:* Permitting the ball to rebound off any part of the player's body in any direction that gives an advantage to that player or her team. The ball may be stopped with an open hand or caught, but it must be dropped directly to the ground. An exception is made in the case of the goalkeeper, who may kick the ball or let it rebound from her hand as long as she does not place or throw it. The goalkeeper loses these privileges when outside the circle or participating in a penalty bully.

4. *Wrong side of stick:* Touching the ball with the rounded side of the stick.

5. *Hitting the ball between own feet.*

6. *Slashing sticks,* or any other interference with opponent's stick.

7. *Personal contact:* Tripping, pushing, shoving, or striking opponent.

8. *Obstruction:* Putting any part of the body between an opponent and the ball (referred to as turning on the ball), preventing her from playing the ball, or running between an opponent and the ball so as to break her stride.

9. *Playing without a stick in hand.*

10. *Delaying the game.*

11. *Offside:* Being ahead of the ball in opponent's half of the field when fewer than three of the opposing team are between you and the goal and the ball is in the possession of your team. An individual cannot be offside when in possession of the ball.

12. *Substituting illegally.*

PENALTIES FOR FOULS

For fouls outside the striking circle:	*The penalty is:*
1. By members of one team	1. Free hit for opponents
2. By members of opposing teams simultaneously	2. Bully on spot
3. By player taking a corner hit	3. Free hit for opponents anywhere in circle

For fouls inside the striking circle:	*The penalty is:*
1. By attacking team	1. Free hit for opponents anywhere in circle
2. By defending team	2. Penalty corner, except for deliberate or repeated fouling or when a sure goal was stopped by fouling, in which case a penalty bully is awarded

Specific Regulations and Penalties

ROLL-IN. Roll-in for opponents if (a) the ball is bounced or spun, (b) the ball does not touch ground within 3 feet of where it went out, and (c) any part of the roller's body or stick crosses side line before roll. The roll-in is repeated if any players are in the alley before roll or if the ball does not enter the field of play. There is free hit for opponents if the roller does not have her stick in her hand or plays the ball before someone else has touched it.

BULLY. A bully is repeated if (a) one of the players is not standing squarely, (b) one of the players moves her feet before the completion of the bully, (c) the bully is incomplete or (d) any other player is closer than 5 yards.

PENALTY BULLY. The bully is repeated if (a) there is interference by any other player, (b) the bully is incomplete, (c) defense sends the ball over the end line not between goal posts, or (d) both sticks simultaneously send the ball over end line not between goal posts. The bully is over and play is restarted with a 25 yard line center bully if (a) the attack sends the ball over the end line not between goal posts, (b) the defense sends ball out of the circle into the field of play or (c) the attack fouls. A penalty goal is scored if (a) the attack or defense sends the ball over goal line between goal post or (b) the defense fouls.

CORNERS AND PENALTY CORNERS. These are repeated if (a) players are not lined up correctly, (b) the defense crosses the end line before ball is hit, (c) a player swings and misses but does not make sticks, or (d) the defending forwards cross the 25 yard line before the ball is out of the circle or before the ball is touched by another player. There is a free hit for the defense if (a) a player taking a hit fouls or (b) plays ball before someone else has touched it.

FREE HIT. A free hit is repeated if (a) a player swings and misses but does not make sticks, (b) another player is within five yards, or (c) the hit is not taken on the spot where the foul was committed. A free hit for opponents occurs if (a) a player fouls, (b) the ball is not motionless, (c) the ball is lofted, (d) the player taking a hit plays it again before it has been touched by another player.

ACCIDENTS AND INTERFERENCE. The umpire may stop the game for not more than 5 minutes in case of injury to a player. She may also stop the game long enough for a player to replace a broken stick or take care of any other matter which may be interfering with the progress of the game. Play shall be restarted with a bully on the spot, unless a foul was involved in the injury or interference, in which case a free hit will be awarded.

SUBSTITUTION. Officially, substitutes may be put in only at half time or in case of injury or disqualification. However, in high school or college games the coaches may agree to allow substitution on corners and bullies. The substitutes must report to the scorers and the umpire. Once a substitute replaces a teammate, that girl may not re-enter the game; however, a player who is winded may drop out of the game and return to it if her team has played short and no one has substituted for her. The penalty for illegal substitution by one team is a penalty corner. The penalty for illegal substitution by both teams is a bully on a spot designated by the umpire.

GAME STRATEGY

There are no rules of thumb governing strategy, for there is great variation based on general team ability and individual playing skill. Certain proven principles are helpful in building a skillful team.

1. Encourage speed, alertness, and creative play on the field.

2. Forwards must create spaces by pulling away from the ball to deceive the defense.

3. Defensive players must constantly observe their forwards and move and position accordingly.

4. When the defense moves with a forward, the ball is hit or rolled to a space; if the defense does not move, the ball is hit or rolled to the forward's stick.

5. Forwards must move on roll-ins and free hits to create a target or space and outwit the defense.

6. Vary style of play by change of speed and strategy, particularly if the team is not functioning well.

Offensive Tactics. At the initial bully players are in positions indicated in Figure 22-19. As the bully is completed the forward line of both teams moves forward and the defense moves to back up forwards and to mark opposing forwards. All forwards not participating in the bully move into opponent's field to receive the ball from teammates or to intercept from opponents. Forwards play in a line, staying 10 to 12 yards apart, with the dribbler slightly ahead. A pass usually should be ahead of the intended receiver and perfectly timed for her to pick up and dribble forward.

The wings should try to move the ball upfield down the alley to keep the defense spread and to move rapidly. As the wing

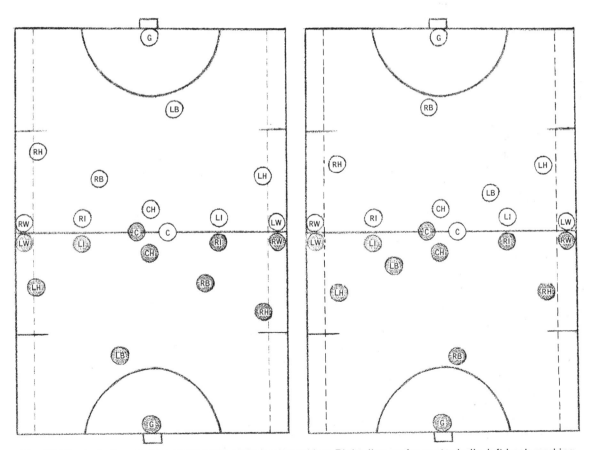

Fig. 22-19. Left, line up for center bully, right back marking. Right, line up for center bully, left back marking.

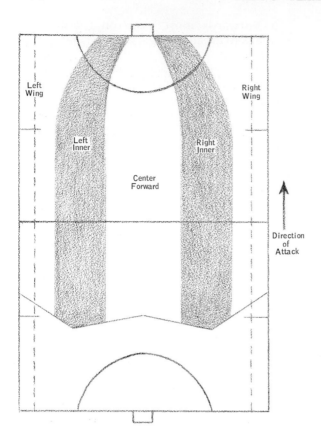

Fig. 22-20. Areas for forwards.

Direction
of
Attack

moves near the 25 yard line she tries to center to an inner or center for a goal shot (see Fig. 22-20).

The forwards converge slightly as they near the circle. At the circle a strong hit should be made for the goal. The inner and the center forward should then rush the center of the goal and the wings should position themselves near the edge of the circle to pick up the goalkeeper's clears to the side.

Wings do not have the opportunity to shoot as frequently as other forwards but occasionally make shots from the edge of the circle.

Defensive Tactics. At the initial bully, players may take positions as indicated in Figure 22-19. The right fullback should be up in marking position, opposing the offense's left inner, as most bullies won by the offense move to the right of the defending team. With more experienced players and more skillful bullies, play may require either fullback to be up. For example, with the right fullback in covering position, the left fullback

moves up to mark the right inner and protect the non-stick side of the center halfback. Initially the forwards tackle back in an attempt to regain the ball. If the ball passes to opponents each defensive player becomes responsible for the area and player she marks.

An aggressive forward line pulls back into its own half of the field in a "W" formation to await a clear from the defense. The center forward is on approximately the 30 yard line in center field, the inners are on their respective sides of the field at about the 25 yard line, and the wings are close to the 50 yard line in either alley.

MARKING. Each back should guard a forward line player, staying close in order to intercept her passes or to tackle. The right halfback should mark the left wing; the right back, the left inner; the center halfback, the center forward; the left back, the right inner; and the left halfback, the right wing.

INTERCHANGING. On the bully, the center halfback should be about 5 yards away in order to intercept an opponent's pass or to gain control of the ball. Although a beginner should learn to play her own position well, advanced players should master the techniques of interchanging and covering, i.e., the defense players change positions either as safety players or as hastily shifted defensive blocks to catch an unguarded, rapidly advancing player with the ball. This tactic is used largely when the forwards have moved down to, or behind, the 25 yard line as the remaining defensive players cover to stop the advance.

Covering. To facilitate the interception of long passes and to cover their own half of the field more adequately, backs (and sometimes wing halfbacks) may play in a deeper defense position. For example, if the ball is on the 50 yard line on the left side of the field, the left back will play up the field, closer to the action of play. The right back covers in a deeper position, closer to the center of the field. Should the ball be passed to the right side of the field, the right back moves up and the left fullback shifts back to a covering position closer to her own goal line and near the center of the field.

Intercepting. Timing is vitally important in gaining possession of a ball being dribbled or passed to others. Team members must quickly move into position to receive the pass or to change the direction of the ball going up or downfield. In order to be adept at such interception, players must watch the ball closely at all times and be ready to move quickly into free space through which a pass might be attempted.

A good defense has all opposing forwards near the ball well marked, with one player in strong covering position. As the attack nears the circle all forwards are closely marked with no covering player. Inside the circle defense players must avoid blocking the goalkeeper's view when a shot is made.

DUTIES AND SPECIFIC SKILLS OF PLAYERS

Attack. All forward players should be fast runners skilled in dribbling, passing, dodging, and goal shooting.

The *center forward* should be an exacting shooter who guides the attack and directs the teamwork. She is responsible for distributing play left and right.

The *right* and *left inners* must work as con-

nectors between the center forward and the wings. They are the "work horses" of the forward line, for they pick up the short clears from their defense and must also be ready to score at the other end of the field. Both should be highly skilled at shooting. The left inner and the left wing must master the trick of turning their shoulders and passing to the right while running.

The *wings* should be the speediest of the line and be skilled in driving the ball to the center of the field as well as in taking it down the alley. They should be able to work effectively with inners on the triangular pass and score from the edge of the circle. On corners, the wing should center a firm drive and move quickly onto the field.

In fulfilling the real job of scoring points as often as possible, the following tips may be helpful to forwards:

1. Move up the field in a line, about a yard behind the ball.

2. Pass the ball when possible so that the defense has less opportunity to "get set."

3. Wings do their hardest work between the two 25 yard lines, moving the ball to keep the defense spread out and setting up other forwards for goal shooting.

4. Be alert to the occasional opportunity to take the ball through the defense alone. This serves to vary the attack as well as to score when other forwards are left behind.

5. It is often a good practice to keep the ball until the opponent is drawn in to tackle. A pass made too soon is easily intercepted.

6. Look for weak players in the opposing defense, as well as for consistent weaknesses in your attack.

7. When the ball is taken, be alert to "tackle back" if it does not interfere with your own defense. If the ball is recovered, pass it ahead quickly to a teammate and regain your place in the attack. A quick pass gains time and lessens the chance of being tackled back.

Defense. A good rule for beginning defense players is for each one to accept responsibility for the same area of the field as that of the forward she marks (see Fig. 22-21). Additional responsibilities are learned later.

The halfbacks should be fast, steady, and versatile players whose task it is to back up, mark, and cover the offense. When their

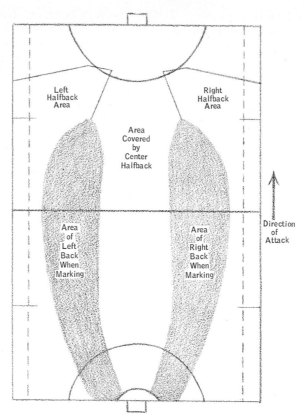

Fig. 22-21. Areas for defense players.

team is attacking, they back up the forwards, often placing themselves between their forward line and their opposing forward to prevent passes from reaching opponents. They feed the ball to their forwards.

The right halfback should be skilled in executing the left drive, left hand lunge and roll-in with the left hand, whereas the left halfback should be adept at using her right hand on the roll-in and at executing the circular tackle.

The backs should work as a pair, each remaining aware of the other's position on the field. They must change quickly from offensive to defensive play. The back on the side of play marks her opponent while the other back covers. If play shifts to the other side of the field, the backs reverse marking and covering responsibilities. The back in covering position is prepared to tackle a forward who has the ball and eludes her defense player. She should time her tackle of an unmarked player at the edge of the circle

so as to give the other defensive player time to cover for her. Each backs up inner bullies on her side of the field. The right back backs up the center bully, behind and to the right of the center half. Both must be skilled tacklers and possess good, accurate driving ability. They must know when to go to the goalkeeper's assistance.

In preventing goals and feeding the offense the following suggestions may prove helpful:

1. Understand the abilities and functions of other defensive players.

2. Mark your opponent and don't interfere with others by trying to do too much.

3. After gaining possession of the ball, try to get rid of it quickly and accurately.

4. Stay about a yard from the opponent you are marking, slightly on the ball side, nearer the goal than the attacker. Try to intercept instead of waiting to tackle.

5. If passed by the opposing forward, first

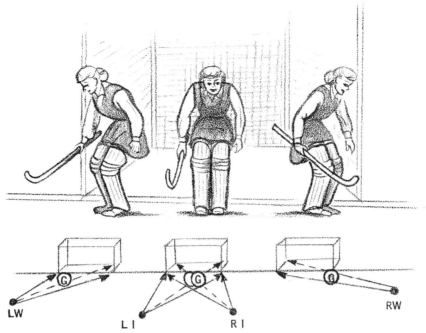

Fig. 22-22. Goalkeeper's positions for various attacks.

try to overtake her and tackle. If another back has moved to tackle, cross over to the side of the field left unprotected. It is usually advisable to interchange only when the goal is threatened or when a defense player is hopelessly behind her opponent.

Goalkeeping. Aside from sound stickwork, goalkeeping requires skills quite different from those of other positions. The goalkeeper's privileges in the circle require that she learn to stop the ball with an open hand (the ball may be advanced but may not be thrown) and with legs and feet. She must be effective and accurate in clearing the ball with her feet and stick.

Awaiting an attack, she stands on an imaginary semicircle that runs from goal post to goal post and extends a yard in front of the goal line. Standing at an angle that gives the best protection from the oncoming attack (Fig. 22-22), she faces the field with feet together, weight on balls of feet, and knees bent, ready to shift position quickly. The stick is held in the right hand, part way down the handle, and used only in an emergency. Avoiding jumping into the ball, she waits, and as the ball strikes her legs she "gives" on impact so that it stops close. She quickly clears it with the inside of the toe to a back or a side halfback waiting to relay it upfield.

When a hard shot is so directed that a two-leg stop is impossible, she must stop the ball with the inside of one foot while maintaining balance to prevent falling and an obstruction.

Although it is safer to stop the ball before clearing, often there is not enough time. Avoid high kicks toward rushing forwards.

The goalkeeper should come out of her position cautiously and only (1) when she can reach the ball before an opponent, or (2) to meet a lone forward if the goalkeeper is the only defense player in the striking circle. She should not come out when two forwards are free in the circle.

If a shot is going to miss the goal, she should hold her position and allow the ball to cross the end line.

Above all, the goalkeeper must be aware that it is the back's job to prevent shooting, but it is *her* duty to stop a shot once made.

Terminology

Advancing—A foul, resulting from moving the ball to one's advantage with any part of the body.

Backing up—Staying close behind a teammate who has the ball or who is tackling an opponent.

Bully—The technique used to start or restart play when both teams are to have an equal opportunity to get the ball. Two players face each other squarely. Each then touches first the ground, then opponent's stick (with her stick) three times, and then tries to play the ball.

Corner—A *long corner* is a hit awarded an attacker on a spot 5 yards from the corner of the field on the side or goal line when a member of the defending team hits the ball over the goal line but not between the goal posts. A *penalty (short corner)* is a hit awarded an attacker at a spot at least 10 yards from the goal post on the goal line when the defense commits a foul in the striking circle or intentionally directs the ball out of play over the goal line but not between posts.

Covering—Playing deep by defense players on the side of the field opposite the ball. A technique that allows the players to intercept, mark, or tackle players outrunning their defense.

Dangerous hitting—Undercutting the ball (hitting it with the stick blade facing up) so that it goes into the air, or hitting the ball into another player even though it remains on the ground.

Dodge—A technique used by a player with the ball to evade an opponent and still retain possession of the ball.

Drawing on opponent—Forcing one's opponent to mark closely or to attempt a tackle so that space will be left clear for a pass to one's teammate.

Dribble—A series of short strokes with the stick used to maintain possession of the ball and move it while running.

Drive—A forceful stroke used for passing, clearing, and shooting.

Fielding—Stopping the ball with hand and stick. Receiving a pass and controlling it close to the stick so that it may be played immediately.

Flick—A stroke in which the ball is pushed with a strong twist of the wrists, putting spin and loft on the ball.

Free hit—A chance to hit the ball with no one nearer than 5 yards; awarded to a team fouled against and usually taken by the nearest back.

Interception—Taking possession of the ball as it is passed from one opponent to another.

Interchange—A temporary exchange of positions between teammates to assume duties of a teammate left behind or out of position.

Marking—Keeping oneself in position in relation to a specific opponent so that one can either intercept the ball intended for her or tackle her once she has it.

Obstruction—A foul resulting when a player goes between an opponent and the ball with any part of her body, hindering the opponent in playing the ball.

Off-side—An infringement that occurs when a player is nearer the opponents' goal line than the ball, with fewer than three opponents between the player and the goal. Occurs only in opponent's half of the field.

Penalty bully—Awarded on a spot 5 yards in front of the center of the goal line to a member of the attacking team and the offending defense player who has violated a rule when a goal might have been scored or who has willfully and repeatedly fouled.

Penalty goal—A score of 1 point awarded the attacking team if a defender fouls during a penalty bully.

Reverse stick—Use of the stick so that its toe points down.

Roll-in—Technique used to put the ball back into play after it has gone out of bounds over the side line.

Sticks—A foul caused by raising the stick above shoulder level when playing the ball.

Tackle—An attempt to take possession of the ball when it is in possession of an opponent.

Tackle-back—Trying to regain the ball from one who has successfully tackled you.

Selected Audio-visual Aids

Filmstrips compiled by Marjorie Pollard. (25 frames, 35 mm.) Sport Shelf, 10 Overbrook Terrace, New York, N.Y. 10033. (Rental.)

Field Hockey Rules Filmstrips. Teaching Aids Service, 31 Union Square West, New York, N.Y. 10003. (Purchase and rental.)

Hockey Basic Strokes. 1956 (18 min., b & w, silent.) Marjorie Pollard Publications, Ltd., The Deanery, Bampton, Oxford, England.

Hockey—Improve Your Game (16 mm., sound, b & w.) Produced by All England Women's Hockey Association. Contact U.S.F.H.A., Film Distribution Chairman Peggy Steig, Eastern Michigan University, Ypsilanti, Michigan 48197.

Suggested Readings

AAHPER: *Field Hockey—Lacrosse Guide*, Division for Girls and Women's Sports, 1201 Sixteenth Street, N.W., Washington, D.C. 20036.

Know the Game, Women's Field Hockey Handbook, Available from Gertrude Hooper, 242 Highland Street, Milton 86, Mass., or Marjorie Pollard, The Deanery, Bampton, Oxford, England.

Lees, Josephine T., and Shellenberger, Betty: *Field Hockey for Players, Coaches and Umpires*, New York, The Ronald Press Company, 1957.

Mackey, Helen: *Field Hockey: An International Team Sport*, Englewood Cliffs, N.J., Prentice-Hall Inc., 1963.

Pollard, Marjorie: *Your Book of Hockey.* Available from Gertrude Hooper, 242 Highland Street, Milton 86, Mass., or Marjorie Pollard, The Deanery, Bampton, Oxford, England.

Richey, Betty (ed.): *Selected FIeld Hockey and Lacrosse Articles*, D.G.W.S., Washington, D.C., 1963.

Periodicals

The Eagle. Official publication of the United States Field Hockey Association, Circulation Manager: Contact U.S.F.H.A. executive Secretary.

Hockey Field. Official Publication of All England Women's

Hockey association. Contact Marjorie Pollard Publications, The Deanery, Bampton, Oxford, England.

Suggested Study Questions

1. Describe and demonstrate three types of tackles. When would you use each one in a game?
2. Why are corners awarded? Explain when a long or a short corner is taken. Sketch a suggested attack play from a corner.
3. Explain (a) backing up, (b) marking, (c) covering, and (d) interchanging.
4. Explain and demonstrate the foul of obstruction.
5. Where is the best place for a goalie to stand for a shot coming (a) to her non-stick side, (b) to her stick side, (c) directly in front of the cage?
6. Select your favorite playing position. Explain the skills, qualifications, and duties of this position.

CHAPTER TWENTY-THREE

Courtesy of Carole L. Mushier, University of Southern California.

LACROSSE

Lacrosse was played on the North American continent long before white men were permanent residents, for the American Indian played the game *baggataway* as a method of conditioning for war and a ritual to gain favor with the Great Spirit. Some historians believe that the Indian game was a development from *knattleikr*, a game brought to the northeast coast of the continent by Norsemen years before.

Baggataway, a rough and dangerous game, drew entire tribes into competition on areas with no boundaries, where goals were often several miles apart. The Indians used a light, strong stick with a hoop or hook at one end. Some competitors carried one in each hand. A net of rawhide strips hung from the end to carry the wooden or deerskin-covered ball. The stick also served to beat off opponents in the heated battle of gaining possession of the ball.

In 1705 Pierre de Charlevoix witnessed baggataway in Quebec and renamed the game "la crosse" for the stick, which resembled a bishop's crozier. Canadians developed rules and safer techniques of play, and lacrosse became the national game of that country in 1867. Introduced in England about 1865, it was spread to all parts of the British Commonwealth and to the United States by Canadian enthusiasts.

The United States women's game came directly from England rather than from the United States men's game. The All England Ladies Lacrosse Association modified rules, eliminated the rough element and sent players and coaches to introduce the game in the United States. By 1931 lacrosse was played in isolated spots in the northeast section of the country, resulting in the formation of the United States Women's Lacrosse Association. This group, like the British association, maintains the game's amateur status, governs all affairs and rules, and provides help through its membership. The popularity of the sport has grown with the exchange of British and American touring teams, annual national tournaments, and clinics.

NATURE AND PURPOSE OF THE GAME

Lacrosse is a field sport played by two opposing teams of 12 members each. It is an extremely fast game in which each team member advances the ball with her crosse by carrying it or passing it. She must move rapidly to a position to pass to a teammate or to score a goal by shooting into the goal net.

Before play begins, field boundaries are established by the team captains. Unlike all other field games, no strict rules govern playing field dimensions, although the goals must be placed at least 90 yards apart and no farther than 110 yards. The minimum width should be 50 yards. An official game has two periods of 30 minutes each (unless shortened by mutual agreement) with no time-outs other than those called by an umpire. A 10 minute rest may be taken between halves.

At the beginning of both periods and after each goal play begins with a center draw by opposing center players. The small hard rubber ball is advanced by the use of the crosse in running, passing, catching, picking up, or shooting. Each team attempts to defend its goal and score against its opponents. At the end of playing time, the team with the larger score is declared winner.

Players. Each team of 12 members has six attacking players and six defense players. The attacks are the center, right attack wing, left attack wing, third home, second home, and first home. Their primary duty is to get the ball into a position for a goal shot as quickly as possible. The defenses—the two defense wings, third man, cover point, point, and goalkeeper—mark closely and attempt to gain possession of the ball by interception or crosse-checking. Once in possession, they move the ball to their own attack players. Distribution of players is not compulsory, and

389

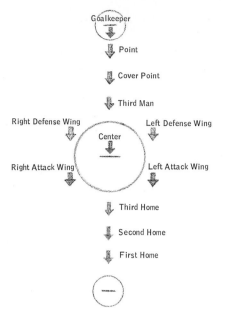

Fig. 23-1. Lacrosse field and playing positions.

all players actually have offensive and defensive responsibilities. Substitutes may enter the game in case of injury and at halftime.

FACILITIES AND EQUIPMENT

One of the advantages of lacrosse is that the field area does not require extensive maintenance or marking and equipment is limited and modestly priced. With proper care, equipment lasts many years.

Field Area. The field is the approximate size of a hockey or football field. A smooth surface, although desirable, is not so necessary as it is in hockey or soccer for true ball roll.

The field has no definite boundary markings, but within the established area are two goals between 90 and 110 yards apart. Each goal consists of two square posts 6 feet high, 6 feet apart, and joined by a crossbar 6 feet from the ground. The goal line is drawn from post to post, and with the 2 × 2 inch wooden frame, forms a square with inside measurements of 6 feet. The wooden posts and crossbar are painted white. Netting, not more than 1½ inch mesh, is attached to the posts and bar and pegged to the ground 6 feet behind the center of the goal line.

The *goal crease* is formed by drawing a circle with a radius of 8½ feet from the center of the goal line.

A center circle with a radius of 10 yards is drawn in the center of the field. Lines are drawn 2 yards on each side from the circle center, parallel to the goal line.

Ball. The ball used in women's lacrosse is made of black, white or yellow rubber sponge. It weighs no less than 4½ ounces and no more than 5¼ ounces, and is between 7¾ and 8 inches in circumference.

Crosse. The crosse is made of a hickory frame with a net-like section of leather and gut on the end for carrying and controlling the ball. It may be any length but may not be more than 12 inches at its widest part nor weigh more than 24 ounces. The wood must be on the right-hand side of the bridge; left-handed crosses are illegal. A string must be brought through a hole at the side of the tip of the turn to prevent the possibility that the point of the stick will catch an opponent's crosse. The leather thongs (lengthwise strings) must be woven to within 2 inches of their termination and tightened sufficiently to prevent a ball from catching in the meshes or resting in a pocket formed by loose lengthwise strings. No metal of any kind is allowed upon the crosse.*

Selection and Care of the Crosse. Special care should be taken in learning the important parts and desirable features in stick selection.

BUTT AND GRIP. End of the handle where one hand is placed. It should be small enough and belled to fit the fingers of the hand.

HANDLE. Usually 25 to 27 inches. Select the length by holding the stick with the right hand at the collar; the end of the handle should touch the armpit.

COLLAR. Point of attachment for the thongs of the gut wall and lengthwise strings; the top of the stick. When held at the collar by two fingers, the head and handle should balance, or there should be only slightly more weight in the head tipping toward the backbone.

BACKBONE. Wooden wall of the face, about 2½ inches wide.

Field Hockey—Lacrosse Guide, August, 1966-68, Division for Girls and Women's Sports, 1201 16th St., N.W., Washington, D.C. 20006.

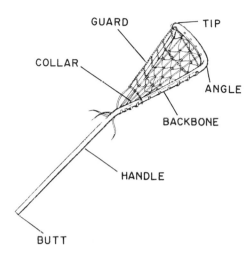

Fig. 23-2. The crosse.

ANGLE. Curved section between backbone and tip. It should be slightly more than a 90 degree angle. As this is the weakest part of the crosse, be sure that the wood is strong and that the grain runs smoothly around the angle.

TIP. Bent portion and end of wood nearest the guard.

GUARD. A heavy mesh of gut approximately 2½ to 3 inches in width. This strong upright runs opposite the backbone. Be certain that the guard is not pulled over on the face of the stick by too tight a bridge or lead string position.

BRIDGE. Thick gut that is placed several inches above the collar and attached to the guard and backbone to prevent the ball from lodging in the crosse.

THONGS. Leather or hide thongs running lengthwise and crosswise to form the netting for controlling the ball. These should be kept taut to avoid a deep pocket.

CARE OF THE CROSSE. Proper care insures a long life. A few rules should be followed:

1. Always loosen the leading strings after playing to relieve strain on the angle.
2. Wipe the stick after playing.
3. Treat the gut and thongs with leather conditioner or white petroleum jelly, the wooden frame with linseed oil. Do not treat the guard or bridge.
4. Hang the stick by the wood across the top when not in use. Store away from heat and dampness.

5. Mend and repair the stick as soon as possible.

Costume. Regular gymnasium costume with socks and tennis shoes or sneakers is appropriate class and intramural attire. For college or club games, tunics and blouses are comfortable and attractive. Canvas or leather-topped shoes with rubber soles are required, but shoes with rubber cleats or studs are preferable. The goalkeeper is the only player who needs additional equipment of leg and thigh pads, chest protector, gloves and a face mask, if desired.

BASIC SKILLS

The Grip. The stick is held by both hands, one at the top of the handle and one at the end. Normally the throwing hand is placed on top. The skills described are for a right-handed player. The beginner can assume the correct hand position by placing the stick on the ground directly in front with the butt end close to the feet. The open part of the head (backbone to the right of player) is facing up. The right hand is placed at the top of the stick so that the "V" of the thumb and forefinger is between the player's face and the stick when held vertically. The knuckles are under the stick as the hand grips firmly. The thumb and forefinger meet to form a permanent ring.

The right hand lifts the stick until the hand is about eye level. With the "V" formed by the thumb and forefinger pointing directly to the crosse head, the *left hand* reaches directly forward to grasp the butt end firmly in the entire hand. The left hand is approximately at waist level. The right elbow is relaxed and, with the forearm, is outside and close to the stick. The upper hand is the guiding hand, the lower the power hand.

Cradling. Cradling is the rhythmical swing of the stick, timed to the action of the player's body, that keeps the ball under control and in the crosse. Beginners should master the vertical cradling position first, as it emphasizes the close position of the stick to the body and the grip and use of the bottom hand.

With the stick in vertical position both hands move in the same direction to the same side of the body. When the cradling motion

Fig. 23-3. Cradling to the left.

reaches either side of the body the open face is away from the body to catch or throw. The face is toward but above the player as it passes across the body. When the stick is on the right, the wood is turned slightly toward the player; on the left, the guard is nearest, to prevent losing the ball.

To begin the cradle to the right side, the bottom arm is at waist level and parallel to the ground. This power arm swings to the right so that it remains close to the waist. The left wrist flexes so that the hand turns in to the body. The right wrist flexes and rotates inward and the forearm remains in back of and close to the stick. There is a rotation (pronation) of the forearm. If the stick were removed at this point, the right arm would look like the outline of a goose, with the head (hand and wrist) moving away from the body.

Both arms work together to swing the stick vertically to the left. The forearm of the lower arm swings outward from the body but remains parallel to the ground at waist level. The entire arm pivots around the elbow that stays close (but not frozen) to the left side of the body. At the end of the swing the wrist extends backward as far as possible.

The top hand guides the stick in front of the body by rotation (supination) of the forearm and by as much flexion of the wrist as possible at the end of the swing left.

As the arms and wrist move, the action is aided by a twist of the body in the direction of the swing. As the stick swings to either side, the body turns at the waist. Leg action when trotting or running is normal and should be unaffected by upper body movement.

Cradling action should be practiced walking, trotting and, eventually, running. As skill develops the ball will swing about halfway up in the stick and the player will find it is possible to cradle with the stick pulled well across to the left or right of the body to protect it from a tackling player.

Footwork. Footwork is extremely important in lacrosse, where so much speed, twisting, turning, dodging, and change of direction are necessary. A player must learn immediately to keep her weight over the balls of her feet and be ever ready to move.

One important footwork maneuver of the field and for passing that deserves special attention is a turn in the opposite direction. When cradling, with right hand uppermost, the turn about to the left is quite natural, for the right foot is forward and the crosse on the right. The pivot and movement of the crosse left is forceful but natural. However, when desiring to change directions to the right, special skill is needed. The left foot must be forward and the stick must be swung left. This is followed by a pivot *on both feet* and a push off the ball of the left foot in conjunction with a strong twist and stick swing to the right. Immediately the player cradles and runs in the new direction.

Picking up the Ball. When the ball is lying or rolling on the ground it must be picked up with the crosse so that passing, running, or shooting can continue. Theoretically, the game is played in the air, but actually many beginners find picking up an important skill, for many balls get free on poor passes and unskilled catches. The player will find situations in which the ball is stationary, rolling away from her, or rolling or bouncing straight or diagonally toward her.

To pick up a stationary ball, the right-handed player moves the crosse to the left of the body. As the ball is approached the feet must be arranged so that the right foot is brought up close to the ball, on the side and pointing forward (advanced players should learn to pick up with either foot forward). The pick-up is done on the move, with the knees, hips, and entire body bent so that the stick can be brought close to the ground. At the moment the stick meets the ball, the hips are twisted to the left. The ball is directly alongside the right foot, and the player's head is over it. A strong bottom hand pushes the stick under the ball. As soon as the ball

Fig. 23-4. Picking up the ball.

Fig. 23-5. Catching.

enters the crosse the player's head rises and cradling begins. In approximately three cradles the crosse will be in a vertical position.

When picking up a ball *moving away from* a player, the same techniques of picking up a stationary ball apply, but the player must increase her running speed in order to catch up with the ball. Since it is moving away, she begins the pick-up action closer to the ball and executes the pick-up movements more strongly and sharply.

A ball *moving toward* a player should be considered an "upside down" catch. The player moves to meet the ball and positions herself behind the path of its approach. The crosse is raised to a nearly vertical position close to the left side of the body. The open face of the stick is behind the ball path as the wood across the top of the stick touches the ground. As the ball enters the stick, the hips are twisted left so that the crosse is close to the side and the feet are up to the ball. The crosse 'gives' as the ball enters, and cradling action begins as the player returns to normal running position.

A ball rolling diagonally which is impossible to get behind must be "captured," using techniques as for a catch. The stick is turned behind the line of the oncoming ball as the body is bent low to bring the stick behind the ball. Cradling begins as the player moves on.

Catching. On all catches the player has the widest part of the face behind the ball, and cradling action begins immediately on contact. Always go to meet the ball and increase speed as it is caught. The grip on the

stick remains unchanged, with the bottom hand turning the stick and the top hand guiding and positioning the face.

When catching a ball on the right (coming from the left), the stick is brought to the front of the body and the head is pointed slightly at the ball so that on contact the ball rolls into the stick. Cradling action by *both* hands begins immediately.

When catching on the left, at any height, cradle to the left and meet the ball with an open face. Continue cradling action.

For all catches feel that the stick is an elongation of the arms and the *top hand* is doing the catching. The player should begin to get the feeling that she is wrapping the stick gently around the ball. The beginner should toss up her own ball, both to right and left sides, while walking, trotting, or running. Later she catches balls thrown from the hand or stick. When catching an extremely high or hard thrown ball, some "give" with the ball may be necessary before cradling.

Passing. Passing must be developed so that the ball travels with speed and accuracy. Two basic passes—overarm and underarm—

are necessary for beginners, while advanced players often use a sidearm pass.

OVERARM PASS. The stick is brought into position by pulling the right shoulder and stick backward to the right from a left cradle position. These preparatory movements imitate the action of an overarm throw. The preparatory cradle should be small and close to the head of the player.

With the stick on the right side, the right shoulder back, and the right (top) hand slightly behind the top of the stick, the bottom hand and stick end lift up and forward to point to the spot where the ball will be sent. The right arm bends slightly, the elbow drops, and the crosse head dips backward. Simultaneously the left hand pulls forcefully to bring the hand into the right armpit as the top hand and arm thrusts forward and upward. When the pass is completed, the head of the stick is pointing to the spot where the ball has been directed.

The length of the throw is determined by the movement of the arms; the speed, by the thrust and stretch of the top arm. A pass to the left requires less swing back of the right shoulder; a pass to the right requires a greater twist of body and shoulder to the right.

The *sidearm pass* is similar to the overarm pass except that the path of the crosse in delivering is in a forward and outward arc, that is, parallel to the ground. The face of the crosse is open and away from the body. The pass moves the head of the stick across the body and the butt end under the right armpit.

UNDERARM PASS. This is used when an overarm pass is hampered by an opponent. The ball is cradled left and the upper body turned strongly left. The lower hand lifts the butt of the stick so that the head swings toward the ground in a semicircular motion. As the body turns left, the stick is nearly parallel to the body, reaching beyond the back leg. The head of the stick, wood toward the ground, swings by the body and forward as the weight transfers and shoulders come forward. The head of the crosse finishes in front of the body and the arms are straight. The higher the head of the stick at the finish, the higher and slower the pass.

Shooting for Goal. Effective goal shooting is the secret to winning lacrosse, for the only way to win is to score. The majority of shots result from passing play around the goal area rather than from a play where one person runs downfield and shoots. Once basic passing skills are mastered, they can become the basis of shots. The overarm, sidearm, and

Fig. 23-6. The overarm pass.

Fig. 23-7. The underarm shot.

underarm shots can be used for effective low corner shots, waistline shots, and high corner shots that "float" into the cage.

OVERARM SHOT. The technique of this shot is similar of that of the overarm pass. It is used far from the goal for a bouncing shot, or closer when the player is approaching straight or diagonally, with the lever action of the lower hand and forceful guiding of the upper, the head of the stick is brought down with a strong follow-through and points in the direction of the ball's intended path.

UNDERARM SHOT. On this shot the player is usually running, with her right side angled toward the goal. As in the underarm pass, there is a big swing to the left. The ball is kept low by a minimal lift of the head of the stick on follow-through. It is an effective shot when the attack has come from behind her defense and moved across with her right side between her opponent and the goal.

SIDEARM SHOT. This is effective on a short play when the attack has dodged to the right of her defense. As in the sidearm pass, the left elbow is out and away from the body and the right (collar hand) arm is back with elbow close to the right side. The ball is shot as the left arm pulls toward the body and the right arm extends in the direction of delivery.

DRAW. The center draw is the method of

A   **B**

Fig. 23-8. The draw. *A*, The ball is placed between the backs of the crosses. *B*, The players lift their crosses up and apart so that the ball rises in the air.

beginning play at each half and after every goal. The draw is used to restart play in the field after a double foul or after an injury when no foul occurred. All players should learn to draw. Opposing players stand with the toe of one foot on the center line. The crosses are held at hip level above and parallel to the center line with the backs of the crosses together, wood to wood, wood to ground, and angle to collar. The rule states that a player's crosse must be between the ball and the goal she is defending. Consequently, if a player holds the collar with the right hand, she faces the goal she is attacking; if the player's left hand is at the collar her back is to the goal she is attacking. The umpire places the ball between the backs of the crosses and on signal the players lift their crosses up and out as each tries to direct the ball, in the air, to a teammate.

Marking.　Man-to-man defense in lacrosse makes marking an important skill. A player positions herself so close to her opponent that she is *almost* touching. In this position she must be able to observe the opponent and the ball, but she remains closer to the goal she is defending than her opponent. From this balanced position she should be able to move for a possible interception or to body check.

Body Checking.　The object of body checking is to impede the course of an opposing player carrying the ball and force her into a hurried and poorly executed pass or shot. No body contact is permitted. If an interception has not been possible, the player checking places herself between the attacking player and her intended goal. The "checker" is on the balls of her feet with relaxed knees and ankles so that the body weight can change quickly as the attacker moves. The defender travels in the same direction as her opponent, always facing her. Often moving backward, she follows each movement by the attack with her body and stick as she crosse checks, slows the opponent, and forces a change of course or a pass.

Crosse Checking.　A player may tap an opponent's crosse in an attempt to dislodge the ball. Players making the check must have the body and stick well under control to prevent dangerous play. Beginners should attempt this skill of firm, small tapping movements downward or sideward *only*. More advanced players may up-check, dislodging the ball so that it may be caught in the air.

Dodging.　This is the most effective technique an attacking player can use to get around an opponent. A player must not rely on her ability to run past an opponent in a wide arc; she must be determined to run as directly as possible to her objective. A smart opponent will place herself directly in the attacker's path; therefore, the attack must camouflage her actions, deceive her opponent, and pass her, or risk losing possession of the ball. In essence, a successful dodge is the result of one or more feints or fakes with stick and body movements. The opponent is pulled out of position or off balance and the attack is allowed to accelerate and run past. As the attack pulls away, she protects the ball by cradling on the side away from the opponent. Once free of the threat of checking, she resumes normal cradling.

Advanced players develop a knowledge and "sense" that tells them an opponent has committed herself to "wrong footing" and a dodge may be accomplished. That is, on a feint by the attack to the right, the opponent pulls to her own left and weights her forward right foot. Similarly, a feint left might draw an opponent to her own right with left foot forward and weighted. A "wrong-footed" opponent can be passed by pulling to the side

Fig. 23-9.　Dodging.

away from the feint and accelerating before she can redistribute her weight or turn and begin pursuit.

GAME RULES AND SCORING

The rules of lacrosse are simple and few. These are designed to protect the player and control the game. An official game has two 30 minute halves with a maximum of 10 minutes between halves. A field umpire and two goal umpires conduct the game with assistance of two timekeepers and two scorekeepers.

The game begins with a center draw. Thereafter each team moves the ball with their crosses in an attempt to position and score a goal. During play the ball may be sent out of bounds and fouls may occur. The simplified rules below control play:*

1. *Stand.* Whenever play is suspended by an official's whistle, all players must stand and hold their positions until directed by an official or play resumes.

2. *Out of Bounds.* When the ball passes out of the established boundaries, the umpire stops play and awards the ball to the player who was nearest to it as it went out. If two players on opposing teams were equally close to the ball as it crossed the boundary, the two players stand 5 yards in and at least 1 yard apart, with the defense player nearer her own goal, to receive a throw-in from the umpire. Play from an out-of-bounds situation must be at least 10 yards from the goal line.

3. *Ball Lodged in Clothing or Equipment.* A ball lodged in the goal netting or in the pads or clothing of the goalkeeper within the crease is removed, placed in the crosse, and played. If lodged in the clothing of other players, it is removed and the umpire calls a draw with the player's nearest opponent.

When a ball is lodged in the crosse, the crosse is struck to the ground to displace it. If this fails, the umpire calls a draw where the ball was caught.

4. *Fouls.* Two type of fouls are recognized: field fouls and crease fouls. In the field of play a player may not:

a. Swing recklessly or check roughly.

b. Reach over her opponent's shoulder to tackle.

c. Hold down or check the crosse of an opponent who is not in possession of the ball.

d. Hold down an opponent's crosse in the air or on the ground when opponent is in possession of the ball.

e. Detain an opponent by contact with her crosse or her body.

f. Deliberately charge an opponent.

g. Trip, push or shove an opponent with body or crosse.

h. Guard her crosse with a raised elbow or with one hand off the crosse.

i. Intentionally touch the ball with her hands except to remove it when lodged in goal netting or clothing.

j. Throw her crosse.

k. Kick the ball intentionally.

l. Dangerously flip the ball into an opponent.

m. Move from her position when the umpire blows her whistle (except for goals) until play resumes or she is directed by the umpire.

n. Play the ball or impede an opponent unless she is holding her crosse.

In and around the *crease* a player must not:

a. When attacking, have any part of her body or crosse over the crease during of after the pass or shot.

b. Check the goalkeeper within the goal crease.

c. When inside the crease, hold the ball in her crosse; it must be passed at once.

d. Draw the ball back into the crease unless both feet are in the crease.

e. When in possession of the ball outside the crease, step back into run across the crease until the ball is passed.

f. When defending, step into the crease if another defending player is in the crease.

The *penalty* for field and crease fouls is a free position. Players "stand." The goalkeeper may return to her position. The umpire indicates where the player taking the free position stands. All players must be at least 5 yards from the player with the ball. On signal "play" the player with the ball may run, pass, or shoot. No free position by an attacking player may be taken within 10 yards

---

*For complete rules, see the current *Field Hockey-Lacrosse Guide* published by D.G.W.S.

of the goal line (measured from the line in any direction). When a foul presents an almost certain goal, the umpire orders any defense player, including the goalkeeper, from between the free position and goal.

When two opponents foul simultaneously, the umpire orders a draw.

Substitutes. Substitutes may enter to take the place of an injured player at any time and the place of any player at half time. If a player temporarily leaves the game and no substitute enters, she may return to play when able. (In high school and college games, substitutions may be made at the umpire's discretion.)

Scoring. The winning team is the one that scores the greatest number of points. A goal counts 1 point and is recorded when the entire ball crosses the goal line from the front and stays beneath the 6 foot crossbar. A legal goal must be propelled by a crosse of the attacking player, or by the crosse or body of a defending player. Tied games are recorded as such.

GAME STRATEGY

The rules of lacrosse permit each player to roam anywhere on the field; consequently, it is the individual's responsibility to fulfill her

duties if a team is to have an effective attack and defense.

The Attack. Attack play is a creative movement initiated by one individual and responded to by the other players. In most games the ease of play and cooperation give the impression that the team is executing a well rehearsed play. This is not true, for the game's fluidity does not allow for set formations. The keys to smooth operation of a game are the result of perfect stickwork, a sense of timing adapted to the speed and skill of teammates, and a total game sense in which all players work to create a space for themselves or team members in which to receive a pass away from opponents.

A defense player often begins the attack with a pass to an attack wing or center about

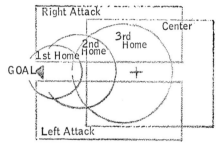

Fig. 23-10. Attack players' territory.

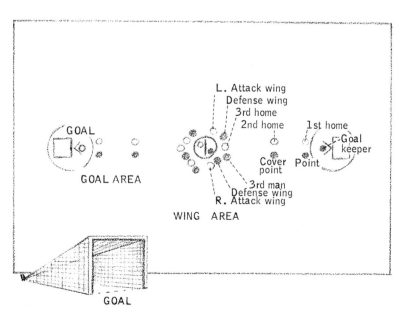

Fig. 23-11. Positioning for center draw.

even with the center circle. Third home often makes the first move to create space, thereby setting a pattern for play.

As an attacking player receives a pass she should start immediately for the goal until checked. A pass to third home might follow, then to second home and then to first home for a shot. For example, center passes to an attack wing, as she should not penetrate too deeply too often. Second home takes the next pass as first home makes a quick dash in front of the goal to shoot as she receives the ball. Second home pulls to one side so that first home will have space in front of the goal.

Beginners will do well to practice a triangular "play" that can be effective anywhere in the field. Player 1 passes to player 2; player 1 dodges her opponent in a path *opposite* to that of the passed ball. Player 2 passes back to player 1 who is moving rapidly for a shot.

An attack player should have the following qualifications:

1. Excellent stickwork with ability to catch, pass, pick up, dodge, and shoot at top speed.

2. Speed and sure footwork with quick, neat, and deceptive steps.

3. Alertness and ability to adapt to play of others.

4. Initiative, presence of mind, and coolness.

5. Knowledge of all positions and areas of their play.

6. Ability to draw her defense (as well as herself) from in front of the goal. At least 10 yards should be kept clear for the shooter.

7. A wide variety of skillful shots, especially a long, low, bouncing shot, which is difficult to defend against.

8. Ability to tackle back if the defense gains the ball.

The following diagrams of attacks illustrate how alert players use passing skill and field positioning to score:*

Official Field Hockey-Lacrosse Guide, 1946-48, pp. 112-113, National Section on Women's Athletics of AAHPER.

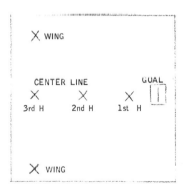

Goal is shot by 3rd H, who cuts in an arc. Play — Wing to 3rd to 2nd to 1st to 3rd. Other possibilities: *1.* Wing to 3rd to 2nd to 1st and back to 2nd on "give and go" around defense. *2.* Wing to 3rd to 2nd to 1st and a high pass over the defense to the opposite wing, who has run downfield and cut into a scoring position.

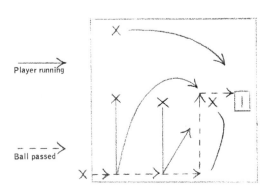

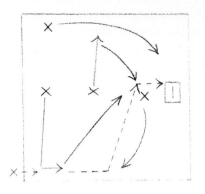

Goal scored by 2nd H, who pulls out to the opposite side of the field from the ball to draw her defense and then cuts into scoring position. Play — Wing to 3rd to 1st to 2nd. Other possibilities: 1. Wing to 3rd to 1st and back to 3rd on "give and go." 2. Wing to 3rd to 1st to opposite wing as in second possibility in previous diagram.

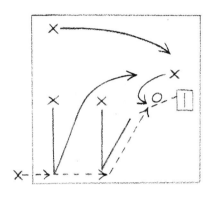

1st H scores goal on pivot shot as she moves from the right of the goal in front of her defense. Play — Wing to 3rd to 2nd to 1st. Other possibility: Wing to 3rd to 2nd to 1st to 3rd on shovel pass.

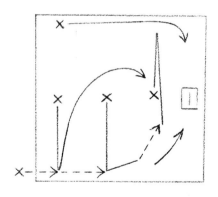

Goal scored by 1st H, who moves to opposite side of field and cuts back in front of defense. Play — Wing to 3rd to 2nd to 1st. Other possibilities: 1. Wing to 3rd to 2nd to 1st and back to 2nd. On this play, 1st blocks out defense and gives pass to 2nd who follows ball to goal. 2. Wing to 3rd to 2nd to 1st to 3rd, who cuts in arc to scoring position.

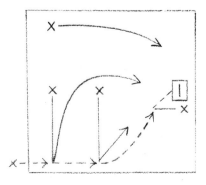

Goal by 1st H on shovel shot from left side of goal. Play — Wing to 3rd to 2nd to 1st. Other possibility: wing to 3rd to 2nd to 1st and back to 2nd or 3rd as 1st screens out defense by moving in front of her. The opposite wing could be used also.

(All these plays may be used on the other side of the field when the ball is brought up there.)

The Defense. The defense player should have sound stickwork, excellent footwork, and the skills of marking and body and crosse checking. Along with these attributes she should have initiative and be able to anticipate both attack and defense maneuvers. The objects of defense play are (1) to prevent opposing players from gaining or keeping possession of the ball and moving it close to the goal, and (2) to gain possession of the ball for her own team's attack.

Individual defense players mark their own opponents, body check, crosse check and intercept the ball whenever possible, pass quickly and accurately, and interchange with each other whenever necessary. Close man-to-man marking enables the defender to have an equal chance of intercepting a pass. Follow the opponent wherever she goes, making certain not to be left behind when she maneuvers and changes directions. The defender stays between the goal and the attacker following her crosse with a hope of checking if she dodges, passes, or shoots.

A defensive player makes decisive tackles without hesitation. The defense never runs up the field to meet the attack, for this makes the attack's dodge easier. She should be met on an angle so that the defensive player can body check and turn to intercept if the attack attempts a dodge.

When a defending player intercepts a ball, she passes it if a player is free, or runs upfield until a safe pass is possible. Help fellow defending teammates by getting free for a pass when no forwards are available.

Interchange is the process by which a free attacking player is intercepted. It requires cooperation, speed, and timing. Third man often makes the initial tackle if she is in good position. When this occurs, cover point takes third home and the nearest defense wing takes second home. If third man stays with third home or is passed, cover point takes the free attack as she approaches the goal. As cover point tackles, the defense wing on the opposite side of the field from the free attack moves to a position in which she is able to intercept a pass to the second home or body check the second home should she receive the ball. Point marks first home. If point had to tackle second home, a defense wing would come in to mark first home.

When interchanging, each player marks closely until the last moment, and then moves definitely. The free defense must get back in the defense as soon as possible by taking the free attack player. The defense players remain in their interchanged positions until a goal is scored or the defense clears.

DUTIES AND SPECIFIC SKILLS OF PLAYERS

First home should:

1. Have the ability to use neat, tight stickwork in a very small space.
2. Be the best shot of all; be skilled in handling catches and converting to shots.
3. Be deceptive in body and cradling action.
4. Tackle goalkeeper out of the crease.
5. Field balls behind the goal.

Second home should:

1. Be able to work in small space.
2. Be an excellent shot from every angle, close and long, and in small spaces.
3. Have deceptive body movements to divert the cover point.
4. Be able to interchange with first home and attack wings.

Third home should:

1. Assist center and attack wings in linking defense and attack.
2. Take a position that will give her working space yet draw the third man from the oncoming player.
3. Be able to rush for goal and pass to a free attack. Move back to position to create space.
4. Be prepared to replace attack wings.
5. Be skilled at triangular pass ("give and go").

Attack wings should:

1. Have speed and endurance.
2. Serve as links between defense and attack.
3. Always be ready to receive goalkeeper and defense's clears.
4. Pass quickly and run rapidly toward goal.
5. Pass accurately to their homes.
6. Play out at their wing positions, cutting in when possible, but moving to create spaces.

7. Shoot well at long and close range, particularly a long bouncing shot.

Center should:

1. Mark center closely to keep her out of shooting range.
2. As a link between defense and attack, go back to help defense bring ball to attackers.
3. Be available to shoot if there is an opening without crowding homes.
4. Intercept and relay passes.
5. Be ready to interchange with third home and act as an extra attack.
6. Learn to control draws—preferably to left attack wing or third home.

Defense wings should:

1. Be exceptionally fast players with stamina.
2. Be both defense and attack players.
3. Always stay between attack wing and goal.
4. Avoid tackling opposing defense wing.
5. Be skilled in the timing and knowledge of defensive interchange.
6. Mark their opponents closely at the draw.

Third man should:

1. Have speed, good footwork, and knowledge and ability to intercept play.
2. Be discriminating and cautious when going into attack area. Return to mark third home quickly.
3. Interchange with center if center is drawn back.

Cover point should:

1. Be the pivot of defense interchange.
2. Be excellent at body checking and close stickwork.
3. Be a steady player with skill at anticipating attacking movements.
4. Never hold the ball, but clear to an attack in good position.
5. Act decisively in defense interchange so wing defenses will know when to come in against second home.

Point should:

1. Be primarily responsible for closely marking first home.
2. Be outstanding at body checking.
3. Be able and ready to attack a player who is free and moving toward goal.

4. Be ready to field ball behind the goal.
5. Be able to start and stop quickly and give long passes.

Goalkeeper should:

1. Have a good, quick eye.
2. Be able to concentrate and anticipate the attack. Find out their strongest shots.
3. Place herself away from the goal line so that she covers every shot with her body or crosse, leaving the smallest possible target area.
4. Be able to catch in limited space in all positions.
5. Be able to give long accurate passes to her attacks.
6. Avoid clearing in front of the goal.
7. Watch first home in order to intercept passes to her.
8. Never leave the crease unless she has a sure interception, or a spoiling play, or has an opportunity to field a ball she is certain to reach before an opponent reaches her.

Terminology

Body checking—Placing one's body between an opponent and her objective so that the opponent's progress is impeded.

Cradling—The action of the body and the rhythmical swing of the crosse that keep the ball under control in the netting.

Crease—A circle 8½ feet in radius surrounding each goal. It serves as a restraining line when shooting for a goal.

Crosse checking—Controlled tapping of the crosse of an opponent in an attempt to dislodge the ball.

Cutting—Movement into a specific location to receive a pass.

Dodging—Getting past an opponent while maintaining possession of the ball.

Draw—The method of beginning play between opposing players at each period and after each goal, and following a double foul or injury.

Free position—A position awarded a player when an opponent has fouled. The player is given the ball in her crosse and may run, shoot or pass. All other players must be at least 5 yards away.

Holding down—Holding an opponent's crosse by one's own crosse—either in the air or on the ground. Unlike legal crosse checking, holding is a foul.

Marking—Guarding an opponent by staying close by and moving as she moves.

Stand—A stationary position all players must hold, unless otherwise directed by the umpire, when the umpire suspends play.

Stick—Another name for the crosse.

Stickwork—Any and all techniques of controlling the ball and stick.

Tackle—Approaching an opponent for the purpose of

body checking or crosse checking to take the ball or impede progress.

Throw-in—Putting the ball in play by having the umpire throw it between opposing players. Used when both players were equidistant from the ball as it went out of bounds.

Selected Audio-visual Aids*

Lacrosse Film Loops. 1961. (9 loops with notes. b & w, silent.) Guy Butler, "Harbledown," Little Hadham, Herefordshire, England.

USWLA Technical Materials. (Bulletin Board Materials, 21 bulletins including skills, coaching notes, etc.) Available from the Technical Materials Chairman, USWLA (See current D.G.W.S. *Guide*).

Suggested Readings

AAHPER: *Field Hockey—Lacrosse Guide*, Current edition, Division for Girls and Women's Sports, 1201 16th St., N.W., Washington, D.C. 20036.

All England Ladies Lacrosse Association: *Lacrosse Do's and Don'ts*, available from Gertrude Hooper, 242 Highland St., Milton 86, Mass.

Boyd, Margaret: *Lacrosse Playing and Coaching*, New York, The Ronald Press Company, 1959.

---

*USWLA is currently developing an instructional film. (16 mm., sound, color.) Information will be available in the D.G.W.S. *Guide*.

Newhof, Caryl, (ed.): *Selected Field Hockey—Lacrosse Articles*, D.G.W.S., 1201 16th St., N.W., Washington, D.C. 20036, 1955.

Reeson, Joan: *Know the Game—LaCrosse*, Obtain from Gertrude Hooper, 242 Highland St., Milton, Mass. 02186.

Richey, Betty (ed.): *Selected Field Hockey and Lacrosse Articles, 1964*, D.G.W.S., 1201 16th St., N.W., Washington, D.C. 20036.

Periodicals

Crosse Checks (yearly), United States Women's Lacrosse Association, Available from Second Vice President USWLA (see current D.G.W.S. *Guide*).

Lacrosse (published several times yearly), All England Ladies Lacrosse Association. (Write Gertrude Hooper, 242 Highland St., Milton 86, Mass.)

Suggested Study Questions

1. Explain defense interchange. What happens when third home is attacking free and unmarked?
2. What skills must a wing attack possess? What of cover point and second home?
3. Describe the parts of the crosse, How do you take care of this stick?
4. Explain and demonstrate the vertical cradle.
5. Trace the historical development of the game of lacrosse.

CHAPTER TWENTY-FOUR

Courtesy of Rice University, Houston, Texas.

SOCCER AND SPEEDBALL

SOCCER

Since the origin of soccer is attributed to such widely separated places as Ireland, Greece, England, and Rome, it is likely that the game developed in several localities at about the same time. The ancient sport of *Harpastrum*, in which a crudely shaped ball was either hit with the hands or kicked, later became *feetballe*, a rough and rugged kicking game played as a mob sport. An inflated animal bladder covered with leather was moved by sheer force through the alleys and streets and out into vacant fields between goals often located miles apart. Although many English monarchs, including King Edward II, Elizabeth I, and James I, passed edicts forbidding their subjects to play this bloody, brawling sport because of the many complaints of damaged property from shopkeepers, the game somehow survived through the centuries. The nobility looked down upon this degrading contest as being for the lowly, rugged commoners. Therefore, it is ironic that it was an Englishman from the upper class, J. C. Thring, who drew up the rules, giving the game respectability. He made soccer safer to play, and introduced it into the private schools and adult clubs of England.

Even though the game was played in America during early colonial times, and in an intercollegiate match for men between Princeton and Rutgers as early as 1869, it did not gain in popularity until after World War I. A modified game for women was first introduced at Bryn Mawr College in 1919 and the first official women's rules appeared in the

Fig. 24-1. Soccer is largely a running and kicking game. It is our most popular world sport. (Courtesy of the Los Angeles Public Schools.)

form of modified men's rules in 1927. Since then soccer for both sexes has become increasingly favored in our school and college programs and has grown as a popular recreation sport for varying ages. As an international game soccer has no equal, for it is the national sport of 53 countries. Truly, the sun never sets on the game of soccer.

SPEEDBALL

At the University of Michigan in 1921 speedball was created by Elmer D. Mitchell for use in the men's intramural program. Although girls and women started playing the game shortly thereafter, it was not until 1930 that the National Section on Women's Athletics (now D.G.W.S.) made the necessary rule changes which popularized the game and tailored it to the specific needs of women instructors and students. Speedball combines basketball passing skills with the drop kick of football and the dribble of soccer. Like speed-a-way,* a relatively new field game which permits running with the ball, speedball appeals most to girls who enjoy playing a game resembling the male sport of football.

NATURE AND PURPOSE OF THE GAMES

Soccer and speedball are active running, kicking, and passing field games played by

---

*For official rules and film write Marjorie Larsen, 1754 Middlefield Road, Stockton, California.

two teams of 11 players each. Although scoring methods differ, the object of both games is to advance the ball down a field 100 yards long and 60 yards wide and to score. The team with the larger score at the end of playing time is declared the winner. The five forward line players—center forward, right and left inners, and right and left wings—are primarily responsible for scoring. The duties of the left, center, and right halfbacks include guarding their opponents and passing the ball to their forwards, as well as scoring themselves. The left and right fullback have duties similar to those of the halfbacks except that they play a more vital defensive role. The goalkeeper's primary task is to prevent the opposing team from scoring.

The field should be no larger than 100 yards in length and 60 yards in width. The minimum for high school play is 80 by 40 yards. The field is divided by a *halfway line*, and the center of this line is marked. Five yards on each side of the center line and parallel to it are two restraining lines.

Specific Soccer Markings. The goal posts are 6 yards apart and joined by a crossbar that is 8 feet above the ground. Fifteen yards in front of each goal line, a line 4 yards long runs parallel to the goal. From this line, quarter circles are drawn which measure 15 yards in radius from a point 1 yard inside the goal post on the goal line. The penalty area includes the lines and space in front of each goal made by these quarter circles. The penalty kick mark is a line 2 feet long, parallel to the goal line, and 12 yards from the center of the goal. Corner kick marks are lines 3 feet long that are marked across goal lines at a point 5 yards from each corner.

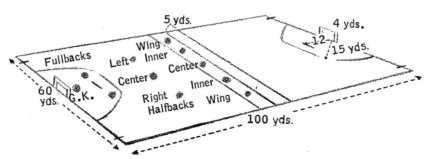

Fig. 24-2. Soccer field and positions.

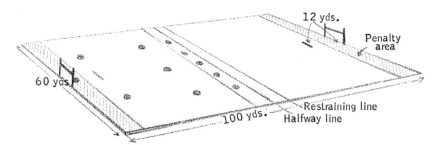

Fig. 24-3.   Speedball field and playing positions.

Specific Speedball Markings.   A line, called the five yard line, is drawn across each end of the field at a point 5 yards from each goal line. The space enclosed by the goal line, side-lines, and 5 yard line is called the penalty area. Penalty kick marks are the same as the soccer markings. The distance between the goal posts and the height of the crossbar are the same as for soccer, but the posts are 20 feet high.

Basic Equipment.   The ball should be a regulation leather-covered soccer ball meas-uring 27 to 28 inches in circumference. For class instruction, there should be one for each group of six to eight players. Tennis, soccer, or hockey shoes may be worn. Light shin guards are helpful for beginners, and those wearing eyeglasses should wear protective guards. Teams should wear costumes of dis-tinguishing colors. A first-aid kit should be handy at all times.

BASIC SKILLS

SOCCER FUNDAMENTALS

Soccer fundamentals include skills nec-essary for controlling, moving, and gaining the ball, as well as scoring. The techniques involved are often referred to as ball-han-dling skills, although the goalkeeper is the only player who may actually handle the ball. Soccer requires endurance and balance, and a conscientious player should strive to de-velop stamina, speed, and skill through a planned conditioning program.

Advancing the Ball with the Feet.   Kicking is the basic technique for moving the ball and for passing and shooting for goals. It is also the primary defense technique of the goalkeeper. Players should strive to become versatile in the use of both feet in as many kicking skills as possible.

INSTEP KICK.   The instep kick is basic to all kicking skills. It is used on both moving and stationary balls as a short pass, a long kick or a shot for goal. It is generally preceded by several running steps. The nonkicking foot supports the body weight slightly behind the ball. As the kicking leg swings backward from the hip, the knee bends and the toe points toward the ground. The arms are away from the body and the body is inclined forward for balance. Watch the ball constantly. The leg swings forward, and as the knee comes in line with the ball, the leg straightens. The toe remains pointing downward so that the ball is met below center by the top of the instep (shoe laces). The knee remains straightened, and the leg and foot extend, thus lifting the ball up and away from the body. A forceful kick will often result in the supporting foot leaving the ground for a moment on the follow-through. A simple instep kick has backspin and remains low. If more height is needed, the kicking leg should be straightened quickly and completely at the moment of ball contact.

Fig. 24-4.   The instep kick.

PIVOT INSTEP KICK.   The pivot instep kick is effective as a place kick and in sending a moving ball in a direction other than the one in which it is traveling. The nonkicking foot is placed 12 to 16 inches behind the ball on the side of the ball in which direction it is to be kicked. The backswing is similar to the simple instep kick, but on the forward movement, the leg swings in a circular motion from the hip, and the body leans slightly backward and *in the direction* in which the ball is to be kicked. The body pivots on the nonkicking toe as the ball is contacted on the instep of the other foot. The ball follows the direction in which the kicking foot points on follow-through.

Fig. 24-5.   The pivot instep kick.

OUTSIDE-OF-THE-FOOT KICK.   The outside-of-the-foot kick is made in a manner similar to that of the instep kick. The difference is that the toe of the kicking foot is turned in so that the ball is contacted by the side and little toe of the foot. For a right foot kick, the ball is met at the center or to the left of the body. The mechanics are described in more detail in the discussion of the outside-of-the-foot pass (see page 410).

Fig. 24-6.   The outside-of-the-foot kick.

TOE KICK.   The toe kick is recommended only for skilled players who are wearing hard-toe shoes. It is used most often for a place kick on a stationary ball. The body mechanics of the kick are similar to the instep kick except that the toe is parallel to the ground and points toward the ball. The toe contacts the ball below center, and the follow-through is in the direction of ball flight.

VOLLEY KICK.   The volley kick is an advanced skill used less frequently by women than men. It is used to kick a ball while it is in the air, either before or after it bounces. The ball must be watched carefully so the kick can be properly timed. The kicking leg is bent and swings from the hip. Allow the ball to drop to about knee level before contacting it with the instep. A ball contacted at too high a point is usually kicked by an extended leg. This results in a skied ball, which offers little control of direction. A *knee volley* may be used on high balls, but control and power are often lost.

Fig. 24-7.   The volley kick.

DROP KICK.   The drop kick is actually a half volley kick which is used to contact a ball the instant it bounces from the ground. In soccer, the drop kick is a goalkeeping skill, but in speedball, it is needed by all players for penalty kicks and scoring. The ball is held at arm's length in front of the body and slightly to the side of the kicking leg. It may be dropped from one or both hands. The kicking leg swings forward, toe pointing toward the ground, and the knee extends as the instep contacts the ball just as it bounces

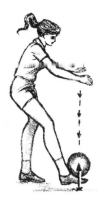

Fig. 24-8. The drop kick.

Fig. 24-10. The dribble.

from the ground. The leg follows through forward and upward.

PUNT. The goalkeeper has the privilege of holding the ball prior to the punt. The ball is held at about waist level at arm's length in front of the body. It is held in this position as a step or weight shift is made to the nonkicking foot. The ball is dropped as the kicking foot begins its forward swing, and the ball kicked by the instep as it reaches a point just off the ground. The higher the point at which the ball is met in the air, and the higher the follow-through, the higher the ball flight will be.

Fig. 24-9. The punt.

Dribbling. Dribbling is the skill by which a moving player maintains control and possession of the ball. It is simply a series of well controlled and timed kicks. A dribble should be used when no opponents are near or when no teammate is clear to whom the ball may be passed. The ball is tapped or pushed along the ground by alternating short kicks which contact the ball below center. Each impetus should move the ball about 10 to 12 inches forward; however, the speed of the runner and the threat posed by the opponents should determine how far in front the ball may be tapped.

The dribble is most easily controlled by alternate taps with the *inside* of each foot. The body is quite erect and the arms are free for balance. The kicking foot is turned outward so that the inside of the foot contacts the ball. This results in the ball having a forward and slightly diagonal path.

Dribbling with the outside of the foot is useful in turning quickly and in keeping one's body between the ball and an opponent. The foot is rotated inward, and the toe is pointed diagonally downward so that contact is made on the outside of the instep.

When moving diagonally across the field or in a circular fashion, the dribbler may alternate an outside tap and an inside tap.

Dribbling with the toes or with the top of the instep with toes forward is a useful skill when running rapidly; however, a "loose" dribble results in a ball that is difficult to control and easily intercepted because of the distance it moves from the dribbler's body. To execute this dribble the toes are pointed forward. Each contact is made with the toes slightly under the ball so that backspin is created and control is maintained.

Short Kicks (Passes). Short kicks, directed with proper power and accuracy, are used for passes, dodges, and goal shots.

INSTEP KICK. The instep kick was described earlier (see page 407). As a short pass, it is most effective when it is deceptively used. That is, the opponents are led to believe a long kick is to be anticipated, but instead a controlled short pass results from less force and limited follow-through.

INSIDE-OF-THE-FOOT KICK. This push pass is accurate but rarely deceptive. The ball is met with the inside of the instep (between the large toe and the heel) and can be directed sideward or forward.

The kicking leg swings diagonally backward and outward. It then swings forward and across the body to contact the ball, which is close to and in front of the body. The knee of the kicking leg straightens, and the ball is swept out and away from the body. The supporting leg is bent to maintain balance and to allow an easy swing of the kicking leg.

Fig. 24-11. The inside-of-the-foot kick.

OUTSIDE-OF-THE-FOOT PASS. The outside of the foot is used for short, deceptive passes and goal shots. Little power is possible because of the limited backswing. The kicking leg swings across and away from the body and passes in front of the bent supporting leg. The knee straightens as the ball is contacted in front of and slightly to the outside of the supporting foot.

Fig. 24-12. The outside-of-the-foot pass.

HEEL PASS. The heel pass is a more skillful pass. The heel is used to prevent a ball from going out of the boundary lines or for a deceptive pass following a feint. The body weight is supported on one leg as the kicking leg, knee flexed, swings backward from the hip. The leg extends slightly as the heel of the kicking foot meets the ball below its center. The knee again flexes to assume the body weight on the follow-through.

Fig. 24-13. The heel pass.

SOLE-OF-THE-FOOT PASS. This skillful maneuver can be executed either from a dribble or on the run. The sole of the foot is placed lightly on the ball and force is exerted by quick flexion of the knee so that the ball is rolled backward. If the passer is running, she may jump, leave the ground, and execute the movement while in the air.

Controlling or Advancing the Ball with the Body. A ball may be trapped by the body or rebounded from the body in order to bring it under control or change its direction.

Trapping. Trapping is the technique for bringing the ball under control. It may result in stopping a ball, bringing it to the ground, changing its direction, or slowing it down. No matter how the ball is to be trapped, the player keeps her eyes on the ball and maintains a relaxed body during performance of this skill so that she is ready for the next play after the ball is controlled.

SOLE-OF-THE-FOOT TRAP. This is a simple and effective trap for low bouncing or slowly rolling balls. It becomes less effective as running speed and ball speed increase. As the ball approaches, the trapping leg extends

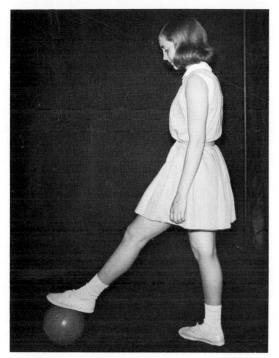

Fig. 21-14. In trapping the soccer ball timing is essential. (Courtesy of Hollis Fait, University of Connecticut.)

forward, the foot is 4 or 5 inches off the ground, and the heel is downward. At the moment the ball touches the foot, pressure is exerted, and the ball is pinned between the foot and the ground.

SIDE-OF-THE-FOOT TRAP. The ball may be trapped by either the inside or the outside of the foot. This trap is not recommended for the goalkeeper, for a misplay could deflect the ball toward the goal. Flex the knee of the trapping leg and raise the foot several inches from the ground. If the ball is to be deflected by the outside of the foot, turn the toe in and downward (pigeon-toed); if the inside of the

foot is used, turn the foot out and let the ankle remain loose and relaxed. The ball will rebound slightly as the body leans in the direction in which the ball is to go.

INSIDE-OF-THE-THIGH TRAP. Trapping with the inside of the thigh is an excellent way of gaining control of a low-flying or rebounding ball. The body weight is shifted to the nontrapping leg. The trapping leg bends at right angles to the line of flight. The foot is several inches off the ground. As the ball strikes the fleshy part of the thigh, the leg "gives" slightly to absorb the impact and allow the ball to fall near the feet.

Fig. 24-16. Inside-of-the-thigh trap.

ONE-LEG TRAP. The player prepares to stop the ball by lining up directly in its path. For a right-leg trap the left leg moves forward, flexes and carries the body weight down and slightly forward. The right knee bends. The shin contacts the ball and forces it to a stop in the wedge formed by the leg and the ground.

Fig. 24-15. Trapping with the sole of the foot.

Fig. 24-17. The two-leg trap.

Two-Leg Trap. The feet are close together. As the ball approaches, the knees bend. The body is inclined slightly forward and balanced on the balls of the feet. The arms are held out for balance as the ball is trapped between the ground and the shins of both legs. Rise quickly and continue play.

Blocking or Trapping with the Abdomen or Chest. These traps are used when the ball is traveling above the ground. As the ball moves to the player, she "gives" or jumps back slightly as she bends forward at the waist. At the moment the ball drops, the body is poised and ready to play the ball. For the abdomen trap, the arms may be extended for balance, but on the chest block, the arms are folded across the chest for protection. The arms and hands must remain in contact with the body throughout the block if they touch the ball.

Fig. 24-18. The chest block.

Volleying. A ball can be rebounded legally from any part of the body except extended hands and arms. Skills of volleying are useful for intercepting or changing the direction of a ball.

Foot Volley. The volley and the half volley kicks are used when a ball has a low trajectory in the air either before or after it bounces. The half volley is performed *just* after the ball strikes the ground (see p. 408).

Knee Volley. The knee volley is used to play a ball descending from a high flight that cannot be played by the more efficient foot volley. The ball must be carefully watched as a step is taken to the supporting leg and the other leg is bent and raised so that the knee contacts the ball from underneath and behind. If the ball is hit directly underneath, it will be skied ineffectively.

Hip and Shoulder Volleys. These volleys are used on balls too low for heading. To execute the shoulder volley, watch the ball flight carefully. Turn the hitting shoulder toward the ball and hold the arm close to the body. As the ball approaches, jump and extend the body to meet the ball with the side and top of the shoulder. The head tilts away from the hitting shoulder.

In executing the hip volley, the arms are away from the body, and the side is turned toward the oncoming ball. The ball is met off the top of the hip, and the body moves laterally to follow through in the direction of ball flight.

Heading. Volleying with the head is an advanced technique used for bringing the ball under control or to the ground and as a method of passing or scoring a goal. With eyes on the ball, place the head so the ball will be met by the forehead. The ball is met by jumping toward it; the neck is stiffened, and contact is made at the hairline on the front of the head.

To head the ball to the side, meet the ball with the side of the forehead and move the head sharply to the side in the direction of intended ball flight.

Fig. 24-19. Heading.

SPEEDBALL FUNDAMENTALS

Many of the fundamental skills of speedball are the same as those of soccer and basketball. All soccer skills and all skills for ball handling in basketball except the bounce to oneself and the dribble may be used. Emphasis should be placed on the drop kick, but the only skills peculiar to speedball are those of converting a ground ball to an aerial ball.

Lifting to a Teammate. The player lifting is about a foot behind the stationary ball. Weight is on the left leg, and the right leg is forward. The knee of the right leg is flexed and the toe is toward the ground. The instep contacts the ball and lifts it by a rapid leg movement, an extension of the knee, and a toe lift. The leg follows through in the direction of the receiver. The lifting of moving balls requires increased speed and accurate timing.

Fig. 24-20. Lifting to a teammate.

Kick-Up or Lift to Self

ONE-FOOT LIFT OF STATIONARY BALL. Standing behind the ball, the player puts the sole of her lifting foot on top of the ball. Applying pressure, she pulls it back toward herself and quickly slides the toes of the same foot under the ball to lift it upward. The toes of the lifting foot turn slightly upward as the

Fig. 24-21. One-foot lift of a stationary ball.

knee bends outward to allow the body and arms to move forward to catch the ball.

LIFT OF A MOVING BALL. The player awaits the moving ball with one leg slightly extended. Her heel is off the ground, and her toe is pointing down. As the ball rolls up and over the toe, the leg is quickly lifted, the knee bends outward, and the body leans forward to catch the ball as it rises off the instep.

Fig. 24-22. Lift of a moving ball.

KICK-UP WITH BOTH FEET. The ball is held between the player's feet by the inside of the feet and ankles. With body weight equally distributed on the outer portion of the feet, the player jumps and bends knees outward to pull the ball up within reach of the hands.

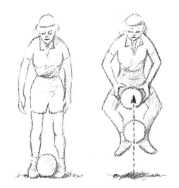

Fig. 24-23. The kick-up with both feet.

TECHNIQUES BASIC TO BOTH SOCCER AND SPEEDBALL

Tackling. The tackle is a technique for taking the ball from an opponent by using the feet. A tackle is considered successful if it causes a dribbler to make a poor pass, overrun the ball, or otherwise play the ball so

Fig. 24-24. Tackling.

Fig. 24-26. The side or hook tackle.

that her opponents gain possession or have an opportunity to set up a better defense. Tackling requires accuracy and correct timing, for the tackler must play the ball, not the player, and body contact must be avoided.

FRONT, OR STRAIGHT, TACKLE. This is used against an opponent who is dribbling. Just after the dribbler contacts the ball, the tackler reaches with one foot, body weight on the other, and places the sole of the foot on the ball. She holds it as the opponent overruns; then the tackler attempts to maintain possession and avoid a tackle back by her opponent.

Fig. 24-25. The front or straight tackle.

SIDE, OR HOOK, TACKLE. This tackle is effective for most field situations. The tackler is positioned to one side of her opponent. Her body weight is supported by the leg away from the ball. As the opponent approaches, the stationary leg bends deeply, allowing the leg near the opponent to extend. The ankle is flexed and the side of the foot is turned toward the ground. The ball is hooked and

pulled toward the tackler as the stationary leg straightens.

As tackling skill develops, players should initiate the tackle from a straight-on position in order to delay relaying their intention to the dribbler as long as possible. When time permits, plan to tackle from the most advantageous position. For example, if the opponent dribbles straight ahead or taps the ball every step, hook the ball to the side of the dribbling foot. The dribbler will find it difficult to tackle back because her weight will be transferred to the foot near the ball. When the dribbler uses a diagonal kick or a skip-foot dribbling pattern, attempt to hook the ball on the side of the dribbler's receiving foot in order to avoid body contact.

SPLIT TACKLE. This is a desperation, or "spoil," play much like the left-hand lunge in hockey. The opponent is almost out of reach as the tackler drops to one knee and extends the other leg and toe toward the ball. If the ball is blocked, the tackler must regain playing position quickly.

Feints and Dodges. Individual ability is greatly improved if a player develops some deception in her play. *Feints* are deceptive moves and tactics which tend to confuse opponents. When possible, passes should be preceded by a feint in order to draw the opponent off balance or out of position. A few common feints are as follows:

1. Feint with the knees in one direction and pass in the other. This is most effective from a stride stand position with the ball in front of and near the feet. Bend the knees, look in one direction and pass suddenly in the other.

2. Feint to pass with the inside of the foot, but stop just before kicking the ball. This is effective on stationary or moving balls.

3. Feint to pass with the inside of the foot, but bring the foot over the ball and pass in the opposite direction with the outside of the foot. It is effective on stationary balls or while dribbling with the inside of the foot.

4. Feint an instep kick but stop or allow the foot to pass over the ball. If the foot passes over the ball, it may be followed by a heel- or sole-of-the-foot pass.

Dodges are individual techniques used by a player with the ball to avoid a tackler. The ability to dodge to either side of an opponent is important. The elements of surprise and speed are important in dodging. The direction of the dodge is determined by the opponent's position two strides away. If her next step will be on the left foot, the dodge should be made to the dribbler's left, as the opponent will be weighted on her right foot and less able to play a ball on her right. The ball is quickly pulled to the left with the right foot. The right foot then takes a long cross-step to the left. The left foot regains control of the ball.

When an opponent approaches before a dodge can be executed, the evasion dodge may be attempted. Push the ball to one side, step to the other side and out of the opponents path, and quickly return to the ball. The speed and momentum of the opponent may carry her out of the play momentarily.

Marking and Interchanging. Marking and interchanging are basic defense tactics. Marking is the ability to stay close enough to an opponent to intercept her passes or tackle the ball. Interchanging is the technique used by the defensive players in changing positions with one another. It is used when an opposing forward evades the defensive player marking her and is moving down the field unguarded. (See Field Hockey, p. 382, for discussion of defense tactics.)

SIMPLIFIED RULES AND SCORING*

RULES BASIC TO BOTH GAMES

1. A team consists of 11 players. Any number of substitutes may enter or re-enter the game unless disqualified.

2. A game is made up of four 8 minute

---

*For complete rules and interpretations see current D.G.W.S. *Soccer-Speedball Guide.*

quarters. There is a 2 minute rest period between quarters and a 10 minute rest between halves.

3. The winner of the toss has the choice of deciding which team shall kick-off or selecting the goal her team defends.

4. Play is started with a place kick by the center forward. Thereafter, the team scored against kicks off, except at the beginning of each quarter, when teams alternate kick-offs. Goals are changed at half time.

RULES FOR SOCCER

1. The ball may be volleyed, blocked, trapped, kicked, dribbled, and passed with the feet, body, and head. Only the goalkeeper (in the penalty area) may use her hands.

2. A player is *off-side* when she is ahead of the ball in the opponent's half of the field and nearer to the goal than any three opponents.

3. A *throw-in* is taken when the ball is kicked over the side line by a member of the opposing team.

4. A *corner kick* is awarded an attacking player when the ball is sent out of bounds over the end line outside the goal posts or over the crossbar by a defending player. A place kick from the end line is made from a point 5 yards from the nearer corner.

5. A *defense kick* is taken by a defending player when any member of the attacking team causes the ball to go over the end line outside the goal posts or over the crossbar. The ball is place kicked from any point on the quarter circle.

6. A *roll-in* results when two opponents cause the ball to go wholly over the side or goal line outside the goal posts. The umpire rolls the ball between the opponents as they stand 5 yards in and directly opposite the point where the ball left the field. If the cause of the roll-in occurs within 5 yards of the goal, the roll-in is taken 5 yards from the goal.

7. A *free kick* is awarded to opponents for a foul or rule infringement. It is a place kick taken at the spot of the infringement. A direct free kick (one from which a goal may be scored directly) is awarded for a foul committed outside the penalty area by either team, a foul committed by the attacking team inside the penalty area, and a foul resulting in player disqualification. An indirect free kick is awarded to opponents when a team improp-

erly takes a corner kick, kick-off, penalty kick, defense kick, free kick, or roll-in. A free kick is also awarded for infringement of goalkeeper's privileges and for off-side.

8. A *penalty kick* is awarded the attacking team from the penalty kick mark when the defending team commits a foul or rule infringement within the penalty area.

9. A *foul* is called when a player trips, kicks, strikes, holds, pushes, or jumps at an opponent, uses unnecessary roughness, or handles the ball.

10. A *field goal* is scored when the ball passes over the endline between the goal posts and under the crossbar. A field goal scores 2 points. A penalty goal scores 1 point.

RULES FOR SPEEDBALL

1. A ball may be advanced with the feet, head, or body when it is a ground ball. An aerial ball may be air dribbled, passed, punted, or drop-kicked. Ground balls may be converted to aerial balls by a lift-up to oneself or another player. Aerial balls become ground balls as soon as they touch the ground.

2. Balls going out of bounds over the side line are put back in play by a throw-in by an opposing team member opposite the spot where the ball went out. When the ball is sent out of bounds over the end line, it is put back in play by an opposing team member by a punt, place kick, drop kick, or throw-in opposite the spot on the goal line where the ball went out.

3. A *tie ball* results when two opponents catch the ball at the same time, cause it to go out of bounds, or commit a double foul. A toss up between the tieing players puts the ball in play.

4. A *free kick* is awarded to an opponent when a foul is committed.

5. A *penalty kick* is given to an attack player when the defense commits a team foul or an individual foul within its own penalty area or behind the goal line.

6. The following are individual fouls: blocking, charging, drop kicking for goal or attempting a forward pass for touchdown within the penalty area; delaying the game; touching a ground ball with hands or arms; holding, tripping, pushing, or tagging an opponent; snatching a ball from an opponent; unnecessary roughness; threatening the eyes of a player; air dribbling more than once; traveling with the ball and holding the ball more than 5 seconds on the field or out of bounds; and taking more than 10 seconds for a penalty kick.

Team fouls are as follows: taking more than three time-outs, having more than 11 players on the field, and making illegal substitutions.

7. The methods and point values given for scoring in speedball are as follows:

Field goal—2 points, made when the ball is advanced across the goal line between the goal posts and under the crossbar.

Touchdown—2 points, made when the ball is thrown by an attack players outside the penalty area in the field of play and is caught by a teammate behind the opponent's goal line.

Drop kick—3 points, made by just dropping the ball and kicking it after it strikes the ground; it must be kicked outside the penalty area, and it must pass over the crossbar and between the goal uprights.

Penalty kick—1 point, made by drop kicking the ball from behind the penalty kick mark; the ball must pass between the uprights and over the crossbar.

A goal cannot be scored directly from a

Fig. 24-27. Methods of scoring in speedball.

kick-off, throw-in, or a ball caught directly from a toss-up play.

GAME STRATEGY

The basic factor in successful and winning strategy is the blending of skillful individual play into a united team effort. If this is to be accomplished, position play is a must. This seems to be a difficult concept for girls and women to grasp, for the problem of players bunching around the ball is one most common in beginning soccer and speedball. (For a more complete discussion of position and team play see Game Strategy in the Field Hockey chapter.)

The basic individual skills necessary for team play are accurate ball handling, skillful blocking and trapping, quick and accurate passing, dodging, marking, and interchanging.

Basic Offense. "Only the team with the ball can score" is a concept which should be instilled in both offensive and defensive players. As the players try to gain control of the ball and pass it to their forwards for a scoring attempt, they should remember the following tenets:

1. Once in possession of it, try to keep the ball. Protect the ball with the body as much as possible.

2. Generally, pass ahead of an intended receiver and out to the side lines until nearing the opponent's goal.

3. Play your own position and avoid bunching near the ball. When interchanging with a teammate, do so quickly, endeavoring to throw the opponent off guard.

4. Look for weaknesses in the opponent's skill and strategy and capitalize on them.

5. Pass to open spaces that can be reached by a moving teammate. Avoid passing to a closely guarded teammate, and never pass *across* your own goal. An interception gives the opponents an immediate scoring opportunity.

6. Master the skills of playing a *long-pass game* out to fast forwards (this is good in soccer when the field is wet); a *short-pass game* quickly, endeavoring to throw the opponents off guard; and a *triangular-pass game*, using any three players (usually a wing halfback and two forwards) to zigzag the ball downfield quickly. Change from one style of attack to another often enough to keep the opponents guessing.

7. Conserve energy whenever possible. Take advantage of "breathers" when the ball is elsewhere on the field and playing it is someone else's responsibility.

8. Be sure all forward line players *know* to whom the ball will be passed and the opponents *do not know* for certain.

Fig. 24-28. In passing, the ball should be kicked in front of the running receiver. (Courtesy of College of Health, Physical Education and Recreation, Texas Woman's University, Denton, Texas.)

9. Take free kicks and throw-ins quickly, before the defense can get organized.

10. Take advantage of wind and all other environmental factors.

11. Be ready to change quickly from offensive to defensive play.

SPECIFICS FOR SOCCER

1. Rush for a goal in the penalty area.

2. Have the wing take a corner kick while her forward line teammates form a semicircle between her and the far side of the goal. Attempt to kick high so that the receiver can get the ball directly in front of the goal and kick it quickly.

3. On a free kick or roll-in it is best to have the forward line ahead of the ball (but onside), and for a right or left halfback to take the kick or roll-in.

SPECIFICS FOR SPEEDBALL

1. Usually an aerial-pass game will move the ball downfield more quickly. Occasionally vary the aerial attack by advancing the ball down the *center* of the field. Pass quickly toward the side line to score a touchdown.

2. Attempt to have two tall forward players who are adept at ball passing and tall enough to catch a ball thrown over the end line players' heads for a touchdown.

3. Plan and practice situational plays from kick-off, free kick, out of bounds, and toss-up.*

4. Quick changes from aerial play to ground play keep defense shifting and often open more scoring opportunities.

5. Know the game score at all times and, when behind, work toward making the type of goal which will give the most points.

Basic Defense. Basic tactics are as follows:

1. Always keep opponents not playing the ball well marked and be alert to intercept passes.

2. The player with the ball should always be tackled or guarded by the nearest defensive player.

3. Plan and practice a plan for interchanging positions.

4. Attempt to keep two strong lines of defensive players plus the goalkeeper between the oncoming attackers and scoring area.

5. Anticipate what a play will be before it becomes a reality.

---

*For additional suggestions, see Margaret Meyer and Marguerite Schwarz: *Team Sports for Girls and Women,* pp. 328-334.

6. On the kick-off, one fullback should move up near the restraining line to intercept if possible.

SPECIFICS FOR SOCCER

1. On a penalty kick, the halfbacks should stand near the forwards they are marking; the fullbacks stand at the outer edge of the penalty area and on each side of the goal posts. The goalkeeper is on the end line, at the moment of the kick, she defends against the kick with the help of the fullbacks. The halfbacks mark to prevent a rush on the goal.

2. On the corner kick, the two fullbacks should be in the goalkeeper's cage. Two halfbacks should be on the same side of the goal as the ball. The third halfback should be in the opposite area. The forward line should be halfway down the field on their respective sides.

3. On the throw-in, one halfback should mark a wing, the center halfback the inner, and the other halfback the center forward.

4. The goalkeeper must always keep her eye on the ball. She usually stands about 6 feet in front of and slightly left of the center of the goal.

SPECIFICS FOR SPEEDBALL

1. Defensive players must be able to shift from ground defense to aerial defense quickly. Basic soccer defense is used for ground play. Aerial play demands a man-to-man or zone defense similar to basketball.

2. On a penalty kick, defending players should stand behind the end line opposite their opponents and rush out to mark their players as the ball is kicked.

DUTIES AND SPECIFIC SKILLS OF PLAYERS

Goalkeeper. The goalkeeper plays near the goal, usually within the penalty areas in soccer and approximately 4 feet in front of the end line in speedball. She leaves her position to attack an opposing forward *only* if the goal area is protected by a fullback.

SKILLS AND DUTIES

1. Primary responsibility is to keep opponents from scoring.

2. Must possess ability to move quickly at all space levels and in all directions.

3. Must possess alertness and judgment in anticipating players and ball flight.

4. Must possess ability to punt, drop kick and throw for distance.

5. Must not be easily upset or panicked by pressure of onrushing players and close play.

STRATEGY

1. Clear the ball down the side lines.

2. Place the ball as close to own forwards as possible.

3. Take advantage of all the privileges of ball handling and moving allowed the goalkeeper.

4. Take the defense kick if a fullback covers the goal.

Fullbacks. In defense play, each fullback plays primarily in one-half the width of the field around the penalty area. In offensive play, one fullback moves near the restraining line and one remains near the goal.

SKILLS AND DUTIES

1. Mark opposing inners.

2. Must be skillful at anticipating the movement and speed of both players and oncoming balls. Move to intercept or tackle quickly.

3. Must be skillful at trapping, volleying, blocking, passing, and intercepting.

4. Must be bold when it is necessary to tackle near the goal area in order to prevent scoring.

5. Must have the ability to execute long kicks when clearing from the goal area or from a defense kick.

STRATEGY

1. Avoid crowding the goal and avoid obstructing the view of the goalkeeper.

2. Be ready to interchange with halfback near the goal if necessary.

3. Be quick to take defense kick (in soccer) if halfbacks are not ready.

4. On offense, one fullback plays near the restraining line to intercept a clear or defense kick. Quickly return to defensive position if opponents get the ball.

Halfbacks. As both attacking and defensive players, the halfbacks over the entire field. In defensive play, they mark the opposing center forward and wings (the right and left halfbacks may be responsible for opposing inners on kick-off or when play is in the center of the field). In offensive play, they follow 6 to 10 yards behind their own forwards.

SKILLS AND DUTIES

1. On defense, marks opposing players.

On offense, works the ball to the forward line.

2. Must have endurance and be able to run fast, dribble, tackle, intercept, and pass accurately. They also must interchange on defense.

3. Must be alert to the occasional opportunity to shoot and score a goal.

4. Must have a working knowledge of their duties and the ability of their own forwards. Must know when to change from offensive to defensive players and the correct playing position to take at all times.

5. Center halfback must have good judgment and the ability to direct the play of her teammates.

STRATEGY

1. Be alert and ready to take throw-ins, free kicks, and an occasional defense kick.

2. Must be able to make accurate kicks and passes to the side lines and to openings created so that forward line players gain quick possession.

Forward Line. The forward line is made up primarily of attack players who generally play from their own halfback area to the opponents' goal.

SKILLS AND DUTIES

1. Must be made up of fast runners and accurate dribblers and passers. Players must be aggressive and deceptive. Players should have the ability to play the ball with either foot, pass and catch under pressure, and kick, shoot, and trap. They must be alert and quick to convert a ground ball to an aerial ball in speedball.

2. Players must be skilled in taking advantage of and creating spaces for passes by rapid and deceptive moves.

3. Players must be able to feint and dodge effectively.

4. Players must be able to change from offensive to defensive tactics and tackle back quickly and effectively.

STRATEGY

1. Short passes toward the side lines are generally the best method of moving the ball toward opponents' goal; however, the center forward often uses long passes to the wings.

2. Center the ball for most shots to the goal in soccer.

3. In speedball, be alert to the *best* scoring opportunity at the moment. That is, if the

defense is out of position, attempt a field goal; if a single defensive player marking the player with the ball is slow in responding or out of position, a drop kick may be attempted. When the defense moves out to mark a play closely, a forward player should break for the end line and a touchdown pass may be attempted.

4. Never miss an opportunity to kick for goal. Follow each kick.

5. Rush the goalkeeper when the ball is in scoring position.

Terminology

Soccer

Blocking—Using any part of the body except the arms and hands to stop the ball.

Clearing—A throw or kick by the goalkeeper after she has stopped a ball in the vicinity of the goal.

Corner kick—Place kick taken on the goal line by attacking team 5 yards from the nearer corner. It is awarded when the ball is sent over the end line or crossbar by a defending player.

Defense kick—Place kick awarded defending team when the attacking team sends the ball out of bounds over the end line not between or over the goal posts.

Direct free kick—A free kick from which a goal may be scored directly.

Dribble—Short series of foot taps used to move the ball.

Drop kick—Dropping the ball and kicking it as it bounces up from the ground.

Free kick—Awarded to the opposing team when a foul or rule infraction is committed (see rule explanation).

Indirect free kick—A free kick from which a field goal may not be scored directly.

Kick-off—Taken by the center forward, who kicks the ball forward or to the sides, at the beginning of the game, at each quarter, and after each goal is scored.

Marking—A back remains sufficiently close to the opposing forward for whom she is responsible in order to intercept a pass, to tackle—should the forward gain possession of the ball—or to prevent the execution of a pass.

Off-side—An infringement that occurs when a player is nearer the opponent's goal line than the ball and fewer than three opponents between the player and the goal. It occurs only in the opponent's half of the field.

Penalty kick—A place kick taken on the penalty kick mark 12 yards from the center of the goal. It is awarded when any member of the defending team fouls in the penalty area.

Place kick—Kicking the ball from a stationary ground position without touching or picking it up with the hands.

Punt—Dropping the ball and kicking it with the top of the foot before it touches the ground.

Tackle—Method of getting the ball away from an opponent without body contact.

Throw-in—Method of putting the ball in play after it has gone out of bounds over the side line.

Trapping—Stopping and gaining control of the ball by use of a foot, one or both legs, or the body.

Volleying—Kicking, kneeing, or otherwise contacting the ball while it is in the air.

Speedball*

Aerial ball—A ball raised into the air by a kick with one or both feet or a thrown ball that has not touched the ground.

Attackers—The team having possession of the ball.

Defenders—The team members who seek to gain possession of the ball.

End goal—A ball that crosses the end line not between the goal posts. It does not count for a score in girls' rules.

Foul—A rule infraction for which a free or penalty kick is given.

Ground ball—A moving or stationery ball on the ground. It may be converted to an aerial ball only by the use of the feet.

Intercept—Catching a pass, a drop kick, or dribble, or getting a passed ball intended for a player on the opposing team.

Kick-off—The way the game is started at its beginning, at each quarter, and after each scored goal. It is done with one foot and is a pass to another player.

Passing—Advancing the ball downfield as in basketball.

Trapping—Stopping a moving ball with the body or one or both feet.

Volley—Playing the ball with the head or any part of the body except the hands, forearms, and feet before it touches the ground. This does not convert a ground ball into an aerial ball.

Selected Audio-visual Aids

Beginning Soccer, 1962. (3 filmstrips, sound, color.) The Athletic Institute, 805 Merchandise Mart, Chicago, Illinois 60654. (Purchase and rental.)

Fundamentals of Soccer, 1964. (16 mm., 13 min., sound, b & w and color.) All American Productions and Publishers, Box 91, Greeley, Colorado. (Purchase and rental.)

Soccer for Girls, 1962. (11 min., sound, b & w.) Coronet Instructional Films, 65 East South Water Street, Chicago, Illinois.

Soccer: The Universal Game. (10 min., sound, b & w.) Hollywood Pan-American Films, 5356 La Mirada Avenue, Hollywood 25, California. (Purchase and rental.)

---

*For speedball examination see Phyllis Roney's A written knowledge examination for speedball in *Soccer-Speedball Guide*, 1958-1960, pp. 91-94, and Rosabel Koss's Speedball quiz in *Soccer-Speedball Guide*, 1964-1966, pp. 100-105.

Speed-A-Way. (b & w.) Marjorie S. Larsen, 1754 Middle-field Road, Stockton, California 95204. (Purchase and rental.)

Speedball for Girls, 1948. (16 mm., 11 min., sound, b & w and color.) Coronet Instructional Films, 65 East South Water Street, Chicago, Illinois. (Purchase and rental.)

Suggested Readings

DiClements, C. L.:*Soccer Illustrated.* New York, The Ronald Press Company, 1955.

Hupprich, Florence L.: *Soccer and Speedball for Girls.* Cranbury, N.J., A. S. Barnes & Co., Inc., 1942.

Meyer, Margaret, and Schwarz, Marguerite: *Team Sports for Girls and Women.* 4th ed. Philadelphia, W. B. Saunders Company, 1965.

Sevy, Ruth: *Selected Soccer and Speedball Articles.* second ed. AAHPER, D.G.W.S., 1201 16th Street, N. W., Washington, D.C. 20006.

Soccer-Speedball Guide. Current ed. AAHPER, D.G.W.S., 1201 16th Street, N. W., Washington, D.C. 20006.

Suggested Study Questions

1. Make a chart with three headings to show the qualifications, specific duties, and areas of the field each should cover for all players on a soccer or speedball team.
2. Some girls are reluctant to play goalkeeper, How would you go about "selling" them on the advantages of playing this position?
3. Draw a sketch showing all player positions for (a) a penalty kick; (b) corner kick; and (c) a kick off.
4. How does one convert a ground ball to an aerial ball in speedball?
5. What are the major differences in the games of soccer, speedball, and speed-a-way?

CHAPTER TWENTY-FIVE

Courtesy of Rice University, Houston, Texas.

SOFTBALL AND SLOW PITCH SOFTBALL

National Ass. for Girls & Women in Sports

Like many other truly American sports, softball just "growed" like Topsy. Softball, so popular with youth and adults in the schools and playgrounds, is a direct descendent of Abner Doubleday's game of baseball. A game of indoor baseball was originated in 1887 by George W. Hancock of the Farragut Boat Club in Chicago. Originally played with a broom as a bat and a boxing glove ball, the game drew on the skills of Rounders, Barn Ball, and One Old Cat. As the game attracted enthusiastic followers Hancock devised rules and provided a large softball and a small-headed bat.

Variations of the game were played under the names of Mush Ball, Pumpkin Ball, and Kitten Ball. Recreation groups moved the sport outdoors under the title of playground ball, and here it gained its greatest popularity as a sport suitable for men and women in an area smaller than that required for baseball.

In recent years still another variation has gained popularity. *Slow-pitch softball* is enthusiastically played by beginners and recreational players. The slow arching delivery, rather than a fast, skillfully placed pitch, equalizes the opportunity of play for the average person.

Softball was officially adopted in 1933 after the first national tournament in Chicago. Walter A. Hakanson of the Denver Y.M.C.A. is credited with naming the present-day game. Since 1927, when the American Physical Education Association adopted softball rules for girls as drawn up by Gladys Palmer, the National Section for Girls and Women's Sports, now the Division for Girls and Women's Sports, has continued its interest in rule development. The Division publishes the rules and strives to insure playing standards for the pleasure and safety of the participants.

The American Softball Association promotes softball through clinics, information services, and sponsored tournaments. In 1951 a Softball Hall of Fame was established to honor outstanding players. In 1950 the International Softball Federation was formed and since that time has encouraged the growth of softball as an international competitive activity. Recently accepted as a sport in the Pan-American Games, softball looks forward to a role in the Olympic games in the years ahead.

Softball is one of the few team games that readily lends itself to informal, co-recreational settings. Played at picnics, play days, backyard gatherings, and in competitive leagues, the game is satisfying to both men and women of all skill and experience levels. It is estimated that 11 million people in 30 countries are softball players; five and a half million of these are in the United States.

NATURE AND PURPOSE OF THE GAME

Like baseball, softball is a game using throwing, batting, catching and running skills by two opposing teams on a diamond-shaped field. Each team of nine players alternates turns at bat and in the field throughout a regulation game of seven innings. Teams remain in the offensive (batting) position until the defending (fielding) team succeeds in getting three of the team members out. Each team member has a specific position to play when on the defense. They are catcher, pitcher, first baseman, second baseman, third baseman, shortstop, right fielder, center fielder, and left fielder. Each position is primarily responsible for covering a specific area of the field (see Fig. 25-1).

Game play begins with one team in fielding position and the other team at "home," one team member preparing to bat. The pitcher, in preparation for delivering the ball, stands squarely facing the batter. She has both feet in contact with the pitcher's plate and holds the ball in front of the body in both hands. The ball is delivered toward the batting area with an underhanded motion so that the hand is below the hip and the wrist no farther

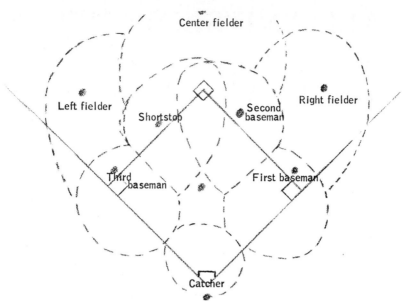

Fig. 25-1. Position play.

from the body than the elbow. The pitcher may take one step toward the batter during the delivery.

The batter attempts to hit the pitched ball with the bat so that the ball travels into the fair territory of the diamond and outfield area. The pitcher attempts to throw the ball so that it is difficult to hit or, if hit, is easily fielded by her defending teammates. They are positioned in the field to catch the ball on the fly, bounce, or roll, and get the batter out.

A player in batting position is "out" if she swings and misses three times, fails to hit after three called strikes, bunts foul after the second strike, hits a fair or foul ball that is caught, or is put out at first base. When the ball is hit foul (and is not caught), the batter may remain at bat.

If the batter is successful in hitting into fair territory, she attempts to run to first, second, third, and home to score a run. She does not have to run all the bases on her own hit, but may stop safely at any of the first three bases and await a teammate's hit to drive her forward. The defensive team tries to tag the baserunner or get the ball to a base ahead of the runner in order to force her out. Players who advance around the bases score runs and further the real team objective of winning the game by scoring more runs than the opponents.

FACILITIES AND EQUIPMENT

Field. A softball game requires a level, unobstructed field area within a radius of 200 feet from home plate between the foul lines. There should be at least 25 unobstructed feet between home plate and the backstop and outside the foul lines. The diamond has 60 foot base lines with a pitching distance of 40 feet (46 feet for men). The field should be free from rocks and holes, and the diamond should be placed so that the players do not have to look directly into the sun.

Figure 25-2 shows the basic layout and

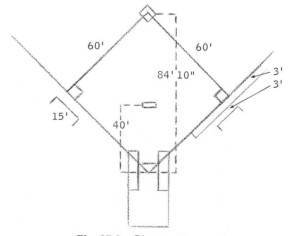

Fig. 25-2. Diamond layout.

Fig. 25-3. Glove and mitts.

measurements of the diamond with:

1. Three foot lines parallel to first base.
2. The batter's box, measuring 3 by 7 feet.
3. The catcher's box, 10 feet by 8 feet, 5 inches.
4. The two 15 foot coaches' boxes.

Balls. Although 14 to 16 inch balls are used indoors and for slow pitch softball, the official softball must measure between $11\frac{7}{8}$ and $12\frac{1}{8}$ inches in circumference. It may weigh between 6 and $6\frac{3}{4}$ ounces. The exterior is smooth horsehide or cowhide seamed with concealed stitches. The center is kapok, cork, or rubber, covered with yarn. The hide cover is glued over the round ball. Rubber-covered balls are often used for practice on damp ground.

Bats. Official bats are made of solid hardwood or laminated wood and must be no longer than 34 inches or more than $2\frac{1}{8}$ inches in diameter at the largest part. Weight is a matter of player preference. A safety grip, at least 10 inches long and of cork, tape, or composition material should not extend more than 15 inches from the small end of the bat. The bat should be marked "Official Softball."

Gloves and Mitts. Protective hand covering that aids in skill development is recommended for all defensive players. Only the catcher and first baseman are allowed to wear mitts — i.e., gloves without separated fingers. The catcher's mitt is heavily padded with a deep pocket, while the first baseman's mitt (often called the claw) is less padded and more flexible. Fingered gloves worn by all other players should be of soft horse, cow, or elk hide. No top lacing, webbing, or other device between the thumb and body of a fielder's glove or first baseman's mitt can be more than 4 inches in length.

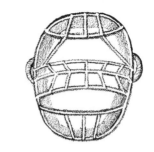

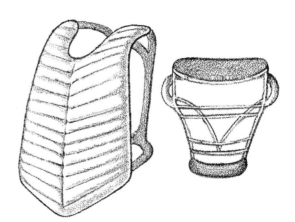

Fig. 25-4. Protective equipment.

Masks and Body Protectors. These must be worn by the catcher and plate umpire. Wire masks are padded with sponge rubber or hair and are adjustable for all players. Body protectors are usually kapok, covered with a dark canvas or check so that the ball is visible against the background. Knickers or full-length slacks should be worn for protection.

Shoes. Canvas-topped or leather-topped shoes with smooth soles or soft or hard rubber cleats may be worn. Metal cleats may be worn, if they are no more than $\frac{3}{4}$ of an inch in length.

Plate and Bases. Home plate is a five-sided figure, made of rubber or comparable material, 17 inches across the edge facing the pitcher. When laid, the 8½ inch sides are parallel to the inside lines of the batter's box. The sides of the point facing the catcher are 12 inches long.

The pitcher's plate is a 24 by 6 inch section of wood or rubber which is placed level with the top of the ground. The front of the plate is 40 feet from the outside point of home plate.

First, second, and thrid base are 15 inch padded squares of hair or felt covered by heavy canvas. Each base has a strap underneath to hold it securely to the ground.

Care of Equipment. Softball equipment is easily maintained and stored. Bats should be wiped, rough edges should be sanded and the wood treated with linseed oil prior to storage. Grips should be repaired or replaced with leather or cork. Store in a dry room at constant temperature.

Leather balls should not be used on damp ground as they absorb water and become misshapen when hit. Both rubber-covered and leather-covered balls should be stitched immediately when split.

Gloves, masks, and body protectors should be hung for rapid drying. All leather surfaces should be cleaned and treated with neat's-foot oil to prevent hardening and cracking.

The pitcher's plate and home plate should be pulled from the ground and stored in a cool place. Canvas-covered bases should be removed after every game to prevent water damage. After brushing and reshaping, they should be stored flat to insure longer life.

BASIC SKILLS

Softball skills require quick reaction time, agility in fielding, accuracy in throwing and hitting, and speed in running. These skills are developed in many activities but are refined for the game of softball only through practice and playing the game.

Catching. The player should be mentally and physically alert so that she can quickly position herself for the catch. The catching position depends both on the height and speed of the ball and the throw the fielder wants to make.

The catching player moves to meet an ap-proaching ball. If the ball is going over the fielder's head, she turns and runs with her back to the ball, looking over her shoulder. (This is faster than running backward.) The height at which the catch is made determines the direction of the fingers. Both hands reach for the ball. The fingers and arms are relaxed and the hands slightly cupped. As the ball hits the glove hand the fingers squeeze and the free hand closes on the top so that the ball is trapped. The ball is caught in the glove pocket, slightly to the thumb side. The hands and arms "give" with the impact of the ball, cushioning the catch.

If possible, the ball should be caught above the waist to facilitate throwing. The fingers point upward and the thumbs are together. For catches below the waist, fingers point downward and the little fingers are together.

Throwing. Throwing is one of the essential skills for a softball player.

OVERARM THROW. This should be a basic skill of all players as it is the fastest and most accurate of all means of ball propulsion. For the right-handed player, the ball is held in the right hand with the first two fingers on top of the ball, the third and fourth fingers spread comfortably to the side with the thumb supporting under the ball. Do not allow any part of the palm to touch the ball.

With the feet in stride position, the weight equally distributed, and the left foot forward, the left shoulder turns toward the target, moving the body at right angles away from the target. As the right arm moves back to a position behind the head at about ear level, the weight shifts to the rear leg. The elbow points away from the body with the upper arm parallel to the ground. The wrist is

Fig. 25-5. Overarm throw.

cocked backward. On the release the forward leg extends in the direction of the target, the shoulders turn parallel to the target as the body rotates, the hips move forward, and the arm is brought forward in a semicircular motion. The hand passes forward past the ear, the elbow straightens, the wrist uncocks, and the ball rolls off the first two fingers. The power of the swing carries the arm down and across the body, rotating the body so that the shoulder of the throwing arm points toward the target.

UNDERARM WHIP THROW.   The underarm throw is used for a quick throw when there is little time to stand or to take a full backswing after fielding a grounder. The ball is held with the thumb on top. The first and second fingers are under the ball, and the third and fourth fingers are on the side of the ball. The body is crouching more than for the overarm throw, and the ball is held below shoulder level. The arm swings back, bent elbow restricting backswing, parallel to the ground, wrist cocked. The forward foot extends and the arm swings across the body at waist level as the body follows.

Pitching.   The well controlled delivery of a ball into the strike zone is one of the highly individualized skills of softball. The pitcher stands on the plate squarely, facing the batter with the ball held in both hands. She must remain motionless for a minimum of 1 and a maximum of 20 seconds before removing one hand. She may use either a slingshot (basic pitch) or a windmill delivery.

BASIC PITCH.   The ball is held in a tripod; the tips of the thumb, index and middle fingers over the seams. It is pushed forward above waist level as the trunk rotates to the right to allow a full backswing and the arm circles downward and backward. While delivering the ball the pitcher may take only one step, which must be toward the batter and taken as the delivery is made. The ball must be delivered with an underhanded motion, the release and follow-through forward, beyond the straight line of the body. "The hand shall be below the hip and the wrist not farther from the body than the elbow."*

On the delivery, the right arm of a right-handed player swings forward as a step is taken with the left foot. The arm follows through in line with the pitch, elbow straight, and the ball rolling off the ends of the fingers. On the follow-through, the right foot moves parallel with the left in a side stride position. Power is gained from a full arm swing, elbow extension and wrist snap, and from body rotation.

For a windmill delivery, the pitching arm makes a complete circle, beginning either in front of the body or on the side. The arm moves rapidly forward, passing straight overhead, then downward away from the batter, then finally forward in the direction of the batter. As the throwing arm moves forward, body weight is shifted to the foot on the pitching arm side. As the ball passes overhead, the right-handed pitcher lifts her left foot slightly in preparation for a step forward. Stepping forward on the left foot braces the body as the pitching arm is thrust forward for the release. The right leg pushes

---

*D.G.W.S.: *Softball Guide*, 1968-1970, p. 117.

Fig. 25-6.   Basic pitch.

against the rubber to transfer weight and add momentum to the swing.

Once a straight pitch is mastered, pitchers should learn other deliveries. The grip and the type and amount of spin the pitcher gives the ball determine its curve, rise, or drop.

DROP BALL.   The ball is held with the thumb to the right, the first three fingers to the left and the little finger back. The palm faces the batter on the delivery and the ball is released with an upward motion of the hand. The ball rolls off the three fingers with a forward spin.

RISE BALL.   The ball is held with the thumb underneath, first and second fingers on top, third and fourth fingers slightly to the left. On the delivery the knuckles are forward. The wrist snaps upward, the fingers pull and the thumb pushes, resulting in a backspin on the ball. When properly executed, the ball rises near the plate.

OUTCURVE.   The palm is turned toward the left as the ball is held in a triangle formed by the thumb and first and second fingers. On the release the second finger is away from the ball. The wrist is snapped sharply to the left, thrusting the ball out of the little finger side of the hand. The ball curves from right to the left — away from a right-handed hitter.

INCURVE.   This pitch curves toward a right-handed batter. The ball is gripped between the thumb and first two fingers. On the release the wrist is snapped from left to right.

Fielding.   Fielding involves the basic skills of catching and throwing. As the ball is hit the fielder moves from a waiting position to a ready position to receive it. At the "crack" of the bat she moves rapidly to position herself. She watches the ball in flight or on the ground and waits to field it with feet in side stride, weight evenly distributed on the balls of the feet and the knees and hips slightly bent.

FIELDING GROUND BALLS.   With the upper body nearly erect, the fielder bends the knees to get down to the ball. The hips are low and the weight is over the feet until the ball is scooped up by the fingers and wrists. If the ball is bouncing, the catch is made as it rises. The fingertips should be touching the ground ready to rise with the bounce. The palm of the left hand is at right angles to the path of the ball, the right hand next to it with little fingers together. The right hand snaps over the left to hold the caught ball, and the natural "give" of the fielding action starts the backswing for a whip or sidearm throw.

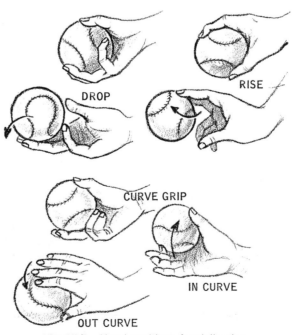

Fig. 25-7. Hand positions for deliveries.

Fig. 25-8. Mastery of the correct grip, stance, stride, and swing is fundamental to success in softball. (Courtesy of College of Health, Physical Education and Recreation, Texas Woman's University, Denton, Texas.)

CATCHING FLY BALLS.   Whenever possible flies should be caught at shoulder level. A catch at this level prevents the fielder from blocking her own vision and puts her in a position for a rapid throw. The fielder tries to position herself so that she will be standing (not running) when the catch is made. The fingers are pointed up, thumbs together, with the palm of the glove hand facing the ball. If the fly is caught at the right shoulder, the hands, arms, and body give backward and are the beginning motion of the backswing preceding the throw. While awaiting the fly, the feet point in the direction of ball flight, and as the ball is caught the trunk turns to the right and the right leg moves back to take the impact. The weight then shifts through to the forward left foot as the throw is made.

Batting.   This is an individual's basic offensive skill. Understanding the basic grip, stance, stride, and swing is fundamental to developing one's own style.

GRIP.   The standard grip is used by most players. A right-handed player places her left hand around the bat several inches above the end. The right hand is placed above the left and touches it. The natural grip is firm but not tense. The second joints of the fingers of the top hand are aligned with the knuckles of the lower hand. Batters attempting a power hit often use the end grip, bringing the hands as far down on the bat as possible. For more accurate and less powerful hits a player may

Fig. 25-9. Hand alignment.

move her hands up the handle of the bat. This "choke" grip is particularly useful to a player who swings late because of weak arm and shoulder strength.

STANCE.   A comfortable, natural stance is taken in the batter's box. The distance from the plate is gauged by the individual's reach and swing. Feet are comfortably spread and knees are relaxed to support the upright trunk facing the plate. The bat is held up and back by an almost straight left arm and a bent right arm. The elbow of the right arm is pointing toward the ground and away from the batter. The batter looks over her left shoulder toward the pitcher.

STRIDE.   Just before the ball reaches the strike zone the batter slides her left leg several inches toward the pitcher. The body moves forward as the swing begins.

SWING.   The bat moves forward in a level plane as the hitter watches the ball moving toward the plate. The hips pivot forward and the body turns toward the pitcher with the bat moving rapidly forward. As the bat meets the ball the arms extend and the wrists snap and roll into the follow-through. As the hands and wrists roll, the body weight shifts to the forward foot. Near the completion of the follow-through the hands are completely over, with the back of right hand uppermost; and the right foot, free of body weight, strides toward first base.

Fig. 25-10.   Stance and swing.

Bunting.   A bunt is a well placed ball that is tapped onto the infield, usually along the first or third base line. It should be a deceptive hit; therefore, the batter should keep her regular batting stance as long as possible. As the pitched ball moves toward the plate the batter pivots on the balls of her feet so that her body and toes turn toward the pitcher. Simultaneously, she slides her right hand up and behind the middle of the bat. (Some batters can bunt effectively with their hands remaining in a "choked grip" position). The bat is in front of the player and parallel to the ground so that the incoming ball is blocked by the bat. There is *no* swing as the head of the bat is turned in the direction of the bunt.

To execute a "drag" bunt along the first base line, the player starts toward first base and *then* contacts the ball late with her bat extended behind her. She pulls the ball along as she runs for first base.

Fig. 25-11.   Bunting.

Base Running.   A batter takes her first stride toward first base as the ball is hit. Short strides and vigorous arm action lead her into a full stride as she crosses first base. Once on base, the runner may stand with one foot on base in a sprinter's start, ready to leave when the ball is pitched. A player can observe the action of the game better if she places her left foot on base and faces the infield. With her feet in side stride position she is slightly crouched, with her weight over the right foot. The runner's arms hang freely down and away from the body to aid in balance and in shift of body weight. The runner takes two or three strides from the base in anticipation of a hit, wild pitch, or catcher's error. If none occurs she returns to base and assumes the starting position. (For a more complete treatment see the section on offensive strategy.)

Stealing.   Stealing bases is a way a base runner may advance on weak defensive plays. Steals most often occur as the ball is missed by the catcher, overthrown at a base, or held too long by a fielder, or as a play is made at another base. Stealing should be done in the interest of team play rather than as a spectacular individual feat.

Sliding.   This is a skill for *advanced players* who are properly dressed in slacks or trousers. Sliding helps runners to evade a tag at second and third base and home and serves as a method of stopping to avoid overrunning second and third base. The two most common slides are the straight and the hook.

STRAIGHT SLIDE.   The straight slide begins from a full stride as the runner tries to avoid a high tag or throw. The take-off leg bends, lowering the body, as the top leg extends directly toward the base. Both legs come together and slide to the base. A quick recovery should be made if the player sees an opportunity to advance farther.

HOOK SLIDE. The hook slide is used to avoid a low tag or to stop an overrun. The base runner goes wide, rather than directly to the base, and extends her right leg so that she slides on the thigh. The left leg bends back and toward the base so that the left foot hooks on the corner of the bag. Both slides should be started early so that the body does not strike the bag at full power.

Fig. 25-12. Hook slide.

SIMPLIFIED GAME RULES AND SCORING*

An official game consists of seven innings. An inning is a portion of the game within which the two teams alternate on offense and defense and in which there are three outs for each team. A full seven innings need not be played if the team second at bat has more runs in six innings or before the third out in the seventh inning. A game tied at the end of seven innings shall continue until one team has more runs at the end of a complete inning or until the team second at bat has scored more runs.

Each team of nine players may have substitutes. Once a player is removed she may not re-enter the game as a player.

The following simplified rules cover the most frequent situations:

Strike. This is called when any of the following situations occurs:

1. A batter swings at a pitched ball and misses.

✳ 2. A pitched ball is delivered over home

_____
*For details of rules and scoring see the D.G.W.S. *Softball Guide.*

plate between the top of the knees and the armpits of the batter.

3. A fly ball goes foul and is not caught, and the batter has less than 2 strikes.

4. A foul tip that remains lower than the batter's head is caught by the catcher.

5. A batter with less than 2 strikes is hit by her own batted ball.

Ball. A ball is any of the following:

1. A pitched ball that does not go over the plate in the strike zone and at which the batter does not swing.

2. A ball that touches the ground before reaching home plate.

3. An illegally pitched ball.

Fair Hit Ball. This is a legally batted ball that:

1. Settles or is touched on fair ground in the infield.

2. Is on fair ground going out of the infield.

3. Touches first, second, or third base.

4. Lands in the outfield in fair territory between the extended lines from home to first and home to third.

5. Lands behind a fence or in a stand at a distance of more than 200 feet from home plate after traveling on or over fair ground.

Foul Ball. A batted ball is foul if:

1. It settles in foul territory between home and first base or between home and third base.

2. It first touches on foul ground beyond first or third base.

3. It bounds past first or third on or over foul ground.

Batter Out. Batter is out when:

1. The third strike is *caught* by the catcher.

2. She has 3 strikes, there are less than 2 outs, and first base is occupied.

3. She swings at and misses the third strike and the ball touches her.

4. She bunts foul after the second strike.

5. A foul ball is legally caught.

6. She hits an infield fly with base runners on first and second or on first, second, and third with less than two outs. (This is the *infield fly rule.*)

Base Runner Out. She is out when:

1. The catcher drops the third strike but the runner is touched with the ball by a fielder before touching first base.

2. The ball reaches first base and is caught and held before the runner reaches base.

3. She is tagged with the ball before reaching first base or at any time when not in contact with a base.

4. Her fly ball is caught.

5. She interferes with a fielder trying to field a ball.

6. When running to any base, she runs more than 3 feet outside a baseline.

7. She is forced out at base.

8. She passes another base runner.

9. She leaves her base before the ball leaves the pitcher's hand.

10. She fails to return to her base before the ball reaches the baseman following a fair fly that is caught.

11. She is hit by a fair batted ball while off base before it is touched by or passes a fielding player.

SLOW-PITCH SOFTBALL

There are several variations of the basic rules of slow-pitch softball, but the rules adopted by the International Joint Rules Committee on Softball are the most commonly used. The game is designed to eliminate the important offensive softball skill of highly effective pitching. The rules of softball are generally applicable; the major rule differences are as follows:

1. The pitcher must deliver the ball with moderate speed underhand, below the hip, with a perceptible arch of at least 3 feet before the ball reaches home plate. The umpire is the sole judge of compliance with this rule.

2. There are *ten* players on a team. The additional player is called the short fielder and usually plays between center field and second base.

3. Bunting and chopping the ball are illegal. They result in an out for the batter.

4. Runners are not allowed to steal bases. A runner may leave her base when the pitch has reached or passed home plate.

Although an official softball is used, a 14 or 16 inch ball is popular with some groups. When a larger ball is used, gloves and mitts are not used by the defensive team.

SCORING

The official scorer has a unique responsibility in softball. She has the authority to make all decisions involving judgment on a play as long as there is no conflict with the official playing rules or the umpire's decision.

The box score is the summary of all action of a player in a game. It is helpful to understand this chart, as a similar form is often used by newspapermen to report the results of baseball and softball games.

The score may be kept in the following manner:

1. Each player's name and position are listed in the order in which she bats or is supposed to bat.

2. The next column (AB) indicates the number of times player is at bat. No turn at bat is charged to player if she hits a sacrifice bunt or fly, is awarded a base on four balls or on called interference or obstruction, or is hit by a pitched ball.

3. Column R indicates the number of runs player scores.

4. Column H is for the number of safe hits.

5. Column PO: number of putouts made by player.

Player	P	AB	R	H	PO	A	E	RBI

P   Position of the player indicated by numbers

1. catcher   5. third baseman
2. pitcher   6. shortstop
3. first baseman   7. leftfielder
4. second baseman   8. centerfielder
9. rightfielder

Fig. 25-13. Box score.

6. Column A: number of assists for put-outs by player.

7. Column E: number of errors made.

8. Column RBI: number of runs batted in by player.

Summary information that must be tabulated after every game includes the score by innings, and final score; runs batted in, and by whom; two and three base hits and home runs; bases stolen, and by whom; sacrifice bunts and flies, and by whom; number of double and triple plays and players participating in them; number of persons left on base; number of bases on balls, batters struck out, and hits and runs given or allowed by the pitcher; winning and losing pitchers; number of wild pitches and passed balls; players hit by pitched balls; the length of the game and the number of innings pitched by each pitcher; and the names of the umpire and scorers.

GAME STRATEGY

The mental concentration and preplanning involved in softball strategy make the game more than a hitting-pitching contest between two teams.

Offensive Strategy. This is built around batting and base-running skills of individuals combined to make a team contribution.

1. The order of batting is one of the first strategic moves a team plans. Generally, the lead-off batter is one who can get on base; the second, a fair hitter and bunter; third, a consistent hitter; fourth, the strongest and longest hitter, who can advance base runners. The weakest hitters hold the seventh, eighth, and last position.

2. Place hitting is more important to a team offensive than inconsistent, spasmodic hits. Generally, a low ball placed straight away through second base serves as a hit. This "spot" is not advised if a runner is on first base, as a weak hit is a perfect set-up for a defensive double play.

3. Bunts and sacrifice flies serve to advance players to scoring position, but both usually result in an out for the hitter. The sacrifice bunt is used when runners are on first, or first and second, and there are no outs. The hitter places the bunt down the first or third base line and tries to "beat it out" to first.

4. Base runners must be alert to the position of all other runners and to any plays called for runners. A few simple guides help the player to anticipate her moves. She should run as fast as possible for first base, touching it and overrunning it along the right field line. If she can advance more than one base on her hit, she moves into foul territory before reaching first and turns toward second base.

The runner must not overrun second or third base. Some teachers suggest the slide for close plays; however, it should be avoided if players' legs are not protected. Players should learn to "pull up short" from a rapid pace without abrupt muscle jerks.

Runners must not lead off bases until the pitcher releases the ball.

On fly balls, other than with two outs, runners advance a safe distance toward the next base so that they can return to their original bases if the ball is caught, or be ready to advance if the ball is dropped. When a fly is hit deep and the runner has time to advance after the ball is caught, she may hold near her base, touch, and then advance. On a fly ball with two out, all runners should advance rapidly, hoping that the ball will be missed.

Runners should advance on wild pitches, overthrows to bases, or a ball dropped by the catcher.

These additional plays are helpful for a basic team offensive:

1. *Double Steal.* Attempted with runners on first and third and one out. The runners on first start a steal. If the ball moves to second base, the runner pulls up and acts as a decoy as the runner on third tries for home. If no play is made at second base, the runner from first advances.

2. *Hit and Run.* A signal from the coach or batter indicates that an attempt will be made to hit the next pitched ball and the base runner thus has additional seconds to run to the next base.

3. *Squeeze Play.* An attempt to score a runner from third by giving the runner a signal indicating a bunt down the first baseline. The base runner moves toward home with the pitch.

Defensive Strategy. A strong team defense depends on individual skills and player cooperation. Strategy is best learned by actual situations that occur during a game. The fielding team must always anticipate and preplan; positioning in the field depends

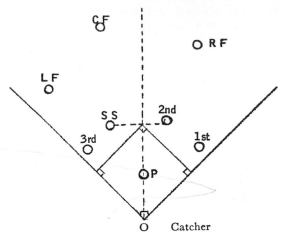

Fig. 25-14. Defensive positions.

upon the offensive situation. For example:

1. Normal playing position (see Fig. 25-14) is assumed when there are no base runners and a straightaway hitter is at bat. Fielders shift to their left for left-handed batters.

2. To combat a sacrifice bunt, the pitcher and first and third basemen move in to field the ball as the second baseman prepares to cover first base.

3. Double play positioning, with a runner on first, brings the first baseman closer to the first baseline as second and third basemen move toward their bases and shortstop moves several steps toward the batter.

Further defensive hints include the following:

1. If possible, put out the runner who is closest to home plate.

2. Make the third out at the nearest and surest point.

3. Consider walking a strong batter when runners are on base and a weak hitter follows.

4. When a runner leaves the base before a fly is caught, attempt a double play by throwing to the base the runner just left. If the runner leaves the base after the fly is caught, throw the ball to the base toward which the runner is advancing.

5. When a runner is on third base, the catcher should not throw the ball to second in order to catch a runner who is stealing. The runner on third may score if the ball is thrown.

DUTIES AND SPECIFIC SKILLS OF PLAYERS

Catcher. Catching is one of the most important and demanding positions on the de-

fending team. The catcher must be able to catch all varieties of pitches, foul tips and pop flies. She must also be able to move quickly and to throw accurately and rapidly to all bases. The catcher is important if pitching signals are used. She evaluates the batter's ability and characteristics and signals for the pitch.

In preparation for the pitch the catcher assumes a semi-erect position directly behind the plate as close to the batter as is possible for safety. The body bends forward, feet parallel. The mitt hand is up as a target for the pitcher, and the right hand is close and ready to close over the ball as it hits the glove. Like all basemen, when making a play at the plate she moves one foot to the corner and stretches to meet the ball so as not to interfere with the runner. The catcher should back up plays at first and third base as the situation demands.

Pitcher. The pitcher must master delivery of a well controlled ball. Her deliveries should include fast balls, curve balls, and slow balls that effectively cross the plate in an area approximately 2 feet above the ground, 3 feet high and 17 inches wide. Aside from fielding hits, she should cover home on a wild pitch or passed ball when runners are on base; cover first or third on hits to these basemen when a base runner is moving toward the base. Pitchers soon learn to throw fast balls to late swinging batters, inside curves to batters crowding the plate, outside curves to those standing away or stepping into the swing, and balls above the waist to batters attempting a bunt.

First Baseman. A tall player with a good reach and ability to catch all types of throws is descriptive of a potential first baseman. She must play off base and field balls with general infield ability, and then place a foot on first base and reach for throws. She must develop a quick pivot and throwing motion to all other bases for effective double plays.

Second Baseman. She must move rapidly and throw accurately to all bases from many fielding positions. She is responsible for the area toward first base, as well as for covering second base on attempted steals and most hits.

Shortstop. The shortstop must be a versatile player of unusual speed. She is positioned between second and third base and receives many hits from right-handed batters. She backs up the pitcher on hits to the mound, and third base on throws from the outfield. She also covers second base when the baseman is fielding.

Third Baseman.   The third baseman plays slightly toward second base for a straightaway hitter. She is resposible for bunts, flies, fouls, and hits in her area (See Figure 25-2). She must be able to throw accurately and fast to first base and recover her position quickly.

Outfielders.   An outfielder must be able to move rapidly to field balls and to throw far and accurately. The center fielder has more territory and should move faster than the left or right fielder. The fielders back up the bases when ground hits come in front of them. The center fielder backs up both other outfielders; the left fielder backs up the infield on hits to the left of the diamond; the right fielder backs up the center fielder and infielders to the right.

Terminology

Appeal play — A play upon which an umpire cannot make a decision until requested by a player. The appeal must be made before the pitcher's next delivery.

Assist — A credit awarded each player who handles the ball in a series of plays that results in a base runner's being put out.

Base on balls — A walk. The batter is allowed to take a position as a base runner on first base when four balls are called before she hits, strikes out, or is put out.

Battery — The pitcher and the catcher.

Batting average — A percentage that indicates a batter's effectiveness at hitting. It is determined by dividing the number of hits by the number of turns at bat.

Double — A two-base hit.

Double play — A defensive play that results in two outs as a result of continuous action.

Earned run — A run scored by a player who reaches first base in any legal manner other than an error made by the defending team.

Error — A misplay on a ball that the scorer rules as avoidable, resulting in advancement of base runner or prolonged life of the batter.

Fielder's choice — An option that a fielder makes in playing a ball — to retire the base runner rather than the hitter.

Fungo hitting — Batter tosses the ball and hits it to fielder for practice.

Hot corner — Third base.

Infield fly — A fly to the infield which is caught or, in the opinion of the umpire, could easily by caught by an infielder.

Inning — One of seven sections of the game in which teams alternate offensive and defensive turns.

Interference — The act of hindering a batter by a defensive player; or an act by an offensive player which impedes or hinders a defensive player who is executing a play.

Keystone sack — Second base.

Line drive — An aerial ball batted sharply and directly into the field.

No hitter — A game in which one team was unable to make a safe hit.

Obstruction — An act by a fielder not in possession of the ball or in the act of fielding a batted ball which physically impedes a base runner.

Pass — A walk or a base given by delivering four balls.

Sacrifice — A bunt, fly, or hit intended to advance the base runner that results in an out for the hitter.

Single — A one-base hit.

Squeeze play — Bringing a player home from third base on a bunt.

Stolen base — A surprise advance to a base closer to scoring position made by a base runner unaided by a hit, error, or putout.

Texas leaguer — A fly ball that drops between infielders and that cannot be successfully fielded.

Triple — A three base hit.

Selected Audio-visual Aids

Beginning Softball. 1954. (8 filmstrips, color.) The Athletic Institute, 805 Merchandise Mart, Chicago, Ill. 60054 (Purchase.)

Fundamentals of Softball Pitching. (12 min., 16 mm., b & w, silent.) United World Films, Inc., 1445 Park Avenue, New York, N.Y. 10029 (Rental and purchase.)

Girls, Let's Learn Softball. (20 min., 16 mm., b & w, sound.) United World Films, Inc., 1445 Park Ave., New York, N.Y. 10029. (Rental and purchase.)

Softball Rules for Girls. 1956. (6 unit filmstrips with captions, color.) School Film Service, 549 W. 123rd St., New York, N.Y. (Purchase.)

Softball Fundamentals. (12 min., 16 mm., b & w, sound.) Young America Films, Inc., 18 East 41st Street, New York, N.Y. 10017. (Purchase and rental.)

Suggested Readings

AAHPER: *Official Softball Guide*, Current Ed., Division for Girls and Women's Sports. 1201 16th Street, N.W., Washington, D.C. 20036.

Kneer, Marian, and McCord, Charles: *Softball*, Dubuque, Iowa, William C. Brown Company, 1966.

Kneer, Marian (Editor): *Selected Softball Articles*, Division for Girls and Women's Sports, 1201 16th Street, N.W., Washington, D.C. 20036, 1962.

Meyer, Margaret H., and Schwartz, Marguerite M.: *Team Sports for Girls and Women*, 4th Ed., Philadelphia, W. B. Saunders Company, 1965.

Mitchell, Viola: *Softball for Girls*, Revised Ed., New York, The Ronald Press Company, 1952.

Suggested Study Questions

1. Explain the techniques of the bunt. When is it advisable to bunt?
2. Explain the infield fly rule. What is the reason for such a rule?
3. When would it be wise to attempt a (a) double steal, (b) hit and run, and (c) squeeze play?
4. What are the fundamental skills necessary for catcher and first baseman?
5. Safety is important in softball. Explain precautions that apply to (a) dress and equipment, (b) batting, (c) base running, and (d) fielding.

CHAPTER TWENTY-SIX

Girls of Edison High School. Courtesy Marjorie S. Larsen, 1754 Middlefield Road, Stockton, California 95204.
Photographed by Robert Hawthorne.

SPEED-A-WAY

This new field game, copyrighted in 1950 by Marjorie A. Larsen of Stockton, California, is the result of ten years of experimentation and development of a lead-up game to hockey that was uncomplicated by difficult rules yet suitable and challenging for all skill levels. Today, speed-a-way, with its simplicity of basic skill requirements and equipment, continues to serve as a hockey lead-up activity but also stands on its own merit as a vigorous, skillful and competitive game for all skill levels from junior high school to college age. It is played throughout the United States, and has also been introduced into England, India, and Canada. It fulfills a need expressed by many girls—to play a game that includes basic football skills.

NATURE AND PURPOSE OF THE GAME

Speed-a-way is an active team game that combines the rules, skills, and techniques of field hockey, soccer, fieldball, speedball, and basketball, with the added opportunity of running with the ball as in touch football. Position and team play resemble hockey; skills of ball handling are similar to basketball and soccer as well as touch football without the hazards often attributed to touch football for women.

Speed-a-way is played by two teams of 11 players each. Each team attempts to advance the ball toward the opponent's goal and score by means of kicking, passing, or running the ball into a designated goal area, while attempting to keep the opposing team from scoring by a similar method.

An official game consists of four quarters of 8 minutes with a 2 minute rest between the first and second and third and fourth quarters. There is a 10 minute halftime interval. Each team is allowed three time-outs of 1 minute each during the game. These may be called only when a team is in possession of the ball or when the ball is dead.

Time suspension may be called by an umpire for injury or game interference.

Each team is composed of five forwards, (a center forward, left and right inners, and left and right wings), three halfbacks (left, center, and right), two fullbacks (left and right), and a goalkeeper. At the beginning of the game and at every kick-off players line up in their own half of the field as indicated in Figure 26-1.

FACILITIES AND EQUIPMENT

Speed-a-way requires a large, level field area similar to a hockey field, with good turf and markings and a goal cage. There is no need for penalty corner markings. Where hockey goals are not available, rules allow the use of soccer, speedball, or football goal standards.

The field is a maximum of 100 yards long and 60 yards wide, and a minimum of 75 by 45 yards. The longer lines are the side lines and the shorter lines the goal lines. The field is divided into four parts by three lines parallel to the goal lines. The middle line cuts the field in half, and the other lines are each 25 yards from the goal lines. When a shortened field is used, the 25 yard line remains 25 yards from each goal. Five yards inside and parallel to the side lines is a broken line running the length of the field. The space between the 5 yard line and the side line is called the alley.

A striking circle is marked at both ends of the field. The circle includes the area described by a 4 yard line parallel to the goal line and 15 yards from it. Using the goal posts as the center, two quarter circles are drawn from the ends of the 4 yard line to a point 15 yards from the goal posts on both sides.

At the center of each goal line is a goal 4 yards wide. Two 7 foot goal posts, 4 yards apart and joined by a crossbar 7 feet from the ground, mark the goal mouth. Four feet behind the goal, other posts and crossbars are

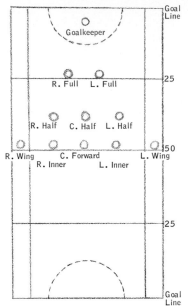

Fig. 26-1. Speed-a-way field and playing positions.

joined to the goal posts and covered with wire or netting.

A regulation leather or rubber soccer ball is the only necessary playing equipment. A well inflated ball, a minimum of 27 inches and a maximum of 28 inches in circumference, is acceptable. Pinnies or other distinguishing apparel should mark opposing teams. Goalkeepers should wear jumpers or additional identification so that their playing privileges will be recognized.

The acceptable seasonal gymnasium costume of shorts, tunics, or warming suits is appropriate dress. Tennis shoes with reinforced toes or canvas rubber-cleated shoes for firm turf are desirable.

Cloth strips tucked in the belt of each player may be a helpful teaching device for beginners. To avoid the shoving that often comes in tagging a player, the one tagging must snatch the streamer for an official tag of the ball carrier.

BASIC SKILLS

One of the unique advantages of speed-a-way is the excitement and fun to the beginning or low-skilled player. A beginning game can be played safely with few skill drills

or new techniques. As team skill develops and individual techniques improve, more satisfaction results from play.

Many of the fundamental skills of speed-a-way are also the basic techniques of soccer, speedball, and basketball. All soccer and speedball skills and all ball handling skills of basketball, except the bounce, bounce pass, and dribble, are used. The unique technique involves catching and running for touchdowns.

Running and Dodging. All players are responsible for moving rapidly, positioning themselves for a pass or kick and for marking and guarding an opponent. Dodging is necessary to avoid being tagged while running with the ball. A high level of fitness, gained through conditioning exercises and distance and obstacle running, develops the stamina for effective play.

SKILLS FOR GAINING CONTROL OF THE BALL

Catching is necessary to control aerial balls (see Chapter 21, section on catching a basketball, p. 345).

Blocking. Thighs, hips, abdomen, shoulder, and chest may be used. The arms and hands should be folded across the chest for protection when blocking with the chest. The player moves into the path of the ball, and when the ball contacts the body, weight shifts to the rear foot and the body "gives" on impact. Holding a slight body bend keeps the ball close to the body and allows better control as the ball is directed downward. (A ball caught in the center of the body often resembles a trap.)

Tackling. This is a technique for taking a

Fig. 26-2. Tackling.

ground ball from an opponent. Tackles are made from the front or side of the opponent without body contact. With weight supported on one leg, the tackler moves the weightless foot to the side of the ball and quickly moves the ball away from the opponent.

Trapping. Trapping is used to gain control of a moving ground ball. The sole of the foot may be used to trap a ball rolling slowly. Standing in the path of the ball the player raises one foot several inches from the ground. The heel remains close to the ground as the ball of the foot is placed firmly on the ball.

Fig. 26-3. Trapping slow ball.

One or both legs are used to trap faster or low bouncing balls. To execute a one leg shin trap with the right leg, the player moves to the ball path and extends her left leg slightly forward. As the ball approaches, the left leg flexes and the body lowers and inclines forward. The toe of the right foot remains in contact with the ground, as the shin touches the ball and wedges it to a stop.

Fig. 26-4. Two leg trap.

When the inside of the leg is used, the right hip rotates outward and the knee and calf force the ball to the ground.

A two leg trap begins with feet close and parallel. Players' arms are extended comfortably at the side for balance. With the weight on the balls of the feet, the knees flex, and the body weight moves down as the shins and ground form a "trap."

Tagging. Tagging a runner with the ball gives the tagging team possession of the ball. Using one or both hands, the tagger approaches the runner from the side or rear. If awaiting her from the front, watch for a dodge and change of direction, then step to the side for the tag. While maintaining running balance to avoid pushing the runner, the tagger makes a quick striking movement and recovers to avoid following through with her weight on her opponent.

ADVANCING THE BALL

A large group of skills are involved in advancing the ball — by oneself, to a teammate, and for a score.

Dribbling. This skill is not used so frequently as in soccer or speedball, for speed-a-way usually becomes an aerial game. At times it is necessary to dribble to maintain possession and advance a ground ball. Legs are rotated slightly outward to play the ball safely off the center of the body. The ball is tapped by the inside of the foot, alternating feet every two or three steps. Dribbling with the outside of the toe and foot is a desirable advanced skill.

Passing with the Hands. Basketball techniques are used. Accurate one-handed and two-handed chest, underhand, shoulder, overhead, and hook passes are important (see Chapter 21, pp. 345-350).

Running with the Ball. Hold the ball securely with both hands or tuck it under an arm against the body. Run when the field is open and no pass receivers are clear.

Passing with the Feet. To pass to the right using the inside of the left foot, the weight is supported on the right leg as the left leg swings diagonally across the front of the body. The knee straightens as the inside of the foot contacts the ball. The leg follows through as far as possible.

To pass to the left with the outside of the left foot, the body weight is on the right leg. The left leg is raised diagonally forward with an easily flexed knee. The left leg swings across the body as the outside of the forward portion of the foot contacts the ball slightly below center.

Place Kick.   This consists of kicking a stationary ground ball with the instep, inside, outside, toe, or heel of the foot. The most basic instep kick is accomplished by shifting the body weight from the right to left foot as the right leg swings through, toe pointing toward the ground. The ball is contacted below center by the instep as the knee extends, lifting the ball up and away on an extended right foot.

Fig. 26-7.   The punt.

Fig. 26-5.   Place kick.

Drop Kick.   A necessary skill for scoring and returning out-of-bounds balls. The ball is dropped from one or both hands at arm's length in front of the body and slightly to the side of the kicking leg. The kicking leg swings forward, toe pointing toward the ground, and the knee extends as the instep contacts the ball just before it rebounds from the ground. The leg follows through forward and upward.

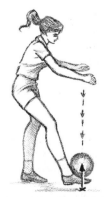

Fig. 26-6.   Drop kick.

Punt.   The ball is dropped from one or both hands from arms extended in front of the body. The kicking leg swings through to

meet the ball with the instep before it touches the ground. The kicking leg follows through.

Lifting to a Teammate.   This is an essential skill for kick-offs, free kicks, out-of-bounds play and a free ground ball. The player lifting is about a foot behind the stationary ball. With the left leg weighted, the right leg is forward, the knee flexed and the toe toward the ground with instep in contact with the ball. The ball is lifted by a rapid leg lift, extension of the knee, and toe lift. The leg follows through toward the receiver. Lift of a moving ball requires increased speed and accurate timing.

Fig. 26-8.   Lift-up to teammate.

Kick-up or Lift-up to Self.   A kick-up with both feet is often too slow to be used unless the player is well away from opponents. The ball is held between the player's feet by the inside of the feet and ankles. With the body weight distributed on the outer portion of the feet, the player jumps and bends knees outward, then reaches down to meet the ball with the hands.

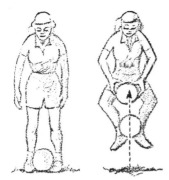

Fig. 26-9. Kick-up with both feet.

A one-foot lift of a stationary ball is begun by standing behind the ball and placing the sole of the lifting foot on top of the ball. Applying pressure to the ball, pull back and quickly slide the toe of the lifting foot under the ball. The toes of the lifting foot turn slightly upward as the knee bends out to allow the arms to move toward the ball.

Fig. 26-10. One-foot lift of stationary ball.

To lift a moving ball the player stations herself in the ball path with the lifting leg slightly extended. The heel is off the ground with toe pointing down. As the ball rolls up and over the toe, the leg is lifted, the knee bends outward, and the body and arms move forward to meet the ball rising off the instep.

GAME RULES AND SCORING*

The rules of speed-a-way are kept as simple as possible yet offer protection for the less skilled players.

*For complete rules see *Speed-A-Way, A New Game for Girls and Boys,* Marjorie S. Larsen, 1754 Middlefield Road, Stockton, Calif. 95204.

The Game. An official game is composed of four quarters of 8 minutes each. Three time-outs of 1 minutes each may be taken by each team.

Substitutes are allowed for players taken out of the game. They enter when the ball is not in play. A player may re-enter the game twice unless disqualified.

The team winning the toss of a coin may choose between kick-off and which goal it defends. At the beginning of each quarter the team that did not kick off the previous quarter will kick. After a score, the team scored against has the option of receiving or kicking off. Teams change goals at halftime.

With opposing teams lined up in their own half of the field the game begins with a place kick (this may be a lift-up to a teammate) from the center of the field in the direction of the opponent's goal. The ball must travel forward at least the distance of its circumference. The player taking the kick-off must not touch the ball again until it is touched by another player.

Players from both teams may cross the center line when the ball is kicked. Players may advance to any point on the field. There is *no* off-sides rule. After a kick-off, a ground ball may be advanced by dribbling, kicking, shouldering, or otherwise volleying with the body, or by a lift-up. An aerial ball (one caught on the fly or after one bounce if kicked) may be advanced by a pass, run, punt, dropkick, or volley.

Scoring. Teams score against their opponents on a field goal or touchdown. A field goal, counting 3 points, is scored when an attacking player kicks a ground ball or does a drop kick from within the striking circle so that the ball travels across the goal line between the goal posts and beneath the crossbar. The goal is scored even if last touched by a defending player. A ball legally touched by the hands (thus becoming an aerial ball) cannot score as a field goal until it is again played as a ground ball. Punts, therefore, do not score as field goals, but a drop kick made from within the striking circle may score.

A touchdown may be scored by a player running across the goal line outside the goal cage area. A touchdown may also be scored by completion of a forward pass from an attacking player in the field to a teammate behind the goal line, but *not* behind the goal cage or post area. A touchdown counts two points.

When soccer, speedball, or football goal posts are used and the crossbar is higher than that used in hockey, an *optional scoring rule* may apply. A drop kick from any place on the field that passes over the crossbar and between the goal posts scores 4 points. If the drop kick passes below the crossbar it must be kicked from within the circle to score 3 points.

Fouls. In speed-a-way any infringement of a game rule is considered a foul. Fouls result when:

1. Any player except the goalkeeper picks up a ground ball.

2. A player holds an aerial ball longer than 3 seconds without passing or running.

3. A player tags an opponent who is receiving or who has possession of a ball before 3 seconds elapse.

4. Two or more players guard an opponent in possession of the ball so that she cannot successfully run, pass, kick, or otherwise play the ball.

5. A player trips, shoves, pushes, charges, or strikes an opponent. (Only an opponent running with the ball may be tagged.)

6. A player knocks or snatches a ball from an opponent's hands.

7. A player kicks an opponent or kicks the ball dangerously into an opponent.

8. A player stands closer than 5 yards to a player taking a penalty corner, throw-in, or free kick.

9. The player executing a throw-in or a penalty kick plays the ball again before it is played by another person.

10. A player receiving a ball from a penalty corner or from a throw-in taken between the goal line and the 25 yard line passes or runs for a touchdown. (There must be three passes before a touchdown is scored).

11. A player scores directly from a free kick, toss-up, or throw-in.

Penalties. Penalties vary according to the place the foul occurs and which player fouled.

1. When any foul occurs outside the striking circle, a free kick is awarded an opponent at the spot of the infringement.

2. When a foul occurs in the striking circle by a member of the attacking team, a free kick is awarded the defending team at any point inside the circle.

3. When the defending team fouls in the circle, the attacking team is awarded a penalty corner. A penalty corner is taken on the end line, where the circle bisects the line. The ball may be put in play by a punt, place kick, drop kick, or throw-in. If a throw-in is used, a minimum of three passes must be completed before scoring a touchdown. Defending backfield players must be behind their goal line; the remainder of the defending team beyond the 25 yard line; and the attacking players outside the striking circle in the field of play.

4. A double foul results in a toss-up between the two offenders on the spot unless it is within 5 yards of the goal or side lines. In such a case it is brought to a place opposite the spot of the foul and 5 yards from the side or end line.

5. A tie ball results in a toss-up at the point of the tie, if more than 5 yards from goal or side lines. Otherwise it is moved 5 yards in from the line.

Out of Bounds. The following rules govern out-of-bounds balls:

1. Balls passing over the side lines are thrown in by an opponent of the player last touching the ball. On a throw-in the player stands outside the side line and throws in any manner. The ball may be played as a ground or aerial ball.

2. Balls sent over the end line outside the goal posts (and not scoring) by either attacker or defender shall be awarded to an opponent at a point on the end line, 15 yards from the nearer goal post, where the circle bisects the end line. The person may put the ball into play by a throw-in, punt, place kick, or drop kick.

3. When a forward pass is intercepted by a defensive player behind the goal, the defending team is awarded an end line out of bounds.

4. If the ball is thrown between the goal posts, out-of-bounds rules are enforced.

5. If the ball goes out of bounds off the bodies or hands of two opponents, the ball is tossed up at a point 5 yards from the side line or end line opposite the spot where the ball went out.

6. If a drop kick initiated *outside* the circle passes below the goal crossbar, out-of-bounds rules apply.

GAME STRATEGY

Speed-a-way tends to be more of an offensive than defensive game. It has developed into a pass and run game. Initially players throw and run with the ball and later develop the skill of punting and kicking for a speedier, more effective game. As there are no off-side rules, any team member may move downfield and score. A more skillful game with more scoring possibilities results if team members play positions and develop skills of that position.

Offensive Strategy. As in all field games team play is the most effective; one person alone has little hope of scoring against 11 opponents.

All forward players should be fast runners, skilled in catching and kicking. They must be alert to their position on the field and aware of the position of other attacking players, trying to scatter in order to keep the defense spread. This allows the attack to pass, run, or kick for a score. Forward line players may rush ahead or remain deep in the opponent's field to set up an attack.

A good offense begins with a successful kick-off. The following is an example of such a play. The center forward lifts to an inner who catches the ball on the fly or after the first bounce. The inner passes to the halfback, who has moved forward. The halfback punts to the wing, who has moved well down into opponents' field. The wing receives the ball on the fly or after the first bounce and runs or passes the ball to the other wing for a touchdown. Many options exist once the wing receives the ball. She may pass the ball toward center field for a field goal attempt by the center forward or pass to either inner for a score.

It is often wise to have one or more players over the goal line waiting to receive a pass. Forwards should vary their attack to divert the defense. As forwards approach scoring position they can expect to be guarded more closely and therefore must become more accurate with short direct passes. More success is gained if the ball remains or is converted to an aerial ball. If positioning is good for a field goal, the ball may be dropped and kicked.

Speed and accuracy in moving the ball downfield are essential. The greater the number of offensive players downfield, the better the opportunity to score.

Forwards and halfbacks should attempt to intercept defense kicks and move them quickly toward the goal before the defensive halfbacks recover to their defense positions.

Penalty corner plays can often result in a score.

The left wing (LW) lifts the ball to her left inner (LI) or left halfback (LH); then that person passes to the center forward, who may kick the ball through the goal or may throw the ball to the right wing, who has come over the goal line for a touchdown pass. The ball could be passed to the LW if she is not too closely guarded (see Fig. 26-10).*

As backfield players gain possession of the ball they pass or kick to the wings, preferably away from the center of the field to avoid interception. Sometimes diagonal passes up-

---

*Description of strategy and figure 26-10 adapted from Kathryn Maloy, "Speed-A-Way Tactics." *Speed-A-Way*, by Marjorie S. Larsen 1960, pp. 11-14.

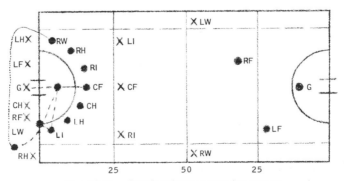

Fig. 26-11. Scoring from a penalty corner.

field are advisable to keep the defense spread. On a ground ball halfbacks should back up the forwards to prevent losing the ball. If a touchdown is planned, the ball may be passed to the halfbacks as forwards try to free themselves for pass reception.

Defensive Strategy. The forwards are the initial line of defense as they attempt to intercept during the kick-off. Once play begins, forwards rarely drop back into their own half of the field.

A defending player attempts to stay between the goal and the player she is marking. On a ground attack the center halfback marks the center forward; left halfback marks the right wing; right halfback, the left wing; left fullback marks the right inner; and right fullback, the left inner. This defense may prove ineffective with an aerial and running attack. A zone defense is recommended.

Using a zone, the center halfback guards the center of the field in front of the goalkeeper; left and right halfbacks guard the area from the side lines 15 yards in; the fullbacks are deeper, guarding the areas between wings and center. If the forwards of the defending team are fast, they may move in to mark the halfbacks. It is rarely necessary for the inners to go back too deeply to guard offensive actions of their fullbacks. Defending fullbacks and goalkeeper must be alert to their wings moving far upfield and kick and clear to them.

DUTIES AND SPECIFIC SKILLS OF PLAYERS

The entire forward line should be fast runners and accurate passers. Their primary responsibility is to move downfield to a position to receive the ball from their backs and ultimately to score.

The center forward is the pivot of the forward line and directs much of their aggressive action. She must be skilled at the kick-off and other directed passes and kicks.

Inners must move rapidly and kick and pass accurately. They move the ball downfield by passing to the wings; they spread the defense to open scoring opportunities. They have many opportunities to score field goals and intercept fumbled balls. Inners rarely move deep into their own half of the field on defense.

Wings must be decisive players who move quickly downfield and who are skilled at catching touchdown passes. They must learn to stay in wide position to keep the defense spread. They must be effective on penalty kicks.

The defense players include the backs and goalkeeper.

The center halfback must have great stamina, for she plays a first line defensive role and follows up the forward line offensively. She must intercept ground and aerial balls and convert to her offensive players quickly. She must be able to lift, kick, and punt accurately, particularly on free kicks. She must create aerial balls for her forward line.

The left and right halfbacks must also be untiring runners who guard the wings defensively and intercept passes in their field positions. They must punt and drop kick well to their forwards, then follow them to the opposing team's circle where they become offensive players.

Fullbacks need strong defensive skills. They are aggressive, but not necessarily fast, players who are strong and accurate punters. On defense kicks they must be effective in lifting the ball to a halfback. Their positioning must avoid crowding the goalkeeper while they guard the area over the end line near the goal.

The goalkeeper has additional playing privileges. She may pick up the ball at any time, anywhere on the field. She must be effective in blocking and clearing the ball to her fullbacks and halfbacks. She must be a strong punter who can reach the wings or inners moving upfield. If a goalkeeper is rushed, picking up the ball may be hazardous and a clearing kick to a back more effective.

Terminology

Aerial ball — A ball that may legally be played in the air. It may be passed, run with, kicked, or reconverted to a ground ball. An aerial ball results from a kick, punt, drop kick, or kick-up caught on the fly or after the first bounce.

Blocking the balls — Using the body to change or direct the progress of the ball. Only the goalkeeper may use hands on a ground ball.

Drop kick — A ball dropped by a player and kicked as it strikes the ground. An optional method of scoring 4 points when soccer or football goals are used.

Dribble — A succession of controlled kicks used to maintain control and advance a ground ball.

Field goal — A score of 3 points made by any attacking player kicking a ground ball or executing a drop kick from within the striking circle so that the ball passes between the goal posts and below the crossbar.

Free kick — Awarded to a team fouled against in the field of play and to the defending team when offense fouls in the circle. An opportunity to kick or lift the ball with no players within 5 yards.

Ground ball — A moving or stationary ball on the ground. As a ground ball it may be kicked, volleyed with the body, or headed. It may be converted to an aerial ball only by use of the feet (except for the goalkeeper, who may use her hands).

Holding the ball — Maintaining possession of an aerial ball for more than 3 seconds without running or advancing the ball.

Murking — Keeping oneself in a position of observation of a specific opponent in preparation for preventing or intercepting a pass, tagging a runner, or tackling the ball.

Passing — A method of advancing an aerial ball with one or both hands.

Penalty corner — Awarded to the attacking team when the defending team commits a foul in its own striking circle. The ball is put into play by a wing of the attacking team from a point on the goal line 15 yards from the nearer goal post by a throw-in, punt, place kick, or drop kick.

Pivot — While maintaining possession of the ball, moving the body around in a circle or part of a circle with any number of steps by one foot while the other foot remains in contact with the ground.

Place kick — Kicking the ball from a stationary ground position without touching it with the hands.

Punt — A ball held and dropped by a player and kicked before it hits the ground.

Shouldering — Meeting and volleying the ball with front, top, or back of shoulder. The arms may be used.

Tagging — A defending player places one or both hands on the back of an attacker who is carrying the ball. A legal tag results in a free kick for the tagging team.

Tie ball — A ball caught simultaneously and held by two opponents. A toss-up results.

Touchdown — A score of 2 points gained by (1) an attacking player's running over the goal line outside the goal cage area, or (2) a successful pass from the field of play to a teammate across the goal line.

Trapping — Stopping and gaining control of the ball by use of a foot, one or both legs, and the ground.

Volleying — Playing the ball with the head or any part of the body except the hands.

Selected Audio-visual Aids

Speed-A-Way film. (11 min., 16 mm., b & w or color.) Marjorie Larsen, 1754 Middlefield Road, Stockton, Calif. (Rental or purchase. Sale, b & w.: $60; color: $105.00. Rental, b & w: $3.00; color, $4.25.

Suggested Readings

Dexter, Genevie (Compiler): *Teachers Guide to Physical Education for Girls in High School,* Sacramento, California State Department of Education, 1957.

Larsen, Marjorie S. *Speed-A-Way, A New Game for Girls and Boys.* 1960. Marjorie S. Larsen, 1754 Middlefield Road, Stockton, Calif. 95204.

Larsen, Marjorie S.: "*Speed-A-Way,*" Journal of the American Association for Health, Physical Education, and Recreation, Vol. 22, No. 2, February, 1951, pp. 46-47.

Suggested Study Questions

1. Select the position you prefer to play. Analyze your defensive and offensive field responsibilities. What should be your strongest personal skills?
2. Sketch five offensive and five defensive plays from the kickoff.
3. Design four plays for the attacking team that could be used from the penalty kick as well as a throw-in within the defenders' 25 yard line.
4. After playing and observing, list 10 helpful hints to pass along to your class to improve the skill and fun of speed-a-way.
5. What unique advantages does speed-a-way have over other field games for the beginning and intermediate player?

CHAPTER TWENTY-SEVEN

Courtesy of Rice University, Houston, Texas.

VOLLEYBALL

Volleyball is an increasingly popular team game which originated in the United States in 1895. Volleyball was originally called mintonette. It was devised by William C. Morgan, a Y.M.C.A. physical director at Holyoke, Massachusetts, for a group of senior men looking for a less strenuous team activity than basketball or football. A rope was stretched across the gymnasium floor and a basketball bladder was batted slowly back and forth across the rope. Later a tennis net replaced the rope, and finally a regulation volleyball net, similar to the one used today, was manufactured by the Spalding Sporting Goods Company. The volleyball replaced the bladder and the game came to require more skill and speed of its players.

The sport has always had the enthusiastic endorsement of the Y.M.C.A., and largely through the efforts of leaders in this organization volleyball has spread throughout the world.

In 1922 men's teams from various parts of the United States gathered to hold a national tournament in Brooklyn. In 1923 the popularity of the game resulted in the adoption of volleyball as an official activity by the National Amateur Athletic Federation.

Although girls and women began playing a modified version of volleyball soon after it was devised, special rules were not published until 1926. During this year they were published in the Red Cover Series of the Spalding Athletic Library. The National Section on Women's Athletics, a division of the American Physical Education Association, set about establishing rules for girls and women that were in keeping with their then current standards and principles of sports and competition. The "two-volley" game, with a maximum of six contacts on a side, was an outgrowth of the planning and thought of the time.

The Division for Girls and Women's Sports of the AAHPER now publishes rules, standards, and guides for volleyball every two years.

These rules are generally accepted in schools and colleges throughout the United States. These guides, a must to each teacher, suggest lead-up games, officiating techniques, and modified rules for younger girls, co-recreational groups, and handicapped students.

The United States Volleyball Association, formed in 1928 under the direction of Dr. George J. Fisher, continues to work on the standardization and interpretation of rules and also sponsors national tournamemts. The organization is composed of representatives of physical education and recreation agencies. The rules devised are intended for use by boys and men and girls and women. Through recent cooperative efforts, the U.S.V.B.A. and D.G.W.S. rules have become more similar, allowing ease of competition between educational and recreational groups.

All international competitive play in foreign countries and during Olympic competition is conducted under rules of the International Volleyball Federation. The major differences between I.V.F. rules and those of the U.S.V.B.A. and D.G.W.S. relate to substitutions, legal hitting surfaces of the body, court positioning during service, spiking position, and player interchange after service. Each year it appears that the rules draw closer. This results in less confusion and more skillful play between competing groups.

Recognized as an Olympic event for women in the 1964 games in Tokyo and won by the host nation's skilled players, volleyball is perhaps the fastest growing women's team sport in the United States. Although as a spectator sport volleyball is not so popular in its land of origin as it is in many foreign nations, among participants it is regarded as a sport with few equals.

NATURE AND PURPOSE OF THE GAME

The game is played by two teams of six players each; each team is placed in its own half of the rectangular court 60 by 30 feet, equally divided by a net 7 feet, 4¼ inches from the floor. Members of a team hit the volleyball across the net and into the opponent's court, using skilled placement and shots and trying to make the ball touch the opponent's area. The opponents attempt to prevent this by hitting the ball up and volleying it back across the net.

Play begins when a server directs the ball across the net with her hand or forearm from a position behind the end line of her own court side. Each server continues serving until she commits a fault or her team fails to return the ball to the opponents and score a point. Only the serving team can score points.

During play, the ball may be batted in any direction with one or both hands or forearms. The ball may be hit three times on each side of the net, only once by each player unless played by another teammate between times. It may be played as soon as any part of it crosses the net and can be recovered from the net.

A game is won by a team if (1) they score 15 points and hold a 2 point advantage over the opponent, (2) they lead by at least 2 points at the end of 8 minutes of play, or (3) they take a 2 point lead after the game was tied at the end of the 8 minute playing period.

FACILITIES AND EQUIPMENT

Court. The rectangular court is 60 by 30 feet, bounded by a 2 inch line, with at least 6 feet of unobstructed area extending from the boundary lines. A minimum of 20 feet of overhead clearance should be allowed. A 2 inch center line divides the court into two playing areas.

Serving Areas. The serving area should be in back of the end lines between the extension of the side lines and should be 6 feet in depth. In a smaller gymnasium, the serving area may extend into the court.

Net. A regulation net should be 32 feet in length and 3 feet wide and is bound at the top and bottom with quarter inch manila rope. The net should be tightly stretched and the height should measure 7 feet, 4¼ inches from the top to the ground at the center of the court. A marker is placed on the tape at the top of the net directly above each side line.

Ball. A round rubber ball that carries 5 to 7 pounds of pressure may be used out of doors, although a ball with a rubber bladder covered with a laceless leather case is required for indoor play. The latter should be 26 to 27 inches in circumference, weigh a minimum of 7 ounces and a maximum of 9, and be inflated to a pressure of between 7 and 8 pounds.

Costume and Accessories. An official gymnasium costume is appropriate for most game situations. Attractive shorts and shirts that allow freedom are desirable for intercollegiate games. A tennis type shoe worn with socks that cushion the feet and prevent blisters is an important safety consideration. Kneeguards are advisable for highly competitive play.

For a regulation game numbered pinnies, and official rule book, scorebook, whistles and horns should be provided.

BASIC SKILLS

Volleys are the basic skills of ball handling and the responsibility of each team member. The type of volley used depends upon the specific game situation, but both the overhand and underhand volleys are used as passes to a teammate, as sets for an offensive play, and as defensive returns to opponents.

Overhand Volley. As a *pass* the overhand volley is basic to all play. It is sometimes called the overhead pass or the chest pass, depending on the position of the ball in relation to the player. This volley often affords the initial contact and control which reduce the spin and force of the opponent's serve or return.

The player moves to a ready position to await the ball. Her feet are apart and parallel or in a slight stride stance (left foot is usually forward for right-handed players) and her weight is supported on the balls of her feet. The heels remain in contact with the floor as knees flex and carry the body downward to a semicrouch position. The trunk is inclined slightly forward and the hips remain under the body. A player may often drop to one knee to get in better position for a low ball.

The hands are at chest level with thumbs pointing toward each other and nearly touching, the palms of the hands are outward toward the ball, and the fingers are well

Fig. 27-1. The overhand volley.

spread and pointing upward. The wrists are flexed, and the arms are in front of the body. The elbows are flexed and elevated. Some players prefer to keep the elbows and arms extended in front of the body and in line with the shoulders, but most carry their arms forward and sideward with elbows pointing slightly toward the ground. As the ball approaches the pocket formed by the fingers and thumbs, the elbows come toward the front of the body. Tension of the arms and hands is evident prior to extension of the body to meet the ball. The head is turned and the eyes follow the flight of the oncoming ball. As the ball is contacted, the arms withdraw to the body, and in one continuous, crisp movement the fleshy parts of the fingers and thumbs simultaneously strike the ball. The body extends upward, with a player often jumping slightly from the ground, to meet the ball. The arms and fingers snap with a coordinated follow-through of the body in the direction of the pass. Wrists extend and rotate inward as the body weight shifts forward behind the ball.

It is imperative that the player position herself so that her feet are pointed in the direction (or 180 degrees opposite for a back set) of the intended volley. This positioning assures simultaneous contact of the ball with both hands. It is very difficult to hit a ball off

of either *side* of the body with simultaneous contact.

Overhead Volley as a Set. The primary purpose of a set-up is to place the ball in the best possible position for an effective spike. The set is usually the second contact, for it usually occurs after the ball has been controlled and passed to a set player. A highly skilled set player will learn to vary sets and produce a mixture of high and low sets, and those close to and back from the net as opponents become more adept at blocking. The beginning set player, usually on the front line, should attempt to set to a height of 10 or 12 feet. The ball should make a short arc and reach its height between the set and spiking players. The ball must be kept parallel to but away from the net.

The set player positions herself for an overhead pass even though she is playing a pass from a teammate which is more easily controlled than the initial volley. Because she must direct the ball in an upward trajectory, she must get under the ball and follow through in a more upward than forward direction. Her feet must be pointed in the direction of the intended pass. This positioning assures simultaneous contact on the ball by both hands. Wrist flexion is important, and the palms and fingers should be allowed to face upward. Prior to contact, the player must be aware of looking up to the ball through the pocket in the hands. At the moment of contact she arches her back to insure an upward ball flight.

Fig. 27-2. The overhead volley as a set.

Cross Set and Over Set. When a set is made from a spiker's left side to be played on her right or set from her right to be played on her left it is termed a *cross set* . An *over set* is made by a set player over the head of one player to be spiked by another; that is, sets from the left forward to the right forward or from the right forward to the left forward that pass over the center forward are *over sets*.

The body positions for these sets should not vary from the routine set, for the cross set and over set have deceptive values, especially in changing or delaying a blocking pattern set by the opponents. When the ball is contacted, the neck and back are sharply arched and the wrists sharply flexed. The fingers control skillful sets more than the thumbs, and this control insures proper height and distance for the spiker without requiring her to cross into the opponent's court.

Reverse Volley. The reverse volley is also called a *back set*. This advanced technique is executed to deceive opponents who are preparing a blocking defense against obvious set-up and spike. For example, a set player (center forward) faces her spiker (left forward) but then sets the ball high over her head and backward to her right forward. The set player's body position is the same as for a conventional set, but as the ball approaches, she tilts her head backward and arches her body backward as she meets the ball over her forehead. She allows her wrists to flex far backward. Her elbows are held up and out, and her fingers point in the direction of ball flight. As the ball is contacted, the fingers are straightened and extend backward as arms and body extend.

Underhand Volley. Although the open

Fig. 27-3. The underhand volley (two-hand bounce pass).

hand, palm-up contact of low balls is frequently used by beginning and recreational players, a wise player and teacher will eliminate the technique as soon as possible. The dig pass is replacing open-hand techniques below the waist, for digs allow more range for the player and eliminate ball handling violations. Even though D.G.W.S. and U.S.V.B.A. rules permit open-hand low volleys and passes, in competitive situations strict rule interpretations often result in calls of holding or lifting violations. It is obvious that a player is more likely to allow the ball to rest on open hands than on closed hands and extended forearms.

Digs. Digs are the most effective techniques for handling powerful serves, spikes, and net recoveries. To execute the *two-hand dig* (or two-arm bounce pass), the body is well balanced in a semicrouch position and the player is prepared to kneel if necessary. The feet are separated, and the weight is on the balls of the feet. One hand is firmly extended with thumb in the palm, facing upward, and the other hand clasps the hand. The thumbs are on top and close together. Some players prefer to make a fist with thumb on top of the index finger and the other hand clasping the fist. The thumbs are firmly pressed together. Other players may choose to form two fists and bring them together in a "hand-heart" position by pressing the knuckles and the heels of the hands together. Although this may be a faster preparation, there is a danger that the hands will not provide a firm hitting surface when not clasped.

In any case the elbows are rotated inward so that the forearms are firm and close. The forearms are low and angled so that the ball will be contacted at its center by the base of the thumbs and lower forearms. As the ball strikes, the body straightens slightly, the arms rise slightly, and the ball rises as a result of its own rebounding force and the small movement of the arms and hands. This technique is frequently referred to as the two-arm forearm bounce (see Fig. 27-3).

One-Hand Dig. This one-hand bounce pass is also effective for net recovery and handling powerful serves and spikes. It is most frequently used in "last ditch" attempts. A player rarely has time to position herself for the play, and she must often rely on practiced skills and reflex action to get her into a crouch or kneeling position similar to that of

Fig. 27-4. The one-hand dig.

three hand positions may be used to contact the ball. In the *open-palm* serve, the fingers are extended and firm and the hand is slightly cupped. The impetus is given the ball by the lower palm and the heel, and the fingers give direction and control.

Greater force is given at ball impact by a *closed palm* position. The fingers are closed forward and in contact with the palm. The ball is contacted by the knuckles and the heel of the hand at the same time. This semiclosed fist position reduces the striking surface and consequently results in some loss of control and direction.

The *closed fist*, often called the *thumb circle* position, results in a striking surface made up of the thumb and index finger. The hand is closed so that a hollow remains inside, and the fully extended thumb grips the first two or three fingers. Power and speed are gained by contact with this restricted hitting surface, but control and accuracy become more difficult.

The *underhand serve* is the easiest serve for beginners to execute. It is easy to learn and to control, but it lacks the force and power of other serves. Standing no more than 6 feet behind the end line and within the extension of the side lines, the right-handed player faces the net with her feet in stride position, left foot forward, knees bent, shoulders square to the net. The ball rests in the palm of the left hand, with fingers pointing to the right and thumb toward the net. The left arm is extended low across the body and forward toward the right.

As the right hand and arm swing backward and upward in a pendulum arc, the elbow is slightly flexed. The trunk rotates to the right to allow for the backswing as the weight shifts back to the right foot. Additional length and height in the backswing result in more power at contact. The right arm and hand swing firmly through to contact the ball as the weight transfers to the forward foot. The ball

the two-arm forearm bounce pass. When the player is well balanced, the weight is equally distributed on the balls of the feet and the trunk is inclined forward. The hand may be in a loosely closed position in which the fingers are in the palm and the heel of the hand is exposed, or it may be in a tightly clenched closed position in which the first knuckles and the heel contact the ball. The arm is near the playing surface and brings the hand directly under the center of the ball. The ball is contacted as close to the ground as possible. As the ball contacts the hand, the wrist snaps upward to counteract the force of the ball and bounce it in the air.

A few players prefer to use the back of the semiclenched hand to contact the ball squarely. In this case, the wrist flips upward to bounce the ball in the air.

The Serve. The serve is a team offensive action which puts the ball in play at the beginning of a game and after every point or sideout. There are three basic serves, and there are varying hand positions and spins that may be imparted to each. Two other serves, the floater and the roundhouse, are gaining popularity among highly skilled competitive players.

In executing any of the basic serves, one of

Fig. 27-5. Hand positions for three basic serves.

Fig. 27-6. The underhand serve.

is struck below the center and lifted from the stationary left hand. (If playing U.S.V.B.A. rules the ball must not be supported at the moment of contact.) The right arm follows through in the direction of the intended ball flight and high enough to lift the ball over the net.

The *sidearm serve* is similar in basic body positioning and timing to the underhand serve; however, the right-handed player stands with her left shoulder toward the net and her feet pointing toward the right side line. The left foot is slightly ahead of the right in stride position. The ball is held in the palm of the left hand with the fingers of the hand directed toward the right side line. The thumb is toward the net. The left arm is fully extended about shoulder level and aligned so that the ball is beyond the left foot.

The extended right arm swings back at shoulder level and parallel to the playing surface. During the backswing, hips rotate and weight shifts to the right foot. The open palm, closed palm, or thumb-circle hand positions may be used as the right arm swings through. The ball is contacted at its center and driven from the holding hand. Weight shifts to the left foot and the right arm follows through past the left shoulder. This serve is difficult to judge by opponents because of its spinning, or floating, action and the angle of entry into the court.

The *overhead serve* is an intermediate and advanced technique that requires movements similar to those of the tennis serve or overarm softball throw. Once mastered, the serve is effective for speed, spin, and placement. The right-handed server faces the net. The left foot is forward, and the right foot is back and angled toward the right side line. Weight is equally distributed. The ball is held by both hands in front of the body. As the left hand tosses the ball 3 or 4 feet above and slightly in front of the right shoulder, the right arm and hand reach backward and then high and upward to contact the ball on its descent. The ball is contacted at a point about 2 feet above the shoulder. In preparation for the hit, the body twists to the right, and weight shifts to the right foot. At contact, body weight transfers to the forward foot. The follow-through is in the direction of the ball flight. Unless one is attempting to impart spin, the

Fig. 27-7. The sidearm serve.

Fig. 27-8. The overhead serve.

Fig. 27-9. The overarm volleyball serve is an advanced technique with movements similar to those of the tennis serve or the overarm softball throw. (Courtesy of the Los Angeles Public Schools.)

ball should be contacted at the center and side rather than underneath or above center.

The *floater overhead serve* was recognized as a deceptive serve after its effective use by the Japanese women in the 1964 Olympics. Preliminary body positioning is similar to the overhead service. The ball may be held high or tossed 2 or 3 feet in the air with no spin imparted. The right arm extends overhead with the elbow slightly bent. As the body weight transfers to the forward foot, the elbow leads the heel of the hand (or a flat fist) to the inert ball. The ball must be contacted squarely in its center if it is to float, bob and weave in flight. No real follow-through takes place, but rather a withdrawal so that the effect is a "punched ball."

The *roundhouse serve* is a highly skillful and powerful hook serve that is difficult to control with consistency. It is recommended only for highly skilled players. The right-handed server faces the side line with feet in a forward stride position, left shoulder toward the net. The ball is tossed by both hands to a position over the right shoulder. The body bends sharply to the right and then twists left as the firmly extended right arm comes out from the right side and over the head. As the ball descends to a level just above the head, the heel of the open hand contacts the ball and the fingers cap the top of the ball. The follow-through is across the body, and forward momentum brings the right foot forward. The ball should rise only slightly, and top spin results in an abrupt drop as the ball crosses the net.

Spins imparted on the ball cause curves, drops and rises and make the serve more difficult to handle. Usually, curved balls are hit with an open hand, for the fingers apply pressure to the ball.

Top spin results in a ball that drops rapidly. In the underhand and sidearm serve, top spin is applied by drawing the fingers upward under the ball. In the overhand serve the ball is hit above center with the fingers on top of the ball.

Backspin is difficult to achieve on the underarm and sidearm serves. On an overhand serve the ball is struck on the back with a forward and downward motion that causes the ball to rise and drop sharply.

For an *outcurve*, a ball that curves to the left in flight, the ball is struck on the right side. The thumb leads in the underhand serve. Overarm, the little finger leads. The wrist rotates inward on contact with the ball.

An *incurve* is a curve to the right in flight. On an underarm serve the ball is hit on the left side with little finger leading. On the overhand serve, the thumb leads the fingers to the ball. The forearm rotates outward on contact.

Spiking. The spike is an important offensive technique used by front line players.* It causes the ball to be driven forcefully into the opponent's court. Spiking becomes a highly individualized skill among those players with coordination, alert reactions, agility, balance, and the ability to jump. There are many variations in hand positioning, approach, and take-off, and individu-

---

*Only front line players may spike under D.G.W.S. rules. See U.S.V.B.A. rules for explanation of spiking by second line from behind 10 foot line.

Fig. 27-10. Spiking.

als must experiment to find their most effective combinations.

The spiker may use either a stationary or running approach with either a double- or single-foot take-off. In competitive play the double-foot take-off and the running approach are more widely used.

The stationary spiker planning a double-foot take-off stands facing the net at a distance of about 18 to 24 inches from it. Her body is tense, and her hips, knees, and ankles are flexed as she watches the approaching ball. As the set-up arcs toward her, she pushes from her crouch by a simultaneous vertical thrust of both legs and the entire body. The spiking arm is lifted behind the head, elbow bent, palm facing the net, and the other arm thrusts upward and across the body. The bent elbow of the spiking arm leads to meet the ball. As the body reaches maximum height in the jump, the elbow extends and the arm comes forward in whiplike fashion. The wrist is cocked. At the moment the ball is contacted on top, the wrist is flexed forcefully, and the hand drives the ball downward. The fingers impart some control and spin to the ball. Follow-through is in the direction of the ball descent but short to avoid net contact. The spiker lands on both feet,

her knees relaxed and her body poised for action in the event the ball is blocked or returned.

If a running approach is used prior to a double-foot take-off, the spiker uses several short, quick steps to gain momentum and proper position. She then brings both feet together for the take-off and continues as described above.

In a *single-foot take-off* from either a running or stationary position, the right-handed spiker faces the direction of the oncoming ball. The right foot leaves the ground, and its upward momentum helps to lift the body upward. As the left foot leaves the ground, the body twists and faces the net as the ball is contacted.

The spiker must avoid too much forward momentum in this take-off, for it would carry her into the net or result in an unbalanced landing. The landing should be on both feet, and the body should be poised for action.

Dink. The *dink*, as a change of pace, must be considered an offensive skill, although it is often used as a "save" when the set comes in too low or too close to the net for a spike. With a closed fist, the player contacts the ball from beneath and "punches" it over the net.

Blocking. Blocking is a defensive technique used to stop a spike at the net. The defending player is opposite the spiking player and facing the net 18 to 20 inches

Fig. 27-11. Blocking.

away. She rises from the ground vertically by simultaneous thrust of both legs as the opposing spiker reaches the height of her jump. As she reaches a point parallel to the net, her arms are vigorously extended overhead with thumbs together, her fingers are firm and slightly flexed, and the heels of her hands are pushed forward. The ball is met by moving the hands into alignment with the wrists so that it is forced back to the court of the spiker. Occasionally it is wise to gain control of the ball by a soft block that deflects the ball high off the fingers into the blocker's own court so that it can be played by a teammate. Blockers should land on both feet and be facing the net in preparation for the next play.

Multiple Blocks. Multiple blocks are more effective than individual blocks against cross court power spikes and spikers that drive the ball along the side line. In forming a *two player block*, the front line players hold in ready position until the ball is set and the spiking position is obvious. The middle player then slides to her left or right to join the outside blocker who has established herself and set the position for the block. The middle player moves until her body contacts the outside

blocker. They leave the ground together — hip to hip, shoulder to shoulder — just after the spiker jumps. Their hands are together so there is no gap between their inside hands.

The *three player block* is effective against an opposing center forward spiker. The block is set by the center player as both side players slide in to contact her and jump together.

Even when blockers are not effective in meeting the ball, their presence at the net often causes the opponent to direct a high, returnable shot.

Net Recovery. Often a ball, poorly delivered on a set-up, a musjudged spike, or an attempted save, hits into the net. Different playing situations are called for if the ball was driven into the net on the first or second contact. (A ball going into the net after the third contact is dead.) If two contacts remain for the ball, the recovery player goes to a deep crouch or a kneeling position facing the ball and side of the court. As the ball drops free of the net she executes a dig, preferably using two hands for control. If the ball rises in the back court, a player delivers the ball deep to opponent's court; if a high recovery near the net is possible, a spike or dink by a net player may follow.

| A | B |

Fig. 27-12. Blocking is a defensive technique used in volleyball against the offensive technique of spiking. *A,* Single block; *B,* double block. (Courtesy of College of Health, Physical Education and Recreation, Texas Woman's University, Denton, Texas, and Rice University, Houston, Texas.)

Fig. 27-13. Net recovery.

When there is only one contact remaining, the net player attempts a defensive "save." Usually a one-hand dig is called for as the ball falls from the net. As it nears the floor, the hand and arm rotate away from the net and contact the ball on the upswing. This stroke imparts upward and forward momentum to the ball.

Players should watch when the ball contacts the net. Balls hitting high on a taut net fall down the net and close to the center line; those hitting the net at center or lower tend to rebound farther into the court.

GAME RULES AND SCORING

The following rules are those recommended by D.G.W.S. See the summary of *major* rule differences between D.G.W.S. and U.S.V.B.A. on p. 458.

THE GAME. A game is completed when one of the following occurs:

1. One team scores 15 points and has a 2 point advantage over the opponent.

2. A team leads by at least 2 points at the end of 8 minutes of playing time.

3. At the end of 8 minutes if the game is tied or there is only a 1 point difference between opponents, play continues until one team has a 2 point lead.

A match is won by the team that first wins two of three games. At the end of each game of a match, teams change courts. In the middle of the third game, teams change after one team has scored 8 points or 4 minutes pass, whichever occurs first.

The captain of the team winning the toss may either take the first service of the first game or have choice of court. The remaining choice goes to the other team. In subsequent games the team that received first in the previous game shall have first serve in the following game.

Players, Substitutes, and Court Position. Six players constitute an official team. If a team is reduced to fewer than six by injury or disqualification, the game is defaulted.

Players may enter the game only twice. Beginning the game is considered one entry. A substitute must take the position and place in the serving order of the player for whom she is substituting. A player reentering the game takes her original position in the serving order and in relation to her teammates. A substitute must take her court position within the 15 second allotted time.

Players assume court positions of left forward, center forward, right forward, right back, center back, and left back. Each player must remain in her own area until the ball is

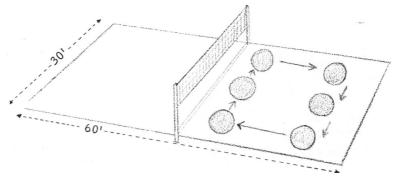

Fig. 27-14. Volleyball player positions, rotation pattern, and court dimensions.

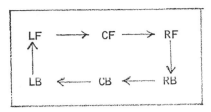

Fig. 27-15. Playing positions and rotation path.

served. She may, however, leave the court to play a ball. The server is the only player allowed outside the court at the moment of service.

Service. Play begins with a serve by the player in the right back position. Thereafter the player continues to serve as long as her team scores points. After loss of service a "side-out" is called and the ball passes to the opposing team. Each player has only one term of service until the serving order is repeated. Players rotate in a clockwise manner to gain their serving position. The following rules govern the serve:

1. A serve may be hit with one or both hands, open or closed, or the forearms. The ball may be held or tossed in the air but must be clearly hit, not thrown.

2. The server stands behind the end line and within imaginary side line extensions. She may step on or over the end line as soon as the ball is hit.

3. A service fault occurs when the ball touches the top of the net, goes into or below the net, fails to reach the net, hits an object over the net or lands outside the court boundaries.

Conduct of the Game. During play the following rules govern the game. If a member of the serving team violates a rule, a side-out is called and the serve passes to the opposing team. If a member of the receiving team is the offender, a point is awarded the serving team.

1. The serve must be legally executed.

2. The ball must be clearly batted with one or both hands (open or closed) or forearms. Contacts with two hands or forearms must be simultaneous.

3. The ball may be volleyed only three times on a side. A player may not have two successive hits. If two or more players contact the ball simultaneously, it is considered only one play and players involved may participate in the next play. If more than one

player forms a block and any of the players is contacted by the ball, any one of the players is eligible to make the next contact (this contact would be considered the second team contact).

4. When players of opposing teams simultaneously contact the ball at the net, the contact is not considered one of the three volleys for either team.

5. Any ball, except a serve, that strikes the net and crosses over is still in play.

6. A ball in play that is not a serve may be recovered from the net if the player makes no contact with the net.

7. A player may not touch the net when the ball is in play. If the ball is driven into the net by an opponent and causes the net to touch a player on the opposing team, play continues and no fault is called. When the play occurs on the third contact, the ball is dead.

8. A player may not reach over the net to play a ball. A follow-through after contact with the ball is permitted.

9. A player may not reach under the net to touch a ball or a player of the opposing team. She may not touch the floor beyond the center line while the ball is in play. A foul is called even if the floor is touched after the ball has hit it.

10. A ball may be played as soon as any part crosses the net.

11. A player may leave the court to play a ball.

12. A ball touching a boundary line is good.

13. A player must be in her own area on the serve. She must not persistently change positions during play or spike at the net when she is a back line player.

14. A team is allowed two time-outs, not to exceed 1 minute each, for rest during a game when the ball is dead. Additional time-outs result in a side-out, or loss of point.

15. A team is penalized by loss of point, or side-out, when a player delays the game by (a) slow preparation to play or serve, (b) delayed recovery of an out-of-bounds ball, (c) slow rotation, or (d) taking more than two time-outs or more than 15 seconds for substitutions after the team has used its two allotted time-outs.

Double Foul. A double foul occurs when opposing players or sides foul simultaneously. The play is repeated when a double foul is called.

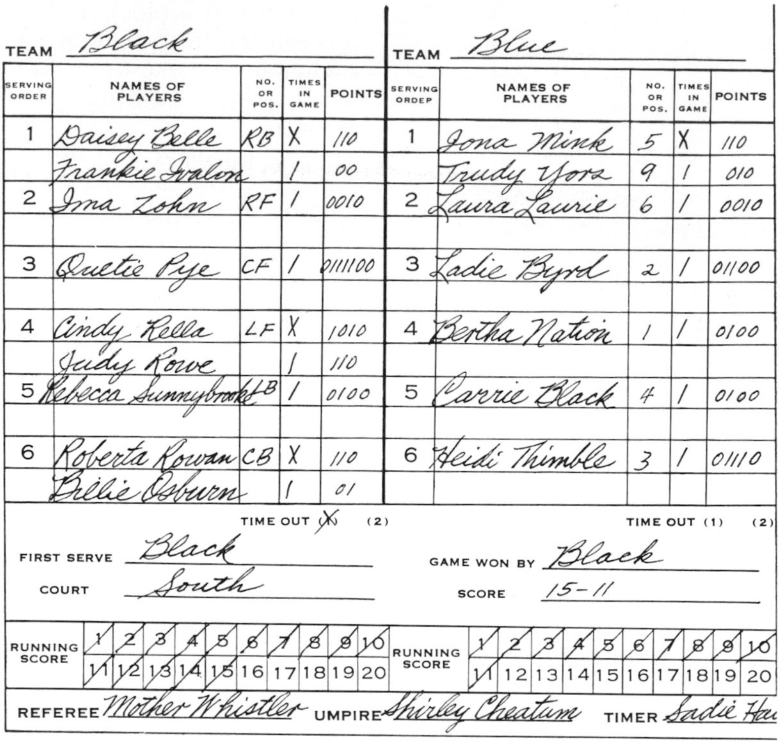

SERVING ORDER	NAMES OF PLAYERS	NO. OR POS.	TIMES IN GAME	POINTS	SERVING ORDER	NAMES OF PLAYERS	NO. OR POS.	TIMES IN GAME	POINTS
1	Daisey Belle	RB	X	110	1	Iona Mink	5	X	110
	Frankie Avalon		1	00		Trudy Yors	9	1	010
2	Ima Zohn	RF	1	0010	2	Laura Laurie	6	1	0010
3	Quetie Pye	CF	1	0111100	3	Ladie Byrd	2	1	01100
4	Cindy Rella	LF	X	1010	4	Bertha Nation	1	1	0100
	Judy Rowe		1	110					
5	Rebecca Sunnybrook	B	1	0100	5	Carrie Black	4	1	0100
6	Roberta Rowan	CB	X	110	6	Heidi Thimble	3	1	01110
	Billie Osburn		1	01					

TEAM **Black**   TEAM **Blue**

TIME OUT ⊠ (2)   TIME OUT (1) (2)

FIRST SERVE **Black**   GAME WON BY **Black**

COURT **South**   SCORE **15-11**

RUNNING SCORE: 1 2 3 4 5 6 7 8 9 10 / 11 12 13 14 15 16 17 18 19 20

RUNNING SCORE: 1 2 3 4 5 6 7 8 9 10 / 11 12 13 14 15 16 17 18 19 20

REFEREE *Mother Whistler*   UMPIRE *Shirley Cheatum*   TIMER *Sadie Hau*

Fig. 27-16. Score card (Adapted from D.G.W.S. Volleyball Guide, 1967-69.)

Scoring. At the beginning of each game, the names of players are entered according to their serving order. Each player's position or number is indicated. Points scored are tallied on the team's running score next to the server's name. A zero (0) indicates completion of a term of service.

A substitute's name is entered below that of the person she replaced in the serving order. When one player leaves and another enters, this is indicated in the column headed "Times in Game." When a player re-enters, indicate this with a "2." If she leaves the game, cross out the "2." This indicates that she may not enter the game again.

Tally time-outs in the proper area.

Information pertaining to first team serving, court area, total score, and victor should be attested to by the official.

MAJOR RULE DIFFERENCES— D.G.W.S. AND U.S.V.B.A.

D.G.W.S.

1. Twenty foot overhead clearance
2. No spiking line (back line players are not allowed to spike)

3. Do not rotate on first serve when ball passes over on side-out

4. Only contacts on the hands and forearms are permitted

5. Allows follow-through over the net following a spike or block but disallows reaching over the net to play the ball

6. Players must be in their own area of play on the service; they must generally play in their own area except to save

7. A clarification with officials should be made prior to setting multiple blocks (this will depend upon interpretation of "one's own area")

8. A player may enter the game twice (beginning the game is counted as an entry)

9. Player may serve at any point behind the end line within the imaginary side line boundaries

10. The ball may be held or be unsupported at the moment of service

U.S.V.B.A.

1. Twenty-six foot overhead clearance is approved but 30 feet or more is recommended

2. Ten foot spiking line (back line players may not spike in front of this line)

3. Team rotates when ball is received for

the first service after opponents have served; a team will not indicate its line-up until the choice of first serve or court is made

4. Ball contact allowed on any part of the body above and including the waist

5. Follow-through across the net is allowed and blockers may reach across the net to contact the ball *after* completion of the opponent's attack

6. The player is in position if she is in proper serving order and there is no overlap of feet positions at the time of service; immediately after the service the players may move within the court, as long as a back line player does not spike in front of the 10 foot line

7. Multiple blocks permitted

8. A player may enter the game three times

9. Allows service only from within ten feet of the right side line and behind the end line

10. Ball must be free of support at the moment it is contacted for service

GAME STRATEGY

Players must understand that the real fun of volleyball comes from skilled team effort. Beginners, in their eagerness to score points all by themselves, will often hit the ball over

the net into the hands of an awaiting opponent instead of using a set-up and a spike for a strong offensive play.

Official rules call for a rotation pattern of play whereby all players eventually play each court position; consequently, all players should develop skill and strategy for each position. These skills include serving, retrieving serves and returns, passing, set-ups, spiking, dinking, blocking, and recovering from the net. The greatest limiting factor for many players is lack of height or inability to jump from the floor. Practice in jumping and timing can do much to help a player "get off the feet" when playing on the forward line. The backs must realize that they rarely send the ball over the net, but that their main job is to place it properly for their forwards.

*Offensive Team Play.** The initial offensive play is the serve. A player should develop varied serves with accurate placement and should become a master at using decep-

---

*If U.S.V.B.A. rules are played, a basic 4-2 offense, using four spikers and two setters and necessitating an interchange, is the most common offensive pattern.

A 5-1 offense is used when a team has five potential spikers and one outstanding setter. Using this pattern, a straight 4-2 is played when the setter is on the front line. When she rotates to a back row position, she is shielded from receiving the serve so that she can move into the front court as soon as the ball is served.

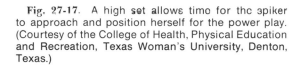

Fig. 27-17. A high set allows time for the spiker to approach and position herself for the power play. (Courtesy of the College of Health, Physical Education and Recreation, Texas Woman's University, Denton, Texas.)

tive body movements, so that the opponents will not be sure which court area the ball will enter.

Both teams try to place their players so that there will always be a spiker and a set-up player on the front line and several strong retrievers and passers on the back line. Every other player, or at least every third player, should be a strong attack player. A basic offensive pattern, the one-two-three, of pass, set, and spike is used by all teams. Generally, the pass goes to a front line player for set, but back line players should be able to set for variety and necessity.

Some teams stress pair-partner play. Each pair has a spiker and a set player, and when they are on the forward line, the one-two-three offense is directed to them. If this pattern is used, variations must be planned for so that the defending team does not come to expect routine plays.

Spikers must be creative and quickly evaluate opponents' court positions and weak areas. A skillful spiker will effectively alternate cross-court spikes, direct spikes and dinks. A further way of loosening the defense is for the set player to spike occasionally on a good pass. A lefthanded spiker or a left-hand spike or dink from an ambidextrous player presents a strong psychological attack.

In the initial line-up, the strongest team spiker should be in the left forward position with a good set-up player to her right. A consistent and forceful server should begin the offense. A fast overhead serve that is placed low over the net with spin on it and lands in a far corner or on a boundary line is usually the most difficult to return.

General playing strategy incorporates playing the ball to the opponent's weaknesses as well as varying the attack by deceptive placement and forceful returns. When possible, place the ball on the receiver's left side. When points are being made, continue the tempo of play. If your team is behind in socre, it may be necessary to speed up play; when ahead and trying to stem an opponent's rally, it is desirable to slow the game with high passes, set-ups, and deep returns.

Defensive Team Play. While awaiting a serve, the left and right forwards pull to the outside and back from the net approximately 10 to 12 feet. The center forward stays about 3 feet from the net until the serve enters the court and then she moves to receive the pass. If the center back moves slightly forward, the five back players form a "W" formation. If the center back stays in line with the other backs, the team position resembles a star (the center forward) and crescent (two outside forward players and the back line).

The individual waiting position is one of poised readiness, with hands up and the body in a semicrouched tensed position. If players forming the "W" or crescent start in rather deep court position they can begin a *creeping movement* forward as the ball is served. Consequently, they are already moving and able to position themselves more easily than if they delayed their movement until the ball is over their court.

When a spike is anticipated, the blockers position themselves across from the spiker, and the remaining front line moves closer toward the blocker or blockers. The back line moves forward and clusters toward the area where the spike, if successful, will drop. Avoid leaving too much back court unguarded.

On defense, individual players watch the ball and the attack players in order to synchronize their movements and anticipate where the ball will land. Generally, the center back should stand nearer the net than the two other defensive players; all three must be watchful of crowding or playing too close to their forwards. Back court players must cover

Fig. 27-18. Power volleyball is increasing in popularity among girls and women. (Courtesy of Rice University, Houston, Texas.)

their part of the court, back up, and get the ball up to the front line quickly and accurately for a spike. It is imperative that players master two-hand and one-hand digs and move quickly for effective defensive play against fast, powerful opponents.

Terminology

Backing up — A planned system of assisting a player who commits herself to making the initial contact on a serve or a spike.

Block — A defensive net play by one or more players who rise with extended arms to return or deflect an opponent's spike.

Cross set — A set which travels parallel to the net and in front of the spiker to her dominant hand side.

Dead ball — A ball temporarily out of play.

Dig — A contact of the ball below the waist with one or both closed hands and extended arms. The ball generally strikes the base of the thumbs and forearms and rebounds in the air. It is used to recover forceful spikes and serves and in net recovery.

Dink — A fake following preparation for a spike which results in a tapped ball that falls close to the net in opponent's court.

Double foul — A foul that occurs when two or more players of opposing teams foul simultaneously. It results in a replay.

Fake — A deceptive movement preceding a shot; for example, apparent preparation for a spike that changes to a high deep hit.

Free ball — An opponent's return which is easily played and controlled.

Holding — A foul which results from allowing the ball to rest on the hand or hands momentarily.

Interchange — Intentionally changing positions with another player to gain advantage in playing the ball.

Lifting — A foul which results from allowing the ball to rest on the hand or hands as they are carried upward.

Over set — A set by either the right or left forward players which passes over the center forward to the opposite forward player.

Pushing — A foul generally called when a two-hand chest volley is not clearly and cleanly batted.

Punched ball — A shot with the fist that returns the ball to opponents following an inaccurate set-up close to the net that did not permit a spike.

Pick-up — The recovery of a forcefully delivered ball. Usually the digging skills are used.

Reverse set — A volley over the head of the set player to a spiker.

Rotation — Clockwise movement of players to a new position at the beginning of a service term.

Spike — An offensive skill, usually the third contact of a ball on a team's own court. The ball is hit above the net and driven downward into opponent's court with power, speed, and accurate placement.

Throwing — A foul resulting from a ball resting in the hand during a throwing motion.

Selected Audio-visual Aids

Beginning Volleyball. (4 slidefilm units, color.) Athletic Institute, 805 Merchandise Mart, Chicago, Ill. 60654. (Purchase.)

Fundamentals of Volleyball. (Revised. 10 min., 16 mm., b & w, sound.) All American Productions and Publishers, P.O. Box 91, Greeley, Colorado 80632. (Purchase and rental.)

Power Volleyball. 8 mm. loop films. Set of five (color). Athletic Institute, 805 Merchandise Mart, Chicago, Ill. 60654 (Purchase.)

Volleyball Drills and Techniques. 1962. (14 min., 16 mm., color or b & w, sound.) All American Productions, P. O. Box 91, Greeley, Colorado 80632. (Purchase and rental.)

Volleyball Skills. 1962. (13 min., 16 mm., color or b & w, sound.) All American Productions, P.O. Box 91, Greeley, Colorado 80632.

Volleyball for Women. (16 mm., 15 min., sound, b & w or color.) All American Productions and Publishers, Greeley, Colorado 80632. (Purchase and rental.)

Suggested Readings

AAHPER, Division for Girls and Women's Sports: *Volleyball Guide*, Current Edition, 1201 16th Street, N.W., Washington, D.C. 20036.

Egstrom, Glen H., and Schaafsma, Frances: *Volleyball*, Dubuque, Iowa, William C. Brown Company, 1966.

La Veaga, Robert E.: *Volleyball*, New York, The Ronald Press Company, 1960.

Thigpen, Janet: *Power Volleyball for Girls and Women*, William C. Brown Company, Dubuque, Iowa, 1967.

Trotter, Betty Jane: *Volleyball for Girls and Women*, New York, The Ronald Press Company, 1965.

Welch, G. E.: *How to Play and Teach Volleyball*. New York, Association Press, 1960.

Suggested Study Questions

1. Describe the skills and techniques necessary for playing center back position.
2. The best team spiker is in center forward position; a set-up player is in right forward position; the ball is served to the left back. What would be a desirable offensive play?
3. Explain the scoring methods used in a volleyball game.
4. Diagram the defensive position of a team awaiting a serve. If the serve is received by the center back, diagram the ball path for the "power play" of pass, set, and spike.
5. Why is volleyball an ideal co-recreational activity?

4

DANCE

*"We are living in a world of beauty
but how few of us open our eyes to see it.
What a different place this world
would be if our senses were trained to
see and hear! We are the heirs of the
wonderful treasures from the past:
treasures of literature and of the arts.
They are ours for the asking—all our own
to have and to enjoy, if only we desire
them enough."*

—Lorado Taft

CHAPTER TWENTY-EIGHT

Courtesy of Dr. Lloyd Messersmith, Southern Methodist University, Dallas, Texas.

SOCIAL DANCE

By Lola Sadlo

The story of social dance is the story of people and the culture from which they come. It is the story of movement in time and space. Follow the dancer and you trace with great difficulty an almost unwritten history: a story that has traveled from the old world to the new and from the new world to the old. One cannot say that social dance is modern or that it is new, for fusion, mingling, mixture, and transportation have created and given life to the Western world's dance of today. The Twist of the Atomic Age is the African witch doctor's gyration of centuries back in steaming jungles. The popular stance, with partner in "shine" position, is medieval in time, for nobles in that period trod their courtly steps in that position. Knee-swaying, hip-swinging, and partner-throwing were a part of the vitality and freedom of one of Europe's most lively dances, the old "Landler," little known outside of Austria until 1770. Democracy today has leveled and banished class divisions of people and their dances. Only desire and taste dictate whether the social dance you do is the inspiration and creation of savages or of dancing masters who have refined or distorted the steps that have evolved through time. Furthermore, in the spread of dance patterns, time has been aided by the media of ships, planes, trains, radio, moving pictures, and television. What happens to dance when millions across the world simultaneously see popular social dances on film? However, what is most important and basic is the human body, aside from the innovations of man's imagination and skill. Its movements remain the same as those of early man. Surely this man, prehistoric man, walked, ran from danger, hopped when pierced by a thorn, jumped to attain his food, leaped across streams and crevasses, slid to dodge an adversary. These locomotor steps, singly or in combination, coupled with rhythm, form, dynamics, and desired pattern are the fabric in social dance today — ageless dance, ageless social dance, "when two are gathered."

PURPOSE

No educational or recreational activity can be said to contribute to the enrichment of lives in our society unless it has objectives. Social dance lays claim to objectives in the following four areas: the physiological, the sociological, the psychological, and the seldom-mentioned spiritual.

1. It contributes to the physical health of the student by providing vigorous exercise.
2. It aids in the development of a well coordinated body.
3. It gives direction to the skills involved in the execution of the most popular dances.
4. It has a health value both physically and psychologically.
5. It gives the individual opportunities to express herself rhythmically.
6. It gives many opportunities for wholesome social relations in controlled situations.
7. It teaches the social skills necessary for comfortable participation in social group activities.
8. It furnishes opportunities for recreation.
9. It is an avenue of expression for the individual student.
10. It is a bridge of experience for the transition from adolescent self-consciousness to adult adjustment in the modern world.

Mediocrity and constant innovations are two of the most pressing problems in the educational social dance area and are of such a nature that principles of basic steps, rhythm patterns and style, proper body alignment, accepted patterns of social dance etiquette and behavior, and a creative approach to *all*

465

social dance should be an integral part of the social dance curriculum.

POPULAR DANCE RHYTHMS

Most of the popular dance rhythms include the basic quarter note, which is equivalent to one walking step.

$$\frac{4}{4} \quad \text{♩} \quad \text{♩} \quad \text{♩} \quad \text{♩} \mid$$
1   2   3   4
walk walk walk walk

Two eighth notes are equivalent to two running steps.

$$\frac{4}{4}$$
1 & 2 & 3 & 4 &
run run run run run run run run

For sustained movement, or movement that has a characteristic hesitation, a half note may be used, which is the equivalent of two quarter notes.

$$\frac{4}{4}$$
1,2   3,4 | 1,2   3,4 ||

The meter is most frequently 4/4, i.e., a strong beat every first note, counted *one*-two-three-four, *one*-two-three-four. It may also be 2/4 (*one*-two) or 3/4 (*one*-two-three). The notation is as follows:

$$\frac{4}{4} \quad \text{♩ ♩ ♩ ♩} \; \| \; \frac{2}{4} \quad \text{♩ ♩} \; \| \; \frac{3}{4} \quad \text{♩ ♩ ♩} \;\|$$

These meters are not necessarily expressed in quarter notes. They may be expressed by a combination of half notes and quarter notes, or by such a combination as an eighth note, dotted to indicate that it is held, and a sixteenth note (one half the beat of the eighth note). There may also be rests between notes, of varying length corresponding to the length of notes.

The following popular rhythms combine the *basic* quarter and eighth notes in various ways.

Box. One slow step, 2 quick steps, 1 slow, 2 quick.

$$\frac{4}{4}$$
S Q Q S Q Q

Magic Step and Swing. One beat is left off the four. Thus count 4 becomes the first step of the repeated dance pattern.

$$\frac{4}{4}$$
S S Q Q S | S Q Q etc. ||

Tango and Cha-cha-cha. Two slow steps, 2 quick steps, and 1 slow step.

$$\frac{4}{4}$$
S S Q Q S

Two-step, Rumba, and Mambo. Two quick steps, 1 slow, 2 quick, 1 slow.

$$\frac{4}{4}$$
Q Q S Q Q S

Waltz. Three even steps in 3/4 time.

$$\frac{3}{4}$$
S S S

Hesitation Waltz. Step and hold for 2 beats.

$$\frac{3}{4}$$
S hold hold

Samba and Bossa Nova. Two quick steps, 1 slow. Note that the meter is 2/4.

$$\frac{2}{4}$$
Q Q S | Q Q S

BASIC SKILLS

BODY FUNDAMENTALS — LEADING AND FOLLOWING

In a social dance class the woman student may sometimes have to lead, i.e., take the boy's part in the dance. The girl who knows how to lead will often be a more sensitive follower but must be careful when dancing with a boy to remember to follow and not to lead.

There are five basic directions for the body to change to for a correct strong lead: forward, backward, right sideward, left sideward and turning (right or left).

ESSENTIALS OF LEADING

1. Do not hold your partner too tightly or too loosely.

Fig. 28-1. Position for forward movement.

Fig. 28-2. Position for backward movement.

2. Listen to the music, identify, and establish the walking beat to the rhythm before starting to dance.

3. Dance confidently on the beat.

4. Step patterns should be anticipated in thought and should be executed with precision and correctness.

5. Begin with simple patterns to establish a firm lead before dancing the more difficult steps.

6. The boy should support his own weight; his balance should be secure.

7. Feel the count internally; do not verbalize it.

8. Slight resistance with the resultant pressure is the principle of the lead.

9. The lead steps out first; the follower waits for the lead before stepping out to follow.

10. Anticipate the next step or move while you are dancing.

11. Elbows should be raised away from the ribs in a buoyant fashion. This is particularly necessary on turning movements.

12. Use the right arm and shoulder as the guiding unit. Do not envelop the girl in too far a reach, for this inhibits her freedom of movement.

13. Know your steps thoroughly.

14. Apply gentle-firm pressure to indicate the body lead, or right arm and hand lead. Release right hand pressure to advance

Fig. 28-3. Position for left sideward movement.

Fig. 28-4. Position for right sideward movement.

forward; tighten pressure to go backward; use the heel to lead into "conversation" or "open" position, and fingers to bring partner into closed position.

ESSENTIALS OF FOLLOWING

1. Since it takes two to tango, maintain a slight resistance to give greater bodily strength and feeling to the leading partner.

2. Weight should not be on heels, but on ball of feet.

3. On backward steps stride with long steps to give freedom to your partner. Be careful not to take the lead.

4. Keep a narrow base; knees should be close together.

5. Do not maintain unusual holds on your partner, cramping his lead.

6. Place your hand and arm firmly on partner's shoulder.

7. Carry your own weight so as not to become heavy in your partner's arms.

8. Reach leg from the hip to step freely.

9. Do not attempt to teach or lead your partner.

OTHER BODY FUNDAMENTALS

Good Posture. This is essential for dancers. Eyes should be kept straight ahead:

head high, chin in, chest out. Carry the shoulders in a free and easy level position. Keep the hips tucked in. Each student should support her own weight with her feet kept close together, except when taking the projected step variation. Stand tall with a straight line going through the ear, shoulder, hip, knee, and ankle. Lean forward ever so slightly to carry most of the weight on the balls of the feet.

Correct Position. Partners should stand with a comfortable distance between them.

BASIC LOCOMOTOR STEPS

No foundation for social dance, or any dance for that matter, would be firm without a knowledge of the following steps:

Walk. The beat is the basic quarter note.

$$\frac{4}{4} \quad \begin{array}{cccc} \text{♩} & \text{♩} & \text{♩} & \text{♩} \\ \text{walk} & \text{walk} & \text{walk} & \text{walk} \end{array} \Big|$$

Run. In 4/4 time, count 1-and, 2-and, 3-and, 4-and.

Fig. 28-5. Position for turning sideward movement.

$\frac{4}{4}$ run run run run run run run run

Hop. Counted like the walk, this is done on one foot or the other.

Jump. This differs from the hop only in that it is done on both feet.

Leap. Counted like the walk, this may be done from either foot.

Skip. Step first with the right foot and hop, then with the left foot.

$\frac{2}{4}$ step R hop R step L hop L

The Slide and the Gallop. When movement is to the side, it is a slide; when forward, the gallop.

$\frac{2}{4}$ step R close L step R close L

These steps may be done alone or in any combination to give a solid and secure feeling for the rhythmic beat of the music played. Do them to records on swing, fox trot, tango, waltz, rumba, cha-cha-cha, mambo. Remember the unit concept, throughout, of the walking step, which is equivalent to a quarter note, or two eighth notes, or a dotted eighth note and a sixteenth note. There is no popular rhythm played to which these locomotor steps cannot be danced.

The student's body movements should coincide with the music. The following progression may be used:

1. Listen to the music.
2. Clap, snap fingers, tap the beat.
3. Walk to the rhythm.
4. Dance to the rhythm.

TRADITIONAL STEPS

Based on the quarter unit, any of the traditional steps such as the two-step, the polka, the schottische, and the waltz can be danced to any popular dance music. All steps are described for the dancer leading.

Two-step. Step with left foot quickly, bring right foot up to close, step with left again, but do not close. Next measure begins with a step by right foot.

$\frac{2}{4}$ step L close R step L

$\frac{2}{4}$ step R close L step R

Polka. The step begins with a hop left. Step with right foot, close left, step again with right foot, and hop on right. Then step with left, and so on.

$\frac{2}{4}$ hop L

step R close L step R hop R

Schottische. Step, step, step, hop. Continue, beginning with other foot.

$\frac{4}{4}$ step L step R step L hop L

Waltz. Begin with a forward step on the left foot, side step with right, close with left. Continue, stepping forward with right foot.

$\frac{3}{4}$ step L side R close L

And now comes the real test of a solid foundation in response to rhythm when locomotor steps and traditional steps are mixed, combined, and danced to any popular music. There is no popular social dance that is performed that does not have any one or a combination of the above steps. When style and characteristics of the dance are added, the student will never be at a loss on the dance floor.

SPECIFIC DANCES

The rhythms of most of the following dances are illustrated in the preceding section on popular dance rhythms.

SWING

Swing is a popular syncopated rhythm dance that has evolved from the lindy and other jitterbug variations. Its meter and rhythm are 4/4. The swim, pony, duck, and temptation, among other popular variations done in "shine" position, are based on this rhythm.

BASIC STEP. Tap-step L, tap-step R, rock L back, rock R forward. These directions are to the boy; the girl does the reverse as she faces boy.

Fig. 28-6.   Closed position.

Fig. 28-7.   Open position.

BASIC STEP CUE.   Tap-step (slow), tap-step (slow), rock rock (quick-quick).

SWING THROW OUT.   Boy does basic step in place while he swings girl with his L hand to position by his L side. Girl travels to this position with basic step, beginning with R foot.

WALK AROUND BREAK.   Boy moves around to girl's original position with basic step while girl travels to boy's original position with basic step.

SINGLE UNDERARM BREAK.   Girl turns clockwise under the boy's upraised L arm with basic step while boy crosses over to his original position with traveling basic step.

FOX TROT

Most dance music today is fox trot. When the tempo is fast, swing is danced; when the tempo is slow, fox trot steps and variations are used. Its name is derived from Harry Fox who introduced the style in Broadway shows of 1913—1914.

Its meter and basic rhythm are 4/4. Most students are familiar with the box and the ladder steps, which now are mixed with the basic step and its variations to give a funda-mental group of steps. The basic rhythm pattern is 4/4.

Fig. 28-8.   Open conversation step.

Fig. 28-9.   Cross conversation step.

BASIC STEP.   Step forward L (S), step forward R (S), step L (Q) diagonally to L, close R (Q). Begin again with L. Girl does step in reverse.

Fig. 28-10.   Position for fox trot or waltz.

BASIC STEP CUE.   Step, step, step-step or quick-quick.

BASIC DIP TURN.   Dip back L, step forward R, step close as in basic step. Move a quarter turn to the R on the quick-quick. Four dip turn steps should complete the full circle in place. Girl dips toward boy with R foot.

CONVERSATION STEP (OPEN POSITION). Boy steps L (S), crosses through with R(S), steps L side (Q), closes R (Q). Girl begins with R.

WALTZ

The waltz, mother of all social dances, continues to be popular. Musical shows on Broadway and movies have brought out each season several new waltz numbers which keep alive its patterns. The waltz rhythm pattern is 3/4.

BOX WALTZ.   Step forward L, step side R, close L. To close the box, step back R, step side L, close R.

BOX WALTZ CUE.   Open open close, open open close.

PROGRESSIVE WALTZ.   Forward L, side R, close L, forward R, side L, close R.

PROGRESSIVE LEFT TURNS.   There is a half turn on each 3 steps. Step out L to L side, facing L, step side R, close L. Step R with toe in, step L side completing turn, close R. Continue revolutions. Begin with R foot, reversing movement, for circles to the right.

CHA-CHA-CHA

The slow two-beat of the Cuban mambo gave rise to the triple hip undulation and shuffle of the cha-cha-cha. Its rhythm is 4/4.

BASIC CHA-CHA-CHA.   Although the true Cuban cha cha cha begins on count 2, it is easier for students to recognize the first beat and marked accent of count 1. Step forward L, step back R, cha-cha-cha shuffle, or step-step-step, on quick-quick's, L R L. Reverse, stepping back on R.

CROSSOVER BREAK.   Cross over L, step in place R, side L, close R, step L in place. Reverse. Girl crosses over with R.

REVERSE CROSSOVER BREAK.   Cross L behind R, step in place R, side L, close R, step L in place. Girl crosses R behind L.

Fig. 28-11. Banjo position.

Fig. 28-13. Dip position.

TANGO

The tango has come to America via the Argentine cowboy, the gaucho. Tango rhythm is 4/4.

Fig. 28-12. Position for tango.

BASIC TANGO PROMENADE STEP. Step forward L (S), step forward R (S), step forward L (Q), step R to side (Q), close L (S). Repeat. Girl steps back with her R foot. The walking step in the tango is marked and heavily accented with a dramatic, continuous, smooth movement. Cushion the supporting foot with a knee bend.

TANGO BREAK. This is forward L (Q), side R (Q), draw L (S). Most variations end with this break.

PROMENADE STEP. Do the first three steps of the basic tango step leading partner in banjo, or right parallel, position. On break bring partner face to face again to closed position.

CONVERSATION PROMENADE. Turn partner into conversation position on open-cross steps. Open L (S), cross R (S). Break to closed position.

CORTE OR DIP TURN. Dip with L knee bent and turned out and body erect (S), step forward R (S), finish with break making a quarter turn to the L.

SAMBA

This movement was originally a tribal dance among African slaves. It was adopted by Brazilians and adapted to a suave, yet gay and lilting, mood. Samba rhythm is 2/4.

SAMBA BASIC BOX STEP. Forward L (Q), side R (Q), close L (S). (This step is similar to a balance step, except that the body sways forward, backward, or sideward in opposition to the direction of the step. The quick weight change may be cued by calling the second step a "limp" step. The weight is there only long enough to transfer to the other foot. The base is narrow. Say to yourself, "Forward, limp, step. Back, limp, step.") This step may be done in "shine" position (Fig. 28-14). It may also be used in the samba box turn to the L in place.

SIDE BALANCE STEP. Side L (Q), behind R (Q), in place L (S). For style look over the shoulder on the side of the foot that is traveling behind. Side R (Q), behind L (Q), in place R (S). Girl does the reverse, beginning with R.

BUTTERFLY, OR COPACABANA. Move into open, or conversation, position with inside hips adjacent to each other and with outside hands released. Do basic samba steps traveling in line of direction, moving diagonally away from partner on QQS and toward partner on QQS. There is a slight rocking movement (forward, backward, forward) on

the QQS. The hips are pushed back in a bustle-lift effect on the second Q step of the pattern. To change, on the forward-limp-step, the boy makes a quarter turn and brings the girl to position facing him in closed position.

RUMBA

The rumba is Cuba's national dance, known there as the "son." Its style is characterized by the smooth rolling undulation of the hips while the upper part of the body is dramatically quiet. Rumba rhythm is 4/4.

THE CUBAN WALK. L foot forward, weight on R. R foot forward, weight on L. Travel on the balls of the feet with relaxed knees. Hold back your weight. The rumba hip motion is in the delayed transfer of weight after the step is taken. After mastering the Cuban walk, combine these to make the following rhythm pattern: walk, walk, walk-hold, or QQ slow. Continue traveling in any direction with QQ slow-hold.

RUMBA BOX STEP. This is the same as the box of the fox trot, adding the hip roll. Side L (Q), close R (Q), forward L (S). Side R, close L, backward R.

RUMBA BREAK. In L or R open, or conver-

Fig. 28-14.   Shine position.

Fig. 28-15.   Rumba position.

sation, position. Side L, behind R, in place L. Side R, behind L, in place R. While the boy does 4 Cuban walk sets (QQS) in place the girl may do 4 Cuban walk sets traveling around the boy, who extends R hand to lead her around, continuing to guide her with his L hand close to waist. He takes her R hand again to complete the circle. Finish phrase of music with 1 complete box pattern.

MAMBO

The mambo, too, is Cuban and the forerunner of the cha-cha-cha. Its distinctive style is derived from the syncopation of setting a 3 beat dance pattern to 4/4 music. The unusual second and fourth beats are accented. The Cuban hip motion, too, is used.

Mambo rhythm is as follows:

MAMBO BASIC BREAK. Lead in step L to side on 4—1. Take two quick steps (RL) together in place in center of pattern on counts 2 and 3. Take slow step to R on count 4 with hold over onto count 1 of the next measure. Reverse movement and continue.

MAMBO BASIC FORWARD BREAK. On count 2 the quick step is either forward L or back R. The feet should not be together in the center; the foot taking the 4—1, or slow count, should be slightly in the lead. Many of the figures and variations are similar to those of the cha-cha-cha, such as the crossover. Say to yourself: "Slow, quick, quick," remembering to close-hold on "slow," break (stepping forward, backward, or sideward) on "quick," and step in place on "quick." The effect is like a bodily whiplash.

BOSSA NOVA

The bossa nova, which means new voice or new beat, came to the United States from Brazil where it has been popular for the last several years.

Its rhythm is Gafiera (like the samba). This has been popular in Brazil for about 100 years. The samba beat allows the jazz musician to put his improvisation to a palatable beat. The beat was innovated by musicians in Brazil's out-of-the-way night club spots off the tourist path. At first the night people lis-

tened; nobody danced. It was not long, however, before the sounds reached the ears of the Brazilian society folk and American tourists. When it did, feet started to tap. The old dances did not fit the new rhythm, so dancers integrated familiar steps with Brazilian folk dances and soon a definite dance pattern emerged. It combines a rumba, samba, and a mild twist with gentle undulation of the hips.

BASIC STEP. Step with L foot to L on count of 1-and. Bring R foot close to (not touching) L foot on count of 2-and. (At the same time lift R hip slightly on the count of 2 and lower on the count of and.) Reverse entire movement.

SECOND BASIC STEP. Do the same step moving forward with L foot and back with R. L foot forward on count of 1. Bring R forward close to L on count of and. Lift R hip on count of 2 and lower hip on count of and. Step R foot back on count of 1. Bring L foot back on count of and. Lift L hip slightly on count of 2. Lower hip on count of and.

OPEN BREAK. Step L on L foot on count of 1. Bring R foot close to L on count of and. Raise R hip (as in basic steps) on count of 2 and lower on count of and. Then boy steps backward on R foot, releasing partner's L hand. Girl steps back on her L foot. Both repeat basic step, raising hip on count of 2 and lowering on count of and.

BOSSA NOVA BOX. Step L foot to L, bring R foot close to it, raising hip and lowering as in basic step. After R foot is brought close to L, dancer turns 90 degrees to R by turning R foot 90 degrees. Repeat this step 3 times to complete a full 360 degree turn. Transition can be into second basic step.

ETIQUETTE

The rules of etiquette are simple, and mostly a matter of common sense. Among the most important on the dance floor are these:

1. Do not teach your partner on the dance floor.
2. Anticipate the next step.
3. Be confident; strive to become a proficient dancer.
4. Do not be a show-off.
5. Be and look interested.

6. Find mutual topics of interest for conversation; *never* gossip.

Suggested Readings

Hall, J. Tillman: *Dance!*, Belmont, California, Wadsworth Publishing Company, 1963.

Harris, June A.: *Dance Awhile*, Minneapolis, Minn., Burgess Publishing Company, 1968.

Heaton, Alma, and Heaton, Israel: *Ballroom Dance Rhythms*, Dubuque, Iowa, William C. Brown Company, 1961.

Kraus, Richard, and Sadlo, Lola: *Beginning Social Dance*, Belmont, California, Wadsworth Publishing Company,, 1964.

Murray, Arthur: *How to Become a Good Dancer*, New York, Simon & Schuster, 1959.

Sachs, Curt: *World History of the Dance*, New York, W. W. Norton and Company, 1937.

White, Betty: *Betty White's Ballroom Dancebook for Teachers*, New York, David McKay Company, Inc., 1962.

White, Betty: *Betty White's Teen-Age Dance Etiquette*, New York, David McKay Company, Inc., 1956.

Suggested Study Questions

1. What are the objectives of social dance?
2. Give 10 suggestions for becoming a good leader in social dancing.
3. How important are the basic locomotor steps of the slide, skip, leap, jump, walk, run, and hop?
4. Explain and demonstrate the traditional steps of the two-step, polka, schottische, and the waltz.
5. What are the basic differences between the mambo and the tango, the bossa nova and the rumba?

CHAPTER TWENTY-NINE

SQUARE DANCE

By Lola Sadlo

Square dancing is a blend of the dancing of many cultures. It began in early French quadrilles and English country dances and was brought to America in the 18th century. Pioneers pushed westward, taking their folk and square dances with them. In the West some of these dances were woven into the fabric of the Mexican and Spanish dances. Thus square dancing today represents democracy in rhythmic action. It is not unusual in various parts of the country to read of 13,000 square dancers convening in one part of a state to "allemande left." In southern California alone there are 68,000 square dancers who belong to organized groups, schools, churches, and other social groups. The friendly spirit among eight people, for that is how many it takes to form a square, is the common denominator that spells one basic form of democracy. Perhaps this is the reason it is called everybody's dance.

NATURE AND PURPOSE

Square Dancing Is for Fun. The basic steps and figures have come down almost unchanged from colonial days, when the square dance was the traditional celebration of work completed.

Only two principal demands are made on the individual dancer: an adequate sense of rhythm and the ability to follow instructions.

Form. The square dance is a definite dance form. Its infinite variety of patterns is achieved by the changing combinations of a relatively small number of basic figures or patterns.

CALL. There are three distinct styles: (1) the "prompt" call, which consists of simple directions called out about a half measure before the pattern or figure is executed, (2) the singing call, and (3) the patter, or chanting, call, which is the most popular.

TIMING. All square dance figures are done in multiples of 4 to 4/4, 2/4, or 6/8 time.

BASIC POSITIONS AND STEPS

GENERAL PRINCIPLES

Relative Positions. Partner changes occur frequently in square dancing; dancers should come to think of "partner" and "corner" not as familiar individuals but as positions relative to themselves.

Position of Hands. Ladies hold skirts when not executing a figure, while gents place backs of hands to their own hips.

The Promenade. In Western square dancing the gentleman always promenades the lady to the gentleman's place in the set. In Eastern square dancing the gentleman promenades the lady to her position in the set when he "picks up" a lady in a figure. Promenades are always *counterclockwise*.

Traffic. Whenever the caller directs a call to 4 dancers to cross the set at the same time and dance with the opposite person, each dancer should allow the person on the left to have the right of way and cross first.

Circles. Circles are always *clockwise* unless directed otherwise.

Outside Ring. Whenever dancers are directed to circle the set on the outside, the standing, inactive dancers should step forward toward the center and then return to position.

Space. All square dance figures and steps should be executed within the limits of the set, which is squared by having partners stand side by side. Their outside arms outstretched should form a perfect square.

Terminology. Square dance terms may change from community to community, from region to region, but the basic and underlying principles remain constant.

477

LADIES AND GENTS. This is the universal vocabulary of the square dance.

FUNDAMENTAL STEPS

A large number of steps may be learned in one large circle. All join hands, with each girl standing on the right side of her partner. There should be an arm's reach between couples.

Circle Left (and Circle Right) Walk (do not run, hop, or skip, but use an easy walking step with but slight up-and-down motion) 8 steps to left. Turn and walk 8 steps to right.

> *Call*: "All join hands and circle left — Back you go and circle right."

Forward and Back. All take 3 steps into the center and hold on count 4. Take 4 steps backing out.

> *Call:* "Into the center forward go — Back from the center and don't be slow."

Call to the ladies; call to the gents.

(They drop hands to execute steps.

Do-si-do (or Do-sa-do). Partners face each other, walk forward 4 steps, pass right shoulders. Continue around partner with 4 steps backward. This should then be done with the corner person who, simply stated, is the person on the other side of you from your partner.

Fig. 29-2. The swing, or buzz step.

The Swing. Partners stand in banjo position (right hips side by side, right feet almost touching.) Using the right foot as a pivot and moving it as little as possible push with the left foot (Fig. 29-2). Offer resistance to each other to do the buzz step in a smooth, fast circle in place. Other swings which may be called are: the one hand swing (a high

Fig. 29-1. Do-si-do.

Fig. 29-3. The elbow swing.

Fig. 29-4.   The two hand swing.

Fig. 29-6.   The promenade.

Fig. 29-5.   The forearm swing.

palm position), the elbow swing, the two hand swing, and the forearm swing.

Call: "Swing with your partner like swinging on the gate."

The Promenade.   The name describes the step, which is a walk (counterclockwise) around the circle (or set) two by two. The skaters or promenade position of the hands is used.

Call: "Promenade home," or "Promenade the circle,"

Grand Right and Left.   Partners in grand circle face each other and give R hands to each other; they walk past each other, drop hands and extend L hands to the next person. Thus they continue around the circle.

It should take 2 counts of music to join hands and pass.

Call: "Right and left grand," or "Grand right and left."

Combine any two or more of the above figures. Then follow these calls:

"Honor your partner—(*Gents bow
    slightly; Ladies curtsey.*)
All join hands and circle wide—
Swing with your partner like
    swinging on the gate.
All join hands and circle right—
Swing your corner with all your
    might.
Into the center—
And back you go.
Ladies to the center—
And don't be slow.
Do-si-do partner—
Do-si-do corner—
Grand right and left—
Swing your partner—
Swing like thunder.
Promenade."

Fig. 29-7. The allemande left.

OTHER FIGURES

Other figures or steps that can be done in a large circle, or square formation are:

The Allemande Left. This is a left hand swing with corner, making a complete turn, always returning to partner with honor or a quick 2 beat balance step. The entire figure requires 8 beats of music. This may be followed by the grand right and left.

Balance. Take partner's R hand, step backward and forward to 4 beats of music. The call may be, "Balance your partners."

Back Track. This is a variation of the popular grand right and left. It is often called, "Meet your honey and turn right back."

The Once-and-a-Half. This movement is danced out of a grand right and left with dancers meeting their partners and taking their partners with a right forearm swing. They swing 1½ times around with partners.

The Sashays. There are four sashay movements in Western square dance.

"SASHAY PARTNERS HALFWAY AROUND." This means to exchange places; the gentlemen dance to the right behind the ladies who dance to their left in front of the gentlemen with 3 small sliding steps (4 beats).

"RESASHAY." This means for the partners to return to original positions over the same path.

"SASHAY ALL THE WAY AROUND." This means for dancers to encircle their partners completely in 8 beats of music.

"ALL AROUND YOUR LEFT-HAND LADY." This means for the gents to circle around their corner ladies passing back-to-back with them. Only they move, while ladies dance 2 steps forward to allow the gentlemen to move more freely; and then ladies return to position.

THE SQUARE DANCE FORMATION

The Set. There are four couples to a set standing in square formation. This square should be no bigger than it takes to circle it with 16 steps. The couples are numbered 1,

Fig. 29-8. The varsouvienne position.

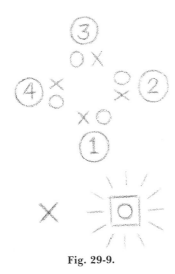

Fig. 29-9.

2, 3, and 4. Couple 1 is the couple whose backs are to the music and the caller (Fig. 29-9).

HEAD COUPLES.   Couples 1 and 3.

SIDE COUPLES.   Couples 2 and 4.

RIGHT-HAND LADY.   The lady to the right past the gent's partner.

OPPOSITE LADY.   The lady directly across the set.

CORNER LADY.   The lady at the gent's left.

HOME PLACE.   The position the gent took when the set was formed.

SQUARE SET PATTERNS

Right and Left Through.   Two couples face each other and dance directly toward the opposite person, whom they pass by the right shoulders. They exchange positions with the other couple and the gents take the left hands of their partners as soon as they have passed through. At the same time each gent places his right hand on the lady's back and wheels his partner counterclockwise to face the opposite couple again. This is an 8 beat phrase. The figure may then be repeated.

Two Ladies Chain.   The two couples called answer the call by exchanging places with each other, extending right hands as they pass. They give their left hands to the opposite gentlemen, who wheel them around as in the right and left through. A chain right back will return the ladies to original positions.

Four Ladies Chain.   This call includes all the ladies, who move to the center, forming a

right hand star and circle clockwise until they reach the opposite gentlemen.

Single Visitor.   One person at a time, either the lady or the gent, leads the figure around the set and visits each couple in turn.

Visiting Couple.   One couple at a time leads the set.

Pick-up Progressive.   Couple leading the figure dances first with one couple, adds another couple, and finally adds the last couple.

Heads and Sides.   Two couples at a time lead the figure.

Breakdown.   All dancers in the set dance the call together.

Hoedown (Hash, Succotash, Chop Suey).   No particular pattern is followed.

PARTS OF THE SQUARE DANCE

There are four parts to a square dance:

The Introduction.   This call introduces the dancers to each other and the music.

The Figure or Main Pattern.   This movement follows the introduction and gives the dance its name. In singing calls the music gives the title to the dance. This principal figure is repeated until all the couples have led it. There is usually a chorus between each execution or round of the figure.

The Chorus.   This pattern usually follows each calling of the figure, or the desires of the caller.

The Finish or Conclusion.   This ending usually follows the final chorus or it may be omitted in a long figure.

"Trimmings" is a word that may describe introductions, choruses, subchoruses, and finishes.

TYPICAL INTRODUCTIONS

"Honor your partner, give her a smile,
Step right back and swing her awhile."

"All jump up and never come down,
Swing your honey around and around."

"Rock on your heel and rock on your toe,
Stomp your feet and here we go."

"Honor your partner and the lady on your left,
All join hands and circle left."

"Home you go from that circle round the
  hall,
Swing your honey; don't let her fall."

TYPICAL CHORUSES (TRIMS, BREAKS, FILLERS)

(For Four)
"Circle four and don't be slow,
'Round and 'round and do-si-do,
Circle four and 'round you go,
Two little ladies go do-si-do."

"Ring, ring, pretty little ring,
Break that ring with a corner swing;
Ring, ring, pretty little ring,
Break that ring with a corner swing."

"Now we swap and now we trade
Your pretty gal for my old maid.
Mine's worth a nickel,
Yours is worth a dime,
You swing yours and I'll swing mine."

(For Eight)
"Allemande left with your left hand,
Right to your partner with a right and left
  grand.
Promenade eight when you get straight,
Home you go and don't be late."

"Left to your corner with your left hand,
Walk right in to a right and left grand.
Meet your honey and everyone swing
Swing, swing, ring-a-ding ding."

"Ring, ring, pretty little ring
Break that ring with a corner swing."
*(This call may be repeated four times until ladies
  have returned to original partners.)*

"Swing on your corner like swinging on the
  gate,
Swing your own and right and left eight."

"Four gents in and listen to my call:
Swing that lady across the hall."

"Eight hands up and away we go,
Circle left and don't be slow."

"Ladies to the center and back to the bar,
  (In and out)
Gents to the center with a right hand star.
  (Gents move once around clockwise.)
Skip your gal and catch the next,
Swing her around on any pretext."
*(This call may be repeated until gents have re-
  turned to original partners.)*

TYPICAL ENDINGS

"Allemande left with your left hand,
  Bow to your partner and take your stand."

"Take your honey right off the floor.
  That's all there is. Do you want more?"

"Swing her high with all your might;
  Kiss her, boys, and say 'Goodnight.' "

"Honor your honey and the girl across the
  hall.
Take your honey to a hole in the wall."

TYPICAL FIGURES OR CALLS

Star by the Right
"First couple out to the couple on the right,
Form a star with a right hand cross,
  (Move clockwise)
Back with the left and don't get lost.
  (Move counterclockwise)
Form a ring and around you go,
Break it up with a do-si-do.
Lead to the next."
*(The call may be repeated for Couples 2, 3, and
  4.)*

Take a Little Peek

"First couple out to the right of the ring,
'Round that couple and take a little peek.
*(Couple 1 separates and peek at each other
  around Couple 2.)*

Back to the center and swing your sweet,
'Round that couple and peek once more,
Back to the center and swing all four.
  (Trim may be added.)
Lead to the next."

Split the Ring

"First and third go forward and back,
Forward again on the same old track.
Right and left through, on you go,
Ladies go gee and the gents go haw
Around   Sally   Gooden   and   around
  Grandma.
Do-si your pretty little Taw,
Do-si the corner girl,
All around that pretty little thing,
Meet your honey with a two hand swing,
Promenade with the corner of the ring."
*(Call is repeated 3 more times to the head
  Couples 1 and 3.*
*Pattern is repeated 4 times to the side Couples 2
  and 4.)*

A TYPICAL DANCE

There are hundreds of square dances, ranging from the above basic figures to the intricate longer figures; however, the pattern and movement principles are the same. Records for square dances, with and without calls, and of varying degrees of difficulty are available at all popular record centers. Directions and calls are fully described and are usually included in these dance albums. Following is a typical grouping of the four parts that go to form the pattern of the majority of square dances:

TEXAS STAR

The Introduction

"All jump up and never come down,
Swing your honey around and around.
Join your hands and form a ring,
Circle left while you call and sing.

The Main Figure

"Ladies to the center and back to the bar,
Gents to the center and form a star.
Right hands crossed and 'How are you?'
Back with the left and 'How do you do?'
Meet your girl and pass her by,
Pick up the next girl on the sly.
Halfway round the ring you go,
Gents swing out and the ladies swing in.
Form that pretty star again,
Turn that star around the ring.
Circle wide till you get straight,
Do-si-do and promenade eight.

The Trim

"Allemande left your corner,
Allemande right your own.
Swing that corner lady,
As though she were your own.
(*This trim may be repeated 3 times to return gentlemen to the original ladies.*)

Conclusion

"Square your sets with a smile on your face,
All jump up and down in your place.
Take your honey to an easy chair —
I don't care; you know where."

ETIQUETTE

Responsibility. When the caller or leader is talking, there should be silence. Responsibility to seven other people is involved.

Listen. Remember that you cannot begin to dance the figure unless you have heard the call.

Respect. Respect the regional differences and colorful colloquialisms in the various sections of our country. There are basic similarities, but all square dancing is not uniform.

Courtesy. Be courteous and thoughtful when new couples are introduced to the set.

Conversation. Since dancers change partners frequently, there is little time to develop the art of conversation; the gent is kept quite busy listening to the calls. Wait until the music and movement come to a stop.

Decorum. Square dancing is not wild and raucous; its decorum requires as much dignity, smoothness, and grace as the social dance.

Suggested Readings

Damon, S. Foster: *The History of Square Dancing*, Barre, Mass., Barre Gazette, 1957.

Gowing, Gene: *The Square Dancers' Guide*, New York, Crown Publishers, Inc.

Hall, J. Tillman: *Dance*, Belmont, California, Wadsworth Publishing Company, 1963.

Harris, Jane, Pittman, Anne, and Swenson, Marlys: *Dance Awhile*, Minneapolis, Minn., Burgess Publishing Company, 1968.

Jensen, Clayne, and Jensen, Mary: *Beginning Square Dance*, Belmont, California, Wadsworth Publishing Company, 1966.

Suggested Study Questions

1. Explain the differences between the prompt call, the singing call, and the patter call.
2. Define the following: (a) head couple, (b) the allemande left, (c) back track, and (d) sashay.
3. What are some of the most important factors that enable a student to learn to dance?
4. What are the four parts of every square dance? What are the differences between each of them?
5. Can you give three typical opening calls and three closing ones while the other members of the class clap the rhythm?

CHAPTER THIRTY

Courtesy Jean Jacobs, Springfield College, Springfield, Massachusetts.

FOLK DANCE

By Lola Sadlo

Folk dance is dancing created and performed by the people of a particular nation. One or any number of persons can perform folk dances, which started and have been developed for many reasons, ranging from entertainment and amusement to a serious part in the religious lives of many peoples. However, many of these folk dances have become more than national or group dances; they have come to be popular in other parts of the world as conquest, colonization, and other major forces have interplayed to shape communication and modes of action.

Today folk dancing is enjoying tremendous popularity in all parts of the world. This is true particularly in the United States, where it has had slow but steady growth. Although European immigrants brought their folk dances along with them, the treatment given to these by outside groups and ethnic societies in the early years was that of "preservation."

In New York in 1905 Elizabeth Burchenal introduced folk dance into the physical education program for girls. Today, with the general acceptance of coeducational dance of all types, much credit goes to the physical and recreation educators who through the years since the turn of the century have kept folk dance alive at all levels and in many places. Travel, television, student exchange, world's fairs, conferences, institutes, workshops, folk dance clubs and camps, and increasing attention to the literature and the recorded music have stimulated interest and growth in this major dance area. (The author includes with great respect and admiration many leaders in the field under whom she has studied, who have given dynamic and devoted lives to the folk dance movement: Vyts Beliajus, Lucile Czarnowski, Anne Duggan, Paul Erfer, Jane Harris, Miriam Lidster, Gertrude Mooney, Lloyd Shaw, Edith Stevenson, and many others.)

NATURE AND PURPOSE

Folk dance, with its singular characteristics that reflect the ideas, the feelings, and the mores of a people, has not, as a rule, been the conscious work of human forces. The new state of Israel is the one contemporary exception. Both the old and the new have emerged in its creation. Folk dance today comes along many avenues: dances from the western world that originated in ancient rituals and customs; dances of the 19th century such as the polkas, schottisches, waltzes, mazurkas, and quadrilles; dances from Europe that we call both recreational and educational; dances with regional characteristics, such as the American square dance, the play party games, the Kentucky running sets, the early California dances, the old time English dances, and the New England longways or contra dances.

Folk dancing gives not only enjoyable, wholesome exercise but is fun to do. Other objectives are:

1. It meets the individual needs of students to become better acquainted with foreign students and to open avenues of interchanged learnings.

2. It affords the opportunity for students to learn folk dances that reflect the cultural-historical background of the different countries in our American heritage.

3. Perhaps its greatest merit is in the field of international friendship and fellowship, understanding, and appreciation.

4. It can be a stimulating, exhilarating experience.

5. It provides a coeducational social outlet and activity.

Exhibitionism, at folk dance festivals, for the tourist, at the theatre, or on the concert stage, has in many instances robbed this form of dance of its simple beauty and authenticity. Folk dancing was meant to be for the en-

Fig. 30-1

Fig. 30-2

Figs 30-1 and 30-2. Folk dancing today is gaining in popularity throughout the world. (Courtesy of College of Health, Physical Education and Recreation, Texas Woman's University, Denton, Texas.)

joyment of the participants, not the observers.

It is difficult today to procure recordings for many of the fine traditional dances; however, many companies are pressing a greater variety of 45 and 33⅓ rpm records with finer tone and reproduction. These frequently have accompanying dance notes and descriptions.

BASIC STEPS

The author's experience has carried her to many parts of the world, to dance with the many ethnic groups she has encountered. Nowhere did she find a single folk dance that did not have as its basic step or steps one or more of the movements described in this section or on pages 468-469 in the chapter on

Fig. 30-3. (Courtesy of Dean Anne S. Duggan, College of Health, Physical Education and Recreation, Texas Woman's University.)

social dance. Many of the positions and figures are described on pages 478-480 in the square dance chapter. Thus a foundation is provided for all folk dance: an international alphabet and language of movement. In order, out of order, in pairs, or in combination one can do these movements to any folk dance music to get the feeling of the

Fig. 30-4. (Courtesy of Dean Anne Duggan, College of Health, Physical Education and Recreation, Texas Woman's University.)

simplicity of the most complex-appearing of folk dances.

In addition to the steps already described in the preceding two chapters the following are used in folk dances.

Buzz. This is the partner (hip-to-hip) swing step commonly used in square dancing (see p. 478, "The Swing," and Fig. 29-2).

Pivot. The dancer places her weight on either foot and takes small "pushing" steps with the free foot to spin in place.

Grapevine. One foot crosses in front of the other alternately, in a continuous movement of traveling steps.

Gavotte. Four counts comprise the time of this step, which moves in any direction, with three walking steps followed by a light tap with the ball of the free foot; the movement is continued, since there has been no change of weight, with this foot.

Mazurka. This step is done in 3/4 time with a diagonal glide step (1), step (2), hop (3), or step-left, close-right, hop-right. On the last hop, after the left foot has been released to swing forward on count 2, the knee is bent while the left foot swings in front, close to the right ankle.

An Experimental Pattern

Experiment with a folk dance traditional step. For example, begin with the basic schottische figure:

1. Schottische forward with partner in open dance position. Starting with outside foot (the foot farthest away from your partner when you stand side by side), step, step, step, hop. Repeat, starting on inside foot: step, together, step, hop. Follow with four hop steps.

2. Try variations on the step itself: for height, for speed, for change of direction or emotion. Experiment with touching the right hand to the left toe and the left hand to the right toe on each step hop. Create your own variations.

3. Try combining five or six of these variations.

4. Change partners frequently while still doing the schottische step and endeavor to make the transition a smooth one.

Learn the background and setting to the dances taught. The literature is replete with materials and information about all countries.

SPECIFIC DANCES

The following dances have been selected for their brevity, beauty, and simplicity to familiarize students with the fundamental steps and to open the avenue toward expanded interest and exploration.

Fig. 30-5. (Courtesy of Dean Anne S. Duggan, College of Health, Physical Education and Recreation, Texas Woman's University.)

Fig. 30-6. (Courtesy of Dean Anne Duggan, College of Health, Physical Education and Recreation, Texas Woman's University.)

JESSIE POLKA (UNITED STATES)

Record: Crystal 108 "Calico Polka" or Educational Dance Recordings FD 2

Formation: Couples facing counterclockwise (CCW) in varsouvienne position (see Fig. 29-8, p. 480).

1. Place L heel diagonally forward L. Close L placing weight on L. Place R toe backward diagonally; extend R heel forward diagonally R. Close R. Extend L toe to side; brush L foot forward.

2. Four two-steps forward, beginning with L foot (polkas may be substituted for the two-steps).

ALL AMERICAN PROMENADE (UNITED STATES)

This is a simple, introductory, progressive mixer that is fun for a beginners' class.

Record: Windsor R 605 "All American Promenade"

Formation: Couples face CCW in circle. Inside hands are joined.

1. Begin on outside foot. Walk forward 4 steps. Turn toward partner on fourth walking step and continue walking CCW, backing up with

4 steps.   Measures 1—4

Repeat Measures 1—4 moving CW.   Measures 5—8

2. Balance (see p. 480) together toward partner, then balance away from partner. Exchange places with partner with the lady passing with 4 steps in front of man, making 1 turn CCW. Measures 9—12 Repeat balance toward partner, then away from partner. Now turn lady under man's arm back to next man. She progresses with 4 walking steps CW. Man progresses and advances forward CCW to next partner taking 4 walking steps.   Measures 13—16

DANISH SCHOTTISCHE (DENMARK)

Record: Columbia 22178 or any good schottische record

Formation: Couple in promenade position (see p. 479 and Fig. 29-6). Face CCW. (The lady is always on the right unless otherwise specified).

1. Two schottische steps forward

beginning with the L foot. Continue forward with 4 step-hops. Repeat 2 schottische steps and 4 step-hops.

2. Face partner. Join R hands. Do 1 schottische step to the left, 1 schottische to the right. Turn with a right hand star* with 4 step-hops. Repeat the entire movement of step 2.

3. Face partner. Place hands on hips. Do 1 schottische to the left, then 1 schottische passing partner in back position. Continue with 4 step-hops to face partner again. Repeat the entire movement of step 3.

LA JESUSITA (MEXICO)

This is a vivacious couple dance which had its origin during the festivities at Christmas time or during "Las Posadas."

Record: Imperial 6082
Formation: Partners face in circle formation. Man has his back to the center.

1. Beginning with the R foot do 7 schottische (Jesusita) steps. Move to the right and to the left, passing partner face to face, then back to back. Continue to alternate for the remaining 5 schottisches. End with 3 stamps, facing partner.

2. Back away from partner with a skip right, skip left, step right, tap left, tap left (these are done quickly). Repeat movement, moving toward partner. Repeat, backing away and coming toward partner.

3. Do 16 grapevine steps, revolving around each other. Cross R foot over L to begin with, touching R shoulders. Alternate, touching L shoulders to continue revolving movement. End with both facing center, lady in front of man with his hands on her shoulders.

4. Back away from center of circle with the same movement pattern of step 2. Repeat in, out, and in again.

5. Partners face in single circle in shoulder-waist position. Move CCW with 6 schottische steps. Man dances forward, swinging leg forward, while lady dances backward, swinging leg to the back at the completion of each schottische. (Tradi-

---

*See Four Ladies Chain, page 481.

tionally, the dance ended with the couples facing the center to kneel in reverence to the birth of Jesus.) Two schottisches may be substituted to complete the phrase of music and the dance.

CORRIDO (MEXICO)

This is an ever-popular favorite at international folk dance recreational gatherings or festivals.

Record: Imperial 1137
Formation: In circle formation of couples. Take a closed social dance position; gentlemen stands with his back to the center.

1. Move sidewards CW with 10 step-close steps. The gentleman begins with his R foot, while the lady begins with her L foot.

2. Move CCW with 7 grapevine steps and end with a step and 2 stamps, alternating feet.

3. Move CW with only 4 step-close steps in preparation to go into the "soldado," which is moving to the center with 4 steps and moving out with 4 steps in a wedge-shaped pattern. The "soldado" is repeated 3 more times.

4. Repeat 2, the grapevine.

Other variations may be substituted for 2 and/or 4.

CUMBERLAND SQUARE (ENGLAND)

This dance is usually done to a quick 2/4 music.

Record: Folkcraft 1143 or other hornpipe tunes
Formation: Four couples in square formation.

1. Head couples slide 8 times across. Head couples slide 8 times back. The men and women pass back to back. Side couples repeat slides across and back.

2. Head couples star by the R with 8 steps. Star by the L with 8 steps. Side couples repeat star movements.

3. Head couples circle to the left (basket) with 16 buzz steps. Keep the R foot in the center. Side couples repeat "basket" movement.

4. Circle L with 8 two-steps, or 16 walking steps, promenading home with elbows linked.

GALOPEDE (ENGLAND)

This is a longways country fun dance and traditionally English in spirit.

Record: Folkcraft 1331
Formation: A column of 4, 5, or 6 couples (men facing the women). Hands are joined, or the arms are linked in lines.

1. The men and women advance forward with 3 steps, bow to partner, retire with 4 steps to original place. Dropping hands, they cross over with 8 steps, passing R shoulders, turning right to stand in the opposite or partner's place. Repeat entire movement, returning to original places.
2. All swing partners CW with a two-hand swing with either 16 skipping steps or 8 Polkas.
3. The first couple (head couple) continue to swing with either 16 skipping or 8 polka steps while the other couples clap and advance lines in preparation for the repeat of the dance with a new head couple. Repeat the three figures until the original head couple returns to original position.

ROAD TO THE ISLES (SCOTLAND)

This is a simple, rather modern Scottish folk dance that introduces the schottische in a charming movement.

Record: Imperial 1005 or Educational Dance Recordings FD 2
Formation: Couples in circle, in varsouvienne position. Face CCW.

1. Place L heel forward and to the left. Walk 3 grapevine steps to the right, L R L. Place R heel forward and to the R. Walk 3 grapevine steps to the left, R L R. Place L heel forward. Then touch L toe in back.
2. Advance or progress forward with 2 schottisches, L R L hop, R L R hop. On the last hop turn halfway to the R to face the opposite direction. The hands remain joined. Repeat this movement, L R L hop, in the opposite direction and turn to face in original direction. Continue with step R L R and hold.

WAVES OF TORY (IRELAND)

Record: Capitol 10250 or "Irish Washer-woman," "Irish Lilt," or "Irish Long Dance"
Formation: Longways—3 couples, lady on the right, facing forward. Each places own hands, palms out, on hips.

1. Move forward with 4 lilting (light running steps with feet raised in front) steps	2 measures
Move backward, 4 lilting steps	2 measures
Step right, swing left (hopping with the right)	1 measure
Step left, swing right (hopping with the left)	1 measure
Turn in place to the right with 4 light running steps	2 measures
Repeat entire movement	8 measures
	16 measures

2. Couples, or lines, face each other. Repeat step 1, passing R shoulders.   16 measures
End facing in original position.

3. The "waves." Head couple (and subsequent head couples), *turn* to face other couples, join inside hands and move forward toward oncoming other couples with running steps. Head couples always raise inside arms to form arch over middle couple who advance to the head to repeat the cycle. Last couple run in place until head couple run *under* the arch that they form as they advance to the head position. The "waves" are always, beginning with the head couple, over, under, over, under, until couples have repeated 2 complete set of "waves." (Back, forward, back, forward.)   16 measures

4. Do half of Step 1	8 measures
Do half of Step 2	8 measures
	16 measures

5. Grand right and left. Head couple join R hands to begin with light running steps the grand right and left. The head couple separates, takes the middle persons' L hands,

and then runs on to the third or last couple. The men move in a circle CCW while the women move CW. Continue grand right and left around in circle.   16 measures

6. All join hands in circle. Glide right 8, glide left 8, run into center of circle 4, run back 4, run in 4.

Hold, shout "Hurrah!"   16 measures

KOROBUSHKA (RUSSIA)

The pedlar's "pack" or "little basket" has given rise to this favorite Russian folk dance, which is also a delightful dance mixer.

Record: Folk Dance MII 1059
Formation: Double circle. Partners face each other with both hands joined. The lady is on the outside.

1. The man, beginning with his L foot, moves forward while the lady, beginning with her R foot, moves backward with 3 running steps and a light hop. Repeat, reversing direction. Repeat again, moving out. Man stamps R foot, points L foot to side and brings feet together. At the same time the woman does the same with opposite foot work.

2. The man folds his arms while the lady puts her hands on her hips. Each partner steps, closes, steps, swings, to the right. (Another variation, more popular, is to turn with 3 steps to the right, ending with a swinging hop-step or a stamp. Repeat to the left. Join R hands; balance, or step toward partner, balance away from partner, change places 3 steps with partner (keeping hands joined and turning lady under arch formed by right arm). Repeat all of this second movement.

Variation: Twirl lady under arm on last 3 steps to next gentleman to his right. Man moves CCW around circle to greet the next lady, who becomes his new partner. Repeat dance to the end of the record, changing partners each time.

VIRGINIA REEL (UNITED STATES)

Record: Folkcraft 1249
Formation: Set of 8 couples with partners facing in two lines. The men are on one side and the ladies are on the other.

1. The Call begins:
"Toward your partner and back you go."
(*Everyone walks 3 steps forward, holds on count 4, then walks back with 4 steps.*)
"Forward again—right hands around.
Forward again—left hands around
Toward your partner—two hands around.
Do-si-do* right shoulders.
Do-si-do left shoulders."

2. Head couple slides (8) down the center and back (8) again.

3. Reel. Head couple reels partner around 1½ times with R elbows linked. The lady reels the gentleman with L elbows linked to return again to partner in the center while the gentleman reels the ladies. Continue to reel to the end of the line with the last couple.

Head couple returns, sliding (8 times) to the head of the two lines.

4. Cast off. Head couples lead their lines around the outside to the foot of the two lines. Here they form an arch. The other 7 couples go under the arch and return to their position. The dance begins again with a new head couple. Cue words and call may be "forward," "slide," "reel," "cast off."

OKLAHOMA MIXER (UNITED STATES)

This American folk dance is sometimes called the "cowboy schottische."

Record: MacGregor 400 or Educational Dance Recordings FD 3
Formation: A circle of couples in varsouvienne position facing CCW.

1. Beginning with the L foot, take 2 schottische steps in line of direction, omitting the hop-swing at the end of each. Hold instead. Continue with 4 walking steps L R L R, swinging foot over each time for the unsteady "wobble" or cowboy walk effect.

2. Place L heel forward, return L toe to side of R foot. Gentleman exchanges places

_____
*See page 478.

with lady crossing to the side with a step, behind, step, while the lady crosses in front of him into the center of the circle with a L R L and hold, facing CW. Drop R hands to make the exchange.

Continue movement with R heel to the side, cross L foot with R toe. Drop L hand while lady walks back to gentleman behind her who takes her into a varsouvienne position on the fourth or last count to repeat entire dance.

SPANISH CIRCLE (UNITED STATES)

This is a contra dance (contra means two lines opposite each other). Contra dances are also known as line, string, or longways dances. This dance probably originated in New England early in the 19th century. It has the elegance and grace of the ballroom dances of the period.

Record: Folkcraft 1047 or Educational Dance Recordings FD 4
Formation: A circle of couples. Two couples face each other; at the completion of the dance they move forward in these directions to meet the next couples. The lady stands to the right of her partner.

1. Couples, with inside hands joined, advance toward each other with 1 waltz step, and back away from each other with 1 waltz step. Take opposite person's hands and waltz a quarter turn. Keep inside hands joined with new partner, waltz forward and waltz back. Give both hands to opposite partner and make another quarter turn. Continue this movement 2 more times until both couples are back in their original positions.
2. Two couples make a star formation with R hands joined and take 4 waltzes around. Star by the left and take 4 waltzes in other direction.
3. Join opposite person with R hands joined and turn completely around with 4 waltzes. Partners join inside hands, waltz forward and back, drop hands and waltz through to meet oncoming couple. As couples go through, the ladies waltz across in the middle of the foursome, while the gen-

tlemen waltz on the outside. Repeat dance from the beginning with new couple.

PHILIPPINE COUPLE DANCE (PHILIPPINES)

The Spaniards, who occupied the Islands in 1505, have given to Philippine folk dancers their sense of gravity, courtesy, and elegance portrayed in this dance.

Record: Folkcraft 1424
Formation: Partners face in two lines.
1. Waltz in place 6 times, turning slightly to the right and to the left with each waltz. Arms are held in ballet 4th position (R arm in a curve overhead, L arm is extended in front, curved in a half circle, chest high).

	6 measures
Turn to the right in place with 3 steps	1 measure
Extend L toe forward and bow to partner	1 measure
Repeat this entire movement beginning with the L foot	8 measures

2. Extend arms to the side and waltz right and left in place.

	2 measures
Take 3 running steps to the right. Point L toe forward and bow to partner.	2 measures
Repeat, reversing Waltzes and running steps	4 measures
Repeat the Waltzes and running steps beginning with the R foot. End with Waltz steps in place.	4 measures

3. Partners waltz around each other CW with 6 waltzing steps.

Begin with R.	6 measures
Turn in place to the right with 3 steps. Step back with L foot and point R toe to end with a bow.	2 measures

MAYIM, MAYIM (WATER, WATER) (ISRAEL)

This is a modern Israeli folk dance, which expresses joy and gratitude in the discovery of water in the desert.

Record: Folkcraft F 1108 A
Formation: Single circle facing center with no partners.

1. The circassia step. Starting with the R foot, progressing CW, cross and step on R foot in front of L, turning slightly to left (counts 1-and).
Step on l foot, beside R, turning to face center (counts 2-and). Cross and step on R foot in back of L, turning slightly to right (counts 1-and). Leap lightly onto L foot, turning to face center (counts 2-and). The entire pattern of measures 1−2 is repeated 3 times. The first step should be accented sharply.

2. Four running steps forward toward center of circle, starting with R foot. The first step should be accented. Knees are bent with body bent forward. Raise arms gradually and upward while moving toward the center. Four running steps (with lowering arms) returning to original position. Repeat 4 running steps in and 4 running steps out.

3. Tap L toe in front and to the side 4 times while hopping 8 times in place with the R foot. Clap in time with the music. Repeat, tapping with R toe, this movement 4 times.

KALVELIS (LITTLE SMITH) (LITHUANIA)

This is a folk dance of the middle 19th century, which followed the introduction of the polka into Lithuania. Prior to this time the dances were slower and less spirited. The hand clapping represents the striking of the hammer on the anvil. The author learned this dance from Vyts Beliajus, who introduced it to the United States.

Record: Sonart Album of Folk Dances M-8 or Educational Dance Recordings FD 3
Formation: Any number of couples in a circle, lady on the right. All join hands.

1. Seven polkas to the right, stamp 3 times. Seven polkas to the left, stamp 3 times. Chorus. Partners face each other. Clap L hand onto R. Clap R hand onto L. Repeat R and L. Link arms and skip around with partners making one complete circle with 4 skips.
Repeat the clapping pattern, link L arms

and skip 4 times in circle. Repeat this entire chorus.

2. All face the center of the circle. The ladies dance to the center of the circle with 3 polkas and then stamp 3 times. They turn and face partners and return to place with 3 polkas and 3 stamps. The men repeat the same movement. Repeat the clapping chorus.

3. Partners face each other. Polka around circle in a grand right and left. Ladies go CW, while gentlemen go CCW. At the end of the polka refrain, face a new partner and repeat the clapping chorus.

Suggested Audio-visual Aid

Dance Films (catalogue). Dance Films, Inc., 25 E. 77th Street, New York, N.Y. 10021.

Suggested Readings

Beliajus, Vyts: *Dance and Be Merry*, Vol. I, New York, Clayton Summy Company, 1940.
Czarnowski, Lucile: *Dances of Early California Days*, Palo Alto, California, Pacific Book Company, 1950.
Dances from Far and Near, Folk Dance Federation of California, 150 Powell Street, San Francisco, Calif.
Duggan, Anne, Schlottmann, Jeanette, and Rutledge, Abbie: *The Folk Dance Library* (five volumes), New York, The Ronald Press Company, 1948.
Fox, Grace, and Merrill, Kathleen: *Folk Dancing*, 2nd Ed., New York, The Ronald Press Company, 1957.
Hall, J. Tillman: *Dance!*, Belmont, California, Wadsworth Publishing Company, 1963.
Harris, Jane, Pittman, Anne, and Waller, Marlys: *Dance A While*, Minneapolis, Minn., Burgess Publishing Company, 1968.
Joukowsky, Anatol: *The Teaching of Ethnic Dance*, New York, J. Lowell Pratt & Co., 1965.
Kraus, Richard G.: *Folk Dancing*, New York, The Macmillan Company, 1962.
Lidster, Miriam, and Tamburini, Dorothy: *Folk Dance Progressions*, Belmont, California, Wadsworth Publishing Company, 1965.
Sachs, Curt: *World History of Dance*, New York, W. W. Norton and Company, 1933.
Tolentino, Francisco R.: *Philippine National Dances*, New York, Silver Burdett Company, 1946.

Periodicals

Let's Dance, Folk Dance Federation of California, 293-299 Broadway, Melbrae, California.
The Folk Dancer, P.O. Box 201, Flushing, Long Island, New York.

Sets in Order, P.O. Box 89, Santa Barbara, California.
Viltis, V. F. Beliajus, P.O. Box 1226, Denver, Colo.

Suggested Study Questions

1. What are the potential educational benefits to be gained in folk dancing?

2. Name a folk dance tradition that has been consciously created. Is there more than one?
3. Describe the following steps: (a) Pivot, (b) Grapevine, (c) Gavotte, (d) Mazurka, and (e) Circassia step.
4. Discuss the universality of folk dancing.
5. What appreciation for peoples of other nations and their cultures can be achieved through folk dancing?

CHAPTER THIRTY-ONE

Courtesy of Agnes I. Michaels, State University College, Fredonia, New York.

MODERN DANCE

By M. Frances Dougherty

NATURE AND PURPOSE

Modern or contemporary dance is a form of activity that uses the body as the instrument and movement as the medium for artistic expression. Dance should provide the student with an opportunity to explore the movement potential of her own unique instrument and to select and organize resulting movements into patterns that provide a satisfying esthetic experience. A rich feeling of well-being, joy, and exuberance comes from moving fully; a fine sense of accomplishment comes from clarity of self-expression. Growth in expression through movement brings about a greater sensitivity to the world we live in and a fuller appreciation for creative expression in other art forms as a part of that world. The function of modern dance in the activity program is to provide an opportunity for each student to move, to sense, to express, to enjoy; to appreciate the worth of her unique expression as well as the expressive efforts of others. Experiences in a dance class should help the student to employ her body as an instrument of expression with increased skill and to understand and apply the principles of selection and organization of movement into effective expressive forms. The photographs in this chapter illustrate some of the many expressive movements and patterns in modern dance.

Some of the activities included in the dance experience have a specific purpose to condition the body to a higher level of its potential for effective movement. Increased strength, flexibility, balance, and relaxation are essential to free the body for use as an instrument of expression. Increased physical

Fig. 31-1. Modern Dance is an art form that uses the body as the instrument for expression. (Courtesy of M. Frances Dougherty, University of Oregon.)

497

Fig. 31-2. In modern dance the body is the instrument for expression. (Courtesy of College of Health, Physical Education and Recreation, Texas Woman's University, Denton, Texas.)

fitness is achieved which contributes to the state of total well-being.

Emphasis on the rhythmic element of movement results in increased agility, coordination, and poise. These qualities combine to extend the range of movement for each individual for more effective motor functioning and for use in communicating ideas and feelings; they contribute to the realization of becoming the kind of person the student wants to be.

FACILITIES AND EQUIPMENT

The basic facilities and equipment needed by the student for participation in modern dance experience is a willing body, an open and curious mind, and unobstructed space in which to exercise them both.

The studio, or dance area, should be large enough so that each person may have enough space to provide for a feeling of freedom to move vigorously. A clean, well sanded, and filled hardwood floor is essential to explore movement fully. Other types of floor covering are apt to result in resistance to movement either by too much texture in surfacing or too little rebound or spring. Full

length mirrors are desirable if they are used for the critical analysis of movement and not solely for admiration. Many movements of the body cannot be viewed by the performer, who can see only those reflections in which she faces the mirror. Other movements either cannot be seen at all or are distorted by trying to see the reflection. The dance area should be well ventilated and kept at a constant cool temperature but not so cool that chilling or muscle stiffness will occur during periods of less vigorous activity such as during the planning and evaluating phases of the class.

The dance costume should be one that allows for the greatest comfort and freedom of movement. A well fitting leotard and tights are usually more comfortable than other costumes and in addition are less apt to obscure the movement. Garments should be kept clean at all times. The esthetic experience must "begin at home." Shoes are not usually worn, although dance sandals or ballet shoes may be used in certain circumstances.

BASIC SKILLS

The skills of modern dance are all those movements the body is capable of per-

Fig. 31-3

Fig. 31-4

Fig. 31-5

Figs. 31-3 to 31-5.   "To the viewer, the dance is a visual image; to the dancer it is an image perceived kinesthetically." —Eleanor Metheny. (Courtesy of College of Health, Physical Education and Recreation, Texas Woman's University, Denton, Texas.)

forming within the limits of its structure. Actually the movements are few and at the same time many; bending, straightening, lifting, falling, twisting, and turning are ways the body can be manipulated through the interaction of the muscular and nervous systems. The variations and combinations of these basic manipulations result in an almost limitless extension of human movement. Variations occur through changes in base, amount of energy expended, rate of speed, and placement in space; selection of combinations are made, both consciously and unconsciously, according to need or purpose.

The body moves from force exerted; movement occupies space and consumes time. Force, space, and time are the dynamic elements of movement. Human movement becomes specific as these elements are applied in varying degrees. Dance experience provides the student with an opportunity to explore these elements in relation to the movement potential of her own body.

Movements occurring from a fixed base are called *axial* movements. Common positions establishing a fixed axis from which movement can take place are lying, sitting, kneeling, and standing; variations on axes are determined by all the different ways one can lie, sit, kneel, or stand. For instance, one might lie face down, with arms and legs outstretched, or on the back with legs together and arms touching the sides of the trunk. Kneeling might be on one or both knees; sitting can be with weight equally distributed or shifted to one side.

Movements propelling the body through space are called *locomotor* movements. The fundamental locomotor movements are rolling, crawling, walking, hopping, and jumping. Variations on these fundamental locomotor movements are achieved by changes in speed, force, and size, and by combining the fundamentals. Among the common variations resulting from these changes are running, leaping, sliding, galloping, step-hopping, and skipping. Variations for phases of movement are achieved by combining locomotor steps, alternating them with axial movement, changing the speed, the force, the direction, and the amount and shape of space used. Explorations into these possibilities create challenging problem-solving experiences for the dance student.

CONDITIONING THE BODY FOR EXTENSION OF THE MOVEMENT POTENTIAL

Effective use of human movement, whether for use in the activities of daily living or as a medium of artistic expression, depends upon the ability of the body to exert power, speed, and agility with a minimum expenditure of energy; to feel a sense of exhilaration and joy from moving rather than a sense of fatigue and lack of coordination. Strength, flexibility, coordination, and relaxation are essential components for producing effective body movement. Some exercises or techniques are submitted as examples of aids to developing these components as basic to realizing the movement potential for each body.

Certain principles provide the basis for selection of the conditioning techniques which follow. These principles are:

1. Extending the range and power of human movement can be accomplished without risk of injury.
2. Each individual possesses a different potential; no two people move exactly alike.
3. Each major part of the body should receive attention during the conditioning period.
4. Activities should provide for alternations in energy output, speed, and the part of the body toward which the exercise is directed.
5. Principles of good alignment and body mechanics must apply in the execution of all techniques.

As a matter of convenience in presentation, the following techniques are grouped together from the position of the body as to axial base; each base includes techniques for different purposes and directed toward different parts of the body. No specific counts are indicated for execution of the techniques in order to allow for a wider range of movement exploration. Variation can be achieved by changing the rate of speed, point of accent, or the quality of the movement. All may be repeated any desired number of times or combined into a continuous series.

I. TECHNIQUES LYING ON THE FLOOR

A. Long Stretch. Position: back-lying, arms extended overhead.

1. Stretch the entire body, extending upward through the fingertips and downward through the toes. Inhale.
2. Hold position.
3. Relax and exhale.

B. Fluid Spine. Position: back-lying, arms extended sideward at shoulder level, palms to floor and legs together.

1. Initiate the movement with a lift of the chest; then, with head hanging and arms trailing loosely, lift the trunk to a sitting position.
2. Let the trunk round forward over the legs as arms come forward to reach toward the feet.
3. Reverse the movement to back-lying position, arms sliding along the floor with head last to touch floor.

Note: Perform with smooth, continuous flow of movement.

Fig. 31-6. Fluid spine.

C. Alternating Spine Extending and Flexing. Position: back-lying (as B).

1. Repeat the trunk lift above to sitting position, with spine extended and arms extended forward, shoulders low.
2. Flex the spine, dropping the head toward knees and reaching with arms toward the feet; bounce from lower back.
3. Pull the trunk back to sitting position with extended spine.
4. Flex the spine and roll back to back-lying position.

D. Lower Back Press. Position: back-lying, arms relaxed at sides of body, feet and legs relaxed.

1. Flex the knees and feet open into "frog" position and press the lower back tightly to the floor.
2. Relax to original position.
3. Repeat, alternately flexing and relaxing.

E. Lower Back Balance. Position: back-lying, arms relaxed, hands resting lightly on thighs.

1. Press lower back tightly to floor.
2. Lift head.
3. Lift heels a few inches from the floor.
4. Hold the position with balance maintained on lower back.
5. Relax and return to position.

F. Leg Stretch. Position: back-lying, one leg extended along the floor; bend the other leg toward the chest and grasp the leg back of the thigh just above the knee. Pull leg to chest.

1. Alternately extend the bent leg upward with straight knee and then flex and pull toward chest.
2. Repeat the alternate leg extension and flexion but without holding the leg with hands. Stress full extension.
3. Repeat alternate leg extension and flexion, but grasp the leg as close to the ankle as possible.
4. On final extension, release hands from the leg and slowly lower leg to floor while pressing lower back tightly to the floor.

Fig. 31-7. Leg stretch.

G. Arm Press with Upper Trunk Lift. Position: back-lying, arms outstretched at sides of body.

Fig. 31-8.   Trunk swing and circle.

1. Keep the head in line with the spine and press palms of hands hard against the floor while lifting head and chest off the floor.
2. Return to position and relax.

II. TECHNIQUES SITTING ON THE FLOOR

A. Hip Rotation.   Position: stride-sitting, legs extended with toes pointed; hands placed on floor behind body for support.

1. Rotate legs inward as far as possible.
2. Rotate legs outward, trying to touch little toe to floor.
3. Hold outward position.

B. Sitting Bounces.   Position: stride-sitting, legs extended, knees straight, toes pointed and spine erect.

1. Flex the spine over the L leg, reaching toward L foot with hands and bounce the trunk close to the leg.
2. Extend the spine and return to sitting position.
3. Twist trunk toward L leg and keep spine extended while bouncing trunk toward L leg.
4. Return to center sitting position.
5. Repeat all over the R leg.
6. Repeat center between legs.

C. Trunk Swing and Circle.   Position: stride-sitting, L hand on floor behind the body for support.

1. Reach R arm toward R foot, drop trunk forward, and swing arm in a circle from R to overhead L as hips are pushed and lifted upward, supporting body weight on heels and L hand (Fig. 31-8).
2. Push body weight forward and into the heels to increase width of the stride position.

3. Return to sitting position and change to R hand in support position behind the body.
4. Repeat, swinging from L to R; then alternate R and L.

D. Thigh Stretch and Trunk Twist.   Position: hurdle-sitting position, L leg bent to side so that the inside of thigh is in contact with the floor, R leg extended diagonally, arms open at shoulder height.

1. R arm lifts in a curve overhead and L arm reaches across the trunk; bounce the trunk over the bent L leg while arms are pulling strongly in an oppositional trunk pull. Avoid collapse in the chest.
2. Return trunk to center as arms return to open position.
3. Initiate movement in the L hip and with a straight spine, bounce the trunk forward over the extended R leg.

Fig. 31-9.   Thigh stretch and trunk twist.

4. Return trunk to center and arms to open position.

E. Thigh Stretch with Spine Flexion and Extension. Position: hurdle-sitting, L leg bent to side with inside of thigh in contact with floor, R foot in front of body with sole of foot in contact with floor.

1. Extend the R leg diagonally upward off the floor as the spine rounds and arms reach toward extended R leg (Fig. 31-10).
2. Replace R foot to beginning position as spine extends, arms open, and trunk returns to beginning position.
3. Repeat R leg extension, but arms remain open and spine extended. Lean trunk diagonally backward, keeping the head in line with the spine.
4. Return to original sitting position.

Fig. 31-10. Thigh stretch with spine flexion and extension.

F. Transition (for repeat of D and E on opposite side).

1. Roll toward extended R leg to a prone lying position, palms of hands under shoulders.

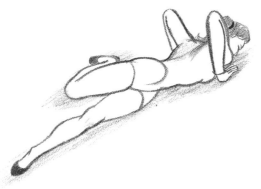

Fig. 31-11. Transition.

2. Bend R leg at knee, lifting the thigh from the hip (Fig. 31-11).
3. Push off with the hands and raise body to hurdle-sit position with R leg bent at side of body, arms open.
4. Repeat D and E on this side.
5. Reverse transition to the L but push off from prone position to upright position on both knees.

G. Spine Flexion and Extension from Kneeling Position. Position: sitting on both legs in a kneeling position, trunk flexed forward with elbows and palms on floor, head hanging forward.

1. Keep the spine flexed, raise trunk from thighs; elbows and palms are thus pulled from the floor.
2. Hands trail to back of trunk as body weight shifts back over the legs.
3. Shift body weight to hands, pushing through the thighs, extend the trunk upward, arching the back.
4. Return body weight to sitting on legs, keeping spine extended.
5. Flex the spine and bend trunk forward to beginning position.

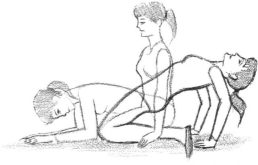

Fig. 31-12. Spine flexion and extension, kneeling.

H. Hip Isolation with Trunk Twist. Position: bent-hurdle position, L leg bent to side of trunk and R leg in front of trunk; body weight is on R hip, thigh, and lower leg with hands resting lightly on R leg.

1. Lift the bent L leg upward from the floor by using only the muscles of the hip and without rocking body forward (Fig. 31-13, A).
2. Replace L leg to floor.
3. Lift L leg from the floor and extend it diagonally forward to the L.

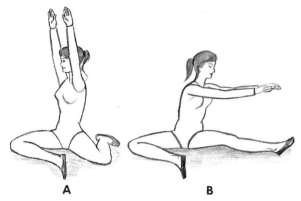

Fig. 31-13. Hip isolation with trunk twist.

4. Repeat 1 and 3 above, and as L leg extends to L twist the trunk toward the extended leg and extend arms (Fig. 31-13, *B*).

5. As L leg returns to floor, twist trunk strongly in opposite direction, arms lifting overhead.

6. Use transition F to change sides or use transition to standing position.

I. Transition to Standing Position. Position: as in H.

1. Extend L leg diagonally to L.

2. Cross L leg over R knee, placing sole of foot on the floor beside knee.

3. Keep spine extended and lift body upward to sit on R heel (Fig. 31-14, *A*).

4. Continue upward lift of the body until weight is on R knee; L foot steps out diagonally forward to L but no weight is placed upon it (Fig. 31-14, *B*).

5. Shift weight onto L foot, and pull R to L into squat position (Fig. 31-14, *C*).

6. Push heels to the floor and slowly straighten knees to bring body to standing position.

7. Continue upward lift onto the toes, allowing body weight to fall forward in lunge position over bent L leg.

8. Flex the trunk low over L thigh, arms and head hanging forward, R leg extended backward.

III. TECHNIQUES IN STANDING POSITION

A. Spine Flexion and Extension. Position: lunge position over L leg.

1. Open arms to side as head lifts and spine extends.

2. Flex the spine and return to trunk-hanging position.

3. Repeat 1.

4. Straighten L knee, extend the spine, shift weight to L foot, bring R to L as trunk lifts to standing position.

Fig. 31-14. Transition to standing position.

Fig. 31-15. Spine flexion and extension, standing.

1. Reach upward by pushing the heel of hands alternately toward the ceiling.

2. Shift the body weight to the heels as arms reach out and downward and trunk flexes.

3. Bounce from lower back to touch palms to the floor.

4. Bend knees, allowing trunk to drop lower, swing arms backward, and bring feet off the floor in a small jump.

5. Swing arms forward as feet return to the floor.

6. Repeat swing and jump.

7. Walk forward four steps as arms swing forward and up overhead.

8. End the phrase by reaching forward with heels of hands and lower arms to sides, emphasizing an oppositional lift of the chest.

5. Continue upward lifting of the trunk until balance is again lost, to fall forward into lunge position, with trunk flexed forward over bent R leg.

6. Repeat sequence with R leg leading.

B. Flexion and Extension of the Spine into Front Fall

1. At step 5 above, continue the momentum of the forward fall, allow hands to slide forward along the floor and push the body into front-lying position by straightening the bent knee. The spine extends fully as front-lying position is reached.

C. Recovery from Front Fall. Position: front-lying.

1. Flex the trunk and pull arms back toward body until they are at the shoulders.

2. Push off with the hands, spine flexed, and rock back over the heels.

3. Slowly straighten the legs and extend the spine to bring the body into standing position.

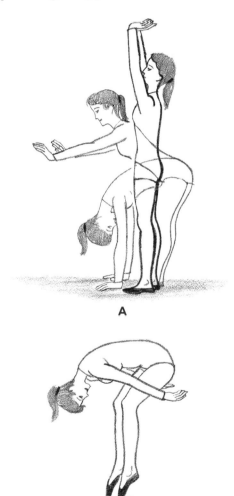

A

B

Fig. 31-17. Reach, touch floor, and swing.

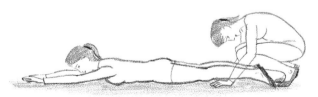

Fig. 31-16. Recovery from front fall.

D. Reach, Touch Floor, and Swing. Position: standing, arms extended overhead.

E. Trunk Twist. Position: standing, feet slightly apart, arms at sides.

1. Keep the trunk erect, spine extended, and bend knees.

2. Stabilize the hips over the bent knees and twist the upper trunk as far to the L as possible; head turns to look backward to L.

3. Flex upper spine, allowing head to drop forward.

4. Return trunk forward over bent knees, flex the spine to drop body to a hang position over knees (Fig. 31-18, *A*).

5. Extend the spine and open arms (knees remain bent).

6. Straighten knees and lift trunk to standing position (Fig. 31-18, *B*).

A

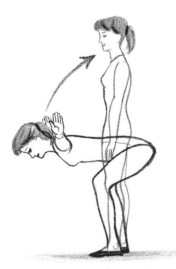

B

Fig. 31-18. Trunk twist.

F. Trunk Twist, Touching Head to Knee. Position: standing with feet parallel in stride position, both arms sideward to the R.

1. Swing arms down across the trunk to L as trunk twists to the L.

2. Bounce forward attempting to touch head to knee (Fig. 31-19).

3. Lift trunk, remaining in twist position.

4. Swing arms and twist trunk to the R. (Repeat 2 and 3).

5. Vary by bending spine backward instead of forward at step 2.

Fig. 31-19. Trunk twist, touching head to knee.

G. Series for Feet. Position: standing in good alignment, heels together, toes slightly apart and knees tightly straightened.

1. Shift weight to balls of feet and bounce heels from the floor.

2. Shift weight to heels and slap toes to floor.

3. Grip the floor with toes and roll ankles outward, then return. Alternate rotation out and in.

4. Shift weight to outer borders of the feet, curl toes, and walk forward.

5. Shift weight to tiptoes and walk back to place.

6. Keep weight R and step diagonally forward with L.

7. Arch over the toes of L foot, bending L knee.

8. Shift weight onto L foot and push "through the arch."

9. Shift weight back to R as L knee straightens.

10. Repeat to the R.

H. Preparation for Elevation (Pliés-Releves)

Plies are knee bends with the movement initiated in the thigh muscles to resist the outward bend of the knees as they are forced outward and as the trunk maintains an oppositional pull upward.

Releves extend the body upward onto the toes, performed by a resistant push into the toes as the heels are lifted from the floor to raise the body vertically.

Fig. 31-22. Fourth plié position.

Fig. 31-20. First plié position.

In the three positions of the feet used in this series, the legs are turned out from the hips, the knees are aligned over the front arches of the feet, and the body weight is centered between the two feet.

1. Plié (1), straighten the knees (2), relevé (3), and return to position by lowering heels. Repeat several times in all positions.

2. Percussive plié-relevé: Plié (1), push weight onto toes by arching the foot as heels are forced off the floor (2), keep weight on toes and relevé (3), lower heels to floor (4).

3. Springing pliés and relevés: move smoothly and continuously from plié to relevé position, repeating four times in each position.

I. Jumps. Positions: First, second and fourth.

1. Apply maximum force to the push-off from the plié to the relevé. The relevé forces the body upward into the air, while the landing is in the plié position. The following controls should be applied during the jumps:

a. Stabilize the spine

b. Avoid relaxing on the landing phase by retaining an oppositional lift in the trunk

c. Keep knees aligned over front arches of feet

d. Utilize the rebound from the floor

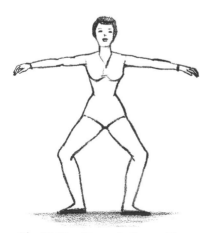

Fig. 31-21. Second plie position.

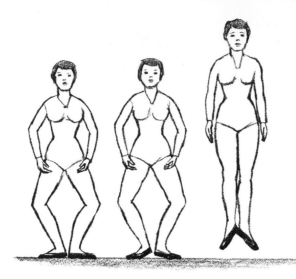

Fig. 31-23. Jump from plié.

2. Do eight jumps in each position.

3. On the landing phase of the last jump in each position, using upward resistance in the body, force the heels off the floor by pressing the knees outward into a deep knee bend. At the same time raise the arms slowly overhead and inhale deeply.

4. Lower arms and raise body to standing position, stepping out to new foot position at the end of the phrase.

LOCOMOTOR MOVEMENTS

Movements that transport the body from one space to another are called *locomotor* movements. The *fundamental* locomotor movements are rolling, crawling, walking, running, leaping, hopping, and jumping. When performed sequentially or continuously, all these have an even underlying rhythm. Combining certain of the fundamentals results in basic locomotor steps having an uneven under-lying rhythm. These are the skip, the slide, and the gallop. Other traditional combinations and rhythmic variations of the fundamental and basic steps result in *derived* steps which may be of the folk dance variety such as the polka, schottische, or mazurka; other combinations result in the social dance steps like the fox trot, waltz, cha-cha-cha, and so on.

Skill in the performance of locomotor movements requires a constant adjustment for balance of shifting the body weight over a moving base. Further adjustments are im-

posed by the following movement considerations: (1) changes in direction and spatial relationships, (2) the application of varying amounts of force, (3) variations in time consumed, and (4) the kinds of movement concurrently taking place in the trunk and arms. For example, one might select the walk as the locomotor movement and build it into a phrase by moving backward in a circular pattern in space, using a heavy step, walking very slowly with the trunk and arms twisted to the left. Or, one could select the skip as the locomotor movement, move forward in diagonals through space, with a light quality and a quick rate of speed, with the trunk lifted high and arms reaching forward.

The possibilities for combining locomotor and axial movements are endless. Variations are derived by changes in spatial, temporal, or force aspects of performance. To explore some of the variations, use the chart in Figure 31-24. To use the chart, place a mark in any square. Each square indicates two locomotor movements to be combined with two axial movements. The example illustrated combines a jump and a slide, which are done with an axial wiggle and rock. The axial and locomotor could be combined or alternated. Variations on these combinations might be achieved by applying changes in space, time, and force. Additional combinations can be indicated graphically by rearranging the horizontal or vertical categories, using more than one square, or by combining patterns chosen by different persons.

Variations in space can be achieved by

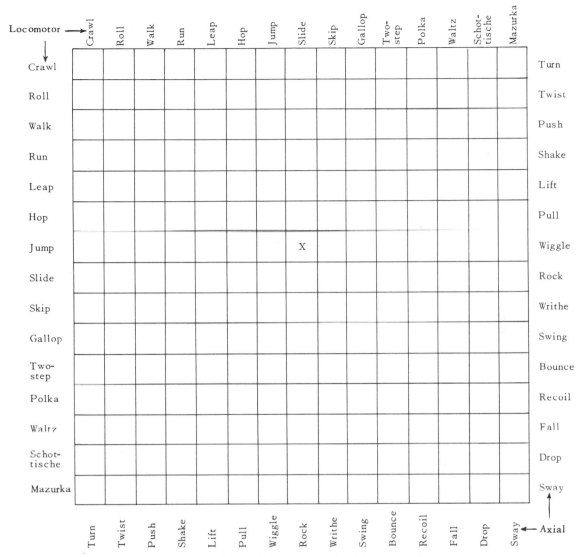

Fig. 31-24. Chart of locomotor and axial movements.

1. Vary space by changing
   a. Range-size
   b. Focus
   c. Level
   d. Direction in body
   e. Direction in area
   f. Floor Pattern

2. Vary time by changing
   a. Tempo (speed)
   b. Accent
   c. Underlying rhythm
   d. Length of phrase

3. Vary force by
   a. Intensity
   b. Quality
      (1) sustained
      (2) percussive
      (3) swinging
      (4) vibratory

changes in focus, area in space toward which the movement is directed, or part of the body surface leading the locomotion. Changes in force aspects are accomplished by varying the amount of energy released to perform a movement. Energy may be released evenly and continuously, quickly and staccato, pulsatingly, or in a single explosive burst. Time differences can be explored by changing the rate of speed, the underlying rhythmic beat, placement of accent, and length of the movement phrase.

MOVEMENT AS EXPRESSIVE COMMUNICATION

An extension of the exploration of movement combinations may serve as a springboard for using movement in a communicative or expressive way. The next step is one of finding and choosing movements, applying the dynamic elements of space, time, and force, and structuring the movements into phrases that have unity. The phrases require a beginning, smooth or logical transitions, and an ending. Such a phrase might be used as a theme or main movement statement. A simple theme, clearly stated, provides the framework upon which a dance is built.

Before attempting to build a dance based on an idea or feeling, it is time well spent to experience manipulating a movement statement or theme by such devices as contrast, alternation, inversion, distortion, diminution, or augmentation. It is through such manipulations that a movement theme is built into a composition.

Ideas for construction of a dance may come from many sources: experience, emotions, literature, poetry, current happenings in the world; from visual, auditory, or textural awareness. Doris Humphrey has referred to these sources as motivations. The student must then search for fresh, original movements that grow out of the motivation, are evocative of the inner feeling, and have significance to the development of the idea. Nonessentials are then eliminated until only the fundamental elements remain upon which the dance structure is built. The movements then need to be arranged in a logical order — given organization, the essence of form in any art. Some of the elements of unified form that are utilized in organization of the movement materials are repetition, transition, contrast, balance, and climax. The resulting form must objectify the idea or evoke the feeling that one wishes to convey to others. These are the processes in the creation of a dance.

The creative process entails a kind of personal discipline. Certain demands are imposed on the creator: (1) the instrument—the body—must be sufficiently equipped with strength, flexibility, and motor control to be able to carry out ideas; (2) the mind must be

Figs. 31-25

31-26.

Figs. 31-25 and 31-26.   To move is to live; to live is to move! (Courtesy of College of Health, Physical Education and Recreation, Texas Woman's University, Denton, Texas.)

actively engaged in developing greater awareness and sensitivity to appropriate thematic materials; (3) one must learn to exercise increasing discrimination and judgment in objectifying these materials in dance form;

and (4) one must be able to perform the dance with a sense of conviction of its worth.

These demands may seem too great; the effort too time consuming. However, the personal satisfaction gained is such that the effort exerted becomes ultimately unimportant and what remains is the exhilaration of having created something meaningful and beautiful. Please give it a try!

Terminology

Alignment—A position of the body in which the body segments are arranged over a supporting base. Good alignment is that position in which the center of gravity of each segment is centered over the base of the segment below or supporting it.

Alternation—An arrangement of movements in an antiphonal form: question and answer, or statement and rebuttal.

Augmentation—The repetitive imitation of a movement pattern in proportionately larger movement.

Balance—Establishing equilibrium of the body over a static or a moving base; an adjustment of the center of gravity over the supporting base.

Beat—A time element that is a felt or seen pulse whose interval of placement determines the rate of speed (fast ....; slow . . . . .).

Bounce—In movement, to execute a bounce is to give in to the pull of gravity and then direct the energy in such a way as to check the fall and bring that portion of the body back to the original position. Bounces are usually done repeatedly.

Diminution—A gradual decrease in size or intensity of a movement.

Distortion—Changing movement from its natural or normal state into a dissonant movement by twisting, elongating, and so forth.

Dynamics—The interplay between the quality and quantity of energy expended; alternations between muscular tension and release.

Elevation—Extension of the body upward vertically in such a way that both feet are off the floor simultaneously as in a jump or a leap.

Extension—A straightening movement at a joint or joints that forces the connecting body parts farther apart.

Flexion—A bending movement at a joint or joints that brings the connecting body parts closer together.

Focus—The direction of the gaze, movement, body part, or attention toward a central point of attraction.

Intensity—The amount of energy expended in performing a movement.

Inversion—To reverse the order of the movements in a phrase; to repeat backward.

Isolation—To move one part of the body while stabilizing the rest of the body.

Lunge—To allow the body to fall with the force of gravity and then to check the fall by stepping out in the direction of the fall. The leg on the step-out foot usually bends at the knee while the other foot remains in the original place.

Percussive—A strong movement in which the force is applied with a sharp impetus and stops suddenly; a striking movement.

Phrase—A unit of movement which has a sense of completion, with a beginning, a middle part, and a full or partial conclusion or completion.

Range—Pertains to the size of movement, and the degree to which the size of the movement can be extended.

Rotation—Movement around an axis.

Spatial pattern—The design of the movement as a result of its placement in space.

Stabilize—To make a portion of the body stationary—immovable—while other parts of the body may be allowed to move.

Sustained—A quality in which the force is exerted smoothly and continuously with no accent at the beginning or at the end.

Swinging—A pendular movement occurring in an arc from a central axis, performed by giving a slight impetus, dropping with gravity, following through, and suspending before the next repetition.

Underlying rhythm—A steady, continuous beat or pulse that occurs because of regular and repeated emphases.

Vibratory—A movement quality in which the force is applied in quick succession, as in quivering.

Selected Audio-visual Aids

Appalachian Spring, Martha Graham and Company. Contemporary Films, 13 E. 37th Street, New York, N.Y.

A Dancer's World, Martha Graham and Company. Dance Films, Inc., 120 W. 57th Street, New York, N.Y.

Modern Dance: The ABC of Composition, Creative Imagination and Choreography. Bailey Films, Inc., 6509 DeLongpre Ave., Hollywood, Calif. 90028.

Modern Dance: Technique in Sequential Form, Narration by Hildegard L. Spreen. Bailey Films, Inc., 6059 DeLongpre Avenue, Hollywood, Calif. 90028.

The Moor's Pavane, Jose Limon. Brandon Films, 200 W. 57th Street, New York, N.Y.

Movement Improvisation, Barbara Mettler Dance Group. Mettler Studios, 242 Newbury Street, Boston, Mass. 02116.

Negro Spirituals, Helen Tamiris. Contemporary Films, 13 E. 37th Street, New York, N.Y.

Night Journey, Martha Graham and Company. Rembrant Films, New York, N.Y.

A Time to Dance, Commentator: Martha Myers (a series of nine programs on kinescope that serve to introduce the audience to the three major dance forms—modern, ballet, and ethnic). NET Film Service, Audio-Visual Center, Indiana University, Bloomington, Ind.

Records

Electronic Music, Columbia-Princeton Music Center. The Dancers' Shop, Childrens Music Center, 5373 West Pico, Los Angeles, California 90019.

Freda Miller Records for Dance, Freda Miller, 131 Bayview Avenue, Northport, Long Island, N.Y.

Improvisations for Modern Dance, Sarah Malament, 3215 Netherland Avenue, New York, N.Y. 10063.

Modern Dance: Music and Materials for Technique, Paul Kuefey, Kimbo Records, Box 55, Deal, New Jersey 07723.

Motivations for Modern Dance, Ruth White. Cheviot Corporation, 9844 Everest Street, Downey, Calif.

Music for Modern Dance, Cameron McCosh. Dance Records Inc., Waldwick, N.J.

Piano for Modern Dance, Quin Adamson Childrens Music Center, Inc., 5373 West Pico Blvd., Los Angeles, Calif. 90019.

Suggested Readings

Hawkins, Alma: *Creating Through Dance*, Englewood Cliffs, N.J., Prentice-Hall, Inc., 1964.

Horst, Louis: *Modern Forms*, San Francisco, Impulse Publications, 1961.

Maynard, Olga: *American Modern Dancers: The Pioneers*, Boston, Little, Brown and Company, 1965.

Methany, Eleanor. *Movement and Meaning*, New York, McGraw-Hill Book Co., 1964.

Mitchell, Jack: *Dance Scene, U.S.A.*, New York, World Publishing Co., 1967.

Norris, Dorothy, and Shiner, Reva: *Keynotes to Modern Dance*, Minneapolis, The Burgess Publishing Company, 1964.

Sorell, Walter: *The Dance Through the Ages*, New York, Grossett & Dunlap, 1967.

Periodicals

Dance Magazine, 268 W. 47th Street, New York, N.Y. 10036.

Dance Observer, Box 473, Madison Square Station, New York, N.Y. 10010.

Dance Perspectives, 1801 E. 26th Street, Brooklyn, N.Y.

Impulse Publications, 160 Palo Alto Avenue, San Francisco, Calif. 94114.

Suggested Study Questions

1. What is the difference between modern dance and other dance forms?
2. Define the following terms: (a) locomotor movements, (b) axial movements, (c) force, (d) time element, (e) space, and (f) derived steps.
3. Give three examples showing how locomotor and axial movements can be combined.
4. How can the body best be trained in order to become an instrument of expression?
5. What is meant by movements that are (a) sustained, (b) percussive, (c) swinging, and (d) vibratory?

5

SPORTS COMPETITION FOR WOMEN

"The only conquests which are permanent, and leave no regrets, are the conquests over ourselves."

— *Napoleon*

CHAPTER THIRTY-TWO

Courtesy of Agnes I. Michaels, State University College, Fredonia, New York.

SPORTS COMPETITION FOR WOMEN

Under wholesome conditions, competition for girls and women *can* be a rich, educational experience. However, all who wish to take part in the program should be given an opportunity to do so, instead of limiting competition to only a few highly skilled players. The intramural program should reach the majority of students who desire to play with and compete against others, either as an individual or a team member. The extramural program according to the recommendations of the Division for Girls and Women's Sports of the American Association for Health, Physical Education, and Recreation (AAHPER), should provide for competition among teams from local schools, community centers, institutions, clubs, or other such organizations. "An intercollegiate athletic program for women should be an extension of an existing extramural program and in addition to established instructional and intramural offerings."*

D.G.W.S. STATEMENT OF BELIEFS*

WE BELIEVE that opportunities for instruction and participation in sports should be included in the educational experiences of every girl. Sports are an integral part of the culture in which we live. Sports skills and sports participation are valuable social and recreational tools which may be used to enrich the lives of women in our society.

WE BELIEVE that sports opportunities at all levels of skill should be available to girls and women who wish to take advantage of these experiences. Competition and cooperation may be demonstrated in all sports programs although the type and intensity of the competition will vary with the degree or level of skill of the participants. An understanding of the relationship between competition and cooperation and of how to utilize both within the accepted framework of our society is

one of the desirable outcomes of sports participation.

WE BELIEVE in the importance of physical activity in the maintenance of the general health of the participant.

WE BELIEVE that participation in sports contributes to the development of self confidence and to the establishment of desirable interpersonal relations.

For these reasons, WE BELIEVE that girls and women of all ages should be provided with comprehensive school and community programs of sports and recreation. In addition, they should be strongly and actively encouraged to take part in such programs.

PROGRAM

We believe that sports programs for girls and women should be broad, varied, and planned for participants at differing levels of skill. There should be full awareness of the wide span of individual differences so that all types, ages, and skill levels are considered in the planning of sports programs. In conducting the various phases of sports programs, principles must guide action. These principles should be based on the latest and soundest knowledge regarding

1. growth and development factors
2. motor learning
3. social and individual maturation and adjustment
4. the values of sports participation as recognized in our culture.

ELEMENTARY SCHOOLS (GRADES 1-6)

We believe in planned, comprehensive, and balanced programs of physical education for every girl in the elementary program. These should provide experiences in basic movements—for example, skipping and simple dance steps, bending, reaching, and climbing—and in a wide variety of activities which require basic sports skills such as catching, throwing, batting, and kicking.

We believe that intramural sports experiences in appropriately modified sports activities should supplement an instructional program for girls in grades 4, 5, and 6, and that in most cases these experiences will be sufficiently stimulating and competitive for the highly skilled girl. We believe

---

*D.G.W.S.: Guidelines for Intercollegiate Athletic Programs for Women, 1965.

†Materials reproduced by permission of Dr. Rachal Bryant and the AAHPER.

extramural sports activities, if included in the upper elementary grades, should be limited to occasional play days (sports groups or teams composed of representatives from several schools or units), sports days, and invitational events.

SECONDARY SCHOOLS (GRADES 7-12)

We believe that in secondary schools a program of intramural and extramural participation should be arranged to augment a sound and comprehensive instructional program in physical education for all girls. Extramural programs should not be organized until there are broad instructional and intramural programs and a sufficient allotment of time, facilities, and personnel for new programs.

COLLEGES AND UNIVERSITIES

We believe that college and university instructional programs should go beyond those activities usually included in the high school program. There should be opportunities to explore and develop skills in a variety of activities, with emphasis on individual sports. It is desirable that opportunities for extramural experiences beyond the intramural program be accessible to the highly skilled young women who wish these opportunities.

FORMS OF COMPETITION

INTRAMURAL COMPETITION is sports competition in which all participants are identified with the same school, community center, club, organization, institution, or industry, or are residents of a designated small neighborhood or community.

EXTRAMURAL COMPETITION is a plan of sports competition in which participants from two or more schools, community centers, clubs, organizations, institutions, industries, or neighborhoods compete. The forms of extramural competition include

1. Sports Days—school or sports group participates as a unit.
2. Telegraphic Meets—results are compared by wire or mail.
3. Invitational Events—symposiums, games, or matches to which a school or sports group invites one or more teams or individuals to participate.
4. Interscholastic, Intercollegiate, or Interagency Programs—groups which are trained and coached play a series of scheduled games and/or tournaments with like teams from other schools, cites, or organizations.

INTERNATIONAL COMPETITION involves players from different nations and provides sports experiences for individuals or groups with exceptional ability and emotional maturity. This type of competition under some conditions could include secondary school girls, but usually it is planned for more mature participants.

CO-RECREATIONAL ACTIVITIES are designed to give boys and girls opportunities to participate on the same team against a team of like composition, provided the activities do not involve body contact. The basis for formation of teams should be to promote good team play. We believe that girls should be prohibited from participating (1) on a boys intercollegiate or interscholastic team; (2) against a boys intercollegiate or interscholastic team; and (3) against a boy in a scheduled intercollegiate or interscholastic contest.

ADMINISTRATION

We believe that certain SAFEGUARDS should be provided to protect the health and well-being of participants. Adequate health and insurance protection should be secured by the institution. First aid services and emergency medical care should be available during all scheduled interscholastic sports events. Qualified professional leaders should ensure a proper period for conditioning of players, a safe environment including equipment and facilities, a schedule with a limited number of games, and similar measures.

We believe that sports OFFICIATING should be the responsibility of those who know and use D.G.W.S. approved rules. Officials should hold current ratings in those sports in which ratings are given.

We believe that the entire FINANCING of girls and women's sports programs should be included in the total school budget. It is suggested that income be handled as a regular school income item.

We believe that the SCHEDULING of sports activities for girls and women should be in accordance with their needs and that their schedule should not be required to conform to a league schedule established for boys and men's sports.

We believe that excellence of achievement should be given RECOGNITION and that the intrinsic values which accrue from the pursuit of excellence are of primary importance. We believe that, when awards are given, they should be inexpensive tokens of a symbolic type, such as ribbons, letters, and small pins.

We believe that expert teaching and quality programs generate their own best PUBLIC RELATIONS. It is suggested that an effective plan be developed for interpreting the values of the sports program to parents, teachers in other fields, and interested members of the school or college community, including the press. A procedure which has proved successful is to invite key groups to a selection of demonstrations and sports events at different levels, so that they may see effective programs in action.

LEADERSHIP

We believe that good leadership is essential to the desirable conduct of the sports program. The qualified leader meets the standards set by the profession, including an understanding of (1) the place and purpose of sports in education, (2) the growth and development of children and youth, (3) the effects of exercise on the human organism, (4) first aid and accident prevention, (5) understanding of specific skills, and (6) sound teaching methods. Personal experience in organized extramural competition is desirable for the young woman planning to become a leader or teacher of women's sports. The leader should demonstrate personal integrity and a primary concern for the welfare of the participant.

POLICY-MAKING

And, finally, we believe that all leaders, teachers, and coaches of girls and women's sports should be encouraged to take an active part in the policy decisions which affect planning, organizing, and conducting sports programs for girls and women. Leaders should make sure that qualified women are appointed to the governing sports bodies at all levels—local, state, national, and international—to ensure that programs are in the best interest of those who participate.

....

D.G.W.S. GUIDES—contain the official rules, articles on coaching, officiating, and valuable information on aquatics, archery, badminton, basketball, bowling, fencing, field hockey, golf, gymnastics, lacrosse, outing activities, riding, soccer, softball, speedball, tennis, track and field, volleyball, and winter sports.

For complete publications list and membership information, write to D.G.W.S.—AAHPER, 1201 Sixteenth Street, N.W., Washington, D.C. 20036.

TYPES OF TOURNAMENTS

Elimination Tournaments. Single and winner-loser tournaments are easily drawn up by using the perfect power of two if the number of contestants is 4, 8, 16, 32, and so on. But when there are more than the perfect power of two, byes are added until this is

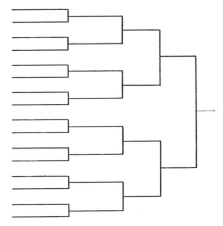

Fig. 32-1. Elimination tournament.

reached. The number of byes should equal the difference between the number of competitors and the next higher power of two. When 15 are entered, there will be one bye (16 − 15 = 1), and so on.

If more than 25 players are entered, two tournaments are recommended rather than one. The best players should be seeded, and if there are four players on teams who are almost equally matched, numbers 1 and 4 should be in the first and eighth positions of the upper bracket, and 2 and 4 in the ninth and sixteenth positions.

In the double elimination tournament, no team is eliminated until it loses twice. The winners move to the right in the first elimination, and to the left in the second elimination. If the winner of the first elimination, however, loses to the winner of the second elimination, she has lost but once, and still another game must be played by the two before a winner is declared.

Round Robin Tournament. Each team plays every other team once, with the final

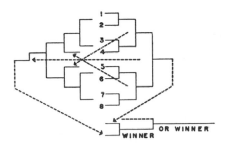

Fig. 32-2. Double elimination tournament.

standing determined on a percentage basis.

The following formula will apply to any number of teams, whether the total is odd or even. With an odd number of teams there is the same number of rounds; with an even number of teams there is one less number of games than teams.

FOR AN UNEVEN NUMBER OF TEAMS. Assign to each team a number and then use only the figures in drawing the schedule. For example, in a league with 7 teams start with 1, putting down figures in the following order:

7	6	5	4	3	2	1
6—1	5—7	4—6	3—5	2—4	1—3	7—2
5—2	4—1	3—7	2—6	1—5	7—4	6—3
4—3	3—2	2—1	1—7	7—6	6—5	5—4

Note that the figures go down on the right side and up on the left. Number 7 draws a bye in the first round and the others play as indicated. With an odd number of teams, all numbers revolve and the last number each time draws a bye.

FOR AN EVEN NUMBER OF TEAMS. With an even number of teams the plan is the same except that the position of No. 1 remains stationary and the other numbers revolve about it until the original combination is reached. For example, with 8 teams:

1—2	1—8	1—7	1—6	1—5	1—4	1—3
8—3	7—2	6—8	5—7	4—6	3—5	2—4
7—4	6—3	5—2	4—8	3—7	2—6	8—5
6—5	5—4	4—3	3—2	2—8	8—7	7—6

Two things only must be remembered: (1) With an even number of teams, No. 1 re-

mains stationary and the other numbers revolve. (2) With an odd number of teams, all numbers revolve and the last number each time draws a bye.

Ladder Tournament. Teams or players are arranged in ladder formation. Any player may challenge another person directly above. If she defeats her opponent, her name is moved up. The final winner stays in the first position longest.

The Pyramid. The number of spaces on the bottom line should be equal to one-half the number of contestants. In the beginning, no contestant has a position on the pyramid, but gains this by challenging another to a match. The winner then takes a place on the lowest pyramid. The loser must challenge another contestant and win before she can gain a position on the pyramid. Contestants advance to the next highest level by winning a match from someone on the same level. Losers change places with the winners. Advancement can be made only when there is a vacant spot on the next higher level (or, if there are no vacant spots on that level, by challenging to the next higher level). The winner arrives at the top first, or can be the one who stays there longest.

TEAM 1
TEAM 2
TEAM 3
TEAM 4
etc.

Fig. 32-3. Ladder tournament.

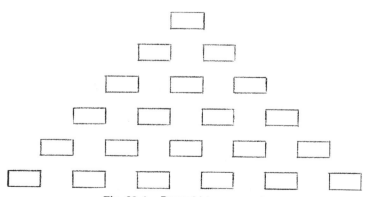

Fig. 32-4. Pyramid tournament.

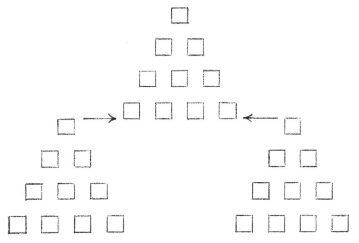

Fig. 32-5. Crown tournament.

The Crown Tournament. Made up of several pyramids, each of ten spaces at different levels, challenging is vertical within each pyramid and horizontal among pyramids. The winner advances first to the top of the highest pyramid. Players may gain their needed first position at the bottom of the horizontal pyramids by lot, challenging another, or by assignment with the better players placed there.

PLAYER CLASSIFICATION

Contestants may be classified according to age, height, weight, skill, physical examinations, or skill tests for competitive purpose. Care must be taken to assure that players are as equally matched as possible and that every safety precaution has been taken in assigning groups to compete against each other in specific areas. The teams should elect their own captains by secret ballot, after listening to a brief talk from their teacher on the duties and qualifications of a good leader, followed by a short student discussion of the main points stressed. Throughout the entire competitive program, emphasis should be placed upon having fun, as well as winning and good sportsmanship.

POINT SYSTEM

A simple system should be devised for keeping points that is not time consuming yet is accurate. Winners should receive the greatest number of points with runners-up the second most, and each participant given entry points for playing in one or more tournament games. The system should be kept on a yearly basis, and will, when used accumulatively over a longer period of time, increase participation. All records might well be kept by elected student intramural managers under close teacher guidance and supervision.

ELIGIBILITY RULES

Although each organization should draw up its own eligibility rules, such a group working on this project should be aware that rules (1) are primarily for the protection of the players, and (2) cover not only participation eligibility but also health requirements, forfeits, penalties for rule infractions, and player conduct. All who take part in the program should have permission to do so from a physician, after having had a physical examination. Those with physical or other types of defects must not be allowed to compete in strenuous sports against more capable and vigorous opponents, but, rather, they should have their own intramural program geared to their limitations. Such a program might include table tennis, shuffleboard, archery, or other similar types of noncombative sports.

AWARDS

If awards are given at the completion of a season, semester, or school year they should be simple and inexpensive, for the major portion of any intramural budget should be spent on leadership and equipment rather than on costly cups or other awards. In granting any award, it should be remembered that every student should have an equal opportunity to earn one. Rotating trophies with winners' names printed on them or on a plate have value, and their use is one way to keep the cost of awards down. A Sportsmanship Trophy should be given yearly and be as valued, or more so, among the players as the first place trophy. An awards banquet is especially attractive to women. It is suggested that the occasion become a most special one to which distinguished guests are invited, and that all who attend it be more dressed up than they are when attending most school functions. Colored slides or action films taken during the season when shown at such a banquet add greatly to a program interest and do much to acquaint the college president, deans, or teachers with the importance, scope, and value of the program. A student committee under the guidance of a selected representative (usually the G.A.A. or W.R.A. president) and the instructor should plan the awards banquet around a unique theme yearly, and the occasion should become a highlighted, eagerly looked-forward-to occasion by every player. Such a dinner can be the "bright red cherry on the vanilla sundae."

THE PARTICIPANTS

The following age classification in grouping girls and women, and suggested activities for each group as endorsed by the Division for Girls and Women's Sports include:*

15 to 18—*Late Adolescent.* This group increases in height and weight rapidly; inaccuracy of movement decreasing, becoming sexually mature, seeking freedom and adventure yet needing surrounding cluster of gang friends. Awkwardness decreases with age, as does insecurity with successful experience; greatly needs approval, understanding; likes team and individual games requiring increasing skill, needs many coeducational game experiences.

19 to 24 — *Young Adult.* Slower, more refined development; period of high physical efficiency; begins to participate more in community life and feels personally more responsibility to society; takes part in more service projects; has multiplicity of interests; prefers coeducational activities.

24 and Over — *Mature Adult.* Increasingly aware of responsibilities to self and others; now matured with fairly definite motor patterns well fixed; vigorous activity is satisfying. Prefers to learn new skills; needs diversified activities in many areas; wants to keep fit; plays mostly for exercise and fun; will seek out places to play and help others to have improved areas for recreation.

PLAY FACILITIES

   I. Public
     a. Schools
     b. Community centers
       1. national
       2. state
       3. local
     c. Parks
  II. Semiprivate
     a. Churches
     b. Y.W.C.A.-Y.W.H.A.
     c. Denominational community centers
     d. Girl Scouts, Camp Fire Girls, Y Teen Clubs
 III. Private
     a. Clubs
     b. Industrial play spaces
     c. Individual play spaces

OUTDOOR FACILITIES

    I. Archery ranges
   II. Beaches and swimming facilities (including outdoor pools)
  III. Bicycle paths
  IV. Bowling greens
   V. Bridle paths
  VI. Camps

---

*Materials reprinted by permission of D.G.W.S. from *Standards in Sports for Girls and Women.*

VII. Courts
- a. Badminton
- b. Handball
- c. Shuffleboard
- d. Squash
- e. Tennis
- f. Volleyball

VIII. Field houses

IX. Fishing streams

X. Golf links

XI. Horseshoe pitching space

XII. Ice skating rinks

XIII. Jumping pits

XIV. Parks

XV. Playfields
- a. Softball
- b. Basketball
- c. Football (used for other games by girls)
- d. Hockey
- e. Soccer
- f. Speedball
- g. Lacrosse
- h. Volleyball

XVI. Playgrounds (including swings, slides, trapeze, and other playground equipment)

XVII. Roller skating rinks

XVIII. Running tracks

XIX. Ski slides

XX. Trails

INDOOR FACILITIES

I. Archery ranges

II. Softball diamonds

III. Bowling alleys

IV. Courts
- a. Badminton
- b. Basketball
- c. Handball
- d. Shuffleboard
- e. Squash
- f. Tennis
- g. Volleyball

V. Ice skating rinks

VI. Rifle ranges

VII. Roller skating rinks

VIII. Swimming pools

THE PROGRAM

(13 to 18 years)

I. Ball games
- a. Softball types
  1. Schlag ball
  2. Hit pin baseball
  3. Soccer baseball
  4. Softball
- b. Basketball types
  1. Dodgeball
  2. Endball
  3. Captain ball
  4. Pinball
  5. Nine court basketball
  6. Basketball
- c. Field types
  1. Corner kickball
  2. Fieldball
  3. Soccer
  4. Speedball
  5. Field hockey
  6. Lacrosse
  7. Speed-a-way
- d. Net games (without rackets)
  1. Newcomb
  2. Giant volleyball
  3. Ring or deck tennis
  4. Volleyball
- e. Net games (with rackets)
  1. Paddle tennis
  2. Table tennis
  3. Badminton
  4. Tennis
- f. Wall games
  1. Handball
  2. Squash

II. Track events
- a. Running
  1. Dashes (up to 75 yds)
  2. Low hurdle relays
- b. Jumping
  1. Running high jump
  2. Standing and running broad jump
- c. Throwing
  1. Basketball—distance
  2. Baseball—distance
  3. Shot put (6 to 8 lbs.)*
  4. Discus throw*
  5. Javelin throw*

III. Swimming
- a. For speed (up to 50 yds)
- b. Strokes for form
- c. Types of diving (high dive not recommended)
- d. Water games
- e. Lifesaving events

IV. Miscellaneous

_____

*Not recommended for junior high school girls.

Fig. 32-6. Competitive swimming for girls and women is rapidly increasing both in intensity and popularity throughout the nation. The majority of America's outstanding swimming champions and Olympic team members are in their early teens. (Courtesy of the Los Angeles Public Schools.)

a. Hiking
b. Skating (roller, ice)
c. Coasting
d. Horseshoe pitching
e. Bowling
f. Shuffleboard
g. Horseback riding
h. Archery
i. Golf
j. Bicycle riding
k. Fencing

(19 to 24 years)
  I. Ball games
    a. Softball types
      1. Hit pin baseball
      2. Softball
    b. Basketball
    c. Field types
      1. Soccer
      2. Fieldball
      3. Speedball
      4. Field hockey
      5. Lacrosse
      6. Speed-a-way
    d. Net ball games (without rackets)
      1. Ring or deck tennis
      2. Giant volleyball
      3. Volleyball

    e. Net ball games (with rackets)
      1. Paddle tennis
      2. Table tennis
      3. Badminton
      4. Tennis
    f. Wall games
      1. Handball
      2. Squash
  II. Track events
    a. Dashes
    b. Relays
    c. Hurdling (2 ft.)
    d. Jumping
      1. Standing and running broad jump
      2. Running high jump
    e. Throwing
      1. Baseball—distance
      2. Shot put
      3. Discus throw
      4. Javelin throw
 III. Swimming
    a. For speed—up to 100 yds
    b. Water games
    c. Diving
    d. Lifesaving events
 IV. Miscellaneous
    a. Hiking
    b. Skating (roller, ice)

c. Coasting
d. Horseshoe pitching
e. Bowling
f. Shuffleboard
g. Horseback riding
h. Archery
i. Golf
j. Fencing
k. Bicycle riding
l. Boating
   1. Sail
   2. Ice
   3. Canoeing
m. Skiing (snow, water)

Although, ideally, a sports and games program should be offered to all participants at regularly scheduled times and be held outdoors whenever possible when vital energy is at a high level, there are also great values to be found in opening up facilities at odd hours so that any spontaneously formed group — such as two would-be badminton players, or a single, lonesome individual looking for companionship and an opportunity to exercise for fun — can be served. Fortunately, today more and more colleges are opening their facilities and furnishing or renting equipment, and providing supervisors or teachers for after-school fun.

Leadership is the real key to the success and value of any physical education or recreation program, whether it be furnished by a school, or any other organization. The real test of the program is in the enjoyment and benefit the participant receives from taking part in it. Any well rounded and conducted program planned to include the previously recommended activities for girls and women and conducted according to the standards devised by the Division for Girls and Women's Sports will have great value, not only to those engaging in it, but to society as well.

Terminology

Play day—Team members are made up of members from several schools or clubs.

Sports day—Each school or team competes as a unit.

Telegraphic meets—Results of competitive events are sent by mail or wire to one designated place and the winner has the best score of all contestants from a widely scattered geographical area.

Elimination tournament—A type of single or double tournament wherein contestants are matched in competing brackets. In the former type only the name of the winner goes out to the right on the chart, whereas in a double elimination tournament the name of the loser goes out to the left of the chart and that of the winner moves out to the right.

Round robin tournament—Each team plays each other team once; the winner of the most games becomes the champion.

Ladder tournament—Teams or individuals are arranged on a ladder type tournament drawing and each player challenges the person above. The winner exchanges places with the loser on the chart.

Pyramid tournament—A type of tournament drawing made up of three pyramids wherein each contestant's name becomes a part of the last line on one of two supporting bases after she has won a challenge match entitling her to enter the tournament.

Crown tournament—A type of tournament drawing made up of several pyramids.

Suggested Readings

AAHPER: *Intramurals for the Senior High School* (1964); *Standards in Sports for Girls and Women* (1961); *Spectator Sportsmanship* (1961); *Girls Sports Organization Handbook* (1961); *Intramural Sports for College Men and Women* (1961); *Guidelines for Intercollegiate Athletic Programs for Women* (1965); *Guidelines for Interscholastic Athletic Programs for High School Girls* (1965); *Procedures for Women's Intercollegiate Athletic Events* (1967), 1201 16th St. N.W. Washington, D.C. 20036.

Barnes, Mildred: *Program in Self Instruction for Officiating D.G.W.S. Volleyball Rules*, Minneapolis, Minn., Burgess Publishing Company, 1965.

Means, Louis: *Intramurals. Their Organization and Administration*, Englewood Cliffs, New Jersey, Prentice-Hall, Inc., 1963.

Vannier, Maryhelen, and Fait, Hollis: *Teaching Physical Education in Secondary Schools*, 3rd Ed., Philadelphia, W. B. Saunders Company, 1968.

Vannier, Maryhelen, and Foster, Mildred: *Teaching Physical Education in Elementary Schools*, 4th Ed., Philadelphia, W. B. Saunders Company, 1968.

Vannier, Maryhelen, and Poindexter, Hally Beth: *Individual and Team Sports for Girls and Women*, 2nd Ed., Philadelphia, W. B. Saunders Company, 1968.

Suggested Study Questions

1. Discuss the place of intramurals in the total physical education program, and in the total educational program of the school.
2. Why should all who participate have a physical examination? Obtain several copies of such examination blanks and choose the best one. Why do you consider it the best?
3. Which seems to you to be the best standard for competition for women drawn up by D.G.W.S.?
4. Discuss which sports you think are best for coeducational competitive events.
5. Some people think that only boys and men should compete in sports. How do you feel about this? Support your reasons in light of the D.G.W.S. recommendations given in this chapter.

APPENDIX

SAMPLE OBJECTIVE TEST QUESTIONS

CHAPTER 1

THE UNIQUE CONTRIBUTIONS OF PHYSICAL EDUCATION TO EDUCATION AND LIFE

PART I **COMPLETION.** Fill in the blanks in each of the following statements with the correct answer.

1. Learning means _____.

2. Experts estimate that by the year 2000 in the United States the life span will be _____ years for males and _____ for females.

3. Most college students have _____ of their lives before them.

4. Total fitness is made up of _____, _____, and _____ well-being.

5. The human body is composed of _____ bones and _____ muscles.

6. Your college physical education program should help you to develop _____ and _____ fitness, movement _____, finer _____ attitudes, knowledges and _____ and better use of _____.

7. Selfish egoistic drives are known as _____ drives.

   One is said to be physically fit when she:

8. _____

9. _____

10. _____

11. _____

12. _____

13. _____

14. _____

PART II. **TRUE OR FALSE** Write + in the blank if the statement is true, 0 if it is wholly or partially false.

_____1. Exercise helps one to build greater resistance to fatigue and disease.

_____2. Exercise and being physically fit increase the recovery rate after surgery and major illness and are aids to ease in childbirth.

_____3. To educate means "to lead forth".

_____4. One always has the same amount of time each day of the week, month, and year.

_____5. Since the body is the fundamental tool for any life task, movement is basic to growth, development, and all learning.

_____6. The primary purpose of all educational experiences is to develop the mind.

CHAPTER 2

BODY MECHANICS AND MOVEMENT FUNDAMENTALS

PART I. **COMPLETION** Fill in the blanks in each of the following statements with the correct answer.

1. The supporting base of the body is the _____

2. _____ can be one of the best means of daily exercise. It is also one of the few cost-free forms of recreation which can bring lifetime enjoyment and healthful benefits.

3. _____ is one of the best hip reducers.

4. According to orthopedic specialists, a woman should not lift or carry any load that weighs more than _____of her own weight.

5. For beauty of movement, the body should be balanced over its supporting base _____, and the center of gravity, which is _____

PART II. **TRUE OR FALSE** Write + in the blank if the statement is true, 0 if it is wholly or partially false.

_____1. How a person moves reveals much about her self-image and personality.

_____ 2. Poor posture can be a contributing factor to menstrual difficulties.

_____ 3. In walking properly the toes should be pointed ahead, and the body weight shifted from the heels, to the outsides of the feet, and then to the metatarsals.

_____ 4. It takes more energy to walk in a straight line than to walk down a flight of stairs.

_____ 5. When standing for a long time it is less fatiguing if the weight is evenly distributed on both feet.

_____ 6. According to Dr. Arthur Steinhaus, a physiologist, women should avoid jumping from heights, heavy lifting, and other activities which greatly increase intra-abdominal pressure.

_____ 7. When pulling heavy objects, you should bend your body slightly toward the direction you are pulling.

_____ 8. It is easier for a woman to carry a heavy load than to push or pull it.

_____ 9. The best way to carry a suitcase is with two hands.

_____10. Pulling is the reverse of pushing.

_____11. Like a set of well-laid bricks, each body part should be balanced, including the feet, hips, chest, and head.

_____12. "Sititis" is not a problem among college students.

_____13. When lifting something heavy, place your feet in a stride position as far away as possible from the object you are lifting.

_____14. When running, it is best to keep your body in a straight line rather than to lean slightly forward.

CHAPTER 3

BODY TYPES, WEIGHT, AND FIGURE CONTROL

PART I. **MATCHING** Place from Column B the letter of the correct answer before each word or statement in Column A.

Column A	Column B
____ 1. Mesomorph	a. A well padded, square body
____ 2. Another name for body build or body type	b. Two thin slices of bread or one pat of butter
____ 3. Estimated percentage of all obesity due to glandular imbalance	c. Thin, frail, pencil like
____ 4. Endomorph	d. Carrying body weight on the outer borders of the feet
____ 5. Number of calories less per week which will enable one to lose one pound of weight	e. Ideal average, inverted triangle
	f. Somatotype
____ 6. Ectomorph	g. 500
____ 7. Ankle pronation	h. 5 per cent
____ 8. Ankle supination	i. Carrying body weight on the inner borders of the feet
____ 9. Number of calories most women students need in their diet daily	j. 8 per cent
____ 10. Foods low in calories	k. Somadamid
	l. 2500 to 3000
	m. 2000 to 2300
	n. 1500 to 1800
	o. Lean meat, skim milk

PART II **MATCHING** Next to the name of the specific exercise listed in Column A, write the letter of the answer in from Column B which describes the body area or the purpose for which the exercise is designed.

Column A

Column B

_____ 1. The scissors kick

a. Body conditioning

_____ 2. The dipsy doodle

b. Hips and legs

_____ 3. The jumping jack

c. The waistline

_____ 4. The curl up

d. Relaxation

_____ 5. Thread the needle

e. Menstrual pain relief

_____ 6. Frog sitting

_____ 7. The camel hump

_____ 8. The Mosher exercise

_____ 9. Running in place

CHAPTER 4

ARCHERY

PART I. **COMPLETION** Fill in the blanks in each of the following statements with the correct answer.

1. An end consists of shooting _____ arrows.

2. Shooting a designated number of ends constitutes a _____.

3. The point of the arrow is called the _____.

4. Additional wrapping around the bowstring where the arrow is nocked is called the _____.

5. When using a bowsight, if arrows group high and to the left of the center of the target, move the sight pin _____ and to the _____.

6. A _____ is the distance between the belly and the string of a strung bow.

7. The call of _____ announces that field archers are ready to shoot.

8. The object of _____ shooting is to send the arrows as far as possible.

9. An arrow striking the target face and rebounding scores _____ points.

10. Field archers generally use the _____ method of aiming, whereas target archers use a point of aim or a _____

11. _____ refers to the number of pounds required to draw the string to a specific distance.

12. Allowing the string hand to move forward before or during the release of an arrow is referred to as _____ .

13. A _____bow is considered the most efficient and smooth set bow.

14. _____ method of aiming is based on the principle of setting the shooter's arm on a plane with the target and in proper position prior to the draw.

15. After the release, the arm and elbow of the string hand move _____ from the anchor position for the afterhold.

PART II. **MATCHING** Select the correct word or term in Column B and place the corresponding letter in front of the statement in Column A.

Column A

_____ 1. Shooting at established targets while walking over a designated course

_____ 2. Value of arrow striking and remaining in the red on the target

_____ 3. Value of arrow penetrating two colors

_____ 4. Archery enthusiast

_____ 5. Bows, bowstrings, arrows, guards, gloves, quivers

_____ 6. Bow made of various materials glued and pressed together

_____ 7. Arching ground

_____ 8. The flight pattern of an arrow

_____ 9. Approximate weight of a bow for a beginning archer

_____ 10. Twenty-four arrows shot from each of three distances — 50, 40, and 30 yards

_____ 11. A game involving shooting at a 48 foot target laid out on the ground

_____ 12. Main portion of the arrow

_____ 13. Presiding official in women's tournaments

_____ 14. Part of the target face which extends beyond the scoring area

_____ 15. Feathers on the arrow

Column B

a. Instinctive aim

b. Range

c. Fletching

d. Tackle

e. Matte

f. Toxophilite

g. Self-bow

h. Clout shooting

i. Five

j. Field archery

k. Seven

l. Kegler

m. Petticoat

n. Laminated bow

o. Trajectory

p. Columbia round

q. Lemonwood

r. Flint round

s. Shaft

t. Lady Paramount

u. Higher value

v. 28 pounds

w. 40 pounds

CHAPTER 5

BADMINTON

PART I. **MATCHING** Place from Column B the letter of the correct answer before each word or statement in Column A.

Column A	Column B
_____ 1. The loss of the first serve in doubles	a. Setting
_____ 2. An infraction of game rules	b. 11
_____ 3. Choosing the number of points to play when the score is tied	c. Rotation
	d. A fault
_____ 4. A defensive shot that travels to the rear court or is used often to change game pace	e. A high clear
_____ 5. The number of points in a women's singles	f. 21
_____ 6. A method of playing doubles	g. Lob
_____ 7. Number of points used for setting a 14-all game	h. One hand down
	i. Hairpin
_____ 8. Type of shot that barely clears the net	j. Long high serve
_____ 9. Type of serve which should be used most often in singles	k. 3
	l. 15
_____10. Number of points used for setting a 10-all game in women's singles	m. The short serve
	n. 5
	o. 2

PART II. **TRUE OR FALSE**   Write + in the blank if the statement is true, O if it is wholly or partially false.

_____ 1. It is a fault for the server to step forward as she serves.

_____ 2. The service area in doubles is short and wide, for singles it is long and narrow.

_____ 3. Cross court smashes are usually the most effective.

_____ 4. Points are scored only by the serving side, with loss of service known as "side out," as in volleyball.

_____ 5. A serve that strikes the net, even if it continues on into the proper court, is a fault.

_____ 6. It is a fault if the server feints a serve or balks her opponent.

_____ 7. The backhand grip is similar to the Eastern backhand grip in tennis.

_____ 8. The smash should be used more in singles than in doubles.

_____ 9. All clears should be placed high and deep.

_____10. "Love all" is a term used for the game score at the beginning of the game and after "setting."

CHAPTER 6

BOWLING

PART I. **COMPLETION** Fill in the blanks with the appropriate word or words.

1. On a _____ball delivery, the ball of a right-handed bowler travels parallel to the right gutter and breaks toward the 1-3 pocket.

2. A _____ball travels in a wide arc toward the pins.

3. _____ and _____ of the thumb and finger holes and span of the bowler's hand determine proper fit of a ball.

4. When players on adjoining alleys address the pins simultaneously, the bowler on the _____ has the privilege of bowling first.

5. In bowling a perfect game of_____, the bowler would deliver _____ balls.

   The maximum number of balls that can be delivered in any game is _____ .

6. The motion of the arm in bowling is best described as a _____ .

7. In a four step coordinated approach, a right-handed bowler moves her _____ foot forward first as she pushes the ball forward. Her last step is taken on the _____ foot in a sliding action and her_____ foot swings behind the body to maintain balance.

8. _____bowling requires the bowler to look and concentrate on the pins during delivery: whereas in_____bowling the aim is a mark or location on the alley.

9. _____is the correct score of the bowler who rolls the following game:

Frame 1 — a strike;   Frame 6 — 2 and 7;
Frame 2 — 8 and 2;   Frame 7 — a strike;
Frame 3 — 9 and 0;   Frame 8 — 8 and 1;
Frame 4 — 2 and 7;   Frame 9 — 8 and 2;
Frame 5 — 6 and 4;   Frame 10 — 9 and 0.

10. Score the first five frames of the following game:

Frame 1 — a strike
Frame 2 — 1st ball knocks down 6 pins; 2nd ball takes two pins
Frame 3 — 1st ball takes 4 pins; 2nd ball takes six pins but the bowler fouls
Frame 4 — 1st ball take 8 pins; 2nd ball knocks the remaining 2 pins
Frame 5 — 1st ball runs to the gutter; 2nd ball knocks down 3 pins

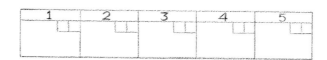

PART II. **MULTIPLE CHOICE** Select the one best answer for the question or situation. Circle the answer.

1. A foul on a delivery results in

   a. loss of half of the pins knocked down
   b. loss of ten points from the total score at the end of the game
   c. the delivery counts, but none of the pins falling is scored
   d. the ball is delivered again with no penalty

2. Which of the following approaches would be in error for a right-handed bowler?

   a. left foot first in a five step approach
   b. left foot first, four step approach
   c. left foot first, three step approach
   d. left foot first, one step approach

3. A style of delivery that results in a bouncing ball on release

   a. bending the knees before the ball swings forward
   b. holding the ball too long before the release
   c. releasing the ball too early
   d. keeping the knees straight and bending only at the hips

4. The distance from the foul line to the head pin on a regulation alley

   a. 55 feet
   b. 60 feet
   c. 72 feet
   d. 48 feet

5. The major advantage of a hook ball delivery is

   a. it curves so it hits the side of the pin
   b. it hits the pins at an angle with a spinning motion
   c. it enables the bowler to "spot" bowl, rather than use direct aim
   d. it makes possible a faster ball delivery

6. The most common reason for a poor release and an erratic aim

   a. releasing the ball too near the center of the alley
   b. too great a force on the forward swing and release
   c. a zig-zag approach

PART III. **MATCHING** Select the correct word or term in Column B and place the corresponding letter in front of the statement in Column A.

<table>
<tr><td align="center">Column A</td><td align="center">Column B</td></tr>
</table>

Column A

_____ 1. Maximum number of pins a bowler can score in one frame

_____ 2. All pins knocked down on the first ball of a frame

_____ 3. Approach area, alley bed, foul line, gutter and pit

_____ 4. Bedposts

_____ 5. A ball which curves to the right from a right-hand delivery

_____ 6. Consistently strong and calm team bowler

_____ 7. A ball that hits the side of the head pin and goes into the 1-2 pocket from a right-handed delivery

_____ 8. A leave of at least two pins after the first ball with the head pin down and at least one pin down between remaining pins

_____ 9. Ball released with the thumb in 12 o'clock position with the fingers under and behind the ball with no forearm rotation

_____10. A bowling type game requiring a ball without finger holds and smaller than the ten pin ball

_____11. Three consecutive strikes

_____12. Spots on the alley bed to aid in aiming

_____13. Name for a bowler

_____14. Wood used for hard surface of the alley bed

_____15. Common weight (pounds) of a woman's bowling ball

Column B

a. Curve ball

b. Martin Luther

c. Kegler

d. Hook ball delivery

e. Straight ball delivery

f. 30

g. 14

h. Candlepins

i. Range markers

j. Brooklyn

k. Turkey

l. Cherry

m. Inning

n. Maple

o. Anchor man

p. Alley

q. Cross alley bowling

r. Split

s. 7-10 split

t. Spare

u. Strike

v. 40

w. Back up ball

CHAPTER 7

FENCING

PART I **TRUE OR FALSE** Write + in the blank if the statement is true, O if it is wholly or partially false.

_____ 1. Women fence competitively with the foil and saber.

_____ 2. The foil target area extends from the collar to a horizontal line across the top of the hip bones on the back and sides to the lines of the groin in front.

_____ 3. In the "on guard" position the feet are at right angles to each other with the forward toe pointing toward the opponent.

_____ 4. There are three fundamental parries for each target area.

_____ 5. A forward recovery following a lunge is useful when an opponent retreats just out of reach.

_____ 6. The winner of woman's standard bout is the person who first scores three legal touches.

_____ 7. A simple attack comprises only a single blade movement.

_____ 8. When advancing, the right-handed fencer moves the left foot forward, then the right.

_____ 9. A beat followed by a disengagement and a lunge is a simple attack.

_____ 10. The cutover is used to change the line of engagement by passing the blade over the opponent's dropped blade.

PART II. **COMPLETION** Fill in the blanks with the appropriate word or words.

1. A lunge is executed in rapid sequence of: (a)_____(b)_____

   _____ .

2. A _____ is an offensive action following a successful parry.

3. Four of the eight fundamental parries are executed with the foil hand in supine position.

   These are parries _____ , _____ , _____ , and _____ .

4. Parries _____ and _____ protect the fencer's low inside line.

5. An _____ parry exerts pressure against an opponent's blade; a _____ parry deflects the opponent's blade.

6. A _____ deviates the opponent's blade and sweeps it into another line of attack with a circular motion.

7. The _____ consists of two rapid disengages followed by a lunge.

8. _____ is gained by the fencer who first extends the foil arm, initiates an attack, or parries an attack.

9. A _____ is a second attack, executed after a parry when the opponent delays or fails to riposte.

10. A _____ is a second action in the same line without withdrawing the extended arm.

11. The four major parts of the foil are _____ , _____ , _____ , and _____ .

PART III. **MATCHING** In the blank at the left of Column A write the letter of the most appropriate term in Column B.

Column A   Column B

_____ 1. Surface area where fencing bout is conducted   a. Engagement

_____ 2. Jump forward combined with a lunge   b. Cutover

_____ 3. Guard position of high inside target area   c. Strip

_____ 4. Forward body movement in guard position   d. Bout
         that brings fencer closer to opponent
                                                             e. Parry of fourth
_____ 5. Return attack after a parry
                                                             f. Parry of sixth
_____ 6. A method of gaining right-of-way from an
         attacking opponent   g. Parry of seventh

_____ 7. Running attack   h. Glide

_____ 8. Crossing blades in guard position   i. Parry

_____ 9. Disengagement of blade over opponent's   j. Retreat
         blade
                                                             k. Advance
_____ 10. Extension of the foil arm as a pretense for
          an attack   l. Lunge

                                                             m. Feint

                                                             n. Riposte

                                                             o. Disengage

                                                             p. Fleche

                                                             q. Balestra

CHAPTER 8

GOLF

PART I. **TRUE OR FALSE** Write + in the blank if the statement is true, O if it is wholly or partially false.

_____ 1. The ruling association for American women amateur golfers is the United States Golf Association.

_____ 2. Approximately half the strokes computed for par are allotted to play on the green.

_____ 3. In tournament play an individual may carry only 13 clubs.

_____ 4. A square or closed stance with a full swing is normally used from the tee when maximum power and distance are desired.

_____ 5. An intentional swing that fails to contact the ball is not counted as a stroke.

_____ 6. The right-handed golfer using an overlapping grip should have the "V" line formed by thumb and forefinger of each hand pointing toward the left shoulder.

_____ 7. In assuming the proper stance for a tee or fairway stroke, the knees should be slightly flexed when addressing the ball.

_____ 8. A player may tee her ball as far back as two club lengths behind the teeing markers without penalty.

_____ 9. A ball lying near an unnatural obstacle may be moved without penalty.

_____ 10. When a ball rests in a bunker, the club must not be grounded in preparation for the stroke.

PART II. **COMPLETION** Fill in the blanks with the appropriate word or words.

1. After the tee shot when progressing to the green the player whose ball is farthest _____ (to or from) the hole plays first.

2. Beginners should remember: "The _____ the iron club number, the _____ the shaft, the _____ loft to the face; consequently, the higher and shorter the ball flight."

3. A beginning set of clubs should include; _____

_____   _____ _____ __   , and

4. Three other essentials for a beginning golf around are _____, _____, and _____.

5. A _____ shot carries the ball high to the green, where it stops quickly.

6. _____ is the most individualized of all golfing skills.

7. _____ is the inclusive term used for sand traps and artificial hazards.

8. The left foot of the right-handed golfer is back from the line of flight and the right hip restricts body rotation. For a short iron stroke the _____ stance may be used.

9. A forward spin and a low ball in flight results from striking the ball as the clubhead travels _____ .

10. In _____ play the winner is the golfer using the least number of strokes over the course. In _____ play, the winner is the person winning the greatest number of holes from her opponent.

11. On a par five hole a player holes out in three strokes. She can boast to her friends she had an _____.

12. On all golf holes, play begins at the _____, progresses up the _____, to the _____ and into the _____.

13,14,15. A golfer with a full set of clubs would use a _____ for the tee stroke on a 380 yard hole. If her first ball traveled 170 yards into the middle of the fairway and she had a good lie and an unobstructed approach to the green, she might use a _____ (or long iron) for her next stroke. The ball traveled 165 yards. She would then use a _____ for a pitch shot or a _____ for a chip shot to the green followed by a roll toward the cup. Once on the green, she would use only a _____.

PART III. **MATCHING** In the blank at the left of Column A write the letter of the most appropriate term in Column B.

Column A	Column B
_____ 1. Theoretical perfect score	a. Birdie
_____ 2. Ball hit by right-handed player that curves right in flight	b. Bogey
	c. Par
_____ 3. Ball hit by right-handed player that goes straight left	d. Driver
_____ 4. One over par	e. Putter
_____ 5. Turf taken by clubhead	f. Number 8 iron
_____ 6. A fairway curving left or right	g. Wedge
_____ 7. Normal stance for middle irons	h. Slice
_____ 8. Club used in deep sand near green	i. Pull
_____ 9. Strokes conceded to a weaker player	j. Hook
_____ 10. Privilege of teeing first	k. Push
	l. Provisional
	m. Honor
	n. Divot
	o. Dog leg
	p. Closed stance
	q. Square stance
	r. Handicap

CHAPTER 9

GYMNASTICS

PART I. **COMPLETION** Fill in the blanks with the proper word or words.

1. Two special events now included in gymnastic competition are _____ and trampoline.

2. In competitive events, _____ must be performed for no longer than 1½ minutes on the floor or a mat within a square area of 39.33 feet.

3. The regulation balance beam is _____ feet from the floor, must be _____ inches wide,

   and _____ feet _____ inches long.

4. The one leg squat is a stunt performed on the _____

5. The most basic vault is the _____ vault.

PART II. **MATCHING** Place from Column B the letter of the most correct answer before each word or statement in Column A.

Column A

_____ 1. The squat stand dismount

_____ 2. The back roll to a straddle seat

_____ 3. The straight arm support

_____ 4. The side cross hand dismount

_____ 5. The side vault

_____ 6. The back shoulder roll

_____ 7. The handstand dismount

_____ 8. The knee scale

_____ 9. The straddle vault

_____ 10. The single leg flank dismount

_____ 11. The swan

_____ 12. The arabesque

_____ 13. The forward shoulder roll

_____ 14. The crotch seat

_____ 15. The yoga handstand

Column B

a. The even parallel bars

b. The horse

c. The uneven parallel bars

d. The balance beam

e. The lower uneven parallel bar

f. Free exercise

CHAPTER 10

REBOUND TUMBLING

PART I. **TRUE OR FALSE** Mark space at left with + if statement is true or with O if false.

_____ 1. Rebound tumbling consists of a series of stunts, usually done between bounces as a person jumps up and down on a springing canvas bed.

_____ 2. Mr. George Nisson has done the most to popularize rebound tumbling, which is · also called trampolining in America.

_____ 3. The best way for a beginner to mount the trampoline is to jump on it.

_____ 4. During World War II trampolining became an important part of the Navy preflight training programs and was used to help orient new pilots to sensations of the many positions in the air they would experience when actually flying.

_____ 5. In the straight bounce the feet should be placed on each bounce far beyond the shoulder line.

_____ 6. On the seat drop the hands, legs, and hips should contact the bed simultaneously.

_____ 7. When in the sitting position on the seat drop, the hands should be placed behind the hips with fingers pointing forward.

_____ 8. The swivel hips is a combination of a seat drop, body half twist and a seat drop landing.

_____ 9. It is imperative that for beginners there should be two spotters at each side of the trampoline and one at each end.

_____ 10. In the pike position the body is bent only at the hips.

PART II. **MATCHING** Place in the space to the left of each item in Column A the letter from Column B that best describes the term.

Column A

____ 1. Bounce

____ 2. Jackknife

____ 3. The tuck

____ 4. Swivel hips

____ 5. Knee drop

____ 6. Front drop

____ 7. Front flip

____ 8. Layout

____ 9. Break

____ 10. Spotter

____ 11. The dismount

____ 12. Suggested number of bounces done before doing a stunt

____ 13. Height of the legs holding the 5½ x 12 feet canvas bed fastened to a steel frame.

____ 14. "Jester leaps"

____ 15. First person to do a triple full twist

Column B

a. Push off with toes, circle arms, flex knees, push heels down

b. Bring both knees up to the chest before the body returns to full extension on to the bed

c. Keep the back straight, knees flexed, return to erect position to bounce three times before repeating movement

d. Extend legs forward, extend legs and arms and touch toes before returning to the bed

e. Circle arms overhead, twist to reverse position on the bed

f. Drop forward on arms, keep body in full extension and come to an erect position on the rebound

g. A position of the body when it is held in full extension

h. On fourth bounce, bend hips and legs, tuck head between the knees and grasp the ankles with the hands; release quickly, extend the legs, and land in an erect position

i. An assistant who helps the performer avoid injury

j. Three feet

k. Roll off the bed to come to a standing position

l. Four

m. Three

n. Five feet

o. First crude trampoline consisting of a pliable board supported at each end on heavy wooden blocks

p. Joe Louis

q. George Loken

r. To lessen the rebound

CHAPTER 11

RECREATIONAL ACTIVITIES

PART I. **TRUE OR FALSE** Write + in the blank if the statement is true, O if it is wholly or partially false.

_____ 1. In horseshoes, the shoe closest to the stake scores 5 points.

_____ 2. In this same game, two ringers thrown by the same player score 6 points.

_____ 3. In table tennis doubles, the service must begin from the server's right-hand court and bounce into the opponent's right-hand court. After the service, partners must alternate hitting any ball returned to their court.

_____ 4. A table tennis game consists of 21 points, and if the score is tied at 20-20 the winner must win two additional consecutive points.

_____ 5. In this same game, a loss of point occurs if a player puts her hand on the playing surface when the ball is in play.

_____ 6. In rope quoits, each player in turn shoots 4 quoits per frame.

_____ 7. A socket team is composed of 10 players.

_____ 8. In the game, Fifteen-Ball, the numbers of the 15 balls total 120, and the player who first scores 61 points is the winner.

_____ 9. In paddle tennis, adults are permitted to have two underhand serves.

_____ 10. Accuracy skish bait casting can be played by any number.

_____ 11. In croquet there are 3 wickets in front of the starting stake.

_____ 12. In this game, two more successive hits are earned if the ball goes through both of the first two arches.

_____ 13. In shuffleboard the black disc must be shot first.

_____ 14. In deck tennis, the server must toss the ring into a minimum flight of 6 inches.

_____ 15. Only one hand may be used in this game to catch or to toss the ring.

_____ 16. An official deck tennis game is composed of 15 points.

_____ 17. Many mixers and easy-to-do games should be included in most social recreational parties.

_____ 18. College recreational club officers and the club sponsor should be elected rather than appointed.

_____ 19. All recreational clubs should be miniature democratic societies.

_____ 20. After-school recreational club activities should include work projects as well as sports and games.

CHAPTER 12

SKIING

PART I. **MULTIPLE CHOICE** Select the best answer and circle the letter preceding the correct statement.

1. Which of the following techniques is executed with the skis across the fall line, the uphill ski advanced, the downhill ski weighted, and the skis parallel?

   a. herringbone
   b. stem turn
   c. side slipping
   d. snowplow

2. Which turn is executed by stemming the uphill ski and then bringing the skis together?

   a. stem turn
   b. stem christy
   c. snowplow
   d. wedeln

3. Which of the following relates to the herringbone?

   a. one ski is perpendicular to the fall line
   b. the skis are flat against the hill
   c. the outside edges of the skis are pushed into the hill
   d. both skis are at an angle of approximately 45 degrees to the fall line

4. In the straight downhill running position, where is the weight?

   a. both skis
   b. inside ski
   c. outside ski
   d. advanced ski

5. Which maneuver requires the least amount of effort to climb a steep hill?

    a.   herringbone
    b.   sidestep
    c.   traverse
    d.   step turns

6. Where is the stem employed in a snowplow?

    a.   with uphill ski
    b.   with downhill ski
    c.   with outside ski
    d.   with both skis

7. What is an important aspect of the traverse?

    a.   keep most of the weight on the downhill ski
    b.   keep most of the weight on the uphill ski
    c.   keep the weight on both skis equally
    d.   keep the downhill ski slightly advanced

8. Which ski carries more weight during the execution of a stem turn?

    a.   inside
    b.   outside
    c.   uphill
    d.   downhill

9. How should the skier care for her boots?

    a.   oil them once a month
    b.   break them in by hiking in them
    c.   protect them with a hard wax
    d.   soften the leather to aid comfort

10. What is the name of the bend or curve that is molded into the skis?

    a.   camber
    b.   shovel
    c.   slalom
    d.   edge

11. When the skis are not sliding, what is the easiest method for the beginner to change direction?

    a.   kick turn
    b.   stepping around
    c.   jump turn
    d.   stepping off

12. Which item of ski equipment is most important?

   a. skis
   b. bindings
   c. boots
   d. ski clothing

13. The use of which uphill conveyance allows the skis to remain on the snow?

   a. chair
   b. gondola
   c. cable car
   d. poma

14. What is the minimum number of persons desirable for a cross country trip?

   a. two
   b. three
   c. four
   d. five

15. What word is used to signify "forward lean"?

   a. vorlage
   b. christy
   c. wedeln
   d. ruecklage

16. What term is used to indicate a fast downhill run?

   a. snowplow
   b. sitzmark
   c. track
   d. schuss

17. What is the average height of ski poles?

   a. from floor to armpits
   b. from floor to chin
   c. from floor to waist
   d. from floor to top of shoulder

18. What name is given to a snow that freezes at night and thaws in the day, that is granular in appearance, and occurs during the spring of the year?

   a. mashed potatoes
   b. base
   c. powder
   d. corn

19. What word is used when you are overtaking another skier on a trail?

    a. fore
    b. track
    c. schuss
    d. back

20. Which of the following terms would not be found in a ski report?

    a. base
    b powder
    c. spring conditions
    d. vorlage

21. What is the name of a series of turns that have no traverse between the turns?

    a. royal christies
    b. rouade
    c. wedeln
    d. ruecklage

22. What must a skier know about release bindings?

    a. the adjustment (tightening) is the same for all skiers
    b. a retaining leash is not essential
    c. safety binding is another name for release binding
    d. adjustments should be made according to skier's weight and ability and the snow conditions

23. How does a novice skier change direction on a hill without using a sliding turn?

    a. stepping around
    b. kick turn
    c. step turns
    d. jump turn

24. What is a rule of safety to follow when using a rope tow?

    a. release bindings should be tightened down
    b. ski poles are carried under the arm
    c. loose fitting clothing should not be worn
    d. the skier leans forward during the ascent

25. Who of the following are directly responsible for administering first aid on the ski slope?

    a. ski instructors
    b. area operators
    c. lift operators
    d. ski patrolmen

PART II. **COMPLETION** Fill in the blanks with the appropriate word or words.

1. Four essential items of equipment for the beginning skier are: _____, _____, _____
   and _____ .

2. The shortest distance from the top to the bottom of the slope is called the _____.

3. Competitive alpine events enclude _____, _____, and _____.

4. Short skis are _____(more or less) manueverable than long skis for a beginner.

5. _____ are spots of accumulated snow resulting from turns made by skiers.

6. Two major factors in the increased popularity of skiing are _____
   and _____ .

7. Jumping events are judged on _____ and _____. Downhill events are evaluated
   on _____ only.

8. A _____ course is set according to contours of the slope. A skier must pass
   through a series of _____ during her descent.

9. Beginning skiers should climb, rather than ride practice slopes for _____ and
   _____ .

10. Many popular artificial ski surfaces are made of _____.

CHAPTER 13

SQUASH RACQUETS

PART I. **TRUE OR FALSE** Write + in the blank if the statement is true, O if it is wholly or partially false.

_____ 1. Squash racquets was devised in England and came to the United States via Canada.

_____ 2 Placing one's body in order to obstruct the view of an opponent is legal.

_____ 3. Balls striking the ceiling are out of play and result in loss of point to the person last playing the ball.

_____ 4. A legal service must travel directly to the front wall and strike above the 6 ½ foot service line.

_____ 5. A deep backswing and follow-through are required for power on the forehand and backhand.

_____ 6. The flat overhead serve resembles a flat tennis service.

_____ 7. When a player is hit by an opponent's ball not traveling directly to the front wall, a let is called.

_____ 8. A point is won or lost by a player after each legal service and rally.

_____ 9. As a safety precaution one should never look at the ball being played from behind.

_____ 10. Singles and doubles courts have identical dimensions and markings.

PART II. **COMPLETION** Fill in the blanks with the appropriate word or words.

1. The effectiveness of the _____ rests upon deception of the stroke execution.

2. A lob service should float back near the side wall and drop _____ to the backwall.

3. To the novice, the squash racket resembles a _____ racket, and its weight is similar to that of a _____ racket.

4. Three basic serves are _____ , _____ , and _____ .

5. _____ shots are low, hard drives that stay close to either the forehand or backhand wall.

6. The _____ shot is a low shot made from one side of the court to the front wall and opposite court.

7. When hit, the _____ resounds to indicate an error and loss of point.

8. The _____ grip of the racket is desirable to avoid shifting the grip during play.

9. When a score is tied at 13-13, the player first reaching 13 may choose to

_____ , _____

or _____ .

10. During a serving series, a player _____ after each successful serve.

PART III. **MATCHING** In the blank at the left in Column A write the letter of the most appropriate term in Column B.

Column A

____ 1. Most consistent service for beginners

____ 2. Hitting the ball before it bounces

____ 3. Hitting the ball immediately after it bounces

____ 4. Ball breaks in play

____ 5. Ideal set position while awaiting a return

____ 6. Place to stand when serving

____ 7. Defensive stroke to gain time

____ 8. A match

____ 9. Player refrains from stroking for fear of striking an opponent

____ 10. Wrist snap used from a close wall position

Column B

a. Near back wall straddling court division lines

b. Near "T" of service and court division line

c. Sidearm smash

d. Lob

e. Volley

f. Half volley

g. Forehand

h. Let

i. Hinder

j. Smash

k. Arc (quarter circle)

l. Chop

m. Flick

n. Drop shot

o. Two out of three games

p. Three out of five games

CHAPTER 14

STUNTS AND TUMBLING

PART I. **TRUE OR FALSE** Write + in the blank if the statement is true, O if it is wholly or partially false.

_____ 1. Americans who first gave educational emphasis to stunts, tumbling, and gymnastics were Peter Ling and Friedrich John.

_____ 2. It is believed that the Chinese developed the first system of gymnastics and tumbling as early as 2600 B. C.

_____ 3. Basic movement skills in stunts and tumbling are rolling, turning, twisting, and jumping.

_____ 4. The squat head balance is also called a "tip-up."

_____ 5. The round off, which may be done to either the left or right, should be learned after the cartwheel is mastered.

_____ 6. In the handstand, the hands should be placed on the mat close together in front of the body.

_____ 7. The cartwheel should always be done on the right side.

_____ 8. In the squat hand balance the head should not touch the floor.

_____ 9. The front handspring should be learned first over a rolled mat.

_____ 10. Another name for the neckspring is a kip or snap-up.

_____ 11. The chest balance is a couple stunt.

_____ 12. In pyramid building, the sturdy persons form the top.

PART II. **MATCHING** In the blank at the left of Column A write the letter of the most appropriate term listed in Column B.

<table>
<tr><td>Column A</td><td>Column B</td></tr>
</table>

Column A

_____ 1. Neckspring

_____ 2. Pyramid building

_____ 3. Dive and forward roll

_____ 4. Spotter

_____ 5. Handstand to forward roll

_____ 6. Foot to hand balance

_____ 7. Elephant walk

_____ 8. Bouncing ball

_____ 9. Dive and forward roll

_____10 Churn the butter

_____11. Chinese get up

_____12. Bear dance

_____13. Squat hand balance

Column B

a. Individual stunt

b. Balances involving two people

c. Person helping the performer in order to prevent injury

d. Picture making with a movement pattern

e. Stunts for two

CHAPTER 15

SURFING

PART I. **COMPLETION** Fill in the blanks with the appropriate word or words.

1. Board selection is based upon the individual surfer's _____ and _____ and the _____ of waves to be encountered.

2. Surfing waves are formed either by _____ across the surface of the water or by a _____ created by a power boat.

3. _____ and _____ are important when rising on the board.

4. The _____ ride is the first in a series of progressions prior to learning to turn the board.

5. The principle of a turn is to create _____ along one side of the board and cause one edge to slide faster.

6. _____ are techniques for steering the board over and through the back of the wave, ending the ride.

7. Three methods, or positions, of paddling the board are: _____, _____, and

_____ .

8. To slow the board, stalling is achieved by applying weight with the _____ foot.

9. For a surfer's personal safety and the safety of other surfers, anticipate wipe-outs and try to

_____ the board.

10. _____ is the skill of walking foot over foot backward to the rear of the board.

PART II. **MULTIPLE CHOICE** Select the word or phrase that best answers the question or describes the situation.

1. A body surfer

   a. should never use fins
   b. may use hands and arms as outriggers
   c. expels all air immediately prior to catching a wave
   d. all the above

2. The best method of transporting a surfboard a long distance is

   a. drag it slowly with the skeg up
   b. drag it slowly with the skeg down
   c. carry it under one arm
   d. carry it on the head

3. In the basic standing turn

   a. the forward foot is the turning foot and the trailing foot the balance foot
   b. the forward foot is the main balance foot and the trailing foot is both a balance and turning foot
   c. the forward and trailing feet are equally responsible for turning the board
   d. none of the above

4. A beginning woman surfer weighing 110 pounds should select a board with the following approximate dimensions

    a. 10' 2" long and 24" wide
    b. 9' long and 22" wide
    c. 6' 6" long and 14" wide
    d. 8' 0" long and 24" wide

5. The prone paddle position is best described

    a. body is centered on the board, toes are approximately even with the end of the board
    b. chin is up with eyes focused on the surf
    c. back is slightly arched and the body weight is resting on the short ribs, stomach, and thighs
    d. all the above

6. To turn the board efficiently while in a prone position

    a. get off the board, swim it around to proper position
    b. drag the arms and toes on the side on which the turn is desired
    c. drag both feet and reverse the pull of the arm on the opposite side of the desired turn
    d. shift the weight of the legs away from the desired turn and continue arm paddling

7. A surfer trying to avoid contact with the cold water in medium surf would probably paddle in

    a. prone position
    b. kneeling position
    c. sit paddle position

8. A surfer with the left foot forward and the right foot as the trail foot would make a standing right turn by

    a. applying pressure with the trail foot on the right rear of the board
    b. shifting the trail foot to the left rear of the board and exerting pressure
    c. cross stepping to right rear of board with forward foot
    d. stepping back to left rear of board with forward foot

9. To accomplish a kick-out or to turn over a wave when going left with the wave

    a. apply pressure through the trail foot on the left rear of the board
    b. apply pressure through the trail foot on the right rear of the board
    c. back pedal and exert pressure on the right rear of the board with both feet
    d. b and c above

10. When trimming a board

    a. use the front foot as a guide as the board comes through the wave
    b. if the board is headed for a nose. dive, back pedal until control is regained
    c. to accelerate the board, step forward foot over foot
    d. all the above

PART III. **MATCHING** In the blank on the left of Column A write the letter corresponding to the most appropriate term or name in Column B.

Column A   Column B

_____ 1. Placing five toes over the nose of the board

a. Ding

_____ 2. The nose of the board drops beneath the surface and continues downward

b. Wipe-out

c. Stringers

_____ 3. The fin of the surfboard

d. James Cook

_____ 4. A break or hole in the surface of the board

e. Pearling

_____ 5. Knocked from, blown or pushed from the board by a wave

f. Duke Kahanamouka

_____ 6. Wood strips used for reinforcing the board

g. Hot dogger

_____ 7. Instrumental figure in the rebirth of Hawaiian surfing

h. Hanging five

i. King Kalakaua

_____ 8. Small board ridden on the chest or abdomen

j. Skeg

_____ 9. Relatively bouyant board

k. Paipo board

_____10. Surfer who concentrates on skills and speed in small and medium surf

l. Pop-out

m. Floater

CHAPTER 16

SWIMMING AND DIVING

PART I. **MULTIPLE CHOICE** Select the correct answer and circle the letter proceding the correct statement.

1. The earliest written swimming instruction, written by a German professor of languages, was description of the

   a. sidestroke
   b. trudgen crawl
   c. elementary backstroke
   d. breaststroke

2. The fastest stroke executed on the back is the

    a.   inverted breaststroke
    b.   elementary backstroke
    c.   backstroke
    d.   none of the above

3. In which of the following strokes is the flutter kick used?

    a.   crawl and inverted breaststroke
    b.   backstroke and crawl
    c.   crawl and elementary backstroke
    d.   crawl and butterfly

4. Which of the following strokes is a restful, powerful stroke that is a necessity in *executing* life-saving skills?

    a.   crawl
    b.   breaststroke
    c.   trudgen crawl
    d.   sidestroke

5. The scissors kick is used in the

    a.   butterfly and trudgen crawl
    b.   sidestroke and trudgen crawl
    c.   crawl and sidestroke
    d.   sidestroke and elementary backstroke

6. In which of the following strokes is an underwater arm recovery used?

    a.   elementary backstroke
    b.   backstroke
    c.   butterfly
    d.   trudgen crawl

7. The single overarm is a comparatively simple stroke and is used following mastery of the

    a.   trudgen crawl
    b.   breaststroke
    c.   sidestroke
    d.   crawl

8. Surface dives are executed

    a.   from the edge of the pool or swimming area
    b.   from any front or back lying position in the water
    c.   from a prone or vertical position in the water
    d.   none of the above

9. When learning the dive from the pool deck, the progression followed is

    a.   standing, sitting, jumping feet first into the water, and diving
    b.   sitting, kneeling, standing on one leg, standing in a semicrouch, and a standing stationary dive
    c.   standing on one leg, kneeling, and a standing stationary dive
    d.   none of the above

10. At the present time, the fastest and most efficient turn for the freestyle swimmer is

    a.   closed turn
    b.   somersault turn
    c.   open turn
    d.   none of above

PART II. **COMPLETION** Fill in the blanks with the appropriate word or phrase.

1. Swimming in a 100 yard individual medley, a competitor would swim the following four strokes:

    (1) _____

    (2) _____

    (3) _____

    (4) _____

2. The property and tendency of the body that makes floating possible is called

    _____.

3. Four strokes basic to other stroke development are the

    (1) _____

    (2) _____

    (3) _____

    (4) _____

4. A trudgen combines an _____ arm stroke and a _____ kick.

5. Four of the five competitive diving groups recognized by the Division for Girls' and Women's Sports are

   (1) _____

   (2) _____

   (3) _____

   (4) _____

6. The _____ is a backward dive executed from a forward take-off.

7. The flutter kick is used in the following strokes:

   (1) _____

   (2) _____

   (3) _____

8. In a back floating position the body may be propelled by _____ or a _____ motion with the hands.

9. The _____ is classified in the cutaway dive group.

10. Three strokes using the sicissors kick are the

   (1) _____

   (2) _____

   (3) _____

11. The phase of arm or leg action which is without propelling force and which follows the power phase is the _____ phase.

CHAPTER 17

SYNCHRONIZED SWIMMING

PART I. **TRUE OR FALSE** Write + in the blank if the statement is true, O if it is wholly or partially false.

_____ 1. Standard strokes are modified and varied to gain effect and further a pattern or a theme.

_____ 2. In the modified crawl the kick is closer to the water surface than in the standard crawl.

_____ 3. Norman Ross coined the term "synchronized swimming" while announcing a water show at the Chicago World's Fair.

_____ 4. A maximum of 4 feet of water depth is necessary for efficient stunt performance.

_____ 5. In sculling, the body moves in the direction of the pressure on the water.

_____ 6. Synchronized swimming is both a sport and an art form.

_____ 7. Synchronization means that all swimmers must do the same thing at the same time.

_____ 8. In the modified breaststroke the head remains above the water.

_____ 9. In a front tuck somersault the legs and feet are extended well out of the water.

_____ 10. The shark figure uses the basic skills of the backstroke.

PART II. **COMPLETION** Fill in the blanks with the appropriate word or phrase.

1. _____ strokes are adaptations of standard strokes for synchronized use.

2. _____ stroking refers to complete strokes performed in a series.

3. _____ strokes combine parts of various strokes.

4. Synchronized swimming must be performed in a definite _____ with selected

_____

5. Five strokes (standard) that are basic to development of suitable synchronized strokes are:

    (1) _____

    (2) _____

    (3) _____

    (4) _____

    (5) _____

6. Standard strokes are modified so that only the _____ and _____ are visible above the water.

7. In solo, duet, and team competition, judging is based on _____ and _____.

8. The shark figure begins in a _____ layout position.

9. The _____ is the official publication of the International Academy of Aquatic Art.

10. Two figures that begin from a back layout position and go immediately to a tuck are _____ and _____.

PART III. **MATCHING** In the blank at the left of Column A write the letter of the most appropriate term or name in Column B.

<table>
<tr><th>Column A</th><th>Column B</th></tr>
</table>

Column A	Column B
_____ 1. Similar to surface dive in pike position	a. Nose Clip
_____ 2. Hips sunk and only head and lower legs seen at the surface	b. Tandem
_____ 3. From back layout with one leg extended vertically the hands force the body directly down	c. Water ballet
	d. Beulah Gundling
_____ 4. Sponsoring body for national competitive events	e. Katherine Curtis
_____ 5. Organization primarily concerned with furthering synchronized swimming in colleges	f. Amateur Athletic Union
_____ 6. Swimmers joined doing identical or complimentary actions	g. Tub
_____ 7. Necessary personal equipment for underwater work	h. Dolphin
	i. Porpoise
_____ 8. Pioneer in development of water ballet and synchronized work	j. Flying porpoise
_____ 9. Begins from back layout before submerging head first in a circle	k. Underwater speaker
_____ 10. Begins from a vertical foot-first surface dive	l. Association of Synchronized Swimming for College Women
	m. Submarine
	n. Ballet leg

CHAPTER 18

TENNIS

PART I. **TRUE OR FALSE** Mark space at left with + if statement is true or O if false.

_____ 1. The alleys are used in playing a singles game.

_____ 2. When the score is deuce a player needs but one more point to win the game.

_____ 3. A set has been completed when the game score is 7-5.

_____ 4. A let serve is called when the ball strikes the top of the net and lands within the proper service court area.

_____ 5. A match has been completed for girls and women when one player has won two out of three sets.

_____ 6. A score of zero (no points) is called "love".

_____ 7. A score of 30-30 is called deuce.

_____ 8. When the score is deuce the service is made from the right-hand side of the court.

_____ 9. In certain cases the ball may be returned legally after it has bounced twice.

_____ 10. In a doubles game either player may return the serve.

_____ 11. A ball that lands on the line is good.

_____ 12. When the server wins the advantage, the score is called "advantage-out".

_____ 13. A volley is a ball that is hit just as the ball contacts the ground.

_____ 14. A lob is a good stroke to use against a net player.

PART II. **MULTIPLE CHOICE** Circle the letter that identifies the correct answer.

1. If the receiver is unable to determine whether a ball is good or not, what should be done?

   a. Continue play
   b. Call the ball good
   c. Call a fault
   d. Ask the server to serve over

2. What is the score of the player who has won three points?

   a. 15
   b. 30
   c. 40
   d. Game

3. What is the score when the server wins the next point after deuce?

   a. Game for the server
   b. Advantage-in
   c. Advantage-out
   d. Love

4. At what point should the ball be hit when serving?

    a. About a foot above the height of the head
    b. As high as the player can reach with racket fully extended in the air
    c. A comfortable reach above the head
    d. Actually is unimportant just so the ball is served before it touches the ground

5. Of the following, what would represent a good defensive stroke against a net player?

    a. Volley
    b. Chop
    c. Slice drive
    d. Lob

6. The game of tennis was originated in what country?

    a. England
    b. United States
    c. Italy
    d. France

PART III. **COMPLETION** Fill in the blanks with the appropriate word or words.

1. Both the server and receiver have made 3 points. The score is _____ or

    _____

2. _____ is hitting the ball before it hits the ground.

3. The _____ is the stroke used for all balls coming to the right of a right-handed player.

4 The stroke comparable to the overhand throw in baseball is the _____.

5. A set must have at least _____ games to be complete, and one player must be_____ games ahead.

CHAPTER 19

TRACK AND FIELD

PART I. **MULTIPLE CHOICE** Circle the letter corresponding to the correct or best answer.

1. In a medium elongated block start the runner places

   a. the foot of the strongest leg in the front block
   b. foot of the strongest leg in the rear block
   c. either leg in the front block
   d. feet in blocks placed parallel

2. In a sprint event the runner pulls from the blocks

   a. by thrusting the body upward and rising immediately
   b. by a long stride that becomes shorter and more choppy as she progresses
   c. by moving the arms in unison to pull the body out at a 45 degree angle
   d. by using the arms in opposition to pull the body out at a 45 degree angle.

3. Identify the one incorrect technique of the sprinter

   a. run relaxed
   b. use a long driving stride
   c. arms swing across the front of the body
   d. breathe as normally as possible

4. Proper description of a portion of an effective sprinter's stride

   a. short, choppy leg action with arms swinging above shoulder level
   b. weight lands on the entire foot and the thrust of the leg is forward and upward
   c. weight lands on the ball of the foot; knee straightens and pressure is applied through the foot
   d. weight lands on the ball of the foot, knee straightens and pressure is applied totally through the heel

5. In a hurdle event, the hurdler

   a. may knock down the hurdles and remain in the race
   b. takes an odd number of strides between hurdles
   c. runs, rather than jumps, over the hurdles
   d. all of the above

6. A hurdler or sprinter in a "get set" position should

   a. have her head raised looking down the track
   b. have her hips lower than her back
   c. have her weight completely on one leg and foot
   d. have her shoulders above her hands

7. In the long jump, as the jumper leaves the take off board

   a. she should keep her head down to avoid fouling
   b. she should grasp her knees to avoid falling backward on landing
   c. the body is propelled upward and outward
   d. the body is propelled upward, perpendicular to the ground

8. In throwing events the series of movements preceeding the release is

   a. hip rotation, shoulder rotation, release
   b. simultaneous hip and shoulder action with the release
   c. shoulder rotation, hip rotation, release
   d. throwing action of the arm and shoulder, hip rotation and release

9. In the high jump, the jumper may

   a. use any method of clearing the bar following a one foot take off
   b. use a two foot take off
   c. use only scissors, straddle and western rolls
   d. none of above

10. In throwing events the measurement is taken from

   a. forward foot of the thrower to the point where the implement comes to rest
   b. forward foot of the thrower to the point where the implement initially strikes
   c. foul line or circle to the point where the implement initially strikes
   d. foul line or circle to the point where the implement comes to rest

PART II. **COMPLETION** Fill in the blanks with the appropriate word or phrase.

1. Track and field activities are grouped into events of _____ , _____ , and

   _____ .

2. Standing starts are used by all but the first runner in a _____ .

3. In track events _____ false starts disqualify a runner.

4. Two types of relays are _____ and _____ .

5. The trailing leg of the hurdler is rotated so that the toes are pointing away from the body

   and the _____ is higher than the _____ and the _____ are higher than the

   _____ .

6. To be a valid throw the _____ of the javelin must hit the ground first.

7. An _____ number of strides is taken between hurdles so that the take off and lead legs remain the same.

8. An outdoor track is usually _____ in length.

9. In throwing events all participants are allowed _____ attempts.

10. In a relay event, the most advantageous placement of runners is to place (answer in relation to their speed) _____ as the lead off runner, _____ as second runner, _____ as the third runner and _____ as the last runner.

PART III. MATCHING In the blank at the left of Column A write the letter of the most appropriate term in Column B.

<table>
<tr><td>Column A</td><td>Column B</td></tr>
</table>

_____ 1. Uncurved side of the track

_____ 2. Fastest runner on a relay team

_____ 3. Cycling action of legs while jumper is in the air

_____ 4. One race with a portion of total race entries

_____ 5. Failure to pass baton in restricted zone

_____ 6. Boundary line within which a throw must land to be fair

_____ 7. Safest baton pass

_____ 8. Hurdle height

_____ 9. Outdoor track surface

_____ 10. Relay in which a runner overtakes a teammate running in the same direction

a. Disqualification

b. Checkmark

c. Sector line

d. Backside

e. Straightaway

f. Shuttle

g. Blind exchange

h. Heat

i. Visual exchange

j. First

k. Anchor

l. Repeat pass

m. Pursuit

n. Hitch kick

o. Tuck

p. Wood

q. Cinder

r. 2 feet 6 inches

s. 3 feet

CHAPTER 20

WATER SKIING

PART I. **TRUE OR FALSE** Write + in the blank if the statement is true, O if it is wholly or partially false.

_____ 1. The slalom ski is usually longer and has a deeper fin than a conventional ski.

_____ 2. To cut across the wake means that the skier has gone to the right or the left of the boat.

_____ 3. It is correct form to bend from the hips while riding two skis.

_____ 4. The beginner is urged to come to a standing position as soon as possible during water starts on two skis.

_____ 5. Skiing at about 15 to 20 miles per hour, the skier will plane 20 to 25 yards before sinking into the water.

_____ 6. During the single ski start, the towline should be on the same side of the ski as the back or dragging leg.

_____ 7. The beginner is encouraged to put the left foot in the back binding of a single ski.

_____ 8. In getting to a standing position on the saucer the right hand and left foot are placed on the saucer at the same time.

_____ 9. Standing too far back from center will cause a saucer to bounce up and down.

_____ 10. Falls on the two ski water start are frequently caused by pulling up on the towline.

PART II. **MULTIPLE CHOICE** Select the word or words that best answer the statement or question.

1. The following is an accurate description of a preparatory position in dry land practice of a two ski start

   a. squat with weight centered over the skis with back straight, knees bent close to chest, arms outside of the knees.
   b. sit down on back of the skis with back straight, knees bent close to the chest, arms inside of knees
   c. sit down on back of the skis with back straight, knees bent close to the chest, arms outside of knees
   d. squat over the center of the skis, back rounded, legs extended with straight knees

2. To turn to the right inside the wake, on two skis, the body

    a. leans left with right knee flexed; push with both ankles
    b. leans right with left knee flexed; push from right ankle
    c. leans right with right knee flexed; push with both ankles
    d. leans left with left knee flexed; push with right foot and ankle

3. To remove slack from the towline

    a. lift the line overhead
    b. pull the line back toward the body
    c. pull the line toward one hip
    d. b and c above

4. When approaching a dock too rapidly after a "whip off," a skier should

    a. dive into the water
    b. squat down and drag cupped hands
    c. sit down in the water
    d. b and c above

5. If possible when attempting water starts, the boat should

    a. be headed toward open water
    b. be headed into the wind
    c. let the towline out full length
    d. all the above

6. A skier wanting to increase her skiing speed signals the boat operator

    a. "in gear"
    b. fist with thumb up
    c. "hit it"
    d. circle with thumb and first finger

PART III. **MATCHING** In the blank at the left of Column A write the letter of the most appropriate word or phrase in Column B.

Column A

_____ 1. Boat speedometer

_____ 2. Turbulence of the water created by the boat

_____ 3. Single ski

_____ 4. Position of skis when running nearly parallel to the water surface

_____ 5. Signal given to have boat move forward to take up slack in the towline

_____ 6. Device for holding the foot in the ski

_____ 7. Skier's signal to stop

_____ 8. Water disk

_____ 9. Stabilizing portion of a ski

_____10. Towline bridle

Column B

a. Palm forward with fingers spread

b. Bridle

c. Pylon

d. Binding

e. Saucer

f. Wake

g. Slalom

h. "Hit it"

i. "In gear"

j. Fin

k. Aquameter

l. Planing

m. Fist with thumb down

CHAPTER 21

BASKETBALL

PART I. **MULTIPLE CHOICE** Circle the letter preceding the correct or best answer.

1. When a field goal is scored, the ball is put in play by

    a. opposing team member at the side line
    b. opposing team member behind the end line
    c. member of the scoring team at the side line
    d. jump ball in nearest restraining circle

2. The jump shot is a desirable offensive skill

    a. when shooting from 20 or more feet from the basket
    b. when loosely guarded in a zone defense pattern
    c. when closely guarded within 15 feet of the basket
    d. none of the above

3. The Thirty Second Rule states that

    a. a team can maintain possession of the ball only 30 seconds in its back court
    b. a team gaining possession of the ball must attempt a goal within 30 seconds
    c. a team must pass the ball a minimum of three times within 30 seconds
    d. none of the above

4. During the last 40 seconds of a game a player was fouled in the act of shooting. Her field goal scored. She is awarded

    a. two free throws
    b. one free throw and ball out of bounds
    c. one free throw
    d. two free throws and ball out of bounds

5. A player-to-player system of defense is best broken by

    a. short quick passes
    b. fast breaks
    c. screens
    d. all the above

6. A forward guarded closely by a tall opponent who keeps one arm overhead will find the most effective pass to teammates is

    a. hook
    b. chest
    c. bounce
    d. overhead

7. Through injury and disqualification a team is reduced to 5 eligible players. The officials rule that

    a. play continues
    b. game is defaulted
    c. game is forfeited
    d. a disqualified player should return to the game and play should continue

8. A toss up is administered between two opposing players

    a. on a tie ball
    b. for a double violation
    c. to begin play after a double foul
    d. all the above

9. The tip-in is a

    a. defensive skill
    b. offensive technique used on rebounding shots
    c. skill used to stop a shot descending into the basket
    d. a and c above

10. On a free throw attempt the ball fails to enter or touch the ring and

    a. ball goes into play
    b. the free throw is repeated
    c. this is a violation; ball is awarded to opponents
    d. none of the above

PART II. **TRUE OR FALSE** Write + in the blank if the statement is true, O if it is wholly or partially false.

_____ 1. Women's basketball is played by two teams of five members each.

_____ 2. During play the court may be "unbalanced," with four players from one or both teams on one half of the court.

_____ 3. When a field goal is scored, the ball is put into play by a member of the opposing team at the side line.

_____ 4. A ball may be rolled to another player.

_____ 5. All players must take their own free throws.

_____ 6. Basketball was originated in England as a woman's game and was later adopted as the "All American Game."

_____ 7. When the ball is dead and time is out, a team may make any number of substitutions, with individual players entering an unlimited number of times.

_____ 8. Any player may shoot for a basket from any court position.

_____ 9. When pivoting, a player is allowed to move both feet, but no more than a yard in any direction.

_____ 10. It is legal for a player to receive a bounce pass, then pivot and perform a limited dribble before passing the ball.

PART III. **COMPLETION** Fill in the blanks with the appropriate word or phrase.

1. A player may legally hold the ball _____ seconds in bounds when closely guarded, _____ seconds out of bounds, and _____ seconds on a free throw.

2. An official game consists of _____ quarters of _____ minutes each.

3. Two basic defense patterns are _____ and _____ defense.

4. A player is awarded _____ when she is fouled in the act of shooting but the shot scored a field goal.

5. A player _____ when she moves to a position where her body protects her teammate's possession of the ball.

6. A time-out may be called by an official for:

   (1) _____

   (2) _____

   (3) _____

   (4) _____

7. When a player gives impetus to propel the ball into the air and then gains possession of it before it is touched by another player or hits the floor, it is called an _____.

8. A violation results in a _____ from out of bounds by the opposing team.

9. Three commonly used two-handed passes are _____, _____, and _____.

10. Teams are allowed two players who _____.

PART IV. **MATCHING** In the blank at the left of Column A write the letter of the most appropriate term or phrase in Column B. A term may be appropriate for one or more statements.

Column A

_____ 1. Two opposing players place one or both hands on the ball simultaneously

_____ 2. A player places one or both hands firmly on a ball held by an opponent

_____ 3. Pushing the ball into an opponent's body

_____ 4. Team takes the fifth time out

_____ 5. On a free throw the ball fails to touch the ring or score

_____ 6. Guarding an opponent without a ball by holding her clothing

_____ 7. Result of intentionally kicking the ball

_____ 8. Player touches the ball to the floor while maintaining possession of it

_____ 9. The half of the court in which a team's own basket is located

_____ 10. Placing two hands on the ball while dribbling

Column B

a. Individual foul

b. Team foul

c. Tie ball

d. Legal, play continues

e. Back court

f. Violation, ball is awarded to opponents

g. Front court

h. Double foul

i. Simultaneous violations

CHAPTER 22

FIELD HOCKEY

PART I. **COMPLETION** Fill in the blanks with the appropriate word or phrase.

1. A hockey team is composed of _____ forwards and _____ defensive players. Name the forwards: _____ , _____ , _____ , _____ , _____

2. The _____ is a series of short taps that move the ball while the player maintains possession of it.

3. _____ are defensive moves to avoid a tackler approaching head on.

4. On a _____ the ball must be motionless before it is hit or pushed along the ground.

5. _____ is a foul resulting when a player places her body between an opponent and the ball, thus hindering play.

6. A _____ is used by a tackler approaching from her opponent's non-stick side.

7. A player is _____ if she is in opponent's half of the field and nearer the goal than the ball with fewer than _____ opponents between her and the goal.

8. A _____ (by opposing team) is used to put the ball into play after it has gone out of bounds over the side line off the stick of a player or players on the same team.

9. The _____ is the area between the side line and the 5 yard line.

10. _____ is credited with introducing field hockey to Eastern college women in 1901.

PART II. **MULTIPLE CHOICE** Select the word or words that best describe the situation or answers the question.

1. The red right halfback makes sticks as she successfully executes a left hand lunge and gains possession of the ball from the white team.

   a. legal
   b. white free hit
   c. red free hit
   d. penalty corner

2. A red forward stops the ball with her feet but does not advance the ball.

   a. legal
   b. free hit white
   c. free hit red
   d. bully on the spot

3. To tackle an opponent coming directly toward you use a

   a. left hand lunge
   b. circular tackle
   c. pull to tackle
   d. straight tackle

4. A stroke in which the ball is pushed with a strong twist putting spin on the ball is

   a. jab
   b. dodge
   c. flick
   d. left hand lunge

5. A stroke in which the ball travels along the ground and there is no backswing is a

   a. scoop
   b. flick
   c. drive
   d. push pass

6. The player who clears to the right and left and marks the opposing right inner is

   a. left inner
   b. left fullback
   c. right fullback
   d. left halfback

7. The player who distributes the play, marks one player only, tackles well, and may shoot for goal is

   a. right halfback
   b. center forward
   c. center halfback
   d. left halfback

8. A white defense player makes sticks as she clears the ball from within the circle.

   a. free hit red
   b. penalty corner
   c. corner (long)
   d. dangerous hitting

9. The white team is taking a penalty corner. The ball is received by the left inner who deflects the ball to the center forward. The center forward shoots immediately.

   a. legal
   b. goal
   c. repeat the corner
   d. red free hit

10. The red left fullback, while in her own striking circle, unintentionally sends the ball over the endline.

   a. white free hit
   b. 15 yard defense hit
   c. penalty corner
   d. corner

11. Which of the following is a special privilege of the goalkeeper?

    a. throw the ball
    b. kick the ball
    c. play with her stick in one hand
    d. stop the ball with her palm and drop it perpendicularly

12. Which members of the team are allowed to drive for goal as long as they are in the circle?

    a. wings, inners, center forward
    b. wings, inners, center forward, center halfback
    c. wings, inners, center forward, any halfback
    d. wings, inners, center forward, any halfback, any fullback

13. What is awarded when a member of the attacking team fouls in the striking circle?

    a. penalty bully
    b. corner
    c. penalty corner
    d. free hit

14. In general, which member of the defensive team should take free hits from the edge of the circle?

    a. center halfback
    b. wing
    c. side halfback
    d. fullback

15. Which of the following describes the most effective roll-in?

    a. feet behind the line, stick into the field, ready to enter play
    b. feet and stick behind the line, stick in hand, blade on the ground
    c. feet and stick behind the line, kneeling on one knee
    d. feet and stick behind the line, stick lying on the ground

16. The defending fullback kicks the ball in the circle. In so doing, she prevents a sure goal from being made. What is the official's decision?

    a. corner
    b. penalty corner
    c. penalty bully
    d. 15 yard defense hit

17. For which of the following would a penalty corner be awarded?

    a. attacking inner makes sticks in the circle
    b. defending fullback sends the ball over the end line intentionally
    c. ball glances off the stick of an attacking inner and goes over the end line

18. In which of the following situations is the corner being taken most effectively?

    a. wing taking the hit is straddling the line, attacking forwards are around the edge of the circle, opposing defense are behind the endline

    b. defending forwards are around the outside of the circle, attacking forwards are behind the end line

    c. wing taking the hit is standing on the end line, attacking forwards are behind the 25 yard line, opposing defense are on the edge of the circle

    d. person taking the hit is straddling the line, opposing defense behind the end line, attacking forwards behind the 25 yard line

19. One fullback plays up when the ball is on her side of the field; the other fullback stays back. This is called

    a. marking
    b. interchanging
    c. covering
    d. backing up

20. When executing the left hand lunge, the tackler should lunge with

    a. a step with the left foot
    b. a step with her right foot
    c. weight on both feet equally
    d. none of these

21. A red left wing shoots for goal in the striking circle. The ball glances off the stick of a defending player and rolls over the goal line between the goal posts.

    a. 15 yard defense hit
    b. goal
    c. corner
    d. penalty corner

22. The game has been suspended because a player has been temporarily incapacitated. How is the game restarted?

    a. penalty bully
    b. bully on the spot
    c. center bully
    d. fee hit

23. A penalty bully has been taken and completed. A goal was not scored nor a penalty goal awarded. How is the game restarted?

    a. 25 yard line bully
    b. 50 yard line bully
    c. corner
    d. 15 yard defense hit

24. A forward shooting for the goal rushes into the goal cage. The goalkeeper clears the first shot, but the ball is hit at her again. During this play, the forward has remained in the goal cage off the field of play.

   a. legal
   b. offsides
   c. corner
   d. penalty corner

25. The left fullback has intercepted the ball near the goal cage and the attacking forwards are all in the circle. Generally speaking, what would be the most effective method of getting the ball to her teammates?

   a. flick to the center forward
   b. drive immediately to the left wing
   c. drive immediately to the left inner
   d. get the ball into a clear space and drive to the left wing

PART III. **MATCHING** Situations that occur during play are listed in Column A. From Column B select the correct method of returning the ball to play after the circumstance described has occurred. A term or word may be used more than once.

Column A	Column B
_____ 1. Sticks in the field of play	a. On the spot bully
_____ 2. Goal scored	b. Center bully
_____ 3. Defense player repeatedly fouls in the circle	c. Penalty bully
_____ 4. Attack fouls in the circle	d. Free hit for opponent at spot of foul
_____ 5. Ball goes over the side line off sticks of opponents	e. Free hit for defense anywhere in circle
_____ 6. Ball goes over side line off stick of single player	f. Bully on alley line
_____ 7. Ball goes over end line off the sticks of two defensive players in the circle	g. Roll-in for opponents
_____ 8. Player trips an opponent in field of play	h. 25 yard bully opposite spot where ball crossed the line (experimental rule change: free hit for defending team 15 yards from the end line opposite place the ball crossed the line)
_____ 9. Defense player obstructs in the circle	
_____10. Ball goes over end line off the stick of an attacking player	i. Long corner
	j. Penalty corner

CHAPTER 23

LACROSSE

PART I. **MULTIPLE CHOICE** Circle the letter corresponding to the correct or best answer.

1. The correct grip of the crosse results in

    a. baseball type grip
    b. throwing hand placed at the butt of the stick
    c. upper hand serving as the guiding hand, the lower hand the power hand
    d. upper hand serving as the power hand, the lower hand the guiding hand

2. In the vertical cradling action

    a. top arm is approximately waist level and parallel to the ground
    b. bottom arm is approximately waist level and parallel to the ground
    c. both a and b above
    d. none of the above

3. For a right-handed player to dodge effectively to the right while cradling, immediately before the pivot, her

    a. left foot must be forward and the stick must swing to the left
    b. left foot must be forward and the stick must swing to the right
    c. right foot must be forward and the stick must swing to the right
    d. right foot must be forward and the stick must swing to the left

4. When picking up a ball rolling away from the player

    a. trap the ball by throwing the crosse on top of it, then scoop it up and begin cradling
    b. overrun the ball and play it as a ball rolling toward the player
    c. use the same technique as picking up a stationary ball but increase running speed
    d. none of the above

5. Learning to catch, beginners should get the feeling that

    a. bottom hand is doing the catching
    b. both hands move together at the collar
    c. top hand is doing the catching
    d. none of the above

6. The preparatory body and arm position for an overarm pass most nearly resembles

    a. overarm softball throw
    b. shoulder (push) pass in basketball
    c. shot-put
    d. b and c above

7. The draw is used

    a. to begin play at each half
    b. to restart play after a goal
    c. to restart play after a double foul
    d. all the above

8. The skill of dislodging a ball from an opponent's crosse is known as

    a. guarding
    b. body checking
    c. dodging
    d. crosse checking

9. A ball legally shot for goal by an attack player, hits the crosse and body of a defense player but continues across the goal line. The official rules

    a. draw, 10 yards from the goal
    b. goal scored
    c. defense takes free position
    d. none of the above

10. The goal keeper is in the crease and her point steps into the crease to stop an almost certain goal by 1st home. The official rules

    a. all defense players move from between attack's free position and goal
    b. free position for defense
    c. ball continues in play
    d. free position for attack with goalkeeper defending

PART II **TRUE OR FALSE** Write + in the blank if the statement is true, O if it is wholly or partially false.

_____ 1. The American women's game of lacrosse came from England rather than from the American men's game.

_____ 2. Offside rules limit defense players to action in their own half of the field.

_____ 3. The crosse is held with the natural throwing hand at the top of the stick and the other hand at the end of the stick.

_____ 4. When cradling action reaches either side of the body, the crosse face is open as if to catch a throw.

_____ 5. When retrieving a stationary ground ball, the right-handed player has the crosse on the right side of her body.

_____ 6. It is a foul for an attacking player to cross into the crease after shooting for the goal.

_____ 7. An attack player may check the goalkeeper in the crease.

_____ 8. As a right-handed player completes an overarm pass the head of the stick points where the ball is intended and the left hand and stick end are in the right armpit.

_____ 9. It is legal for a tired player to leave the game and return later if she has not been replaced by another player.

_____ 10. Required field dimensions are 60 by 100 yards.

PART III. **COMPLETION** Fill in the blanks with the appropriate word or phrase.

1. There are _____ attack and _____ defense players.

2. The three attack players who most frequently have a shot for goal are _____ , _____ and _____ .

3. The two deepest defense players are: _____ and _____ .

4. _____ is the rhythmical swing of the stick in time with the player's body that keeps the ball under control in the crosse.

5. Two types of fouls are the_____ and_____ .

6. Penalty awarded for a field foul is a _____to the person or team fouled.

7. The game of _____ , often thought of as the parent of lacrosse, was popular with American Indians centuries ago.

8. A player may_____ or _____ with the ball.

9. Three defensive skills needed by all defense players are_____ ,_____ , and_____ .

10. After the ball goes out of bounds equidistant between two opposing players, the official executes a _____ .

PART IV. **MATCHING** In the blank at the left of Column A write the letter of the most appropriate term or statement in Column B.

Column A

_____ 1. Begins play at each half and after every goal

_____ 2. Closely guarding an opponent

_____ 3. Placing one's body between an opponent and her objective to impede her progress

_____ 4. Attack skill used to evade a player marking

_____ 5. Holding position on an official's signal (whistle)

_____ 6. Minimum distance between goals

_____ 7. Attack player

_____ 8. Out of bounds

_____ 9. Method of restarting play in the field after a double foul

_____10. Interruption of a free attack player

Column B

a. 110 yards

b. Stand

c. 90 yards

d. Interchange

e. Marking

f. Body checking

g. Draw

h. Center draw

i. Point

j. Interchange

k. First home

l. Ball given to player closest to ball as it went out

m. Free position

n. Crosse checking

o. Dodging

CHAPTER 24

SOCCER AND SPEEDBALL

Soccer

PART I. Give the penalty for the following infractions.

1. Ball is kicked out of bounds at the side lines _____

2. Ball is kicked over the cross bars or over the goal line outside of the goal posts by the attackers _____

3. Ball is kicked over the cross bars or over the goal line outside the goal posts by the defenders _____

4. Foul committed by either team outside the penalty area or by attackers inside the penalty area _____

5. Team mate stands closer than 5 yards on a free kick _____

6. Foul committed by defenders inside penalty area_____

7. Foul committed simultaneously by both teams _____

8. On a free kick, penalty or defense kick player kicks ball a second time before it is played by another player _____

9. Off-side _____

10. Ball is sent over side lines by two opposing players _____

PART II. **TRUE OR FALSE** Write + in the blank if the statement is true, O if it is wholly or partially false.

_____ 1. Dribbling is a defensive tactic used to get the ball around an opposing player.

_____ 2. The corner kick is usually taken by the wing.

_____ 3. The goalkeeper may drop-kick or throw the ball.

_____ 4. An inner should always take the free kick.

_____ 5. A throw-in is taken by the team that causes the ball to go out of bounds.

_____ 6. On a kick off the ball may be kicked into the opponent's side of the field or it may be kicked backward to one's own backs.

_____ 7. The goalkeeper may not leave the goal mouth at any time.

_____ 8. A regulation soccer team is composed of 11 players.

_____ 9. The game is started by a kick off by the right inner to the center forward.

_____ 10. A player is on side if she is in her own half of the field.

PART III **MATCHING** In the blank at the left of Column A write the letter of the most appropriate term in Column B.

<table>
<tr><td colspan="2" align="center">Column A</td><td align="center">Column B</td></tr>
<tr><td>_____</td><td>1. Awarded when a defending player fouls in the penalty area</td><td>a. Blocking</td></tr>
<tr><td></td><td></td><td>b. Trapping</td></tr>
<tr><td>_____</td><td>2. Given for a foul committed by the attacking team inside the penalty area</td><td>c. Attacking team</td></tr>
<tr><td>_____</td><td>3. The team in possession of the ball in the defense area of the opposing team</td><td>d. Corner kick</td></tr>
<tr><td></td><td></td><td>e. Drop kick</td></tr>
<tr><td>_____</td><td>4. Rebound kick made after the ball touches the ground</td><td>f. Dribbling</td></tr>
<tr><td>_____</td><td>5. A short series of foot taps used to move the ball</td><td>g. Heading</td></tr>
<tr><td></td><td></td><td>h. Roll-in</td></tr>
<tr><td>_____</td><td>6. Used to get the ball away from an opponent</td><td>i. Indirect free kick</td></tr>
<tr><td>_____</td><td>7. Using any body part except the arms and hands to stop or deflect the ball while it is in the air</td><td>j. Kick-in</td></tr>
<tr><td></td><td></td><td>k. Off-side</td></tr>
<tr><td>_____</td><td>8. A kick taken by the center forward to start the game, at each quarter, or after a goal is scored</td><td>l. Penalty kick</td></tr>
<tr><td></td><td></td><td>m. Direct free kick</td></tr>
<tr><td>_____</td><td>9. Only player who can touch the ball with her hands without penalty</td><td>n. Punt</td></tr>
<tr><td></td><td></td><td>o. Place kick</td></tr>
<tr><td>_____</td><td>10. Stopping a rolling or rebounding ball with the body or feet</td><td>p. Tackle</td></tr>
<tr><td></td><td></td><td>q. Goalkeeper</td></tr>
<tr><td></td><td></td><td>r. Wing</td></tr>
</table>

Speedball

PART I. **MULTIPLE CHOICE** Circle the letter preceding the best answer.

1. Which player most frequently takes the free kick?

   a. right or left wing
   b. center forward
   c. right or left halfback
   d. right or left inner
   e. right or left fullback

2. Which team puts the ball into play after a score has been made?

    a. the team that scored
    b. the team scored against
    c. the team with the higher score
    d. alternate teams

3. What is the decision when the defense sends the ball over the goal line but not between the goal posts?

    a. throw-in
    b. place kick
    c. punt
    d. drop kick
    e. all the above

4. Who marks the left wing?

    a. opposing left wing
    b. opposing right wing
    c. opposing left halfback
    d. opposing right halfback
    e. opposing right fullback

5. Which group in the following list is the best combination of players who play both offensively and defensively?

    a. center forward, right inner, left fullback
    b. center halfback, right halfback, goalkeeper
    c. center halfback, right halfback, left halfback
    d. center halfback, right halfback, center forward

6. What is the decision if the center forward on the kick-off lifts the ball diagonally forward and directly to the left inner?

    a. legal play
    b. repeat with corrections
    c. jump ball
    d. free kick to opponents
    e. none of these

7. How is the ball put into play if two opponents send the ball out of bounds simultaneously?

    a. toss-up
    b. free kick for team behind in score
    c. throw-in for team behind in score
    d. repeat kick-off

8. Which opposing player is marked by the right fullback?

   a. right inner
   b. left inner
   c. right halfback
   d. left wing
   e. left halfback

9. A running player catches the ball and takes three steps which constitutes

   a. juggling
   b. traveling
   c. charging
   d. obstructing
   e. blocking

10. The center halfback kicks her own right inner; this is

   a. charging
   b. obstruction
   c. team foul
   d. unfortunate

PART II. **TRUE OR FALSE** Write + in the blank if the statement is true, O if it is wholly or partially false.

_____ 1. A bouncing ball, having been blocked with the body, may be caught and played as an aerial ball.

_____ 2. There are four backfield members on a speedball team.

_____ 3. A player having caught an aerial ball while standing still may progress in any direction with two steps.

_____ 4. It is a foul to hold the ball out of bounds longer than 5 seconds.

_____ 5. The kick-off is used only to start the game.

_____ 6. When a member of the defending team fouls in their own backfield outside the penalty area, a free kick is awarded the attacking team.

_____ 7. A drop kick for a goal must be started from outside the penalty area to score.

_____ 8. A player with the ball in her hands may move one foot in any direction while maintaining contact with the ground with the other foot.

_____ 9. A touchdown scores 3 points.

_____ 10. The goalkeeper may pick up a ground ball with her hands and convert it to an aerial ball.

PART III. **MATCHING** In the blank at the left of Column A write the letter of the term associated with the statement in Column B.

<table>
<tr><td>Column A</td><td>Column B</td></tr>
<tr><td>_____ 1. Free kick</td><td>a. Man-to-man marking</td></tr>
<tr><td>_____ 2. Time-outs</td><td>b. 8 Minutes</td></tr>
<tr><td>_____ 3. Throw-in</td><td>c. All players 5 yards away</td></tr>
<tr><td>_____ 4. Penalty kick</td><td>d. Foul</td></tr>
<tr><td>_____ 5. Attackers</td><td>e. Out-of-bounds ball</td></tr>
<tr><td>_____ 6. Defenders</td><td>f. Opponents 5 yards away</td></tr>
<tr><td>_____ 7. Tripping</td><td>g. A defensive player</td></tr>
<tr><td>_____ 8. Defensive tactic</td><td>h. Team attempting to gain possession of ball</td></tr>
<tr><td>_____ 9. Length of quarters</td><td>i. Three</td></tr>
<tr><td>_____ 10. Fullback</td><td>j. Team in possession of ball</td></tr>
<tr><td></td><td>k. 5 Minutes</td></tr>
<tr><td></td><td>l. Charging</td></tr>
<tr><td></td><td>m. Two</td></tr>
<tr><td></td><td>n. Touchdown</td></tr>
<tr><td></td><td>o. Foul by defense in its penalty area</td></tr>
</table>

CHAPTER 25

SOFTBALL AND SLOW PITCH SOFTBALL

PART I. **MULTIPLE CHOICE** Circle the letter preceding the best answer.

1. The most important throwing skill for a fielder is

   a. sidearm
   b. overhand
   c. pitch
   d. underhand

2. In delivering a ball to the batter, the pitcher

   a. must remain motionless for one second before delivery
   b. may take only one step toward the batter
   c. may use a slingshot or windmill delivery
   d. all the above

3. Which of the following statements concerning the skills of catching a fly ball is false?

   a. Fingers of both hands are extended and tense
   b. The ball is caught at shoulder level, if possible
   c. The ball contacts the glove hand first
   d. The player moves to meet the ball

4. In slow pitch softball

   a. the pitcher must release the ball at shoulder level
   b. the pitcher must arch the ball at least three feet from the point of delivery to home plate
   c. every other batter must bunt
   d. rules of base stealing are the same as in regulation softball

5. A situation that could result in the application of the infield fly rule would have

   a. bases loaded and no outs
   b. bases loaded with two outs
   c. runner on first base only with no outs
   d. runners on first and third bases with no outs

6. A batter who normally swings late at a pitch should

   a. separate her hands in the grip
   b. choke the bat
   c. move forward in the box
   d. move hands to the end of the grip

7. In the "hit and run" play with a runner on first base, the batter should attempt to

   a. hit a ground ball ahead of the runner
   b. hit a fly ball
   c. bunt
   d. hit a ground ball behind the runner

8. The major difference between the slingshot and windmill deliveries is

   a. the path the ball travels to the plate
   b. the way the ball curves or drops
   c. the windup for release
   d. all the above

9. A pitch that curves from right to left, away from a right-handed hitter is called a

   a. drop ball
   b. fast ball
   c. incurve
   d. outcurve

10. With the bases loaded and two players out, the defensive team should attempt to make the third out at

   a. nearest and surest point
   b. home plate
   c. first base
   d. third base

PART II. **TRUE OR FALSE** Write + in the blank if the statement is true, O if it is wholly or partially false.

_____ 1. On a count of two balls and two strikes the batter bunts foul on the next pitch.

_____ 2. Runners may not lead off of bases until the pitcher releases the ball.

_____ 3. When preparing to deliver, the pitcher must hold the ball no less than 1 second nor more than 20 seconds before taking her two step delivery toward the batter.

_____ 4. With no outs and runners on first and third, the defense should try to put out the runner closest to home plate.

_____ 5. The pitcher usually covers first base when the first baseman fields a bunt.

_____ 6. For power hits the bat should be held with hands touching the lower hand at least 8 inches from the end of the bat.

_____ 7. After four balls are called on the batter, she moves to first base and all other baserunners advance one base.

_____ 8. To catch a ball going far overhead, the fielder turns her back to the hit and runs, looking over her shoulder to keep the ball in view.

_____ 9. A batted ball that hits in the infield and rolls across the baseline from home to first before being touched is a fair ball.

_____ 10. There are 10 defensive players on a slowpitch softball team.

PART III. **COMPLETION** Fill in the blanks with the appropriate word or phrase.

1. A regulation _____ inning softball game is played on a _____ shaped field by two teams of _____ players each.

2. To make a pitch curve outward and away from a right-handed batter, a right-handed pitcher snaps her wrist from _____ to _____ on delivery.

3. Sliding is never necessary when approaching _____ base.

4. The strike zone is over home plate between the _____ of the knees and the batter's

   _____

5. The _____ and _____ may use mitts.

6. The strongest and longest hitter should be the _____ batter in the lineup with the three weakest batters in _____ , _____ and _____ positions.

7. The _____ covers second base when a left-handed hitter is at the plate and the hit goes between first and second bases.

8. A baserunner is _____ when hit by a batted ball before it is touched by or passes a fielder.

9. A _____ is used by a batter to advance a baserunner from first to second, resulting in the batter's being put out.

10. An attempt to score a runner from third by signaling an intended bunt down the first-base line is called a _____ .

PART IV. **MATCHING** In the blank at the left of Column A write the letter of the most appropriate term or name in Column B.

Column A   Column B

_____ 1. Author of first softball rules for girls   a. Bunt

_____ 2. Ball swung at and missed by batter   b. Line drive

_____ 3. Pitcher and catcher   c. Pitcher and catcher

_____ 4. Second base   d. Battery

_____ 5. Responsible for more territory than any other   e. Gladys Palmer
         player
                                                          f. Amos Stagg
_____ 6. Team in field
                                                          g. Ball
_____ 7. Ball on fair ground going out of infield to
         outfield   h. Strike

_____ 8. Ball hit foul in the outfield   i. Fair ball

_____ 9. Pitch that hits the ground before reaching   j. Foul ball
         the plate
                                                          k. Infield fly
_____10. Deceptive, easy hit that usually travels home
         to third or home to first   l. Keystone base

                                                          m. Center fielder

                                                          n. Shortstop

                                                          o. Defense

CHAPTER 26

SPEED-A-WAY

PART I **TRUE OR FALSE** Write + in the blank if the statement is true, O if it is wholly or partially false.

_____ 1. Speed-a-way is one of the oldest women's field sports in the United States.

_____ 2. During play the ball may be kicked, passed, or carried.

_____ 3. Offside rules are identical to those in field hockey.

_____ 4. A runner may be tagged with one hand.

_____ 5. On the kick-off the ball may be passed or lifted in any direction.

_____ 6. An aerial ball is one caught on the fly or if kicked, after one bounce.

_____ 7. Fouls occurring in the striking circle carry a greater penalty than field fouls.

_____ 8. Speed-a-way is more an offensive than a defensive game.

_____ 9. After a goal, the scoring team kicks off.

_____ 10. The goalkeeper may pick up a ground ball anywhere on the field.

PART II. **COMPLETION** Fill in the blanks with the appropriate word or words.

1. It is a foul to hold an _____ ball longer than _____ seconds without passing or running.

2. When _____ , the ball is dropped from the hands and kicked as it rebounds from the ground.

3. Skills of Speed-a-way are similar to those of other field games: position and team play resemble _____ ; ball handling skills are like _____ and _____ , with the unique ball carrying of _____ .

4. There are _____ players on a team: _____ forward(s), _____ back(s), and _____ goalkeeper(s).

5. A field goal scores _____ points; a touchdown, _____ points; and a drop kick over the bar from outside the circle scores _____ points.

6. When a forward pass is intercepted by a defensive player behind the goal, the _____ team is awarded _____ .

7. Out-of-bounds balls over the side lines are put into play by a _____ .

8. In _____ , the ball is dropped and kicked before it hits the ground.

9. An _____ ball may be advanced by pass, run, punt, drop kick, or volley.

10. Double fouls result in a _____ .

PART III. **MATCHING** In the blank at the left of Column A write the letter of the most appropriate term or name in Column B.

<table>
<tr><td>Column A</td><td>Column B</td></tr>
</table>

Column A

_____ 1. Originator of Speed-a-way

_____ 2. Forward line player

_____ 3. A method of putting the ball in play at kick-off

_____ 4. Stopping the ball with one or both legs

_____ 5. Awarded to attacking team when defending team fouls in the circle

_____ 6. Penalty for foul outside the circle

_____ 7. Penalty for double foul

_____ 8. Taking a ground ball away from an opponent

_____ 9. Awarded when ball goes out of bounds off two opposing players

_____ 10. Playing the ball with the head or shoulder

Column B

a. Tackle

b. Trapping

c. Blocking

d. Volleying

e. Abner Doubleday

f. Marjorie Larsen

g. Left inner

h. Goalkeeper

i. Lift-up

j. Penalty corner

k. Drop kick

l. Punt

m. Toss-up

n. Tie ball

o. Free kick

CHAPTER 27

VOLLEYBALL

PART I. **MULTIPLE CHOICE** Circle the letter preceding the answer most correct for the statement.

1. When two opposing players contact the ball simultaneously over the net this is a

  a. double foul
  b. foul on one of the players
  c. legal play and the contact is not counted as one of the three volleys for either team
  d. legal play and the hit counts on either side as play continues

2. A game is won by a team if

  a. they score 15 points and hold a 2 point advantage over the opponent
  b. they lead by at least 2 points at the end of 8 minutes of playing time
  c. a and b above
  d. all the above

3. Players A and B on the receiving team contact the service simultaneously. A contacts the ball again as she sets to B (front line player) who spikes it over the net. The referee's decision is

  a. point; too many contacts
  b. point; too many contacts by Player A
  c. side-out
  d. legal; play continues

4. The center front receives a pass from the back line. She is preparing to set to the left front spiker when she observes a strong two-man block prepared for her left front player. The best offensive play would be

  a. dink
  b. bump to midcourt
  c. back set to right front spiker
  d. "shoot" the ball to deep court

5. If the served ball is played by the receiver off her upper arms, this is

  a. legal — U.S.V.B.A. rules
  b. legal — D.G.W.S. rules
  c. illegal — D.G.W.S. rules
  d. a and b above
  e. a and c above

6. On a second contact, the ball is delivered too low and too close to the net for an effective spike. The player should

   a. use underhand volley
   b. head the ball
   c. block
   d. dink
   e. dig

7. The term "power volleyball" refers to the skilled offensive pattern of

   a. pass, set, spike
   b. pass, set, dink
   c. set, set, shoot
   d. bump, set, bump

8. One of the following statements is false; identify it

   a. a volleyball team has six players
   b. a player may leave and enter the game any number of times
   c. a game may be played by either time or score, whichever is reached first
   d. a team rotates each time it receives the ball (except on first service of a game of D.G.W.S. rules)

9. The center forward of the team receiving the serve is the team's best set. On service she should

   a. move back in her area and attempt to receive the serve
   b. remain about 3 feet from the net and move forward as soon as the ball passes over
   c. remain about 3 feet from the net and move back as the serve enters the court
   d. remain as close to the net as possible throughout the serve

10. A 3-player block on an opposing right front spiker might be called illegal by a D.G.W.S. official on the basis of the rule stating that

   a. each player must remain in her own area until the ball is served
   b. a player may not reach over the net to play a ball
   c. a player must not persistently change positions during play
   d. a player must not spike at the net when she is a back line player

PART II. **TRUE OR FALSE** Write + in the blank if the statement is true, O if it is wholly or partially false.

_____ 1. All players must be on or inside the boundaries of the court when the ball is served.

_____ 2. A served ball that goes into the net is automatically a side-out.

_____ 3. A team rotates each time it loses the ball.

_____ 4. The forearms or fists may be legally used to play the ball.

_____ 5. Time-out for substitution may be taken when the ball is dead and shall not exceed 1 minute.

_____ 6. The server may step over the end line as soon as she strikes the ball.

_____ 7. A ball touching the top of the net and continuing into the opponent's court on service is called a "let" and is replayed.

_____ 8. In D.G.W.S. rules a player must be in her own area on service; thereafter during play she is free to move anywhere on her side of the court.

_____ 9. If two or more players on one side contact the ball simultaneously during play, it is considered only one hit.

_____ 10. It is permissible to put in a substitute for a player just as she is ready to serve.

PART III. **COMPLETION** Fill in the blanks with the appropriate word or phrase.

1. Intentionally changing positions with another player to gain advantage in playing the ball is

   called an _____ .

2. The most effective technique for handling power serves and spikes is the _____ .

3. The "W" and crescent formations refer to a team's _____ position.

4. Assisting a serve is _____ .

5. When a server steps on the end line during service it is a _____ .

6. When a net player steps on the center line during play it is _____ .

7. Players _____ in a _____ movement to a new position at the beginning

   of a service term.

8. The most effective power play after receiving with a bump pass is a _____ for an effective

   _____ .

9. The top of the net is _____ from the floor.

10. A set made by a set player over the head of one player to be spiked by another is called an

    _____ .

PART IV. **MATCHING** In the blank at the left of Column A write the letter of the most appropriate term or phrase in Column B. A term may be appropriate for one or more statements.

Column A	Column B
____ 1. Serving team delays the game	a. Two
____ 2. Double foul	b. Side-out
____ 3. Ball retrieved from net during play	c. Dig
____ 4. Foot fault on service	d. Service
____ 5. Illegal ball handling by member of receiving team	e. Repeat play
____ 6. Defensive skill	f. Play continues
____ 7. A team's initial offensive skill	g. Out of bounds
____ 8. Maximum number of games in a match	h. One
____ 9. Both an offensive and defensive skill	i. Point for serving team
____10. A contact of the ball below the waist by one or both closed hands and extended arms.	j. Spike
	k. Three
	l. Volley
	m. In bounds
	n. Block
	o. Dink

CHAPTER 28

SOCIAL DANCE

PART I **MATCHING** Place from Column B the letter of the correct answer before each word or statement in Column A.

Column A   Column B

_____ 1. Two eighth notes   a. Equivalent to one walking step

_____ 2. The basic quarter note   b. The box

_____ 3. A half note   c. Equivalent to two running steps

_____ 4. One slow step, 2 quick, 1 slow, 2   e. Equivalent to two quarter notes
        quick
                                                          f. The waltz
_____ 5. Two quick steps, 1 slow, 2 quick, 1
        slow   g. The two-step, rhumba, and mambo

_____ 6. Three even steps in 3/4 time   h. The hesitation waltz

_____ 7. Step and hold for two beats   i. Samba and bossa nova

_____ 8. Two quick steps, 1 slow in a 2/4   j. The schottische
        meter
                                                          k. The two-step
_____ 9. Step l, close r, step l

_____ 10. Step, Step, Step, hop

PART II. **TRUE OR FALSE** Write + in the blank if the statement is true, O if it is wholly or partially false

_____ 1. The twist of today was originally the ancient African witch doctors' gyrations.

_____ 2. The swing, a popular syncopated rhythm dance, has evolved from the Lindy and other jitterbug variations.

_____ 3. Most dance music today is the rhythm of the cha cha cha.

_____ 4. The mambo is Cuban in origin.

———————— 5. The samba was originally a tribal dance among African slaves.

———————— 6. The tango comes to us via the Argentine cowboy, the Gaucho.

———————— 7. The basic rhythm of the bossa nova is gafiera.

———————— 8. The meter of the Argentine samba is 2/4.

———————— 9. Rhumba rhythm is 3/4.

———————— 10. Tango rhythm is 4/4.

CHAPTER 29

SQUARE DANCE

PART I. **COMPLETION** Write the ending of these typical square dance calls or patterns.

1. Honor your partner, give her a smile, ————————————————————— .

2. Ladies to the center and back to the bar, ————————————————— .

3. First couple out to the right of the ring, ————————————————— .

4. Circle four and don't be slow, ————————————————— .

5. All jump up and never come down, ————————————————— .

PART II. **TRUE OR FALSE** Write + in the blank if the statement is true, O if it is wholly or partially false

———————— 1. All square dances are done in 8 or multiples of 8 to 4/4, 2/4, or 6/8 time.

CHAPTER 30

FOLK DANCE

PART I. **MULTIPLE CHOICE** Circle the letter of the correct answer.

1. Mayim, mayim is a dance from

   a. Lithuania
   b. Israel
   c. Russia
   d. Egypt

2. In the Spanish circle, the dancers are in

   a. a square
   b. circle
   c. two lines facing opposite each other
   d. social dance position

3. Korobuska is a Russian dance meaning

   a. the peddler's pack or little basket
   b. a shoemaker's tools
   c. little donkey
   d. a farmer's hayrack

4. Galopede is a longways dance from

   a. Ireland
   b. Scotland
   c. England
   d. France

5. The mazurka step is done in

   a. 1/4 time
   b. 2/4 time
   c. 3/4 time
   d. 4/4 time

PART II. **MATCHING** Place from Column B the letter of the correct answer before each word or statement in Column A.

Column A

_____ 1. La Jesucita

_____ 2. The Jessie polka

_____ 3. Corrido

_____ 4. Cumberland square

_____ 5. Waves of Troy

_____ 6. Road to the Isles

_____ 7. Kavelis

_____ 8. Buzz step

_____ 9. Gavotte

_____10. Grapevine

_____11. The Virginia reel

_____12. Contra formation

_____13. Mayim, Mayim

_____14. All American promenade

_____15. Pivot

Column B

a. Poland

b. England

c. The United States

d. Scotland

e. Lithuania

f. Mexico

g. Ireland

h. Partner hip-to-hip swing

i. Three walking steps followed by a light tap of the ball of the free foot

j. One foot crosses in front of other alternately in a continuous movement of traveling steps

k. Square dance

l. Also called the Cowboy schottische

m. Two lines opposite each other

n. Expresses gratitude and joy for finding water in a desert

o. A mixer

p. Spinning step done by small pushing steps

CHAPTER 31

MODERN DANCE

PART I. **COMPLETION** Fill in the blanks with the appropriate word or words in each of the following statements.

1. Movements which propel the body through space are called _____ movements.

2. Movements that employ any range of movement from a stationary base are known as _____ movements.

3. Modern dance is a form of creative expression that uses the _____ as the instrument, and _____ as the medium for artistic expression.

4. Movements which begin from common positions such as lying down, sitting, or kneeling are examples of _____ movements.

5. Walking, jumping, hopping, and running are _____ movements.

PART II. List 6 techniques for conditioning the body to produce effective movement while in a standing position

1. _____

2. _____

3. _____

4. _____

5. _____

6. _____

PART III. **DEFINITIONS** Define the following terms.

1. Focus _____

2. Percussive movement _____

3. Rotation

4. Inversion

PART IV. **TRUE OR FALSE** Write + in the blank if the statement is true, O if it is wholly or partially false

_____ 1. Modern dance and social dance are basically the same art forms.

_____ 2. Force, space, and time are the dynamic elements of movement.

_____ 3. Sliding, galloping, step-hopping, and skipping are all variations of fundamental locomotor movements.

_____ 4. Effective use of human movement depends upon the ability of the body to exert power, speed, and agility with a minimum expenditure of energy.

_____ 5. Releve's extend the body upward onto the toes.

CHAPTER 32

SPORTS COMPETITION FOR WOMEN

PART I. **DEFINITIONS** Define the following terms.

1. Sports day_____

2. Telegraphic meets_____

3. Round robin tournament_____

4. Crown tournament_____

PART II. **COMPLETION** Fill in the blanks of the following statements with the correct answers.

1. Players challenge another person directly above in the_____tournament.

2. In the elimination tournament if 15 are entered, there should be_____bye.

3. In the same type of tournament, if 28 are entered, there should be_____byes.

4. If 58 are entered, there should be_____ byes.

5. In the round robin tournament, with an_____number of teams there is the same number of rounds.

6. In the same type of tournament, there is_____less number of games than teams if an even number of teams are entered.

PART III **TRUE OR FALSE** Write + in the blank if the statement is true, O if it is wholly or partially false.

_____ 1. For competition the best selection of a team captain is appointment by the teacher or coach.

_____ 2. All game and eligibility rules are basically for the protection of the players.

_____ 3. In extramural competition, teams or individuals play a series of games with like teams from other schools, cities, or organizations.

_____ 4. The division of Girls' and Women's Sports is a part of the American Association for Health, Physical Education, and Recreation and the National Education Association.

_____ 5. In a doubles elimination tournament, no team is eliminated until it loses four times.

_____ 6. In a round robin tournament wherein there is an odd number of teams, all numbers revolve and the last number each time draws a bye.

_____ 7. In the pyramid tournament, the number of spaces on the bottom line should equal 1/2 the number of contestants.

_____ 8. In the same type of tournament, losers change places with the winners.

_____ 9. All eligibility rules for competitive events should be drawn up primarily for the spectator so that all who come to watch a competitive game see only well-matched, skilled contestants compete against each other.

_____ 10. The first women's game of basketball was played at Smith College in 1899.

_____ 11. Contestants may be classified according to age, weight, skill, physical examination results, or skill tests taken for competitive purposes.

_____ 12. All awards should be simple and inexpensive, for in women's competitive events emphasis should be placed upon the joy of participating as well as on winning, rather than upon receiving an elaborate award.

_____ 13. Among other things, in the competitive program the type of activities selected should be of educational as well as of physical value.

_____ 14. Women's teams or individuals should be taught and coached and games officiated by qualified women whenever and wherever possible.